ECONOMIC DEVELOPMENT
FOR AFRICA
SOUTH OF THE SAHARA

Other International Economic Association symposia

*

Edited by Kenneth Berrill
ECONOMIC DEVELOPMENT WITH SPECIAL REFERENCE TO
EAST ASIA

Edited by Howard S. Ellis and Henry C. Wallich
ECONOMIC DEVELOPMENT FOR LATIN AMERICA

Edited by D. C. Hague
STABILITY AND PROGRESS IN THE WORLD ECONOMY

Edited by F. H. Hahn and F. P. R. Brechling
THE THEORY OF INTEREST RATES

Edited by Sir Roy Harrod and D. C. Hague
INTERNATIONAL TRADE THEORY IN A DEVELOPING
WORLD

Edited by Erik Lundberg
THE BUSINESS CYCLE IN THE POST-WAR WORLD

Edited by F. A. Lutz and D. C. Hague
THE THEORY OF CAPITAL

Edited by R. A. Musgrave and A. T. Peacock
CLASSICS IN THE THEORY OF PUBLIC FINANCE

Edited by E. A. G. Robinson
THE ECONOMIC CONSEQUENCES OF THE SIZE OF NATIONS
PROBLEMS IN ECONOMIC DEVELOPMENT
THE ECONOMICS OF EDUCATION

Edited by W. W. Rostow
THE ECONOMICS OF TAKE-OFF INTO SUSTAINED GROWTH

Edited by Brinley Thomas
ECONOMICS OF INTERNATIONAL MIGRATION

ECONOMIC DEVELOPMENT
FOR AFRICA
SOUTH OF THE SAHARA

Proceedings of a Conference held by
the International Economic Association

EDITED BY

E. A. G. ROBINSON
(PRESIDENT 1959–62)

MACMILLAN
London · Melbourne · Toronto

ST MARTIN'S PRESS
New York
1965

First Edition 1963
Reprinted 1965

MACMILLAN AND COMPANY LIMITED
Little Essex Street London WC2
also Bombay Calcutta Madras Melbourne

THE MACMILLAN COMPANY OF CANADA LIMITED
70 Bond Street Toronto 2

ST MARTIN'S PRESS INC
175 Fifth Avenue New York NY 10010

PRINTED IN GREAT BRITAIN

CONTENTS

		PAGE
LIST OF PARTICIPANTS		vii
INTRODUCTION		ix

PART I

CHAP.

1. ECONOMIC DEVELOPMENT IN AFRICA : AIMS AND POSSIBILITIES. G. J. Ligthart and B. Abbai (UN Economic Commission for Africa) — 3

2. PROBLEMS OF AFRICAN ECONOMIC DEVELOPMENT. E. A. G. Robinson (University of Cambridge) — 48

3. PROBLEMS OF ECONOMIC DEVELOPMENT OF CONGO. F. Bézy (University of Lovanium, Congo) — 71

4. PROBLEMS OF ECONOMIC DEVELOPMENT OF EAST AFRICA. D. Walker (University College of East Africa) — 89

5. PROBLEMS OF ECONOMIC DEVELOPMENT OF FRENCH-LANGUAGE COUNTRIES AND TERRITORIES. L. de Carbon (University of Nancy) — 138

6. PROBLEMS OF ECONOMIC DEVELOPMENT OF GHANA, NIGERIA, SIERRA LEONE, LIBERIA, SPANISH TERRITORIES. J. W. Williams (University of Ghana) — 184

7. PROBLEMS OF ECONOMIC DEVELOPMENT OF ANGOLA : POLES AND PROSPECTS. L. M. Teixeira Pinto and R. Martins dos Santos (University of Lisbon) — 198

8. PROBLEMS OF ECONOMIC DEVELOPMENT OF THE FEDERATION OF RHODESIA AND NYASALAND. W. L. Taylor (University College of Rhodesia and Nyasaland) — 222

9. PROBLEMS OF ECONOMIC DEVELOPMENT OF THE REPUBLIC OF SOUTH AFRICA. C. S. Richards (University of Witwatersrand) — 246

PART II

10. POPULATION MOVEMENTS AND PROBLEMS. J. J. Spengler (Duke University, U.S.A.) — 281

11. THE PROBLEMS OF LABOUR IN AFRICAN DEVELOPMENT. D. H. Houghton (University of Rhodes) — 312

CHAP.   PAGE

12. EDUCATION IN AFRICAN ECONOMIC GROWTH.   J. Vaizey
    (University of London)   340

13. CREATING INCENTIVES FOR ECONOMIC DEVELOPMENT.
    S. Enke (Duke University, U.S.A.)   361

14. PRICES AND PRICE FORMATION IN AFRICAN ECONOMIES.
    G. Leduc (University of Paris)   382

15. CAPITAL AND CAPITAL SUPPLY IN RELATION TO THE DEVELOP-
    MENT OF AFRICA.   S. H. Frankel (University of Oxford)   407

16. CAPITAL AND CAPITAL SUPPLY IN RELATION TO THE
    DEVELOPMENT OF AFRICA.   L. B. Rist (World Bank)   444

17. TROPICAL AFRICA AND THE WORLD ECONOMY.   W. E.
    Moran (University of Stanford, U.S.A.)   475

18. COMMODITY AND TRADE POLICY IN AFRICA.   L. H. Dupriez
    (University of Louvain)   503

19. ISSUES IN COMMODITY STABILIZATION IN AFRICA.   P. T.
    Bauer (University of London)   532

20. SOME ASPECTS OF AFRICAN AGRICULTURAL DEVELOPMENT.
    M. Yudelman (World Bank)   554

21. PROBLEMS OF THE AFRICAN MINING ECONOMY.   Roland Pré
    (Paris)   588

22. PROBLEMS OF LARGE-SCALE INDUSTRY IN AFRICA.   D. J.
    Viljoen (University of Potchefstroom, South Africa)   616

23. SMALL-SCALE INDUSTRY IN AFRICAN ECONOMIC DEVELOP-
    MENT.   H. W. Singer (United Nations, New York)   638

24. MONETARY AND FISCAL POLICY IN RELATION TO AFRICAN
    DEVELOPMENT.   A. T. Peacock (University of Edinburgh)   654

25. MONETARY AND FISCAL POLICY IN RELATION TO AFRICAN
    DEVELOPMENT.   L. H. Samuels (University of Cape Town)   677

26. THE CONTRIBUTION OF ECONOMIC RESEARCH TO AFRICAN
    DEVELOPMENT.   W. P. Stolper (Massachusetts Institute of
    Technology)   712

    INDEX   735

vi

LIST OF PARTICIPANTS

Mr. B. Abbai, UN Economic Commission for Africa, Addis Ababa.

Professor R. E. Baldwin, University of California, Los Angeles, U.S.A.

Mr. M. Beheiry, Bank of Sudan, Khartoum.

Professor F. Bézy, University of Lovanium, Léopoldville, Congo.

Dr. Forrest Cookson, Arlington, U.S.A.

Mr. M. Dowuona, University College of Ghana.

Professor L. H. Dupriez, University of Louvain, Belgium.

Professor S. Enke, Duke University, U.S.A.

Professor L. Fauvel, Faculté de Droit et des Sciences Économiques, Paris.

Professor S. H. Frankel, Oxford University, England.

Dr. N. Gavrilov, African Institute, Moscow, U.S.S.R.

Ato Taye Gulilat, University College, Addis Ababa.

Ato Tekle Haimanot, Ministry of Finance, Addis Ababa.

Professor D. H. Houghton, Rhodes University, Grahamstown, South Africa.

Mr. S. Hymer, University College of Ghana.

Mr. K. G. V. Krishna, The Royal College, Nairobi, Kenya.

Mr. G. Lardner, UN Economic Commission for Africa, Addis Ababa.

Professor G. Leduc, University of Paris.

Mr. G. J. Ligthart, UN Economic Commission for Africa, Addis Ababa.

Mr. P. S. Menon, UN Economic Commission for Africa, Addis Ababa.

Mr. William E. Moran, Jr., School of Foreign Service, Georgetown University, Washington, U.S.A.

Mr. Selby B. Ngcobo, University College of Rhodesia and Nyasaland.

Dr. P. N. C. Okigbo, Government of Eastern Nigeria, Enugu, Nigeria.

Mr. H. M. A. Onitiri, University College, Ibadan, Nigeria.

Professor A. T. Peacock, Department of Political Economy, University of Edinburgh, Scotland.

Professor Roland Pré, Bureau géologique et minier français, Paris, France.

Mr. Leonard B. Rist, International Bank for Reconstruction and Development, Washington, U.S.A.

Professor E. A. G. Robinson, Cambridge University, England.

Professor L. H. Samuels, Witwatersrand University, Johannesburg, South Africa.

Dr. H. W. Singer, Department of Economic and Social Affairs, United Nations, New York.

Dr. G. Skorov, UNESCO, Paris.

Professor J. J. Spengler, Duke University, U.S.A.

Professor S. Stanley, University College, Addis Ababa.

Professor W. P. Stolper, Ministry of Economic Development, Lagos, Nigeria.

Mr. John Vaizey, Institute of Education, University of London, England.

Professor D. J. Viljoen, Potchefstroom University, South Africa.

Professor E. Vopicka, Institute of Economic Planning, Prague, Czechoslovakia.

Dr. Abdoulaye Wade, Université de Dakar, Sénégal.

Professor D. Walker, University College of East Africa, Makerere, Uganda.

Professor J. W. Williams, University of Otago, New Zealand.

Ato Mezmur Yeheyes, Ministry of Agriculture, Addis Ababa.

Dr. M. Yudelman, Center for International Affairs, Harvard University, U.S.A.

INTRODUCTION

By AUSTIN ROBINSON
(President I.E.A. 1959-62)

THE Conference on Economic Development for Africa, held in Addis Ababa, represented the third of such regional conferences organized by the International Economic Association. The first, concerned with Latin America, was held in Rio de Janiero ; the second, concerned with East Asia was held in Gamagori in Japan. The central purpose of such conferences has been to bring together leading economists of the region to examine with specialists from outside the region the problems of economic development as they apply to that part of the world.

In the case of the African conference, it was unique in another sense. It represented the first occasion on which academic economists from all over Africa had met together to discuss the problems of African development. It was the first opportunity for many of them to meet simultaneously their colleagues from other African countries and to discover from joint discussion how far the problems of the countries of Africa are similar and how far dissimilar.

As a background to our discussions we persuaded the experts of the Economic Commission for Africa to prepare for us a general paper on African development and various authorities on different parts of Africa to write their views on the problems confronting the development of these particular areas. These various studies are printed here as Section I of the present volume.

The ECA paper was exceptionally interesting in its attempt to use Mexico as a bench-mark of a country just reaching the stage of 'take-off'. (I shall not engage in argument regarding the detailed validity of that concept ; those issues were very fully threshed out at another conference of the IEA.) Mexico, with agriculture representing only about 20 per cent of gross domestic product, despite an excess of primary exports over primary imports, and with some 18 per cent generated in manufacturing, was clearly far more advanced in most respects than any African country north of the Zambesi. Thus it was clear that African countries were starting in almost all cases from very low levels of development and of income per head and had a long way to go to reach 'take-off'.

On the other hand all of these studies served to emphasize the very rapid current economic growth of most of the countries of Africa.

The rates of growth of total gross domestic product (including the subsistence sector) has in most cases been between $4\frac{1}{2}$ per cent and 6 per cent per annum. Africa, with a very few exceptions, has certainly not been stagnant. The problem is not to stimulate growth where it has been lacking, but to maintain and increase it in rapidly changing circumstances. The coming of independence to many of the countries of Africa has made Africans more conscious of their poverty and more anxious to exercise their new responsibilities to overcome it ; and political ambitions have inevitably emphasized the desirability of achieving solutions, if that is possible, more quickly than in the past.

Independence has at the same time affected in a number of ways the flow of resources for development. In the past, the countries of Africa south of the Sahara which have developed furthest — notably South Africa, the Rhodesias, and what was formerly Belgian Congo — have achieved it largely with an inflow of private foreign capital. With independence, foreign enterprise is in many African countries regarded much more critically and is at the same time somewhat more shy of accepting the risks involved. The papers by Professor Frankel, M. Rist, Professor Taylor and Professor Richards all bring out in different ways the dilemma here and the dangers of conflict between maximum economic development and maximum fulfilment of political aspirations.

Independence has also had its effects on the channels of transfer of technical knowledge to Africa. In the past the foreign administrator and the foreign entrepreneur have brought to Africa the experience and the techniques of the more advanced countries and have helped to apply them to African conditions. It is now necessary to construct new channels for this transfer of knowledge ; international aid, both financial and technical, is increasingly supplementing and taking the place of private investment and private enterprise. All this is the more important because Africa is in many respects the test case of whether or not it is really practicable to short-cut the long processes of history in other continents and achieve results in substantially shorter periods of time.

From these background studies certain common features and issues quickly emerged : the heavy dependence of all these African countries on primary production and primary exports ; the great advantage accruing to those countries which had mineral resources to add to agricultural resources ; their sensitivity to fluctuations of primary product prices; their very small scale, almost without exception, both as markets for the development of local industries and as nations attempting to carry the administrative burdens, national and international, of nation-hood ; in most cases also, the paucity of educated manpower to carry the responsibilities of national and industrial administration, and of the skills needed for industrialization.

It was not to be expected that all the forty or so participants would agree on every issue and every possible solution. A body of academic economists makes its contribution to the realities of economic development not by reaching verbal compromises but by crystallizing issues and by clarifying differences of opinion. The Conference was hard-hitting and no respecter of persons ; it was the better for that. It included both participants who believed strongly in the virtues of liberal policies and private enterprise, open equally and without discrimination to all persons of all races, and also participants who believed with equal sincerity in the virtues of planning economic progress, of using statistical analysis to foresee the trends and the problems of the future, and of removing obstacles to progress by careful forethought and timely action. Conflicts of judgment made themselves evident, for example, in relation to social expenditures on education, where one school of thought emphasized that expenditure must not run so far ahead of income that industrial growth is inhibited by shortage of capital ; the other school emphasized the contribution of education to the 'unspecified factor' in growth and the importance of balancing investment in fixed capital with human investment.

Differences were obvious, again, in relation to trade policy. One school, strongly represented among West African participants, emphasized the damage done by the tremendous oscillations of the terms of trade, the dangers of their long-term movement adversely to primary products, the apparently low income-elasticities of demand for primary products, and was thus led to advocate diversification of African economies, and their rapid industrialization. Others again saw dangers in this : that the comparative advantages of Africa still lay in primary production ; that the longer-term trends of primary product prices were by no means certain ; that African economies and national markets were of insufficient scale for efficient industrialization. The obvious truth is that it is almost impossible to prove with any certainty a generation in advance which infant industries are ultimately likely to justify themselves and which are likely to be failures. Most of the West African economists present were particularly anxious to take risks and to push industrialization to the limit, in the belief that their traditional exports were unlikely to expand sufficiently to meet the constantly increasing needs for capital equipment in a rapidly growing economy, and that import-saving wherever practicable would permit the expansion of other imports and fewer brakes upon growth from balance of payments difficulties.

It was natural that we should be concerned primarily with the basic issue why African countries are poor. We were, I think, most of us persuaded that Africa is a tough and hard continent, with large areas of not very fertile soils, with uneven and not very rich mineralization (though there are obvious and important exceptions to this), with great distances between centres of production and those of consumption or export. While populations are growing in some cases with alarming rapidity, there are large areas that are under-populated rather than over-populated. In many respects Africa is more truly under-developed than most of the areas that are so described. While many of the railway systems were built around the turn of the century to facilitate export and to serve mineral production, road transport is only now beginning to become adequate. Other public utilities, and particularly energy supplies, are just in process of development. Industrialization, outside of South Africa, the Rhodesias and the Congo, is only beginning. The limiting factors, in Africa as everywhere, are three : capital, a skilled labour force and a sufficient body of entrepreneurs.

Considering the average levels of income, the volume of saving in Africa is surprisingly high — the consequence in part no doubt of very unequal distribution of income, in part of involuntary saving enforced through commodity boards, company savings, fiscal policies and the like. Domestic saving has been around 10 per cent in a number of countries and over 20 per cent in Congo and the Rhodesias. Including foreign finance, gross capital formation has been between 25 per cent and 30 per cent of gross domestic product in several countries and around 15 per cent in many others. It has been possible, that is to say, to support growth rates of 5 per cent or thereabouts.

From many points of view the limitations of skilled labour and entrepreneuring have been more serious. Here it is very difficult, however, to generalize. In South Africa, as Professor Houghton's most interesting paper shows, there is growing up round the firms which are better employers a stable body of regular employees, with increasing skills and responsibility. The bad employers, on the other hand, suffer from high labour turn-over and employees with little or no sense of involvement or ambition to achieve success and promotion. It was not easy to judge how far this reflected the special circumstances of an individual country. In Congo, for example, Professor Bézy suggested that labour turn-over was small and productivity had responded to increases of wages ; when Belgian supervisors had been withdrawn, Africans had successfully taken their places. But it was clear that, even in the countries that were wholly African and where opportunities were unlimited, there remained short-term problems, at least, of inadequacy of skills and of lack of full sense of involvement in the skilled crafts needed for modern development.

The problems of entrepreneuring are even more complex. In the past industrial development has mostly depended on ex-patriate firms, often importers who, cut off from sources of imports, have attempted local manufacture. These have included not only nationals of the various metropolitan powers but also Levantines and Syrians in West Africa, Asians in East Africa and numerous refugees from Central Europe and elsewhere. To their drive and ingenuity the rapid progress of industry, large and small, in Africa has largely been due. It is far from clear at present how far the various countries of Africa visualize the continuation of multi-racial societies, with much more equal opportunities for all, Africans as well as ex-patriates, than has sometimes existed in the past; or how far on the other hand they may be intending to impose increasing pressures on those of non-African origin. This is not the sort of question on which it is to anyone's interest to force the issue. But it is natural that a group of economists should ask themselves where, in the long run, the entre-preneurs of Africa are going to be found.

In the field of trading there is a long history of African entre-preneuring; it is most manifest in West Africa. But in many respects entrepreneuring in the field of trade is a less demanding activity than the organization of production, with the various problems of tech-niques, the purchase of equipment, and the organization of supplies of materials that are involved. But this problem is obviously closely interconnected with that of large-scale and small-scale industry that we discussed with the aid of papers by Professor Viljoen and Dr. Singer. There are obvious reasons why large-scale industry in Africa should tend to rather large size. But the larger the business, the more remote from African experience and opportunity. It is less easy in Africa than in most advanced countries, or for that matter than in India or Japan, for the successful craftsman to start up on his own, outside of a few such industries as, say, building or printing. It is clear that improved machinery is needed for helping the African small-scale industrialist to start up on his own. But we could not but be aware of the many difficulties — technical, financial, and educa-tional — involved.

Inevitably much time and thought was given to the problems of agriculture and the development of African agriculture from pure self-subsistence to complete participation in the monetary economy. We owed to Dr. Yudelman (see p. 555), the division of African agriculture into four phases : pure subsistence production for direct consumption ; primarily subsistence production with a small production for the market ; mostly for the market with some production for direct consumption ; specialized production for the market. It seemed to us more valuable and more realistic to think in terms of the whereabouts in this framework of particular groups in particular countries than to treat of dual economies, with groups wholly engaged in self-subsistence or wholly in the monetary economy.

But however defined, African 'self-subsistence' agriculture plays a very large part in the economic life of Africa today ; as Dr. Yudelman's figures show, it employs over half the male population in all except a few countries and over two-thirds in a number of them ; it contributes 30 per cent or more of gross domestic product in a majority of countries. Economic development, if it is to be realistic, must include a policy for its improvement. But in many respects this is the most difficult task of all. The present market is the producer's stomach. Where is the market to be found for increased production ? In those regions in which profitable cash crops can be grown, there has almost everywhere been a significant response to price incentives to expand production. But not all regions are suitable, either in soil or in geographical location, to export crops. The growth of urban populations has been slow and the cities have been fed in many cases by expansion of European rather than African production.

Thus it is almost certainly true to say that in many parts of Africa the desired improvements and transitions of African agriculture can come only with increasing demand as a consequence of the removal of large numbers out of African agriculture and of the growth of urban markets for foodstuffs and agricultural materials. If, as is much to be hoped, world demands both for staple exports and new agricultural products develop and can be stimulated by lower prices, the resources almost certainly exist in Africa to meet them. They could be greatly increased by more regional specialization of production, the use of favourable soils and locations more exclusively for cash crop production combined with the purchase of food crops from other areas. But it is just in respect of the probability that markets will at all quickly expand sufficiently to solve these problems throughout Africa that many of us feel sceptical. Meanwhile we found ourselves concerned with the disruption of the traditional economy as the consequence of education and other trends and with the dangers of pressures towards more rapid absorption of individuals into the monetary economy than is consistent with the growth of that economy and the difficulties of finding capital resources to expand it.

Introduction

We ended by asking ourselves, with the help of a paper by Professor Stolper what contribution economic research might make to African development. Professor Stolper's paper illustrates the many purposes for which those engaged in planning economic development or making economic policies require knowledge, and if possible statistical knowledge. Without it an administrator is fumbling in the dark. With it he is half-way to a solution. It is very remarkable how the statistical knowledge of Africa has increased during the twenty-five years since the present writer found himself collaborating in Lord Hailey's *African Survey* ; at that time national income statistics were virtually non-existent. One knew very little quantitatively regarding Africa beyond the erratic and incomparable trade statistics, the uncertain guesses of populations and the heroic attempts of Professor Frankel to estimate capital investment. But even today there are serious *lacunae*. To take but a few examples, one knows almost nothing about the educational or professional qualifications of immigrants and emigrants and thus far too little about the actual stocks at any time of high-level manpower and entrepreneuring capacity. Far too little is known about the subsequent employment of Africans who have received education to different levels. Far too little is known, again, about the production of the self-subsistence economy and the extent of its transition towards the monetary economy. Very little is known about the volume of internal trade. Very little is known about costs of transport and handling to regions remote from the ports and the effects of these on prices. Very little is known quantitatively about small-scale industry in Africa or about the origins of the entrepreneurs of small-scale industry.

Some of these are *lacunae* which could be filled by suitable questions in the population censuses of Africa. Some could be filled by better industrial censuses. Some represent questions on which individual research by academic economists could throw valuable light. Some of the major issues of African development — the better understanding of the problems of balance, for example, between fixed capital investment and investment in education — depend on more research outside Africa as well as inside it.

To this growing body of knowledge, both academic economists in Africa and in other countries are making their contributions. An even greater contribution is coming from the work of the Economic Commission for Africa established in Addis Ababa and to whose studies this Conference was deeply indebted. Their stimulus to more and better statistics and more comparable statistics has been invaluable. But there remains great scope for further work and the encouragement to it that more detailed knowledge and understanding of the problems of Africa can greatly contribute to African development and welfare.

The success of the Conference owed much to the help and hospitality of the Economic Commission for Africa and its then Director-General Dr. M. Abbas. The Conference was held in the newly opened Africa Hall, built for the use of the Commission by the Government of Ethiopia, where we enjoyed all the advantages of a conference-room completely equipped for simultaneous translation. It owed much also to the welcome and encouragement of H.I.M. The Emperor Haile Sellassie and the Ministers and Officials of his Government. To all of these we express our very grateful thanks.

PART I

Chapter 1

ECONOMIC DEVELOPMENT IN AFRICA: AIMS AND POSSIBILITIES

BY

G. J. LIGTHART and B. ABBAI

UN Economic Commission for Africa : Addis Ababa

I. INTRODUCTION

MUCH that has recently been said and written with respect to economic development, particularly in a semi-popular vein, is connected with Rostow's *Stages of Economic Growth*.[1] It is not our intention to start another 'Methodenstreit' when we say Rostow's main weakness is in his method. In a gathering of professional economists it certainly need not be repeated that historical observation is necessary to bring together facts and describe situations as a starting-point for analysis, but that the inductive method, consisting of generalization of common elements in observed situations, does not necessarily lead to an effective explanation of events.

It will be recalled that Rostow distinguishes five stages of growth : (1) the 'traditional society', in which a 'ceiling exists on the level of attainable output per head' resulting from 'the fact that the potentialities which flow from modern science and technology were either not available' (the pre-industrial revolution case) 'or not regularly and systematically applied' [2] (the under-developed country case) ; (2) the 'pre-conditions for take-off', where the traditional society is transformed in the ways necessary to start application of modern technology in production ; [3] (3) the 'take-off', where 'old blocks and resistances to steady growth are finally overcome' and where 'the forces making for economic progress . . . expand and come to dominate the Society. Growth becomes its normal condition' ; [4] (4) the 'drive to maturity', where 'the now regularly growing economy drives to extend modern technology over the whole front of its economic activity' ; [5] (5) the 'age of high mass-consumption', where the 'resources tend increasingly to be directed to the production

[1] W. W. Rostow, *The Stages of Economic Growth* (Cambridge University Press, 1960).   [2] *Op. cit.* p. 4.
[3] *Op. cit.* p. 6.   [4] *Op. cit.* p. 7.   [5] *Op. cit.* p. 9.

of consumer durables and to the diffusion of services on a mass basis'.[1]

Already from this summing-up it appears that the crucial concept in Rostow's structure is his 'take-off' stage, which can be defined only in terms of the state of steady growth which follows it. Unfortunately this state of growth 'sustained and self-reinforcing' is not defined, nor is it proven that it indeed is or can become a normal condition and, with respect to the advanced countries, it certainly seems a bold assumption. The weakness shows particularly in Rostow's discussion of the first 'take-off': the 'take-off' of the industrial revolution in England (which might more properly be regarded as the 'take-off' of the leading industrial countries, which achieved their rapid industrial growth as a group rather than as individual cases, although the starting-point varied somewhat from one country to another), where neither the 'take-off' nor the necessity of the ensuing economic growth is explained: the entire process as depicted remains very much of a historical accident.[2] Indeed, why England in the 1780's, why not Ancient Egypt or Imperial Rome or China many centuries ago, as Lewis asks implicitly in the preface to his book?[3] Was it Arkwright's mechanical spinning or the invention of the steam engine, or did the others experience one or more last inhibiting factors which they could not overcome? Answers to these questions would be exceedingly interesting; but although their solution obviously cannot be left to the economic historian alone, they need not concern us here.

Looking at the process of economic development and the stages it passes through — if, in principle, there are such stages, sufficiently clear-cut to be recognized at all times — it seems useful to distinguish between two different cases: (1) the historical development of the now leading industrial nations, and (2) the process of catching up by less developed countries, which is at present under way in a few instances. In the former case, the criticism of Rostow's argument has its full validity; in the latter, however, it can be argued that the example of relatively advanced economies and the existence of stores of knowledge and experience exert a continuous pull on the less developed economies, thus creating a force which may cause a sustained growth process if no bottlenecks or other obstructions develop. But, even in these cases, the necessity for sustained growth until the backlog is recovered is not proven and does not seem to exist: the strictly logical objections inherent in the method applied

[1] W. W. Rostow, *The Stages of Economic Growth* (Cambridge University Press, 1960), p. 11.
[2] *Op. cit.* p. 31.
[3] W. A. Lewis, *The Theory of Economic Growth*, p. 6.

by Rostow remain, though his concepts acquire greater acceptability here than they have in the former case.

The overall growth of an economy is composed of forward thrusts of separate industries gaining in impetus and levelling off, not only stimulating and strengthening but also, at times, obstructing each other's growth.[1] Lack of expansion of certain industries or certain facilities may put a brake on the forward surge by causing bottlenecks. If the impetus of the advancing industries is great enough, this by itself will provide an expansionary force for the lagging sectors ; however, if it is not, or if removal of the bottleneck needs a long gestation period (*e.g.* in the case of education), the general growth process may be stopped altogether. Hence it is generally necessary for possible bottlenecks caused by such facilities (mainly education, transport, energy, etc.) to be sufficiently cleared before the growth process starts in the more directly productive industries. Therefore, it seems true that a 'pre-condition for take-off' stage has to precede a period of growth if the latter is to be sustained ; but this is Rostow's argument in reverse.

Perhaps one reason why, in observed history, economies which have once started a process of expansion either experience a more or less sustained growth or at least resume interrupted growth more easily, may be the fact that any bottlenecks encountered are likely to be fewer and less serious, hence more easily removed, than those existing before 'take-off' (to use the term loosely), the economy thus resuming its growth under weaker exogenous impulses.

Subject to the qualifications regarding theoretical validity mentioned above, it may perhaps be assumed that there exists some sort of course of development for under-developed countries making up their backlogs roughly along the lines described by Rostow. In the following pages an endeavour will be made to chart the early stretches of that course and to fix the position of a number of selected African countries along the route. Subsequently the aims of governments and their efforts to move forward will be discussed and linked with the existing situation and apparent possibilities.

The countries selected and discussed in the following pages are :

[1] On p. 53, after he has developed his stages of growth in terms of the overall economy, Rostow brings up the aspects of separate sector growth saying : 'At any period of time it appears to be true even in a mature and growing economy that forward momentum is maintained as the result of rapid expansion in a limited number of primary sectors whose expansion has significant external economy and other secondary effects'. Then, however, he suggests that sector growth is only a special case of overall growth rather than that overall growth is composed of growth of individual industries : 'From this perspective the behaviour of sectors during the take-off is merely a special version of the growth process in general ; or, put another way, growth proceeds by repeating endlessly, in different patterns, with different leading sectors, the experience of the take-off'.

Cameroun, Congo (Léopoldville), Ethiopia, Federation of Rhodesia and Nyasaland, Ghana, Guinea, Ivory Coast, Kenya, and Nigeria : a sample of nine countries out of more than thirty major countries and territories between Sahara and Limpopo, giving a coverage of 55 per cent in terms of population. The inclusion in a number of cases of indicators for Mexico in the early 1950s may give a rough pointer to the way ahead. Since that country is believed to have entered the 'take-off' stage during that period, it provides a convenient bench-mark against which the situation in the selected countries may be compared.

II. THE WAY AHEAD

A. *Structure of Production and Trade*

Economic development is normally associated with structural changes in the economy. Given a balanced distribution of resources, development usually involves, in the course of time, a growing share of non-agricultural output and services in the total gross national product. It may probably be assumed that in the relatively less-developed countries' development follows a path of diversification of production from a closed agricultural economy to, roughly, the situation which prevails in the leading industrial nations of the world. This assumption should, however, be handled with caution, particularly as the end-phase is not very precisely defined and may in fact show rather wide variations due to resource endowment and to the growth process itself, as well as to the community's conscious or unconscious preferences and valuations with regard both to final aims and to the means of achieving them. But it may still be useful as a working hypothesis for the purposes of this study.

When production per head increases, in a closed economy changes in the production pattern are necessarily determined by changes in the expenditure pattern. If development is to continue, the increase in income, identical with the increase in production, must be split in some proportion between increased capital formation and increased consumption, so that the expenditure pattern, in turn, is determined by the rate of expansion of the economy and by changes in the consumption pattern resulting from the increase in income. Assuming that consumer preferences of different peoples at each income level are fairly similar, it cannot be too difficult to determine what stages the expenditure pattern, and consequently for a closed economy the production pattern, will pass through during its process of growth. Owing to the limitations on our

6

physical capacity to consume, and from past experience, we can expect the production pattern to shift away from basic foodstuffs and semi-durables such as textiles and shoes to durable consumer goods and products entailing increasing ratios of machine processes. In addition, an increasing rate of capital formation will reinforce the shift towards metal and electrical manufacturing industries. In the following pages the production patterns of the selected countries will be used as an indicator to fix their position in the development process.

In an open economy — and the economies concerned are quite open — things are considerably less simple than in a closed one, as the domestic patterns of production and expenditure can, to a large extent, be adjusted to each other by exports and imports. Consequently, certain corrections will have to be applied to the indicators based on the production patterns mentioned above. It will be clear that a country which exports part of its agricultural production in exchange for industrial products is at a different stage of development from the country which consumes its entire agricultural production locally, all other things being equal. In principle a country which exchanges a considerable part of its national product need not be considered to be behind another country which produces locally the different product categories which the former imports. However, this other country does not depend for its expansion so much on foreign demand for its main export commodities and has, because of its more diversified production pattern, greater opportunities for developing an indigenous process of reciprocal stimulation of industries. Thus, the fact that a country has a mining industry producing for export does not indicate the same degree of advancement as where such an industry also provides for the domestic market and is integrated in the industrial establishment of the country. Therefore in the tables below the pattern of foreign trade will be linked to the pattern of production to give as complete a picture as possible of the structure of the economies under discussion.

It seems appropriate to start the statistical comparison with some general data. Table 1 (see p. 8) lists a few aspects of population and population density.

It is a commonplace among students of African conditions to say that it is impossible to make generalizations. This is unfortunately no less true for individual countries than for the continent as a whole : wide and profound regional variations in characteristics exist in almost every respect within national boundaries as much as among different countries. Differences in population density — as shown in the table, and particularly in the column for range of

7

TABLE 1

POPULATION AND POPULATION DENSITY

	Area (000 sq. km.)	Total Population (in. mil.)	Non-Indigenous (in % of total)*	Population Density (p. sq. km.)	Range of Density	National Increase (in %)
Ethiopia	1,184	20·0	0	17	—	1·6
Guinea	246	2·6	0	10	5–169	2·2
Nigeria	878	31·2	0	36	7–157	—
Cameroun	432	3·2	0	7	1–94	2·1
Ghana	238	6·7	0	28	2–71	3·1
Ivory Coast	322	3·1	0	8	2–25	3·1
Congo (Léopoldville)	2,345	12·0	1	6	—	2·0
Kenya	583	6·4	4	11	1–49	—
Rhodesian Federation	1,253	7·0	3	6	—	—
Northern Rhodesia	746	2·3	3	3	—	2·5
Southern Rhodesia	387	2·0	9	5	—	3·0
Nyasaland	119†	2·7	0	23	—	—

* 0 means less than ½ per cent.   † 20 per cent of which consists of lake surface.

density — are a first indication of such variations. None of the countries under discussion has, as yet, achieved the state of a single integrated economy, or even nation, the typical feature being that of weakly linked and more or less self-sufficient local economic units. Pockets of development exist alongside areas living in different degrees of isolation. Consequently, in the case of all country averages shown below, the uneven distribution of economic activity should be kept in mind.

With regard to Table 1, attention should also be drawn to the distribution of the non-indigenous population, which does not appear from the table. In most cases these groups are concentrated in a few urban or sub-urban communities or rural areas, which of course considerably alters the percentage for any particular region. But for a given country as a whole the size of the non-indigenous community has rather far-reaching effects on the type and pattern of economic activity as well as on the social structure and political situation, to which allusion will be made below.

The size and characteristics of the primary production sectors agriculture and mining are considered in Table 2 (see p. 10), in addition to two indicators for the degree of monetization of the economy : wage and salary earners as a percentage of total population and the value of exports per head in U.S. dollars.

It should be kept in mind that estimates of national product and its breakdown over the major sectors are on the whole subject to rather wide margins of error. Estimates for agricultural production, particularly subsistence production, as well as for commerce or trade and 'other services' are inevitably rather conjectural. Arbitrary variations in those estimates therefore necessarily affect the percentage shares of all other sectors. This should be taken as an explanation of certain seemingly inexplicable variations in the percentage shares of agriculture in GDP between countries (Table 3 shows that high estimates for commerce and services in the cases of Guinea and Cameroun depress the shares for agriculture).

Similarly, rather serious qualifications attach to figures for active population engaged in agriculture, as much depends, *e.g.*, on the estimate of women engaged ; the figures should accordingly be taken with a grain of salt. It seems reasonable to assume that, on a comparable basis, this percentage may be somewhere between 85 and 95 for the first six countries in Table 2.

Exports of agricultural produce as a percentage of GDP show an interesting trend. They rise, as agricultural production develops and more of it is traded, up to a certain point beyond which they start to decline as non-agricultural exports are increasingly taking

9

TABLE 2

PRIMARY PRODUCTION SECTORS

	Primary Production % GDP	Mining % GDP	% Active Population engaged in Agriculture	Agricultural Sector			Wage and Salary Earners as % of Total Population	Value, in U.S. $, of Exports per Head of Population
				% GDP	Agricultural Exports % GDP (% of Agr. prod.)	Subsistence Production % of GDP		
Ethiopia	62	0	90	62	9(15)	50	0	3
Guinea	50	2	87	48	9(19)	36	4	9
Nigeria	64	1	78	63	12(19)	30-33	2	14
Cameroun	52	3	91	49	18(37)	34	4	35
Ghana	64-69	4	70	60-65 *	18(30)	30-33	5	45
Ivory Coast	65	0	91	65 †	30(46)	30	6	49
Congo (Léopoldville)	47	16	85	31	15(48)	12	8	35
Kenya	43	1	80	42	13(31)	25	9	21
Rhodesian Federation	34	14	80	20	8(40)	9	13	70
Mexico, 1950	24	4	58	20	3(15)	...	15	20

* Estimates. † For the entire A.O.F.

their place. This trend is roughly followed by the percentage of agricultural production exported, since with the expansion of other sectors of the economy surpluses from the agricultural sector are more and more needed for the domestic market.

The pattern for Mexico shows interesting differences with those of the selected African countries. Its inclusion, however, does not necessarily mean that countries reaching the 'take-off' stage will all have more or less the same structural aspects, though it will be agreed that both the global shifts (from primary to secondary and tertiary activities) and the structural shifts of individual sectors (from food processing, textiles, etc., to durable consumer goods) of countries in the 'take-off' stage are probably of the same order of magnitude. Apart from the global and sectoral shifts in the composition of output, it will also be agreed that a minimum degree of saturation in the economy of infra-structural investments is an essential condition of the 'take-off'.

Thus such comparisons with Mexico — in terms both of structural levels and of levels attained in the provision of basic facilities, *e.g.* transport, consumption of electricity and fuels, as well as a degree of literacy and higher education — as will be made later on, will fix the probable stage each country has reached on the path of development. There is another advantage in these comparisons, namely, that when a country reaches the 'take-off' stage we can assume that the right balance has been achieved among the various structural levels which may be described as the 'conditions of take-off'. This assumption of the 'right balance' in the total 'conditions of take-off' is important because of the danger of thinking that, because certain sectors or basic facilities have reached an advanced stage of development, irrespective of the levels reached in other spheres, 'take-off' is likely to occur.

Table 3 (see p. 12) shows the percentage distribution of industrial origin of GDP by broad categories. As already mentioned, wide margins of error in the estimates, particularly for agriculture and for transport, commerce, and services, introduce certain arbitrary elements into this table. The smaller figures, however, are less affected by these 'incomparabilities' than the larger ones.

If for the first five countries of this table the totals for transport, commerce, and services were taken to be 23, the agricultural sectors would be 72, 65, 63, 66, and 66 per cent respectively, which would probably less approximately reflect the relative positions of the respective countries. The relatively high figure for electricity production in the Federation is due to high consumption by the mining industry. Congo (Léopoldville) would have shown a high figure,

TABLE 3

DISTRIBUTION OF INDUSTRIAL ORIGIN OF GDP

(Percentages)

	Total	Agriculture	Mining	Manufacturing	Building and Construction	Electricity, Gas, and Water	Transport and Communications	Commerce	Services	Total of Transport, Commerce, and Services
Ethiopia	100	62	0	2	3	0·2	5	13 §	15	33
Guinea	100	48	2	2	7	0·7	24		16	40
Nigeria	100	63	1	2	11	0·0	15		8	23
Cameroun	100	49	3	5 †	3	0·0	6	36	18	40
Ghana	100	60–65 *	4	3	4	0·3	24–29 *	24–29 *	23	24–29
Congo (Léopoldville)	100	31	16	10	4	‡	9	7	23	39
Kenya	100	42	1	10	4	1·0	8	13	21	42
Rhodesian Federation	100	20	14	12	8	2·3	6	16	22	44
Mexico, 1950	100	20	4	18	2	0·5	4	31	20	55

* Estimates. † Includes handicrafts. ‡ Included in mining and manufacturing. § Includes handicrafts : 5.

too, but for the fact that the contribution by this branch of industry is not shown separately. The high figure for construction in Nigeria is connected with a building boom experienced in that country during the late 1950s.

As can be readily seen, the level of manufacturing output for all the countries selected compared with Mexico (about 20 per cent) is generally low. The relatively 'more developed group' of countries, including the Federation of Rhodesia and Nyasaland, Congo (Léopoldville), and Kenya, have reached the level of net output in total GDP ranging from 10-12 per cent. The rest of the group may well be regarded as still 'undeveloped', the level of net output for these countries in total GDP lying well below 5 per cent.

As the process of industrialization continues, the composition and scope of manufacturing output also alters in the following successive, fairly recognizable, stages :

   (i) food processing and textiles ;
  (ii) intermediate products for further processing (chemicals, metals, and building materials) ;
 (iii) various kinds of consumer goods ;
 (iv) capital goods.

A breakdown of manufacturing industry should show a shift from light consumer goods to heavy industries as industry develops.

An analysis of the composition of manufacturing output by kinds of products processed (see Table 4, p. 14) also shows a clear distinction between the more developed and undeveloped groups of countries. The percentage of net manufacturing output indicates that in the case of the former a sizeable proportion of industrial output is devoted to the production of intermediate products and basic materials, such as industrial materials, metal processing and building materials. In these countries, the proportion of food production and textiles in total manufacturing output is somewhat smaller than in the case of the undeveloped group of countries, where industrial production is still largely confined to the production of foodstuffs and to some extent textiles, etc. It may therefore be said that the more developed countries have entered the second production phase while the undeveloped ones are still in the first phase.

A few remarks with regard to disturbances in the pattern may, however, still be in order. A main disturbing factor arises from the chemical industry in the Cameroun, as soap manufacturing and to some extent oil expressing are included in it. In Cameroun only one factory of the chemical industries group, one for liquefied gas,

TABLE 4

COMPOSITION OF MANUFACTURING OUTPUT
SELECTED AFRICAN COUNTRIES

(Percentages)
1958

	All Manufacturing	Food, Beverages, Tobacco	Textiles, Footwear	Wood, Furniture	Paper, Printing	Leather, Leather Goods	Construction Materials (non-metallic products)	Chemicals	Metals, Metal Goods and Repairs	Miscellaneous
Ethiopia (1958) Net output	100	58	19	3	2	3	7	..	..	8
Guinea (1956) Employment	100	23	7	60	..	..	..	..	10	..
Cameroun (1956) Gross output	100	44	8	15	1	1	2	17	12	..
Ghana (1958) Net output	100	41	..	34	7	1	1	3	7	6
Congo (1959) Employment	100	16	11	8	8	..	4	46	12	..
Kenya (1958) Net output	100	25	6	9	8	..	8	7	31	6
Rhodesian Federation (1958)	100	20	11	6	7	..	11	5	28	2
Mexico (1950)	100	30	17	5	4	1	4	9	27	3

TABLE 5

COMPOSITION OF IMPORTS : SELECTED COUNTRIES

	Year of Reference	Value of Imports by Major Commodity Groups				Percentage Distribution of Imports by Major Commodity Groups			
		Total	Food, Beverages, Tobacco	Materials and Fuels	Manufactures	Total	Food, Beverages, Tobacco	Materials and Fuels	Manufactures
Ethiopia	Av. 1956/7–1958/9 (millions Eth. $)	187·1	16·2	33·5	137·4	100	9	18	73
Guinea	Av. 1956/8 (billions F. CFA)	8·0	0·5	1·8	5·7	100	6	23	71
Nigeria	Av. 1956/8 (billions F. CFA)	148·0	24·3	23·8	100·0	100	16	16	68
Cameroun	Av. 1958/9 (millions £)	21·7	3·6	4·2	13·9	100	17	19	64
Ghana	Av. 1956/8 (billions F. CFA)	88·3	19·5	15·7	53·1	100	22	18	60
Ivory Coast	Av. 1957/8 (millions £)	12·3	3·3	2·9	6·1	100	27	23	50
Congo	Av. 1957/8 (billions F. Congolese)	18·4	2·7	2·4	13·4	100	14	13	73
Kenya	Av. 1957/8 (millions £)	71·4	10·6	15·3	45·5	100	15	21	64
Rhodesian Federation	Av. 1956/8 (millions £)	160·7	15·9	35·6	109·2	100	10	22	68
Mexico	Imports: Av. 1955/8 (millions of pesos)	12,070·0	927·0	3,468·0	7,674·0	100	8	39	53
	Exports: Av. 1955/8 (millions of pesos)	9,436·4	2,438·8	3,221·6	3,771·0	100	26	34	40

manufactures producer materials. Such, however, is not the case in Congo (Léopoldville), where, apart from soap and perfumes, the chemical industries produce a whole range of producer goods — from explosives, sulphuric acid and insecticides to glycerine, paints and varnish, and bottles. A high percentage of metal goods industries in Cameroun, due to the special resource position, is largely accounted for by one enterprise producing aluminium articles based on the country's aluminium industry.

The percentages for the production of food, beverages, and tobacco, and of textiles and footwear for Guinea, Cameroun, and Ghana are lower than they normally would have been, owing to a rather important wood industry working for export. If wood production is excluded, for those countries the shares of the food and textile industries are 58, 52, and 62 respectively.

Analysis of the structure of imports is made difficult by the fact that in the process of development several shifts between commodity categories are superimposed on each other, while the actual resource endowment of the countries also puts its mark on the trade pattern.

Data on import patterns indicate significant differences among the countries selected and these differences would appear to be very closely related to the countries' industrial output patterns. In general, their import patterns are characterized by a high level of processed food products, beverages, and tobacco ; a low level of imports of industrial materials ; a high level of imports of building materials and fuels ; a moderately low level of machines and equipment ; and an excessively high level of textiles, footwear, clothing, and other consumer goods. Shifts that can be expected to take place more or less simultaneously would be : (1) an increase in imports of industrial materials due to increased domestic production, (2) a decrease in imports of finished consumer goods, and (3) an increase in imports of capital goods ; (4) relative changes in food imports would depend on production margins existing in agriculture, but would normally be in a downward direction owing to the simultaneous modernization of that sector.

Table 5 (see p. 15) shows the value of imports by broad commodity groups as well as the percentage distribution of these commodity groups in total imports for the nine countries and Mexico. A glance at this table shows that the level of imports of food, beverages, and tobacco is rather high compared with the corresponding level for Mexico (8 per cent). At the same time, the level of imports of industrial materials and fuels is generally low compared with Mexico (39 per cent), although the proportion of mineral fuels and building materials in the total imports of materials is much

TABLE 6

COMPOSITION OF IMPORTS OF MATERIALS AND FUELS

Country	Year of Reference	Total	Mineral Fuels	Industrial Materials	Building Materials	All Materials and Fuels	Manu-factures
Ethiopia	Av. 1956/7–1958/9	100	12	4	3	19	81
Guinea	Av. 1956/8	100	6	11	6	23	77
Nigeria	Av. 1956/8	100	7	8	5	20	80
Cameroun	Av. 1958/9	100	7	15	0	23	77
Ghana	Av. 1956/8	100	9	8	6	23	77
Ivory Coast	Av. 1957/8	100	16	10	6	32	68
Congo	Av. 1957/8	100	10	4	2	16	84
Kenya	Av. 1957/8	100	15	8	4	27	73
Rhodesian Federation	Av. 1956/8	100	6	14	4	24	76
Mexico	Imports : Av. 1955/8	100	6	24	—	30	70
	Exports : Av. 1955/8	100	8	38	—	46	54

TABLE 7

COMPOSITION OF IMPORTS OF MANUFACTURES
(As % of total manufactures)

	Year of Reference	Total	Textiles, Footwear, etc.	Consumer Goods (excluding Textiles, etc.)	Machinery and Equipment	Transport Equipment	Not specified
Ethiopia	Av. 1956/7–1958/9	100	35	28	15	17	5
Guinea	Av. 1956/8	100	26	10	38	16	9
Nigeria	Av. 1956/8	100	41	19	15	22	3
Cameroun	Av. 1958/9	100	22	52	6	20	—
Ghana	Av. 1956/8	100	38	25	15	19	3
Ivory Coast	Av. 1957/8	100	35	24	27	14	—
Congo	Av. 1957/8	100	14	44	23	18	1
Kenya	Av. 1957/8	100	17	32	17	22	12
Rhodesian Federation	Av. 1956/8	100	22	22	33	23	—
Mexico Imports:	Av. 1955/8	100	5	20	50	25	—
Exports:	Av. 1955/8	100	77	21	1	1	—

higher than that of Mexico. The result is that the proportion of manufactures in total imports for all the countries is as high as 70 per cent, compared with about 50 per cent of that of Mexico. In the case of the more developed group of countries (Congo (Leopoldville), Kenya, and the Rhodesias) a shift would appear to have taken place from food imports to imports of materials, whereas in the case of the undeveloped group of countries food imports still account for a high proportion of total imports.

Table 6 (see p. 17) shows the level as well as the composition of imports of fuels and materials in total non-food imports. The percentage shares of fuel imports naturally reflect the domestic resource position in that category. This is particularly clear in the case of the Federation and Congo (Leopoldville). The years covered for Nigeria are not sufficiently recent to reflect the development of an oil industry.

The level of industrial imports varies considerably from country to country. In general, imports of industrial materials are of considerably less importance in these countries than in Mexico (24 per cent), although Mexico has reached a stage at which it exports significant quantities of industrial materials (some 38 per cent of total non-food exports). Among the developed group, Congo (Leopoldville) and Kenya have the smallest proportion of imports of industrial materials, largely because in these two countries' domestic production of industrial chemicals, metals and related materials plays a significant rôle in their total manufacturing output. It may be that there has been considerable substitution in domestic production of industrial materials in the more developed group of countries, or else that domestic raw materials are processed.

All countries depend to some extent on imported building materials, those least so dependent being the more developed countries. But, on the whole, the level of industrial materials is low and the level of manufactures still high in total non-food imports, reflecting the fact that, given the structure of domestic industrial production, only minor quantities of manufactures are produced for the domestic market.

Table 7 (see p. 18) shows the percentage distribution of imported manufactures. It can be seen from this table that the level of imported textiles, footwear, etc., is on the whole excessively high as compared with Mexico (5 per cent). In the case of the more developed countries (Kenya, Congo (Leopoldville), and the Federation of Rhodesia and Nyasaland), the level of textile imports is somewhat lower than for the rest of the group. This would appear to be reasonable, since the textile industries have reached a somewhat advanced stage in these countries and domestic production of textile goods accounts for a much higher proportion of total apparent consumption than in the case of the undeveloped group of countries.

Imports of machinery and equipment vary considerably from country to country, but the general level in all countries is decidedly lower than that for Mexico (50 per cent). It would appear from the table that the more developed group of countries, as well as Ghana and Guinea, import fairly high proportions of machinery and equipment as compared with the rest of the group.

The level of transport equipment in total imported manufactures would appear to be reasonable as compared with Mexico (25 per cent). Imports of consumer goods, excluding textiles and footwear, are still high, reflecting the fact that hardly any of the countries have reached the stage of producing consumer goods and depend almost exclusively on imports. It is clear from Tables 5-7 and from the comments in the preceding paragraphs that a close relationship exists between the pattern of imports and the structure of industrial output. A fair conclusion from the analysis contained in the tables would be that the relatively more developed group of countries show quite a favourable structure of imports from the angle of industrial development, namely, a rather lower level of imports of food, beverages, and textiles, a higher level of imports of machinery and equipment, and a somewhat lower level of imports of building materials. This indicates both an increased level of industrial activity and a relatively wider range of industrial production in the countries concerned.

B. *Infrastructure*

In the previous section some basic tables were elaborated with a view to determining levels of economic progress in terms of the structural changes achieved by selected African countries. The present section will deal with the provision of basic facilities, *i.e.* energy, transport, and education (levels of school enrolment and literacy).

From the point of view of government policy, it is obviously important to know what kind of situation is required for some sort of self-generating process of expansion (loosely, a 'take-off stage') to start, not as a reflection of what happened elsewhere in the past but as a logical minimum requirement in the present. A more precise study of 'take off' requirements in all or most relevant aspects, with a stronger theoretical basis than Rostow offers, and a closer analysis of the 'take-off stage' itself, with its process of reciprocal generation of expanding industries, would be of great

value for the policy-makers in under-developed countries. Pending
systematic analytical work in those directions, the following pages
can offer only some haphazard and provisional aspects of the problem,
even omitting certain vital — socio-political — aspects relating to
human attitudes and reactions, social structures and social values,
and social and economic institutions, in favour of aspects which
can be expressed quantitatively at present : energy, transport, and
education.

Some basic tables have been elaborated for the purpose of comparing selected African countries in the matter of provision of basic
facilities. These tables are again cast in comparative terms and
contain generally accepted global indices, though these are by no
means exhaustive. Data on Mexico relating to corresponding levels
in the provision of basic facilities are also incorporated in the tables.

Energy and Fuel Consumption. As the level of energy and fuel
consumption is normally taken as an indicator of the degree of
urbanization and industrialization, it would be of interest to compare
the selected African countries in that respect.

Table 8 (see below) summarizes the position of these countries
regarding electricity consumption, installed capacity and total energy
consumption in kg. coal equivalent. Here the disparities between

TABLE 8

ELECTRICITY AND ENERGY CONSUMPTION

	Electricity Con- sumption (mil. KWH)	Electricity Con- sumption per Head of Population (KWH)	Installed Capacity (KW per 000 of popula- tion)	Energy Consumption per Head of Population (kg. coal equivalent)
Ethiopia	87	5	2	8
Guinea	17	7	6	..
Nigeria	430	14	4	42
Cameroun	53 *	17 *	40 †	77 †
Ghana	340	51	14	52
Ivory Coast	48	15	4	..
Congo (Leopoldville)	1,890 †	158 †	58 †	109 †
Kenya	328	51	13	150 ‡
Rhodesian Federation	1,320 §	189 §	129 †	557 †
Mexico, 1950	5,074	197	48	590

* Excluding consumption by metal-refining industries ; total consumption : 675;
electricity consumption per head : 211.
† Including capacity used for and consumption by metal-refining industries.
‡ Consumption, 1954.
§ Excluding consumption by metal-refining industries ; total consumption : 3,540;
consumption per head : 506.

countries are considerable. As can be seen from the table, the leading countries in total energy consumption are the three in the relatively more developed group, viz. the Federation of Rhodesia and Nyasaland, Kenya, and Congo (Leopoldville) in that order, and the total energy consumption recorded by the first-named of these is about the same as that of Mexico in 1950.

In the case of the Federation of Rhodesia and Nyasaland and Congo, the bulk of total energy consumption consists of electricity ; this fact is reflected in their higher levels of installed capacity per head. It is to be noted that most of the electricity produced in the Federation of Rhodesia and Nyasaland and Congo is consumed by the mining and metal-processing industries. Something very similar applies to Cameroun, with its aluminium-processing industry.

The level of installed capacity in Kenya is low because that country imports electricity from Tanganyika and Uganda.

Transport. Adequate provision of transport facilities, with consequent lowering of transport costs, constitutes perhaps the most important single prerequisite for economic progress. Furthermore, the lack of adequate transport facilities inhibits the mobility of goods and services and thus 'polarizes' the domestic markets by creating spatial discontinuity. Division of labour and specialization become restricted. The 'polarization' of domestic markets exercises an unfavourable influence on industrial growth, as it normally makes for lower capacities and high costs.

In the case of the selected African countries, mention must be made of some special factors which have a bearing on the overall problem of transport. The generally low income levels in these countries result in what are often called 'thinner' markets. Population densities are also low, which would imply that a given level of transport facilities in these countries is much less effective than it would be in populous regions. These considerations suggest that an appraisal of the present levels attained by these countries in the provision of transport facilities is of paramount importance.

Table 9 (see p. 23) shows available transport facilities in the selected African countries. It should be noted that the data relate only to railroads, roads, and commercial vehicles. The omission of water transport constitutes a serious gap, as that mode of transport is especially important in some countries, like Congo and Nigeria. Coast-wise shipping, which is important in some West African countries, has also been disregarded. As can be seen from the table, railroad densities (lengths of railroad per 1,000 sq. km.) are extremely low compared with Mexico. The leading countries in railway development include Ghana, the Ivory Coast, and the

TABLE 9

TRANSPORT FACILITIES

	Length of Railroads (km.)	Length of Railroads per 1,000 sq. km.	Length of All-weather Roads (km.)	Length of All-weather Roads per 1,000 sq. km.*	No. of Commercial Vehicles	No. of Commercial Vehicles per 1,000 sq. km.	No. of Commercial Vehicles per 000 of Population
Ethiopia	784	0·7	4,761	4	6,434	5	0·3
Guinea	696	2·8	7,600	31	5,000	20	1·8
Nigeria	2,880	3·3	21,144	24	23,000	26	0·7
Cameroun	500	1·2	3,918	9	12,000	28	3·8
Ghana	1,198	5·1	7,200	30	14,434	61	2·2
Ivory Coast	1,307	4·1	16,740	52	13,119	41	4·2
Congo (Leopoldville)	5,822	2·5	27,062	12	23,000	10	1·6
Kenya	1,600	2·7	15,129	26	11,180	19	2·0
Rhodesian Federation	4,841	3·9	70,000	56	45,300	36	6·5
Mexico, 1950	23,259	11·8	24,864†	13†	130,000	66	5·1

* Equals per cent of country within 5 km. of a road.

† Hard-surface roads only.

Federation of Rhodesia and Nyasaland; but in provision of railroads even these countries fall from 2 to 3 times below the level attained by Mexico.

The spatial distribution of railroads shows about the same pattern for all the countries. Most of the railroads link the ports to certain focal points in the interior, because, by and large, railroad construction has been closely associated with the development of foreign trade in general and of mining in particular (FRN, Congo). Foreign trade still plays a dominant rôle in the overall commerce of these countries. The spatial densities of railroads (ports-oriented) reflect the existing imbalance between the export sector and domestic trade and suggest that domestic markets are still insufficiently developed.

As far as road transport is concerned, a figure for the length of roads per sq. km. (see Table 9, column 4) can also be interpreted as the percentage of the country lying within 5 km. of a road. According to that index, there are considerable variations from country to country in the provision of roads. The leading group in this respect are the Ivory Coast, Ghana, and Guinea, 52, 30, and 31 per cent respectively of whose areas are accessible. Countries in the lowest category are Congo, Cameroun, and Ethiopia, with only 12, 9, and 4 per cent respectively, which indicates that a considerable part of the interior of these countries, even excluding uninhabited regions, is far from accessible.

Another important consideration is the quality of the roads. In general, the proportion of first-class asphalted roads in the total road network is small. Again, road haulage depends almost entirely on imported fuel and spare parts, so that maintenance costs and depreciation rates are high. Data on road transport freight rates for these countries are fragmentary; but all available evidence suggests an extremely high level of transport costs.

Data on numbers of commercial vehicles (per 1,000 sq. km. and per 1,000 inhabitants) (see Table 9) are closely related to the length and quality of road networks. Here again the leading countries are Ghana, the Ivory Coast, and the Federation of Rhodesia and Nyasaland. The data on numbers of commercial vehicles per 1,000 of population give another picture and bring out differences in population density.

In conclusion, it may be said that Ghana, the Ivory Coast, the Federation of Rhodesia and Nyasaland, and Kenya constitute the leading group in the provision of transport, while Ethiopia and Cameroun are lowest as regards fixed facilities, and Ethiopia, Nigeria, and Congo (Leopoldville) show the lowest figures for commercial motor vehicles. However, it should be borne in mind that inland

24

water transport, which is of some importance precisely in Nigeria and Congo (Leopoldville), has been omitted from this comparison.

Education. The need to relate educational development to economic development in general is, perhaps justifiably, felt more in less developed than in developed countries. At a recent conference on African education, it was held that African educational programmes should be more and more related to current and prospective skill requirements of developing economies.

Brief mention must be made of two aspects of education and their significance for development, viz. the extension of education (adult and universal primary education) and the 'deepening' of education (expansion of secondary and higher levels).

(a) *Extension of Education.* While it is desirable to extend universal education to as many people as possible, experience has shown that it is costly and would lay a considerable burden on the resources of these countries. Furthermore, wholesale extension of universal education without a corresponding expansion of employment opportunities can create more problems than it solves.

However, the importance of mass education (especially adult education) for economic development is fairly well recognized. By far the greater part of the active population in these countries is still illiterate, thus constituting a mass of undifferentiated and hence much less productive labour. Adult education, appropriately planned, converts this mass of labour into a more productive co-operative factor in production. Again, as economic development and urbanization are still in their early stages, the vast majority of the active population in these countries are engaged in rural activities, mainly agriculture. Considerations regarding the value of adult education in improving productivity are therefore closely related to the appropriate methods of improving agricultural productivity. In the words of the report on African education, adult education 'produces most rapid and considerable results'[1] for economic development.

It is generally agreed that the imparting of knowledge to the adult rural population should not be confined to the mere extension of formal education (reading and arithmetic), but rather that the content of adult education should be so integrated as to take account of the complex, mostly non-economic, variables which govern the rural outlook in traditional societies. However, the view that economic development in such societies should be associated with the changing of the general 'way of life' and outlook has given rise

[1] UNESCO/EDAF/REP/6, Outline of Plan for African Educational Development.

25

to considerable problems regarding the type of education to be offered and the techniques to be used in promoting it. The new dimensions this will involve, such as the impact of modern technology on old values, etc., are likely to preoccupy governments for some time to come.

The problem created by primary education is twofold. In countries where elementary education has not reached an adequate level, a balanced expansion of secondary and higher education has been impossible, and this has created an educational bottleneck for economic development. On the other hand, in those countries where elementary education is pushed too far ahead a problem of migration to the towns has arisen, because education gives the rural child expectations of a 'way of life' that is unattainable in prevailing rural conditions.

(b) *'Deepening' of Education.* Higher education of all kinds at all levels creates specialized skills, thus increasing and extending division of labour and productivity. Specialized and higher instruction in particular are essential for structural change and overall growth. The importance of secondary education, for instance, can hardly be overemphasized : '. . . There is a whole range of jobs for which the qualification is a secondary education, with or without one or two years of specialized training to follow — secretaries, nurses, laboratory assistants, book-keepers, printers, elementary school teachers and the like. The middle and upper ranks of business consist almost entirely of secondary school products, and they are also the backbone of public administration.'[1] For that reason, secondary education is to be regarded not just as a transition to higher education but as a self-contained unit with its own goals. As one survey puts it, 'it justifies itself as an element in raising the nation's cultural level and also, as African educationalists emphasize, as a factor in economic, social, and political development'.[2]

Table 10 (see p. 27) shows the ratios of enrolment to corresponding school age groups of the population for various levels of education including primary, secondary, and higher levels. Data on primary and secondary level enrolments are based on calculations made by UNESCO.[3] As the table shows, while there are variations from country to country, the general level of primary education in selected African countries compares favourably with that attained by Mexico in 1950. As regards second-level education, the enrolment ratio

[1] W. A. Lewis in a letter to the *Economist*, London, January 10, 1959.
[2] UNESCO, Secondary Education, *African Trade & Development*, February 1961.
[3] UNESCO, *The Educational Situation in Africa Today* (UNESCO/EDAF/S.4).

attained by Ghana (29·4) is quite high compared with the ratios reached by the other countries, including Mexico (4·9). Arthur Lewis, in his letter quoted above, says : 'By back-of-the-envelope methods I have reached the conclusion that countries in our [Ghana's] state of economic development are not self-sufficient in secondary school products until about 4 per cent of each generation is entering

TABLE 10

SCHOOL ENROLMENT AND LITERACY

	First Level: Ratio of Enrolment to Population 5-15 (adjusted for duration of schooling)	Second Level: Ratio to Enrolment to Population 15-19 (adjusted for duration of schooling)	Higher Level: Ratio of Enrolment to Corresponding Age Group	Estimated Percentage of Adult Literate Population
Ethiopia	4	0·5	0·1	1–5
Guinea	19	1·1	..	..
Nigeria	43	2·9	0·1	10–15
Cameroun	78	3·0	..	5–10
Ghana	67	29·4	0·4	19–23
Ivory Coast	33	1·4	..	..
Congo (Leopold- ville)	72	3·0	..	35–40
Kenya	52	3·9	0·2	20–25
Rhodesian Federation	54	2·6	0·0	15–20
Mexico, 1950	47	4·9	1·4	57

secondary schools'. This seems to have been borne out by Mexico's experience of a decade ago. The figure of 4 per cent is admittedly arbitrary ; but the conclusion is clear. Secondary education, which Lewis calls 'one of the keys to economic development', is in varying degrees lagging behind in some of the countries listed.

It can also be seen from the table that higher education (see column 3) is still in its early stages of development. The leading country in this respect is Ghana (0·4 per cent). The other countries are well below the level reached by Ghana. When we compare this level with that reached by Mexico (1·4 per cent), it seems safe to say that the gap in African education is much more marked and much more serious in the sphere of higher education than in second-level education.

The level of literacy (see column 4) is significantly lower than that attained by Mexico (57 per cent). In general, it may be said

27

then that the standard of education achieved by the selected countries compares favourably in primary education, lags somewhat behind in secondary education (with the significant exception of Ghana), and is well behind in higher education as compared with the corresponding levels attained by Mexico.

Another problem noted in higher education is its distribution over the various fields of study. The different forms of specialized training should obviously accord with current and prospective demand for skills. A view commonly held is that higher education in Africa tends to overstress the traditional fields of arts and law to the detriment of economics, science, and engineering, the need for which will be much greater in countries undergoing industrialization.

C. *Prevailing Growth Forces*

The important point under the above heading is to ascertain whether changes are already taking place and, if so, at what speed. Supporting statistics are particularly hard to come by in Africa ; even figures for economic expansion over the last ten years are not available for more than one or two countries. In general, it can be assumed that growth rates at present are not high and that any growth over the last ten years has been rather irregular owing to fluctuations in crops and export prices, while production increases in real terms have been limited and confined to a few industries or areas. Production of export crops has expanded in some of the selected countries. The mining industry has increased its output, particularly of copper, in Congo (Leopoldville) and Northern Rhodesia, and industrial production in general has risen in Congo (Leopoldville), Southern Rhodesia, and Kenya. Any expansion in most industries other than mining has followed a rapidly dwindling impetus given by high export earnings or increased demand due to population growth (*e.g.* food crop production and domestic trade). However, as actual growth forces may supply pointers to future developments and to the relative positions of countries now and over the next few years, some figures on capital formation and savings are presented below (see Table 11, p. 29).

Ratios of capital formation and savings, being structural features of the economy, except where conditioned by fluctuating export earnings, do not readily change overnight. Savings depend on income and expenditure patterns, which are normally rather stable, and capital formation (perhaps with the sole exception of public capital expenditure) largely depends on the rather rigid given investment opportunities of the economy itself. Savings and capital

TABLE 11

RATES OF CAPITAL FORMATION AND SAVINGS

| | Gross Capital Formation as % of GDP | | | Financing of Investment in % of GDP | | | |
| | | | | Foreign | | Domestic | |
	Total	Public	Private	Public	Private	Public	Private
Ethiopia	6	3	3	2	0·5	2	2
Nigeria	11	4	7	3		8	
Cameroun	14	5	9	6	3	4	1
Ghana	13	6	7	..	..	..	..
Congo (Leopoldville)	29	11	18	6		5	18
Kenya	27	11	16	..	..	..	*
Federation of Rhodesia and Nyasaland	31	12	19	11		12	8
Mexico, 1950	14	6	8	2	0·2	11	1

* Owing to the existence of a common East African currency, no separate figures could be established for Kenya.

formation ratios are therefore an important index not only to any
change occurring but also to its scope. A breakdown of capital
formation will show whether investments are directly or indirectly
productive or largely consumptive, while a study of the financing
of investments and the composition of savings will bring out the
sources of finance (foreign or domestic) and the origin of savings,
i.e. whether voluntary (typifying popular preferences) or imposed
by the government.

Table 11 indicates a clear difference between the selected
countries and at the same time shows a shift to private investment

TABLE 12

COMPOSITION OF CAPITAL FORMATION

(In percentages)

	Building and Construction			Machinery and Equipment	
	Residential	Non-residential	Other Construction	Machinery and Equipment	Transport and Equipment
Nigeria, 1952/6	19	42		14	25
Ghana, 1953/7	58		6	36	
Kenya, 1954/8	17	17	23	22	21
Federation of Rhodesia and Nyasaland, 1954/ 1958	8	11	15	48	
			18 *		

* Investment in the mining industry.

as the rate of capital formation rises, as well as an increase in private
domestic savings. The relatively high figure for domestic savings in
Nigeria is due to high marketing board savings ; it is undoubtedly
duplicated in Ghana. The figures for Mexico in 1950 seem rather
low in comparison with Congo (Leopoldville), Kenya, and the
Federation, perhaps because Mexico during its 'take-off' had no
specially close links with a metropolitan country which could provide
the necessary additional financing.

Rostow suggests that 'the rate of net productive investment at
take-off should rise to over 10 per cent of N.N.P.'. [1] Unfortunately,
the figures in Table 11 are gross. Nor is it clear what part of investments is to be considered productive. However, generalizing this

[1] Rostow, *op. cit.* pp. 37, 39 *et seq.*

rule of thumb it appears that Congo (Leopoldville), Kenya, and the Federation have reached this stage as regards the rate of capital formation. That these countries are not in fact 'taking off' suggests that some of the other conditions for 'take-off' are not fulfilled.

Table 12 gives the composition of capital formation for four of the selected countries. It shows that as the rate of investment increases the proportion of productive investment rises also. In countries with higher rates of capital formation the share of machinery and equipment is also higher, while in those with a lower rate greater shares are taken up by public building and construction, residential building, and possibly transport equipment.

III. AIMS AND EFFORTS

A. Plans and Policies [1]

The traditional controversy regarding the rôle of the government sector and the extent as well as the character of government intervention in the operation of the national economy is well known. At the heart of this controversy lie considerations of economic welfare and the social interest. During the process of economic change, however, and especially during the earlier stages, there would appear to be additional technical reasons why the rôle of government in its capacity as an agency of growth should be emphasized. There is emerging a body of opinion in favour of relating the rôle of government to the various phases of growth and of establishing a greater degree of public intervention in the initial stages of economic progress, designed to create the basic facilities which are of crucial importance for development, especially in the 'pre-conditions' period. The argument is that in the early stages of growth the operation of the price mechanism is so limited in scope that it cannot be relied on to ensure orderly development in those sectors of the economy which require 'inputs' that are not directly profit-bearing. Even in the private sector there are strong arguments for the view that, particularly where there is a lack of domestic entrepreneurial skill and capital, the co-ordinating and promotional functions of government as well as their direct participation, are essential for industrial and commercial growth. Variations of this view would seem to have taken root in Africa.

Changes in social and political processes consequent upon and/or entailed by economic development further enhance the need for more

[1] See also *Economic Bulletin for Africa*, Vol. 1, No. 1, pp. 74-89, 'Survey of Development Programmes and Policies'.

active government participation than would normally be supposed. These changes are much more severe and likely to be more disruptive when economic progress, associated with modern technology and related 'modes of thought', impinges upon traditional societies with their own indigenous cultural values as well as self-contained social and political organizations. Smooth and appropriate changes in the social infrastructure consistent with economic change and technological progress are important and indispensable before the 'take-off' stage is reached. But since the required basic physical facilities and, more so, the social infrastructure cannot be measured in terms of gain and loss, the need for and the importance of government intervention in the development of the national economy prior to take-off assume considerable significance.

Most of the selected countries which have only recently gained their independence are undergoing among other changes a change of attitude regarding government participation in, and plans and policies for, national economic development. The present period is one that may be described as a 'formative' stage in the process of framing government plans and policies as well as experimenting with various tools and techniques, and very much will depend on social and political developments in those countries. All that can reasonably be said at the moment is that the countries are in varying degrees aware of the need for public action. They all have plans, at any rate for public capital expenditure, which indicate the emphasis to be put on each of the sectors to be developed. Table 13 (see p. 33) shows the percentage distribution of public capital expenditure under the development programme as well as government capital expenditure per head per annum in U.S. $.

If the data in columns 4, 5, and 6 of this table are related to the indicators given in Tables 8, 9, and 10 of Section II *B*, it will be noted that — with a few exceptions, such as electricity generation in the Ivory Coast, which indicates that country's concentration on agricultural exports (Nigeria is well advanced in the preparation of a hydro-electric scheme to be carried out under its next few development plans and also has substantial reserves of natural gas), and education in Ethiopia — planned action and apparent needs in infrastructure seem to match fairly well.

In general it appears from Table 13 that all the selected countries put the greatest emphasis on the development of their transport systems. This suggests that transport is the major need for the development of most African countries and that its improvement is certainly a prerequisite for any degree of growth. Inadequacy of the transport system is the main obstacle to the development of

TABLE 13

GOVERNMENT CAPITAL EXPENDITURE IN DEVELOPMENT PROGRAMMES

	Government Capital Expenditure (in U.S.$ per head per annum)	Percentage Distribution						
		Agriculture	Industry	Electricity	Transport and Communications	Education	Health	Other
Ethiopia, 1957/61	2	7	10	11	54	5	3	10
Guinea, 1960/3	15	26	21	—	18	5	4	21
Nigeria, 1955/62 †	1	1	1	7	56	10	2	27
E. Nigeria, 1958/62	2	4	8	—	25	21	5	37
W. Nigeria, 1960/5	5	23	14	2	15	8	2	36
Cameroun, 1960/5	8	32	—	—	48	8	4	8
Ghana, 1959/64	40	7	8	31	15	9	13	17
Ivory Coast, 1958/62	10	33	3 *	2	30	12	4	16
Congo (Leopoldville), 1950/9	7	6	—	7	44	5	6	32
Kenya, 1957/60	3	38	—	1	14	9	—	34
Rhodesian Federation, 1959/63 †	7	2	—	44	35	8	6	5
S. Rhodesia, 1957/61	9	13	—	28	19	2		38

* Expenditure on mineral prospecting.

† Excluding plans for regions or territories.

33

internal markets and the integration of the indigenous inhabitants into the economic vortex. Transport programmes have been prepared to open up new areas and bring them into contact with the money economy, and to create new possibilities for the evacuation of the increasing surplus production to the markets. Inadequate transport facilities may also militate against the promotion of exports. Although most existing transport systems in Africa were originally developed to serve foreign trade, they cannot cope with heavy traffic. In Guinea, for example, a road on which traffic averaged five trucks a day in the past cannot now take about five hundred trucks.

For their electricity the selected countries mostly depend on hydro-electric schemes, which have the advantage that the electricity generated is usually cheap but the disadvantage that they absorb substantial capital over a relatively short period, during which expenditure in other directions must be considerably curtailed. Most of the countries under review have recently emerged from such a period; Ghana and Nigeria are about to enter it; Kenya is fortunate enough to be able to profit from generating capacity in Uganda.

The provision of an infrastructure in transport, electricity generation and, in particular, education needs not only money but also time. These facilities must therefore be largely available before the development process can be expected to start in the more directly productive sectors of the economy. In general, however, infrastructure investments and basic facilities, although a necessary, are not a sufficient condition for economic development. The economy must begin its development process through other factors, as the mere existence of an infrastructure will not induce growth. This leads to the question whether and, if so, when developing countries should allocate a larger share of their investments to more directly productive sectors. The second and third columns of Table 13 show interesting differences in policy from one country to another with regard to these sectors. Existing plans reflect in their emphasis the political philosophies of the governments concerned.

In Congo (Leopoldville), Kenya, and the Federation the governments have followed a rather *laissez-faire* policy with regard to industry and large-scale or so-called 'European' agriculture, perhaps because the latter showed some vitality under private initiative, but probably also because of the political preferences of the predominant settler groups. In Ivory Coast and Cameroun no public capital is spent on industry either. In the remaining countries, however, and particularly in Guinea, the governments feel that a positive effort

34

on their part is required to stimulate a more rapid rate of growth. Whether this is premature, leading to subsidized industry or capital loss or both, or whether the governments concerned will succeed in simultaneously removing all remaining obstacles to take-off, only time and experience or a much more thorough analysis than can be offered here will show.

Agriculture is the remaining sector to which all governments give at least some attention in their programmes. In Congo (Leopoldville) and the Federation (as distinct from Southern Rhodesia) that attention is limited to research, with a view to improving yields and quality of production for export as well as for the domestic market. The other countries which devote more money to the agricultural sector can be roughly subdivided into : (1) those concentrating on production techniques and the production structure of traditional agriculture and going so far as to provide for agrarian reform, such as Kenya and Southern Rhodesia, and to some extent Guinea ; and (2) those concentrating on increasing and improving export crops, such as the extreme case of the Ivory Coast. Most of the others follow a blend of these two policies. Except where, as in certain cases, a country's plans are concentrated on increasing and diversifying export crops, in which case success depends on foreign markets, agricultural development need only follow *pari passu* development in other domestic sectors — after any existing deficiencies have been covered. As is well known, it is the other sectors that have to lead the way to rapid growth, permitting a shift of economically active population away from agriculture, creating domestic demand for agricultural produce and increasing productivity and income per head in the agricultural sector, and thus creating markets for their own products. However, the agricultural sector obviously not only needs to but also must develop simultaneously with the rest of the economy lest rapid growth be obstructed by agricultural bottlenecks. Some governments therefore rightly devote special attention to the necessary changes in rural life, particularly as some of them take a long time and may almost be classified as elements of the required social infrastructure.

B. *Instruments of Economic Policy and the Impact of Government*

Owing to the typical structure of the economy of the countries under review the impact of government action is much less marked than it is in the more advanced countries of the world. Many of the traditional fiscal and monetary instruments of government policy

have far less effect or none at all. Large sections of the population
pay no direct taxes, the banking system has practically no hold on
economic activity, government expenditure rapidly leaks away in
increased imports or transfers abroad, and so on. It is therefore
understandable that during the early stages of development governments look for more effective policy instruments and are increasingly
resorting to non-financial and more direct measures to improve
conditions, expand production, and stimulate growth.

Measured by public expenditures in relation to national product,
the scope of the government sector in the selected countries varies
substantially from country to country (see Table 14), although some

TABLE 14

GOVERNMENT REVENUE AND EXPENDITURE

	Revenue in % of GDP	Expenditure in % of GDP		
		Total	Current	Capital
Ethiopia (1957)	8	8	6	2
Guinea (1956)	..	9	8	1
Nigeria (1958)	10	12	9	3
Cameroun (1956)	11	17	16	1
Ghana (1958)	15	15	14	1
Ivory Coast (1956)	4 *	7	6	1
Congo (Leopoldville) (1958)	21	27	18	9
Kenya (1958)	17	21	17	4
Rhodesian Federation (1958)	18	19	11	8

* In 1958 export duties increased so much as to make revenue equal to expenditure.

of the differences are due to foreign financial assistance and consequently not reflected in the figures for revenue given in the table.
In the latter case, the higher figures on the whole reflect somewhat
more advanced economies. One necessary qualification attaching to
the figures in Table 14 concerns the fact that not all expenditures
over which the government has control are registered in government
accounts. This applies particularly to the activities of public corporations and state-owned enterprises ; but there is also some capital
or current spending by foreign governments outside the national
budget. In Nigeria and Ghana, marketing board levies can be
compared to an export tax, in so far as the reserves are used for
purposes other than price stabilization. Substantial amounts from
these reserves are spent outside the government budget, which
further qualifies the figures in the table.

Not only the levels but also the structures of revenue and expenditure are relevant when measuring the impact of government action on the economy. This is not the place for a detailed analysis of government finance, particularly of current expenditure. (For that the reader is referred to the *Economic Bulletin for Africa*.[1]) But a few remarks on the structure of revenue may be in order. Table 15 gives a percentage breakdown between direct taxes, indirect taxes, and non-tax revenue and shows that most of the selected

TABLE 15

STRUCTURE OF REVENUE IN PERCENTAGES

	Direct Taxes (income and others)	Indirect Taxes				Non-tax Revenue
		Import Duties	Export Duties	Other	Total	
Ethiopia (1956)	22	27	10	31	68	10
Guinea (1959)	25	56	9	4	69	6
Nigeria (1956)	12	41	20	10	71	17
Cameroun (1956)	21	32	25	8	65	14
Ghana (1957)	14	31	43	3	77	9
Ivory Coast (1959)	24	18 *	45	*	63	13
Congo (Leopoldville) (1956)	32	17	25	5	47	21
Kenya (1956)	32	27	5	5	47	21
Rhodesia and Nyasaland (Fed.) (1956)	56	19		4	23	21

* Including other indirect taxes.

countries derive about 70 per cent or more of their revenue from indirect taxes. Only the three last-named countries, with large companies and sizeable high-income settler communities, show somewhat higher percentages for direct tax income and lower figures for indirect taxation. A high rate of indirect, as opposed to direct, taxation has, *prima facie*, the effect of obstructing development. While a certain inequality of income is admittedly an important stimulus to economic development and excessive income taxes may be a serious brake on initiative and risk-taking, a lower rate of indirect taxation should normally spread purchasing power over the mass of consumers and thus tend to expand markets on which a domestic industry could be founded.

Apart from capital expenditure for the provision of basic facilities to induce development, as discussed in previous sections, governments have aimed at the expansion of agriculture and industry.

[1] *Economic Bulletin for Africa*, Vol. 1, No. 2 : 'Public Finance in African Countries : Some Trends and Problems'.

Policy measures designed to increase agricultural production range from research and extension, price stabilization schemes, regulation of the collecting trade, the organization of co-operative movements, credit facilities, the dissemination of improved processing methods and simple processing machinery, to land reform and reorganization of the rural production structure. A number of governments actively engage in agriculture through public corporations and develop and manage plantations or other agricultural enterprises, usually growing new or improved crops, or have established processing industries for local agriculture or livestock products to improve their quality and expand outlets for them.

As mentioned above, divergences in political philosophy play a greater rôle in government policy with regard to industry than with regard to other sectors. Although all countries try to stimulate industrialization, some do not go beyond traditional measures, such as exemption from income and other taxes and from import duties on machinery and equipment and/or raw materials, or a measure of Customs protection, actually leaving the establishment of industries entirely to private initiative. Countries going a little further create special financing institutions offering credit facilities on easier terms, while other countries still have established industrial research institutes, industrial extension services, and industrial estates for large-scale or small-scale industry. The most determined governments actively try to induce foreign firms to establish themselves in the country, offering them all sorts of incentives as well as guarantees regarding re-transfer of profits and the like, participate with private, foreign, or domestic interests in joint enterprises or invest directly in state-owned industries.

So much for the political instruments now in use in the selected countries. But, even with the most energetic measures, experience has shown that expansion of the non-agricultural sectors cannot be achieved until all other conditions for it have become so favourable that government assistance is no more than a marginal consideration. Private capital needs rather large safety margins, particularly when operating in a foreign country ; often write-off periods as short as three to five years are demanded. Government assistance can, by decreasing risks or by taking some of them over, accelerate the growth process. However, the fundamental conditions for establishment have to be sufficiently favourable to offer a chance of success. Cost-return relationships (on the basis of economic calculations) are therefore the crucial aspect to which all attention has to be first devoted, and they depend on a whole range of factors of which those discussed above are only a few.

IV. REMAINING OBSTACLES

A. *Structural Imbalance*

From the second section it would appear that the selected countries fall into roughly two groups, the one comprising Congo (Leopoldville), Kenya and the Federation being in some respects more advanced than the other. It can probably be assumed that in the first of these groups communities of European and other settlers, providing larger reservoirs of skill and capital, have given an initial impulse to development. At this point the question might arise whether these countries have reached or nearly reached the take-off stage. Despite any conclusions that might be drawn from the data on structure and infrastructure presented in Section II, the general impression created by the economies concerned would suggest a negative answer. Industrial expansion seems to lack the typical reciprocal generation and to depend too much on exogenous stimuli.

One striking feature in all the countries under review is the considerable disparity in income levels among the population. Leaving aside the subsistence sector, the differences in levels of income between different social groups within the monetary sector are immense. A convenient distinction can be drawn between a high-income and a low-income group, the former consisting of the merchant and the business class in urban areas, together with holders of senior positions in both public and private sectors (disparities in incomes and their persistence being due to the inelastic supply of skills and 'know-how'), on the one hand, and to the abundance of unskilled African labour on the other. The differences in income levels are even more marked in the three countries mentioned in the previous paragraph, where significant foreign settlement has taken place and where the high-income group is relatively larger than in the other countries.

Since the volume of personal money incomes shapes the domestic market, the ways in which these incomes are spent are characteristic for that market, and therefore important for economic development. Disparities in incomes between the two broad groups correspond very closely with two different patterns of consumption. Earnings in the low-income group are such that most of them are spent on domestically produced food and clothing, shelter and 'cheap' imports, while incomes are so high in the other group as to open up the entire range of consumer goods and services to its members and also permit of considerable savings. This means that the high-income group spends a substantial proportion of earnings on consumer luxuries, consumer durables, and services. The demand for services, including housing, public utilities, health, schools, etc., has led to a considerable development of the infrastructure in urban areas. The construction of urban dwellings and other buildings in most of the cities is but a reflection of this demand.

Table 16 gives an example of such disparity in consumption patterns for a country where such data were available :

TABLE 16

CONGO (LEOPOLDVILLE): PATTERN OF CONSUMPTION
IN PERCENTAGES

	African	Non-African
Subsistence	27	—
Goods, domestic	40	8
Services	5	38
Imports	22	24
Taxes, savings, other	6	30
	100	100

As regards demand for consumer goods and consumer durables by the high-income group, the internal market would appear to be too narrow to provide sufficient basis for the production of a variety of goods, so that practically all consumer goods for this class of consumer are imported without much hope of import substitution. Incomes earned by this group therefore largely leak away through imports and transfers of savings abroad, instead of increasing the size of the domestic market. This phenomenon must be even more marked in the countries with large settler communities, where there are more high-income earners and consumption patterns more rigidly follow traditional foreign customs. This may partly explain why the three selected countries with high investment rates have not yet been able to achieve self-generating growth.

On another level income differences — this time between industrial labour and other indigenous income earners — adversely affect industrial development through costs. Given a fixed level of production costs, the higher the wage quota the greater normally the advantage to the community, as other cost elements can be assumed to be largely foreign. However, where the foreign cost quota in a definite production process can be taken as constant or even decreasing with expanding production, the lower the local wage bill the higher production can be, if price elasticity for the product can be taken as greater than 1. Industrial wage increases relative to other income tend to limit industrial expansion in the domestic market and to reinforce further leakage through higher imports, this time for the low-income group.

In some countries the matter is further complicated by the desire to achieve increased productivity through increasing wages. In Congo (Leopoldville) and the Federation, for instance, productivity was stepped up by fixing minimum wages and increasing African wages in general. This has led to greater mechanization and, in Congo, to an absolute decline in the volume of employment, which in 1959 returned to the 1950 level, despite the rapid increase in production. At the same time some income redistribution took place as the proportion of African wages in total national income increased. This reinforced the dichotomy between the modern and the traditional sectors ; unemployment and a return to the countryside became normal features on the eve of independence.

Associated with disparities in income levels is the emergence of urban centres with an adequate infrastructure and services of all types, which in a second phase attract new industries. The large share of high incomes devoted to services considerably or even, in view of the overall state of the economy, disproportionately stimulates the growth of the tertiary sector and creates the anomaly of very advanced agglomerations amidst a primary sector largely producing for subsistence. While it is recognized that economic growth must start in nuclei of development, which will expand to include larger and larger parts of the country in the process of economic growth, it seems doubtful that the sharp contrasts existing between modern and traditional sectors in almost all of the selected countries will contribute to that process. A certain degree of integration of the entire economy must prevail. Disparities in income and consumption patterns may well be taken as a substantial obstacle to the growth of industrial production.

B. *Social and Political Bottlenecks*

Beyond the purely economic aspects of growth lie social and political aspects. These are not merely relevant to the problem of economic development ; what distinguishes them from other equally relevant forces is their decisive bearing on the process of economic change. As has been reiterated, the pace and the very fate of economic development are in the end determined by how profoundly and quickly the political and social environments change.

Large sections of the populations of many of the selected countries find themselves in a social and cultural framework that is hardly suited to the dynamics of development. Traditional loyalty to a particular religious or social clan is in no sense compatible with a unified effort to overcome the pressing problems of economic under-development. Then also, loyalty may be directed merely to the old order of things, rather than to specific religious or social groups; while this may be less serious, where it exists it is still serious enough. The reasons may be varied; but behind an apparent nostalgia for the good old days loom quite concrete pecuniary interests. The incompatibility of ancient manners and attitudes with the transition into industrial society quite often creates serious obstacles to growth. These are by their very nature many and varied and cannot be gone into here.

Politically, a Western-oriented indigenous *élite* must have emerged, as it is the most crucial element in the break-up of the traditional tribal-cum-spiritual authority based on land. The transfer of that authority to the Western-oriented *élite* will provide a unifying force in these countries.

It is true that in West Africa the indigenous merchant and business class is as yet limited and that there exist more or less distinct cultural and ethnic identities which may still make for social and political conflicts. However, the mere presence of a colonial authority has given rise to 'reactive' nationalism, which has provided a force for national integration. On the other hand, social and political relations in countries with settler communities do not as yet appear to contain enough unifying elements for national integration. The availability of European skill in these countries has retarded the creation of an indigenous *élite*, as the merchant and business class largely consists of non-African identities and cultural and historical differences present obstacles to vertical social mobility. In addition, owing to the social and economic importance of these minorities, metropolitan countries have delegated a varying amount of authority to them which, under present political trends, gives rise to conflict and to social and political instability.

Finally, once there is a well-established and centralized political authority determined to embark on economic development it has to be able to rely on a competent and devoted civil service to carry out its policies. Although this seems to be related to the educational levels reached in the country, there is the additional requirement of an administrative tradition, which cannot be taught in universities but which has to be acquired through time and experience and fundamental adjustments to another way of life.

In general, as a slight variation of Rostow [1] we may say that economic development requires 'a definitive social, political and cultural victory of those who would modernize the economy over those who would either cling to the traditional society or seek other goals'.

DISCUSSION OF THE PAPER BY THE STAFF OF THE ECONOMIC COMMISSION FOR AFRICA

Professor Robinson, opening the discussion of the paper prepared by the Staff of the Economic Commission for Africa, expressed the gratitude of all the participants for a study which provided an admirable and wide-ranging introduction to the work of the Conference and would greatly help to establish their perspectives. He suggested that in the sessions of the first day they should seek to establish what were the major economic problems of Africa, what were problems common to a majority of the countries of Africa — the similarities and the differences ; that they should reserve till later sessions more detailed discussion of particular problems.

He applauded the use made by the writers of the paper of the concepts of 'take-off' developed by Professor Rostow. The IEA, he recalled, had held a Conference on this topic the previous autumn and the papers and discussions of it were to be published. He thought that the broad outcome of the Conference was that, while there was a good deal of statistical evidence to show that some of the processes were more gradual than some of the advocates of the concept of 'take-off' suggested, and while several of the earlier countries seemed to have 'taken-off' without achieving Professor Rostow's critical 10 per cent ratio of net capital formation to gross product, yet there had been a fair consensus of opinion that there was value in attempting to learn the lessons of past history for the now developing countries in some such generalized framework.

Professor Robinson emphasized a point mentioned in the paper : that the pre-conditions were supposedly cumulative, in the sense that the un-fulfilment of any one of them might hold up further progress. He took Rostow's five pre-conditions in succession and attempted to apply them to Africa, emphasizing the wide differences between different regions. While psychological attitudes to change were very different from those that had existed a generation earlier and a belief in the importance of progress was more common, it would, he suggested, be untrue to say of many areas that the abandonment of traditional outlooks was anything like complete. The broadening of education was beginning, but this was still a major problem. The strengthening of the body of entrepreneurs,

[1] *Op. cit.* p. 59.

43

outside the regions where most entrepreneuring was expatriate, was proceeding, but was still, he thought, one of the chief limiting factors on development. Equally the revolution of agricultural methods and productivity, which Rostow treated as a pre-condition, though obviously proceeding apace in parts of West Africa, was far from universal. Finally, as the ECA paper brought out, the African infrastructures of transport and energy, despite tremendous advances in recent years, remained substantially below the levels of most countries at what had been regarded as the period of 'take-off'. He thought that, if one was determined to be realistic, large parts of Africa were still almost a generation removed from actual 'take-off'.

He found the discussion of the relation of economic structure to 'take-off' the most novel and exciting part of the paper. He was particularly interested in the treatment of Mexico as a bench-mark of the type of economic structure which might need to be achieved before 'take-off', implying that it might be an additional pre-condition that employment in agriculture might have to be reduced to some 20–25 per cent of total employment. He would have liked to see a more wide-ranging analysis of the structures of other countries at the supposed time of 'take-off'. The United Kingdom, so far as his memory served, was close to the present Mexican figure by the last quarter of the eighteenth century. But he would very much have liked to have seen the comparable figures for Japan at the turn of the century. Would they have supported this generalization ? And, if it were supported, could one use the difference between the existing and the pre-conditional scale of agriculture (adjusted, he assumed, for resources used in agricultural exports) to give some order of magnitude of the time-scales by estimating the approximate annual movement out of agriculture ?

Finally, he expressed surprise that the ECA paper had not discussed more fully the part played by leading sectors, and in particular the need to see the transmission of the initial expansive forces of a first leading sector to other leading sectors successively if growth was to become self-sustained. He thought this was one of the chief impressions that he had drawn from the IEA Conference on 'Take-Off'. The treatment of leading sectors, and the dangers of treating them to too great an extent as milch-cows to nourish general social policies was, he thought, an important issue of practical policy in Africa.

The subsequent discussion, in its first stages, was largely concerned with the possible inferences that might be made from the economic structures of countries that had 'taken-off'. *Dr. Singer* emphasized the dangers of relying on the data of contributions of sectors to gross domestic product, unless valuations of resources used reflected their true economic scarcities. He was doubtful whether the valuations of African labour in fact did so. *Professor Dupriez* similarly stressed the differences between physical measures and monetary valuations. *Professor Williams* illustrated the same point from the high value productivity of labour in Ghana growing cocoa and the low productivity growing foodstuffs. *Professor Samuels* doubted the value of sector figures ; the value of the product of any one sector was greatly dependent on the demand generated in other sectors ; he preferred either a more detailed analysis or a broader analysis distinguishing only primary and secondary production.

Professor Frankel was sceptical of any process of using national income data in a causal sense. If one considered either agriculture or mining, the income generated bore no direct relation to what they might have contributed to the establishing of the environment in which the given national income could be generated. Could one say what the value of output of agriculture would be if the mining industries had not existed ? It was, in his view, very dangerous to use sectoral data to show trends. He thought there was a confusion between the integration of the sectors of the economy and the process of creation of income.

Dr. Singer and *Professor Robinson* did not think that there was any intention to use these data in a causal sense. They both agreed that the generation of incomes operated reciprocally. But they thought, none the less, that consideration of the changes of structure, through changes of productivity, could provide valuable information regarding the degree of development of an economy.

Dr. Yudelman thought the authors had been well advised to use Mexico as a bench-mark. It was a country which had exhibited an explosive history with remarkable economic progress, largely based on rapid agricultural development during the past decade.

Mr. Moran wished to know whether the Rhodesia-Nyasaland Federation had 'taken-off'. Was not that implied by Table 3 ? *Mr. Ligthart*, speaking as one of the authors of the paper, agreed that this might be inferred, but suggested that though this pre-condition had been fulfilled, others had not. *Mr. Ngcobo* thought that the structural analysis had only limited value. It overlooked the fact that structure was only partly economic and partly non-economic. He thought it could not explain dynamic change. *Professor Bézy* similarly emphasized the importance of social factors. Often these presented obstacles; sometimes they were favourable to change. He was not sure whether the data relating to sectors were sufficiently reliable to bear the conclusions that were being drawn.

Professor Walker drew attention to the limitations of the size of the domestic markets of many of the African countries and the remainder of the discussion was largely concerned with issues of the effects of this and other considerations on industrialization and on commercial policies. *Professor Walker* himself drew attention to the relevance of this to proposals for customs unions ; he thought the smallness of existing African markets a critical obstacle in present circumstances.

Dr. Singer argued that the smallness of markets for African industrial products arose partly from the fact that multiplier effects of African leading sectors tended to escape across national boundaries. While he realized that he was making a value judgment, he thought that the value of such multiplier effects was negligible to the United Kingdom or the United States but of immense significance to African countries. He very strongly agreed with Professor Walker in emphasizing the limitations of African markets.

Professor Frankel commented that if Dr. Singer carried his argument to its logical conclusion he would close the markets of all under-developed countries. Import-saving industrialization would take place where it was economic, as was shown by its history in the Union of South Africa. The multiplier effects across boundaries was a two-way process, and Africa, as in the case of copper, had benefited from the multiplier effects of growth outside Africa.

Professor Robinson thought that it could not be assumed that Africa could depend exclusively on growth of export markets and could employ manpower increasingly in that way. Estimates of future copper exports from Northern Rhodesia, and of the manpower needed to produce them, suggested that employment was more likely to decline than to rise because the growth of productivity was outstripping that of demand. He regarded industrialization for domestic consumption as ultimately, if not immediately, likely to become economic.

Mr. Onitiri thought that the primary objective should be to discover the most economic fields for diversification. Structural change was needed, he argued, because economies were too open. The integration between the leading sector and the economy as a whole was very small because profits were largely remitted abroad and the consumption of expatriate senior staff was largely upon imports. If one wished to enlarge the reciprocal generation of income, one must be prepared to make closer the relations between the leading sector and the rest of the economy.

Professor Frankel said that if one sought diversification at the expense of the main existing source of livelihood it would do damage. *Professor Robinson* thought Mr. Onitiri had no such intention. He assumed him to be considering the whole problem dynamically. A more rapidly growing economy would, other things equal, have greater demands for imports of machinery, equipment, and materials. It was obviously desirable to do everything possible to maintain or enlarge the existing sources of export earnings. But if, as was not unlikely, these were insufficient to cover both increased imports of capital goods and increased imports of consumption goods, it would not, in his view, be improper to divert expenditure on imports from luxury consumption goods to capital goods by suitable import duties. *Professor Frankel* was not prepared to agree.

Dr. Singer thought there were two separate problems involved for under-developed countries : the creation of wealth ; the creation of the capacity to create wealth. The latter was essentially a long-term problem, and it was this problem that was intimately connected with diversification.

Mr. Ligthart, concluding the discussion, commented that he had used Mexico as a bench-mark because it was a country, evidently in the process of 'take-off', with increasing reciprocal generation of incomes, with which he had the good fortune to be personally well acquainted. He agreed with the view that the critical phase was the transfer from the first leading sector to the second. African countries were very isolated and very dependent on exogenous factors, generally and in particular on export markets. He could find no example in Africa of one leading sector setting off a second. While he appreciated Professor Frankel's arguments about multipliers exerting their effects across boundaries, he was primarily concerned with the problem of whether African countries could catch up. From that point of view he thought that the significant consideration was the extent of the multiplier effects within their boundaries.

Chapter 2

PROBLEMS OF AFRICAN ECONOMIC DEVELOPMENT

BY

AUSTIN ROBINSON
University of Cambridge

I. INTRODUCTORY

MY purpose in this paper is to look in very broad and necessarily rather superficial terms at the problems of economic development in Africa regarded as a whole. I shall inevitably traverse many of the problems that the Conference will consider in more detail at a later stage with the individual papers on particular topics. I suggest that the full detailed discussion of these topics be reserved for that stage. I had originally hoped that it would be possible to write this paper in the light of the many background studies that are being prepared for the Conference on the problems of development in particular countries and to draw on them for the purpose. In the event it has, to my regret, been necessary to write this before the majority of them were available. But I hope the Conference itself will make the discussion of this paper the opportunity to consider, in the light of those papers, what are the common problems of development of Africa as a whole.

II. THE SPECIAL FEATURES OF AFRICA

The problems of economic development are remarkably different in different parts of the world and the application of a single uniform model — if it is to be regarded as a guide to action — may be very misleading in relation to a particular country or even a particular continent. Some of the countries which, by an oversimplification, are termed under-developed are poor, as are several of those in Asia, because they are over-densely populated in relation to their endowments of soil and rainfall. Some, on the other hand, are poor because their resources have not yet been at all fully exploited and they lack the capital development of transportation and of industrial

48

equipment, and in some cases also a sufficient population, to achieve a high level of productivity. Some of these countries, as India and China, have a long history of sophisticated education and craftsmanship, but have yet to be permeated by twentieth-century Western technology. Others have no comparable history of education and craftsmanship and both have to be created *de novo*. Some are potentially rich, if the problems of education in modern technologies and the problems of the acquisition of transport facilities and of capital equipment can be solved. Some, for lack of natural endowments of resources and climate and because of a dense population in relation to these limited endowments, present problems very much more difficult even of long-term solution.

Where in this spectrum does Africa stand? If one is to be so brave as to generalize about Africa, one must, I suggest, categorize Africa today as an economically backward continent, with a low present standard of life for its inhabitants, principally, but by no means wholly, because its populations have not yet mastered the modern technologies and applied them to their problems and conditions. One must ask — that is to say — how this process of assimilation and education can best be speeded up.

By the criterion of density of population I believe that, if one looks at the continent as a whole, it would be true to say that it is underpopulated rather than overpopulated. There are, of course, limited areas in the Union of South Africa and possibly in West Africa, where local concentrations of population are, given present agricultural methods, almost certainly excessive in relation to resources. But over the greater part of the continent it would, I think, be truer to say that, given a more advanced agriculture, a larger population could make possible a better and cheaper provision of transport, of energy supply, of distribution and a larger-scale and more efficient industrial organization, so that average income per head would be higher rather than lower. But even if that is disputed, Africa is surely much nearer to, let us say, South America than to, let us say, India or China, in the sense that the problems of overpopulation do not obtrude themselves at every turn.

By the criterion of natural resources it is more difficult to generalize. Over many parts of Africa land, as such, is so plentiful as to be almost a free good, and its abundance has led in the past to inherited methods of agriculture which have treated it as such. But neither African soil nor African rainfall is such as to make Africa, outside of limited areas, potentially a rich agricultural country and much remains to be done to master the technical problems of crop-growing and of animal husbandry in African conditions and of the

c

control of the many diseases which affect both. In terms of agricultural resources I hesitate to say more than that the differences of yield of similar soils handled by expert farmers using modern

TABLE 1

POPULATIONS OF AFRICAN COUNTRIES SOUTH OF THE SAHARA, 1956
(Millions)

	African	European	Asian	Total *
South				
South Africa †	12·2	2·97	0·42	15·6 *
Central				
Congo	12·7	0·10	0·01	12·8
Rhodesia and Nyasaland	7·0	0·25	0·01	7·3
Ruanda Urundi	4·4	0·01	—	4·4
East				
Ethiopia	20·0	..	..	20·0
Kenya	5·9	0·06	0·19	6·2
Madagascar	4·8	0·07	—	4·9
Mozambique	5·9	0·07	0·02	6·0
Sudan	10·3	..	..	10·3
Tanganyika	8·3	0·03	0·09	8·5
Uganda	5·5	0·01	0·06	5·6
West				
Angola	4·2	0·11	—	4·4
Cameroons ‡	3·2	0·02	—	3·2
Equatorial Africa ‡	4·9	0·02	—	4·9
West Africa ‡	18·8	0·09	—	18·9
Ghana	4·7	0·01	—	4·7
Nigeria	31·8	0·01	—	31·8
Sierra Leone	2·1	..	..	2·1
Approximate Totals §	172	4	1	177

* Including 'others'; the largest element is 1·28 m. 'coloured' in South Africa.
† Including populations of Basutoland, Bechuanaland, Swaziland, and South West Africa.
‡ Former French territories.
§ Including other countries in the Region with populations totalling about 5·8 m.; Somaliland, Togoland, and Liberia are the largest of these.

methods and by the average of African cultivators shows that the more widespread application even of existing knowledge could considerably increase yields.

If one turns to mineral endowments, one cannot forget the extent to which the economic advance of the Union of South Africa has been dependent on gold and diamonds, that of Northern Rhodesia and the Congo on copper, and of the part played by these and other minerals in the development of Ghana and other parts of West

TABLE 2

NATIONAL INCOMES OF SELECTED AFRICAN COUNTRIES
(U.S. $ converted from national currency units at official exchange rates)

	Year	U.S. $ per head
East Africa		
Kenya *	1957	78
Madagascar ‡	1956	119
Mauritius	1957	232
Tanganyika †	1957	48
Uganda *	1957	57
Central Africa		
Congo	1957	76
Rhodesia and Nyasaland	1957	132
West Africa		
Cameroons ‡ §	1956	142
Equatorial Africa ‡ §	1956	126
West Africa ‡ §	1956	133
Gambia ‡	1957	56–70
Ghana	1957	194
Nigeria	1956	69
Sierra Leone ‡	1957	70
North Africa		
Egypt ‖	1956	109
Tunisia	1957	176

Source : *Economic Survey of Africa since 1950* (ultimate sources there given).

* Net domestic product at factor cost.
† Gross domestic product at factor cost.
‡ Gross domestic product at market prices.
§ Former French territories.
‖ National income at 1954 prices.

Africa. None the less, if one compares African endowments of minerals with those of Europe or America, it is their limitations and remoteness rather than their generosities which need to be stressed.

If I may sum up, I would say that Africa, while not as richly endowed as North or South America, or as the more favoured parts of Europe, is potentially much richer than those parts of Asia where more severe limitations of resources and rainfall are allied with grave overpopulation. Africa started at the beginning of this century with very low standards of life, based on primitive methods of agriculture and rudimentary techniques of manufacture. Even now the African standards of life in the more backward areas are among the lowest in the world. Thus the problems of raising these standards in Africa resolve themselves into the twin problems :

(*a*) the assimilation of modern methods of production and of the power to create and maintain a modern organization of industry, commerce, and government ;

(*b*) the creation and financing of the necessary capital equipment of a modern economy.

One's optimism or pessimism regarding the future development of Africa depends on one's assessment of future progress in solving these two problems. The central problem, as I see it, is that of enabling the African to master the problems of a modern civilization and to control his environment in the same way that members of more advanced countries can already do. In small numbers and where opportunity has been given, Africans have shown their capacity to do this. The need is to spread this capacity as widely as it is spread in the advanced countries.

III. RECENT RATES OF GROWTH

Before I go on to discuss what may be the future of African economic development and what may usefully be done to encourage it and, if possible, to speed it up, may we first consider what have been the rates of growth in the recent past. In Table 3 are given estimates prepared by the Statistical Office of the United Nations of the annual geometric rates of growth of real gross domestic product of a number of African countries. I have added some guesses for certain countries for which estimates of GDP at constant prices were not available to the UN and where one can do no more than use rather rough-and-ready methods to correct current price estimates to allow for price changes.

While the official estimates of gross domestic products, and indeed of population changes, are not firm enough to permit any absolutely confident judgment, and *a fortiori* the unofficial guesses of orders of magnitude, it seems clear that African territories have been advancing in recent years at rates of growth fully comparable

Robinson — Problems of African Development

with those of much of the rest of the world. Indeed the impression left on any visitor to the modern enclaves of Africa is of the tremendous speed of expansion. The problem is in no small degree that of maintaining this impulse if the circumstances that permitted it are changed.

TABLE 3

AVERAGE ANNUAL RATES OF GROWTH OF REAL GROSS
DOMESTIC PRODUCT
1950–59 *

	Rate of Growth of Total GDP	Rate of Growth of GDP per Head
UN estimates		
Congo	4·5	2·1
Former French West Africa	4·1	..
Rhodesia and Nyasaland	6·0	3·4
Orders of magnitude for other African countries		
Union of South Africa	5·0	..
Uganda	5·0	..
Kenya	6·0	..
Tanganyika	4·5	..
Nigeria	5·0	..
Ghana	6·0	..
For comparison †		
U.S.A.	3·3	1·6
France	4·0	3·1
West Germany	7·5	6·3
India	3·5	2·2
Egypt	2·1	− 0·3
Tunisia	3·3	2·0
U.S.S.R. ‡	10·5	8·7

* Or nearest available period of years.
† UN Estimates.
‡ Rate of growth of real net material product only.

The rates of growth of domestic product are considerably higher than those of population in all of the territories given and, if maintained, would probably double income per head in most cases in a period of between 25 and 30 years. But three things need to be remembered. First, that in some of the territories with a high rate of growth, a large part of the income has gone to those receiving profits and the growth of African incomes has in some cases been

53

slower. Second, that the growth has been associated with a very large inflow of capital from abroad. Third, that African incomes per head are at present so far behind the incomes of European nations that a very long period of rapid growth — nearer to 100 than to 50 years — would be necessary to reach the present standards of Europe.

IV. THE ASSIMILATION OF MODERN TECHNIQUES

If one considers the economic growth of the most advanced nations, the continued maintenance of high rates requires not only the better application of known techniques but also the continuous creation of new techniques by new research and development. From the point of view of Africa, by contrast, there is in existence an immense body of relevant knowledge in the possession of the advanced countries and potentially applicable to Africa. Some of this requires further research into specific African problems of application. This is probably truer of agriculture than of industry — but in general the task is one of transferring and applying available knowledge rather than of creating it.

In all countries, this process of assimilating and using knowledge is the most important factor in economic progress. In the United Kingdom the increase of capital per head can probably account for no more than a quarter of the increase of output per head. The remaining three-quarters of the total increase must be explained by better and more scientific 'know-how', better organization, better training and better health of workers, and by similar factors. New capital investment is important in permitting the application of these new methods; it acts as a catalyst in this respect. But capital investment is not in itself enough. I stress this, because some of the recent writings on growth seem to me to put exaggerated emphasis on capital formation and to treat it, not (as I think it should be) as a necessary condition of growth, but as in itself a prime and sufficient cause of growth.

The transfer of knowledge has in the past usually been a very slow process. The transfer from the Mediterranean basin to Northern Europe would appear to have been spread over centuries rather than decades. The transfer of techniques from China and India to Europe was equally gradual. The problem of today is whether and how this process can be greatly speeded up in the case of Africa.

It is important in this respect to have in mind the great differences within Africa itself. A large part of Eastern and Central Africa has been in effective touch with the outside world for no more than eighty years. Small areas on the West Coast have had associations with Europe for two centuries or more. Ethiopia has had associations that go far back in time. Some of these areas have had a long history of learning and education. In others formal education is a matter largely of the past three or four decades.

In the phase of the rapid development of Africa in this century, the main channel of the transfer of knowledge has been the European or Asian, working and making his home in Africa. It is through them that the modern techniques have principally been brought in and applied. They have known them and have been enabled to visualize them in the countries of their origin. But the process has been an essentially different one in Africa from that which has operated in other under-developed areas. In India and Pakistan, and to a notably greater extent in Japan, the educational background and experience in the countries concerned made it possible to graft the new European techniques on to traditional indigenous crafts, and there was a sufficient indigenous financial system to permit the relatively quick emergence of local entrepreneurs, able to absorb and utilize the new methods. In Africa the process of absorption of the new techniques by Africans has been much more difficult. The gap between their own traditional methods and those employed in European or Asian factories or farms was too wide for them to bridge by a change of their own practices, except in a few cases, such as building, or clothing, or service industries. The problems of finance have also been more difficult, though exceptions can readily be found in West Africa. Thus, as Professor Houghton [1] has made clear, African workers have too often accepted a position of detachment, of non-involvement, in their employment and have carried little or nothing over into a more permanent technical assimilation. The result has been that African economies almost throughout the continent have largely depended on non-African entrepreneurs for all except a few small-scale activities.

One may perhaps regard this problem of developing a modern African industrial organization in part as being another aspect of the issue of the choice of techniques that has been so much discussed in relation to India. The European techniques, outside the few cases of building, clothing, and the services industries that I have quoted, are probably too capital intensive for immediate absorption by African small-scale craftsmen-entrepreneurs. But almost more important, outside of the Union (and in many cases inside it also) the European unit of organization in Africa tends to be large and

[1] See below, pp. 326-7.

to require forms of organization and control and amounts of capital that are beyond the present capacity of all but a few Africans. There are here, it seems to me, two major problems : one short-term and one long-term. The short-term problem is how African economies shall be kept operating and African economic growth maintained over the next ten or twenty years. Africa has been developed hitherto on a multi-racial basis. This has implied that Europeans, or in some regions Asians, have been encouraged or permitted to fill the gaps in African skills, qualifications, and resources. As a result Africa has progressed far more rapidly. The Europeans and Asians have, of course, benefited. But they have benefited because they were benefiting Africa. They may have secured some-times in the past more than their fair share of the gains. Privilege and monopoly are in process of disappearing. But on a basis of equality, the foreign expert, prepared to work continuously and for long periods in Africa, seems indispensable to continued African progress for a good many years to come. It is difficult to see how large-scale industry, banking, and finance, or foreign trade, can be efficiently conducted without a considerable measure of outside assistance. The central problem is how to create a climate of mutual confidence in which, without privilege, and with equal opportunity for all, a multi-racial society can operate, with all concerned making their appropriate contributions and receiving their appropriate rewards.

The longer-term problem is to make it possible for Africans at every level to assimilate more rapidly the techniques and the ways of thinking of the modern world. This is partly a problem of formal education. At present almost throughout Africa education beyond the elementary stages is inadequate to produce a sufficient number of educated technicians, technologists, professional experts, the administrators and the teachers, to satisfy the probable demand at the time that this generation of students will be required to meet it. The problems, as has emerged from the studies made in Nigeria and from studies in progress in Rhodesia and Nyasaland, are extra-ordinarily difficult to solve quickly.

But formal education is only a part of the problem. A greater part is represented by the necessary creation of a craft-conscious body of skilled workers and of responsible foremen. Some of this may be the task of technical colleges, but the main problem is 'on the job' education and the creation of a sufficient first generation of African craftsmen. It is here that the difficulty is greatest. The problem is potentially most soluble where there are numerous European craftsmen, but very understandably it is precisely here that colour-bars are most likely to be demanded to protect the non-African craftsmen against competition. The problem is politically easier of solution but practically more difficult where European craftsmen are few.

The problems of higher administration both in government and in industry are most acute of all. The demand for educated and qualified Africans of sufficient maturity to carry responsibility is far in excess everywhere of demand. In industry and commerce, in particular, plans to 'Africanize' staffs are in many cases held back by lack of sufficient trained personnel rather than by deliberate intention.

Most African countries are now putting education very high in their development programmes. I believe they are right in doing so, not only as an element in welfare but also as a means of raising productivity and income. If it is proper to think in terms of African 'take-offs', I would regard the improvement of education as an essential part of the preliminary phase of creating the pre-conditions.

V. THE EXISTING ECONOMIC STRUCTURE

If I may turn next to the present economic structure of African economies, one must emphasize the extent of its present dependence on agriculture. Even if one recognizes, as has been insisted by Professor Bauer, that much of the agricultural population is concerned in other functions, and particularly in distributive activities,

TABLE 4

DISTRIBUTION OF GROSS DOMESTIC PRODUCT BY
INDUSTRIAL ORIGIN
(Percentages)

	Year	Agri-culture	Mining and Manu-facturing	Others
Congo	1959	26	35	39
Kenya	1959	41	15	44
Mauritius	1958	30	27	43
Nigeria	1956	63	15	22
Rhodesia and Nyasaland	1959	19	40	41
Tanganyika	1959	59	18	23
Union of South Africa	1959	12	38	50

it is still relevant to have in one's mind that, while in 1959 only 4 per cent of the domestic product of the United States was generated in agriculture and 7 per cent of that of West Germany (both of these countries not far from self-sufficiency), in few African countries does the proportion fall below 25 per cent. In Sudan the proportion of gross domestic product generated in agriculture in 1959 was 61 per cent, in Tanganyika 59 per cent, in Kenya 41 per cent, in Nigeria (in 1956) 63 per cent, in Congo 26 per cent; the only territories falling below 25 per cent were the Rhodesias and Nyasaland, heavily dependent on mineral production, where the proportion was 19 per cent and the Union of South Africa where it was as low as 12 per cent.

To take the obverse of this, there are few countries in Africa where mining and manufacturing at present contribute more than 25 per cent of the gross domestic product, whereas in more advanced countries this proportion is usually close to or over 40 per cent ; in the United States 39 per cent, in West Germany 53 per cent, in the United Kingdom 48 per cent. The highest African proportions were 38 per cent in the Union of South Africa, 40 per cent in Rhodesia and Nyasaland, and 35 per cent in Congo. More typical were 11 per cent in Sudan, 18 per cent in Tanganyika, 15 per cent in Kenya, and 15 per cent in Nigeria (in 1956).

The normal trend of development in this respect is well illustrated by the figures for Italy. As recently as 1950, 29 per cent of gross domestic product was generated in agriculture, and only 38 per cent in manufacturing and mining, the remaining 33 per cent being generated in the other tertiary activities. By 1959, only 19 per cent of the product was generated in agriculture, and the proportion from manufacturing and mining had risen to 43 per cent, with an increase of tertiary activities to 38 per cent. One would expect African development to follow a similar pattern : that improved efficiency in agriculture should provide the food needs of African populations as well as growing agricultural exports from the work of a smaller proportion of the national manpower (and woman-power), having regard to the relatively low income elasticity of demand for food. But the primary importance of agriculture needs always to be borne in mind. It is only if the productivity of African agriculture can be increased that resources can be found to expand other activities. Moreover, the experiences of a number of under-developed countries in other parts of the world, particularly in Asia, have provided a warning that the income elasticity of demand for food, though low, is still high enough, when associated with the large element that food normally represents in total expenditure and with growing population, to make the danger of insufficient expansion of agriculture and inflation in the food sector one of the most severe limitations on economic development.

There has, it is true, been a very considerable growth in the volume of agricultural production for Africa as a whole; it has been estimated (*UN Economic Survey of Africa since 1950*, p. 98) that it had increased by 40 per cent between pre-war and the average of the three crop years 1955–8, and that *per capita* agricultural production in tropical Africa in 1958 was 20 per cent higher than pre-war. But such a rate of long-term improvement is scarcely sufficient to support the general rates of growth of African territories. Two-thirds to three-quarters of the total land area cultivated by Africans in tropical Africa was, and almost certainly still is, used for subsistence production, and it is here that advance, though by no means negligible, is inevitably slowest.

VI. THE PATTERNS OF AFRICAN ECONOMIC DEVELOPMENT

If one attempts to study the main patterns of African economic development, two stand out most clearly. The initiating force in some of the regional developments has been mineral discoveries and the subsequent mining development. Outstanding examples are the gold and diamond discoveries in the Union, the copper-mining in Rhodesia and Katanga. These mining developments have had consequential effects far beyond the actual direct production involved. In the first place, they have required transport facilities and their traffics have justified the creation of railways; but the railways, once built, have enabled all kinds of other developments to take place; they have made possible the expansion of agricultural production and exports and a greater degree of exchange and specialization throughout the region. Secondly, the mining communities have required and have gradually helped to build up an infrastructure of other public utility services. Thirdly, they have required a variety of engineering services and facilities both for capital construction and for maintenance. All of these have served to create an enclave of modern technology within a particular small region of Africa and have given Africans an opportunity to acquire skills in two occupations — mining and civil engineering — where, at an early stage in national education, their comparative advantages have probably been greatest. Fourthly, the exports of minerals have provided a relatively easy solution for the problems of the balance of payments and have permitted the inflow both of capital goods needed for further development and of consumer goods which have raised African as well as non-African standards of living.

Finally, by the usual multiplier process, the incomes thus created have generated demands which found their satisfaction first in imports, but which in recent years have been beginning to lead to developments of manufacture for the local market not only in the Union and Southern Rhodesia, where the process has gone furthest, but also in the Congo, in Kenya, and in West Africa, where the process is in its earlier stages. Thus in Africa, the mining industries have predominantly played the part of leading sectors and the industrial developments have largely grown outwards from mining.

But it is well to remember that there are likely to be limits to the power of the mining industries themselves to expand and absorb manpower. If I may illustrate from the case of Northern Rhodesia, the annual growth of demand for copper in the future does not seem likely to be greater than the annual increase of productivity. Thus while copper production, if all goes well, may continue to contribute to the solution of the balance of payments problems of the Rhodesias, the progressive absorption of Africans into the modern economy must come from other developments. The initial push may come from mining, but at a later stage the continuation of growth must usually depend on a wider-based industrial and agricultural development.

The second main pattern of development has been the grafting on to African agriculture of the production of cash crops for export. This has been the line of development of Uganda, Tanganyika, and Kenya in the East, of Ghana, Nigeria, and the former French territories in the West; it has played a large part also in the development of the Congo. Within this process of development, two rather different patterns have emerged. In Uganda, Tanganyika, Ghana, and Nigeria the cash crops have come principally, though not exclusively, from African peasant cultivation. In the Congo, in Kenya, and in the Portuguese territories a chief part has been played by estates or large farms on which techniques have been those of large-scale agriculture, and the management has, in the initial stages at least, been non-African. There have, in addition, been interesting attempts, as at Gezira, to find a compromise between the two.

The history of Ghana has shown that in Africa, as outside it, the successful cultivation of a profitable export crop can form the basis of a considerable economic advance. But for a variety of reasons the development is more difficult than that which can flow from mining. The bulky export crops do not provide as remunerative a freight for a railway. While agricultural development has followed where railways have been built, it has been more difficult to justify railway building in advance on the basis of agriculture alone. Moreover, a widespread agricultural development does not create, as mining does, a small enclave of advanced techniques which can spread outwards. Nor is it so easy to teach and sustain the new techniques to a widespread agricultural population as to a concentrated body of mining or industrial workers organized by a small staff of trained experts.

VII. CAPITAL AND ECONOMIC DEVELOPMENT

I turn next to the part played by capital in development, and the problems of capital supply. I shall not attempt to anticipate in detail Professor Frankel's discussion of this and shall confine myself to certain essentials.

I have said earlier that there has been some retreat, in recent years, from the exaggerated emphasis that was earlier placed on the rôle of capital. There is now, perhaps, a greater belief that, if technical progress is rapid, capital will become available, either from domestic sources or from overseas, so that it is more important to concentrate on the creation of the conditions in which technical progress is rapid. But it would be equally mistaken to under-rate the importance of capital.

It has sometimes been suggested that for 'take-off', or indeed for rapid progress, a net fixed capital formation of the order of 10 per cent of gross domestic product is required. With a capital/output ratio of 3, that would be consistent with a growth rate slightly above 3 per cent per annum. To secure a net fixed capital formation of that order it is necessary to have a gross fixed capital formation of the order of 20 per cent.

Estimates of gross domestic fixed capital formation as a percentage of gross domestic product are given in Table 5 for a number of African countries. It is clear that the levels of fixed capital formation in most of the countries shown have been close to the level postulated. Indeed if, as is the case in many countries, depreciation has been as high as the normal 10 per cent of gross product, the marginal capital/output ratio has been well below 3.

It is, perhaps, interesting to see what has happened in the Federation of Rhodesia and Nyasaland, where the statistics are more than usually complete. For the whole period 1954–9, gross fixed capital formation at 1954 prices represents 27 per cent of gross domestic product. Depreciation is estimated at 6 per cent. The net capital formation of 21 per cent provided an average growth rate of 6 per cent compound. Thus the marginal capital/output ratio was about 3½. If the rates of growth of Kenya and Uganda were as high as I believe, the capital/output ratio in their cases must have been considerably lower.

TABLE 5

GROSS DOMESTIC FIXED CAPITAL FORMATION
AS PERCENTAGE OF GROSS DOMESTIC PRODUCT

	1959 %
Congo	17
Ghana	13
Nigeria *	12
Rhodesia and Nyasaland	24
Tanganyika	15
Union of South Africa	21
For comparison	
Italy	21
France	17
United Kingdom	16
U.S.A.	17
Egypt	9

* 1956.

A large part of the capital has come from outside of Africa. In the case of Rhodesia and Nyasaland nearly 30 per cent of investment was financed by the capital inflow, and a large proportion of the remainder represented the ploughing back of profits accruing to overseas investors.

The recent study, *The Flow of Financial Resources to Countries in the Course of Economic Development, 1956–1959*, by the OEEC, shows that of some $27·3 billion of contributions to under-developed countries and multilateral agencies during that period, $12 billion came, either directly or through multilateral agencies from private investors, and the remaining $15·3 billion represented official grants and loans. These proportions, which refer to the whole under-developed world, cannot be applied directly to Africa. But the importance of private investment to Africa is evident. In the absence of private investment, an immense increase of government grants or loans would be necessary, if present rates of growth were to be maintained.

Much of this private investment is the investment of the large international concerns which have, in recent years, increasingly expanded by building subsidiaries in African countries. Much of the industrial development has been due to them. And they have been in a particularly good position not only to finance development but also to provide the technical 'know-how' and to recruit the overseas experts who were necessary to staff the undertakings. In many cases also these international concerns have been extremely anxious to train African staff for responsibility, and to reduce their overseas recruitment where possible.

One of the most important problems for African development is to find ways in which, within and consistent with the political development of Africa, these industrial concerns can satisfactorily operate. They have represented the 'leading sectors' in African economic development and a principal way of introducing modern techniques of production into Africa.

Almost more important than the aggregate of investment is its distribution between different uses. The first stage of industrialization is inevitably the creation of a minimum infrastructure of transport, energy supplies, and public utility services generally. In addition, health and education make substantial demands for capital equipment. The greater part of Africa has been provided with a minimum equipment of railway services, mainly during the past fifty years. Road transport and the necessary roads have been built, many of them within the past twenty years. Though much remains to be done to improve road surfaces and to build permanent long-distance roads, there is, in most areas, now a sufficient infrastructure in this respect.

The supply of cheap energy, largely in the form of hydro-electricity, has absorbed in some areas, notably Uganda and Rhodesia, a large share of the available capital. While the absence of reasonably cheap energy can be an obstacle to economic development, the results, hitherto, of the Owen Falls Scheme do not appear to support the view that cheap energy is in itself sufficient to promote economic development. Large investments in such very long-lived equipment would seem to be only doubtfully of value in promoting development, if similar amounts of capital can equally be made available for shorter-lived industrial equipment and opportunities can be created for their profitable investment.

Government investment in the creation of an infrastructure which might play the double rôle of providing necessary facilities for industrialization and an expenditure which, through multiplier effects, might create further incomes, expenditure, and industrial

63

investment, has been a feature of the Italian development plan and might provide an interesting example for similar application in parts of Africa.

None the less, it is industrial and commercial investment on a larger scale that Africa seems most to need, and channels for the transfer of credit and capital resources into credit-worthy African hands are only now beginning to be created. One of the most difficult things to visualize at present is the necessary structure of capital market and credit facilities to channel foreign capital into African development. The present structure of large international concerns, in itself, provides a present solution of this problem for a substantial part of industry. In East Africa, Asian money is channelled through Asian banking and credit institutions into Asian development.

VIII. SOME CONCLUSIONS

I have put the emphasis in this paper on the transfer of knowledge, of modern technology, and of organizing experience to the populations of Africa. I believe that this is the first and major task.

The future economic development of Africa, as I see it, will depend on the rate at which Africa can learn to use and to absorb the knowledge already existing in the outside world. In this process of transfer and absorption, non-Africans, working and living in Africa, have played a very important part. If they cannot continue to make their contribution to African development, on a basis of equality, I believe that the rate of progress will be greatly slowed down.

If the necessary entrepreneuring ability, initiative, and responsibility can be found to absorb it, large amounts of capital will continue to be required from outside Africa. The channels through which this may be secured may need much modification if the part played by international concerns is reduced.

DISCUSSION OF PROFESSOR ROBINSON'S PAPER

Professor Frankel, in opening the discussion, emphasized that the purpose of the meeting was to clarify minds and not to describe a particular economy. There were a wide variety of African countries. Nothing could be decided by the analogy of 'take-off'. No reference had been made to the possibilities of substantial declines, and history was full of instances of decline as well as growth. He thought it more valuable to concentrate attention on the obstacles to growth. Why does growth not continue indefinitely ? In his view most of the so-called 'take-offs' had been fortuitous. They had resulted from the discovery of gold in the Union, from similar discoveries of copper in Northern Rhodesia, and from the introduction of cocoa in Ghana. Many of the improvements, moreover, were due to the personal energies of particular individuals. One must consider the obstacles to growth and the chances of decline. Just as families moved from clogs to clogs in three generations, so the nations grew and declined, often from non-economic reasons. It had been said that African economies were open and that it was easy to secure growth and change. He believed that the opposite was, in fact, the case : that Africa was at present enclosed and the problem was to open it.

He thought it was important to clarify certain concepts. Were we trying to develop Africa for political or for economic reasons ? It was not enough to take the attitude that we should attempt to increase everything, all along the line. It was not useful to talk about education in the same terms as one spoke about investment in tangible things. Investment was a matter of the use of time, and the time at our disposal was limited. One should concentrate first on those things which produced income. He agreed with what Professor Robinson had said about entrepreneurs benefiting Africa because they benefited themselves; by making the right decisions they gained from it and created the resources available. They were discussing a period when such resources would decline. It was important therefore to distinguish between facts and fantasy.

Professor Frankel emphasized that in his view economists should remember the limitations of their responsibilities. They should confine themselves to examining the inter-actions of people in their economic studies. They should not be occupied in prediction. He was concerned that many of the papers of the Conference seemed to be full of the sheerest fantasy. African territories which had secured independence had got to realize that their demands cannot exceed their resources. Many of their fancies of the future had little to do with fundamentals.

Africa, he emphasized, was a very hard continent, and the Africa of tomorrow would be up against the same realities that had limited its development in the past. The world had come to realize that the greatest resource of Africa was the experience of the Africans. They had learned a great deal about Africa. But whereas at an earlier stage the entrepreneurs had exercised great influence on African development potentials, it was now believed that the resources of industry could be diverted to other schemes for the development of Africa. His own investigations made it clear that it was not true that more funds had been drawn out of Africa than the capital that had been put into Africa.

Professor Frankel ascribed the backwardness of Africa to the absence of a large foreign immigration of trained and educated Europeans, such as had happened in the development of South America. Those continents which closed their doors against immigration tended to be poor ; those that threw open their doors found themselves rich.

He emphasized again that economists should not identify themselves with the tasks of the government. If Adam Smith had been writing today he would have emphasized the dangers of the increase of the power of the governments as against their peoples. There were indications of the peoples of Africa being saddled with bureaucracies that they could not afford. He suggested that the beautiful building in which the Conference was meeting was inappropriate to the existing resources of Africa. He emphasized, finally, that economic growth was, in his view, largely to be ascribed to fortunate accidents. Africa's greatest need was the guidance of administrators and entrepreneurs.

Mr. Beheiry agreed that the great need of Africa was for trained manpower. He regarded this as the most urgent need of all. There was a very widespread shortage of trained men in the professions and of foremen and technicians in industry. The great problem was how to secure the skills and the know-how. His experience in the establishing of the Central Bank of Sudan had shown that, with a great deal of help from the Central Banks of other countries, it had been possible within two years to get a nucleus of Sudanese trained. He emphasized also the value of expatriate experts who were made available to help African countries, with the knowledge that they could return to a post in their country of origin. It was very necessary to create a sense of service and to supplement, for the time being, local skills with foreign skills.

Dr. Enke suggested that it was necessary to bear in mind that Africa was emerging from a period of history from which a complete break was impossible. After a period of colonialization it was necessary to have a phase of de-colonialization. Professor Robinson had suggested that, through a deterioration of the terms of international trade, foreign enterprises might have secured too large a share, both as a result of monopoly and because the experts in a leading sector of the economy and the government officials were very close together. Independent African territories were moving into a new era, when the close relation between the government and leading sectors no longer existed. The problem in the immediate future was the integration of these foreign sectors into the overall planning for economic growth. He believed that foreign enterprise had an assured place in which it could serve as a leading sector provided Africans were in a position to secure that it did not get an excessive share of the gains from trade. But he was concerned about the leaks from the foreign enclave. In Australia and New Zealand the effects of the development of foreign trade went right down to the lowest levels of the economy ; whereas in West Africa they largely disappeared, either into profits remitted abroad or into the imports of consumer goods for expatriate employees. In his view, only the governments of the territories concerned could effectively integrate these foreign concerns into the economies.

Dr. Singer argued that all the newly independent countries had governments that were determined to try to plan. He thought that the discussions from the terms of trade were irrelevant. He argued that there were two overriding things : first, the capacity of African countries to repay borrowings, which was largely a problem of balance of payments ; and second, that the governments, and ultimately the peoples, of the more advanced countries were necessarily forced to vote and devote part of their national incomes to aiding the under-developed world. In his view the aid-giving capacity was likely to grow more rapidly in the immediate future than the capacity to receive and absorb such aid by under-developed countries. There was likely to be a tremendous disequilibrium in this respect. He thought that it was important that very much more attention should be paid to the possibilities of increasing these flows of public capital and their full absorption by the under-developed countries.

Professor Peacock raised the question of the usefulness of the concept of the capital/output ratio in trying to think about the possible rates of growth of African economy. He argued that, if one studied year by year figures for the Federation of Rhodesia and Nyasaland, there were fluctuations from year to year explained by external forces. He doubted the value of this ratio for planning purposes. *Professor Robinson* replying to him said that he agreed entirely with Professor Peacock that capital/ output ratios could not safely be used to explain changes of income over short periods. He regarded them only as a useful long-period guide to the probable amount of capital required if income was to be raised by some given annual ratio. Experience in India had shown the limitations of overall capital/output ratios, and that any detailed analysis required the use of sectoral capital/output ratios or detailed studies of the capital costs of individual projects.

Mr. Moran emphasized the important part that foreign capital could play in bringing into under-developed countries know-how, capital, and expertise together. He was more sceptical than Dr. Singer about the prospects of very large increases of public aid advanced to under-developed countries. He certainly did not expect this to grow to such an extent as to make private investments more important. He thought that the advanced nations were still very far from agreement in making large and regular contributions of foreign aid.

Professor Frankel again emphasized the importance of economists refraining from engaging in prediction. While it might be proper for entrepreneurs to attempt to predict the size of their markets, this was not, in his view, the matter in which economists should concern themselves. He found it impossible to make sense of the use of the capital/output ratio. *Mr. Lardner* in turn also expressed the view that it was better to rely on detailed data of particular projects.

Professor Robinson found himself in vigorous disagreement with Professor Frankel. He believed that economists had a contribution to make in the development of under-developed countries by seeing the limitations of the available resources and by judging the ways in which public expenditures should best be balanced against each other. He thought Professor Frankel was leaving out of account the important contribution which investment in human capital formation could make to African progress. He was under the impression that Professor Frankel assumed that investment in fixed capital formation was all important while investment in human capital formation gave no return at all. *Professor Frankel* denied this.

Dr. Wade argued that economic statistics had an important part in establishing certain relationships which subsequently could form the elements to be used in planning economic development. It was urgent to establish these relationships but he did not think it was right to start with such concepts as the capital/output ratio which would later have to be determined in relation to African countries. In working out the basic conditions of economic development he thought economists should be prepared to accept the necessity for planning even if they did not regard it as their own work. One of the major problems of Africa was how far the state should intervene by creating a plan and by performing certain functions. If it were Professor Frankel's view that it was not important to encourage education, he did not agree with him.

Professor Bézy argued that it was important that economists and sociologists work together in their studies of Africa. He thought there was not yet sufficient integration of the two approaches. It was necessary to study intensively the demographic patterns of Africa, and the other elements in the structure of society. In considering any society it was important, first to consider its structure, and then to see what developments in the social structure were necessary to economic development. It should be remembered that when the classical economists wrote there had already been major changes in the social structure of Europe, and in framing their economic theories they were able to assume that these social changes had already taken place. In African society changes had scarcely begun. He thought that Karl Marx had shown the way that economists should follow in combining a social and economic approach. This integration was important not only for theory but also for policy. In choosing patterns of investment it was desirable to see that economic projects would not conflict with social objectives. It was important to consider the means of changing outlooks in Africa. It would be necessary to achieve complete mutation of African civilization and its assimilation to what had become a universal world type. Economic policies should take this into account at all stages. *Professor Samuels* thought that there was a tendency towards confusion as to what was meant by education. It was important to distinguish vocational training from general education. He suggested also that in any discussions of the functions of an economist one should remember that there were three broad but distinct groups of economists: the purely academic economist, the economist who acted as adviser to governments and one who had been trained as an economist but was now serving as an administrator. The degree of detachment of economists from actual determination of policies was clearly different in the three cases.

Professor Dupriez agreed at once to the distinguishing of different forms of education. He was in agreement also with Professor Bézy in stressing the importance of change and education to a new phase of African development. He thought that it was desirable to develop general education as well as technical education.

Dr. Singer wished to consider the problem of the transfer of knowledge. He argued that there was a huge stock of available knowledge but most of this took the form of knowledge of how to organize abundant capital with limited labour. A great deal of research, he thought, was necessary to create autonomous systems suitable to the relative factor supplies.

Professor Robinson argued that Western countries possessed large supplies of fundamental knowledge which could readily be embodied in different actual technologies suitable to these different relative scarcities of supply of factors : that it was not only knowledge but application of knowledge that was wanted. *Mr. Yudelman* agreed that limits existed relevant to African agriculture.

M. Roland Pré thought that it was important that under-developed countries should continue to send an intellectual *élite* abroad for education. Unless their best students went to universities and research institutes abroad there was an indication that the gaps of knowledge would widen rather than narrow. He thought that mass education was necessary in order that Africans at all levels should acquire not only more know-how and technical knowledge but also a more general understanding of conditions of a modern society in order that they might be integrated into it. He thought that it would be necessary also to get teachers from more advanced countries. He quoted the example of the contribution which the people from Northern Italy had made towards the development of Southern Italy. By making intensive studies of the people of the South they found ways of helping them. He thought that the task of education in Africa was vitally important, but that it was essential to distinguish between the problems of assimilating an African *élite* into the *élites* of developed countries and the problems of the general education of the African masses.

Mr. Lardner suggested that one should distinguish the process of training an African *élite* to the point at which Africans might be able to research on the problems of Africa from the transfer of ready-made knowledge from advanced to under-developed countries. One had to ask what resources of knowledge, they could get into African countries and the channels through which the knowledge could flow.

Mr. Moran believed that much research being done in Western countries would not be adaptable immediately to under-developed countries but he thought there was advantage in thinking in terms not only of the latest recipes but also of earlier recipes. One had to remember that the advanced countries had more than a century of recipes, and out of their past history recipes suitable to under-developed countries could often be found. *Professor Frankel* agreed that the most valued knowledge was secured in doing the job. Africa should start by seizing the opportunities that were ready at hand. A certain amount of knowledge could readily be transmitted. He thought that the readiest knowledge to transmit was how to govern. The art of government at local and regional levels, the arts of treasury control and of economic planning were things which expatriates living in Africa were best prepared to teach to African populations. They could also teach the arts of living in the modern world and of decision making. The most necessary thing was to teach people to be adaptable. The African had always succeeded to a remarkable extent in dealing with his own very difficult African environment, but *Professor Frankel* believed that teachable knowledge of how to handle some of the problems of Africa itself was almost non-existent.

Professor Houghton thought that the recipes of obsolete technology were of very limited value. One had to take the most modern techniques and work them out afresh in the light of relative factor endowment. He quoted an instance in which obsolete equipment in a factory had made it wholly unproductive until modern techniques were introduced. *Mr. Moran* stated that he was not suggesting that one should use the actual equipment of the past but modern equipment with a modern interpretation of earlier techniques. One needed a flexible method of approach. Many United States industries were, in fact, of small scale and flexible. *Mr. Beheiry* argued that there was a continuous process of learning and of discovering the best and most appropriate methods. *Dr. Singer* thought that we had come back to the problem of investment by the back door. There was a capital cost of building up a body of knowledge by experience and Africa had to be prepared to invest in this kind of human capital formation. *Professor Robinson* ended by commenting that he thought that the transferability of knowledge was very different indeed in the two cases of industry and agriculture. In the first there was a great deal of knowledge which was readily transferable from the advanced countries to Africa. In the case of agriculture very much utilization research had to be done. But he wished to re-emphasise the importance of learning on the job and of increasing the assimilation of craftsmanship and competence, and responsible foremanship throughout Africa. It was these qualifications in which he thought that African countries generally fell most greatly behind.

Chapter 3

PROBLEMS OF ECONOMIC DEVELOPMENT
OF CONGO

BY

FERNAND BÉZY
University of Lovanium, Congo

I. INTRODUCTION

THE Congo [1] is a vast Central African territory situated astride the equator. It is 2·3 million square kilometres in area — that is, a third of the size of the United States. It has only 13 million inhabitants — that is, 8 per cent of the United States' population. The average density of population is thus only 5 inhabitants per square kilometre.

H. M. Stanley's explorations opened the way for civilization in the country at the end of last century. The Congress of Berlin (1885) granted it the status of an independent State, under the sovereignty of Leopold II, King of the Belgians. He granted it to Belgium in 1908. On the 30th June 1960 the Congo gained its independence.

Up to the First World War, economic activity in the Congo was limited to the commercial development of collected produce and crops, the construction of roads into the interior, and the exploration of the natural wealth of the country. A vast network of communications covering 15,000 kilometres is provided by the river Congo and its tributaries. Navigation is, however, impeded at several points by rapids. Railways were, therefore, designed to make up for the deficiencies in river communication, and to connect with the river important economic regions — especially Katanga Province (in the South-East) where rich mineral deposits were discovered. In 1918 almost 2,000 kilometres of railway track were open to traffic ; today 5,000 kilometres are available.

It was only after the First World War that the economy of the Congo really sprang to life. Since that time, the national product (at fixed prices) has been increasing exponentially at an annual rate of 4·7 per cent. The 'trend' is a perfect expression of the

[1] I am discussing the former 'Belgian' Congo.

71

TABLE 1

MAGNITUDE OF FOREIGN TRADE IN THE CONGO, 1950–8

(Thousand millions of francs)

	1950	1951	1952	1953	1954	1955	1956	1957	1958	Average
(a) Value of production	23·8	32·7	37·1	36·9	38·9	42·3	45·1	42·3	40·9	
(b) Value f.o.b. of exports	16·3	21	23·3	21·6	24·7	26·7	30	26·8	25·2	
(c) Value c.i.f. of imports	8·6	14·5	19·2	17·2	18·2	18·1	19.14	21	16·9	
(d) Value of imported goods used in production	1·1	2·6	4·1	3·4	3·9	4·6	5·3	5·5	4·6	
(e) Disposable goods: $(a)+(c)-(d)$	31·3	44·6	52·2	50·7	53·2	55·8	59·2	57·8	53·2	
(f) Proportion of production destined for export: $b/a \times 100$	68	64	63	59	63	63	67	63	62	64
(g) Proportion of imports in total of disposable goods: $c/e \times 100$	27	33	37	34	34	32	33	36	32	33

Statistical source: *Bulletin de la Banque Centrale du Congo Belge et du Ruanda–Urundi*, the October number of which, in all years, contains estimates of the national income. The estimates given in Table 2 concern only production of goods; services are excluded.

continuous and fairly constant pressure of the factors conditioning growth. Indeed, the figures show little deviation from the general trend, and what deviation there is derives merely from the effect of cyclical fluctuation. If we leave out of account subsistence production and limit our investigation to market production, the 'trend' for the thirty-five post-war years shows an annual increase of 6 per cent.[1] As far as I know, such a marked and continuous growth has rarely been attained elsewhere in the world.[2]

II. EXTENT OF DEVELOPMENT

May I begin by enumerating briefly the various criteria by which one may judge the importance of the factors of growth at work in the Congo, and the level of development attained ?

TABLE 2

COMPONENTS OF FOREIGN TRADE IN CERTAIN AFRICAN COUNTRIES
(Average of years 1954–7)

	Proportion of Capital Goods in Imports (%)	Value of Exports per Head (in dollars)
Congo	35	35
French Equatorial Africa	30	16
Cameroons (under French protection)	24	27
French West Africa	19	17
Madagascar	18	18
Algeria	17	46
Morocco	15	33
Togoland (under French protection)	14	
Tunisia	12	32
Ghana		53
Kenya-Uganda		17
Nigeria		12
Tanganyika		13
Egypt		18

Statistical source : *Étude sur la situation économique de l'Afrique depuis 1950*, New York, Nations Unies, 1959, pp. 166-9. (*Economic Survey of Africa since 1950*, pp. 160-6.)

[1] On the method of calculating the national product, cf. 'Quelques Considérations sur le développement de l'économie congolaise', *Bulletin de la Banque Centrale du Congo Belge et du Ruanda-Urundi*, Vol. 3, mars 1961, p. 100.
[2] Cf. F. Bézy, *Principes pour l'orientation du développement économique au Congo*, Léopoldville, Éditions de l'Université, 1959, pp. 3-8.

(a) *The Congo as an Open Economy*

The part played by foreign trade in providing a market for the national product and in supplying disposable resources gives some idea of the state of development of an economy. In a state of complete under-development, the whole of production is devoted to consumption, in a subsistence economy, and income is extremely low. At the other extreme, in an advanced state of development, production is fairly diversified and productivity high enough to ensure an appreciable average income per head, without dependence on foreign countries.

In the Congo, development takes the form of a huge export of primary goods, financing for the major part the import of capital goods, which strengthen the factors of growth. On an average over the last ten years, imports have formed about a third of available goods and two-thirds of production has been exported.

(b) *Size of Industry in the Congo*

Another way of measuring, on an international level, the stage of development of the Congolese economy, is by comparing, for different countries, the proportion of the gross domestic product provided by agriculture and industry :

TABLE 3

CONTRIBUTION OF AGRICULTURE AND INDUSTRY
TO THE GROSS DOMESTIC PRODUCT IN 1956 (%)

	Agriculture	Industry
Ethiopia	78	9
Tanganyika	68	10
India	64	11
Burma	52	15
Philippines	40	19
Kenya	39	20
Colombia	36	21
Egypt	35	15
Morocco	34	26
Congo	24	39
Netherlands	11	43
West Germany	9	49
Belgium	7	48
United Kingdom	7	39
United States	5	38

Statistical source : *Bulletin Mensuel de Statistiques des Nations Unies*, XIII, 1, janvier 1959, pp. x-xiv.

It seems that, if we use the progressive substitution of industry for agriculture as an index of development, the Congo is about half-way between highly under-developed and highly developed countries. For more accurate comparison with the latter, we should also take into account the structure of industrial production. In 1957, this was made up as follows : mining and metal extraction and basic refining, 51 per cent; industrial processing of agricultural products, 12 per cent; manufacturing industries, 21 per cent; building and production of building materials, 16 per cent. The passage from agricultural to industrial activity is the first mark of development, as it indicates that the country is being liberated from a subsistence economy. But, for the most part, industrial production has not yet passed the primary stage. It is in this respect that the Congolese situation differs from that of highly developed countries. In manufacturing industries proper production is, however, expanding vigorously.

TABLE 4

COEFFICIENT OF INCREASE OF PRODUCTION OF MANUFACTURED
GOODS IN 1957 COMPARED WITH 1938 AND 1949 *

	1957/1938	1957/1949
World	2·42	1·66
Class I	2·49	1·60
Class II	2·11	1·70
Class III	2·22	2·39
Class IV	2·38	1·81
Africa		
Tunisia	..	1·35
Egypt	3·22	1·53
Morocco	..	1·53
Union of South Africa	3·80	1·68
Algeria	..	1·96
Rhodesia	7·48	2·31
Angola	..	2·32
Congo	12·58	3·21

* Countries are arranged in Classes according to the size of their output of manufactured goods, in dollars per head, in 1953. Class I, $200 or more ; Class II, $100 to $199 ; Class III, $50 to $99 ; Class IV, less than $50.

Cf. *Bulletin Mensuel de Statistiques des Nations Unies*, XIV, 11, novembre 1960, pp. viii et xvi. For Africa, see *Étude sur la situation économique de l'Afrique depuis 1950*, New York, Nations Unies, 1959, p. 146.

(c) *Size of the Volume of Employment*

In forty years the labour force employed in Congolese enterprises, outside the subsistence economy, has increased considerably, so that in 1955 it comprised nearly 40 per cent of the adult male population. Today the Congo has by far the largest industrial working class of Central Africa.

TABLE 5

POPULATION AND INDIGENOUS LABOUR-FORCE IN THE CONGO

(000's)

	(a) Labour-force	(b) Able-bodied Adult Males	a/b %
1915	37	—	—
1920	125	—	—
1925	292	2,138	13·6
1930	399	2,419	16·5
1935	377	2,499	15·1
1940	536	2,607	20·6
1945	700	2,656	26·4
1950	962	2,843	33·8
1955	1,183	3,043	38·9

Cf. F. Bézy, *Problèmes structurels de l'économie congolaise*, Louvain, Éditions Nauwelaerts, 1957, p. 101.

TABLE 6

NUMBER OF AFRICAN WAGE-EARNERS

(1954–7)

	(000's)
Congo	1,083
Algeria	1,035
Morocco	928
Southern Rhodesia	610
Kenya	555
Tanganyika	431
Northern Rhodesia	263
Ghana	262
Madagascar	248
Uganda	226
Nyasaland	164
Ruanda-Urundi	114

Statistical source: *Étude sur la situation économique de l'Afrique depuis 1950*, New York, Nations Unies, 1959, p. 48.

(d) *Size and Increase of Urban Population*

In the Congo there is a marked discrepancy between the distribution of population and resources. As a result of development, which groups men together in places of work and communication, there have been, in a short time, considerable migrations of population. Before the war only 8 per cent of the total population lived outside their traditional areas. Now one-quarter of the population does so. In fifteen years, the urban population proper has increased fivefold, and it is more and more tending to concentrate in large towns.

TABLE 7

GROWTH OF URBAN POPULATION IN THE CONGO, 1940–55
(Indigenous population — 000's)

Inhabitants in 1955	Number of Urban Centres	1940 (a)	1955 (b)	b/a
More than 100,000	2	74	505	6·8
50,000 to 100,000	4	50	252	5·0
20,000 to 50,000	7	51	183	3·6
10,000 to 20,000	9	38	129	3·4
Total of urban centres	22	213	1,069	5·0
Total population living outside traditional habitat		1,133	2,850	2·5
Total population		10,328	12,563	1·2

Cf. F. Bézy, *Problèmes structurels de l'économie congolaise*, Louvain, Éditions Nauwelaerts, 1957, p. 59.

III. FORMS OF DEVELOPMENT

(a) *The Congo: a Dual Economy*

More than any other Central African country (except perhaps Northern Rhodesia), the Congo is an economy of a 'dual' type. That is to say, everywhere outside the subsistence economy, development of production has been brought about by enterprises of a capitalist type, under the management of Europeans. In most of the neighbouring countries the contribution of foreigners has been limited to the development of transport and marketing of produce, while most of the production is carried out by enterprises of a traditional type, under indigenous control. In the Congo there has been active European participation even at the primary stage, not only in industry (mining or manufacturing), but also in agriculture.

TABLE 8

SIZE OF INDIGENOUS ENTERPRISES AND INCOME OF AFRICAN
WAGE-EARNERS IN THE CONGO

(Millions of francs)

	1950	1954	1958
(a) Gross national product	30,480	49,350	55,850
(b) Marketed product of indigenous enterprises	3,600	4,950	6,230
(b)/(a) as %	12	10	11
(c) Monetary income of indigenous population	8,780	15,910	20,330
(d) Wages paid to indigenous population	5,180	10,960	14,100
(d)/(c) as %	59	69	69

Statistical source : 'National Product, National Income and National Expenditure in the Belgian Congo in 1958' in *Bulletin de la Banque Centrale du Congo Belge et du Ruanda-Urundi*, VIII, 11, novembre 1959, *passim*.

The above table shows how independent indigenous producers in the Congo play only a small part in the production of goods that pass through commercial channels. Thus, it is not surprising that such a large part of the active population should have been absorbed into the working class, and that such a considerable proportion of the monetary income of the Congolese is made up of wages.

(b) *Structure of the Western-type Economy and Formation of Capital*

As much as two-thirds of the capital invested in the Congo comes from the private sector of the economy. The main contribution of the state has been the carrying out of the ten-year plan, 1950–9. In the private sector, a detailed examination of company balance sheets and of issues of shares and debentures shows that as much as 60 per cent of the funds invested comes from the undistributed profits of the large firms. In a period of investment, for several years running, up to 40 or 50 per cent of annual profits have been ploughed back :

We should ask how such a high coefficient of reinvestment can have been attained. To answer this question we have to survey briefly the whole process of the domestic accumulation of capital. The first element that we have to consider is the dichotomy of the

TABLE 9

DISTRIBUTION OF PROFITS IN CONGOLESE COMPANIES
(Millions of francs)

	(a) Total Profits	(b) Gross Distributed Dividends	(c) $\frac{(a)-(b)}{(a)} \times 100$
1950	7,887	1,877	76
1951	4,738	2,599	45
1952	6,731	3,417	50
1953	6,765	3,837	43
1954	7,197	4,383	39
1955	8,105	4,978	38
1956	9,642	6,032	37
1957	10,839	6,608	39
1958	8,490	5,541	35
1959	7,258	5,570	23

'Profits of joint-stock companies where main activity is in the Congo', *Bulletin de la Banque Centrale du Congo Belge et du Ruanda-Urundi*, IX, 5, mai 1960, p. 231.

structure of Western-type economy in the Congo. No organized capital market exists in the country : there is no stock exchange ; commercial banks have hitherto hardly ever granted long-term credit, and the 'investment banks' (notably the Societé de Crédit au Colonat et à l'Industrie) have absurdly limited scope for action. If an enterprise wishes to buy plant, it can attract capital only by working through a European stock exchange. Naturally, only the biggest firms, with established reputations, subsidiaries of the large Belgian trusts, have access to the European capital market. Small and middling enterprises, unknown outside the Congo, have no chance of acquiring fresh capital from abroad.

The result is an uneven distribution of capital in the market economy of the Congo. Whatever the sector — mining, manu-facturing, agriculture, commerce, banking — activity is divided between two groups of enterprises of very different character : on the one hand, a small number of firms of very large size, highly integrated on the financial level ; on the other hand, a host of small or medium-sized units with little relation between each other. The first group is responsible for a proportion of production or activity which ranges from 50 per cent to more than 80 per cent of the total, according to the sector. In the mining industry, for instance, five large firms, financially integrated, account for four-fifths of total production, employing only one-quarter of the labour force. In banking, one single organization holds 80 per cent of the deposits (end of 1955). As far as import trade is concerned, activity is distributed as follows:

TABLE 10

STRUCTURE OF IMPORT TRADE IN THE CONGO IN 1957
(Distribution of firms according to size of turn-over)

Size of Turn-over (m. francs)	Numbers of Firms	Turn-over (m. francs)	Percentage of Turn-over
Above 500	6	5,026	27
100–500	32	5,835	32
50–100	38	2,505	14
10–50	155	3,353	18
5–10	105	736	4
1–5	423	970	5
Total	759	18,425	100

Statistical source: 'The structure of the import trade in the Belgian Congo and in Ruanda-Urundi', *Bulletin de la Banque Centrale du Congo Belge et du Ruanda-Urundi*, IX, 3, mars 1960, p. 95.

Out of 759 businesses examined (account was taken only of traders with a turn-over of more than a million francs a year), 38 large firms — that is, 4·5 per cent — had the monopoly of 60 per cent of the activity, 528 firms — that is, 70 per cent of the enterprises examined — only accounted for 9 per cent of the import trade.

Because of their access to European capital markets, large firms have been able to finance fairly modern techniques from the very beginning. They have created powerful sources of energy.[1] The quantity and quality of their equipment have enabled them to effect considerable increases in labour productivity. Thus, while their position on the production market is important, on the labour market they occupy a comparatively insignificant place. Much of the Congolese labour force is scattered through a host of small enterprises that, lacking financial means, are forced to use (or even abuse) highly labour-intensive methods, to the detriment of labour productivity. There is, therefore, a great difference in the structure of costs in the two groups of enterprises. Thus, in the mining industry, wages make up less than 10 per cent of costs in Upper

[1] Total output of electricity is higher in the Congo than in any other African country, apart from the Union of South Africa. The production per head, in kilowatt hours, is 194 in the Congo, while in Algeria it is only 106, in Morocco 97, in the Cameroons 75, in Tunisia 67, in Ghana 60, in Kenya 44, and less everywhere else. Cf. *Étude sur la situation économique de l'Afrique depuis 1950*, New York, Nations Unies, 1959, p. 36. (*Economic Survey of Africa since 1950*, p. 35.)

Katanga Province, but more than 70 per cent in most enterprises in Kivu.

On the labour market, the general level of wages has been very low for a long time, for the following reasons. On the one hand, demand for labour comes mainly from a large number of small and medium-sized enterprises which can offer only poor wages because of the low productivity of their labour force. On the other hand, the supply price of labour is low for sociological reasons,[1] and because, not being organized, labour has had, until recently, no power as a pressure-group.[2]

As the large firms pay their workers the market-price, and no more, they can profit from the enormous difference they maintain between labour productivity and labour remuneration; the difference that Marx would have called 'surplus value'. It is from this difference that the sums for financing programmes for improving plant are extracted. In the Congo, such programmes have been concentrated into certain fields, as a consequence of the investment policy of the trusts; the way in which they complement each other has been turned to the profit of the enterprises, as a result of greater and greater external economies. Within these poles of growth, enormous liquid assets have been accumulated, especially in periods of cyclic prosperity. It is thus that the ploughing-back of profits has set off an autogenous development of the Congolese economy.

The main components of the mechanism of the formation of domestic saving are, then, briefly :

(1) the size of organized production, in the form of Western-type enterprises ;
(2) the dichotomy in distribution of capital ;
(3) the great difference in labour productivity — the result of (2) ;
(4) the size of the mobilized labour force — the result of (1) ;
(5) the maintenance of low wages, resulting from prevalent conditions of the labour market—the low rate of wages has favoured
    (a) the survival of marginal enterprises that provide the greater part of the labour force with work,
    (b) the self-financing of enterprises with high productivity ;

---

[1] A large number of workers are still integrated in the traditional social structure. Hence, these workers do not regard their wages as providing the main source of their essential consumption, for which, in principle, they still look to the clan. The wage, then, is no more than an extra : the Congolese, therefore, are not hard bargainers on the labour market.

[2] This fact stems, to a large extent, from the restrictive laws on trade unions, which were repealed only in 1957. Before then, out of more than a million Congolese workers, less than 10,000 were union members.

(6) the polarization of investments into sectors in which growth is centred, which are now spreading out.

As a matter of fact, Congolese economic development has been financed to a large extent by the forced saving of a generation of workers, and even of those of independent means. Indeed, economic policy has kept agricultural prices artificially low, for fear that a rise in the cost of living might bring with it an increase in wages. Thus, inflationary periods, as well as those following devaluation, have, until recently, always worsened the position of peasants and workers, thus increasing — temporarily at least — the possible mobilization of forced saving.

IV. THE ECONOMIC EFFECTS OF DE-COLONIZATION

The establishment and functioning of the Congolese economic system was possible only under a political régime of the colonial type. There can be no doubt that such a system has real advantages. Within the framework of economic liberalism it can even be considered to have been successful, if the only criterion we apply is that of the impetus given to development, and the spontaneous rhythm of expansion in the economy. No other Central African country has achieved as marked results in so short a time.

But soon after the declaration of independence (June 30, 1960) other criteria come into play, showing up the disadvantages of the present economic structure. Success in efficiency and productivity could best be assured by the organization of the market economy entirely into Western-type enterprises. But, because no initiative was left to the indigenous population (either genuinely because of their incapability, or as a consequence of racial discrimination, or in the vain hope of perpetuating economic domination), an 'enclave economy' has been created — now, by the very fact of its independence, subject to a foreign power. It is fair to say that, on June 30, 1960, no enterprise in the Congo was in the hands of nationals, and that, in the enterprises that were to be proclaimed 'alien', no Congolese had been trained to any post above that of mere foreman.

Independence has meant for the Congo, then, merely the substitution, for political allegiance, of an apparently autonomous régime which is, in fact, still economically dependent, as in many Latin-American countries. But the situation will be even more unstable in the Congo, for — unlike the countries that have been independent for a long time — it has no nationals who have been prepared to act as intermediaries and/or interlocutors with the foreigner. In the short run, only disorder can result from the co-existence of a new political order alongside an economic structure of a colonial type that has not been altered to fit the new situation. The disorder is taking the following form.[1]

Under the old order there was only one pressure group : the large capitalist enterprises, which dictated the course, directly or indirectly, of all economic policy. Since independence this group has lost a great part of its power of influence, because of the 'alien' nationality of its principal representatives. Other groups have sprung up, now exerting almost unbridled pressure : first, the police force and army ; and, secondly, the civil service. The first group gains its power by force of arms ; the second, by political pressure. Indeed, after the hurried departure of almost all the Europeans in public administration, political criteria alone have determined the choice of Congolese to replace them.

Less than a year after the advent of independence, the new pressure groups have managed to change, to their advantage, the monetary relationships of the old order. The appointment of Africans — overwhelming in public administration, less so in the private sector — has brought about the birth of a new middle class, which has inherited, to a large extent, the purchasing power of the Europeans who have now fled the country. In the national army, the average pay has increased fivefold. In the police force, the average salary has been multiplied two and a half times. In public administration, the remuneration of the lower grades was increased by a third on the declaration of independence, and new salary scales are planned for July 1961. In the private sector of the economy, wages have increased by a quarter.

On the other hand, great pressure is being placed on business firms to prevent them raising their selling prices in order to 'repress' inflation. Till now (May 1961) it is true to say that the volume of means of payment has not increased particularly.[2] But, because of the differentiated evolution of the power of social pressure groups, the global constancy of the volume of money has concealed significant changes in component monetary flows. A considerable redistribution of wealth is to be noted. Under the old order, it must be admitted, the inequality of distribution was extraordinary, even

[1] At the end of the second six months of 1961.
[2] The (fiduciary) note issue rose by 20 per cent in the year ending February 1961. But it is possible that this growth was offset by a fall in bank deposits belonging to Europeans. Actually, the Congolese, who have replaced the Europeans, prefer to use notes, even when the method by which they are paid requires them to keep a bank deposit.

given the different position of the main social groups in the hierarchy of aptitudes and wielding of responsibility.

TABLE 11

DISTRIBUTION OF NATIONAL INCOME IN THE CONGO
IN 1950 AND 1958

	Total Income (000 m. francs)		Population (000's)		Income per Head (000 francs)	
	1950	1958	1950	1958	1950	1958
Congolese population :						
Wage earners	(5·2)	(14·1)	(2,485)	(3,445)	2·09	4·09
Non-wage earners	(8·3)	(13·8)	(9,015)	(9,913)	0·92	1·39
Total	13·5	27·9	11,500	13,358	1·17	2·09
European population	8·3	16·5	56	110	148·20	150·00
Companies (undistributed profits and direct taxes)	7·2	3·4				
State (net income on property)	0·3	0·3				
Total	29·3	48·1	11,556	13,468	2·54	3·57
Income received by outside world	1·5	3·8				

Statistical source: 'National Product, National Income, and National Expenditure in the Belgian Congo, 1958', *Bulletin de la Banque Centrale du Congo Belge et du Ruanda-Urundi*, VIII, 11, novembre 1959, p. 416.

Before independence, the relationship between social classes in the Congo was poisoned by the fact that two types of discrimination were superposed one on the other : the managers and executives of enterprises were practically all white, whereas the workers and the mass of the consumers were coloured. The accession to independence brought with it yet a third type of discrimination : the difference between aliens and nationals, which has been added to the other two and arises within the same social groups. Moreover, this third type of discrimination has upset the balance of forces between the groups. Because of these factors, decolonization could not take the form of a mere evolution, on the economic level. It is, therefore, a revolution that is taking place now — one which will overthrow the economic structure of the country, in the medium long run.

In the immediate future, it is to be feared that the pressure of the new dominant groups will rapidly bring about monetary disorders. Indeed, inflation cannot for long be held back by a freezing of prices. In the small badly equipped firms, employing a great proportion of the total labour force, wages account for such a large percentage of cost-prices that an increase, at constant selling-prices, would inevitably bring about an increase in unemployment. This is, in fact, happening already. If, through lack of understanding of the inevitability (in the short-run) of this prospect, the dominant group increase their pressure, the government will have to permit a rise in prices, in order to avoid an insoluble problem being created in a short time by the extension of unemployment. And it is not only the domestic situation which will suffer from the monetary disorders. Indeed, the rise in prices will weaken the position of export firms, on the foreign market. Then there will be a depreciation — no doubt, irreversible — of the exchange rate, resulting sooner or later in devaluation.

The evolution of the situation, as I foresee it, need not be considered as inevitably consequent on the granting of independence to *any* ex-colony. The Congo is a special case, because of the singular incompatibility between its particular economic structure and its new political structure. This lack of harmony is in itself dynamic: it postulates a series of bilateral adjustments, which will doubtless follow the line of least resistance.

But we must ask how decolonization can be expected to affect the rhythm of economic development in the Congo. In the immediate future, advantageous results, as well as negative effects, are to be seen. Unfortunately, it is difficult to see whether the net effect will be positive, because of the intervention of political disorders, which can account, in part, for the deterioration of the economic situation.

I must examine the effects that can be produced, and have indeed already been produced, by inflation. These effects are evident in the way partial monetary flows have become disaligned, in that a large part of the domestic purchasing power has been transferred from the entrepreneurs to consumers favoured by the régime. Because of the demonstration effect — important in the Congo, as in all colonial societies — the new consumers have extremely little propensity to save. Two dangerous consequences are to be expected.

(*a*) In agriculture and manufacturing industry the consumer goods sector will be favoured at the expense of the sector concerned with capital goods and exports. In the enterprises in which production will be rigorously stimulated by excess demand, expansion will soon be hindered by bottle-necks, because of the inelasticity of the system of short-period production. This has already happened in manufacturing industry in Leopoldville: notably in textiles, boots and shoes, and in the soap and margarine industries.[1] It is to be feared that the excess demand might then take on abnormal forms, with the consequent risk that activity might be developed in the wrong direction, attracting investment whose future profitability is doubtful.

(*b*) The disalignment of monetary flows can endanger the development of saving, at least of the type known under the old order. Later we shall see that this difficulty can be remedied to a certain extent, even in the immediate future.

On the positive side, the following advantageous effects are to be noted :

(*a*) Imports of consumer goods are strictly controlled. The old order exercised a liberal policy in this matter, partly for the benefit of the metropolitan economy. At the present time, the decrease in exports has noticeably reduced the exchange reserves and, consequently, the volume of imports has been severely reduced. The demand for products of local manufacture has consequently been greatly stimulated, not only for substitutes for goods previously imported, but also for other products, on which an otherwise unusable purchasing power can be expended. Obviously this is an artificial diversion of demand, due to inflation, which will be temporary in so far as it goes against the preferences of the consumer.

(*b*) In European-type enterprises, Africanization of management is proceeding on a large scale and at a rapid rate. At present, half of the Europeans previously employed in the private sector of the Congo economy (not including Katanga Province) have been retired. Only the lower grades have, of course, been affected ; because of their lack of training, the Africans are not really fit for responsibilities at a high level. It seems, however, that progress will necessarily be made in this field before very long. Up to now, the dismissal of some of the European management does not seem to have had harmful repercussions on productivity. On the contrary, productivity is increasing, at any rate in manufacturing industry.[2] This shows that Africanization of management offers possibilities which the enterprises did not recognize, before they were forced to do so.

In contrast with the orderly, though rapid, evolution of Africanization in industrial management, where the best elements have been promoted, there has been excessive Africanization in public administration : only 1,100 Belgian civil servants are left in the Congo, out of 8,500 (not including Katanga Province) — that is, 13 per cent.

---

[1] Cf. F. Bézy and J. L. Lacroix, ' La Production des industries manufacturières à Léopoldville et dans le Bas-Congo ', *Notes et Documents de l'Institut de Recherches Économiques et Sociales*, No. 15/SE-11, Léopoldville, Université Lovanium, juin 1961, *passim*.   [2] *Ibid., passim.*

Africanization has not insured the appointment of the best candidates, for it has been based almost wholly on political criteria. It can be claimed without exaggeration that it is only the solidity of the economic structure that prevents the Congo from collapsing into complete anarchy.

(*c*) The demand for local products, already stimulated by import restrictions, is increased even more by the rise in wages in both private industry and public administration. Up to the present, the enterprises seem to have 'digested' the rise in wages ; this rise in purchasing power will no doubt significantly widen the domestic market, if inflation does not wipe out its effect. The rise in wages, however, will reduce the repatriation of profits but will also reduce investment if something is not done.

And even without increasing purchasing power, the Africanization will, nevertheless, increase the demand for home-produced goods, because the newly-appointed Africans have a lower propensity to import consumption goods (and to remit profits) than the Europeans, whom they replace.

Even if one neglects the influence on effective demand exerted at the moment by a degree of inflationary pressure, there is no doubt that there exist in the Congo profitable investment opportunities in the consumption goods industries. There is a potential derived demand for the capital goods industries, where activity at the moment is very low. As long as the political climate calms down, such investment can have multiplier effects to give new impetus to the economy.

(*d*) But where can the capital be found ? As a result of the substantial redistribution of purchasing power from producers to consumers, it might be argued that the principal source of investment funds has been dried up ; perhaps we are killing the goose that lays the golden eggs.

It can be replied, first, that the effect on total profits of the rise in average costs has been offset, at least in part, by a considerable increase in output, above even full employment output. Moreover, exchange control is restricting the repatriation of profits, which under the old order was virtually limitless. Thus, at the moment, the Congolese private sector has considerable excess liquidity. If investment is not being carried out, it is because of the political situation and the shortage of foreign currency. In the future it will be necessary, by skilful policy, to allow sufficient profits to be repatriated, to attract foreign funds, but to restrict these remittances sufficiently to encourage the financing of internal development. It seems, to the present author, that a solution can be found which will

87

require no reduction in reinvestment, despite the present re-distribution of wealth.

In the long run, we must hope that the state will be able to redress, by appropriate investments, the present disadvantages of the Congo economy. In my opinion the remedy should lie less in an immediate transformation of existing enterprises, than in the creation of a new type of economic sector which will be able to co-exist economically with the old one. In any case, it is the existing economy which will provide, as in the past, the financial means for the realization of this policy.

Between 1950 and 1957 the Congolese companies provided more than half of the tax receipts of the state by paying in taxation more than 42 per cent of their income. During this period taxes have absorbed 20 per cent of national income [1] — a figure considerably higher than that for most under-developed countries. Nevertheless, it will be remembered that, during this period, self-financing was very substantial in the Congo. For the economy as a whole gross capital formation has therefore exceeded 25 per cent of national expenditure, while in other African countries (except Rhodesia where the economy is similar to that of the Congo) less than 15 per cent was invested.[2] Even in People's China, accumulation has not reached such proportions, since it has varied, from 1952 to 1956, between 18·2 and 22·5 per cent of the National Income.[3]

The ideal solution for the Congo would be to preserve such an effective device for the creation of domestic saving. Perhaps this aim is not incompatible with the necessary adaptation of the economic structure of the country to the requirements of the new political order.

---

[1] H. Leclercq, *Principes pour l'orientation d'une politique fiscale au Congo*, Léopoldville, Éditions de l'Université, 1959, p. 16, *et seq.*

[2] *Étude sur la situation économique de l'Afrique depuis 1950*, New York, Nations Unies, 1959, p. 98.

[3] Ch. Bettelheim, 'Accumulation et développement économique de la Chine', *Économie Appliquée*, XIII, 3, 1960, p. 351.

Chapter 4

PROBLEMS OF ECONOMIC DEVELOPMENT OF EAST AFRICA

BY

DAVID WALKER

University College of East Africa

INTRODUCTORY

FOR the purposes of this paper East Africa is defined to mean the three adjacent British dependent territories of Uganda, Kenya, and Tanganyika. These three territories constitute an area which is bounded: in the north by the Sudan, Ethiopia, and Somalia; in the west by the Belgian Congo; in the south by Nyasaland and Portuguese East Africa; and in the east by the Indian Ocean. In total: the three countries have an area of about six hundred and fifty thousand square miles; a population of about twenty-two million people; and a combined domestic product of £544 million. By comparison with the really big countries of the world such as the United States, which has an area of about three million square miles, East Africa is not a large country. Nevertheless, distances are very considerable; from the north of Kenya to the south of Tanganyika is about a thousand miles; the width of Tanganyika is about six hundred miles; and her land area alone is about the same as Nigeria, and almost as much as Pakistan.

Each of the three territories has its own government and legislature and each will, in the none-too-distant future, emerge as a separate independent state — Tanganyika by the end of 1961. There is, however, some chance that after obtaining independence they may decide to come together in some sort of federation or union.

Yet, though separate countries with separate governments which often pursue diverse policies in all sorts of ways, they combine to run a number of enterprises and services on an East African basis, notably the railway and postal services and many research services. They also come together to form what does — with very few exceptions — constitute an East African Common Market or Customs Union. There is also a common monetary system and freedom

89

for capital and people to move freely from one territory to another. A number of important economic problems flow from these inter-territorial links and arrangements, and we shall be touching on them later in the paper.

Though there are many similarities between the three countries there are also significant differences both as regards their present economic characteristics and problems and also as regards the development paths they have followed. It will be necessary, there-fore, to consider, in part at any rate, the three territories separately.

In the first main section of the paper I briefly describe the main characteristics of the three economies at the present time, and in the second and third sections I briefly look back on the economic development that has occurred and indicate some of the points which seem to me to emerge from a study of the growth and present position of the three East African economies.

I. MAIN CHARACTERISTICS OF THE EAST AFRICAN ECONOMIES

In the Appendix I provide some statistics which summarize the main economic characteristics of the three economies. I would like here only to mention the really key characteristics and call attention to some factors which cannot easily be indicated in statistical tables.

The first point to emphasize is the poverty of the three countries. Even when the subsistence sector is included, average *per capita* incomes are low, varying from about £33 per head per year in Kenya to less than £20 in Tanganyika ; and these figures do not really reveal clearly the typical position, for a relatively small non-African population earns a disproportionate part of the total income. No satisfactory racial breakdown of the domestic product is available, but the average employee income is a good indication of the racial in-equality ; European wages averaging about £1,250 a year, Asians about £500, and Africans about £60 per year.

A second point is the dependence on agriculture and related forms of economic activity. This is so both with respect to domestic product and — even more so — with respect to exports. In Kenya — the least dependent on these forms of activity — the agricultural, livestock, etc., sector of the economy constitutes some 42·5 per cent of the total product and some 22 per cent of the monetary product. In Tanganyika the corresponding figures are 59 and 41 per cent, and in Uganda 54 and 50 per cent ; and of course if one takes into account the indirect contribution to the domestic product through the processing and transport activities connected with the agricultural industries the percentages would be even higher. As regards exports, with the exception of about £4·5 million of diamonds and £1 million of gold from Tanganyika, £2·5 million of copper from Uganda, and about £1·5 million of sodium carbonate from Kenya, agricultural products dominate the scene. Out of a total East African export figure of about £120 million there is no product other than agricultural products — except the four mentioned above — which contributes more than £1 million to exports.

The third point it is desired to stress is the importance of foreign trade in the three economies. Exports constitute nearly 40 per cent of East Africa's money domestic product and imports about 37 per cent. Kenya is, *prima facie*, less dependent on exports and more dependent on imports than the other two territories. However, the statistics may be misleading; since many firms have their head offices in Nairobi, goods destined to be used elsewhere in East Africa may sometimes appear as part of the Kenya import bill.

It is also important to note the relative degree of specialization in export production of the three territories. In the case of Uganda, cotton and coffee completely dominate the scene, and though a growing contribution is being made by tea and copper the country is very much at the mercy of the world demand for two crops. In contrast, the position of Kenya and Tanganyika is a good deal better from a stabilization point of view, for their exports are much more diversified.

I should now like to turn to something which is not brought out in the statistics. I have stressed the importance of agriculture, but have not said anything about the type of agriculture. In all three countries the employment sector is small and most people earn their living as peasant farmers producing their own food and also a surplus for sale — either for export or for the domestic economy. In Kenya the estimated number of employees is about 600,000 out of a population of about six and a half million. In Uganda about a quarter of a million people have jobs out of about the same total of population. It is doubtful if more than 5 to 7 per cent of the population of East Africa as a whole work as employees for wages or salaries as compared with the 40 per cent or so in the United Kingdom. Thus the vast majority of the working population are working for themselves — and as the number of independent traders and businesses is small they are working on the land. And the high estimate of the contribution of the subsistence sector to the total domestic product is evidence of this.

What is interesting is the very different contributions made to the production of export crops and cash crops generally by the ordinary African peasant.

In Uganda he is responsible for most of the agricultural cash income. All the cotton and more than 90 per cent of the coffee is produced in this way and we have noticed how these crops dominate the export sector. Non-African plantation enterprises are responsible for the important sugar industry (value of sales about £4 million in 1959), the tea industry (£1·5 million), and part of the coffee industry (£1·5 million), but the income of African producers is far greater ; that from coffee and cotton alone amounting to some £25 million in 1959 and in addition there were important sales of tobacco, livestock products, and foodstuffs probably amounting to over £10 million. The value added in the monetary sector from agriculture in 1959 is estimated at about £50·6 million ; of this total only about £5 million or 10 per cent arises in non-African enterprises and if the subsistence sector is included the share is very much lower.

When we turn to Kenya the position is entirely different. For reasons which we will notice later Kenya became, from an early stage, a country of European settlement with an agricultural economy based upon plantations, large ranches, and farms. And though African agricultural production is now developing extremely quickly the export and the cash sector generally is still dominated by non-African (European) enterprises. In 1957, for example, the contribution to the cash economy of agriculture was about £25 million, of which non-African enterprise contributed nearly £20 million. The livestock sector contributed about £8 million, of which the non-African share was nearly £6 million. Thus, unlike Uganda, non-Africans dominate in agricultural production which is sold for cash, and even more so the export trade.

And the method of production in the non-African sector is of course very different. The great mass of peasant cash production in Uganda is from small-holdings and activity complementary to, and in many cases subsidiary to, the production of subsistence food crops. And the tools of production are few and simple, often only a knife and a hand hoe. In Kenya, on the other hand, the units of production in the non-African sector are often very large and are quite highly mechanized.

In Tanganyika the position is roughly half-way between that of Kenya and Uganda. The important sisal crop is produced on large plantations as is most of the tea and some of the coffee. The cotton, cashew nuts, and most of the coffee is produced on African small-holdings in the same way as in Uganda. Though non-African estates occupy less than 1 per cent of the land, they account for some 45 per cent of her total agricultural exports and about 35 per cent of the total value of marketed agricultural produce. They are, therefore, most important, but, unlike Kenya, African production of coffee, cotton, and other cash crops has been at least equally as important as non-African production for about twenty years.

Another important characteristic is that over the years Kenya has come to occupy a key position in the East African economy. Most of the major firms which operate in the East African Common Market maintain head offices and warehousing and handling facilities for breaking bulk and distribution in either Nairobi or Mombasa. Kenya undoubtedly enjoys natural advantages within the three territories for the performance of this entrepôt function and especially *vis-à-vis* Uganda. It is interesting to note in Table 2 in the Appendix the relationship between Kenya's direct import and her net imports. The difference between these two figures represents the quantity of goods ordered by Kenya firms from outside East Africa which are eventually sent on to Tanganyika and Uganda. Kenya receives a substantial income by performing these entrepôt activities and it is perhaps significant that no less than 15 per cent of Kenya's domestic product is derived from commercial and financial activities — a much higher percentage than either of the other two territories. The Kenya Minister of Commerce has recently stated in an address to the Economics Club of Kenya (*East African Economics Review*, June 1960) that : 'The total value of the services rendered by Mombasa and Nairobi to territories other than Kenya must be an invisible export of the order of £45 million per annum'. When one recalls that the money domestic product of Kenya is only about £165 million this is a strong — probably a too strong — claim. Nevertheless, there is no doubt of the importance to the Kenya economy of this activity.

Kenya has also developed a substantial visible export trade with the other two territories. Table 2 in the Appendix shows that Kenya exported about £12 million of goods to the other two territories and had a favourable balance of trade with them of about £7 million, and Table 4 provides more information of the growing share in such trade which she is now taking. These exports consist both of agricultural products and also — and this is becoming increasingly important — of manufactured goods. It is clear from the domestic product estimates set out in Table 1 that the manufacturing sector of Kenya is much more important than the manufacturing sectors of the other two territories and a substantial proportion of this output — possibly as high as 25 per cent — is exported to Uganda and Tanganyika.

We will be looking at some of the problems that arise out of these two rôles that are being fulfilled by Kenya later in the paper. The point it is desired to make at this stage, however, is a simple one ; that Kenya is performing certain functions for the other two territories. Though East Africa as a whole is very much an export-orientated economy this is much more true of Tanganyika and Uganda than it is of Kenya. Though Kenya does export to the rest of the world a substantial proportion of her domestic product she is also an important supplier of goods and services to her East African neighbours, and this activity is a vital element in her economy.

I have touched on the importance of exports in the East African economy. This point and certain related matters need to be stressed very strongly.

In a very real sense Kenya, Tanganyika, and Uganda are dependent economies in that the level and growth of their incomes depend to a very substantial extent upon happenings outside East Africa. This is so in two important respects. First is the high proportion of money domestic product arising directly or indirectly from the production, transport, processing, and selling of exports. Changes in the world demand and supply position of the goods East Africa produces can easily affect this very large source of income and this in turn can affect other sectors of the economy.

The other reason why the term 'dependent economy' is appropriate is that a second key variable determining or influencing the level of incomes is the level of (autonomous) capital expenditures ; which investment is almost entirely carried out by the government, by other public or quasi-public bodies, or by large expatriate firms financed, for the most part, by sources of finance external to East Africa and thus dependent in the last resort upon the views of people outside the territories.

The emphasis upon the key rôle of the export and investment sectors is based upon the (observed) close association between changes in these two elements and the level of domestic money incomes.

It is perhaps appropriate to mention here that the East African governments have very little flexibility as regards running budget deficits financed by increases in the quantity of money as the three countries are all on a Sterling Exchange Standard with the money supply being provided through the East African Currency Board. This means that though balance of payment difficulties cannot really arise there is little flexibility for deficit financing.

The foreign trade position of East Africa also needs to be noted. Table 2 in the Appendix shows the position for 1959. East Africa as a whole had a surplus on the balance of trade of £7·3 million, but this overall position concealed important differences between the three territories, Kenya having a deficit of £23·1 million and Tanganyika and Uganda having surpluses of £12·8 million and £17·7 million respectively. (I have already mentioned how the published statistics may exaggerate Kenya's unfavourable balance and the favourable balances of Tanganyika and Uganda.) Kenya, moreover, had a substantial favourable balance of trade with Uganda and Tanganyika, and when one takes this inter-territorial trade into account her deficit falls to £16·3 million as compared with surpluses of £7·3 million and £16·4 million for Tanganyika and Uganda.

No territorial estimates of invisibles are available and the latest estimate for East Africa is for 1958. In that year, however, there was an overall deficit on East Africa's invisible account of about £18 million. Though it is not possible to deploy statistics in support of the following view, it is believed that Kenya has a large overall deficit on both visible and invisible account with the rest of the world offset by imports of capital and exports of goods and services to the rest of East Africa. It is believed that Tanganyika is roughly in balance with the rest of the world (including the rest of East Africa) and that Uganda has a substantial surplus with the rest of the world and with Kenya.

One final point. The racial composition of East Africa's population is given in Table 1. It is perhaps necessary, however, to mention the key rôle the small number of non-Africans fulfil in the economic life of the territories. I have already mentioned their rôle in agricultural production.

What is striking is their dominance in the non-agricultural sectors. Almost all the wholesale trade and industrial and financial services are in their hands and a good deal of the retail trade. The country's export and import trade, its electricity industry, its manufacturing industries, its banks, its railway system, etc.: these are owned or controlled by non-Africans. And in the Public Services too non-Africans fill most of the technical positions and a high proportion of the senior administrative posts. And even though the educational system has expanded very rapidly during the last fifteen years, it is almost certain that the country's administration and economy would break down if a high proportion of the non-Africans were removed. In this — as in so many other ways — East Africa is unlike the former British territories in West Africa — though the position is in no sense as bad as it was in the Belgian Congo a year ago.

II. ECONOMIC DEVELOPMENT IN EAST AFRICA

In this section an attempt is made to sketch the way in which economic development has occurred in the three territories and to indicate some of the factors that have been important in this development. No effort has been made to be complete, nor has an attempt been made to treat the three territories in the same way or at the same length.

(i) *Uganda*

From the time of Stanley's visit in 1875 Buganda — now one of the four provinces of the Protectorate of Uganda — was the centre of British and European interest in East Africa. Though Arab traders had reached Buganda at least twenty-five years before and the explorers, Speke and Grant, had discovered the source of the White Nile in Lake Victoria in 1862, it was Stanley's visit and his account of his trip which first really interested the outside world in the country. Anglican missionaries reached Buganda in 1877 and the Roman Catholics followed in 1879. Not until 1894 was the country formally taken over by the British as a Protectorate ; indeed it is from 1900, with the signing of the Uganda Agreement of that year, that one can really date the beginning of effective British administration. Uganda has thus been in contact with the world economy for a very short time.

When Speke and Grant reached Uganda it had taken them nearly two years to get there. They had travelled across what is now Tanganyika and had approached Uganda around the southern end of Lake Victoria. This was the route subsequently followed by the missionaries and traders for many years, for the direct route west across what is now Kenya was impassable because of hostile tribes and difficult country. As contact with the outside world developed and as there became established in Uganda missionaries and traders and, finally, government officials, it became clear that the only effective way to link the country with the outside world was by building a railway, and the United Kingdom government agreed to do this at the Brussels Conference of 1890 with the main objective of putting down the slave trade by opening up the country.

The Uganda railway took a long time to plan and build. Work upon the line began at Mombasa in 1895 and in December 1901 the first locomotive ran through to Kisumu on Lake Victoria, the journey to Uganda being completed by lake steamer. It is difficult to exaggerate the economic effect on Uganda of this 580-mile single track line. Before its completion the cost of moving goods to and from the coast was quite prohibitive for all except a very narrow range of goods ; ivory of course being the classic example of a commodity that could bear the cost of transport. Before the line was built the cost of moving goods to and from the coast was about £240 per ton or about 6s. per ton-mile. At the present time, with much higher wage and fuel costs than in 1902, the average cost of transport by rail in East Africa is about 20 cents per ton-mile. Transport costs were spectacularly reduced by the building of the railway.

The railway having been built, it was important to use it and find something which could be exported and thus earn money with which to purchase imports and provide the government with tax revenue so as to reduce its dependence on a rather parsimonious British Treasury ; also to prevent the British Treasury having to cover the operating costs of the new railway as well as the interest charges.

In 1902 it was by no means clear what was to be the export commodity. No minerals seemed to exist. Many attempts were made by the government and by private European entrepreneurs with tea, cocoa, sugar, coffee, ground-nuts, rubber, and other crops. After many attempts and experiments cotton turned out to be the winner ; cotton produced by peasant farmers as an addition to their subsistence activities.

Cotton production and exports expanded very rapidly after about 1905. In that year 241 bales of cotton were exported, representing about £1,000. Five years later the total had risen to over 13,000 bales of a value of £165,000. By 1925 nearly 200,000 bales of cotton were being exported down the railway line, yielding over £4 million. Money flowed back into the country and though some of it was immediately spent on imported goods, some went to the government and financed public expenditure and some was spent on home-produced commodities, thus leading directly to the expansion of the domestic money economy.

Cotton dominated the Uganda economy right up to the last war. In 1937 cotton exports were some 82 per cent of the total export income and worth over £4 million at even the low level of prices then existing and, as we have seen in Section I, cotton is still a most important income earner.

However, even in the pre-war years coffee was becoming established, also as a peasant crop. By 1937 there were about 50,000 acres planted to coffee. In that year some 13,000 tons were exported yielding about £420,000 — about a tenth of the value of cotton exports. The basis for a great advance in coffee had, however, been made. Uganda was in a good position at the end of the war to take advantage of the great upsurge in prices and under its impetus acreages and production expanded rapidly. At the present time the coffee crop is about 100,000 tons a year, and as we saw in Section I its contribution to both exports and production is now greater than cotton.

In 1904 Uganda's exports amounted to about £50,000. In 1959 domestic and inter-territorial exports combined were around £50 million, a thousandfold increase, and though there have been considerable increases in both the level of prices and the size of the population there can be no doubt of the very great real increase in export income per head, domestic income per head, and in the standard of living. In 1959 nearly 100,000 tons of coffee, 1½ million 100-lb. bales of cotton, a quarter of a million hundredweight of copper, and 66,000 hundredweights of tea were exported. In 1904 such goods were hardly being produced at all. And it has been the growth of production for export from small peasant farms that has been the main force in the development of the economy and that has provided the wealth to support the social services on the one hand and the demand for home-produced goods and services on the other, as well as the demand for a substantial flow of goods into the country from overseas. Uganda provides a text-book example of a country whose economic development has depended, and indeed still depends, upon the grafting on to a traditional and indigenous system of subsistence agriculture the production of an export crop.

Though peasant agriculture is of overwhelming importance in the economy, attempts have been made to develop and encourage other forms of economic activity, particularly in recent years. A major attempt was made in the 1950s to provide the basis for modern manufacturing industry. Very large sums of money were invested in the Owen Falls Hydro-electric Scheme in the expectation that the provision of power would remove the most important factor preventing industrialization. This has not happened and today half the capacity of the dam is unused. Though a number of individual industrial projects have been established and are now making a useful contribution to the economy, the policy as a whole has not succeeded and as yet the large sums of money expended have not yielded a very high return. The geographical isolation of the country, the smallness of the market, competition from Kenya (important because of the East African Common Market), lack of raw materials and skilled labour ; all these make it difficult for industry, unless there are special reasons, to establish itself in Uganda without very great government help. And though the rate of growth has been quite large in recent years the manufacturing sector is still very small, constituting about 6 per cent of domestic output.

In recent years, too, there has been development in plantation agriculture — particularly in tea — but as noted above such activities still constitute only about 10 per cent of the output of the monetary agricultural sector.

In looking at the economic development of Uganda an obvious question which arises is why — in contrast to Kenya and, indeed Tanganyika — plantation and settler agriculture did not get firmly established in the early years of the century. There is no simple or single explanation. One reason was the lack of a suitable crop. Tea and Arabica coffee which were tried are not really suitable for Buganda and the Eastern Province and those parts of the country which are suitable, notably the Western Province, were not well served from a transport point of view. Considerable acres were put to rubber, but except when the world price is very high Uganda cannot grow rubber at a profit. Another reason was the general policy of the government. After the First World War, and indeed before, no special attempts were made to attract settlers and this, combined with the attractiveness of Kenya and the attempt of the Kenya authorities to attract settlers, was an important reason for the lack of settlers in Uganda. Another reason was the lack of labour. Peasant cash farming having got established early on there was an unwillingness to work on the plantations. Finally, just as the small number of plantations were getting established after the First World War, they were badly hit by the world slump.

During the inter-war years sugar plantations developed to serve the home market and as already stated in more recent years there has been a development of tea plantations in the Western Province, which is now linked to the main transport system.

We have noticed the dominance of cotton and coffee in the Uganda economy. The marketing of these two crops has been very closely controlled by the government for many years. This has had a number of effects, but I have space to consider one aspect only : that (as in West Africa) very large sums of money were accumulated as marketing board surpluses during the war and early post-war years.

Due in part to the war-time bulk purchase agreements with the U.K. the Uganda government took full control over export marketing in the early war years. From 1943 onwards the prices obtained under these contracts were reasonably high and the government took the view that if they were passed on to the peasant growers the effect would be inflationary. Other reasons also led to the building up of a surplus ; the desire to have a reserve for price stabilization purposes in the future, the desire to build up a reserve to assist government capital spending in the future, and the feeling that higher prices would discourage food production.

It is not possible to be at all certain what was the main reason behind the accumulation of funds, but the upshot was that by the end of 1953 the cotton and coffee growers of Uganda had contributed nearly £30 million to price assistance funds and about £22 million to development projects of various kinds in addition to about £30 million in export taxes — very large sums indeed.

In 1953 the broad policy was changed to an attempt at deliberately forecasting the price for a season and paying the grower accordingly. The position since 1950 is, with respect to the two main crops, set out in Tables 7 and 8 in the Appendix. It will be noted that over the whole period of 1950 to 1959 coffee growers have received something like 74 per cent of the income they might have received, and in the case of cotton about 66 per cent. However, in some years the growers received very low proportions indeed. In the case of cotton, for example, in 1951 they received only 38 per cent of what they might have received and in 1952, 45 per cent. In the case of coffee they received 27 per cent only in 1950, 31 per cent in 1951, and 43 per cent in 1952. However, since the policy was changed in 1953 the position has been a good deal better and in a number of years growers have been receiving a subsidy from the price assistance funds.

At the end of 1959 some £11·6 million and £16·3 million remained in the price assistance funds with respect to coffee and cotton respectively, which is probably more than sufficient to implement the 1953 policy.

Transfers from the state marketing of cotton and coffee have enabled the government to spend on capital and current account more year by year than they would have been able or willing to raise in taxation. Most of the money was spent on relatively non-productive things : some £10 million, for example, being spent on education. Though this spending has been useful in many ways it has contributed to the very serious public finance position which now exists as it lifted government expenditure to a level which it is difficult to finance from ordinary taxation sources.

It is difficult to be sure of the general economic effects of the severe 'taxation' levied on the peasants, but in my view it damped down the development of African agriculture and the expansion of the money economy at 'the grass roots level'. In recent years, however, there is no doubt that the existence of the funds and withdrawals from them have played an important part in maintaining the level of economic activity.

(ii) *Kenya*

Though British rule was established in Kenya in 1895 the country's birth from an economic point of view really dates from 1902, when the first trains began to travel regularly from Mombasa to Kisumu and when its borders were advanced at the expense of Uganda from the Rift Valley to the present frontier, thus including all the 'Highlands' within her borders.

As in Uganda, economic development was necessary to reduce the country's dependence on the U.K. Prospects did not seem bright. There appeared to be no great sources of minerals and — unlike Uganda — much of the country seemed barren. Moreover, there seemed to be a great shortage of indigenous people and these — again unlike the people of Uganda — seemed to be extremely backward ; thus rapid development by peasant farmers seemed unlikely. On the other hand, there did seem to be some considerable stretches of land — what is now called the 'Highlands' — which appeared both more or less devoid of people and potentially attractive to Europeans from a farming point of view.

Given this assessment it seemed to the early visitors and administrators that the only hope for rapid economic development was through immigrant farming enterprise ; that the Kenya path should be similar to that of Canada and Australia. Their view was perhaps fortified by the knowledge that at the time great expansion was taking place in those countries and it seemed that if wheat and/or sheep could produce a good living in Canada and Australia, then similar activities could produce a good living in Kenya. Thus European immigrants were encouraged to come both by the administration and by the very early pioneers to develop the country on a wheat/sheep, Canada/Australia basis.

But in fact the Kenya Highlands were not really suitable for this type of farming and even today, after a century of farming and scientific effort, knowledge of how to deal with the environment so as to produce regularly good crops of wheat, etc., is not complete. And the early settlers suffered severely.

Nevertheless, by the start of the First World War economic development had got under way, though not on the basis of wheat and wool. Two other crops were crucial. First and most important, coffee. It soon became clear that parts of the Highlands — from 5,000 to 6,000 feet — were ideally adapted to growing high-grade Arabica coffee and from 1910 onwards, under the stimulus of rising world prices, considerable acreages were put to coffee and exporting began. The second crop was maize. Relatively high world prices for maize enabled farmers to make some profits from its production and export and this was a great asset to those whose land was not suitable for coffee or who could not afford its long period of gestation. There was also some planting of sisal.

In 1914 the total value of agricultural exports was about £208,000 — nearly all of it from European farms — and this was nearly double the value of total exports ten years before. By 1914 too the government was matching expenditure with revenue from Kenya and was no longer dependent on the U.K. grants.

What of African agriculture? Only in one province had any special effort been made and that had on the whole been a failure. Cotton was introduced into the Nyanza Province of Kenya where conditions seemed very similar to those in Buganda and Busoga in Uganda where cotton production was going ahead rapidly in the years before the First World War. But in Nyanza it did not catch on at this time. It is not very clear why this was so, but one answer would seem to be that there were greater opportunities for wage labour in Kenya and men preferred earning wages to producing cash crops. If the experiments in Nyanza had been successful the economic development of Kenya in succeeding years might have followed a different course, for there might have been a good deal more emphasis on African peasant agriculture.

The First World War greatly affected the Kenya economy, for most of the European farmers left to take part in the East African Campaign against the German forces in Tanganyika.

At the end of the war Kenya profited out of the short post-war primary commodity boom, but was seriously hit by the collapse of prices at the end of 1920.

During the depression years of 1921/3 government decisions were taken which were to set the pattern of the Kenya economy for many years.

Three important policy decisions may be distinguished. First, that for the foreseeable future economic development would depend primarily upon European agricultural enterprise and that such enterprise must, therefore, be encouraged and supported by government activity. This was probably good economics at the time, but it was also a reflection of the political power and influence of the European settler community. The other two decisions related to this basic one.

The second conclusion was the need to develop export crops. Coffee and sisal were to be developed on land which was suitable and by farmers who had the capital, and maize was to be grown by farmers who were not in this position. Every effort was to be made to enable farmers to make a profit on these crops by charging very low railway freight rates and by building road and railway branch lines so as to reduce costs to farmers as much as possible.

The third decision was with respect to such commodities as wheat, meat, cheese, milk, butter, etc. By the 1920s Kenya farmers could produce these commodities — though with some risks — but not at a price that could compete with imports. It was therefore decided to introduce a protective tariff on them to secure the East African market for them. Thus, the consumers in Uganda and Tanganyika as well as in Kenya were to be forced to pay higher prices for these commodities in order to provide income for the Kenya settler farmers. This early interest in protection was a forerunner of things to come. Kenya has always had a much greater interest in protectionist measures both with respect to agriculture and industry than the other two territories and this has led, from time to time, to conflicts.

During the 1920s steady progress was made. Government revenue doubled in seven years, rising from 1·6 million in 1922 to 3·3 million in 1929. By 1929, too, exports had reached £2¾ million (by the same year Uganda's exports had reached £4¼ million) almost all produced by European enterprises, of which coffee yielded about £700,000, sisal £550,000, maize £310,000, sodium carbonate £277,000. And production for the East African market also increased. Output of wheat rose from 28,000 bags in 1922 to 174,000 bags in 1929; milk production rose from 242,000 gallons in 1922 to 422,000 gallons in 1929.

In contrast to the development of European enterprise the development of African agriculture during the 1920s continued to be slight.

The great slump of the 1930s hit Kenya very badly. Its impact was accentuated by desert locust visitations which had a most serious effect on the economy. The 1930s as a whole were not good years though towards the end of the period, with the improvement in the world market position, developments along the same line as in the 1920s were bringing about a revival. Tea and pyrethrum exports were also developing in the years before the war and were beginning to make a useful contribution to the economy.

Though not affected to the same extent as in the First World War the economy was considerably affected particularly in the early years during the Second World War. And the fact that imported goods were difficult to obtain gave a fillip to the development of manufacturing industry.

Considering the post-war period in Kenya it is desired to draw attention to the following points.

First is the continuance and growth of the European agricultural sector. Figures of production and exports are set out in Tables 9 and 10 in the Appendix.

Second, very great efforts have been made in the last few years or so to develop African farming. The so-called Swynnerton Plan, a five-year plan for the development of African agriculture, was accepted in 1954 and is still continuing. Since then very large amounts of capital have been put into African farming and a complicated system of land consolidation and farm planning has been carried through. Results are now becoming clear and there is evidence of an agricultural revolution taking place in the African areas of Kenya. Between 1958 and 1959 there was a 19·5 per cent increase in the value of African agriculture and livestock. Coffee planting, so long forbidden to Africans in Kenya, has gone ahead extremely quickly and by the end of 1959 26,000 acres had been put to coffee and production, which was a thousand tons in 1954, was running at the rate of 6,000 tons valued at £2·2 million. Other crops too, including pyrethrum and tea, are also being produced by Africans. From 1957 to 1959 the cash income of farmers increased from £6·8 million to £9·1 million and all the evidence there is suggests that this rate of increase is going to continue. Change in agriculture is a fairly slow process, but with the capital expenditure already incurred or planned the economic foundations have been laid for rapid expansion. Very much higher cash incomes should be earned by African farmers during the next decade or so.

The third point to make concerning the Kenya economy is the remarkable development of secondary manufacturing industry that has taken place since the war. During a little over a decade whereas the domestic income increased three times, the manufacturing industry increased by about six times. For the most part this growth in industry has not been brought about by a policy of protection, though there have been protective measures in a number of individual commodities. The Kenya government, however, has been extremely solicitous towards potential industrialists and has done everything it can to make such people feel welcome and at home. For the most part, however, the growth in the industrial sector has been a reflection of a growing demand in East Africa for industrial products.

The fourth characteristic of the Kenya economy has been the growth of exports from Kenya to her neighbours. These movements are shown in Table 4 and it is clear that this trade is important to her. Traditionally Kenya's exports to Uganda and Tanganyika have been dairy products, but in recent years there has been a substantial growth in exports of manufacturing industry. There has also been a substantial growth in invisible exports to the other two territories.

(iii) *Tanganyika*

German rule began in Tanganyika in 1885. Before that date the principal contact of the inland parts of the country with the outside world had been with the Arab trading caravans who had been trading — mainly in slaves and ivory — for a good many years before. In the thirty years of effective German occupation a tremendous amount was done. Much money and energy was devoted to research and development in plantation agriculture and much was discovered and put into effect concerning not only sisal, but also coffee, tea and rubber. Two railways were built — one line from Tanga to Moshi and one from Dar-es-Salaam to Kigoma on Lake Tanganyika.

By the beginning of the First World War a pattern of exports had been built up which, in its emphasis on sisal, oil seeds, coffee, and cotton, has persisted to the present day. In 1913 about 20 million tons of sisal, 9 million tons of ground nuts, 1 million tons of coffee, 2 million tons of cotton, and 6 million tons of copra were exported; sisal exports alone amounted to over £500,000. All this production was from alienated land and no real attempt was made to induce the Africans to turn to the production of cash crops. However, unlike the early days in Kenya, emphasis was upon plantations rather than upon farming in the European sense.

Tanganyika suffered badly during the First World War. Many plantations were abandoned and considerable destruction took place. Thus, when the British received the Mandate from the League of Nations in 1919 they took over a country in a pretty parlous state from an economic point of view.

During the 1920s there was a period of quite rapid development during which public expenditures increased and there was considerable private investment. Exports which were around £1 million in 1921 rose to £4 million in 1928. Progress, however, was not continued at the same rate in the 1930s. There was the setback of the world slump and then, as the Hitler régime rose to power in Germany, there was considerable political uncertainty as to whether Germany would take over again. This was not good for economic development. Nevertheless, by 1937 exports were back around the £4 million mark.

During the inter-war period as a whole there were some important developments. The transport system was greatly improved, a new railway line being constructed to Lake Victoria from Tabora and the Moshi line extended to Arusha, and a number of new roads built. The most important developments, however, were the great efforts made to induce African production of cash crops. The most significant of these were concerned with the growing of high-grade coffee by the Chagga on the slopes of Kilimanjaro (as early as 1924 the Kilimanjaro Native Planters' Association, the forerunner of the famous Kilimanjaro Native Co-operative Union, was formed), the planting of Robusta coffee in the Bukoba District, and the considerable planting of cotton in the Lake Victoria Basin generally. By the end of the inter-war years African peasant production of cash and export crops was quite considerable, probably amounting to almost 50 per cent of such agricultural produce.

However, though great progress had been made it is important not to exaggerate the impact that had been made on a poor subsistence economy. By 1938 there was probably a population of about 6 million people. In that year exports and imports were about £4 million each and thus *per capita* less than 13s. per annum. Government expenditure was running around £2 million a year, representing a *per capita* expenditure of about 6s. per year. There can be little doubt that the money economy was relatively small and the amount of goods the typical Tanganyikan was able to buy was miserably low.

During the period since the war development has gone ahead rapidly as shown in the Tanganyikan tables in the Appendix. Increases in production and the favourable movements of the terms of trade have increased the standard of living of the ordinary man and have also enabled the government to acquire more resources to assist economic development. And in very recent times the generally good political atmosphere, due to the absence of racial and tribal conflicts and the inspiring leadership of the present Prime Minister, have made Tanganyika the most favoured of the East African territories for foreign investors.

To some extent the improvements in Tanganyika have been in commodities that were important before the war — sisal, cotton, and coffee — but new commodities have also come into prominence, notably diamonds, cashew nuts, and ground-nuts, and in recent years the manufacturing sector has been growing fast though it is still in aggregate very small.

Although official and continuously comparable domestic product calculations go back only to 1954 it is possible to make rough estimates of the economy's rate of growth during the last ten years. In Tanganyika, as in so many economies that are dependent on exports, the rate of growth of exports is a fair indication of the rate of growth in the economy as a whole. From 1948 to 1959 both volume and value of exports increased about 2·7 times or about 10 per cent per annum. The export sector is about 25 per cent of domestic output. In contrast, production in the subsistence sector probably advanced at only a slightly faster rate than the population increased — say by 2½ per cent per annum. Aggregating these growth rates it is reasonable to estimate that Tanganyika's real domestic product may have increased by about 5 per cent per annum since 1948. Since the annual population growth was about 1·7 per cent per annum it is clear that there has been a very real gain in *per capita* incomes, although that income may still seem very low.

III. SOME LESSONS FROM EAST AFRICAN EXPERIENCE

I want in this third section to try to indicate some of the points of general interest to those concerned with the problems of economic development which seem to emerge from a study of the development paths and present development position of the East African territories. Some of these points emerge fairly naturally and directly out of the material deployed in Sections I and II, but others will not and my claim that they are significant will have to be taken on trust — for there is not space to set out all the evidence.

(i) *Natural Resources*

In considering the development problem in East Africa it is vital to appreciate some of the physical and geographical features of the area.

On the whole, the East African environment is a harsh one from an economic point of view. First, there is a lack of minerals. The only minerals that have played a significant part in the economic development of the area are the diamonds, soda ash, copper, and gold that we mentioned when we discussed the structure of East African exports earlier in the paper and the internal use of local rocks for the production of cement, bricks, etc. There have been small amounts of other metals mined — notably wolfram in Uganda — but not in significant quantities over the years. It is known that there is coal in Southern Tanganyika, but it is away from the coast and it has not yet been worth while exploiting. There is, too, a complex of minerals in Eastern Uganda which may at some date provide the basis for a fertilizer and chemical industry. The oil companies have spent considerable sums of money looking for oil, particularly in the coastal regions, but so far without success.

The absence of minerals implies the need for agriculture to be of first importance and yet — and this is my second point — rainfall and other natural factors drastically limit the land area that is really suitable for intensive agricultural development. About two-thirds of the land area of Kenya, one-third of Tanganyika, and a small part of Uganda have at best rainfall suitable only for an unintensive type of pastoralism. Rather less than one-quarter of the total land area of East Africa has a good chance of obtaining regularly year by year more than 30 inches of rain, and from a rainfall point of view this is what is required to enable intensive agricultural development to be viable. There is probably scope for development of the area's water resources through irrigation schemes and the like, but not only is this extremely expensive, but a good deal more basic scientific knowledge is required before many areas could be so opened up.

The soils of East Africa too pose their problems to the potential user. It is often thought that soils in tropical countries are of very high fertility. This is not so. In East Africa some soils are as good as any in the world, but for the most part there is a deficiency of minerals or of humus and soils are on the whole less durable than those of the temperate latitudes.

Then there is the presence of numerous diseases. Malaria, for example, is endemic throughout East Africa and this has a weakening effect on the population. Also very important are the diseases caused by the tsetse fly. At the present time about 40 per cent of the land area of East Africa is tsetse infected ; about two-thirds of Tanganyika, about one-seventh of Uganda, and about one-tenth of Kenya (there being few occurrences of the fly in desert and semi-desert areas).

To really rid an area of tsetse fly requires amongst other things a fairly dense and permanent settlement of farmers. In this connection, and indeed in many other ways, progress is hindered in many parts of East Africa by the lack of people! Though there are some areas, particularly in Kenya, where there is a fairly high population density — though not by Asian or West Indian standards — most of the area is under-populated and economic development is hindered thereby.

Closely connected with the basic natural endowments of the region is a general lack of knowledge as to how to deal with many of the problems, particularly those concerned with diseases of men, animals, and plants. There is also a lack of knowledge of the social structures and ideas that are prevalent in the economic structure of the main productive unit — the farm. In comparison with the research that has been done in the Western world relatively small amounts have been done on problems of tropical agriculture and diseases. There is also a shortage of trained and skilled manpower at almost all levels and of entrepreneurial ability.

One final point concerning natural endowments. Geographical factors are such as to make the transport of goods and people a relatively difficult and costly operation. There is only one river of major importance from a transport point of view — the Nile — and though it is used for part of its course, long hauls are not possible because of rapids, etc. Railway costs both for building and of operation tend to be high, for lines have to cross difficult country and also have to pass through long stretches of country which because of lack of water or tsetse fly are not developed and from which no traffic originates. In Tanganyika, for example, most of the centre of the country is arid and the more productive parts are concentrated in rather disconnected areas around the periphery of the great central arid area. And although roads and railways link the main concentrations of production and population, distances and dispersion make costs high.

High transport costs also make the development of a complete East African market much more difficult. There is, for example, a modern textile factory in Uganda. The capital of Tanganyika, Dar-es-Salaam, is nearly a thousand (transport) miles away and the cost of transporting cotton goods from the mill in Uganda to Dar-es-Salaam is far greater than the cost of transporting goods there by sea from Bombay.

(ii) *Exports*

It will be clear from what has been written above that the dynamic element in the development of all three territories has been the production and sale of goods in the overseas market. And it is difficult to see how it could have been otherwise. Moreover, it seems to me that the expansion of agricultural and mineral exports is still a prerequisite of any major attempt to increase *per capita* incomes.

The development process in East Africa seems to have taken place in the following way. An export crop or crops are developed or are expanded and money flows into the country from outside. A substantial part of this money is spent directly or indirectly upon imports ; the remainder plays a significant rôle in the development of internal trade. As the export sector grows and the inflow of money increases there is a tendency for local industries to be established in response to the increase in the size of the market and such growth can be encouraged to some extent by government action. With the growth of local industry the level of inter-regional trade grows, but growth depends in the last resort on the growth of export earnings.

With the present low level of money incomes and the general poverty from the point of view of natural resources not only is there no magic factor which could dramatically transform the region's economy, but in my view a 'boot-strap' operation is not possible and the only likely way to reach a situation where it might be possible is by expanding exports.

To increase the level of exports requires of course increases in agricultural production and we shall be looking at this in the next section. But it also requires both a reasonably developed marketing system and a cheap and efficient transport system, not only with respect to the long main-line rail hauls to the coast, but also on the branch lines and the feeder roads that bring the produce to the main centres. The marketing function — the provision of proper facilities linking buyers and sellers — is extremely important when one is dealing with traditionally minded producers, particularly if it is desired to bring about the production of a new crop or a change in the appearance or type of crop that is being produced.

I have suggested that exports have been and are the dynamic element in connection with the economic development of East Africa. What is important, however, is not so much the quantity of exports that is produced, but the amount of money that is received for them. If export prices rise the increase in revenue resulting can have just as stimulating an effect on the development of the economy as can an increase in revenue due to an increase in production; though, of course, if the prices of imports have increased *pari passu* and the country requires the same quantity of them then there will be a much larger leakage and the stimulating effect will be that much reduced. Periods of rising export prices have on the whole been good for economic development and periods of low or falling export values have been poor.

In so far as exports and imports constitute an important part of the domestic product it follows too that changes in the terms of trade have important effects on the quantities of resources available for use in the countries and, therefore, upon the standard of living in a broad sense. There is no direct link between increases in production and changes in the standard of living. It is possible for movements in the terms of trade to offset increases in production.

One final point concerning exports. At the present time there is concern in East Africa with respect to the Common Market/Free Trade area issue in Europe. East Africa as a whole exports roughly the same value of exports to the six as to the seven; in Kenya, however, 35 per cent of exports go to the six and only 26 per cent to the seven; corresponding figures for Tanganyika are 25 and 38 per cent and for Uganda 19 and 21 per cent. If the effect of the European Common Market arrangements is to protect the ex-French and Belgian colonial producers at the expense of other producers, then this will be very serious for East Africa.

(iii) *African Agriculture*

If my view of the importance of exports is correct it follows, given the present structure of the East African economy, that a great expansion in the output of the African agricultural sector is required. How far is this likely?

From one point of view the achievements of the ordinary African peasant farmer in Uganda and Tanganyika are very great. As stated above the Uganda farmers, using very simple implements, produced (and exported) some 400,000 bales of cotton and some 90,000 tons of coffee in 1959 as well as great quantities of foodstuffs and livestock products both for on-the-farm consumption and for sale to the urban population and those working on the non-African plantations. And the achievements of Tanganyikan farmers too with less good natural conditions are also great.

Yet it is important to get things into perspective. *Per capita* incomes are low and *per capita* incomes of ordinary peasant farmers are even lower. And though there has been growth during the last fifty years and in many cases very rapid growth, the absolute level reached is not high and compared with the aspirations of the people, it is extremely low. Moreover, and this is a key point, it seems very doubtful if a continuation of the paths that have followed will produce a rate of improvement similar to that obtained in the past. There is some evidence that something like a limit in *per capita* output in the peasant sector with present methods may have been reached in recent years in Tanganyika and Uganda — though this is a rather bold and rash judgment to make as it has been said and proved wrong so often in the past!

I have already stated that the production of export and cash crops by African farmers has been done without any real change in the farming system; by adding on an acre or two of cotton or coffee or ground-nuts cultivated in the traditional manner with hoe and axe and knife. Increases in production have been achieved primarily by increasing acreages rather than by raising yields; though whilst productive and accessible land is abundant this is of no great account, for what matters in these circumstances is yield per man, rather than yield per acre ; and over the long run yield per man has certainly gone up.

The building of railways and the establishment of an effective market demand for crops caused the farmers to work harder, though essentially in the same way. Farmers gave up leisure to produce crops for sale. They took advantage of new market opportunities to bring themselves to a new production/leisure equilibrium.

Now this method of expanding agricultural output is becoming difficult. On the one hand the availability of good and accessible land is no longer as easy as it was. Second, the scope for increased production by having less leisure is now by no means great given East Africa's climatic conditions and the heavily concentrated demands it makes at harvesting and planting time. Moreover, the development of educational facilities is reducing the availability of child labour to the farmer.

Agricultural acreage and production statistics are not sufficiently good to establish beyond reasonable doubt many propositions. But it is fairly clear to me that, for example, cotton yields per acre in Uganda have hardly altered during the last thirty years. And as this is a crop to which a very great deal of attention has been given by the research services and by the field extension services this is significant. Then in more recent years there is some evidence that acres per man and production per man has not been rising. During the last ten years total acreages in Uganda under crops have gone up by about 26 per cent whereas the population has increased by about 30 per cent. Average cultivated acres *per capita* have remained more or less constant at around 1·4 acres, whereas up to the early 1950s *per capita* acreages were increasing.

In my view the scope for increases in production with existing methods and arrangements is not great. However, to drastically alter the farming system is no mean task. The production of food crops is even today regarded as the first priority by most farmers. Though most farmers produce a cash crop for the world market or for sale in the towns, and are, therefore, part of the money economy, all are subsistence farmers in the sense that they grow their own food and there is no sign of any real change in this position. And, though simple cost/benefit analysis suggests that in many cases specialization on cash or export crop production would increase net incomes, many farmers are reluctant to do this for reasons which are often neither irrational nor social.

There is a great demand by farmers for security and they are prepared to pay a substantial insurance premium for the security which, they believe, production of their own food provides. And there are very grave risks in African conditions, where so much is unknown, of putting all one's eggs in one basket. Then very often additional capital is required in order to expand production for the cash sector and this is not very easy to obtain. Thirdly, there is the very high subjective rate of interest which African farmers have, and given the various risks and uncertainties to which he is subject this is not surprising, but it makes it difficult to persuade him to invest.

Given that the subsistence sector is likely to persist for a good time to come, it is important that attention be given to increasing labour productivity in it, as very often the peak period of planting or harvesting coincides with the peak period for harvesting or planting an export or cash crop. On the whole, agricultural departments have not paid a great deal of attention to the productivity of the subsistence sector.

It is fairly easy to list what is required to bring about a fairly substantial increase in production in the peasant sector. It is necessary for farms to be consolidated and fenced and for there to be changes in the land tenure system designed to give security so as to ensure that a farmer has a real interest in developing his land. It is necessary for the plough to replace the hoe; to get rid of tedious and time-consuming hand-weeding. Livestock needs to be fully integrated in the farm so that animals may be used for ploughing and carting and use made of manure. Spraying and fertilizers need to be used and in some areas new land needs to be opened up, possibly involving the use of tractors and irrigation. On the whole these methods are known and recent work in Kenya in connection with the Swynnerton Plan has shown what are the necessary ingredients in order to get the changes brought about. First, there must be co-operation between the people and the various government departments. Second, there must be farm plans drawn up on the basis of experience in the field and not just on the research farm ; and the farm plan needs to be explained carefully to the individual farmer by an agricultural officer whom he trusts. Third, the farmer must be followed up very frequently by the agricultural officer to ensure that the farm plan was really understood and is being carried out. Fourth, which follows from the previous points, capital has to be injected into peasant farming for tools, fencing, and land consolidation and where necessary for feeder roads and for water. And quite a part of this capital must be available either as a gift or at extremely favourable rates of interest. Finally, the farm plan must be geared to the market. There is no point in having plans to produce commodities for which there is no demand.

Now, as I have said, the ingredients are known and the success of the Swynnerton Plan has demonstrated that such a policy can be carried out under East African conditions. But there are many factors which have to exist simultaneously and in so many parts of the area these do not exist. In some there is a lack of capital or of revenue money for extension workers. In others there is lack of knowledge as to an appropriate farm plan. In others there is no co-operation between the people and the government. In all areas there is great conservatism and inertia.

It is not easy in my view to visualize a situation in which agricultural output from peasant agriculture will grow very rapidly during the next five to ten years, though it may well be that new African governments will be able to enthuse their people and obtain funds and staff to bring about an agricultural revolution. But there is no real evidence to support this hope.

(iv) *Non-African Agriculture*

I propose to comment on Tanganyika and Uganda first of all and then to take Kenya for, as mentioned in an earlier section of the paper, Kenya's development in this respect has been different from the other two territories.

There is no doubt in my mind that economic development has been held back during the post-war years in Tanganyika and Uganda by the unwillingness of the governments to allow more land to be alienated to non-Africans for estate development. For essentially political motives the colonial governments have allowed relatively small amounts of land to be alienated during this period. In this they have been fulfilling the apparent wishes of the majority of people, but they have not been prepared to try and persuade the people that development of plantation agriculture was very much in their own economic interests. They have been — as is so typical of colonial governments — more interested in the political and emotional response to suggestions on alienation rather than in the economic benefits likely to follow and have pursued, therefore, rather negative and conservative policies. Whilst appreciating the government's difficulties, it is my view that much greater efforts should have been made to persuade African District Councils, politicians, and the people of the benefits likely to follow from plantation agriculture. In Uganda production and output of tea and sugar and coffee could have been greater than it has been and in Tanganyika similarly. It is appreciated that profits may flow overseas, but to some extent this problem is overemphasized in present circumstances when there is so little scope for reinvestment, further land alienation not being permitted. One of the great advantages of plantation development is that it brings into the country (and keeps in the country) capital and enterprise which are in very short supply. Indeed, plantation development is one of the few sectors in the economics of Tanganyika and Uganda in which external finance, or indeed non-African local finance, is likely to be interested, and because of the limitations of such investment outlets a good deal of Tanganyikan and Ugandan savings may have moved either to Kenya or outside East Africa altogether.

It may well be necessary, in order to make alienation of land palatable to African governments, that there should be joint projects associating a plantation company with a public corporation, the government, the African local government, and perhaps individual African entrepreneurs or capitalists. Some considerable progress along these lines has been made in recent years in Uganda in connection with the tea schemes of the Uganda Development Corporation but it has been a very slow process.

With this as a background, it was to me very surprising that the recent Economic Survey Mission to Tanganyika of the International Bank did not face up to the problem of estate development at all. They emphasized that the estates were making a very large contribution to the economy and that it would be disastrous if they were allowed to disintegrate, but they did not take the point any further and indicate whether in their view further estate development would be desirable.

In Kenya, of course, the position in regard to land alienation has been very different and we have noticed the overwhelming predominance of European enterprise. Production there has been held back by lack of immigrants, lack of capital, and to some extent lack of labour, rather than lack of land. Given reasonable political conditions and the continuation of something like the present land arrangements, there seems no reason why the coffee, sisal, and tea plantations and the farmers producing wattle and pyrethrum for export should not all expand. As regards farmers providing for the local market, the future depends in part upon the general policy of protection of the government both as regards tariffs and as regards the intricate system of marketing boards that have been developed there during the last twenty years.

There is very little reliable statistical information concerning the relative merits of non-African and African farming in Kenya, but a most interesting table can be constructed out of the work recently done by Mr. Davidson of the Edgerton Agricultural College in

Economic Development for Africa South of the Sahara

Kenya. Table 14 in the Appendix is derived from his work and though there are a large number of assumptions behind the statistics it seems to me that the broad conclusions that emerge from the table are most suggestive. The following are the points that seem to emerge :

(a) That there is no evidence that land is used more efficiently in the sense of there being higher yields per acre in the smaller African holdings than in the larger European holdings.

(b) That output per man is higher in the larger European farms than in the African farms. And this, moreover, when the number of workers per acre is not substantially different in the two types of farming though in the European areas, of course, the workers are organized in bigger units and are assisted with larger amounts of capital.

(c) That even in the European areas gross output per man is not very high and is not sufficient to afford anything like the standard of living that can be afforded to an agricultural labourer in the United Kingdom or in the United States. In this significant sense both sets of farming are inefficient by the best world standards and need improving.

It should be noted that the comparison is one between averages and that a comparison between the average European farm and a new 'Swynnerton Farm' might not show exactly the same position. Nevertheless, there does not seem much economic sense in breaking up the larger capitalized non-African farming units on economic grounds though there may be a case for action designed to increase the proportion of value added going to labour.

(v) *Government*

The rôle of government has been important in the economic development of East Africa. This has been so not only with respect to the performance of the generally accepted functions of government — the maintenance of law and order, provision of a road and rail network, the carrying out of basic surveys and research, the establishment of schools, technical colleges, and farm institutes, etc. — but also in ways of more direct economic importance.

There is little doubt, for example, that the speed with which cotton took on in Uganda as a peasant crop was due to the fact that the government was very much behind it. In contrast to the position in — say — the Nyanza Province of Kenya there was available in Uganda in the early years of the century a fairly complete and tight system of administration. The Central Protectorate government was able to use this administrative system to get things done. And this sort of government coercion continued in Uganda up to the 1920s, if not beyond. One of the reasons often given for the expansion of coffee planting in a particular county in Buganda, for example, in the 1920s is that the local chief, with the full support of the District Commissioner, gave the local people the choice between planting coffee trees or going to help build the railway line then being constructed to Kampala. Many coffee trees were planted ! In recent years the government and the chiefs have lacked the power (or the will) in both Uganda and Tanganyika to 'persuade' in this way. The recent World Bank Economic Survey Mission to Tanganyika, for example, stated that by the end of 1958 because of lack of co-operation of the people with the administration 'in many areas where soil conservation measures and good husbandry practices had been making progress the people ceased to carry them out and exhibited a widespread reluctance to listen to any advice offered by the extension staff'. In Kenya, on the other hand, the government in the early days of the Swynnerton Plan did have the will to carry through certain measures, and the success of the new approach having been demonstrated, developments were rapid.

Looking backwards in Kenya there is no doubt of the importance of the rôle of government. The whole immigration policy, the railway rate reductions, and the protective tariff policy of the 1920s ; the structure of marketing boards designed to help the European farmer ; the recent efforts by government to establish industry and to seek external markets for agricultural products : all these as well as the recent Swynnerton Plan are clear evidence of the massive rôle of government.

In Tanganyika, too, there were the efforts to get African cashcrop farming established in the 1920s and the great amount of effort put into the development of co-operative activity which has been bearing fruit in recent years.

One could list many other activities of the government in the economic field which have been important. The provision of rural water, of cattle dips, of helping Africans to establish themselves in trade and industry, the provision of improved seeds and the demonstration of the possibilities of new crops ; the establishment of marketing boards : these and many other actions of government have been important. European farmers and business men have played a great part in the development process, as have Asian traders and business men and African farmers and workers, but it is difficult to exaggerate the positive rôle of government.

Looking to the future, it seems to me that the rôle of government is still of overwhelming importance in connection with the development process. Whenever one considers the various things that might be done to speed up economic development, so many of them require government action and the spending of public money on current or capital account whether it be to provide more extension officers, or feeder roads, or to make loans to progressive farmers, or establish a major irrigation scheme. And the present political climate of opinion which makes private investors rather chary of investing in Africa makes the rôle of government even more important.

In relation to the needs governments' resources are slight. All the East African governments are spending a high proportion of the gross domestic money product: Kenya about 26 per cent, Tanganyika about 24 per cent, and Uganda about 23 per cent, and yet because of the poverty of the countries these considerable efforts represent only £7, £3, and £4 per head of the population respectively. Tables 15 and 16 in the Appendix indicate the level and distribution of total government expenditure and current revenue in 1959/60.

I should like to make three points with respect to recent trends in public finance.

First, the very considerable growth in the level of government spending during the past ten years : by over three times in Kenya, by nearly four times in Tanganyika, and by more than four times in Uganda. Part of this increase is a reflection of price changes, but over the period expenditure per head of the population has probably doubled as has the importance of government spending in relation to the gross domestic product. Second is the increasing emphasis in the period on the social services. Current expenditure on health and education rose from 13 to 22 per cent of expenditure in Kenya, from 16 to 26 per cent in Tanganyika, and from 22 to 33 per cent in Uganda. There are enormous social needs to be met and great political pressures that they should be met. Arguments can be deployed in support of social service expenditure, particularly education, on economic grounds. However, in my view, and given the economic structure of the country, it is doubtful if on economic grounds this great emphasis can be justified. Expenditure yielding money returns in the shorter run would seem to be required. The third point is the somewhat precarious state of all the budgets at the present time. Current revenue is hardly sufficient to meet a level of current expenditure which is being held back with great difficulty. It seems doubtful, given the existing percentage of money incomes being raised in taxation, if much additional revenue should be collected by increasing tax rates, though revenue yields might, by drastic tax changes, be raised by 15 per cent or so by a tough-minded African government commanding the enthusiastic support of the people during a three- to five-year period. But even this would bring in only an additional £5 million in Kenya and £3 million in Tanganyika and Uganda, and in all add about 10s. per head per annum to government spending.

Uganda is fortunate in having a very small national debt, having financed most of her post-war capital development out of revenue obtained during the time when cotton and coffee prices were booming, but both Kenya and Tanganyika have national debts with interest charges amounting to some 8 and 6 per cent respectively of current expenditure.

The cost of borrowing is very high at the present time. The London market is effectively closed to African borrowers and the cost of borrowing from the British government may be as much as 6 per cent with a repayment period of 15-20 years which means a net service charge of about 8¾ per cent per annum. International Bank loans have similar charges. This sort of burden, given the precarious state of the current budgets of the territories, makes external borrowing difficult and puts an effective limit on the amount that the countries can afford to borrow.

If development during the next five to ten years is to proceed at a fairly rapid rate, external assistance in the form of grants or loans with low interest charges and long repayment periods will be necessary.

The financial stringency that all three countries are now faced with makes even more necessary the establishment of effective long-term fiscal and perhaps economic planning so as to avoid waste of scarce resources. To some extent the present financial difficulties of both Uganda and Tanganyika, for example, stem from wrong decisions taken a few years ago when the prices received for export crops were better than they are today. Government expenditure became geared to a terms of trade position which was not, and should not have been, expected to continue. But given the needs of the situation there is a great temptation to spend up to the hilt.

(vi) *Inter-territorial Problems*

In earlier sections of the paper we have noted the economic links existing between Kenya, Tanganyika, and Uganda ; the level and recent growth of visible trade between the territories ; and the fact that visible and invisible inter-territorial exports are an important element in the Kenya economy.

Here it is desired to mention some of the economic problems that have arisen in recent years due to these economic links and arrangements. These have recently been under examination — and a report produced — by a small committee under the chairmanship of Sir Jeremy Raisman.

A number of the problems raise no questions of general interest to economists. On a number of agricultural commodities some territories — Kenya in particular — impose import restrictions which reduce the reality of the common market. Then there are detailed financial problems as to how the costs of the various common services should be apportioned between the three territories. Then, too, there are differences as to the degree of consultation and agreement there should be between the governments on a number of issues and as to which services should be common and which not.

Others do have more general interest, however. There are, for example, problems arising out of the export of agricultural products from Kenya to the other territories which are associated with the marketing-board structure and system of protection. When Kenya exports to Uganda or Tanganyika she charges a price based on the controlled internal Kenya price which is usually a good deal higher than the price she is able to get when exporting the goods to the world market ; the difference being made possible by the high protective tariff. For instance, in the middle of 1960 the export price received for bacon and ham was about 178s. per cental and for butter about 244s. per cental ; whereas the price charged to Uganda was 326s. and 318s. respectively. Part of this difference may be accounted for by differences in quality and transport costs, but by no means all.

At first sight it would seem that Uganda is being 'exploited'. Kenya, however, claims that over the long run the price at which her products are sold to Uganda and Tanganyika is lower than the price they would have to pay for imported goods of the same quality. She does not deny that the f.o.b. export price is lower than the price at which the goods are sold to Uganda but claims that comparisons should not be with Kenya products f.o.b., but with imported products c.i.f. Whether or not this claim is true it is by no means clear that the argument stands. If there was no central marketing organization in Kenya presumably the price to Uganda (and Kenya) citizens would tend to approximate to the f.o.b. export price as there would be no incentive for any particular farmer to export at a lower price than he could sell locally. If producers were selling in competition, then local prices would approximate to f.o.b. prices given — as seems reasonable — that supply would not be seriously affected. It is the central marketing system that prevents this happening. Now in a unitary state there may be a case for having a central marketing organization and having the differential prices. So long as this policy is generally accepted by the inhabitants of the country it is just another form of agricultural protection and income redistribution. However, problems arise when one is not dealing with a unitary state, for whereas the disadvantage to the Kenya consumers is offset to some extent by an advantage to the Kenya producers in the case of Uganda and Tanganyika there is no offsetting advantage to the high prices suffered by the consumers.

The main problems that have arisen in recent years, however, have centred around industrial developments. During the last fifteen years Kenya has built up a substantial manufacturing sector and a fairly high proportion of the output goes to the other two territories. This leads to two problems. First, there is a public finance problem. We have seen that customs revenues constitute a high proportion of total government revenue. All manufacturing goods for consumer use — and most Kenya industry is of this type — are taxed. As the products of such industries are substituted for goods formerly imported from outside East Africa all the territories lose customs revenue from the displaced imports, but whereas the producing country gets offsetting indirect benefits through higher incomes and thus higher income tax proceeds and customs and excise tax proceeds resulting from the spending of such incomes the other two territories do not, except in so far as the increased Kenya incomes lead to an increased demand for goods from the other two territories; and on the whole Kenya's marginal propensity to import from them seems fairly low.

The second problem emerges directly from the growth of industry in Kenya. There has been a feeling in both Uganda and Tanganyika that they have been losing through membership of the common market in that industrial development has taken place in Kenya designed to serve the whole area, whereas if they had had their own separate customs barriers additional industry would have come to them. It seems extremely doubtful if this is so, for the size of the Uganda and Tanganyikan markets is so small.

Almost certainly the existence of the common market has caused more industrial development to take place than would have taken place if there had been three separate markets. There is little doubt that the great bulk of the advantages flowing from these developments have come to Kenya. It is not, however, clear that the other territories have in any sense lost by these developments. The gain has been unequal, but all have gained. Inequality in the distribution of the common market benefits is the problem.

Economic Development for Africa South of the Sahara

With a unitary state or a federal state such differences in relative benefits can be reduced by transfers through the public finance system.

East Africa has been in the rather unusual and somewhat unstable position in that though having a customs union there is no overall fiscal or governmental authority and, therefore, no way of rectifying through the public finance system any of the inequalities arising through the operation of the common market. The recommendations of the Raisman Commission, if accepted, would mark a beginning of such a public finance process. They recommend that a distributable pool be established, formed by having percentages of the income tax proceeds and the customs and excise proceeds put into a central pool out of which the expenses of the common services would be taken and also payments made to the exchequers of Uganda and Tanganyika to compensate them (at the expense of Kenya) for some of the direct fiscal and other losses that they suffer through being members of the common market. If accepted, this will be a very important step forward.

One other point, though not directly related to what has gone before, may be noted here. Within each of the territories there are important regional differences. In Uganda, for example, African cash incomes per head in 1959 varied from about £20 *per capita* in the richest districts of Buganda to about £3 per head in the poorest district of Kigezi. Now such differences are important to any country, but are even more important, I believe, in African countries which lack the homogeneity we associate with many developed countries. Tribal allegiances are strong and the existence of very different income levels raises extremely difficult problems for those responsible for policy with respect to economic development. Should the main objective be to concentrate resources in the less developed areas so as to increase the *per capita* incomes in these areas ? Should all parts of the country have an equal allocation of development finance ; or should a purely national view be taken and investment concentrated in these areas where it would yield most profit — often these will be the areas already most developed. It is not easy to give a definite affirmative answer to the last question in view of the very strong tribal and regional feelings that exist.

(vii) *Population and Land*

It would be wrong in a paper of this type not to make some reference to population problems. Yet in view of the mass of literature in this field (notably the report of the East African Royal Commission, 1953) it is difficult in the space available to discuss the question and I will be briefer and even more dogmatic than I have previously in this section.

The first point to make is that unlike so many under-developed countries there is no obvious and general problem of unemployment or under-employment — no general problem of land hunger or land shortage. Throughout East Africa's economic history labour shortage has been a problem rather than the abundance of labour. It has always been difficult, for example, to recruit workers for the sisal plantations in Tanganyika and the coffee and tea plantations in the other territories. One of the reasons why Kenya and, to a lesser extent, Tanganyika European farmers tended to oppose the introduction of coffee into African farming was because they feared the effects of such a lucrative cash crop on the supply of labour to non-African farms. Total population is about 22 million and total land area about 650,000 square miles. Population is increasing fairly rapidly by about 1·7 per cent in Tanganyika, about 2·5 per cent in Uganda, and — though more doubtfully — by about 1·6 per cent in Kenya. Nevertheless, there seems little serious problem of land shortage for a number of years to come.

The second point to make is that as stated in the first part of the paper, East Africa is primarily a peasant country, the number of wage earners being very small relatively to the size of the adult population. Given this it follows that the existing low level of wages is primarily a reflection of low opportunity earnings in peasant agriculture. And on the whole this is not due to lack of land.

The third point is that the increase in the number of jobs does not seem to be keeping up with the increase in the population. In Uganda, for example, the number of employees has remained roughly constant during the last ten years, whereas it is estimated that the number of adults in the population has increased by over 50 per cent. Even in Kenya where the wage sector is most highly developed, the number of employed males has only gone up about 17 per cent during the last ten years whereas it is probable that the number of adult males in the population has gone up by the order of 40 per cent. This produces a problem in that there is an increase in the demand for jobs as more and more people are becoming dissatisfied with life in the countryside.

The fourth point is that it is difficult for men in areas where there is land shortage to move to areas where there is no such shortage and this aggravates the problem where it exists. In very broad terms land areas are divided on tribal lines and though by means of special effort and arrangement it is possible for men from one tribe to move into land 'belonging' to another tribe it is not a completely free-and-easy operation. This makes local land shortages a much more difficult problem to deal with than would otherwise be the case.

A fundamental point concerns the carrying capacity of land. This is of course a function of, amongst other things, the amount of capital that is available, transport facilities and the desire to use the land intensively. One of the results of the intensive development in Kenya through the Swynnerton Plan has in fact been a shortage of labour on certain farms even though the Central Province of Kenya as a whole is one of the areas which is most over-populated.

In very broad terms I would argue that given reasonable amounts of capital available for the development of African agriculture and given that there is greater mobility of peoples from tribal area to tribal area and a desire to use the land reasonably intensively I do not feel that there is an overall land problem.

There are, however, two problems which have been giving special trouble in recent years. The first arises out of the great growth of education that has taken place which produces for the labour market each year a very large number of boys who have had four to eight years of education, but have not reached the Senior Secondary Schools. In the past, students with this period of education have usually obtained white-collar jobs. With the growth of the educational system and the failure of the number of jobs to grow at anything like the same rate, these boys are not now obtaining such jobs. A clear imbalance now exists both within the educational system in that there are plenty of jobs for students with School Certificate or with higher qualifications but not for students who have not reached this level. It is difficult to see how this problem can be solved until universal primary education exists and when, therefore, it becomes clear that all such people cannot obtain white-collar jobs and must be absorbed into the agriculture sector, or unless there takes place a very rapid growth in the economy and, therefore, in the number of jobs available.

The second problem is not unconnected with the first. There does seem to be a reluctance to work in agriculture. To an outside observer the overall net advantages of a particular job may seem similar in a particular agricultural activity to an activity in a town, but normally the potential worker prefers the job in the town to the job in agriculture. There are presumably many reasons for this. There is excitement and bright lights in the town, and medical services, schools, and opportunity for political discussions, whereas in the country these things do not exist to the same extent. There does seem to be a very real preference for work in the towns and this is something which needs to be taken into account when considering the relative expansion, under government support, of employment opportunities in different industries.

IV CONCLUDING NOTE

Though this paper is long it has not been possible to touch directly on all the points which it would have been desirable to touch upon though some of them are implicitly covered. Notable omissions are : detailed discussion of the scope for industrial development ; particular reference to the economic rationality of peasant cultivators ; consideration of the general rôle in economic development of foreign enterprise and capital ; the discussion of scope for major irrigation schemes ; discussion of the monetary, credit, and banking structure ; discussion of the problems of migrant labour and labour supply generally ; and discussion of the present and prospective balance of payments position.

Nevertheless, I believe I have stressed most of the key and significant elements in connection with the economic development of East Africa. I lay great emphasis on the following factors. The unfavourable natural resources position ; the lack of a serious population problem ; the rôle of non-Africans in the economy ; the dependence upon exports ; the different ways in which development has occurred as between the three East African countries ; the limitations on peasant agriculture with existing methods ; the problems arising out of the East African common market ; the importance of government action and the need for external financial assistance if the development rate is to be rapid ; and the importance of the basic transport network and marketing facilities in development.

Economic Development for Africa South of the Sahara

STATISTICAL APPENDIX

TABLE 1A

KENYA : GROSS DOMESTIC PRODUCT BY INDUSTRIAL ORIGIN, ETC., 1959

Industry	Total Product		Monetary Product	
	£m.	%	£m.	%
1. Agriculture	63·8	29·7	26·1	16·0
2. Livestock	20·5	9·5	9·3	5·7
3. Forestry	3·8	1·8	0·8	0·5
4. Fishing and hunting	1·1	0·5	0·9	0·5
5. Mining and quarrying	1·2	0·5	1·2	0·7
6. Manufacturing	20·2	9·4	20·2	12·4
7. Construction	8·3	3·8	8·3	5·1
8. Electricity and water	2·3	1·1	2·3	1·4
9. Transport, storage, and communications	18·9	8·8	18·9	11·6
10. Wholesale and retail trade	27·1	12·6	27·1	16·6
11. Banking and insurance	3·5	1·6	3·5	2·1
12. Rentals	8·4	3·9	8·4	5·1
13. General government	21·5	10·0	21·5	13·2
14. Services	14·6	6·8	14·6	8·9
Totals	215·3	100·0	163·2	100·0

Gross Capital Formation = £m. 43
As % of Gross Domestic Product, 20%
As % of Gross Money Product, 26%

Estimated population 6·45 million, of which there were :
66,400 Europeans,
169,900 Asians, and
6,171,000 Africans

Per capita incomes :
Total product, £33·4
Monetary product, £25·3
Number of employees, 596,897
Average wage of Europeans, £1,223
Asians, £486
Africans, £64

TABLE 1B

TANGANYIKA : GROSS DOMESTIC PRODUCT BY INDUSTRIAL ORIGIN, ETC.,
1959

Industry	Total Product		Monetary Product	
	£m.	%	£m.	%
1. Agriculture	79·6	44·8	36·8	34·7
2. Livestock products	17·4	9·8	4·4	4·1
3. Forest products	4·6	2·6	2·4	2·3
4. Hunting and fishing	3·5	2·0	0·3	0·3
5. Mining and quarrying	6·4	3·6	6·4	6·0
6. Manufacturing	6·9	3·9	6·9	6·5
7. Craft industries	5·8	3·3	—	—
8. Construction	11·3	6·3	6·9	6·5
9. Public utilities	1·0	0·6	1·0	0·9
10. Transport, storage, and communications	11·7	6·6	11·7	11·0
11. Distribution	8·3	4·7	8·3	7·8
12. Ownership of dwellings	3·6	2·0	3·6	3·4
13. Public administration and defence	12·5	7·0	12·5	11·8
14. Miscellaneous services	5·0	2·8	5·0	4·7
Totals	177·6	100·0	106·2	100·0

Gross Capital Formation = £m. 22·9
As % of Gross Domestic Product, 14·1%
As % of Gross Monetary Product, £21·6%

Estimated population 9·08 million, of which there were :
21,800 Europeans,
84,100 Asians, and
8,942,000 Africans

Per capita incomes :
Total product, £15·6
Monetary product, £11·7
Number of employees, 433,268 (Africans only)
Average wage of Europeans, NA
Asians, NA
Africans, NA

UGANDA : GROSS DOMESTIC PRODUCT BY INDUSTRIAL ORIGIN, ETC., 1959

Industry	Total Product		Monetary Product	
	£m.	%	£m.	%
1. Agriculture	88·6	58·8	50·6	46·7
2. Forestry, fishing, and hunting	6·5	4·3	2·0	1·9
3. Mining and quarrying	2·0	1·3	2·0	1·8
4. Cotton ginning, coffee curing, and sugar manufacture	4·2	2·8	4·2	3·9
5. Manufacture of food products	1·3	0·9	1·3	1·2
6. Miscellaneous manufacturing	4·6	3·0	4·6	4·3
7. Electricity	2·1	1·4	2·1	1·9
8. Construction	3·8	2·5	3·8	3·5
9. Commerce	14·1	9·4	14·1	13·0
10. Transport and communication	5·5	3·6	5·5	5·1
11. Government (administration and miscellaneous)	3·9	2·6	3·9	3·6
12. African local government	2·1	1·4	2·1	1·9
13. Miscellaneous services	8·5	5·6	8·5	7·8
14. Rents	3·5	2·3	3·5	3·2
Totals	150·7	100·0	108·3	100·0

Gross Capital Formation = £m. 17·0
As % of Gross Domestic Product, 11·3%
As % of Gross Money Product, 15·7%

Estimated population 6·52 million, of which there were :
           11,000 Europeans,
           72,000 Asians, and
           6,429,000 Africans

Per capita incomes :
           Total product, £23·1
           Monetary product, £16·6
           Number of employees, 239,460
           Average wage of Europeans, £1,249
           Asians, £537
           Africans, £60

NOTES ON TABLES 1A, 1B, AND 1C

1. Sources : *Annual Statistical Abstract*, Uganda, 1960 ; *Annual Statistical Abstract*, Tanganyika, 1959 ; December 1960 issue of the *East African Statistical Department's Quarterly Bulletin* ; *Economic Survey*, Kenya, 1960.

2. The estimates of the Gross Domestic Products are drawn up on the same basis with two exceptions. In Tanganyika estimates are made of the contribution of craft industries (mainly beer brewing) and African hut construction in the non-monetary sector. This amounts to some £5·8 million in the case of the former and about £4·4 million in the case of the latter. To achieve as an exact comparability as possible it would be necessary either to deduct these two items from the Tanganyika estimates or else attempt an estimate on a similar basis for Kenya and Uganda. This has *not* been done. The Tanganyika estimates of capital formation have, however, been adjusted so as to exclude capital formation in the non-monetary sector.

3. Population censuses were held in Tanganyika in 1957 and in Uganda in 1959. No census has been held in Kenya since 1948, and it is believed that it is quite possible that the population may be some 7 or 8 per cent higher than the current estimate thus reducing income per head by a corresponding amount.

TABLE 2

BALANCE OF TRADE, ETC., 1959

(£m.)

Item	Kenya	Tanga-nyika	Uganda	East Africa
(1) NET IMPORTS	61·5	34·5	25·5	121·5
(Direct Imports)	(78·8)	(28·3)	(14·4)	(121·5)
(2) DOMESTIC EXPORTS	33·3	45·3	42·1	120·7
(3) RE-EXPORTS	5·1	1·9	1·1	8·1
(4) TOTAL EXPORTS	38·4	47·2	43·2	128·8
(5) Visible Balance of External Trade (4) – (1)	– 23·1	+ 12·8	+ 17·7	+ 7·3
(6) Inter-territorial Imports	5·5	8·1	6·5	20·1
(7) Inter-territorial Exports	12·3	2·6	5·2	20·1
(8) Inter-territorial Balance (7) – (6)	+ 6·8	– 5·5	– 1·3	—
(9) TOTAL BALANCE (5) + (8)	– 16·3	+ 7·3	+ 16·4	+ 7·3
Total Exports (4) + (7) as % of GDP	23·5%	28·0%	32·1%	27·4%
of Money Product	31·1%	46·9%	44·7%	39·4%
Total Imports (1) + (6) as % of GDP	31·1%	24·0%	21·2%	26·0%
of Money Product	41·0%	40·1%	29·5%	37·5%

NOTES ON TABLES

1. Sources : As for Tables 1A, 1B, and 1C.

2. Direct Imports. Goods imported into East Africa from outside the territories for consumption or warehousing in East Africa including in both cases goods which are subsequently re-exported (*i.e.* sent outside East Africa) or transferred (*i.e.* goods sent on to another East African territory).

3. Net imports. Direct imports minus transfers to other East African territories plus transfers from other East African territories.

4. Domestic exports. East African products exported to countries outside East Africa.

5. Re-exports. Imported goods subsequently re-exported without change of form to places outside East Africa.

6. Inter-territorial imports and exports. Trade in goods produced in East Africa.

7. Valuation methods. External imports and exports are valued at port of entry or exit to East Africa. Transfers where possible are valued at original cost, but where this cannot be done an estimate is made. It follows for example that the balance of trade of Uganda is not really a true balance of trade in that it is not valued at the point of entry to Uganda, but at the point of entry to East Africa, normally Mombasa, which is some 400 miles away. Thus Uganda's exports are over-valued by the amount of the transport costs from her borders to Mombasa and her imports are under-valued in the same way.

TABLE 3

DISTRIBUTION OF EXPORTS, 1959

(Only items in excess of £1 m. are listed)

Item	Kenya £m.	Kenya % A	Kenya % B	Tanganyika £m.	Tanganyika % A	Tanganyika % B	Uganda £m.	Uganda % A	Uganda % B
Meat and meat preparations	1·99	6·0	4·4	1·51	3·3	3·1			
Cashew nuts				1·56	3·4	3·2			
Coffee (not roasted)	10·58	31·8	23·2	5·75	12·7	12·0	18·69	44·4	39·5
Tea	3·60	10·8	7·9				1·19	2·8	2·5
Animal feeding stuffs							1·65	3·9	3·5
Hides and skins	1·63	4·9	3·6	1·92	4·2	4·0			
Raw cotton				6·66	14·7	13·9	15·43	36·7	32·6
Sisal	3·46	10·4	7·6	13·06	28·8	27·3			
Pyrethrum and pyrethrum extract	2·19	6·6	4·8						
Sodium carbonate	1·71	5·1	3·7						
Wattle bark and extract	1·23	3·7	2·7						
Diamonds				4·55	10·0	9·5			
Copper							2·78	6·6	5·9
Gold				1·07	2·4	2·2			
All other Domestic Exports	6·9	20·7	15·1	9·23	20·03	19·3	2·35	5·6	5·0
TOTAL DOMESTIC EXPORTS	33·3	100·0		45·3	100·0		42·09	100·0	
INTER-TERRITORIAL EXPORTS	12·3		27·0	2·60		5·4	5·20		11·0
TOTAL EXPORTS	45·6		100·0	47·9		100·0	47·3		100·0

A = % of *Domestic* Exports.
B = % of *Total* Exports (including inter-territorial exports).

NOTES

1. Sources : As for Tables 1 and 2.
2. Values at Port of Exit, *i.e.* F.O.B.
3. Items of value amounting to more than the £1 million are included. No inter-territorial export exceeds £1 million.

TABLE 4

EAST AFRICA'S INTER-TERRITORIAL EXPORTS, ETC., 1950–9

Item	Kenya %	Tanganyika %	Uganda %	East Africa £'000
1950				
Foodstuffs	59	9	32	3,463
Beverages and tobacco	10	8	83	1,689
Other	70	23	8	1,980
Total	50	13	37	7,132
1959				
Foodstuffs	66	17	16	6,188
Beverages and tobacco	52	8	40	4,724
Other	62	12	25	9,186
Total	61	13	26	20,098
The Increase 1950–9				
Foodstuffs	76	28	3	2,725
Beverages and tobacco	75	8	17	3,035
Other	61	9	30	7,206
Total	67	13	20	12,966

NOTES ON TABLE 4

1. Sources: *Annual Statistical Abstract of Kenya, Uganda and Tanganyika,* and *Annual Trade Reports.*
2. The figures published on inter-territorial trade in the above publications until 1958 include excise and import duty components which are eventually transferred to the receiving territory. The 1950 figure has, therefore, been roughly adjusted to take account of this. This makes the 1950 and 1959 figures able to be compared in a crude sort of way.
3. The Uganda inter-territorial export figure for 1959 includes the value of electricity sold by the Uganda Electricity Board to Kenya though in some sense this is not technically a visible export. This amounted to some £2,000,000 in that year.

TABLE 5

UGANDA'S IMPORTS AND EXPORTS, ETC., 1904/5–1935

Year	Imports	Exports		Government £'000	
		Total	Cotton as % of Total	Revenue	Expenditure
1904/5	115	60	85	60	173·0
1909/10	403	176	90	165	240·1
1914/15	589	523	84	282	289·2
1925	2,678	5,097	94	1,479	1,108
1930	1,614	2,060	82	1,412	1,640
1935	1,704	3,630	83	1,500	1,350

Source: H. B. Thomas and R. Scott, *Uganda,* C.U.P., 1935.

TABLE 6

UGANDA'S IMPORTS AND EXPORTS, ETC., 1946–60

Year	Imports £m.	Exports		
		Total £m.	Cotton as %	Coffee as %
1946	5·1	9·0	62	20
1947	6·5	10·9	65	14
1948	9·0	13·9	54	23
1949	12·5	23·5	74	12
1950	15·4	28·9	58	29
1951	22·1	47·4	60	29
1952	24·3	47·7	63	26
1953	25·7	33·6	50	35
1954	25·2	41·0	51	33
1955	34·0	42·3	39	48
1956	28·1	41·5	48	39
1957	28·9	46·8	38	47
1958	27·0	46·3	40	46
1959	25·5	43·1	37	44

Source : *Uganda Statistical Abstracts.*

TABLE 7

UGANDA : STABILIZATION AND THE COFFEE SECTOR, 1950–60

Year	Growers' Incomes		Export Taxes		Marketing Board Surplus		Ex-Farm Income Amount
	Amount £m.	% of Ex-Farm Income	Amount £m.	% of Ex-Farm Income	Amount £m.	% of Ex-Farm Income	
1950	1·7	27	1·2	19	3·3	53	6·2
1951	3·0	31	1·9	19	4·9	50	9·8
1952	3·8	43	1·7	19	3·3	37	8·8
1953	5·1	67	1·3	17	1·2	16	7·6
1954	8·6	80	1·8	17	0·4	4	10·8
1055	16·4	111	2·9	20	−4·6	−31	14·7
1956	9·7	86	1·9	17	−0·2	−2	11·4
1957	11·0	73	3·8	25	0·2	1	15·0
1958	11·9	77	2·8	18	0·7	4	15·4
1959 1960	14·1	93	2·2	14	−1·2	−8	15·1
1950/59	85·3	74	21·5	19	8·0	7	114·8

TABLE 8

UGANDA : STABILIZATION AND THE COTTON SECTOR, 1950–60

Year	Growers' Incomes		Export Taxes		Marketing Board Surplus		Ex-Farm Income Amount
	Amount £m.	% of Ex-Farm Income	Amount £m.	% of Ex-Farm Income	Amount £m.	% of Ex-Farm Income	
1950	7·3	50	2·9	20	4·1	28	14·6
1951	10·4	38	5·9	22	10·4	38	27·0
1952	11·9	45	6·0	22	8·4	32	26·7
1953	10·4	74	2·9	21	0·4	3	14·0
1954	12·9	71	3·5	19	1·5	8	18·3
1955	11·6	73	3·1	20	0·8	5	15·8
1956	12·6	76	3·4	20	0·3	2	16·7
1957	13·0	77	3·4	20	0·1	1	16·9
1958	12·8	101	2·3	18	− 2·8	− 22	12·7
1959	11·7	101	2·0	17	− 2·5	− 21	11·6
1960							
1950/59	114·6	66	35·4	20	20·7	12	174·3

NOTES ON TABLES 7 AND 8

1. Sources : 'The gross domestic product of Uganda, 1954/9', Uganda unit, East African Statistical Department, 1961. The geographical income of Uganda, 1950/6, East African Statistical Department, July 1957.

2. In Table 7 the statistics up to and including 1953 are not strictly comparable with those in 1954 and after.

3. Ex-Farm Income/Proceeds. This is the gross proceeds of the sale of exported produce minus the costs of processing, transporting, and marketing. The item is equal to the proceeds to the grower plus export tax and marketing surpluses ; it represents what the growers *could* have received if these two items had not been levied.

4. In addition to the items mentioned in 3 above there is included in the Ex-Farm Income/Proceeds total of Table 8 an amount of about £m. 0·3 or £m. 0·4 a year as 'bonus to African Local Governments'. Over the whole period this levy amounted to £m. 3·6 out of the total Ex-Farm Income/Proceeds of £m. 174·3, *i.e.* it represented about 2 per cent of the total.

TABLE 9

NON-AFRICAN AGRICULTURAL PRODUCTION : KENYA

Production/Sales	1946	1950	1955	1959
Wheat : 000 tons	73	127	120	126
Coffee : 000 tons	9	10	24	19
Sisal : 000 tons	27	38	38	54
Factory butter : million lbs.	5	6·0	10	12
Milk : million gallons	5	8	14	18
Cattle : 000's	18	28	46	97
Pigs : 000's	47	48	49	92

Source : *Kenya Statistical Abstracts, 1955,* to date.

TABLE 10

KENYA : IMPORTS AND EXPORTS, ETC., 1946–60

Year	Imports Amount £m.	Exports Amount £m.	% Composition of Exports						
			Coffee	Sisal	Tea	Cotton	Maize	Hides and Skins	Sodium Carbonate
1946	15·0	6·3	14	14	8		3	6	6
1947	20·8	8·9	15	16	10		8	8	7
1948	30·2	10·3	19	23	6		2	9	10
1949	38·9	11·0	14	26	6	2	—	11	4
1950	34·1	17·1	21	24	8	1	4	11	5
1951	53·9	20·1	17	29	6	4	3	9	5
1952	59·3	25·8	28	17	5	4	9	4	5
1953	51·7	19·5	34	13	5	3	2	8	4
1954	60·3	20·3	28	10	10	4	5	7	6
1955	71·5	25·7	35	8	11	6	6	5	5
1956	69·8	29·0	47	7	9	3	—	4	5
1957	72·0	26·4	41	8	11	1	2	6	5
1958	60·9	29·3	36	8	11	2	6	4	4
1959	61·5	33·3	32	10	11	2	3	5	5
1960									

Source : *Kenya Statistical Abstracts, 1955,* to date.

TABLE 11

TANGANYIKA : IMPORTS AND EXPORTS, 1920–59

(£m.)

Year	Imports	Domestic Exports
1920–4 (average)	1·7	1·7
1925–9 (average)	3·5	3·4
1930–4 (average)	2·5	2·3
1935–9 (average)	3·3	4·2
1948–50 (average)	25·5	19·8
1955–9 (average)	35·8	42·8

Sources : *Tanganyika, a Review of its Resources and their Development*, edited by J. P. Moffett, Tanganyika Government, 1955 ; *Tanganyika Statistical Abstract, 1959* ; *Quarterly Bulletins of the East African Statistical Department*.

TABLE 12

TANGANYIKA : GOVERNMENT FINANCE, 1920–58

(£m.)

Year	Total Revenue	Total Expenditure
1921	0·8	1·1
1925	1·5	1·4
1930	1·7	2·2
1935	1·9	1·7
1938	2·0	2·1
1947	5·6	5·5
1950	11·5	11·6
1955	19·5	22·6
1958	22·3	27·0

Source : As for Table 11.

135

TABLE 13

COMMODITY COMPOSITION OF TANGANYIKA'S DOMESTIC EXPORTS,
1920–59
(% of Total Value : main items only)

Year	Sisal	Coffee	Cotton	Diamonds	Gold	Hides and Skins	Cashew Nuts	Ground-nuts
1920–4	24	12	11	—	—	6	—	12
1925–9	32	16	14	—	1	7	—	6
1930–4	37	17	9	—	6	5	—	5
1935–9	37	11	13	—	14	5	—	4
1948–9	57	7	10	8	3	3	—	
1952–3	43	14	12	7	2	3	1	1
1957–8	24	18	17	9	2	3	3	2
1959	29	13	15	10	2	4	3	6

Source as in Tables 11 and 12.

TABLE 14

PRODUCTIVITY RATIOS, ETC., IN KENYA, 1957

| Item | European Arable Land | | | African Arable Land |
	Planta-tions	Mixed Farming	Total	
	£'000	£'000	£'000	£'000
Total gross output	12,871	15,698	28,569	58,223
Total costs	8,496	13,586	22,082	37,733
Profit	4,375	2,112	6,487	20,490
	£	£	£	£
Gross output per acre	58·24	6·45	10·76	7·28
Gross output per male employed	148·00	165·00	154·00	99·00
Profit per acre	19·79	0·87	2·44	2·56
			Acres	Acres
Area available for cultivation			2,654,330	7,992,320

Source : B. R. Davidson, 'The Economics of Arable Land in Kenya', *East
African Economics Review*, June 1950. Full details of definitions and statistics can
be found in the article.
By 'Arable Land' is meant land with a regular rainfall of at least 30 inches
excluding forests and national reserves.

TABLE 15

TOTAL GOVERNMENT EXPENDITURE, 1959–60

Item	Kenya Amount £m.	%	Tanganyika Amount £m.	%	Uganda Amount £m.	%
General Administrative Services Law and order, defence, etc.	13·2	28	6·7	27	5·7	23
Community Services Roads, Township developments, etc.	3·7	8	2·2	9	3·5	14
Social services	10·3	22	6·5	26	8·2	33
Economic services	6·6	14	4·7	19	3·3	13
Recurrent Financial Obligations Public debt, pensions, etc.	7·0	15	3·4	13	2·0	8
Other	6·0	13	1·7	6	2·2	9
Total expenditure	46·8	100	25·2	100	24·9	100
Per head of population	£7		£3		£4	
% of GDP	20%		12%		16%	
% of gross money product	26%		24%		23%	

Source : *Quarterly Statistical Bulletin.*

TABLE 16

CURRENT REVENUE, 1959/60

Item	Kenya £m.	% of Total Taxation	Tanganyika £m.	% of Total Taxation	Uganda £m.	% of Total Taxation
Income tax	10·5	36	3·8	22	3·6	21
Poll taxes, etc.	2·0	7	1·6	9	0·6	4
Other direct taxes	0·4	1	0·2	1	—	—
Total direct taxes	12·9	44	5·6	33	4·2	25
Import duty	10·1	35	7·8	46	5·6	33
Excise duty	3·6	12	2·5	15	2·3	14
Export duty	—	—	(...)	(...)	4·0	24
Other indirect taxes	2·4	8	(1·2)	(7)	0·8	5
Total indirect taxes	16·1	55	11·5	67	12·7	75
Total taxation	29·0	100	17·1	100	16·9	100
Other revenue	8·9		5·0		5·0	
Total revenue	37·9		22·1		21·9	

Source : *Quarterly Statistical Bulletin.*

Chapter 5

PROBLEMS OF ECONOMIC DEVELOPMENT OF FRENCH-LANGUAGE COUNTRIES AND TERRITORIES[1]

BY

L. B. DE CARBON
University of Nancy

I. GENERAL BACKGROUND

THE French-language countries and territories south of the Sahara cover an area of eight million km? (fifteen times the size of France) and their population in 1956–7 was 33 million (see Annex I for separate figures). Of the fourteen countries concerned,[2] three (Mauretania, the Central African, and the Gabon Republic) each have well under one million inhabitants : Madagascar, the most populous, has five ; most others have somewhat more than two and a half million. It is true that these countries have often retained or re-established certain earlier links which have the effect of pushing out the frontier (customs union, common currency for several countries) ; nevertheless, the first question that comes to mind is whether any of them have the 'minimum demographic size' necessary in relation to the general costs and expenses of economic development. For France's division into 21 economic regions, it was held that 'the size of the regions must not be arbitrary. For example, if a development corporation is to function properly, it has to employ first-class personnel, and to do so it generally has to be able to count on work worth at least 2 billion old francs a year'.[3] A population of one million was then considered the minimum, but this figure is not really meaningful without an analysis in terms of income,

[1] Translation from the French by Elizabeth Henderson
[2] The two former trust territories of the French Cameroons and Togo ; seven countries of the former Federation of French West Africa, namely the Republics of Sénégal, the Ivory Coast, Mali, Mauretania, Volta, the Niger, and Dahomey ; four countries of the former Federation of French Equatorial Africa, namely Gabon, Congo, the Central African Republic, and Chad ; and the Malagasy Republic.
[3] B. de Maud'huy, *Problèmes administratifs posés par la mise en œuvre des plans régionaux*, Report to the Economic and Social Council of France, March 1960.

saving, entrepreneurial capacity, and the availability of top-level executives capable of assuming the responsibilities of administration and development. The African countries here under discussion have even harder problems to solve than the under-developed regions of France, but they can count on ample technical and financial aid from outside, especially from France ; and if they may appear to have the size of a region rather than of a country, they will no doubt sooner or later form suitable groupings by free agreement.

The economic history of French-language Africa south of the Sahara and Madagascar is marked by two waves of radical change in the former patterns and processes of the economy. The first followed the Second World War, which led France to reconsider the principles of development of the overseas countries and territories for which she was responsible. The second has the same origin, but can be more closely identified as the recent years of political liberation, when aid to the young African nations has become an internationally recognized obligation.

If we are to describe the economic situation of a group of countries which, while evolving on roughly parallel lines, do not by any means have identical problems, there is not much point in describing each separate case with the help of detailed statistics ; it will be more helpful to trace the general direction in which these countries are moving and the driving forces behind the movement, to identify durable relationships, and to stress the latent but already operative factors of transformation : French Africa opened out towards the world at large just when France opened out towards the European Economic Community — a double impetus of interest for our purposes.

We shall therefore not marshal a lot of figures to pinpoint present problems, especially since the statistics often lag behind the facts. We shall try, rather, to take a dynamic view of the past so as to get a better understanding of the problems of today. A close fabric of economic and financial relations has been woven, first on liberal principles by the sole pay of private enterprise, then by the centripetal forces of the excessively self-centred franc area, and finally by the mechanism of a system of planning which was, for a long time, autarchic with respect both to the sources of finance and to sales markets. The enormous financial machinery created for the modernization of the overseas territories still exists and has been adapted to new tasks, but the problems which came in the wake of independence are no longer subject to centralized decisions.

II. ECONOMIC DEVELOPMENT BEFORE INDEPENDENCE : ITS MECHANISM AND STAGES

The period prior to 1940 was not comparable with the post-war period with respect to either the rate or the structure of investment nor were investment methods and investment returns the same. Nevertheless, it would be both incorrect and unjust to deny or belittle the results obtained in several decades of economic liberalism.

The exports of the former Federations of French West Africa and French Equatorial Africa, together with those of Madagascar, amounted to 230 million gold francs in 1913 and to 2,565 million current francs in 1938. Neglecting the four years of the First World War and the four or five years of the great depression which destroyed more capital overseas than was newly invested, and allowing for the loss in the value of money which reduced the franc to one-fifth of its former value, the rate of expansion of exports during the remaining sixteen years was more than 5 per cent annually, in value terms.[1]

This expansion was largely due to a flow of investment into the major infrastructures required for export development. It cannot be gainsaid that investment fell far short of what other metropolitan countries did in their overseas territories, which, however, were more richly endowed with natural resources then in demand on Western markets ; but France has since done much to close the gap. Basing himself on S. H. Frankel's work,[2] Lord Hailey writes : 'He has estimated that a total of about £1,222 million had been invested from abroad up to the end of 1936. Of this, about £564 million took the form of loans and grants to governments ; about £581 million took the form of 'private listed capital', the public issues, that is, of companies ; about £95 million was the estimated total of non-listed capital. . . . Of the total of £1,222 million about £523

[1] Value of exports in million current francs :

	1913	1938
French West Africa	126	1,416
French Equatorial Africa	37	264
Madagascar	56	819
Cameroons	.. 46 (1920)	252

Bournier, *Statistiques du commerce extérieur des possessions françaises en 1938*, Secrétariat d'État aux Colonies, 1941.

[2] Lord Hailey, *An African Survey*, 1st Edition, 1938, pp. 1317-18 ; cf. 2nd Edition, 1956, p. 1321 ; derived from S. H. Frankel, *Capital Investment in Africa*, 1938.

million is the estimated share of the Union of South Africa, which is 42·81 per cent of the investment in all territories, and 55·54 per cent of that in British territories. Of other British territories, the most important fields of investment have been : the Rhodesias, which have taken about £102 million ; Nigeria, £75 million ; Tanganyika, £52 million ; Kenya and Uganda, £46 million ; the Sudan, £43 million ; the Gold Coast, £35 million ; and South-West Africa, £32 million. The total investment in all British territories is estimated to have been some £941 million to the end of 1936, which is about 77 per cent of the whole.

'In non-British territories the greatest investment has been in the Belgian Congo, where it is estimated to have been £143 million. In the French territories the estimated total is £70 million, of which about £30 million is in French West Africa, and £21 million in French Equatorial Africa. The estimated investment in the Portuguese territories is about £67 million, divided fairly equally between Angola and Moçambique. Thus in the Belgian territories there is about 11·73 per cent, in the French 5·76 per cent, and in the Portuguese 5·46 per cent of all the capital invested.

'The meaning of these figures, so far as they concern economic development, can most clearly be seen by calculating the investment per head of population. . . . The foreign investment in the Union amounts to about £55·8 per head of total population, European, Asiatic, coloured, and native. It is about £38·4 per head in the Rhodesias, about £8·1 per head in British East Africa, about £4·8 per head in British West Africa, about £13 in the Belgian Congo. In Angola and Moçambique it is about £9·8 per head, though the railway and port developments in both these territories serve much more than the local populations. It is lowest in the French colonies, about £3·3. In French West Africa it is no more than £2·1 per head. . . .

'. . . investment controlled by governments has been a very important part of the whole, about 44·72 per cent for all these territories together. . . . The proportion tends to be lowest in the more highly mineralized territories, where there has been extensive borrowing for mining undertakings, and highest in those territories where railway construction controlled by the government has been almost the only important form of economic development. . . . In the French territories the proportion is in general close to the latter group. It was 71·72 per cent in Equatorial Africa, 60·71 per cent in Togo and the Cameroons, and 54·15 per cent in French West Africa.'

A lot of comments could be made on the preceding figures and on the low level of public capital invested in the Belgian Congo and in the Portuguese territories, for example. One might, in particular, establish a connection between the volume of investment and the ensuing advantages to the investing countries ; it is not by accident that the dollar earners came off best. On the other hand, the above estimates probably understate the situation considerably.

Be that as it may, the £70 million of French investment in Africa mentioned above for 1936 are equivalent to some 3,000 billion old francs at current prices. It was largely infrastructure investment and strongly capital-intensive. Public and private investment between 1946 and 1958 is estimated to have amounted to more than one-third of the above figure ; this was investment of low capital-intensity (between 2 and 3) and the figure for total national income (French West and Equatorial Africa, Cameroons and Madagascar) works out at something in the neighbourhood of 1,200 billion old francs in 1958.[1]

The liberal system which left direct development to private capital certainly had its disadvantages. Foreign capitalists were mostly interested in investment for exports with assured markets, especially to supply the metropolitan countries. This growth process increased social welfare in the overseas territories only as a by-product. The creation of schools, public health improvements, town planning, housing, all the things that are the very base of social progress, can in such circumstances be financed only by budget surpluses, and budgets fill out only in the measure that taxable wealth increases. In the new era following upon the Second World War the process of social advance was reversed. The fundamental social objectives were determined first, and rapid economic development came to be seen as a means to achieve social progress. In the old system, social action soon reached its capacity limits. In 1935, for example, the public debt constituted a very heavy charge on ordinary budgets overseas and was responsible for one-fifth of budgetary expenditure.[2] It must be said that France helped the economy of the territories in question in many ways ; the statistics all too often only show the amount of the loans floated by each territory or Federation on the French capital market with the guarantee of the French government, but say nothing about other aid such as premiums paid out to overseas producers (more than 500 million current francs between 1932 and 1936 for rubber, cotton, sisal, coffee, bananas, and oil seeds).

[1] Cf. *Outre-mer 1958*, Service des Statistiques d'Outre-mer, 1959, Recueil de Statistiques et d'Études. Cf. R. Gendarme, *L'Économie de Madagascar*, Institut des Hautes Études de Madagascar, 1961.
[2] Cf. L. B. de Carbon, *L'Investissement dans les territoires dépendants*, Cahiers de l'Institut de Science Économique Appliquée, Series A, n°. 8, 1951.

I shall have more to say later about the arrangements and institutions which were set up after 1945 and which continue, after various re-adjustments, to promote economic growth in the overseas countries of French language ; but before we do so, it may be useful to set out a few figures relating to the line of development before the new period of growth set in and to the situation at the eve of independence.

III. EXPORTS

Let us first consider the export figures (quantum), which are significant in so far as national income largely depends on foreign sales. These often account for more than one-third of national income, or, if non-market production is excluded, to half of it or more ; they furthermore are the focus of many economic activities, keep transport going to and from the ports, and constitute the prime source for the formation of purchasing power and investable saving, at least in the countries here under consideration.

TABLE 1

INDICES OF EXPORT QUANTUM

1925 = 100

	1911	1938	1950	1957
French West Africa	51	193	197	313
French Equatorial Africa	57	185	182	300
Cameroons	..	299	295	451
Madagascar	42	185	100 *	140 *

(Cf. Bournier, *op. cit.* and *Outre-mer 1958.* An asterisk denotes that the figure is an estimate of the writer.)

The oft-maligned 'colonial' system can, in exaggerated caricature, be summed up in the four commandments of the colonial pact : sell exclusively to the mother country, buy exclusively in it, export in the raw, serve the flag monopoly. The first thing to be done was to build the infrastructures and to develop raw material resources. In the countries here under discussion local public works budgets rose from 13 million gold francs in 1913 to 180 million in 1920, which indicates the nature of the initial investment drive.

That exports went mainly to metropolitan markets was an insurance rather than a handicap in this phase of development, which continued into the fifties — witness the table below, with its often remarkable growth figures.

TABLE 2

IMPORTS INTO FRANCE

(thousand tons)

	1913	1929	1938	1949	1959
Bananas : Total	3	128	178	184	341
Of which from French over-	—	5	178	180	341
seas territories					
Cocoa : Total	27·6	35·8	42·5	66	56
French overseas territories	0·7	24·6	38·7	66	48
Coffee (not roasted) : Total	115	170	186	88	197
French overseas territories	1	5	59	61	150
Timber : Total	1901	2230	545	1707	1063
French overseas territories	35	120	206	161	646
Groundnut oil : Total	..	..	3	18	94
French overseas territories	..	..	..	16	94
Groundnuts (unshelled): Total	256	309	388	272	421
French overseas territories	177	286	376	232	371
Groundnuts (shelled) : Total	238	366	459	..	..
French overseas territories	..	4	192	..	..

Although we shall see that great changes took place in the principles of development at the key dates of 1946 and 1958–9, there was never any discontinuity in the growth trends; only the great depression and the two wars temporarily introduced a halt or a setback into an otherwise progressive rise.

TABLE 3

ANALYSIS OF EXPORTS OF CERTAIN FRENCH OVERSEAS TERRITORIES

	1938 %	1959 %
Groundnuts	22·5	27
Coffee	19·4	22·5
Cocoa	18	21·7
Timber	12·5	15·1
Cotton	6	6·8
Palm kernels and palm oil	4	4·2
Bananas	1·6	2·7

The considerable increase in exports did not change their structure. A calculation relating to all the territories concerned except Madagascar, and comprising 83 per cent of the value of exports in 1938 (when total exports were worth 2·5 billion) and 87 per cent in 1959 (115 billion), shows the following percentage distribution.

Four major commodities still account for three-quarters of exports today, just as twenty or thirty years ago. One of the consequences of this state of affairs is obviously that the economies concerned are highly sensitive to fluctuations in the price of these products; such fluctuations were frequent in the past and were often made up of short commercial oscillations (monthly fluctuations) superimposed upon a strong upward or downward trend over one or several years.[1] More recent years were not much more favourable from the point of view of export price stability, which in any case would need to be assessed not only in nominal terms but also in real terms. Some stabilization measures have been put into effect, but only domestically and not on the international plane, which is what matters for these commodities. This is, of course, a problem which cannot be solved in the absence of real international co-operation, such as we are still far from having achieved. When a Committee of Experts of the Council of Europe examined the development of Africa and the means of European co-operation, it held that price stabilization for the major export commodities would be one of the most effective ways to aid developing countries.[2] This was some years ago, but no progress in this direction has since been recorded.

The exports of Madagascar are more diversified than those of the other African countries discussed above. In Madagascar the four

---

[1] C.i.f. price per kg. in francs (annual averages):

	Cocoa *	Coffee *	Groundnuts †	Palm kernels ‡
1921	260	113	554	107·8
1926	772	305	1290	304
1931	310	139	574	117·8
1936	263	152	486	94
1939	364	228	800	154
1949	165·3	75·8	152·6	92·6
1953	257·3	94·5	397·7	89·5
1954	432·6	96·7	418·6	90·7
1955	278	96·2	297·9	86·9
1957	255	95·6	339·2	90

* Ivory Coast.   † Sénégal.   ‡ Dahomey (*Outre-mer 1958*), *op. cit.*

[2] *Le Développement de l'Afrique*, Strasburg, 1957.

Economic Development for Africa South of the Sahara

major export products accounted for barely more than half the total value of exports in 1959.[1]

In Annex II, a number of tables show the development of foreign trade in the countries concerned since 1950, when pre-war exports were reached once again. It can also be seen from these tables that during the past ten years the terms of trade were generally favourable, though unevenly so for the different countries; the best year was 1954. Some figures indicating the range of these movements are given below.

TABLE 4

TERMS OF TRADE

(1949 = 100)

	1950	1954	1957
French West Africa	106	143	120
French Equatorial Africa	112	109	108 (117 in 1955)
Cameroons	109	148	117
Madagascar	145	176	177

(*Outre-mer 1958, op. cit.*)

While exports increased, imports expanded even more rapidly. For example, between 1950 and 1959 all the French-language overseas territories together ran up a balance-of-payments deficit of about 31 billion new francs on a cumulative value of imports of 88 billion new francs. The countries here under consideration account for 24·5 billion new francs of these total imports, and their balance-of-payments deficit comes to nearly 6 billion new francs.

TABLE 5

IMPORTS OF FRENCH-LANGUAGE AFRICA SOUTH
OF THE SAHARA AND MADAGASCAR

(m. tons)

	1938	1950	1959
Condensed milk	1·54	4·88	14·1
Rice	46·7	63·3	180·1
Wheat flour	15·9	59·1	41·0
Sugar	23·0	43·5	109·5
Wines and spirits	15·4	51·0	40·0

[1] The total c.i.f. value of exports was 18·6 billion francs, distributed as follows : coffee (not roasted), 5·97 ; vanilla, 2·23 ; rice, 1·24 ; sugar, 1·14 ; tobacco, 0·87 ; raffia, 0·79 ; cloves, 0·71 ; hides and skins, 0·53 ; sisal, 0·45 ; and finally minerals : graphite, 0·25 and mica, 0·29.

However, if the franc area is excluded, the Cameroons actually had a small surplus in their trade with other foreign countries during the same period (although the surplus amounted to only half their deficit with the franc area).

The import surplus certainly had to meet capital goods requirements, but also served a considerable improvement in the supply of consumer goods, especially staple foods.

The indices of the value of imports show the improvement of the standard of life.

TABLE 6

INDICES OF THE QUANTUM OF IMPORTS

(1949 = 100)

	1913	1938	1950	1952
A.O.F.	26	58·6	112	200
A.E.F.	10	31	107	185
Cameroon	15 (1920)	30	106	167
Madagascar	11	66	120	255

These figures testify to the rise in the standard of living. But they are largely the result of public capital flows from France, not only to finance investment but also to defray the expenses of suzerainty, administration, and defence. French supply votes for all these current expenses represented an addition of four-fifths to the investment expenditure financed by French budgetary funds. The net balance of public transfers from France to overseas countries and territories from 1953 to 1959 inclusive amounted to 34·5 billion new francs, which was twice as much as the beneficiaries' trade deficit ; for French West and Equatorial Africa, the Cameroons, and Madagascar the net balance of such transfers came to 8 billion new francs during the same period (see Annex VI).

It is these transfer surpluses which explain the import surplus. They were channelled into local development in various ways and even contributed to quite a sizeable extent (probably more than 15 per cent) to the coverage of ordinary local budgets. Financial aid was distributed under a number of different headings, but mainly under that of financing development programmes. While a country like Nigeria was able to finance more than 80 per cent of its development expenditure between 1955 and 1961 (and in 1962) from domestic resources, this was not so in the case of the countries here under consideration ; on the contrary, the proportion was just about the inverse of the Nigerian, since the French-language countries south of the Sahara require foreign funds for at least four-fifths of their development expenditure.[1]

IV. INSTITUTIONS FOR ECONOMIC DEVELOPMENT

May I now briefly survey the institutions set up to promote the economic development of these countries ? The existing institutions were all remodelled when French Africa attained independence in 1958-9 and new ones were created ; but far from diminishing, French financial and technical aid to the same beneficiaries has actually increased.

The principles and methods of operation of the new development drive were laid down in the basic law of April 30, 1946, which defined the methods of planning, financing, and executing invest-ment programmes 'designed to fashion the future of 51 million people in the Overseas Territories'. Before that, there had indeed existed development plans, but they were concerned mainly with exports, disposed of no certain sources of finance and were made up of isolated projects rather than of co-ordinated programmes designed to raise the standard of living. From 1946 onwards, the needs of the local population and social progress became the prime preoccupation. In the early stages, there were also some immediate and temporary concerns, like closing the dollar gap and a rather ill-defined attempt at consolidating relatively complementary structures to form a French Union primarily interested in its internal relations.

[1] For purposes of comparison, I give the detailed figures by source of funds for Nigeria during the period 1955-62 ; these are taken from D. T. Healey's study for the Institute of Commonwealth studies.

Domestic Sources (million £)		%
Budgetary funds	137·3	55·2
Domestic loans (from Marketing Boards and Central Bank)	47·7	19·2
Grants by Marketing Boards	12·8	5·1
Miscellaneous	5·0	2·0
Total	202·8	81·5
Foreign Sources (million £)		%
IBRD loans	10·0	4·0
UK government loans	15·0	6·0
Colonial development and welfare grants	19·4	7·8
Miscellaneous	1·7	0·7
Total	46·1	18·5

The new law had a preamble announcing certain principles which have lost none of their force today. The preamble spoke of high social purposes, of the insufficiency of private enterprise, of the need for permanent reconciliation between metropolitan and local interests, of the desirability of drawing to the largest possible extent on private capital however much the public sector invested, of planning under the auspices and on the responsibility of government, of the determination to undertake irrevocable commitments, of the obligation to engage the co-operation of the local populations, of the deficiency of loan capital but at the same time also of the importance of not relying too much on grants but to the greatest possible extent on financial contributions from the Territories themselves, whose own development efforts were ultimately the true pledge of success.[1]

The main outlines of the new arrangements were as follows. The law created an Investment Fund for Economic and Social Development (FIDES), to receive and distribute among the overseas countries and territories for which the Ministry of Overseas France was responsible all the budgetary funds appropriated for development plans. A public institution called the Central Finance Corporation for Overseas France (CCFOM) was set up as financial agents for FIDES and also put in charge of all other financial operations designed to contribute to the implementation of the plans.

The Board of Directors of FIDES at the same time had the function of authorizing the operations of CCFOM. The majority of the board were Members of Parliament generally selected (by the two Chambers' Committees for Overseas Territories or by the Ministries for Overseas France and Finance, as the case may be) for their interest in questions of overseas development — which meant in practice very often a member elected overseas ; the rest were senior civil servants, such as the Commissioner-General of Planning, and representatives of the ministries concerned. Was this really, as it was meant to be, a 'true Board of Directors under the chairmanship of the Minister for Overseas France ?'[2] This is a debatable question, both from the point of view of the principles of decision guiding the vote of each member and from that of the responsibilities incurred ; the civil servants were concerned with questions of economic efficiency, the other members were free to follow parliamentary, that is electoral concerns.

In principle, the fund's resources were not limited to annual

[1] Cf. L. B. de Carbon, 'Principes et méthodes d'expansion économique dans les territoires d'outre-mer', *Chroniques d'Outre-mer*, No. 25, May 1956.
[2] 'La Caisse centrale de la France d'outre-mer', *Documentation Française, Notes et Études documentaires*, No. 1, 393, October 1950.

budget appropriations under the finance act, but it was also to receive contributions made by the territories themselves out of their own resources. In practice these contributions also came from the metropolitan power in the form of long-term advances made to the territories by the CCFOM, which in turn received its funds mainly from the Exchequer.

While it was the responsibility of the Board of Directors of FIDES to approve CCFOM operations from the point of view of their usefulness to development in the overseas territories, these operations had ultimately to be approved by the Council of CCFOM itself from the more strictly financial point of view. The Board and the Council met jointly about once a month.

The Finance Corporation had more than the mere passive functions of a financial agent ; it was in reality a development bank with very wide responsibilities : [1] it was to help the territories to cover investment expenditure under their development plans, to help local authorities, public firms, and mixed companies with their development projects, and finally to provide financial aid for the creation or extension of private firms. It granted many medium- or long-term low-interest loans (sometimes interest at 2 per cent or less covered barely more than the lender's administrative cost) to municipal authorities, chambers of commerce, railway administrations, electric power companies, real estate companies, agricultural or social credit institutions, etc. Apart from FIDES funds, in respect to which CCFOM acted merely as agent, the loan operations of the Finance Corporation were based on an endowment fund provided by the state (25 million new francs), plus reserves and profits carried forward, and above all on advances by the Exchequer or the Modernization and Development Fund (which has since been renamed the Economic and Social Development Fund). These advances were the main source of finance for the Finance Corporation and enabled it to operate on the large scale required by the development problems of the public and private sector. The CCFOM was also authorized to raise finance on the market by inviting the public to subscribe loans, but no use has so far been made of this faculty because of the high cost of borrowing on the French capital market.

Backed by all these financial resources, the CCFOM was able to grant, on its own account, new loans of some 20 billion old francs per year. But these figures do not do justice to the opera-

---

[1] A. Holleaux, 'Rôle de la C.C.F.O.M. dans le financement des plans de développement économique et social', *La France d'Outre-mer, Études et Informations*, No. 148, November 1950.

tional capacity of that institution, in so far as they neglect the more or less rapid turnover of prior credits in the amount of more than 200 billion old francs as well as technical aid provided by the corporation on the occasion of granting a loan and during its whole period (which means keeping a watch over the borrower's business management and situation). Finally, mention has to be made also of the contribution of private capital, which was generally a condition of any CCFOM loans to private firms ; as a rule private capital had to make at least a matching contribution.

The annual programmes of the territories formed part of development plans extending over several years, of which there were two between 1936 and 1960. These plans were first drawn up for each territory separately and then put into effect, in agreement with the Ministry for Overseas France through constant consultation with local legislatures, which were so enabled to assume their responsibilities in full and to take their decisions at all times in full knowledge of the facts. At first, France contributed about 55 per cent to the finance of each programme in the form of grants ; later, around 1953 and 1954, the grant rose to about 90 per cent, since it became apparent that the territories, with their heavy long-term commitments for economic and social development and modernization, had little over to repay any loans.

The development programmes were made up of two sections :

(*a*) a *general section*, where all expenditure was government-financed and the entire implementation of which, at the stages of decision, construction, and finance alike, remained the sole responsibility of the metropolitan power. The expenditure in question concerned mainly very broad projects involving the interests of the French Union as a whole or of France in particular ; [1]

(*b*) an *overseas section* for each territory, which comprised local development projects, to be approved by local legislatures and by the governing bodies of FIDES and CCFOM as described earlier.

When many overseas territories became independent in 1959, far-reaching changes had to be made in the institutions through which France helped to plan, implement, and finance the development programmes of the new sovereign states. FIDES carried on

---

[1] 'This section covers expenditure for scientific research, capital endowment for public firms, government equity-holdings in mixed companies, and projects which, by their nature or effects, interest the metropolitan power and several overseas territories.' (A. Holleaux, *op. cit.*)

for those countries which decided to maintain their status as French Overseas Territories, and a new Aid and Co-operation Fund (FAC) was set up for the new states of the Community. The CCFOM now acts as agent for both, as well as for a fund (FIDOM) set up in 1950 for the development of the new overseas *departements* of Martinique, Guadeloupe, Guiana, and Réunion.

'The resources of these Funds come from French government subventions appropriated each year by the Finance Act. The *Caisse Centrale* acts merely as a paying-out agent, and as such carries out decisions taken by the governing bodies of the Funds and by the Ministers who are their chairmen.' [1] The CCFOM itself was renamed (on Dec. 31, 1958) Finance Corporation of Economic Co-operation.

Apart from the French overseas departments and territories, the Finance Corporation extends its activities independently to the sovereign states of the Community, to the Cameroons and Togo and the other countries with which its Council authorizes it to deal. It handles the operations of the three Funds FAC, FIDES, and FIDOM and administers the National Price Stabilization Fund for Overseas Commodities and the Overseas Textile Support Fund.[2] Finally it handles the payments of the European Development Fund (FEDOM) to overseas countries and territories, by virtue of an agreement concluded with the Commission of the European Economic Community.

The Finance Corporation's financial operations since the law of April 30, 1946, up to the end of 1959 amounted to 937 billion current francs, of which 222·4 billion were on its own account and 714·6 on account of the development Funds (FIDES, FIDOM, FAC). Africa south of the Sahara and Madagascar received during the same period 173·1 billion old francs on the Finance Corporation's own account and 574 billion old francs on account of FIDES and later FAC. The bulk of this latter amount consisted of grants.

The distribution of allocations for development programmes was not always the same, but infrastructures always absorbed much of the money, especially in the initial phases. For the two economic plans covering, respectively, the periods 1947–53 and 1954–9 and

---

[1] A. Postel-Vinay, Director-General of the Caisse Centrale, *La Caisse Centrale de Coopération Économique: étages sur les problèmes de planification*, mimeographed document, August 1960. The figures quoted in what follows and the results of the Finance Corporation's activities are mostly taken from this document.

[2] 'These Funds are authorized to grant advances (and sometimes subsidies) to the price stabilization funds which have been set up in most overseas countries and territories to dampen the effects of price fluctuations for agricultural products on the economy and on the standard of living of agricultural producers and planters.' (A. Postel-Vinay, *op. cit.*)

involving much the same total amounts in constant francs, the percentage distribution was roughly as follows :

TABLE 7

DISTRIBUTIONS OF DEVELOPMENT EXPENDITURES

	1947–53 %	1954–9 %
Transport investment	49	21
Educational and social investment	15	24 (15% for housing)
Mining, power, and manufacturing industry	11	25
Agriculture	12	19
Research	6	11
Miscellaneous	7	—
Total	100	100

Financial aid granted to Africa south of the Sahara and Madagascar by the Finance Corporation from its own resources between April 30, 1946, and December 31, 1959, amounted to 173·1 billion old francs and was distributed as follows :

(*a*) Loans to local communities or public institutions : 44·2 billion. These were low-interest loans (2·5 per cent) and served to finance infrastructures, such as port installations, roads, and highways, water supplies, rural investment, etc.

(*b*) Equity or loan capital for government-owned or mixed companies : 58·5 billion. These companies, which were set up under the law of April 30, 1946, operate in the field of electricity generation (seven companies), building construction (six), agricultural and social credit (eleven). The Finance Corporation either grants them long-term loans (generally at a rate of 2·5 or 3 per cent) or subscribes to some of their capital, or finances the respective governments' contributions to the companies' capital.[1]

This kind of financial aid is often linked with arrangements for technical aid — Electricité de France, for example, has furnished valuable help in planning and executing particular projects. Its effects are often a multiple of the original sum ; by short-term lending of funds borrowed at long term, for instance, social credit

[1] The Finance Corporation's financial aid was distributed as follows : electricity companies, more than 36 billion ; building construction companies about 8 billion ; credit institutes about 14 billion. See on this subject Gaston Leduc, 'Les Sociétés d'état instruments de mise en valeur', *Archives de Philosophie du Droit*, Sirey, 1952.

institutions have been able to grant advances of 51·7 billion.[1]

(c) Aid to 246 private firms, mostly in the form of medium- or long-term loans : 70 billion old francs, of which 36 billion to seven large industrial and mining companies, 20 and 34 billion to 239 medium-sized undertakings in the field of agriculture, industry, and forestry (textile and saw mills, breweries, flour mills, oil mills, sugar refineries, etc.). The interest rate is generally 5·5 per cent.[2]

The Finance Corporation never substitutes itself for private enterprise ; on the contrary, it makes every effort to make private enterprise possible and to stimulate it. L. Rey writes : 'The *Caisse Centrale*, which is a kind of banking institution operating under the direction of a Council including representatives from big banks, has never tried to compete with the banks themselves. When it lends to private companies, it provides money which could not have been obtained from any other but a public source, given the risks involved. . . . French aid has never aimed at creating a state economy, and it has always been the intention that private enterprise should one day take the place of public capital in the development of French Africa.'[3]

Taken as a whole, the results achieved with this system were often excellent, notwithstanding certain misjudgments and mistakes on the part of FIDES.

The annual rate of investment in French-language Africa south of the Sahara and Madagascar during the last ten years was 22 per cent of gross domestic product, and nearly 30 per cent of national income in money terms, that is, excluding non-market production.

Gross domestic product rose by 9 or 10 per cent on the average over the ten years, though there were marked fluctuations due to crop and price variations. According to the calculations of the Overseas Statistical Office (*Outre-mer 1958*) the capital/output ratio reached the extraordinary low value of 2.[4]

[1] 'These institutions are now subject to the law of their country. Some of them have become joint-stock companies, although their shareholders are almost exclusively public authorities. Others have become public or semi-public institutions. These changes were made by agreement between the governments concerned, the Finance Corporation, and the other shareholders.' (A. Postel-Vinay, *op. cit.*)

[2] Mining of iron ores at Fort-Gouraud (Mauretania), phosphate at Taiba (near Dakar) and Akoupame (Togo), alumina works at Fria (Guinea) and aluminium industry at Edea (Cameroons), manganese at Franceville (Gabon), and uranium mining at Mounana (Gabon).

[3] *L'Aide de la France à l'Afrique Noire et à Madagascar* : lecture delivered at the University of Basel, January 1961.

[4] This is the capital/output ratio Brazil had during the period 1945-54 (cf. United Nations, *The Economic Development of Brazil*, 1956). But this stage of development in Brazil included no construction of transport facilities which have

As L. Rey stressed in the lecture quoted above, the principal feature of these recent developments is that Africa has been opened out to the world at large. Factors of progress began to penetrate far into the bush, rural conditions began to change as agricultural production grew, the bases of industrialization were laid, a few large and modern production centres were constructed which should radiate economic, technical, and social progress and even become true 'development poles' by calling forth induced, complementary, or associated investment. Finally, the conditions of human life are being improved in the key sectors of education, health, and housing.

But everywhere much remains to be done. The characteristics of the local economies are still the same and bear witness to the precariousness of the situation and to the long road that still has to be travelled. Non-market production still amounts to 25 to 35 per cent of domestic product, according to the country concerned ; exports still contribute more than one-fifth to national income and still concern only a few staple commodities ; the foreign trade deficit in 1958 still amounted to 112 million new francs in French West Africa (without Guinea), 192 million in Equatorial Africa, and 128 million in Madagascar. Foreign aid is more necessary than ever.

V. PROSPECTS AND PROBLEMS

In 1960 the Cameroons, Togo, and eventually the nations of the Community attained full internal and external sovereignty. 'Nothing was lost of what had been created for African development, but everything was transformed. In spite of institutional changes, French aid continues undiminished in volume and is directed to essentially the same purposes. Financial aid has never been more extensive : the 1961 French budget is providing 1,528 million new francs for civil expenditure alone, excluding any loans which the Finance Corporation may grant on its own account. As in the past, these funds will serve to put French technicians at the disposal of African governments — at their request, to arrange for fellowships and training courses in France, to finance fundamental research, to execute the large construction programmes which are France's gift to her partners. . . . They will also help to balance national budgets, but this form of aid should disappear in time, since it would not be in order for the new nations to run permanent budget deficits.' [1]

a high capital/output ratio. It is true that development in the French-language countries was initially concerned mainly with the restoration and extension of existing installations, which would bring down the average capital/output ratio. See Annex III for national income statistics.   [1] L. Rey, *op. cit.*

Future prospects thus rest on two facts : the new nations are in a difficult financial situation, and French aid continues. But French aid is now set in a rather different context, in so far as it has to take account, on the one hand, of the implementation of the Rome Treaty and, on the other, of the consequences of the political independence of the overseas territories. All this raises very important problems for the economic development of the new states.

Speaking at the Weizmann Research Institute in Israel in August 1960, W. A. Lewis said : [1] 'If the ambition is to grow as rapidly as the countries of Europe and North America have grown during the past century, the desired growth rate is about 2 per cent per head per annum. Allowing for population growth, this means that in most new states national output should grow by about 4 per cent per annum. Higher rates than this are stated as objectives in some development plans, but 4 per cent is so difficult to obtain that it is really quite an ambitious target. Economic growth at about 4 per cent per annum requires that new states withhold from personal consumption about a quarter of the national output. One-half of this, or about 12 per cent of national output, is needed to provide an adequate framework of public services ; the other half is required for capital formation.'[2]

Actually, in the French-speaking African countries the tax burden, as a proportion of money income, is heavier than it used to be and yet ordinary budgets are still in deficit.[3] In 1955 fiscal revenue absorbed 18 per cent of national monetary income in all of French Africa south of the Sahara together. Between 1958 and 1961 ordinary expenditure increased considerably, as is only to be expected in countries where new sovereignty entails new expenses, *e.g.*, for the diplomatic service, the army, the breaking up of formerly federal services, etc. A young nation, eager to plan for the development of its resources and to raise the standard of life of its population has to answer many calls for more and better central and regional services. During these last few years, ordinary budget expenditure rose by 48 per cent in the Cameroons, and by 68 per cent in the group of countries formerly belonging to the Federation of French Equatorial

[1] W. A. Lewis, 'Problèmes des états nouveaux', *Bulletin de la Banque Centrale des États de l'Afrique de l'Ouest*, No. 66, January 1961.
[2] 'The governments of under-developed countries should each year spend about 3 per cent of their national income on education, 2 per cent on public health, 3 per cent on economic services such as communications, agriculture and geology, and about 4 per cent on general administration and social assistance.' (W. A. Lewis, *op. cit.*)
[3] Cf. L. B. de Carbon, 'Politique fiscale et croissance économique', *Bulletin de la Banque Centrale des États de l'A.E.F. et du Cameroun*, May 1961.

Africa. Three-quarters of revenue come from indirect taxation, and the need to attract private investment leads to tax concessions which put a severe limit on any increase in direct taxation for many years to come. As a result, fiscal policy is exceedingly hard to adapt to development policy, the pressure of indirect taxation being particularly inflationary in countries where large trading concerns occupy a dominant and often powerful position. There can be no doubt that fiscal policy will have to be reconsidered in the light of equity no less than in that of greater economic and financial efficacy. But in an under-developed economy income distribution is so unequal, fiscal control so weak, the means of tax evasion so numerous, foreign economic relations so predominant, the pressure of privileged groups so strong, and the poverty of the masses so prohibitive of any increase even in indirect taxation, that the greatest difficulties are to be feared for these young democracies which need so many and have so few resources.

I have said that French aid at the moment still bolsters ordinary budgets. Is this not a somewhat embarrassing situation from the point of view of political independence? The Cameroons had a budget deficit of 37 per cent in 1961!

On the other hand, even if total French aid remains the same, will not its relative weight alter now that we have the European Economic Community? In *per caput* terms, French foreign aid is the highest in the world.[1]

In a study of the franc area as it was a year ago, P. Moussa stressed what he called its 'compactness',[2] meaning the preponderant part of France played in the internal commercial and financial relations which link the countries of the franc area to their former mother country. The franc area was for a long time strongly self-centred and its development owed nearly everything to France herself.

According to Moussa, the reasons for this 'compactness' were the complementarity of the franc area's economies, legislative and administrative provisions such as preference tariffs and quotas for imports from elsewhere, the organization of certain markets in the area, and the coupling of certain foreign imports with imports from French overseas countries and territories. Furthermore, French companies add to this 'compactness' by buying their supplies and

[1] 'In 1959 it amounted to 84 new francs as against 77 in the U.S., 43 in Soviet Russia, 23 in the United Kingdom, 19 in Canada, 18 in Australia, 12 in the Netherlands, 11 in Western Germany. In absolute terms, 3·7 billion new francs of French aid rank third after American (13·2 billion) and Russian (8·5 billion) foreign aid.' (L. Rey, *op. cit.*)

[2] P. Moussa, *L'Économie de la zone franc, Séries Que sais-je?* Presses Universitaires, 1960.

selling their products in the protected markets of the franc area and by relying on a private banking system to back these operations. But how long will this 'compactness' survive once foreign sellers can freely offer better prices and qualities and once the obstacle of exchange difficulties is removed ?

Protectionism and French capital flows in the overseas territories together created a dense network of internal trade in the franc area, in which France accounted for two-thirds or three-quarters of the foreign trade of each of the countries of French Africa south of the Sahara and Madagascar.

Transfers between France and the other countries of the franc area are in remarkable equilibrium, both in the aggregate and with respect to each country (see Annex VI).

TABLE 8

ANNUAL SETTLEMENTS BETWEEN COUNTRIES OF THE FRANC AREA
(millions of N.F.)

	1953	1954	1955	1956	1957	1958	1959
Public transfers (balance)	+2546	+2738	+3727	+5667	+6375	+6667	+7141
Private transfers (balance)	−2414	−2498	−3147	−5491	−5284	−6192	−2247
Net balance	+132	+240	+580	+176	+1091	+475	−106
Trade balance with franc zone	−1762	−1723	−1924	−1836	−2491	−2962	−4082
Counterpart of foreign exchange settlements :							
on current account	−264	−92	−167	−509	−764	−821	−279
on capital account	+145	+202	+160	+131	+182	+283	+396
Invisibles	−533	−887	−1230	−3332	−2281	−2809	−3491

Plus (+) means surplus of transfers from France; *minus* (−) means surplus of transfers to France.

Source : 1960 Report of the Monetary Committee of the Franc Area.

The large 'invisibles' item in the table represents freights and all forms of insurance, holiday expenditure in France, investments on the French capital market, the expenses of overseas students and trainees, etc. . . . All these tend to tighten the commercial and financial relations between France and the other countries of the franc area.

French aid, which is expressed by the rather high balance of public transfers thus comes back to France and gives work to French firms. The budgetary sacrifice which France makes for the sake of its overseas partners is reduced by the amount of additional tax revenue from incomes created in France by the return flow of the aid funds (budgetary revenue absorbs some 20 per cent of national income in France).

158

This mechanism has led to a sort of symbiotic development of certain economic sectors in France and overseas.[1] Now, the application of the Rome Treaty will enable the overseas countries financed by France to use the purchasing power they owe to France for ordering from suppliers who compete with French suppliers and these latter will cease to enjoy any protection *vis-à-vis* the other countries of the European Economic Community. Some foreign exchange disequilibrium might also result from the opening up of the closed trading system resting on French aid. This latter danger is not without remedy : the best solution would no doubt be if other Common Market countries took on a sufficient part of public investment overseas.

There is good reason to believe that the factors making for equilibrium of transfers within the franc area will be affected by present-day political developments. Some of the things that come to mind in this context are the disappearance of imperial preference ; the transfer of responsible functions into African hands, which will put an end to the repatriation of the savings of the formerly French officials ; fiscal pressure on companies to discourage repatriation of profits to France ; protection for nascent local industries and import restrictions on consumer goods ; increase in foreign exchange deficits as a result of autonomous commercial policies ; and a loosening of control over overseas issuing banks.[2]

With most of the French-speaking countries overseas France has signed more or less long-term co-operation agreements which are more in the nature of declarations of intent than of precise commitments. The climate of independence requires tactful procedures, especially when foreign aid is still so necessary.

In a recent memorandum to the Academy of Moral and Political Sciences, entitled 'La politique de l'Occident vis-à-vis du Tiers Monde', Maurice Allais made a number of recommendations : a

[1] 'In many branches, the overseas franc area absorbs more than 50 per cent of exports. This happens in cotton, staple fibre and printed piece goods, household linen, hosiery goods ; sugar, confectionery, beer, vegetable oils, cheese ; certain engineering products such as refrigerators, metal safes and furniture, lighting and heating fixtures, lorries ; in the chemical industry for soap, compound and nitrogen fertilizers, paints and varnishes, rubber articles, petroleum products, lime and cement ; footwear ; furniture and other wooden articles. . . . 2·3 per cent of the French agricultural population and 5 per cent of the industrial population, 36 per cent of the fixed personnel of the merchant fleet and more than 50 per cent of that of the air fleet — that is, respectively, 120,000, 300,000, 20,000, and 10,000 people making up a total 450,000 — work in France to sell overseas or to carry passengers and goods overseas.' (P. Moussa, *op. cit.*)
[2] Cf. L. B. de Carbon, 'Implications des zones monétaires et situation de la zone franc', *Bulletin de la Banque Centrale des États de l'A.E.F. et du Cameroun*, February 1961; cf. also G. Leduc, 'Coordination de la politique monétaire dans l'Union Française', *Revue des Sciences Financières*, November 1952.

liberal exchange policy should be adopted under which purchases can replace grants; guarantees should be stipulated to protect private investments against political risks ; [1] future markets covering several years ahead should be organized for a number of commodities ; arrangements should be made to help the currencies of under-developed countries to become convertible ; and finally, economic information about the under-developed countries should be publicized in business circles. France is actually doing several of these things and, as we have seen, she adds the essential element of powerful technical and financial aid. The task is enormous, and there would be no hope of accomplishing it without a common ideal, which alone is the basis of true co-operation among peoples and individuals alike.

But if a common ideal is a necessary condition of success, it is not a sufficient one. Private capital will not feel safe under any system of guarantees against political risks, which in any event is difficult enough to establish, so long as the governments of the overseas countries fail to furnish proof of prudent conduct. Even inter-governmental public capital flows are not likely to be large in the absence of assurances about the efficient use of the funds. Should it be stipulated that foreign aid funds be used for investment, and if so, according to what priorities ? Should aid be given annually or for a number of years at a time ? Which is better : multilateral or bilateral aid ? Is it reasonable to finance patently unbalanced plans which might do more harm than good to further progress ?

I can attempt only a few general comments. Grants are still indispensable in the weak economic situation characteristic of the initial stages of development in under-developed countries. The fundamental principles and purposes of development lay down certain social priorities which might serve as a basis of co-operation agreements from case to case. It should be possible to study development objectives together with beneficiary countries without detriment to their sovereignty. No method of financing can work properly without the good faith of both parties. Finally, there is no reason why bilateral aid should not be given in addition to multilateral aid. Aid to the Third World must not be allowed to become a matter of rivalry and competition, or else we shall never achieve our aim of spreading civilization, strengthening international solidarity and assuring peace ; on the contrary, all we would get is disorder, conflict, and strife.

[1] Cf. L. B. de Carbon, 'La Garantie des investissements étrangers, son importance et ses problèmes', *Bulletin de la Banque Centrale des États de l'A.E.F. et du Cameroun*, February 1960.

de Carbon — Development of French Africa

ANNEX I:

AREA, POPULATION, AND POPULATION DENSITY
OF OVERSEAS TERRITORIES
(latest estimates *)

Territory (Capital)	Area (1000's of Km.²)	Population French of Metropolitan Stock and Foreigners*† (Units)	French of Local Stock ‡ (1000's)	Total (1000's)	Density of Population (Persons per Km.²)
A.O.F. (Dakar) Total	4,634	88,240	18,982	19,070	4·1
Sénégal (Saint-Louis)	197	48,593	2,270	2,319	11·8
Soudan (Bamako)	1,204	7,382	3,701	3,708	3·1
Guinée (Conakry)	246	9,500	2,482	2,491	10·1
Côte-d'Ivoire (Abidjan)	322	11,638	2,471	2,483	7·7
Dahomey (Porto Novo)	116	2,767	1,710	1,713	14·7
Niger (Niamey)	1,189	3,040	2,412	2,415	2·1
Mauritanie (Saint-Louis)	1,086	1,627	614	615	0·6
Haute-Volta (Ouagadougou)	274	3,693	3,322	3,326	12·1
République autonome du Togo (Lomé)	57	1,277	1,093	1,094	19·2
État du Cameroun (Yaoundé)	432	16,515	3,170	3,187	7·4
A.E.F. (Brazzaville) Total	2,510	25,236	4,849	4,874	1·9
Gabon (Libreville)	267	3,984	400	404	1·5
Moyen-Congo (Brazzaville)	342	10,429	749	759	2·2
Oubangui-Chari (Bangui)	617	5,939	1,121	1,127	1·8
Tchad (Fort-Lamy)	1,284	4,884	2,579	2,584	2·0
Madagascar (Tananarive)	590	74,085	4,848	4,922	8·3
Comores (Dzaoudzi)	2	995	177	178	89·0
Côtes des Somalis (Djibouti)	22	4,422	63	67	3·1

* For French of metropolitan stock and foreigners, results of census of 1956, except for Guinée and the Autonomous Republic of Togo, for which the figures show the current administrative estimates. For the native populations, estimates for 1957, except for Côte d'Ivoire, Mauritanie, Haute-Volta, and État du Cameroun, for which the figures are for 1956.
† Including native citizens of French overseas territories other than the one immediately concerned.
‡ Or citizens of Togo or Cameroun.

ANNEX II: TRADE STATISTICS

TABLE 1

EXTERNAL TRADE OF THE FRANC ZONE EXCLUDING FRANCE
(Millions of N.F.)

	1950*	1951*	1952*	1953	1954	1955	1956	1957	1958	1959
Imports	5,954	8,191	9,411	7,054	7,529	7,871	8,233	9,772	11,454	12,542
Exports	3,952	4,804	5,196	4,848	5,446	5,593	5,684	6,260	7,553	7,806
Balance	2,002	3,387	4,215	2,206	2,083	2,278	2,549	3,512	3,901	4,736

* Including États d'Indochine.

TABLE 2

MOVEMENTS OF THE TERMS OF TRADE

(1949 = 100)

	1950*	1951*	1952*	1953	1954	1955	1956	1957
A.O.F.	106	124	106	117	143	130	119	120
Cameroun	109	128	105	111	148	136	115	117
A.E.F.	112	132	110	112	109	117	114	108
Madagascar	145	167	138	149	176	135	151	177

TABLE 3

TRADE BALANCES OF AFRICAN COUNTRIES OF THE FRENCH ZONE

(millions of N.F.)

	1950*	1951*	1952*	1953	1954	1955	1956	1957	1958	1959
A.O.F.										
Imports	843	1,227	1,220	1,105	1,330	1,344	1,335	1,550	1,499	1,602
Exports	621	774	804	935	1,165	1,066	1,200	1,209	1,373	1,376
Balance	− 215	− 453	− 416	− 170	− 165	− 278	− 135	− 341	− 126	− 226
Cameroun										
Imports	211	330	373	283	325	363	333	363	449	403
Exports	164	227	221	262	305	331	263	300	486	535
Balance	− 47	− 103	− 152	− 21	− 20	− 32	− 70	− 63	+ 47	+ 132
A.E.F.										
Imports	268	365	468	296	334	367	411	522	539	626
Exports	159	228	205	201	256	274	283	308	398	451
Balance	− 109	− 137	− 263	− 95	− 78	− 93	− 123	− 214	− 191	− 275
Madagascar										
Imports	300	458	468	453	481	428	462	523	531	300
Exports	243	267	328	297	321	285	326	325	405	373
Balance	− 57	− 191	− 140	− 156	− 160	− 143	− 136	− 198	− 126	− 217

TABLE 4

CUMULATIVE TOTALS 1950–9 OF IMPORTS AND TRADE BALANCES

(millions of N.F.)

	Imports	Trade Balance
All overseas countries and territories	88,011	− 30,869
of which		
A.O.F.	12,085	− 2,525
Cameroun	3,433	− 354
A.E.F.	4,196	− 1,518
Madagascar	4,995	− 1,524

Volumes of Exports
(1949 = 100)

	1950	1951	1952	1953	1954	1955	1956	1957	1958	1959
A.O.F.	103	97	105	124	136	133	166	163		
Cameroun	98	107	108	134	125	143	136	153		
A.E.F.	98	109	111	113	158	169	163	176		
Madagascar	107	100	123	117	115	136	144	143		

TABLE 6

IMPORTS AND BALANCES IN EXTERNAL TRADE*
(millions of N.F.)

	1950	1951	1952	1953	1954	1955	1956	1957	1958	1959
Overseas Countries and Territories	1,315 / -90	1,895 / -405	2,234 / -649	1,720 / -440	1,820 / -360	1,978 / -358	2,185 / -715	2,555 / -1,021	2,672 / -939	2,904 / -654
A.O.F.	196 / -71	209 / -88	267 / -104	232 / -52	285 / -21	283·35 / +2·83	326·26 / -74·02	382·18 / -161·34	428·70 / -142·80	409·80 / -81·88
Cameroun	52 / +12	73 / +9	120 / -22	96 / +33	105 / +31	110·88 / +48·90	102·57 / -8·42	110·80 / -6·53	132·79 / +18·01	125·24 / +96·42
A.E.F.	86 / -48	121 / -69	143 / +157	107 / -55	115 / -46	133·79 / -49·61	158·10 / -75·32	175·58 / -71·43	196·72 / -79·70	106·49 / -41·26
Madagascar	55 / -20	81 / -46	114 / -52	92 / -56	87 / -26	87·22 / -27·27	106·70 / -24·34	117·46 / -22·96	125·77 / -28·19	122·34 / -24·54
Total Deficit of Franc Zone including France	-1,070	-3,795	-4,785	-2,510	-1,820	-1,178	-4,856	-5,965	-4,531	-769

* Line 1 = exports; line 2 = trade balances.

163

TABLE 6 (*continued*)

TOTALS OF DEFICITS FOR PERIOD 1950–9
(Millions of N.F.)

Total of franc zone	− 30,207
Overseas countries and territories	− 5,631
of which	
A.O.F.	− 800
Cameroun	+211
A.E.F.	− 377
Madagascar	− 326

TABLE 7

INDICES OF VOLUMES OF EXPORTS IN 1957
(1949 = 100)

Territories	To France	To Rest of Franc Zone	To Foreign Countries
A.O.F.	145	155	317
Cameroun	114	285	288
A.E.F.	147	395	252
Madagascar	105	192	420

TABLE 8

INDICES OF VOLUMES OF IMPORTS IN 1957
IN CERTAIN CATEGORIES
(1949 = 100)

	A.O.F.	Cameroun (1956)	A.E.F.	Madagascar
Non-durable goods (food)	279	337	228	340
Durable goods	237	133	274	281

TABLE 9

INDICES OF VOLUMES OF TOTAL IMPORTS
(1949 = 100)

	1950	1951	1952	1953	1954	1955	1956	1957
A.O.F.	117	152	135	136	175	171	174	200
Cameroun	106	153	146	123	152	164	152	167
A.E.F.	107	133	138	107	129	151	154	185
Madagascar	120	178	151	166	189	170	193	255

ANNEX III: NATIONAL INCOMES

TABLE 1

Gross National Products of Certain African Countries. Averages of Years 1946–8 and 1952–4

(Millions of N.F. at constant prices of 1955)

	A.O.F.		Cameroun		A.E.F.		Total		Madagascar (1947)
	N.F. m.	%	N.F. m.	%	N.F. m.	%	N.F. m.	%	N.F. m.
Average 1946–8									
Production for export	35·5	11·4	8·2	12·3	13·3	16·1	57·0	12·4	23·2
Importing activities	32·6	10·5	6·8	10·2	8·6	10·4	48·0	10·5	16·1
Food production	139·4	45·0	34·0	51·1	28·6	34·5	202·0	44·0	52·9
Animal husbandry *	37·4	12·1	5·8	8·7	14·9	18·0	58·1	12·6	15·7
Domestic investment activities	32·6	10·5	8·2	12·3	10·2	12·3	51·1	11·1	17·4
Net output of public sector not included elsewhere	32·5	10·5	3·6	5·4	7·2	8·7	43·3	9·4	19·3
Gross national product	310·0	100·0	66·6	100·0	82·8	100·0	459·4	100·0	144·78
									1953
Average 1952–4									
Production for export	93·4	16·7	25·3	20·2	21·3	13·5	140·0	16·6	29·6
Importing activities	81·6	14·6	21·9	17·4	23·0	14·6	126·5	15·0	32·4
Food production	201·0	35·8	37·6	29·9	55·0	34·8	293·6	34·8	73·5
Animal husbandry *	44·1	7·9	6·5	5·2	17·6	11·1	68·2	8·1	21·0
Domestic investment activities	68·9	12·3	20·4	16·2	18·2	11·5	107·5	12·7	31·0
Net output of public sector not included elsewhere	71·6	12·7	13·9	11·1	22·9	14·5	108·4	12·8	33·9
Gross national product	560·6	100·0	125·6	100·0	158·0	100·0	844·2	100·0	221·68

* Excluding exports.

TABLE 2

TOTAL GROSS NATIONAL PRODUCT OF A.E.F.,
CAMEROUN, AND A.E.F.
(Moving averages of three years)
(milliard francs of 1955)

Year	GNP	Year	GNP
1944	381	1950	677
1945	385	1951	757
1946	400	1952	807
1947	462	1953	860
1948	522	1954	901
1949	603	1955	953

TABLE 3

INCREASES OF GROSS NATIONAL PRODUCT
OF A.O.F., CAMEROUN, AND A.E.F.
(milliard francs at constant prices of 1955)

Country	Average 1947–9	Average 1954–6	Percentage Increase
A.O.F.	349·5	628·0	79
Cameroun	79·3	138·7	75
A.E.F.	89·5	167·4	87
Totals	518·3	934·1	80

TABLE 4

SECTORAL RATES OF GROWTH, 1947–53, OF A.O.F.,
CAMEROUN AND A.E.F. TOGETHER
(milliards of francs)

Sectors	Average 1946–8	Average 1952–4	Ratio of Increase
Export production	57	140	2·45
Importing activities	48	127	2·63
Food production	202	294	1·45 } 1·39
Animal husbandry *	58	68	1·18
Domestic investment activities	51	108	2·10
Net output of public sector not elsewhere included	43	108	2·51
Gross national product	459	844	1·84

* Excluding exports.

TÀBLE 5

SHARES OF AGRICULTURE AND RURAL ACTIVITIES
IN GROSS NATIONAL PRODUCT
(milliards of current francs)

	A.O.F. (1951)	A.E.F. (1956)	Algeria (1953)	France (1954)
Product of agriculture and rural activities	224	100	164	1,420
Gross national product	444	203	571	15,790
Agriculture, etc., as percentage of GNP	50·5%	49·0%	29%	9%

TABLE 6

SHARES OF NON-MONETARY SECTOR IN GROSS DOMESTIC PRODUCT
(milliards of current francs)

Country	GNP	Non-Traded Production*	Monetary Sector	Percentage Non-Traded
A.O.F. (1951)	444	164	280	37
Madagascar (1953)	180	49	131	27
A.E.F. (1956)	203	77	126	38

* The non-monetary or non-traded sector corresponds in general to self-subsistence, but includes in principle also direct real investment (in cattle, land-improvement, or housing). This item has been undervalued in some of the studies quoted (in A.O.F. only the investment in cattle, estimated at 6 milliard current francs, has been included). The combined study of A.O.F., Cameroun, and A.E.F. shows, however, that the total of such direct investment has been considerable. A note indicates that for the three territories together the values in milliards of constant francs of 1955 were as follows in the years 1951 to 1955 inclusive : 29, 38, 50, 39, 40 milliards.

TABLE 7

TOTALS OF WAGES PAID BY GOVERNMENTS, CORPORATIONS,
AND PERSONS
(milliards of current francs)

Total of Wages Paid by	A.O.F. (1951)	A.E.F. (1956)	Madagascar (1953)	Cameroun* (1951)
Governments	38	15	16	4 †
Public and private enterprises and persons	54	23	32	7
Totals	92	38	48	11

* For Camerouns wages paid to Africans only.
† Adjusted for partial inclusion of public enterprises.

TABLE 8

GROSS NATIONAL PRODUCTS OF A.O.F. 1947–56
(1949 = 100)

Years	Index	GNP at Constant Prices of 1955 (milliard f.)	Year	Index	GNP at Constant Prices of 1955 (milliard f.)
1947	68	308	1952	118	535
1948	77	349	1953	127	575
1949	100	453	1954	141	640
1950	112	507	1955	132	598
1951	114	517	1956	142	644

TABLE 9

INDICES OF GROSS NATIONAL PRODUCT
(1949 = 100)

Years	Indices of GNP in Real Terms	Percentage Increase of each Year over preceding Year
1947	68	..
1948	77	+14
1949	100	+30
1950	112	+12
1951	114	+2
1952	118	+4
1953	127	+8
1954	141	+11
1955	132	−6
1956	142	+8

TABLE 10

VOLUME OF EXPORTS, TERMS OF TRADE, AND NATIONAL PRODUCT, 1949–56
(1949 = 100)

Years	Index of Volume of Exports	Terms of Trade	Index of Gross National Product
1949	100	100	100
1950	103	107	112
1951	97	125	114
1952	105	106	118
1953	123	117	127
1954	136	142	141
1955	131	131	132
1956	160	121	142

TABLE 11

GROWTH AND EXPENDITURE ON PUBLIC SERVICES IN A.O.F.
(Milliards N.F.)

	1951	1956	Index (1951 = 100)
At current prices	444	656	148·5
At constant prices	517	644	125

Note.—The above figures may be compared with the growth of the staffs of the various public activities given in the next table.

TABLE 12

PERCENTAGE GROWTHS OF STAFFS OF PUBLIC SERVICES IN A.O.F.
SEPTEMBER 1, 1951, TO JANUARY 1, 1956

	%
Education	119
Agriculture, animal husbandry, etc.	58
Law and justice	54
Public works, mines, geology	41
Health and sanitation	40
Ports and communications	24
Fiscal and financial services	22
Security	15
General administration and miscellaneous	9
Total of all services (general average)	35

Note.—It will be seen that the staffs have grown very differently in different types of service, showing a wide dispersion around the general average. The largest increases have been in the social and technical services, which represent a form of human investment.

ANNEX IV: PUBLIC INVESTMENT

TABLE 1

INVESTMENT OVERSEAS FINANCED BY METROPOLITAN FUNDS
(FIDES, CREDITS, AND CCFOM)
FROM THE ESTABLISHMENT OF FIDES TO 1958
(milliards of N.F.)

Territories	1951 *	1952	1953	1954	1955	1956	1957	1958
A.O.F.	75·0	43·0	31·0	19·0	26·0	36·2	35·7	34·2
Togo	3·72	0·75	0·69	0·86	1·32	1·00	5·75	1·54
Cameroun	27·9	17·7	11·3	22·3	9·7	7·59	8·65	6·32
A.E.F.	36·1	18·9	14·0	9·2	10·5	13·4	18·9	10·2
Madagascar	19·2	11·9	12·9	6·3	7·8	10·6	9·40	7·27
Comoro Is.	0·83	0·48	0·83	0·29	0·38	0·38	0·28	0·25
Somalis	3·74	0·9	0·9	0·35	0·41	0·20	0·19	0·16
New Caledonia	3·02	1·6	0·75	0·17	7·6	1·18	3·31	2·29
Polynesia	2·24	0·65	0·35	0·24	0·46	0·47	0·77	0·79
Saint-Pierre-et-Miquelon	0·91	0·08	0·22	0·19	0·19	0·32	0·14	0·06
New Hebrides	—	—	—	—	—	0·19	—	0·12
Total †	190·0	100·0	83·0	67·0	72·0	75·3	83·1	63·2

* Total to December 31, 1951, from the establishment of FIDES.
† Including former French stations in India and general expenditure which cannot be allocated to particular territories. (General Section of FIDES.)

TABLE 2

LOCAL PUBLIC INVESTMENTS 1944–55 OF A.O.F., A.E.F. AND CAMEROUN

(millions of current N.F.)

	1944	1945	1946	1947	1948	1949	1950	1951	1952	1953	1954	1955
A.O.F.												
Local budgets *	595	719	940	1,262	1,535	2,375	5,349	5,128	6,603	6,139	6,179	6,808
Railway and ports †	92	83	250	59	167	57	369	816	1,380	1,063	1,364	1,702
Contributions to FERDES ‡	..	..	..	..	..	70	112	175	158	375	509	330
By Cocoa Fund §	..	..	..	..	..	..	10	277	330	465	360	364
By Coffee Fund §	..	..	..	..	..	..	104	222	158	527	521	559
Road Fund	..	..	..	..	..	..	..	..	..	1,500	1,350	1,600
A.E.F.												
Local budgets *	143	218	387	495	421	592	1,052	2,801	1,668	1,639	472	290
Railway and ports †	3	3	..	..	..	..	89	220	422	127	119	167
Cameroun												
Local budget	127	84	102	105	352	481	499	637	1,754	1,269	253	552
Railway and ports †	24	15	23	14	..	..	38	182	338	234	578	751
P.E.R. ‖	..	..	..	..	..	..	..	..	..	15	40	60
By Cocoa Fund	..	..	..	..	..	82	195	324	369	..	..	..
Joint A.O.F., A.E.F., and Cameroun												
Various contributions to investment	5	10	21	81	183	207	788	337	241	281	378	415
Communes and chambers of commerce ¶	..	..	..	..	..	25	50	50	100	150	230	250
Total	989	1,132	1,723	2,016	2,658	3,883	8,655	11,169	13,521	13,784	12,353	13,848

* Total of federal and territorial budgets.
‡ Contributions of native authorities to FERDES in A.O.F. from 1949.
¶ Investments financed through Communes and Chambers of Commerce excluding those financed by advances from CCFOM.

† Investments financed from internal resources.
§ Investments financed from the Cocoa and Coffee Funds from 1950.
‖ Fund for Petit Équipement Rural established in 1953.

TABLE 3

PUBLIC AND PRIVATE INVESTMENT, 1944–55
IN A.O.F., A.E.F., AND CAMEROUN
(N.F., milliards at prices of 1955)

Years	Construction and New Works *	Equipment	Research and Pilot Studies †	Investment in Traditional Forms of Capital	Total
1944	6·1	1·3	—	18·8	26·2
1945	7·6	1·5	—	13·1	22·2
1946	8·8	2·4	—	15·5	26·7
1947	12·7	5·2	1	16·1	35·0
1948	19·3	9·8	1	17·5	47·6
1949	27·6	14·3	1	20·2	63·1
1950	38·5	19·2	2	22·3	82·0
1951	45·9	22·6	2	14·3	84·8
1952	47·6	22·9	2	18·9	91·4
1953	44·4	22·5	3	24·8	94·7
1954	42·8	22·9	3	19·7	88·4
1955	44·2	27·3	3	20·1	94·6
1956 ‡	51	28·5	3·5	17	100

* The method of estimation of investment in construction and new works, based on the use of cement and materials, does not permit distinction between civil and military works. Thus the latter are included in the estimate for this territory.
† Excluding materials.
‡ For 1956, estimate made by M. Branchu, administrateur I.N.S.E.E., by the same methods employed by M. Maldant.

ANNEX V: BUDGETARY STATISTICS

TABLE 1

BUDGETS OF GROUPS, TERRITORIES, AND PROVINCES OF OVERSEAS
TERRITORIES : INITIAL ESTIMATES

(millions of N.F.)

	1953	1954	1955	1956	1957 §	1958
A.O.F.						
Current expenditure	68,938	77,016	86,414	103,972	110,990	127,188 (p.)
Capital equipment, etc.	19,978	22,248	16,568	13,168	15,460	15,618 (p.)
Gross total	88,916	99,264	102,982	117,140	126,450	142,806 (p.)
Net total *	82,002	93,022	97,448	112,758	122,918	135,828 (p.)
Togo						
Current expenditure	2,992	3,152	3,572	4,126	4,581	5,547
Capital equipment, etc.	590	684	743	396	300	953
Gross total	3,582	3,836	4,315	4,522	4,881	6,499 †
Net total *	3,396	3,652	4,072	4,396	4,881	6,389 ‡
Cameroun						
Current expenditure	15,348	16,118	19,639	19,756	21,998	19,015
Capital equipment, etc.	6,738	4,106	3,704	2,264	1,444	975
Gross total	22,086	20,224	23,343	22,020	23,443	19,990
Net total *	20,288	19,918	22,275	21,592	22,958	19,687
A.E.F.						
Current expenditure	17,368	15,906	17,160	19,454	21,836	22,788
Capital equipment, etc.	5,972	5,276	5,630	4,508	4,700	3,424
Gross total	23,340	21,182	22,790	23,962	26,536	26,212
Net total *	23,006	21,148	22,394	23,672	26,068	25,786
Madagascar						
Current expenditure	24,168	29,342	33,626	33,970	36,728	40,374 (p.)
Capital equipment, etc.	6,344	7,234	7,180	5,318	3,562	3,408 (p.)
Gross total	30,512	36,576	40,806	39,288	40,290	43,782 (p.)
Net total *	28,616	33,798	37,564	37,346	39,798	43,148 (p.)
Total of Overseas Territories						
Current expenditure	134,779	148,240	167,527	189,450	205,705	225,626
Capital equipment, etc.	40,834	41,568	35,167	27,091	26,817	25,970
Gross total	175,613	189,808	202,695	216,541	232,522	251,596
Net total *	164,468	180,196	192,167	209,305	227,396	242,681

Source : Direction du Contrôle ; Ministère de la F.O.M.

* After deductions of transfers from current to capital budgets.

† Togo failed in fact to approve a balanced budget on current account : 1,916 million francs of receipts against 2,773 millions of expenditure. It was hoped to cover the deficit with equivalent financial aid from the French state.

‡ Togo approved a single total for its general budget and its railway. The figure of 953 million francs includes 2 millions for the railway.

§ For 1957 all figures are those of budgetary estimates before their revision to take account of state services.

(p.) Provisional.

N.B.—For A.O.F., A.E.F., and Madagascar the figures are those for the grand total of the budgets of the group, and the territories or provinces, after adjustment to exclude double counting and transfers.

TABLE 2

TOTAL OF CURRENT BUDGETS OF ALL OVERSEAS TERRITORIES : *
PRELIMINARY ESTIMATES
(millions of N.F.)

	1953	1954	1955	1956	1957	1958
Total of fiscal receipts †	115,338	130,035	144,156	158,385	166,777	191,363
of which :						
Direct taxes	(37,646)	(39,629)	(43,890)	(44,989)	(46,566)	(48,215)
Indirect taxes	(73,205)	(84,519)	(94,874)	(107,584)	(113,711)	(136,195)
Registration fees, etc.	—	—	(3,220)	(3,759)	(4,257)	(4,516)

* Double counting and transfers excluded.
† *I.e.* A.O.F., Togo, Cameroun, A.E.F., Madagascar, Comoro Is., Somalis, French Polynesia, New Hebrides (except for 1953 and 1954). Wallis and Futana (except for 1953 and 1954) and Saint-Pierre-et-Miquelon.

TABLE 2A

TOTAL OF CURRENT BUDGETS OF ALL TERRITORIES :
SOURCES OF INCOME
(millions of N.F.)

	1953	1954	1955	1956	1957	1958
Receipts from state property	2,614	2,299	2,406	2,803	2,801	3,374
Receipts from operations and services	12,088	12,424	14,382	16,346	17,914	13,121
Contributions, grants, and reimbursements †	2,912	3,452	4,412	10,020	16,156	14,135
of which :						
State budget	—	—	—	—	(13,146)	(6,217)
Advances	—	—	1,200	—	—	—
Drawings on reserves	185	30	971	1,414	1,368	1,920
Total current receipts	134,749	148,240	167,527	188,968	205,016	223,912

TABLE 2B

TOTAL OF CURRENT BUDGETS OF A.O.F. : *
SOURCES OF INCOME
(millions of N.F.)

	1953	1954	1955	1956	1957	1958
Fiscal receipts : Total	59,410	67,518	76,518	88,088	94,616	111,378
of which :						
Direct taxation	(20,682)	(22,396)	(24,022)	(24,592)	(25,496)	(25,832)
Indirect taxation	(37,216)	(43,318)	(50,382)	(61,220)	(66,302)	(82,022)
Registration fees, etc.	(6)	(86)	(1,236)	(1,388)	(1,792)	(2,342)
Receipts from state property	1,692	1,242	1,118	1,110	1,226	1,504
Receipts from operations and services	6,362	6,726	7,474	8,364	9,262	5,238
Contributions, grants, and reimbursements †	1,320	1,500	1,302	4,906	6,190	8,810
of which :						
State budget	—	—	—	—	(4,956)	(3,324)
Drawings on reserves	154	30	—	1,022	—	258
Total current receipts †	68,938	77,016	86,412	103,490	111,294	127,128

* Total of group and territorial budgets.
† Including reimbursements of loans and advances.
‡ For detail of territories see Annex V, Table 2, footnote †.

TABLE 2c

CURRENT BUDGETS OF INDIVIDUAL TERRITORIES: SOURCES OF INCOME
(millions of N.F.)

	1953	1954	1955	1956	1957	1958
Republic of Togo						
Fiscal receipts: Total	2,776	2,964	3,343	3,742	3,146	3,394
of which:						
Direct taxation	(548)	(610)	(603)	(360)	(350)	(319)
Indirect taxation	(2,156)	(2,302)	(2,683)	(3,308)	(2,728)	(2,985)
Registration fees, etc.	(54)	(32)	(39)	(50)	(51·4)	(70)
Receipts from state property	18	18	19	34	24·4	29·2
Receipts from operations and services	172	140	178	250	332	351
Contributions, grants, and reimbursements *	26	30	32	100	86	58·4
Drawings on reserves	—	—	—	—	—	—
Total current receipts	2,992	3,152	3,572	4,126	3,589	3,833
State of Cameroun						
Fiscal receipts: Total	13,918	14,832	17,578	17,412	15,534	16,187
of which:						
Direct taxation	(3,670)	(3,642)	(3,610)	(3,246)	(3,582)	(3,800)
Indirect taxation	(9,430)	(10,452)	(13,180)	(13,482)	(11,194)	(11,601)
Registration fees, etc.	(516)	(432)	(488)	(640)	(720)	(747·8)
Receipts from state property	86	98	91	176	248	209
Receipts from operations and services	1,344	970	1,274	1,740	1,675	1,918
Contributions, grants, and reimbursements *	—	218	296	428	4,542	702
of which:						
State budget	..	..	400	..	(4,100)	(260)
Drawings on reserves	—	—	—	—	—	—
Total current receipts	15,348	16,118	19,639	19,756	21,998	19,105

* Including reimbursements of loans and advances.

TABLE 2c (*continued*)

CURRENT BUDGETS OF INDIVIDUAL TERRITORIES: SOURCES OF INCOME

(millions of N.F.)

	1953	1954	1955	1956	1957	1958
A.E.F.*						
Fiscal receipts: Total	15,060	13,268	13,820	15,094	16,186	18,174
of which:						
Direct taxation	(4,280)	(3,334)	(4,358)	(4,940)	(4,994)	(5,338)
Indirect taxation	(10,140)	(8,388)	(8,902)	(9,504)	(10,544)	(11,956)
Registration fees, etc.	—	—	(402)	(450)	(486)	(714)
Receipts from state property	502	536	720	1,012	858	1,170
Receipts from operations and services	1,440	1,254	1,514	1,654	1,718	1,080
Contributions, grants, and reimbursements †	340	848	784	1,330	1,772	1,218
of which:						
State budget	..	(800)	..	..	(1,645)	(889)
Drawings on reserves	26	..	322	366	1,302	1,146
Total current receipts ‡	17,368	15,906	17,160	19,456	21,836	22,788
Madagascar §						
Fiscal receipts: Total	21,394	26,738	27,856	28,390	30,352	34,092
of which:						
Direct taxation	(8,054)	(8,852)	(10,440)	(10,902)	(11,096)	(11,776)
Indirect taxation	(12,040)	(16,472)	(15,864)	(15,718)	(17,432)	(21,220)
Registration fees, etc.	—	—	(840)	(1,000)	(1,000)	(415)
Receipts from state property	280	310	378	364	346	358
Receipts from operations and services	1,816	1,998	3,028	3,110	3,664	3,651
Contributions, grants, and reimbursements †	678	296	1,022	2,106	2,340	2,113
of which:						
State budget	..	..	1,200	..	(1,640)	(851)
Advances	—	—	142	—	26	160
Drawings on reserves						
Total current receipts	24,168	29,342	33,626	33,970	36,728	40,374

* Total of group and territorial budgets.
‡ For detail of territories see Annex V, Table 2, footnote †

† Including reimbursements of loans and advances.
§ Total of territorial budget and provincial budgets.

TABLE 2C (continued)

CURRENT BUDGETS OF INDIVIDUAL TERRITORIES: SOURCES OF INCOME
(millions of N.F.)

	1953	1954	1955	1956	1957	1958
Comoros						
Fiscal receipts : Total	270	324	413	424	454	495
of which :						
Direct taxation	(134)	(154)	(192)	(190)	(198)	(200)
Indirect taxation	(128)	(162)	(215)	(228)	(248)	(284)
Registration fees, etc.	(8)	(6)	(5)	(5)	(7)	(9·3)
Receipts from state property	1·4	2	3	3	3	5
Receipts from operations and services	28	30	23	35	37	36·8
Contributions, grants, and reimbursements *	—	—	—	—	10	9
Drawings on reserves	5	—	18	18	40	32
Total current receipts	304	356	456	480	544	578
Côte des Somalis						
Fiscal receipts : Total	613	623	642	619	710	781
of which :						
Direct taxation	(85)	(108)	(115)	(115)	(120)	(130)
Indirect taxation	(482)	(466)	(480)	(452)	(531)	(584)
Registration fees, etc.	(41)	(42)	(39)	(44)	(53)	(59·3)
Receipts from state property	13·1	14·8	17	21·6	19	17·4
Receipts from operations and services	644	756	282	480	462	352
Contributions, grants, and reimbursements *	1·6	1·6	307	379	328	219
Drawings on reserves	—	—	15	—	—	—
Total current receipts	1,273	1,396	1,264	1,500	1,519	1,369

* Including reimbursements of loans and advances.

Economic Development for Africa South of the Sahara

TABLE 3A

TOTAL OF CURRENT BUDGETS OF ALL OVERSEAS TERRITORIES *
EXPENDITURE : PRELIMINARY ESTIMATES †
(millions of N.F.)

	1953	1954	1955	1956	1957	1958
Debt service	5,374	8,073	10,206	11,119	13,794	16,570
of which :						
Reimbursement of CCFOM	..	..	..	..	(6,272)	(8,576)
Salaries and wages of staff	64,638	71,166	80,436	94,931	105,300	99,859
Materials	27,333	27,494	32,109	34,906	36,395	35,506
Operational expenses	11,122	11,845	18,826	12,989	13,771	11,474
of which :						
Communications	..	..	..	..	(6,207)	(7,631)
Grants, contributions, advances, reimbursements, etc.	13,555	20,049	21,423	28,169	31,319	53,302
of which :						
Contribution to metropolitan budget	..	..	..	..	(394)	(12,841)
Transfers to capital budget	11,005	9,612	10,527	7,236	5,126	8,915
Total current expenditure	134,779 ‡	148,240	167,527	189,450	205,705	225,626

Source : Direction du Contrôle. Ministère de la F.O.M.

* *I.e.* A.O.F., Togo, Cameroun, A.E.F., Madagascar, Comoros, Somalis, French Polynesia, New Hebrides, New Caledonia, Wallis and Futana, Saint-Pierre-et-Miquelon.
† Excluding transfers and double counting.
‡ French Polynesia is included in the total figures but not in the detail.

TABLE 3B

CURRENT BUDGET OF A.O.F.* EXPENDITURE :
PRELIMINARY ESTIMATES
(millions of N.F.)

	1953	1954	1955	1956	1957	1958
Debt service	3,164	4,264	5,200	6,094	6,354	10,556
of which :						
Reimbursement of CCFOM	..	..	..	..	(2,128)	(4,200)
Salaries and wages of staff	31,572	35,178	40,098	49,284	55,364	51,604
Materials	14,554	14,416	16,603	18,564	19,374	19,386
Operational expenses	5,934	6,736	7,242	7,850	8,236	5,998
of which :						
Communications	..	..	..	..	(2,710)	(4,260)
Grants, contributions, advances, reimbursements, etc.	6,800	10,182	11,737	17,798	18,126	32,666
of which :						
Contribution to metropolitan budget	..	..	..	..	(90)	(8,860)
Transfers to capital budget	6,914	6,244	5,533	4,382	3,532	6,978
Total current expenditure	68,938	77,014	86,413	103,972	110,990	127,188

* Total of group and territorial budgets.

TABLE 3C

CURRENT BUDGETS OF INDIVIDUAL TERRITORIES. EXPENDITURE: PRELIMINARY ESTIMATES

(millions of N.F.)

	1953	1954	1955	1956	1957	1958
Republic of Togo						
Debt service	72	116	266	178	205	229
of which:						
Reimbursement of CCFOM					(155)	(152)
Salaries and wages of staff	1,802	1,870	1,966	2,404	2,841	3,319
Materials	434	460	537	628	761	930
Operational expenses	234	220	207	130	190	197
of which:						
Communications					(156)	(157)
Grants, contributions, advances, reimbursements, etc.	264	302	353	660	584	761
of which:						
Contribution to metropolitan budget					(—)	(—)
Transfers to capital budget	186	184	243	126	—	111
Total current expenditure	2,992	3,152	3,572	4,126	4,581	5,547
State of Cameroun						
Debt service	644	1,738	2,263	2,008	3,812	1,849
of which:						
Reimbursement of CCFOM					(1,250)	(1,247)
Salaries and wages of staff	7,388	8,280	9,486	10,488	11,074	10,080
Materials	2,738	2,622	3,202	3,400	3,111	2,305
Operational expenses	1,748	1,680	1,755	1,442	1,230	1,157
of which:						
Communications					(855)	(869)
Grants, contributions, advances, reimbursements, etc.	1,032	1,492	1,865	1,990	2,287	3,321
of which:						
Contribution to metropolitan budget					(92.2)	(129)
Transfers to capital budget	1,798	306	1,068	428	484	303
Total current expenditure	15,348	16,118	19,639	19,756	21,998	19,016

TABLE 3c (*continued*)

CURRENT BUDGETS OF INDIVIDUAL TERRITORIES. EXPENDITURE : PRELIMINARY ESTIMATES
(millions of N.F.)

	1953	1954	1955	1956	1957	1958
*A.E.F.**						
Debt service	834	852	1,050	1,202	1,510	1,672
of which:						
Reimbursement of CCFOM					(1,172)	(1,348)
Salaries and wages of staff	9,162	8,818	9,255	10,736	12,128	11,060
Materials	3,794	3,310	3,357	3,714	4,040	3,502
Operational expenses	1,276	1,024	1,151	1,130	1,272	1,368
of which:						
Communications					(620)	(768)
Grants, contributions, advances, reimbursements, etc.	1,968	1,870	1,951	2,384	2,418	4,760
of which:						
Contribution to metropolitan budget					(84)	(1,386)
Transfers to capital budget	334	32	396	290	468	426
Total current expenditure	17,368	15,906	17,160	19,456	21,836	22,788
Madagascar †						
Debt service	464	754	961	1,084	1,294	1,638
of which:						
Reimbursement of CCFOM					(1,062)	(1,168)
Salaries and wages of staff	12,530	13,546	16,016	17,858	19,179	18,782
Materials	4,728	5,084	6,631	6,602	6,679	7,210
Operational expenses	1,630	1,770	2,058	2,080	2,250	2,374
of which:						
Communications					(1,400)	(1,417)
Grants, contributions, advances, reimbursements, etc.	2,918	5,410	4,717	4,404	6,734	9,736
of which:						
Contribution to metropolitan budget					(12)	(1,889)
Transfers to capital budget	1,898	2,778	3,242	1,942	492	634
Total current expenditure	24,168	29,342	33,625	33,970	36,728	40,374

* Total of group and territorial budgets.

† Total of territorial budget and provincial budgets.

TABLE 3c (continued)

CURRENT BUDGETS OF INDIVIDUAL TERRITORIES. EXPENDITURE: PRELIMINARY ESTIMATES
(millions of N.F.)

	1953	1954	1955	1956	1957	1958
Comoros						
Debt service	8	26	59·4	68·8	72	77·6
Salaries and wages of staff	220	222	280	282	322	319
Materials	80	80	78·6	92·4	92	107
Operational expenses	12	20	28·4	28·4	32	33·6
Grants, contributions, advances, reimbursements, etc.	8	8	10	8·8	26	41
Transfers to capital budget	6	—	—	—	—	—
Total current expenditure	334	356	456	480	544	578
Côte des Somalis						
Debt service	70·5	116	134	149	155	180
Salaries and wages of staff	736	777	686	831	875	642
Materials	328	377	334	350	363	317
Operational expenses	50·8	54·1	50·7	49·5	56	42·8
Grants, contributions, advances, reimbursements, etc.	44·3	54·1	58·9	120	67	186
Transfers to capital budget	42·6	16·4	—	—	3	1·5
Total current expenditure	1,273	1,396	1,264	1,500	1,519	1,370

ANNEX VI: BALANCES OF PAYMENTS

TABLE 1

BALANCES OF PAYMENTS BETWEEN FRANCE
AND FORMER A.O.F. AND TOGO
(millions of N.F.)

	1953	1954	1955	1956	1957	1958	1959
Public transfers (Net balance)	+413	+376	+549	+579	+705	+763	+930
Private transfers (Net balance)	−351	−459	−521	−471	−686	−752	−771
Net balance of transfers	+62	−83	+28	+108	+19	+11	+159
Balance of visible trade with the franc zone	−105	−116	−279	−48	−161	−141	−268
Balance of monetary transfers							
On current account	−36	−8	−2	−80	−186	−221	−72
On capital account	+7	+5	..	+27	+52	+158	+301
Balance of invisibles	−217	−342	−254	−379	−391	−548	−732

Source : Comité Monétaire de la zone franc.

Plus (+) represents a balance due from France.
Minus (−) represents a balance due from the African territory.

TABLE 2

BALANCES OF PAYMENTS BETWEEN FRANCE AND CAMEROUN
(millions of N.F.)

	1953	1954	1955	1956	1957	1958	1959
Public transfers (Net balance)	+69	+72	+51	+120	+124	+76	+99
Private transfers (Net balance)	−80	−78	−60	−147	−99	−91	−55
Net balance of transfers	−11	−6	−9	−27	+25	−15	+44
Balance of visible trade with the franc zone	−53	−51	−44	−53	−57	+19	+35
Balance of monetary transfers							
On current account	+5	+53	+56	+14	−9	+26	+131
On capital account	+2	..	+3	+2	+2	+3	+4
Balance of invisibles	−34	−80	−75	−110	−35	−139	−225

Source : Comité Monétaire de la zone franc.

Plus (+) represents a balance due from France.
Minus (−) represents a balance due from the African territory.

TABLE 3

BALANCES OF PAYMENTS BETWEEN FRANCE AND FORMER A.E.F.
(millions of N.F.)

	1953	1954	1955	1956	1957	1958	1959
Public transfers (Net balance)	+150	+178	+195	+216	+265	+306	+329
Private transfers (Net balance)	−152	−159	−208	−212	−228	−279	−315
Net balance of transfers	−2	+19	−13	+4	+37	+27	+14
Balance of visible trade with the franc zone	−40	−32	−81	−62	−143	−111	−133
Balance of monetary transfer							
On current account	−68	−62	−52	−42	−76	−78	−26
On capital account	+4	+4	+6	+3	+6	+12	+24
Balance of invisibles	−48	−69	−81	−111	−15	−102	−201

Source : *La Zone franc en 1959.* Comité Monétaire de la zone franc, Rapport 1960.

Plus (+) represents a balance due from France.
Minus (−) represents a balance due from the African territory.

TABLE 4

BALANCES OF PAYMENTS BETWEEN FRANCE AND MADAGASCAR
(millions of N.F.)

	1953	1954	1955	1956	1957	1958	1959
Public transfers (Net balance)	+181	+156	+222	+215	+220	+255	+300
Private transfers (Net balance)	−187	−168	−161	−201	−285	−256	−288
Net balance of transfers	−6	−12	+61	+14	−65	−1	+12
Balance of visible trade with the franc zone	−103	−136	−119	−115	−178	−101	−196
Balance of monetary transfers							
On current account	−51	−23	−29	−11	−38	−1	−23
On capital account	+1	+2					
Balance of invisibles	−34	−11	−14	−77	−72	−156	−70

Source : *La Zone franc en 1959.* Comité Monétaire de la zone franc, Rapport 1960.

Plus (+) represents a balance due from France.
Minus (−) represents a balance due from the African territory.

Chapter 6

PROBLEMS OF ECONOMIC DEVELOPMENT OF GHANA, NIGERIA, SIERRA LEONE, LIBERIA, SPANISH TERRITORIES

BY

J. W. WILLIAMS
University of Otago, Dunedin, New Zealand [1]

I. INTRODUCTORY

THE four countries of West Africa with which we are concerned face much the same problems as do other under-developed countries, with the exception of those which arise from a great density of population. In this paper, I treat the problems of the four countries together, dealing with particular countries only when the difference between them is sufficiently great to make this treatment seriously misleading. The countries are considerably alike in climate and in natural resources ; the traditional economies and social institutions are also very similar. Their principal differences arise mainly from the fact that they are at different stages of economic and political development.

By economic development, I understand changes in an economy which are likely to result in higher incomes per head, or which at least make higher incomes possible. Development problems are of two kinds : 'what to do' and 'how to do it'. 'What to do', includes broad problems — such as whether to encourage a high degree of industrialization or not, how far growth must be balanced and so forth — and narrower problems concerned with the actual techniques to be adopted. 'How to do it' is concerned with problems of organization. What sort of political and social arrangements are most likely to encourage growth ? What incentives can induce people to adopt changes which will increase production ? How can a static economic and social system be changed to a dynamic one ? In the main I shall be concerned with the second type of problem. The first kind of problem is one with which both developed and

[1] Lately of the University College of Ghana.

under-developed countries are faced. The second kind of problem is more sociological in nature, but is still, I think, within the field of economics, and it is where I feel someone who has some first-hand acquaintance with these countries can have some comparative advantage.

II. THE SPECIAL FEATURES OF WEST AFRICA

Geographically, there are two distinct regions in West Africa — the rain forest and the coastal plains of the South, and the semi-arid and arid areas in the North. In Nigeria about half the population lives in the Northern Region, which lies largely in this dry area, but in the other countries most of the people live in the forest or on the coastal belt. By European standards, West African soil is for the most part shallow and poor and, except under forest cover, lacking in humus. Water is either deficient or over-abundant, depending on the area and time of the year. The technique of shifting cultivation, or bush fallow, is an essential soil conservation practice for peasant farming under these circumstances. Any change in existing practices must be carried out with great care if adequate fertility is to be preserved in the long run. The land is economically most productive in tree crops — timber, vegetable oils, rubber, tropical fruit, and cocoa — which are the important cash crops. Grains can be produced in some areas — millet, maize, rice — but the yield is rather low. The most important food crops in the South are yams and cassava.

Population density, regarded simply as a ratio of population to land area, is low by European and Asian standards — typically 30 to 100 per square mile. There are a few limited areas of denser population which have developed not so much because of particularly favourable economic circumstances, but as a consequence of political and social history. In relation to agricultural resources and to techniques actually in use, there are areas where the density of population may be past its optimum point. In these areas the period of bush fallow has been reduced to too short a period to allow for adequate maintenance of fertility. The situation could, however, be remedied by internal migration, the better utilization of land without a change in techniques, or by the expansion of food-crops, such as rice in swampy areas, which would call for no radical changes in techniques. To effect these changes is not, of course, easy, and a number of resettlement schemes have proved to be failures. In the recent past, population has probably been stationary at a high birth rate–high death rate level. No adequate vital statistics exist and census data is not sufficiently accurate to deduce rates of population growth. There is an official estimate of 2 per cent for the rate of growth of Nigeria's population, but it is based on no firm figures. In Ghana vital statistics are available for the larger towns and they give the very high rate of natural increase of $3\frac{1}{2}$ per cent. It seems unlikely that this can be the rate for the country as a whole. The towns have been growing rapidly and probably have a younger population, including women of child-bearing ages, than the country as a whole. It is also probable that most old people return to the villages before they die. Still the likelihood of a rate of growth of 2 per cent or more seems high. No statistics are available for Liberia but the rate of growth is probably still at a low level. Sierra Leone is probably at or near a period of rapid growth.

III. THE PROBLEMS OF AGRICULTURE AND FOOD SUPPLY

The governments in the four countries have usually seen the agriculture problem as one of a sufficient supply of food to feed the growing population in the country as a whole and especially in the towns. In Ghana the rapid growth of cities — Accra, for instance has grown from about 120,000 in 1950 to 400,000 in 1960 — does not appear to have led to any absolute shortage of food. It is true that imports of food have increased, but it seems that the economy still has a reserve of production sufficient to meet its food needs without any great changes in agriculture. The same appears to be generally true of Nigeria. Opinions of agriculturists, as to how far production can be raised by the application of improved techniques, range from very optimistic to very pessimistic. Whatever the ultimate possibilities, a change-over from traditional to more scientific methods will be difficult. Slogans such as 'mechanization' will not help very much. For nutritionists, the problem of food supply presents itself in terms of quality rather than quantity. There is a general shortage of protein to remedy which, a large increase in cattle population would be necessary. Other deficiencies are largely a matter of food habits and can, no doubt, be remedied by education.

Many economists have looked to improved efficiency in agriculture to release supplies of labour for industry. It is a widely held view that even with present techniques there is sufficient disguised unemployment in agriculture now to provide labour for industry and to continue to provide it at any rate of expansion which is at all likely to be attained in practice for many years to come. Whether this is in fact so is difficult to find out in West Africa ; there are no farm management studies of traditional agriculture. Evidence for the theory is in the form of 'casual empiricism' which mainly consists of observing that a lot of people seem to be sitting around in the villages without a great deal to do. Perhaps the villagers make the same deductions about the visitors ! In Ghana considerable use is made of migrant workers from the North, including French-speaking territories — one writer has estimated the numbers to be of the order of 100,000 a year — not only in cocoa farms but also to assist in food growing. On the other hand workers do migrate to the towns during a building boom and return again to the country when it is over, which would seem to point to a surplus. I shall take up this point again when dealing with the traditional economy. In view of the large proportion of the population engaged in agriculture however, we need postulate only quite modest improvements in agricultural methods and productivity to allow for quite large transfers of labour to industry and there is no reason to expect that the supply of unskilled labour will be a limiting factor on industrial expansion for many years to come.

Substantial improvements in the cultivation and processing of the standard export crops are apparently possible. Some apprehension is felt in Ghana about the market prospects for cocoa, which is far the most important export crop. The demand is inelastic and a relatively small increase in the crop leads to a heavy fall in prices. The marketing board system which operates in Nigeria, Ghana, and Sierra Leone prevents internal prices from fluctuating to the same extent. Attempts have been made to reach agreements with cocoa buyers for a stable price, but without success. Whether the producing countries would gain from such an agreement is at least open to doubt ; it would be very much a gamble and a gamble in which they would not know whether they were gaining or losing. Control of supplies has been attempted by Brazil but not by Ghana and Nigeria except within the crop year. Control is difficult. The cocoa crop varies a good deal from year to year according to the weather ; the area under cultivation is dependent on decisions made at least five or six years earlier and the storage of cocoa is difficult and expensive for more than a year. In Ghana an important aim of agricultural policy has been to broaden the range of exports and attention is being paid to the production of rubber and coffee. In Nigeria cocoa is also important but does not dominate the export trade to the same extent. Palm products are the most important export, and groundnuts come a close third, after cocoa. The wide range of uses for vegetable oils means that the demand is more elastic for Nigeria's exports as a whole. Sierra Leone is mainly dependent on palm products on the agricultural side and to that extent shares with Ghana the disadvantages of being a single crop exporter. The equivalent export crop in Liberia is rubber, the greater part of which is grown on plantations, but of which a proportion comes from peasant producers.

IV. OTHER NATURAL RESOURCES

The four countries have a limited range of minerals. Nigeria produces tin and columbite and small quantities of lead, zinc, and gold. It also has coal but the output from coal mines is not large and in recent years the industry has been faced with increasing costs and diminishing output per head. Demand is small and declining. Iron ore exists, but has not yet been worked on a commercial scale. On the whole there does not seem to be much future for mining in Nigeria. Ghana still exports gold to the value of £8 m. a year but some mines have closed down and others are marginal. Diamond exports amount to £5 m. annually and seem likely to continue at about this level. Manganese is also mined. There are no coal deposits. Iron ore is known to exist but the extent and richness of the deposits is not fully known. It is at present rather inaccessible but will become much less so when the Volta lake comes into existence. Mining is likely to make a useful contribution to the national income for some time to come but is likely to diminish in importance. Liberia has extensive deposits of high-grade and easily worked iron ore and Sierra Leone also has good deposits which are being worked. The most important minerals in Sierra Leone are diamonds and present production is about £12 m. a year.

Prospecting for oil has gone on in each of the four countries. After a twenty-year search it has been discovered in Nigeria in sufficient quantities to supply all local requirements and leave a large surplus for export. Production costs are, however, rather high and sales may be confined to neighbouring countries. A refinery is being built in Nigeria and also in Ghana where it will use imported crude.

Forests are an important source of wealth. Timber is produced in each country both for local use and for export. Methods of working the forests have been wasteful from a long run point of view as only selected species have been cut out. Large areas of forest have also been destroyed to make farms. The problem of forest conservation is to regulate cutting and to provide for replanting where necessary so that timber may be grown as a crop rather than exploited as a wasting asset. Nigeria's reserves of good timber are rather small ; Ghana's are larger in relation to its size ; Liberia's forests still await exploitation, while in Sierra Leone the trees are mainly second growth and not of first quality.

In general, natural resources, with existing techniques, are sufficient to support the existing populations at a reasonable standard. It also seems likely that the adoption of better methods, improvements in breeding of cattle, and greater efficiency of distribution could maintain and probably increase the standard of living of a rising population for a good many years to come. Expansion in the production of the traditional export crops and the export of new crops is also possible and agricultural exports are likely to remain the mainstay of the economies for a long time yet. Industrialization is not likely to be based on the exploitation of minerals.

V. THE TRADITIONAL ECONOMY

By the traditional economy I mean the system of production, distribution, and exchange which has existed in West Africa for hundreds, perhaps thousands of years. In its pure form it probably now exists only in the more backward areas, but the great majority of the population in each of the countries still live in ways which have changed in only minor respects from those of their grandparents and great-grandparents. Traditional economies have been described as subsistence economies and contrasted with market or with monetary economies. While these terms do point to certain characteristics of the traditional economy they do not adequately describe it even in broad outline. It is, I think, necessary to spend a little time in examining it, because if change is the essence of development it is important to know what is being changed.

What we might call the pure form of the traditional economy of the West African type consists of independent small communities each of which is very nearly self-contained and whose economic system has reached a state of static equilibrium. Population is stationary or growing very slowly. Its size is determined not by the availability of natural resources, as in the classical stationary state, but is at a biological balance determined by a high death rate and the maximum attainable birth rate. In general, land is sufficiently abundant in relation to the population to make it a free asset. The practice of shifting cultivation makes even its site value unimportant. The marginal productivity of capital has fallen to zero as with known techniques further investment in tools would yield no advantages. Each man needs a hoe and a cutlass and can make no use of more. Consumers' capital goods are few and simple so that each household can make its own without reducing the amount of time spent in agriculture. Labour is very nearly homogeneous — each man can do all the usual jobs of the community. Only a few specialists — chiefs, priests, and a few craftsmen — receive 'wages'. Other members of the community receive a share of the community's real income equal to the average product.

Under normal circumstances in West Africa, labour produces a surplus in agriculture so that time and resources are available for providing entertainment, education, art, literature, music, and religious activities. It is only if we regard the provision of these services as the use of leisure time — and the only justification for this view seems to be that they are not provided by specialists — that we can regard work in agriculture and in the maintenance of capital as the only form of employment. In this case, of course, the existence of any surplus in agriculture implies 'under-employment'. But why should we look at the traditional economy in this way? There is no reason to believe that labour resources are being distributed in an undesired way between agriculture and other activities. Nor is there any reason to suppose that the productivity of labour is zero or less. If a certain amount of labour — so many hours' work — is withdrawn from agriculture we must expect the product to fall. It is of course possible to imagine circumstances in which it would not and these circumstances may prevail in countries with a very high density of population, but there are good grounds for supposing that they do not in West Africa. The productivity of labour proposition is, however, sometimes confused with another one which is that if we withdraw a man from the community the agricultural product might not fall as the rest of the community would maintain output, but only of course at the expense of their other activities. It follows that labour is in no sense a free good or in unlimited supply. It must be attracted to work in industry by the offer of higher wages or better conditions.

In practice, however, in West Africa the 'young men' — a term which applies to all 'progressive' elements in the traditional economy — have ceased to value the traditional way of life and they want to get away from it. They possibly over-rate the advantages of town life, but at present they do not require much attracting. Most 'young men' have a primary education — if they have more they have already left the traditional economy. It is also true that anyone who has been educated to this level is expected by the community to get a job suited to his education. To remain in the village, or to return to it unsuccessful, would involve a loss of social prestige. The value of such educational attainments today is of course very much overrated by the villagers, who are thinking in terms of the very recent past when the ability to read and write would be enough for a white collar job. The problem of unemployment of school-leavers who have come to the towns looking for jobs is in fact a serious one particularly in Nigeria where the southern regions are spending more than 50 per cent of their budget on education. Office jobs are now requiring a high school education and the primary school boy is forced to compete with illiterates for jobs such as garage assistants, motor-drivers' mates, and even ordinary labouring. A number do finally accept this status, but the majority, for some years at any rate, regard themselves as 'applicants' seeking something better and hanging on in towns in the hope of it turning up.[1] In Ghana the position does not appear to be so serious as the expansion of education took place over a longer period and has not yet gone so far. The problem has also been partly solved by the setting up of the Builders' Brigade, in which young men and women have been organized on quasi-military lines, partly for training in crafts and partly to undertake building, public works, and agricultural projects. The Brigade has, however, not been very successful in finding worthwhile occupations for its members and it has been run at considerable cost to the taxpayer. 'Back to the land' and settlement schemes have been tried out on a small scale both in Nigeria and Ghana without much success. One trouble is that they are expensive in terms of capital expenditure and supervision. Another is that the training has been rather too effective in that the trained men have been able to get supervisory jobs on government employment and do not wish to stay on the land. In Sierra Leone and Liberia education and educated jobs have been confined to the town people but a similar position will no doubt arise.

In the traditional economy, although each community may be more or less self-sufficient, there is room for trade within the communities, as households may have surpluses or deficits at different times — deficits, for example, when celebrations are called for. Trade between communities is, however, confined to luxuries or to the specialities of particular areas, such as salt. In general the economy of a large area will be fragmentary with no economic advantages arising from centralization. We saw in Ghana a political framework parallel to the economic one. The country — especially

[1] I am indebted to Dr. A. Calloway who is working on this problem for information about Nigeria.

in the South — was divided up into a large number of petty states and even small villages had their own chiefs and had a good deal of political independence.

The traditional economy is, then, a static and fragmentary one and the problem of development is to turn it into a dynamic and integrated one. Some degree of integration has of course already been achieved in the more advanced areas. Towns are not a new thing in West Africa and they have been supplied with food from the country. In the past, however, and to a considerable extent today, it is an undesigned surplus which is sold. That is, no individual farmer is dependent for his income on a town market, but a community as a whole may have a regular surplus to sell. In Ghana these surpluses are collected by itinerant market women who travel from place to place buying and reselling in different small markets and sending the overall surplus to the towns. Commercial food farming is, however, now more common and may be expected to keep pace with the growth of towns. Political integration has been largely achieved in the four countries. The introduction of new techniques and new social relationships will lead to greater specialization and a wider market.

The extent to which the traditional economy can resist change must, however, not be underestimated. It might have been expected that the large additions to cash resources which have come from production of cocoa and oil palm products would have had a marked effect on the traditional economy, but, in fact, it has had remarkably little. Some of the money has been used to raise the level of consumption and some has gone into prestige expenditure on funerals, litigation, and the building of large houses which either stand empty or are only partly used. But the typical farmer has hardly altered his way of life. He has no better drainage, water supply or other amenities than his fathers had and he lives in the same type of compound house where fufu is pounded and cooking done over charcoal pots. Much investment is in fact outside the economy. Sending sons or nephews to be educated abroad is a favourite use of money, but educated men never return to the village so that this expenditure is a net cost to the rural community. Transport is another common form of investment, but the market is over-supplied and it is commonly operated at a loss.

VI. THE MODERN SECTOR

The modern economy of cities, factories, cinemas, and so forth, where people live by earning wages or by setting up as capitalist entrepreneurs, is small in each of the four countries. Although Nigeria has a lower *per capita* income than Ghana it probably has a more advanced non-traditional sector than Ghana. In Liberia one must count the rubber plantations as part of a modern economy in respect of their organization, but outside this the modern economy is very small and confined to a small area. The Colony of Sierra Leone is essentially 'modern' in thought and outlook but appears to have become stagnant at a relatively low level.

In the past, expenditure in the modern sector on directly productive investments has been carried out by private capital. Except in Liberia plantations have played a very minor rôle. Processing of primary products — timber milling, oil-palm pressing, nut crushing — is of some importance, but processing is not carried far for most exports and there appear to be difficulties in carrying it further. What manufacture there was was either on a very small scale — at the craft level — or was in localized industries such as brewing and brick-making. Colonial governments confined their activities to public works. Investments by Africans were almost entirely in building, transport, and minor craft industries. The colonial governments saw their job as one of maintaining law and order and towards trade and industry adopted in general a *laisser faire* attitude. European settlement was strongly discouraged and in recent years certain fields have been reserved for Africans by strict control of migration. It was, however, on the initiative of colonial governments that the first development plans were drawn up. The plans were for the most part plans to expand the sort of activities which were already being carried out and consisted mainly of public works. In Ghana, the first development plan was started in 1951 at which date the country had internal self-government. In Nigeria the International Bank mission drew up a plan in 1955 and in Sierra Leone the Child plan goes back to 1949. Liberia has no specific plan but the Tubman government has undertaken a number of development projects in recent years.

The first major problem in carrying out a plan — how to find the money — was not an immediate one in Ghana, which had accumulated considerable funds in the hands of the marketing boards and was enjoying a buoyant revenue from cocoa. Nigeria was not quite as well off, but had reserves adequate for considerable development. The supply of foreign exchange was not a serious limiting factor in any of the countries. There were important limitations in the ability to mobilize resources — shortages of skilled manpower, lack of entrepreneural ability and experience, delays in the delivery of equipment, and bottlenecks of various sorts. Most of these difficulties are being gradually overcome, but they still limit the speed at which development can be carried out.

VII. PLANNING FOR DEVELOPMENT

It is rather easy to criticize both the development plans which have been adopted and also the general approach to planning in Ghana and Nigeria. There appear to be two basic approaches possible to planning, one which might be called the micro-economic and the other the macro-economic. The first looks on development as part of the general solution to the basic economic problem — how to make the best use of what you have got. In producing a plan, then, all investment possibilities should be divided into a number of projects, the division being as fine as it is practical to make it. Each project should then be assessed in terms of social benefits and social costs, and investment undertaken up to the limit of resources available, in such a way as to equate marginal social benefits and marginal social costs in each line. This procedure may not always be practical in the time available for planning, but the procedure actually adopted, which consists of saying 'so much for agriculture, so much for industry, so much for education, 'is a very crude approximation to it, and it allows only for suboptimization within the broad fields covered. It could therefore easily happen that the funds allotted to one field had run out before projects which had a higher net benefit than those which were still being undertaken in another field had been carried out. Fortunately, from this point of view, common sense has been allowed to break in and plans have not been treated as hard-and-fast restrictions.

The other general approach is concerned more with the macro-economic aspects of planning development. This is the realm of the theories of balanced growth, or of unbalanced growth, of the 'big push' and the 'take-off' into sustained growth, of comparative advantages, high and low capital intensities, and so forth. Consideration of these matters is not precluded by the first approach as they would come within the general considerations of social benefits, but to take them systematically into account in the cost-benefit type of approach would be extraordinarily difficult. There is little discussion of such matters in practical planning, but they are of course in the minds of politicians even if in a muddled way. They also lurk behind a general problem which on the face of it is more straightforward. This is the decision as to whether it is better to concentrate investment in either the modern or the traditional sector or to divide the available funds in some way between the two.

If we take a short-run view of the greatest direct benefit for a given level of expenditure we might well conclude that improvements in the conditions of life in the rural areas should be given first priority. A supply of good drinking water, medical services, sanitation, better housing, some improvement in roads, and so forth would go a long way to improving the health and well-being of the population. If this were combined with a great expansion of agricultural extension services offering improved methods, better varieties of crops and advice on better farm management, the village might become a pleasant place to live in. If we consider that in the tropics only the simplest type of housing and furniture is necessary in the villages as life is lived largely out of doors, that clothing is a luxury, and that though the productivity of the soil is limited there is at present no great difficulty in getting a living, one might well ask what are the advantages of changing it for the very doubtful advantages of life in an industrial civilization. This solution would, however, be quite unacceptable to present African opinion which, with the rest of the human race, are firmly convinced that distant fields are greener. In any case such a policy would probably founder on the rocks of population growth.

A directly opposite approach is to concentrate effort entirely in the modern sector and to build up an efficient industrial society. The rest of the economy would benefit from this growth in several ways. First, the modern sector would provide employment with a higher productivity than the traditional economy ; second, it would provide a market which would encourage the growth of commercial farming ; and third, it would enable capital to be accumulated, which could be used eventually to provide the amenities which the rural sector requires. The availability of capital and the drawing away of labour to the towns might also force the introduction of more efficient methods in the rural economy. The rural sector might have to wait some time for these benefits, but it would be better off in the end and anyhow it has waited a good many thousands of years already. It is along these lines that African leaders are thinking, but political considerations have and no doubt will in the future force them to compromise by spending at least some development funds on rural amenities. There is a danger that the available funds may be spread so thinly that it will be impossible to achieve anything worthwhile in either sector. The building up of a modern sector is easier said than done and the amount of investment which is required to attain even a modest rate of growth is usually greatly underestimated in West Africa. The rate at which foreign capital and entrepreneurship has flowed into Ghana has been very disappointing, although it has increased considerably in the past two years. Nigeria with a later start has done relatively better. Direct investment by the State in industry has also not been very successful largely owing to the lack of efficient managers.

A particular difficulty in development planning which has already been mentioned in connection with education, is the fact that growth becomes unbalanced very easily. I am aware of, and sympathize with, the view that unbalance may be a good thing, but unfortunately the balance is likely to be tipped in the wrong direction. Plans may provide for the growth of industry, for example, and for the growth of the infrastructure necessary to support it. If, however, the industries do not arrive it is almost inevitable that the rest of the programme will be carried out and we shall have fine roads, new harbours, and large administrative buildings with very little industry for them to serve. Another danger is that if industrial growth is not up to expectations any proposals will be seized on and given all sorts of encouragement, such as tax concessions, special railway and harbour rates, and so forth, even if they are of doubtful merit. We may find adjacent territories setting up very similar industries on a scale which would be adequate to serve the whole of West Africa. A case in point is the building of oil refineries by both Nigeria and Ghana.

VIII. THE PROBLEM OF ENTREPRENEURING

Ghana has short-circuited the problem of entrepreneural incentives internally by moving towards a socialist system. While I do not want to take up any position in this paper on the general issue of socialism versus capitalism, my experience of conditions in Ghana rather inclines me to the belief that little reliance can be placed on the Ghanaian entrepreneur for rapid development. There are many Ghanaian traders and a few who have small manufacturing businesses. But the Ghanaian businessman's attitude to growth is very different from that of the typical entrepreneur in the eighteenth and early nineteenth centuries in England, for example. He remains, even when trading on a fairly large scale, in his approach essentially a petty trader. He is in business primarily to make money and to spend the money as he makes it on a higher standard of living and (somewhat unwillingly) in support of his numerous relations. No doubt a government firmly convinced of the virtues of private enterprise could achieve something in the way of encouraging the capitalistic virtues in the course of time, but the tendency must always be for the new governments to want to achieve their aims more directly. Nigeria is rather different. There have been larger urban communities for a longer time than in Ghana, and some quite large-scale entrepreneurs are operating mainly in trading. The political philosophy of the Nigerian government has been more attractive to overseas firms, and has provided more encouragement for local business men. Liberia is firmly on a free enterprise basis, but the important industries are in the hands of foreigners. It appears that Sierra Leone may follow the Ghana pattern. Nigeria also has a better basis for expansion of small-scale and craft industries than the other countries.

There is, I think, no reason to feel pessimistic about the future of the West African countries. Change is under way and steady growth in income is likely to be accomplished. On the other hand the exaggerated expectations of political parties are not at all likely to be realized. To do as well in the twentieth century as Europe did in the nineteenth is about the maximum we can expect.

Chapter 7

PROBLEMS OF ECONOMIC DEVELOPMENT OF ANGOLA: POLES AND PROSPECTS [1]

BY

L. M. TEIXEIRA PINTO and R. MARTINS DOS SANTOS

I. THE IMPORTANCE OF AFRICAN DEVELOPMENT

THE problems stemming from economic development are still among the most important topics of discussion in the world today.[2] The subject itself is far wider and more complex than might appear at first sight since the human, social, and political aspects of economic development must not be forgotten. It would naturally be much more convenient for economists if they could juggle with figures at leisure in a universe composed exclusively of products and quantities, but this it not possible. Instead, they have to attempt to improve conditions in poorer areas, and to prevent the imbalance that already exists from deteriorating. The task is, in fact, so urgent and important that it has been labelled the 'twentieth-century crusade'. The more highly developed countries are placing their sympathetic aid at the service of this crusade and are offering to become centres of technical, economic, and financial co-operation for the purpose of combating the threat of famine and under-development. International organizations of a regional or world-wide character are studying the problems more and more closely, and can now offer assistance to almost every nation on a scale which, although it may appear minute in relation to world demand, is, nevertheless, the outcome of praiseworthy endeavour.

The African continent has come to occupy an increasingly larger part of the economic life of the world, and it is hardly surprising, when we consider the links we have with this continent, that we should have devoted so much attention to it. The most striking

[1] Translated by R. S. Griffiths.
[2] Cf. papers by the present authors on tropical Africa and, in particular, 'Problèmes du développement de l'Afrique tropicale', Lisbon, 1959, 'Analyse des possibilités d'un marché commun portugais', Lisbon, 1960, by L. M. Teixeira Pinto, and 'L'évaluation du revenu national dans les économies africaines' (assessing national income in African economies), Lisbon, 1959, by R. Martins dos Santos.

political development is the movement towards independence of territories which had formerly been governed as colonies and — if we make an exception for certain extreme cases where disorder and chaos have ensued — this movement has been accompanied by considerable expansion of economic activity. Realizing this need for economic progress, an African statesman has declared that it would be a 'fundamental mistake' to suppose that the proclamation of independence would mean the end of the struggle for these new states. He is not the only person to hold this view, and both earlier and recent African history make it clear that economic, social, and political factors are interdependent in these countries.

In spite of all the human and cultural resources that Africa may possess or claim to possess, we feel that it is impossible for the continent to reach a stage of development where it can provide a reasonable standard of living for its inhabitants on its own initiative.[1]

II. THE PROCESSES OF CHANGE IN AFRICA

If we consider the economies of the African countries, we notice a feature which is common to almost all under-developed areas, namely the predominance of primary-producing activities. This is due not only to the fact that the inhabitants depend on such activities and devote their time to them, but also because of the income they provide. The economies cannot be defined, however, solely as primary ; it has often been said that Africa has a dual economy, and that modern and traditional sectors exist side by side, with governments and foreign trade playing a more or less decisive rôle.

Even this definition does not seem complete to us, since it does not take into account the deep-seated relationship between social and economic life any more than it singles out the specific aspects of the private sector.

There is no need for us to explain why Africa is an under-developed area with the economic and social structure typical of such areas. The reasons are well known by now [2] and we shall therefore try to avoid unnecessary repetition by taking for granted the numerous statistical factors, as well as the usual 'vicious circles' of development.

On the other hand, it is essential to stress the fact that, in Africa, economic development, in which a great many production factors

---

[1] It remains to be seen, of course, how co-operation between the more advanced countries and the African nations will develop.

[2] Cf., for instance, the reports by the Economic Departments or Commissions of the United Nations Organization.

play rôles of varying importance, necessarily has a dual character, one of the elements — the ownership of capital and techniques — being contributed by European or American groups, and the other — land and labour — being sold or provided by the local population. This has resulted in the creation or perpetuation of social distinctions similar to those that exist in other parts of the world,[1] but corresponding in some areas of Africa to ethnical divisions. This duality is extremely important in that it can lead to a state of extreme social tension if distribution is too unbalanced, or if the dominant groups either gain control of the production factors or misuse them for their own benefit. This is why land and labour problems can have a considerable influence on trends in African economic development. If this aspect of the subject is neglected, there is a danger of relations between the different ethnical or social groups deteriorating considerably or possibly even to an irremediable degree.

There is nevertheless no reason to believe that the problems arise solely from the distribution of property. A number of other difficulties arise when the local inhabitants are obliged to contribute to production in a new way. A typical example is to be found in the concept of services rendered, which traditionalists and Europeans view in very different ways.

In addition, the notion of investment in Africa came to be linked with 'the opening-up of means of communication to prospect and create outlets for an empty continent so that more advanced production agents could penetrate and develop its resources *naturally*'. Obviously it subsequently became necessary to define the spheres of influence of the different sectors of investment, and the public sector became responsible for creating an infrastructure, while the private sector dealt with foreign trade.

The exploration of the continent should have been followed by an increase in population and initiative in the newly explored areas, but in some cases this did not occur and local labour had to be used under conditions which were far from ideal psychologically or economically, as is always the case when a group does not mingle with the rest of society.[2]

European techniques have mainly been introduced in sectors

---

[1] In different countries, these social distinctions correspond to a more or less intensive stratification of social classes and to a greater degree of ease in obtaining access to higher classes.

[2] This was the case, for instance, in the towns and in certain agricultural and mining centres. In addition, when African peoples find themselves included in a market-type or monetary economy, they realise that the society they are trying to imitate, although it is geographically near at hand, is nevertheless remote and closed from the sociological point of view. The consequences of urban development in Africa cannot be too greatly stressed and provide a strategic element which should not be underestimated.

concerned with exploiting the natural resources of the soil and sub-soil, and, as a consequence, they are also being used by the processing industries. This is why we find highly developed extraction industries working in isolated enclaves ; they have links with the outside world, but little influence on development in their own area.

The introduction of these methods into traditional rural life is a far more complex process than where mining industries are concerned, and the direct and indirect consequences may vary to a wide extent. In some cases, the traditional form of subsistence agriculture tends to take a commercial turn, with all the difficulties this implies in respect of adaptation to human and economic relations based on a different set of values. In other cases, the methods are introduced more directly by the creation of farming on an industrial scale — an entirely new form of agriculture — and give rise to all the problems, of labour, salaries, adaptation to new techniques, and so on, that are encountered in the mining areas.

It is difficult, if not impossible, to assess the relative importance of the various forms of production ranging from the closed, subsistence economy to the plantation-type economy.[1] However, from the dynamic standpoint, it is safe to say that a large proportion of agricultural production has entered the market economy circuit, with the result that the balance between subsistence and commercial farming has tended to be destroyed and that agrarian and, consequently, social structure has been altered in a number of important ways.[2] These changes have led to a different attitude towards the land, and have thus contributed to urban development and to the rapid growth of an increasingly large proletariat.

It is also a fact that the plantation-type economy — which entails the direct introduction of new techniques — implying, as it does, the acquisition of large areas of land and large numbers of employees, gives rise to difficult sociological problems with particular emphasis

[1] We have no intention of discussing the advantages and drawbacks of the plantation system ; we simply wish to point out that this system has specific features which can prompt us to consider large plantations as 'poles of development', the influence of which within a country's economy may not be very widespread. A 'plantation' economy is one which engages in mass-production using modern technical methods. Of course, native 'planters' may exist, but their commercial output generally co-exists with subsistence farming and their marketing patterns are not independent of the latter. The examples of coffee, cocoa, cotton, rubber, sugar, and oil production are characteristic and some observers such as Lewis (*Tropical Agriculture*, 1950) state that : 'The combination of a large area of land and plentiful labour is always desirable from a technical point of view but the political obstacles in the way of these two conditions required for a plantation-type economy are almost insurmountable'.

[2] There are a great many cases which could be chosen as examples of the reactions of local societies to the penetration of European farming. A particular study has been made of reactions to the introduction of cotton, coffee, and cocoa cultivation in Central Africa.

on those connected with social, racial, and institutional co-existence.

In any event, on nearly every occasion when European techniques have been introduced into African territories and modern methods of economic organization are applied, this has been followed by a rapid and even more intensive disintegration of the local economic and social structure.

Through lack of any appropriate social policy, a vacuum was created in local society; traditional structures were emptied of their economic and social content without undergoing any formal modifications. Battered from the outside by changes in the marketing and production of merchandise, and sapped from within by the introduction of new cultures and new values, traditional societies are altering at varying tempi; even when their superficial features appear unchanged, they are founded on different social relations which create serious human and sociological problems. This is a characteristic trait of African life and corresponds to the deformation of traditional structures; if the aim is for social and economic development to make rapid progress new institutions must be provided.[1]

Any alteration in a society, any changeover from one form of society to another implies that help and assistance should be given to those who have to fit in the new social framework. Few people can live or survive if they are not well adapted to their environment, and this applies to social, as much as to actual physical, surroundings.

This is why it is necessary to make 'social' investments for the large section of the population which is undergoing this transformation and which feels the need for 'support' in the widest and highest sense of the term.[2]

Finally, another important economic fact is that trade is dominated by large firms which have their headquarters abroad, some of which contribute to the trading circuit while others deal with production. This system means that a great deal of the profits made are exported and that the local effects of investment decrease,[3] regardless of the question of the strategic part played by these firms in development.

---

[1] The example of the 'native woman' and of her place in society suffices to give an idea of the importance of the problem.

[2] These investments cannot be subjected to the normal rules of profit and loss accounting — their cost must be calculated in human terms and it should be borne in mind that what the African masses desire is civilization, not forced Westernization.

[3] In addition, as a result of the development of the villages and certain agricultural areas where small landowners are common, an African middle class is emerging. Its members are few in number, but they engage in agriculture as well as in trade, and they handle an appreciable portion of the money circulating in the local economy. The attitude of this middle class can have an enormous influence on development trends.

Although they remain in contact with the various sectors of the economy, these firms naturally find their place in the monetary and market economy. Another important factor — the structure of the existing or future monetary economy — therefore has to be borne in mind as well. We have already mentioned key-sectors such as foreign trade and the public sector, but if we consider the way the foreign trade sector is made up, we find here too an example of the high concentration of economic power. In other words, whatever the type of development for which plans are being made, the possibility of opposition or co-operation from these firms must be considered.

A large number of public functions are, in fact, the responsibility of a small number of large units, and the result is that increases in productivity are not automatically followed by higher wages or lower prices, because the firms concerned have the final word on these matters. There is also the fact that, by affecting export prices, these major firms influence the currency exchange rate for the territory, and, furthermore, they are free to export capital which could be used to finance other local undertakings.

Since these big firms often import and export in under-developed areas and are importers in developed countries, the choice as to where they will use their profits depends more on the firm's overall policy than on the country's needs. A rapid analysis of the economies of African countries — even the independent ones — makes it clear that certain firms more or less control the existing markets.

In fact, the economic backwardness of such territories can be attributed both to the internal structure of the economy and to the way in which it is deformed or thrown off balance by foreign trade, with the resulting stagnation or even setbacks in some sectors, while others grow too quickly and to too great an extent. In a monetary economy, this type of imbalance can be countered by 'opening up' the economy, allowing foreign trade to deal with bottlenecks, but an open economy controlled from the outside implies the creation of payment problems that are far from negligible.

III. POLICIES FOR DEVELOPMENT

In order to draw up an economic development policy, we must for the moment concentrate on the following points :

(a) The aims in view and the means to be used so as to achieve them ;

(b) the assessment of these aims and means, as well as of the efficiency of the development model, from a financial standpoint;

(*c*) the social consequences of the projected development;

(*d*) the foreseeable consequences of the transformation of the structures.

We can assume from the start that African economic development should correspond to a plan [1] prepared so as to correlate both economic and social matters, making allowance for the fact that it will be necessary to raise capital of all kinds rapidly, and that qualified economic agents will be required to use this capital.

Among these problems, we shall first deal with those which concern the development model, not only because they are bound up with the theoretical problems we have examined, but also because a possible policy can thus be incorporated into the comprehensive model.

There are numerous known examples of economic growth, all more or less based on standard Keynesian economic theory, but all of them dominated by the need for a strategy relating to a fundamental variable factor : the investment or creation of capital. Setting aside a whole series of different conditions, we admit that, in some of the models, there is a direct and constant relationship between the annual volume of investment in fixed capital and the increase in output. These models have, however, been applied in areas governed by a monetary economy which provides the vehicle necessary to transmit the direct or indirect effects of investment.

We do not claim in this paper to set up models as simple as this or to forecast to what extent they can be applied to the implementation of economic development. It is enough for the present to acknowledge that these models presuppose the existence of institutions and well-defined attitudes on the part of the economic agents, and that they have hardly ever proved suitable for poorly developed economies, which lack not only the conditions required to propagate the effects, but also the statistical elements essential to the planning itself.

Furthermore, there is no general agreement on the factors most favourable to growth, since some people advocate a disseminated development with simultaneous expansion by sectors, while others stress the advantages of concentrated growth, or growth by 'poles', which creates imbalance between the sectors within an economy.

[1] A plan is not a universal panacea the results of which are foreordained since, if it is to be implemented, it calls for the active participation, and even in extreme cases, almost the mobilization, of the population. It is nevertheless quite obvious that little progress will be made at the stage where the choice is made between active and traditional planning methods.

History gives us both practical and theoretical examples of unbalanced concentrated growth situations, from the English industrial revolution up to the Soviet industrialization policy. However, the political repercussions of certain forms of imbalance, and the ever-present uncertainty as to the variable factors of the external sector (payment difficulties and the cost of commodities or exports) are such that it is impossible to have too marked a discrepancy between output and consumption without running the risk of the country involved finding itself too dependent on other countries or obliged to have recourse to various forms of controls which are incompatible with the existing political institutions.

It does happen, however, above all for technological reasons,[1] that concentrated growth is advocated in under-developed economies because of the interdependence between production and the external economies which has to be taken into account.

In such cases, growth appears as a process of agglomeration and of propagation. The agglomeration depends initially on the existence of a pole of development situated or set up in a geographical space or region, and this implies a number of conditions such as technical infrastructure, transportation, substantial capital, and a whole series of motive units capable of stimulating the expansion of other undertakings, and of altering the economic structure. All this requires a certain amount of reorganization.

In order to assemble the essential basic conditions, it is necessary to possess above all not only power, human, agricultural, and mineral resources, but also reserves of capital and technical ability. The existence of motive units follows and means that they

reduce cost and sale prices ;
increase supply and demand, even if this should involve the risk of exhausting resources and of creating certain social drawbacks such as water pollution, atmospheric pollution, noise, radioactivity, and, above all, new social categories ;
attract credits, since they are the basis from which investment will multiply.

Taking into account the problem of Africa as described above, it is easy to understand that the existence or creation of poles and motive units engenders social tensions and may even pose political problems.[2]

[1] Africa also reveals examples of growth by poles, but almost always bound up with the outside world by the internal logic of mercantile capitalism which prevents the profits made from being used in the producer country itself.
[2] Consider, for instance, the relationships between certain large foreign firms and African governments.

Whatever the outcome, the creation of a pole implies a choice, since several sets of alternatives exist :

the protection of subsistence production or the expansion of output for trading purposes ;
or the substitution of local products for imports or the stepping-up of exports ;
or the immediate disintegration of the traditional sector or the co-existence of techniques.

In view of the shortage of qualified economic agents in Africa and the direct or indirect disintegration of traditional sectors, the policy of development poles means that the introduction of elementary education programmes and increased settlement by white people will have to be accompanied by direct support to areas which are not polarized or have few poles, by means of a common development policy. A policy based solely on the second terms of the alternatives listed above would be destined to failure from the outset because of the political and social problems it would raise. Here again, we discover another feature of development poles, namely that the problem is not only one of creating and spreading them, but of understanding their 'meaning' and 'purpose'.

In the presence of a set of resources which would enable one or several motive units to be set up, a decision has to be taken on whether the installation is to be individual or collective. If a development pole policy is adopted, it has to be thought of in terms of a series of units and of co-ordinated agglomerations so as not to deprive the population of the possible advantages to be derived from outside economies. After the running-in period, however, additional investment must start to multiply, prices must be reduced, and new products put on the market. This will give rise to several problems including that of the permissible degree of monopoly [1] and of balancing factors, and also that of the existence of a human society responsive to the innovations being made.

The propagation of the effects on a domestic level is also essential, and is the consequence of the spread of a flow which creates in turn a whole pattern of price and credit currents. The most typical example is that of a dam which distributes energy in all directions and facilitates the setting-up of industries and agricultural output,

---

[1] For instance, if a firm being set up in Portugal is to prove a good business proposition, it must cause a greater reduction in domestic prices than if it had been set up in another country. It would be pointless to give concrete examples of cases where this has been so, and of others where results have been different because of factors which were favourable to monopolies spurred on by a mercantile mentality.

depending on the form of energy. Monetary currents tend to veer away from the traditional sectors to swell the new currents created, hence causing multiplication phenomena. This is on the assumption, of course, that firms do not withhold the overall profits of creation and innovation either directly or indirectly through pressure groups or national or international interests.[1] Once the poles have been created and their benefits distributed, their social and human implications still have to be defined and this will depend on the change in behaviour of the economic agents. All innovations that have a far-reaching effect modify society and lead to changes and adaptations of behaviour. Here the problem is on a much vaster scale since it involves creating new ideas and new values, setting up new institutions, opening up new horizons to all members of society, and, above all, taking economic decisions that the latter will be capable of understanding.

Descriptions of several concrete cases of development poles in Africa are to be found in earlier works.[2] If we return to this question, it is because under any régime the intensity and speed of industrial effort are vitally important factors requiring an enormous influx of real capital and technical ability. Among the numerous patterns of productive units, we shall choose the most simple in order to ensure the cohesion of the activities and units meeting the conditions of poles of development such as those we have described above, *i.e.* where, at one and the same time, there are energy-producing centres, raw materials, agriculture centres, and means of transport.

In addition, the experience acquired in many areas proves that the production period can be greatly reduced by means of certain kinds of national and international co-operation, and the existence of a volume of capital that can be mobilized. These production complexes modify and educate the society in which they grow up, and they have a dual effect : as an additional agglomeration, by settling the population, and as a junction, by attracting new industries. Lastly, they create centres for communication networks.

In the African context, another problem arises, however : that of the relationship between the sectors of a dualistic economy with all the economic and social consequences of a development based on poles where modern production methods are applied. Technical progress is not, in fact, transmitted alone ; it is accompanied by

[1] This attitude of firms has caused a great deal of controversy, but it is now common practice for many independent countries to demand 'payment' for the working of national or regional resources by foreign firms, and efforts have been made to spread motive units by applying different formulae ranging from partnership to the levying of 'exhaustion taxes' for national or local development funds.

[2] Cf. Rui Martins dos Santos, *Alguns polos de desenvolvimento éconómico africano*.

changes in the economic structures of output and trade which, in turn, are inseparable from the social and mental structures. We must therefore create zones of progress, *i.e.* human complexes which are capable of adapting, co-ordinating, and assimilating technical progress and Western structures. This development of human society is essential if there is a desire to make real progress without destroying men and ideals.

It is surely not necessary to insist on the need for planning in Africa, but the necessity of determining priorities and achieving an overall equilibrium must be stressed. It would be pointless to attempt to make a strictly accurate estimate for the latter since no data are available and nothing is known of the resources and human scope of certain kinds of community development.

The priorities, on the other hand, are as follows :

(*a*) As radical a transformation as possible of structure, the appointment of competent and efficient local authorities and the promotion of the concept of co-operatives, as well as their creation ;

(*b*) improvement of the standard of living of the populations by supporting subsistence agriculture so as to achieve higher productivity and by attempting to foster community development ;

(*c*) provision for collective needs in public health, education, and culture through an attempt to train men and technicians more quickly, by combating illiteracy and making elementary education more widespread ;

(*d*) the distribution of foreign trade by products and countries ;

(*e*) lastly, the setting-up of poles and zones of development, taking particular account of the hydro-electric and mining resources.

It is in this last respect that we are endeavouring to apply this simplified model to the case of Angola, by outlining, albeit roughly, the possible zones of development or pointing out possible poles and motive units.

IV. MODEL OF ECONOMIC DEVELOPMENT FOR ANGOLA

There would be no point in discussing whether a disseminated or polarized growth model would be most appropriate for the Angolan economy, since the path to be taken is already marked out by the natural, human, and historical features of the country.

Several inter-related factors militate against any inclination to apply a disseminated development model to the Province. These are :

(1) The size of the Province : about 1,250,000 square kilometres, *i.e.* an area greater than that of all the Common Market countries ;

(2) the sparse population of only 4,500,000 inhabitants, representing half that of European Portugal ;

(3) the uneven distribution of the population (average densities by cantons ('concelhos') and districts ranging from 0·19 people per square kilometre in Porto Alexandre to 106·03 people per sq. km. in Luanda ;

(4) the co-existence of different and extreme types of economy (only a very small percentage of the aboriginal population presumably takes part in the monetary economy, but a very large proportion of this population is more or less regularly in contact with the market economy sector) ;

(5) the absence of 'monetary' currents and of a domestic market which is essential if the effects of monetary investment are to be propagated ;

(6) the diversity of the natural resources and aptitudes in the different areas of the Province ;

(7) the existence of a few highly developed pockets essentially concerned with mineral resources, but almost exclusively orientated towards the outside world.

It is therefore necessary to choose a polarized growth model, of which we shall now outline the general features.

Poles of Growth and Polarized Areas

We shall begin our analysis by describing the present poles of development and the effects of polarization, basing our description on the study made of the economic, political, and administrative life of Angola. The main poles are as follows :

(i) *International*

(*a*) Polarization directed towards the Congo Republic (Brazzaville) : the northern part of the Cabinda district.

(*b*) Polarization directed towards the Congo Republic (Léopoldville) : a few administrative posts at the Cabinda frontier,[1]

---

[1] This polarization is to some extent reciprocal since Congolese workers are found in the mines.

a frontier strip in the Zaire and Uîge districts, which may be as much as 100 kilometres wide, and a few posts to the north and south-east of the Lunda, as well as a small part of the Moxico.

(c) Polarization directed towards Northern Rhodesia : attraction is exerted on the posts of Lévua, Calunda, and Macondo in the Upper Zambesi district, and even more on the post of Mussuma (Bundas) and the south-eastern point of Moxico (post of Luiana).

(d) Polarization directed towards South-West Africa : mainly noticeable in the Lower Cubango and part of the Cuando districts.

(e) Polarization directed towards South-West Africa : this is perhaps a new phenomenon which is witnessed above all at the frontier of the Huila with this territory.

(ii) *National*

Strong polarization directed towards Portugal. This is an indisputable fact, the reasons for which are many and varied : more than 30 per cent of the foreign trade of the Province is concerned with transactions with European Portugal ; a large proportion of private investment is from Portugal ; the most important planning centres are in Lisbon, it is there that the decisions are taken and impetus given to the different sectors of the economy, to public works, to local authorities, and to labour.

(iii) *Provincial*

Most of the poles of attraction of the Province are in Luanda. The rapid development of this town demonstrates the demographic aspects of this polarization ; from 60,000 in 1940, the population rose to 200,000 in 1960.

If we consider the production activity, we come to the conclusion that the most important Angolan industries are in Luanda ; it is the leading industrial centre of the territory, and it is also the headquarters of many of the large firms which dominate the import and export trade as well as the wholesale domestic trade. It is the centre of air communications in the Province, accounting for about half of the passengers embarked and disembarked in all the airports and landing strips served by the domestic air lines, it is at the head of a railway line into the interior, the second port of the territory, and also the centre of the civil, social, and cultural life of a vast region.

There are two motive units at some distance from the town (50 to 60 kilometres), in the Dande and the Bon Jésus, which have not yet become centres of agglomeration, the 'Fazenda Tentative' with sugar and palm-oil factories, and a sugar plantation. In studying the 'zones of development', both have been considered as being attached to the pole of development of Luanda, and their intrinsic polarizing functions have been taken as constituting an extension of those of the urban centre.

(iv) *Regional*

In addition to the pole we have just mentioned, there are a number of urban poles, some of which also have other agglomerative functions (administrative, economic, cultural, etc.). The regional attraction they exercise varies somewhat ; it is slight and restricted in the North because of the proximity of the capital, but more pronounced in the Centre and the South where the attraction of Luanda is hardly felt. These poles are :

(a) *Lobito-Benguela*. Lobito is a town which is developing rapidly ; it now has more than 40,000 inhabitants whereas it had only 14,000 in 1940. It is the main port of the Province, and the volume of merchandise handled is more than twice that passing through Luanda. It lies at the head of the longest railway in Angola, and is the trading centre for a very vast area which extends, in Angolan territory, as far as the Lunda and Moxico boundaries. It is also one of the large industrial centres of the Province. Not far — 30 kilometres — away is the town of Benguela, which is organically linked to Lobito. Although it is the capital of a district and is an important cultural centre, it does not have the characteristics of an urban pole, as can be seen from its slow development ; with 14,000 inhabitants in 1940, it had only 15,000 in 1955. This is why it has been considered preferable to speak in terms of a single Lobito-Benguela pole. The Catumbela, which has a large sugar and alcohol factory as well as other industrial units such as a castor-oil factory, and the Dombe Grande with its sugar and palm-oil factories, have also been incorporated into this system. If we add the industries of Lobito and Benguela to these industries, they constitute an industrial pole which is as important as that of Luanda without being as concentrated.

(b) *Nova Lisboa*. This is the second largest town of the Province. In 1960 it has 48,000 inhabitants, three times its 1940 population.

(c) *Sà da Bandeira*. This town does not have the features needed to attract a large population. It has an excellent climate, however, and its influence as a cultural pole —although still regional — could be considerably developed.

(d) *Malange.* According to recent statistics, the town probably had 20,000 inhabitants in 1960. As far as industry is concerned, it has very few factories, most of which process the raw materials of the region.[1] The distance separating it from Luanda and transport difficulties have enabled Malange to begin, albeit modestly, to play the part of a tourist pole because of the numerous attractions within its zone of influence.

(e) *Silva Porto.* This is a town which is slightly less populated than Malange and which is developing at more or less the same rate.

We might also mention several centres which, although not strictly urban poles, nevertheless exercise a certain power of attraction on a regional level. Two of them are practically reduced to a single production unit which might even be considered a motive unit. These are :

(a) *Moçâmedes–Porto Alexandre.* The town of Moçâmedes, which had 7,000 inhabitants in 1955, is too subjected to the social and cultural life of Sà da Bandeira for it to be included among the urban poles. Together with Porto Alexandre, however, it exercises a kind of centrapetal influence owing to the abundant supply of fish in its waters. This has given rise in both towns to a flourishing industry depending on fish.

(b) *Dundo* (Angola Diamond Company). In view of the amount of labour absorbed by the diamond mines and the numerous services connected with their workings, such as administrative and domestic services and food supplies, a somewhat more mobile nucleus of population than that of some towns has been created in the Lunda. Although this is an export-biased motive unit and therefore does not have the means of domestic propagation required to produce large-scale development or economic agglomeration, the size of the markets where it acquires the produce and materials required for its subsistence (for example, the large number of cattle regularly bought from the Lower Cubango) and the importance of its social and cultural work is sufficient to explain why the Company's influence as a pole is not merely local.

(c) *Boa-Entrada.* This is the leading coffee producer of the Province, having produced 10,000 tons, *i.e.* one-tenth of the total production, in 1960, and it is also one of the top palm-oil producers. Connected by a few kilometres of road to Gabela with its oil, soap, and food industries and linked, above all, by railway to Porto Aboim,

[1] A sugar factory, which is obviously considered as being connected to the Malange pole, is being reorganized at Quissol.

Boa-Entrada can certainly be classed among the Angolan poles of regional development, for more or less the same reasons and to the same extent as the Diamond Company.

(v) *Local*

There are still a number of poles that can be mentioned, such as administrative, trading, agricultural, or stock-breeding centres. Their influence is, however, more limited, since it is practically confined to the centre's own canton or district or to a few neighbouring villages.

Among the agricultural and stock-breeding poles of development, we should mention several colonization centres, the most important of which is obviously Cela, if only because of the value of the work accomplished there and because of the great things expected of the present policy of average plantations,[1] chiefly devoted to dairy produce, citrous fruits, coffee, and pig-breeding.

There are also a number of indigenous colonization centres (Caconda, Vale do Queve, Vale do Loge, Damba, etc.), where there are thousands of settlers working the land and with revenues higher than those of the greater part of the aboriginal population.

At first sight, since these are essentially closed societies with little influence on neighbouring populations, it does not seem that they are destined to act as poles even on a local level. And yet this could be the case, in that endeavours are being made, with the support of the authorities, to solve a number of problems connected with the scientific study of farming and the most suitable cultivation methods for certain areas, with the elementary transformation of farm produce or with the marketing of this produce — problems which affect all local producers who have to face up to the same difficulties. If these groups of settlers are to fulfil their mission, they must allow others to benefit from the solutions found and must provide the basis for improving farming and stock-breeding methods in the areas where they are installed.

A number of laboratories and experimental stations have fulfilled motive functions similar to those of an 'open' colonization centre from the technical and scientific standpoints. Mention should be made, in particular, of the Laboratorio Central de Patologie Veterinaria, of the Serviços de Veterinaria e Indùstria Animal in Nova Lisboa, the Estaçâo Zootécnica Central of Ganda, the Station Zootécnica do Sul at Humpata, the Estaçâo de Melhoramento de Plantas, de la Junta de Exportaçâo dos Cereais of Chianga (Nova Lisboa) ; the Estaçâo Experimental of Onga-Zanga (Catete), the

[1] 120 hectares.

Centro de Investigaçâo Cientifica Algodoeira, the Estaçâo Agricola Central at Salazar, the Posto Experimental do Caracul and the Direcçâo dos Serviços de Veterinaria near Moçâmedes, etc. However, all these units come within the scope of the poles of development already mentioned.

In order to define the limits of the zones of influence of the different poles, we shall begin by analysing only the two largest centres : Luanda and Lobito–Benguela. Although the importance of Luanda as a pole is essentially provincial in character, its influence extends over only a quarter of the Province. In the other three-quarters of Angola, the dominating influence is that of the Lobito–Benguela complex.

The economic life of these two centres is bound up with the existence of a railway into the hinterland — from Luanda to Malange in the first case and from Lobito to Texeira de Sousa in the second — and of a port centralizing almost all the trade movements between the corresponding zone and the outside world. In order to obtain an idea of this centralization, it is sufficient to know that the port of Luanda handles 80 per cent of all the merchandise passing through the ports of Zone A and that the ports of Lobito and Benguela — above all Lobito — represent 90 per cent of the port traffic of the South (Zone B).

Once the extent of these two zones has been defined, and if we bear in mind what was said above about the particular structure of the Province, we are forced to conclude that, in Zone A, there is only a single pole outside Luanda, namely Malange. There are several sub-poles, usually administrative centres, which actually fulfil the function of poles only in so far as they cater for the requirements of the local inhabitants (social life, trade, food, and drink industries). With their plantations and industrial units, some firms also play an important rôle. The Cela colonization centre, for instance, can be considered as a local pole of development.

In Zone B, in addition to the urban and industrial complex of Lobito–Benguela with its sub-poles Catumbela and Dombo Grande, there exist three urban poles of regional importance — Nova Lisboa, Sà da Bandeira, and Silva Porto, and a motive unit at Dundo. There is also another pole at Moçâmedes–Porto Alexandre, where the main activity is fishing.

V. THE BROAD OUTLINES OF A DEVELOPMENT POLICY

Now that we have described the location, importance, main functions, and attraction potential of the poles of development and have roughly set limits to the zones of influence, with their centres at Luanda and Lobito–Benguela respectively, we can sketch the outlines of a possible growth policy for the Angolan economy.

In addition to the priorities listed in the first part of this report, the main directives will be as follows :

(a) The concentration of the dynamic factors (capital and technical assistance), preferably in the privileged zones which already exist or are about to be created, since they will then complement each other and benefit will be derived from them ;

(b) the creation or preservation of a number of secondary poles so as to avoid proletarianization or over-population of the towns ;

(c) the creation or development of communications and means of transport to provide links between additional development zones.

In order to achieve the aims listed in paragraph (a), two basic zones of development are contemplated : Luanda–Dondo–Malange (two existing and one projected) and Lobito–Benguela–Upper Catumbela–Nova Lisboa (two well-defined poles and one being formed). Each of them will support zones or poles within its sphere of influence (Zones A and B) ; Lândana and Cela–Gabela for the first ; Sà da Bandeira — the Cunene Colonization Centre Moçâmedes–Porto Alexandre and Luso for the second (paragraph (b)).

The function to be given to each of these poles and the problems to be solved in order to ensure the development of each zone in the most satisfactory manner possible are as follows :

Zone A

(i) *Luanda–Dondo–Malange Development Line*

Luanda would continue as a pole, but would also fulfil a more important function, as the result of the development of an industrial belt corresponding to the requirements of the town and the availability of raw materials in the zone.[1]

In view of its location in relation to the Cambambe Dam, the powerhouse of which (together with the Mabubas Dam on the Dande and two other structures that could be contemplated to harness the middle and upper stretches of the Cuanza) can also supply power to the other poles of the line, Donde is obviously the

[1] In this 'belt', industries such as coffee processing and copper refining could be contemplated.

most suitable place for setting up industries consuming large amounts of electricity. It is here that it will be necessary to install aluminium and ferro-alloy plants, the annual output of which are estimated at 370 million [1] and 140 million escudos respectively, a plant for nitrogen and other chemical products related to petroleum refining, a phosphate fertilizer plant, and so on. Some of these units will use the raw materials of the zone — iron and manganese ores, natural limestone, quartz, and phosphates — thus giving new impetus to the mine workings. It can be anticipated, furthermore, that the creation of the first industries will set off a very large local movement towards centralization, not only economic and technical, but also demographic in scope.

Malange could become the main centre of the cotton textile industry of the Province by using the raw-material resources of the north-eastern part of the district (55 per cent of the Angolan cotton production). Of the two spinning and weaving units which exist at present, only one would remain in Luanda to process the raw material produced in the areas of Ambriz and Catete ; the other should be transferred to Malange where it would be modernized and extended. It would also be necessary to take an interest in the other industrial sectors already installed in the town such as the oil fats (ground-nuts and cotton seeds) and starch (manioc) industries.

Profit could be derived from the combination of several favourable factors — water and power resources, communications, and mineral wealth — to undertake the development of a vast area situated between the above-mentioned poles along the Luanda railway and the Cuanza, Bengo, and Lucala rivers. The following workings, in particular, could be used to good effect : the iron mines on Mounts Tumbi and Saia in the Lucala/Pungo–Adongo area, where output should reach one million tons by 1965 and could be transported by a railway line to be built on the left bank of the river Lucala ; the iron and titanium mines in the area of Zenza de Itombe, which should have an annual output of 180-240,000 tons by 1962 ; the iron and manganese-iron mines in the area of Cacuso–Lucala– Quitota, where production should reach 50,000 tons by 1962 once the present experimental stage is over, as well as at Camame (Quilombo) ; the libolithic deposits and other asphaltic or bituminous formations in the Dande area (first producing area), at Cassoneca (Icolo and Bengo) and Calucala (near Zenza d'Itombe) ; the mica deposits in the regions of the Dande and Quiçama ; oil wells at Benfica (Belas), Calinda, Cacuaco, and perhaps at other places where prospecting is under way. In addition, other interesting work

[1] During the first stage.

can be contemplated, this time, however, in agriculture, stock-breeding, and forestry : sugar in the low-lying land of Caquembe (Muxima zone) ; tobacco at Cacuso–Duque de Bragança to support the European colonies of the plateau of Malange and in the areas of Lucala–Cambo and Muxima–Cassoalala ; fruit, especially oranges and bananas, in the regions of Cambambo–Massangano–Zenza d'Itombe, and of the Quiçama and the Dande–Babiri ; horticultural produce in the watered areas of Cuanza–Bengo ; palm kernels in the valley of the Cuanza, particularly between Muxima and Cambambe (in addition to the 'Tentativa' working in the Dande) ; beef from the bar of the Dande to that of the Cuanza, although production covers only part of local needs ; timber in the area of Zenza, Cerca, and the Upper Golungo.

(ii) *First Auxiliary Pole: Cela–Gabela*

Essentially, this would consist of the European colonization centre midway between Luanda and Nova Lisboa, the town of Gabela and Boa–Entrada, plus several interesting agricultural and stock-breeding points in the Quibala region.

At Gabela, which is the centre of the important coffee-producing region of Southern Cuanza, it would be possible to set up a factory to manufacture powdered coffee instead of, or at the same time as, that suggested for Luanda which would soften the possible effects of the coffee crisis.

(iii) *Second Auxiliary Pole: Lândana*

The works planned on the Chiloango and the construction of the port of Lândana will certainly create a pole capable of competing with those which now exist in the adjoining territory of the ex-French Congolese Republic and with the town of Cabinda. In fact, due to the use of the Chiloango for transportation of timber from Maiombo and the location of the phosphate deposits — at Câcata, Chibuste, Cambo, and other points in the Lândana hinterland — it is not difficult to forecast the important rôle that this port will be called upon to play in the development of Zone A.

(iv) *Propagation of the Development*

Links between the central line of development for Zone A and its supporting poles will be ensured by a number of centres which are not poles in themselves, such as towns and villages not included in the pattern already described, as well as by a few isolated workings of relative importance such as copper mines, for instance.

The transportation network will have to be extended, and if a more rapid development of the entire zone is to be promoted, it will not be sufficient merely to make far-reaching reforms with a view to improving the cultivation methods of the basic produce such as coffee, palm kernels, cotton, rice, beans, manioc, ground-nuts, and tobacco,[1] to facilitate marketing by using industrial methods as far as possible and to ensure a better distribution of agricultural income (reforms under which co-operatives of Europeans and Africans will have to be created). In addition, it will be necessary to encourage and develop other kinds of produce which may be of great value for the economy of the Province as a whole including, among other things, 'hard fibres', 'caju', and fruit, especially bananas.

ZONE B

(i) *Line of Development Lobito–Benguela–Upper Catumbela–Nova Lisboa*

This line, which is based on the centres of Lobito–Benguela, Nova Lisboa, and possibly the Upper Catumbela, extends along the Benguela railway almost as far as Chinguar. It has the advantage, therefore, of possessing rapid means of transport almost everywhere, not only towards the sea but also into the interior, while the dams of Biopio and Lomaum on the Catumbela provide it with an appreciable amount of energy.

The rôle of the town of Lobito as a pole has remained unaltered in the plans outlined for this line. In respect of Benguela, it might be possible to attempt to solve the crisis created by the shortage of fish in one of the following two ways (unless both are used together) : the creation of a fishing fleet with a larger radius of action equipped with modern means of detecting shoals of fish, as well as with cold-room installations, or else research into the prospects of industrialization (sisal production, agricultural equipment, and shipyards for instance) so that the town will not have to depend on the fishing industry to so great an extent.

In the Upper Catumbela, a cellulose and paper-making factory is being set up. On the regional level, the presence of this factory will certainly have a considerable effect on the development of economic activity and living standards in view of its volume of out-

---

[1] We shall not discuss sugar which is produced by industrial methods on a very localized basis.

put, the amount of European and African labour of high technical standard it will require and, above all, because it will inevitably promote the development of a great many other activities such as forestry, salt-mining, lime production, paper industries, and so on in adjacent areas. There is reason to hope that a new pole of attraction will be created, since, in addition to the motive functions of this new unit, a number of conditions that are propitious to agglomeration are present, including the proximity of the Lomaum powerhouse on the Catumbela, the privileged position of the locality in relation to the markets of neighbouring poles and the natural wealth of the area.

Along the line connecting the three poles over a strip of territory 140 kilometres wide, a large number of primary installations are to be found : iron at Cuima, where more than 500,000 tons per year are already being produced ; [1] manganese near Caala and Longonjo ; salt on the coast at Lobito and Benguela ; beef at Ganda, Bailundo, and Caala, and pork in the same areas ; maize (more than 50 per cent of the entire Angolan production) on the plateaux of Benguela and Huambo ; wheat, especially in the Huambo (two-thirds of the total production) ; sisal in Ganda (first zone of cultivation, representing 75 per cent of total output), the Boccio (second producing zone), and the Balombo ; fruit, especially citrous fruits and pineapple, in the Balombo along the railway from Benguela (beyond Ganda) and bananas in the valley of Cavaco ; castor-oil (80 per cent of total production) in the region of Balombo, Boccio, and Chila, the production of which would be sufficient to supply the whole Catumbela factory working at full capacity ; [2] the 'alunites' in the same area ; timber, coffee, beans, etc. There are also extensive sugar plantations in the same areas and at other locations in the Benguela district.

(ii) *First Auxiliary Pole: Sà da Bandeira–Colonization Centre*

In spite of all its features as an urban pole of distinctly European tendency and as a very promising agricultural and stock-raising zone centre, Sà da Bandeira does not combine all the conditions required to set up a large industry.

It would nevertheless be advisable to support a few industrial undertakings which might be of value for the local food supply or particularly suitable for the region such as agricultural equipment, fruit canning, and sausage-making, for instance, and to attempt to

[1] A branch of the main line from Benguela is to be built from Robert Williams (Caala) to Cuima so as to facilitate evacuation of the output.
[2] Processing capacity : 20,000 tons.

give the town the character of an important technical centre.

The Colonization Centre in the Valley of the Cunene, which specializes in stock-breeding, tobacco, and wheat, could become an instruction centre for modern agriculture methods for the Africans and a pole of attraction for European farmers.[1]

(iii) *Second Auxiliary Pole: Moçâmedes–Porto Alexandre*

It is here that would be concentrated the greater part of the industry devoted to fish products (canning, fish flour and oil, dried fish, etc.). Using modern methods to obtain the raw materials and to process and pack the final products, this industry would continue to be almost entirely given over to the export trade since the task of supplying fish for the domestic market would be left to the Benguela factories. The single exception would be that of fish flour which could be used to provide foodstuffs for the cattle of the neighbouring plateau and would provide a substantial domestic market for the industry.

(iv) *Third Auxiliary Pole: Luso*

Without mentioning Dundo, where the Angolan Diamond Company will naturally continue to act as a 'motive unit' and exercise some influence over the regions of the interior to the north of the Province, there is everything to be gained from possessing a supporting pole to promote the development of a vast part of the territory within Zone B. All the factors seem to point to Luso, the capital of the Moxico, for this position.

The first product to be developed is certainly manioc. In fact, the Moxico and Lunda districts are best suited to this plant and Moxico alone can produce 60,000 tons.[2] The conditions in the Bié are also highly propitious.

The local production of starches can therefore be contemplated. However, if a regular and cheap supply of raw material is to be ensured, it is absolutely essential, at least for the present, to attempt to produce it directly so as not to depend too much on native production in the early stages. On this point, the experience of Mozambique is very instructive.

The ground-nut production is also considerable, and there is a large ground-nut and sesame-seed oil factory which should absorb a large part of the present output.

---

[1] The centre is mixed.   [2] Present output is about 30,000 tons.

(v) *Propagation of Development*

A regional urban pole (Silva Porto), several local centres and a number of motive units disseminated over Zone B should facilitate the spread of development from the poles and main zones listed above.

In addition to the Angolan Diamond Company, whose polarizing functions we have mentioned, and the industrial complex of the Upper Catumbela, which we have connected to one of the poles of the Lobito–Nova Lisboa line of development, there is one more motive unit that should be mentioned, since it may form an additional unit for the spread of development. This is an undertaking which we were unable to include in the structure we outlined at the beginning of this paper because it does not have a fixed location. It is the concessionary of the Cuima iron mines and the Moxico coal deposits which has recently started to work the iron in the Chilesso mountains and in the Andulo and is preparing to start extraction operations in the Cassinga–Dongo–Artur de Paiva–Cuchi region.

There would certainly be advantages to be derived from concentrating investment efforts on certain poles or certain regions of Zone B, since the labour requirements would then be seen to rise and the yearly migration towards the North would slow down ; the general polarizing effect exercised by Zone A on Zone B would be reduced. In addition, as a result of the creation of new centres of attraction, internal movements would probably increase in the latter zone and the beneficial effects of the development would be more widely felt since the distances are shorter and it would be easier for the workers to have more frequent contact with their original environment.

Chapter 8

PROBLEMS OF ECONOMIC DEVELOPMENT OF THE FEDERATION OF RHODESIA AND NYASALAND

BY

W. L. TAYLOR

University College of Rhodesia and Nyasaland

> We must always remember that economic forces are only the manifestation of the ever-changing wants and desires of ourselves and of our fellow-men. When we are in conflict with economic forces we are in conflict with ourselves. By changing ourselves and others we can radically modify the forces that encompass us.[1]

I. INTRODUCTION

LIKE the rest of tropical Africa, the Federation of Rhodesia and Nyasaland is grappling with the fundamental economic problem of transforming rapidly and effectively the traditional subsistence economy — of which agriculture is the mainstay — into a modern exchange economy. This transformation process constitutes the basic characteristic of economic development in the greater part of Africa.

The Federation also shares in common with the rest of tropical Africa a great dilemma. How best to resolve the conflict arising from the necessity for rapid economic progress — in the light of rising political expectations and social and population pressures — with the obstacles imposed by a harsh physical environment, together with the need for time for scientific research to solve these physical problems. The political power of the large European minority group, furthermore, makes this dilemma more acute in the Federation than elsewhere in tropical Africa.

The barriers to economic development in the Federation are many but they are not all unique. By comparison with much of the rest of tropical Africa, the Federation possesses, for example, a reasonably well-developed infrastructure. It is the broad range of

[1] Quoted from E. A. G. Robinson's essay 'Difficulties of Economic Transition', p. 224, published in *Modern Industry and the African*, ed. J. Merle Davis, 1933, Macmillan, London.

political, social, and racial difficulties linked inextricably with the physical environmental challenge that presents the Federation with its greatest problem and which consequently constitute the most intractable impediments to economic growth. These human problems are proving more difficult, obstinate, and perverse than the physical ones.

African society in the Federation is undergoing a process of rapid, forcible transformation comparable only to the violent changes of a revolution. Although the motives of the dominant European group are clearly economic, and the disintegration of the traditional subsistence economy is caused by the collapse of its inferior economic institutions, the main problems arise because the new economic institutions are not fully assimilated by African society, which disintegrates and decays without being replaced easily by the new system of values.

The real problem and danger is that a cultural and economic in-between is created in the attempt to harmonize what are essentially two incompatible institutional systems. In this process of transformation Africans are forced to decline from a position of cultural maturity as Africans to cultural insecurity as Europeans.

Nevertheless, this condition is not due wholly to economic exploitation by Europeans in the accepted sense in which exploitation means an economic advantage of one partner at the cost of another, though, of course, it is closely joined with changes in the economic conditions connected with land tenure, marriage, and so on, each of which influences a large number of social habits and traditions of all kinds. When a cash economy is imposed on the traditional African economy, it is not poor or low wages that result in the low incomes per head ; African institutions simply employ a different system of values ; they are at the same time both thrifty and non-market-economy-oriented.

In the Federation, too, major development problems arise because the forms of land tenure are the focus of interest as the basis on which social organization directly depends. What seem to be economic conflicts are almost exclusively forms of economic pressure designed to induce Africans to give up their traditional way of life and thus to compel them to adjust to the mechanisms of the cash economy — to work for wages and buy goods in the marketplace. Thus, the transition to the cash economy creates serious problems by destroying the traditional fabric of the rural economy : the village group ; the family ; the old forms of land tenure and all the customs and standards that supported life within the traditional framework.

Economic Development for Africa South of the Sahara

In the final analysis, it is these human factors emerging from the political, cultural, and social conflicts of the Federation which have retarded economic growth, possibly more than any other factor. It is the pressure of the politically dominant European minority, actively pursuing an economically orthodox development policy which, paradoxically, creates the country's grave social and political problems and which thereby retards overall economic development. This constitutes the Federation's major development handicap.

While European skills, initiative, techniques, capital, and economic drive have been the chief stimulants of growth in the past — while they have been the key elements leading to the present high level of economic development in the Federation — they are no longer sufficient, *in themselves*, to stimulate greater economic development in the future. They are necessary, and indeed vital ; but until the politically dominant European minority shares their fruits with the African majority, on a basis of greater equality for all, development will continue to be retarded and fitful.

The Federation exhibits several features which highlight the necessity of European settlement in the country. The African way of life is still basically traditional, with the great majority of Africans still active participants in the subsistence economy, but the impact of the European way of life has had shattering consequences for the traditional pattern of existence. Except, for example, for the Republic of South Africa the transformation and modification by the subsistence economy has proceeded further in the Federation than anywhere else in Africa.

The process of change has developed most rapidly in the last decade and has been based chiefly on the growth of agricultural and mineral exports engineered with European skills, capital, and techniques coupled with African labour. And it is precisely here — namely in the disintegration and decay of the traditional economy and the channelling of its resources into the modern economy — that the crux of the country's major development problems lies.

Concomitant with this change has been the emergence of African political nationalism and the drive to secure a large share of political control over the destinies of the federal area. Thus, in addition to what might be called the 'normal' structural development problems common to most under-developed African countries, the Federation grapples with development problems flowing directly from the political conflict, problems which are aggravated by the racial composition and political imbalance of the country's population. To this important extent, the Federation's development problems are unique in tropical Africa.

The consequences for economic development which will flow from this most dynamic of all 'variables' are impossible to predict with any degree of precision. As and when Africans assume political control of each territory, however, the African governments will still be forced to work within the physical limitations imposed by each territory's resource base and economic potential. African political independence will not, of itself, guarantee economic development. Indeed, for a period, economic development might well be retarded by the attainment of independence. The most important task will still be the expansion of the cash economy. With the advent of independence this problem will assume even greater importance, since Africans will feel freer to press for a more rapid reorganization of social and economic life, and indeed, demand that reorganization.

The Federation, then, faces a most complex set of development problems. Exacerbating the purely objective economic problems — more or less common to all countries of tropical Africa — are the problems arising from the fluid nature of the political upheaval the country is experiencing and will continue to experience for many years ahead. The solution to the many-faceted economic development problems confronting the Federation and its constituent territories lies largely with the European minority recognizing that the awakening will of the Africans is the basically significant factor for the future. Until Africans are able to assume much more of the direction and control of the speed of political and social advance, economic advance will continue to be depressed and unpromising, and may only be resuscitated when Europeans and Africans learn to work together for the common weal.

II. THE RATE OF ECONOMIC GROWTH

The Federation of Rhodesia and Nyasaland was created as a new and separate nation on September 3, 1953. The total area of the new state is some 486,000 square miles, equivalent to about one-sixth of the area of the United States of America. Three-fifths of the total area is accounted for by Northern Rhodesia, three-tenths by Southern Rhodesia, and only about one-tenth by Nyasaland. In the first few years after its establishment the fledgling state achieved a rate of economic growth which, whether measured in money or real terms, was extremely rapid. At the outset, however, it should be emphasized that the very rapid rate of economic expansion was not due simply to the creation of the Federal state. It was the cornerstone of the Monckton Commission's assessment of the economic advantages which flow directly from Federation that the present Federal structure itself was directly responsible for the rapidity of the country's economic growth.[1]

This superficial view of the country's economic development will be discussed later. In the meantime, it should be borne in mind that the main impetus to rapid development was supplied basically by the operation of two conjoint economic forces : viz. the increase in the volume and value of the country's exports and the high rate of investment, financed largely by the inflow of considerable external investment funds. Luck, too, played its part in securing rapid growth of the domestic product. The price of copper, the country's major export, for example, as a consequence of favourable external market conditions reached the unusually high average price of £267 per ton in the seven-year period, 1953–9, compared with £196 per ton in the preceding seven-year period.

That the primary influences in the growth of the economy have been the expansion of exports and the heavy injection of investment capital is revealed by the following table.

TABLE 1

INDICES OF SELECTED ECONOMIC INDICATORS

Year	Export of Goods and Services		Gross Investment		Export plus Investment	GDP in Money Economy	
	Value	Volume	Value	Volume	Value	Value	Volume
1954	100·0	100·0	100·0	100·0	100·0	100·0	100·0
1955	85·8	110·2	127·0	131·2	117·2	117·3	103·4
1956	95·8	115·6	161·7	175·2	135·2	134·7	119·2
1957	110·9	106·1	161·2	180·7	130·7	131·9	125·2
1958	113·5	96·1	132·8	155·8	115·8	130·2	126·5
1959	131·9	123·6	129·4	148·6	131·7	150·8	138·8

It is not surprising in an under-developed economy like the Federation's that the value and volume of exports, together with investment, should be the dominating influences and the main engines of growth. Even in 1958 when both these forces were considerably depressed, exports accounted for roughly 44 per cent of GDP, measured at current prices, while investment was equivalent to about 30 per cent of GDP. An examination, therefore, of the future prospects for these forces will provide the best indication of future rates of growth and, thus, some inkling of the typical development

[1] See *Report of the Advisory Commission on the Review of the Constitution of Rhodesia and Nyasaland*, Cmnd. 1148, Oct. 1960, chap. 4.

problems which lie ahead for the Federation and which it shares with many other African countries.

Over the period 1954–9 the total increase of GNP in the money economy was 60 per cent (38 per cent in real terms), equivalent to an annual rate of increase of 6 per cent. This rate of growth reflects favourably on the productive capacity of the Federation's economy, but it does not indicate accurately the increase in economic 'welfare' of the population as a whole. A much more illuminating statistic is the increase in national income per head which, in real terms, was no more than 3 per cent per annum. This mediocre rate of increase left the Federation, for example, with a *per capita* income at the end of 1960 of £55, considerably below the Republic of South Africa and even lower, than Ghana's.

Table 1 also shows that the economy's pace of development has been of a spasmodic, erratic character. 1954–6 was a period of substantial growth, but in 1957–8 the impetus was lost and a much slower rate of growth was experienced ; the value of GDP in the money economy fell by $3\frac{1}{2}$ per cent while showing only a slight increase in volume. In 1959, however, GDP rose significantly because of favourable 'windfall' external conditions in the shape of increased demand for, and the high price of, copper exports. Herein lies one of the key economic questions from the point of view of the future problems of economic growth and development of the Federation. Do these developments indicate no more than a temporary decline in expansion or do they presage a shift to a permanently lower level of expansion ?

In my view, this marked slowing-down in the rate of growth of the economy during the last few years has been caused, not solely by the operation of short-lived factors, but rather by the inevitable operation of more long-lived fundamental economic forces, clashing with social and political problems largely ignored by those responsible for guiding development. The forces which were chiefly responsible for imparting thrust to the economy are losing their momentum, and, consequently, it seems probable that the Federation's future economic growth over the coming decade — to look no further ahead — is likely to be on a much lower level than in earlier years.

Fundamentally, the reasons why it is to be expected that the Federation's future rate of growth is likely to be much less spectacular than in its earlier years, hinge around the prospects for growth in capital investment and the likely future rate of increase in exports. The main concern lies with the outlook for capital investment.

At the present stage of its economic development the Federation necessarily relies to a considerable degree on external sources for its supply of capital. The Federation has not reached, or even nearly reached, the 'take-off' stage into self-sustaining economic growth. Its domestically generated earnings are insufficient to maintain an adequate rate of domestic capital formation. Furthermore, the future outlook promises little hope that domestic savings can be increased sufficiently to replace the decline in external capital inflow which has occurred during the last two years. The Monckton Commission does not seem to have appreciated this fact, for it erroneously concluded that

'the rising percentage of gross investment financed from domestic savings' has 'strengthened the Federation's capacity to increase and sustain its economic growth and made it less dependent on external capital'.[1]

An analysis of the source and use of capital funds in the period 1954–9 is given in Table 2 below.

TABLE 2

SOURCE AND USE OF CAPITAL FUNDS, 1954–9

Source of Finance		Use of Capital	
	%		%
Savings			
Government and statutory bodies	19·9	Central and Local Government statutory bodies	24·4
Companies	12·9	Transport	5·6
Persons, etc.	18·7	Electricity	8·1
Depreciation	20·7	Other	2·0
Total domestic savings	72·2		—— 15·7
Net Borrowings Abroad		Business	
Official	9·5	Mines	15·8
Private	16·6	Other	44·1
Net drawing on reserves	1·7		—— 59·9
Total	27·8		
Total available finance	100·0	Total gross capital formation	100·0

It will be seen from this table that a substantial proportion of 'domestically created savings' has been provided by a surplus of

[1] See *Report of the Advisory Commission on the Review of the Constitution of Rhodesia and Nyasaland*, Cmnd. 1148, Oct. 1960, Chap. 4. p. 24. Even if the official figures are taken at their face value they do not bear out this conclusion. As shown below, the considerable annual variation casts doubt on the Commission's assump-

government and local authorities' incomes over current expenditure. Now that taxation (direct and indirect) has been increased — with detrimental effects on other forms of savings and on capital inflow — there exist only limited prospects of any substantial increases in the public sector's source of income.

This presents a serious problem for the future since a rapid rise in investment on such items as education, health, social services generally, and social investment as a whole, is almost certain to occur for political and social reasons, if for no other. External debt-servicing in the future will also absorb a larger 'chunk' of investment expenditure than in the past. Thus, it seems likely that the amount of capital formation created by the public sector, in the future, is likely to decline as the available sources of finance created out of budget surpluses diminish, unless there are swingeing increases in taxation, or governmental resort to inflationary financial measures.

Until recently, personal savings have shown a tendency to rise, although their magnitude is still small in relation to overall capital requirements. Concomitant, however, with the present unsettled political climate, personal savings have dropped off considerably. Furthermore, it is legitimate to assume that the rate of 'domestic savings' will continue to fall. As an inevitable by-product of the increasing participation of Africans in the machinery of government, it may be assumed that a substantial redistribution of income between the racial groups is likely to occur. Such a redistribution of income is both politically and economically desirable, but such action will necessarily lead to a reduction in the aggregate savings propensities of the community.

Although business savings constitute a substantial source, and have amounted to as much as 33 per cent of capital funds available, their future outlook is also unpromising. Total business earnings may be expected to grow with the expansion of the economy, but it does not follow that the margin of available savings will increase proportionately, since, almost certainly, wage-costs as well as taxation will be bound to rise. Furthermore, it is to be expected that aggregate African incomes (in money and real terms) will rise considerably faster than aggregate non-African incomes. For these

tion of a rising percentage of domestically financed investment. Moreover, it is clear that annual changes in 'domestic savings' are caused chiefly by variations in the externally held balances of foreign-owned subsidiary companies.

Total Domestic Savings as a Percentage
of Gross Capital Formation

	%			%
1954	84	1957		54
1955	86	1958		55
1956	76	1959		86

reasons it may be concluded that the aggregate propensity to save in the community is unlikely to rise and may well decline as time goes on.

III. THE PROSPECTS FOR THE CONTINUED INFLOW OF CAPITAL

This prospect would be less disturbing if the country had reasonable expectations of attracting, in the future, the same large volume of external capital it has succeeded in obtaining in the past. But this prospect is highly unlikely. The whole investment environment of Africa has changed for the worse. In world capital markets, Africa, with few exceptions, is regarded as a dubious investment risk.

Before Federation, investment prospects in the Rhodesias had attracted overseas investors. The great Northern Rhodesian copper deposits were developed in this period. In Southern Rhodesia, with the possibility of Federation in the air, foreign investors took an active interest in industrial investment and in the real-estate market. The agricultural sector, especially investment in tobacco production, also attracted considerable attention.

When the Federation was established the conjuncture for foreign investment was decidedly favourable. The Federation held out the promise of political stability and racial harmony. Unfortunately, the high hopes held for peaceful political evolution in the Federation have been dashed. Today, the country faces a widespread feeling of uncertainty, which has led to a sharp contraction in the inflow of capital. In the last year capital seepage of considerable magnitude has occurred and, during the last quarter of 1960, threatened to become a flood. To halt the outflow, exchange control was imposed in February 1961 with the aim of preventing the export of 'resident' companies and individual funds to safer areas. Thus, although the country enjoyed a rising trend in export earnings and healthy trade balances, its foreign reserves were heavily eroded as political unrest developed. This outflow of capital should be regarded fundamentally as an expression of decreasing confidence in the country's immediate prospects and, dispassionately viewed, there is little prospect of the situation improving without fundamental changes occurring in the political arena.

In one major field of past investment, namely, property development, which has been the magnet for disproportionate amounts of developmental capital — especially in Salisbury, the capital city — the future outlook is also discouraging. Much of this development has been financed by external capital from Britain. The incentive has usually been twofold : a lucrative investment venture with expectations of capital appreciation, and the chance to escape high United Kingdom taxes and death duties. The empty office blocks of Salisbury are a mute testimony to this type of 'milk bar' economy, and a monument to mismanaged investment priorities. The real-estate boom has been seriously deflated by the excess supply of accommodation coupled with a sharp drop in immigration and a sharp increase in emigration. Moreover, British taxes have been steadily reduced and the opportunities for more fruitful investment elsewhere in the world have improved.

Industrial development, however, might still prove capable of attracting further investment funds from external sources after the present monetary controls are abolished. It is unfortunately true that the imposition of exchange control not only tends to act as a psychological deterrent to new investment but it also restrains domestic funds from fleeing to 'greener pastures'. If and when the present exchange controls are lifted, and if the economy is to be jerked out of the depression into which it has been sliding, the private investor might be induced to re-enter the industrial sector of the economy. In this area the omens appear fairly propitious. With the expansion of the domestic market and, in particular, the African market — where by 1965 total African purchasing power will probably exceed total European purchasing power — the prospects for a growing local manufacturing industry will certainly be enhanced.

To be successful the output of locally based manufacturing industries must be able to compete in price and quality with imported articles. Although local industry has the advantage of a relatively cheap labour supply, this advantage is often outweighed by the adverse factors of distance, poor communications, and the relative smallness of the extent of the market. Thus, it seems likely that the prospects for the eventual rapid expansion of local industry — which would help to regenerate the inflow of external capital — depend on government acceptance of a greatly increased protective policy, even at the cost of adding still further to development problems by increasing production costs and reducing the country's ability to export.

Until 1960 the Federation had enjoyed remarkable success in obtaining official capital from abroad — both from international organizations and from public issues on foreign capital markets. The past record has been dominated by the giant Kariba Hydro-Electric Scheme, for which some £45·6 million was raised from the

International Bank, the Colonial Development Corporation, and other similar organizations. This sum represented a large commitment : of the total loans granted to African countries by the International Bank, the Federation has received a stimulating 36 per cent of the total ; of the CDC's total loans and investments in African countries, 41 per cent has gone to the Federation. Expenditure of this magnitude has been of enormous value, but in view of the now lengthy queue of potential borrowers in Africa it is doubtful, to say the least, whether the Federation will continue to receive such 'favourite-son' treatment in the future. It seems certain that the supply of institutional capital in the next decade will be on a much lower scale than in the past.

The Monckton Commission, in discussing the Federation's need for capital inflow in the future, estimated that

> to maintain the impetus of recent years the Federal Government must be able to raise regularly in the London market or in other overseas capital markets sums of the order of £10 million a year.[1]

This goal has been well within the Federation's capacity in the past. From 1954 to March 1959 a total of £42 million was raised by public issues abroad. Since that date no additional external public issues have been possible. Ability to raise large sums abroad depends not only on the borrower's credit-worthiness, a term which embraces financial and economic considerations, but also on general political conditions prevailing in the country. Until, therefore, the present political difficulties have been resolved, it is unrealistic to assume that it will be possible for the Federation to attain the Monckton target.

IV. THE PROBLEM OF DEBT REPAYMENT

A more substantial reason, however, exists for expecting a reduced net inflow of official capital in the years ahead. Previously borrowed capital must be repaid and the time is fast approaching when the Federation's debt repayments will begin to assume heavy proportions. The following table illustrates the magnitude of the problem.

It will be noted that by 1966 the Federation will be required to find an average of about £10 million per year for repaying its external debt (in addition to which almost 20 per cent of the so-called internal debt is held by foreigners). With this commitment, even if successful in borrowing as much on overseas capital markets in the future

[1] See *Report of the Advisory Commission on the Review of the Constitution of Rhodesia and Nyasaland*, Cmnd. 1148, Oct. 1960, p. 96.

as it has done in the past, the Federation will be getting little or no new capital — new borrowings will be consumed by the repayment of maturing debts. In addition to this debt repayment burden, there is a growing weight of interest payments, which even with the present level of national debt, absorbs approximately 25 per cent of the Federal Government's revenue.

TABLE 3

AMOUNT OF NATIONAL DEBT * DUE FOR REPAYMENT †

Period	Internal ‡	External	Total
1960–5	£14,914,207	£15,110,659	£30,024,866
1966–70	9,263,912	46,589,263	55,853,175
1971–5	25,134,414	29,619,297	54,753,711
1976–80	45,030,218	23,122,881	68,153,099

* As at end — 1959. Figures are gross ; no allowance made for Sinking Fund operations.
† Roughly 20 per cent of internal debt is held externally.
‡ At last date of payment.

Thus, for these reasons it seems certain that capital investment, whether from external or internal sources, is likely to be on a much lower level in the future, which will result in a lower rate of economic expansion unless the lost momentum is compensated for by increases in other sectors of the economy.

V. THE PROSPECTS FOR EXPORTS

The most promising avenue is from an increase in exports. The Federation's economic expansion in the past has been generated by the twin determinants of expanding exports and the highly favourable rate of foreign capital investment. The prospects for the latter are gloomy : hence, the burden thrown on income derived from exports will be considerably increased.

It is impossible to predict accurately the future level of exports, especially for a raw-material producing economy ; but it would be less than prudent to expect a rate of growth of the expansion of exports any greater than was achieved in the relatively favourable conditions of the period 1954–60.

The Federation's export trade is dependent on the sale of copper, gold, asbestos, chrome, lead and zinc, and tobacco to the industrialized countries of Europe and North America, which usually absorb some 80 per cent of the country's exports. Future export prospects for most of these commodities are fairly bright. Only tobacco, which accounts for roughly 15 per cent of export sales, appears to face a slower increase in demand. From the demand side it seems likely that the future course of the volume of the Federation's exports should be relatively favourable. As regards values it is reasonable to assume that average prices realized in the next decades will be roughly the same as in 1960. This implies for the country's two main exports, copper and tobacco, average prices of approximately £240 per ton and 30d. per lb., prices which are generally regarded as 'normal' in the respective industries. It is, furthermore, unlikely during the next decades that the export prices of these commodities will fluctuate so wildly as in the last five years, which promises to make for more stability in the Federation's export trade.

On the supply side, however, physical limitations, especially labour scarcity in the agricultural sector, might exercise a dampening influence in the future. Finally, the composition of the Federation's export trade might be widened as new mineral deposits, which include iron, bauxite, and nickel, are exploited. All in all, it seems reasonable to expect 3 per cent as the minimum annual rate of increase in the Federation's total exports, measured in constant prices, which would approximate the rate achieved in the period 1954-7. Thus, then, although the future rate of increase in exports may be at least as high as the average of the past few years, exports will probably not provide the additional required thrust to the economy to replace the diminished momentum occasioned by the depressed prospects for capital investment.

VI. THE IMPLICATIONS FOR FUTURE GROWTH

Many important consequences and a large number of difficult economic problems flow from this forecast of a lower rate of increase in the economic development of the Federation. Two aspects of these problems, namely, the employment question and the income redistribution question are amongst the thorniest and most deserving of closer examination.

The Federation's population is growing apace. The present total population of 8·4 million is likely to reach 9·5 million in 1965 and be fairly close to 11 million by 1970. The African population may be expected to reach 9·1 million by 1965 and over 10 million by 1970. Figures relating to present total employment (including the subsistence sector) are uncertain ; but, ignoring the subsistence sector, it may be assumed that the total number of Africans in paid employment in 1960 was approximately 1·1 million, or roughly 50 per cent of the total number of African adult males. Even if this very low ratio does not increase in the years ahead, there will be about 175,000–180,000 Africans increasing the supply of African labour between 1961 and 1965.

It may well be that this figure seriously underestimates the magnitude of the employment problem. For, in addition to those in employment, there are many thousands more unemployed and active job-seekers. The extent of African unemployment has, furthermore, become even more serious during this last year as the general economic plight of the economy has weakened.

The problem, then, of finding jobs for the rapidly expanding African urban population will become even more serious in the future, since, as has been demonstrated above, the rate of general economic progress will probably be at a lower rate than in the past.

Ways and means of ameliorating this situation are being explored along many different paths. The most generally favoured course is to provide increased employment opportunities via policies designed to stimulate industrial development.

It is, however, unrealistic to place too much emphasis on manufacturing industry as the means for coping with this problem. For example, between 1954 and 1960 the numbers employed in manufacturing rose from 127,000 to 144,000, an annual increase of only 2 per cent. During the same period, the net output of manufacturing industry rose from £25·7 million to £51·9 million, an annual increase of over 12 per cent, and Gross Fixed Capital Formation totalled £100 million. On this basis, then, an absorption of a further 50,000 Africans into manufacturing would involve a rise in industrial output of over 200 per cent and an investment of nearly £300 million. Thus, as a short-term solution to the Federation's unemployment problems, manufacturing industry will be of only minimal assistance.

Governmental preference, furthermore, to implement rapid industrial growth is to rely largely on tariff protection as the main instrument. While this preference is easily understandable, it does not seem to be widely appreciated that such a policy is two-edged. In a country like the Federation, possessing few natural advantages favouring industrialization, with poor internal and external communications, a tariff wall, to be successful, would have to be both wide and high. A real dilemma exists here. Accepting the need to stimulate rapid industrial growth, must protection be discarded as a weapon to achieve the desired ends? There is no clear and satisfactory answer to the question : the most that can be asked is that general recognition be given to the fact that the implementation of such a policy necessarily involves a cost which will have to be borne subsequently by the community in the form of higher prices.

A policy, however, of actively promoting the growth of secondary industry is not certain of success in solving the urban African unemployment problem. Income redistribution is becoming, and will become, a more potent factor in the total situation. A considerable redistribution of income between European and African is likely to take place in the coming decade and so precipitate more serious problems, particularly in the social and political fields.

It is likely that this redistribution of income will occur from two different directions. On the one hand, increased African employment with the accelerating shift of Africans out of the subsistence economy to the cash economy, is one major cause. On the other hand, increasing educational standards, the provision of more and different kinds of educational facilities, and the acquisition of industrial skills, are all enabling Africans to demand higher wages. A supplementary reason is the advance of African trade unions and the consequent strengthening of their bargaining positions. These developments are operating with increasing effect to raise the share of the national income accruing to Africans. Past evidence shows that the share of national income earned by Africans has been rising slightly faster than the national income itself — implying a degree of income redistribution. This trend will probably continue and, even though the national income will probably rise more slowly in the future, an ever-increasing share will tend to go to African income earners.

There is evidence, too, that total European money incomes have been rising more slowly and might even cease rising in the future, if the rate of overall economic growth continues to fall off sharply. In real terms it seems likely that the European section of the community will suffer not only a relative decline, but probably an absolute fall in its share of national income. This surprising conclusion raises many serious questions. In the main, this result is likely to occur via a rise in the price of consumer goods which will be an inevitable consequence of the implementation of protection policies designed to increase African employment. The magnitude of European purchasing power and the pattern of European expenditure mean that the impact of higher prices will fall more heavily on European than on African incomes.

In addition, the expectation that aggregate European real income in the future is likely to show a relative decrease is strengthened by the likelihood that the level of taxation will have to rise to meet the additional expenditure on social services and to maintain development expenditure, and that the major source of revenue for these developments will necessarily have to be the higher income group. It can be held that such a readjustment of relative monetary and real income levels between the main racial groups is desirable. Equally, it can be held that such a realignment is undesirable. Either way the process raises serious problems.

The European group is not prepared to stand by helplessly in the face of an erosion of its income. Various European sectional interests vigorously propound policies aimed at maintaining European employment and incomes, such as 'the rate for the job'. It is a quixotic fact, moreover, that such a policy directly contributes to the general reduction in European real incomes via the raising of costs. It can be expected, furthermore, that the interested parties will strive with all the power at their command to resist what seems to be an attack on their standard of living. In the nature of things, attention will be on money incomes : meanwhile, the relentless erosion of European real incomes will continue.

VII. THE CONTRIBUTION OF FEDERATION TO DEVELOPMENT

It will now be appropriate to consider the effects which Federation has had on the development problems of the area. This question has many facets. I should make it clear that I am in full agreement with the maintenance of a larger political and economic entity in Central Africa. There can be no doubt from an economic viewpoint that such an enlarged unit has many economic advantages, not least in its enhanced ability to raise overseas finance. A wider market for the products of local industry is another major advantage and I would hesitate to recommend the reversion to separate territorial tariff barriers.

Nevertheless, in what follows it will be seen that I criticize, rather harshly, the actual form which Federation has taken, because it seems to me that the current form of federation has been an economic liability and magnified the difficult development problems confronting the area as a whole. To justify this criticism I propose to examine, first, the growth of personal incomes of European and Africans, and then review the industrial and commercial background against which these incomes were earned.

The table shows an increase of 8 per cent in European incomes between 1954 and 1960 while African incomes increased by 33 per cent. When expressed in money terms these rates are not unusually high. The rate, while encouraging in itself, means, of course, very little in absolute terms since the increase is calculated on such a small base. It is significant, furthermore, that there has been no meaningful increase in the proportion of cash incomes to total African incomes, which points to the conclusion that there has been

TABLE 4

PERSONAL INCOMES PER HEAD IN THE FEDERATION

	1954	1955	1956	1957	1958	1959	1960
	£	£	£	£	£	£	£
Europeans	552	586	616	625	596	586	600
Africans Cash Subsistence	10 8	11 8	12 9	13 9	13 9	13 11	14 10
Africans Total	18	19	21	22	22	24	24

little progress in the aggregate economic advancement of the African section of the population.

Recent welcome developments in African job advancement on the railways and copper mines might seem to indicate that the future rate of increase in the incomes of African wage earners will be more rapid. But this is doubtful. Although a relatively highly paid African *élite* labour force is emerging and earning remuneration comparable with Europeans, this has had little impact on the bulk of the African labour force. Increase in real income can only be achieved through productivity increase, while the latter is dependent on a rise in the value of production per head of the employed population. What are the prospects for this development?

In primary industry the two main products — copper in Northern

TABLE 5

EXPORTS OF COPPER AND TOBACCO

	Copper		Tobacco
	000 tons	£ million	million lb.
1955	383	117	122
1956	429	121	209
1957	466	89	180
1958	420	71	194
1959	600	120	228
1960	...	122	242

Rhodesia and tobacco in Southern Rhodesia — account for the bulk of the area's economic activity and are the chief items in its exports. Being export products their value is dependent upon demand and supply conditions in world markets. This applies particularly to copper ; the average flue-cured tobacco price having remained fairly stable between 35d.-40d. per pound in the last few years.

The copper price now seems to have stabilized at around £220-£230 per ton. The amount which the market can absorb limits the supply which the Northern Rhodesian mines can profitably produce and, while this limit may rise as time goes on, it is unlikely to rise sufficiently to permit production to expand at rates enjoyed in the late 1950s. Tobacco production has expanded steadily, but for technical and marketing reasons it is held that the limit is around 230 million lb.

Over the whole field of primary industry the economic effect of Federation has been slight. It has had no important effect on the investment and production policies of the mining houses, though it may have helped somewhat to raise the output of tobacco farmers, who are mainly concentrated in Southern Rhodesia.

It is significant to note also that primary industry absorbs the major part of the African labour force. In Southern Rhodesia there are about 640,000 Africans in employment, of whom just over two-thirds are employed in industry. The rest are employed in commerce and domestic service. Of the industrial labour force, 294,000 are employed in European agriculture and in mining, totalling 46 per cent in primary industry.

Secondary industry in the Federation has made considerable progress in recent years. Net output, for example, increased from £25·7 million in 1954 to £51·9 in 1959–60, an annual increase of over 12 per cent compound. Of greater interest, however, is the territorial distribution of secondary industry. Of the total output, 76 per cent was produced in Southern Rhodesia, 20 per cent in Northern Rhodesia, and 4 per cent in Nyasaland. This violently skewed distribution of manufacturing industry cannot be explained in purely economic terms when it is borne in mind that the populations of each territory are roughly equal ; that the bulk of the secondary industry is devoted to the production of consumer goods ; and that, with the exception of grains, tobacco, and dairy products, nearly all the raw materials used by manufacturers have to be imported.

The relative backwardness of Northern Rhodesia's (especially the Copperbelt's) industrial development is significant in this regard. The Copperbelt is a compact area containing about 40,000 Europeans and 300,000 Africans (cf. Salisbury : 82,000 Europeans and 190,000 Africans) with the highest average income of any community in the Federation. The total wages bill of the mines alone totals some £20 million per annum and yet the whole of Northern Rhodesia produces only about £16½ millions gross of manufactured goods.

These facts are striking, for they illustrate the magnitude and gravity of the problem which flows directly from the existing political relationship between the three territories. This relationship has tended to distort the pattern of territorial industrial development in favour of Southern Rhodesia, and disrupt the optimum allocation of the country's resources. These problems arise principally from Southern Rhodesia's pre-eminent position, achieved by virtue of the constitutional provisions that give it representation in the Federal Assembly out of all proportion to the relative size of its population. Thus, the national problem of the location of industry and territorial industrial development has been bedevilled by the conflict between the optimum allocation of resources and the politically encouraged pattern of the distribution of manufacturing industry.

It has been strongly argued by pro-federationists that the fact of federation has created new opportunities for employment. In facilitating the transition from a subsistence-type economy to a cash economy, secondary industry has a vital rôle to play, in that it can potentially provide greater rewards than those to be earned in the subsistence economy. Yet secondary industry in the Federation has not fulfilled this rôle to any significant extent. It is a remarkable fact that, despite their very different levels of economic development, almost the same proportion of the African population in each territory is in paid employment. This can be seen in the following table.

TABLE 6

AFRICANS IN EMPLOYMENT, 1957-8

	Southern Rhodesia	Northern Rhodesia	Nyasaland
Number employed (000's)	300	285	300
Percentage of total population	11	12	11
Percentage employed in home territory	100	77	33

Thus, neither Northern Rhodesia nor Nyasaland is able to provide employment for all who seek work. Nyasaland, where about two-thirds of all job-seekers are forced to migrate to Southern Rhodesia or the Republic of South Africa, is in an especially serious position. No doubt this problem would still exist even if the territories had remained separate political entities, but it is hard to imagine that the degree to which it exists under federation would still be so serious. In the case of Northern Rhodesia normal economic forces alone would have opened up considerable development opportunities which, in the event, have accrued to Southern Rhodesia's benefit. In Nyasaland special financial assistance is, in any case, necessary and would probably have been forthcoming from the United Kingdom Government.[1] That approximately 200,000 Africans from Nyasaland are forced to seek work outside their own territory — 50,000 of them outside the Federation — is an indication of how little has been done by the Federal planners to develop alternative job opportunities in Nyasaland.

In terms of development projects in Africa, the Kariba Hydro-Electric Scheme occupies a unique place. As a feat of engineering — despite the unfortunate necessity to build a prop to the dam-wall — it stands supreme. In the Federation itself the scheme has a vital economic and political significance. And yet it is open to question as to whether it is a sound economic enterprise. Two questions must be answered before doubts about its value can be set at rest. Will it prove an economic asset and contribute significantly to the solution of the Federation's economic problems ; and will it benefit the whole Federation ?

Usually, the answer to the first question is a resounding 'Yes!' supplemented by references to its beneficial effects on industrial development. This answer is difficult to understand since the cost of power averages only some $1\frac{1}{2}$ to 2 per cent of the total costs of manufacturing industry. In addition, the availability of power plays only a minor rôle in the location of industry. Mining, however, is another matter, since here power costs may represent as much as 10 per cent of total costs of production, but there are only mines where there are minerals.

An alternative justification is to point to the rate of growth of power consumption. In the Federation, the rate of growth has been such as to indicate that increased supplies of power were needed, but not necessarily on the scale of Kariba. The published scale of charges is unlikely to encourage industry since it will be seven years or more before the lower tariff becomes operative. Thus, serious grounds exist for doubting the worthwhileness of the Kariba Scheme as a necessary investment to encourage economic development in the Federation.

[1] From 1953 to 1957 Colonial Development and Welfare grants totalled some £2·4 million compared with £1·8 million in 1949–52. See *Report on an Economic Survey of Nyasaland*, 1959, C.Fed. 132, p. 65.

The second question can only be answered negatively. Kariba power will be supplied only to Southern Rhodesia, Lusaka, and the Copperbelt centres of Northern Rhodesia, and not at all to Nyasaland. It is for these reasons that one doubts whether the Kariba Scheme will be the 'open Sesame' to industrial expansion which its advocates claim. If it is not, then its development has done a positive disservice to the economy in diverting attention and resources away from more urgent economic priorities.

The real cost of the Kariba Scheme is the opportunity cost of development projects forgone elsewhere in the economy. The most significant loss here has been in the field of transport. Development of this section of the infrastructure is woefully inadequate. The road system between the territories has been badly neglected. The roads from Salisbury to Blantyre, from Lusaka to Zomba, and the Great North Road from Kapiri Mposhi to Tunduma, the Federation's only link with East Africa, are in a parlous state.

The railway network is much more efficient, but since 1953, when the Federal Government assumed control over Rhodesia Railways, there have been no major extensions to the system, except the completion in August 1955 of the line from Bannockburn in Southern Rhodesia to the Mozambique border, which was initiated by the Southern Rhodesian Government. Of the railway system's total route mileage of 2,628 miles, with the exception mentioned above, the total mileage was completed by 1932. Although Lord Lugard's view that 'the material development of Africa may be summed up in one word — transport'[1] may be an over-statement there can be little doubt that improved and more extensive railway links are fundamental to development in the Federation. Considerable investment has been carried out on improved methods of operation, but these have still to be reflected in lower costs or significantly faster services. Goods, for example, travelling from Salisbury to Ndola must still travel 1,100 miles via Bulawayo and Livingstone, as they did half a century ago, although the road journey is only 500 miles.

Thus, for the above general reasons it is open to serious doubt whether Federation has contributed towards the solution of the area's major economic problems. Railway development played a key rôle in the expansion of the U.S.A., the U.S.S.R., Canada, and Australia and there is no reason to suppose that the rôle would have been very different in Central Africa. Yet this vital work has gone by default. When the Salisbury–Lourenço Marques railway was constructed, Southern Rhodesia was relatively well supplied with a

[1] Sir F. D. Lugard, *The Dual Mandate in Tropical Africa*, Edinburgh, Blackwood, 1922, p. 5.

transport network. The advent of Federation — with political control vested in Southern Rhodesia — has diverted resources which could have been applied to transport needs generally in Northern Rhodesia and Nyasaland, to a project whose chief benefit is to Southern Rhodesia — Kariba. By neglecting to develop its transport system the Federation has failed to lay that solid base on which sound industrial growth can hope to rise.

VIII. CONCLUSIONS

Paternalistic relationships do not produce the type of environment in which a market economy can best flourish.[1]

We have seen above that the Federation is experiencing a rapid economic transformation, the impact of which is being felt, to a greater or lesser degree, by every inhabitant of the area. The old forms of economic production, distribution, and exchange are being ruthlessly modified and transformed in a relatively short space of time.

The main lesson emerging from this violent clash of the old and the new is to appreciate that this process of change may be best assimilated to the country's ultimate advantage, if the process of innovation and adaptation moves in such a way that African interests and institutions are not wholly destroyed.

The danger of the moment is that . . . for lack of the necessary change in native methods, industry after the European model may grow faster and more generally than is in the ultimate interests of the country.[2]

Although written more than a quarter of a century ago this view is as apposite today as it was then.

The problems facing the Federation's economy are many. Some of these problems are typical of any under-developed economy, some have a purely African cast and some are but manifestations of the problems which arise from attempting to control, co-ordinate, and direct an economy growing at a most rapid pace.

The most difficult problem of all, however, is that of developing successfully the type of society in which there is equality and justice for all black, brown, and white men in the country. It may well be asked if it is possible to control and direct the growth of the society and the economy towards this goal. In answering this question

[1] W. J. Barber, *Dollar Investment in Central Africa*, New Commonwealth, v. 31 (April 30, 1956), p. 212.   [2] Robinson, *op. cit.* p. 204.

value-judgments must inevitably play a considerable part. In the Federation, the evidence indicates that the major aim of European policy has been to effect the most rapid rate of economic growth possible in the European-controlled sector of the economy. This has carried the corollary that it has been deemed necessary to intervene with this process on as few occasions as possible. From the standpoint of orthodox economic theory this form of development may be judged to be sound and normal.

But I suspect that the Federation's main problems have been exacerbated by allocating and encouraging public investment in those projects which seem to yield the highest short-run returns. Such a policy has flowed from a tragic misreading of the needs of the area, a misconception by the Federal planners of the most effective way to cope with the process of change. Dedicated in its Constitution to the concept of racial partnership in the political and economic spheres, the Federal planners might well have produced better 'welfare' results if they had applied criteria consonant with these aims, not criteria wholly consonant with the dictates of orthodox economic arguments. When viewed in this light, the problems of the Federation assume a different and more vital significance.

Some writers on the Federation's affairs have been all too ready to assume, uncritically, that the Federal planners have deliberately set out to achieve the highest growth rate for European interests only, and that the goal of economic and political partnership has been sheer hypocrisy. This is, I feel, a much too shallow and naïve conclusion. Granted that there is an element of truth in this approach, it may well be, however, that, dominated by the world-wide post-war drive for rapid economic growth, the politicians and the civil servants have — like their counterparts in Western Europe and the U.S.A. — hesitated to take any steps that might appear to inhibit the greatest possible increase in productivity in those sectors of the economy most obviously susceptible of rapid growth. Surrounded by poverty on all sides, convinced that 'what is right for Europe and the U.S.A. is *a fortiori* right for a much poorer country like the Federation', it is an understandable error that economic policy should have been oriented towards the almost total exclusion of any appreciation of the social and political problems that such a policy might create.

We cannot argue against this policy only by an appeal to logic. It is partially a matter of value-judgments as to whether problems — other than purely economic — do not demand more attention. In the Federation the die has been cast ; it is now of paramount importance that a re-orientation of policy takes place. That 'man does not live by bread alone' has not been sufficiently recognized in the Federation.

The problems arising from rapid economic development will be the more easily coped with in the years ahead if those responsible for guiding economic development realize the full consequences of economic change for the political and social life of the country. The most effective future economic policy may be regarded as the one which, while vigorously tackling the problem of raising income per head, at the same time consciously attempts to ameliorate the almost intractable problems of a political, social, or racial nature that inevitably arise.

Such a policy entails a deliberate reshuffling of priorities, a recognition that the goals of economic policy are not necessarily only economic in character, and a national awareness that the structural economic problems presently confronting the country are of far less importance and are far outweighed by the political, social, and racial problems that a purely economically orthodox development policy engenders. It must be recognized that policy decisions based on economic efficiency and the criterion of directing investment resources into projects which yield the highest short-run returns — without regard to the inequalities such policies create in other fields — are themselves inhibiting growth in the future. The cost, of course, will be an apparent retardation in the rate of growth of the economy ; the advantages, however, will be the stimulation of a rate of growth which will better serve the longer-term social and political aims of the Federation, and better promote the economic interests of all its inhabitants.

Chapter 9

PROBLEMS OF ECONOMIC DEVELOPMENT OF THE REPUBLIC OF SOUTH AFRICA[1]

BY

PROFESSOR C. S. RICHARDS

University of the Witwatersrand, Johannesburg

I. THE GENERAL SCENE

AFRICA south of the Sahara comprises that area of the continent approximately south of latitude 20° north, and therefore includes all the more recently set-up new states evolved from the former British, French, and Belgian Colonies or dependencies as well as those states or dependencies (*e.g.* Liberia, Angola, South Africa, etc.) previously existing.

Of all these areas the Union (now Republic) of South Africa is, economically, by far the most advanced, its expansion and development in the last fifteen years having been phenomenal judged by any standard.

It measures approximately 1,500 miles north to south and 1,250 east to west, and covers an area of almost 473,000 square miles, or between one-seventh and one-eighth the area of the United States. It consists of a high (6,000 ft.) land mass separated from a long but relatively narrow lush coastal area on the east and south by the Drakensberg Mountains (rising to 11,000 ft.), and gradually verging towards drier and semi-arid country on the west towards south-west Africa. In consequence it has no navigable rivers from its main ports all on the east or south coast (Cape Town, Port Elizabeth, East London, and Durban), and this has vitally affected communication with the drier interior, and costs, since this must all be done by rail or road and now partly by air.

Because of its latitude and varying altitude, climatic conditions show considerable variety, and the crops and agricultural products reflect these conditions. Its social conditions, its peoples, and its economic system exhibit equally striking contrasts — the static and

---

[1] I am greatly indebted to my Research Assistant, Miss Mary Piercy, who has assembled all the statistical material, drawn the graphs and assisted all through in the preparation of the paper.

the dynamic, the primitive and the modern, the handcraft and the highly technical, subsistence economy side by side with an advanced industrialized society, primitive native villages in close proximity to modern skyscraper cities. Particularly is this so in the contrasting elements of its population. It has a total population (1960 Census, preliminary figures) of 15·841 million made up of 3·068 million Whites and 12·773 million Non-Whites : the latter composed of 10·807 million indigenous African (predominantly Bantu) from many different tribes and ethnic groupings, 1·489 million Coloureds and 0·477 million Asiatics. The White population is made up of about 1·718 million of indigenous Afrikaner descent (56·0 per cent) and 1·350 million English-speaking indigenous or immigrants, including 4 per cent foreign languages, and an appreciable percentage of Jews, and representing elements from almost every white country in the world.

The population is probably relatively more heterogeneous than that of any other country. Africans from innumerable tribes and at varying stages of culture and economic development, from the raw native living in the reserves to the highly educated sophisticated professional, distributed approximately half in the Native Reserves, one-quarter on White farms and in small towns, and one-quarter as permanent urban dwellers and migrant labourers in large towns : Asiatics mainly concentrated in Natal and the Coloureds mainly in the Cape.

Its mineral wealth in precious and base metals is considerable and varied — gold, diamonds, platinum, osmiridium, uranium, etc., coal, iron, manganese, lead, copper, asbestos, tungsten, phosphates, chrome, etc. Similarly with agricultural products — cattle, sheep, pigs, wool, mealies, wheat, oats, groundnuts, timber, fibres, sugar, tobacco, cotton, wines, all types of citrus and deciduous fruits, etc.

Its industrial complex shows similar range and variety and embodies techniques highly modernized (as in the steel industry), as well as those relying on the employment of large numbers of un-skilled workers. The whole economy is based on a large participation in international trade. Thus in 1960 :

Gold exports £268·0 m.[1]
Trade exports (excluding gold and 394·7 m. } £662·7 m.
ships' stores)
Imports (excluding gold) 555·7 m.

The importance of international trade to South Africa is clear when these figures are compared with the net national income (£2,017·5 m.

[1] The currency unit £ is used in this paper for convenience, although a decimal currency system of Rands and Cents was introduced on February 14, 1961. R2 = £1, R1 = 100 cents.

1959–60) and with the value of manufacturing output of £1,210·6 m. (1959). It has now a highly developed commercial and reserve banking system, modern highly technical steel and engineering industries, diversified manufacturing industries, a diversified money market, modern Stock Exchange facilities, and virtually all the institutions of a developed financial economy. Its geographic national income for 1959–60 was estimated at current prices as £2,239 m. (an increase of 7·2 per cent over the previous year), the sector disbursement of which is shown later.

The population composition as shown is such that race questions, not surprisingly, compound virtually all its problems : political, philosophic, ethical, religious, and economic — especially the latter. They colour every question, obtrude in every discussion (with innumerable views on their 'solution'), and constitute the fundamental problem of the Republic not only in regard to internal relations but to relations with the rest of Africa, and with the rest of the world — the latter (external) mainly as regards the Republic's policy concerning Non-Whites, the former (internal) concerning the ruling political policy towards other Whites and all Non-Whites. These aspects will be touched on later.

II. ACTUAL GROWTH SINCE 1910

The above brief account sets the stage : but an essential prerequisite to any discussion of *problems* of economic development, whether past, present, or future problems, is a pretty clear idea of the economic development which has actually taken place in recent years. This is especially so as regards South Africa, since many current and future problems have their roots deep in the past. In the case of the Republic of South Africa the half-century from 1910, spanning the period from the Union of the former four separate colonies, Cape, Natal, Orange Free State, and the Transvaal, to 1960, forms a suitable background picture. This section, with the aid of the appended graphs and statistics,[1] attempts a short sketch of events and development, the results of which were the formative material

[1] The relevant statistics from which the graphs have been derived are in some cases indicated on the graphs or can be inferred from them. They are, however, mainly, but by no means exclusively, obtained from the official Jubilee Issue, *Union Statistics for Fifty Years, 1910–1960*. Details of the basis upon which the statistics are drawn up and qualifying notes will be found in this publication. Most of the graphs dealing with value or wages are drawn after conversion of the relevant statistics from current to constant prices, in which cases the choice made for this purpose from the official price indexes is indicated. In all cases the base year is 1938.

for the difficult problems of the immediate past and constitute the soil from which must develop the problems of the future. It should be added that, as subsequently shown, economic development in the last fifteen years has been spectacular. There follows brief comment on the changes in the major economic factors in the last fifty years.

(a) *Population : Graph 1*

Total population has grown in the fifty years 1910–60 from 5·878 m. to 14·928 m., white population having increased from 1·257 m. to 3·123 m. The following table shows the percentage racial composition of the population 1910–60.

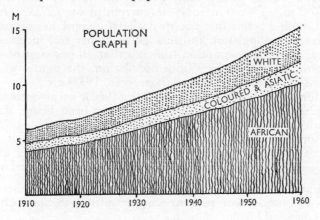

TABLE 1

RACIAL COMPOSITION OF THE POPULATION

YEAR	WHITES		NON-WHITES						Total	
			Africans		Coloureds		Asiatics			
	No.	%	No.	%	No.	%	No.	%	No.	%
	(m.)		(m.)		(m.)		(m.)		(m.)	
1910	1·3	21·4	4·0	67·3	0·5	8·8	0·1	2·5	5·9	100
1920	1·5	21·9	4·6	67·7	0·5	7·9	0·2	2·4	6·8	100
1930	1·8	21·1	5·6	68·6	0·7	8·0	0·2	2·3	8·5	100
1940	2·2	20·9	7·1	68·7	0·8	8·1	0·2	2·4	10·4	100
1950	2·6	20·9	8·4	67·7	1·1	8·6	0·4	2·8	12·5	100
1960	3·1	20·9	9·9	66·3	1·5	9·7	0·5	3·7	14·9	100

The significant feature over the whole period is, contrary to general belief, the steadiness of the proportions of Non-Whites, especially African, to Whites, the only increasing proportion being those of Coloureds and Asiatics. This misconception regarding the increasing proportion of Non-Whites appears sometimes to be used as part justification for existing attitudes and policy.

(b) *National Income : Graphs 2, 3, and 4*

Graph 2 shows the growth of National Income (Geographic and Nett) at both current and constant prices. Its significant growth periods have been from the end of 1932, after the abandonment of the gold standard, to 1960 (fivefold, geographic, at constant 1938 prices), and 1949 to 1960 (one-third and two-thirds) — the actual figures at constant prices being, £226·6 m. in 1932 (current prices £217·1 m.), £585·6 m. in 1949 (current prices £897·2 m.), £995·0 m. in 1960 (current prices £2,239·0 m.).

Graph 3 : this increase in national income has outpaced the increase in population and has led to higher real incomes *for all races*. On the assumption (official) that 70 per cent of national income accrues to the White population, the figures of income *per capita* at constant prices (base year, 1938) are :

for Whites, £115 (1938), £201 (1960), or at current prices £452·2, the increase in real income per head being, therefore, approximately 75 per cent over this period ;

for Non-Whites, £13 (1938), £22·8 (1960), or at current prices £51·3, also an increase in real income of 75 per cent. In connection with this Non-White share it must be pointed out that :

(i) about half the African population lives in the reserves and the product of subsistence agriculture is not included in national income statistics ;

(ii) (a) the (money) incomes of Africans are, in many cases (*e.g.* in agriculture, in the mines, and in domestic service) increased by goods and services in kind and (b) are augmented as a result of state or municipal paternalistic policy in providing goods and services, including housing at uneconomic rates ;

(iii) on the other hand, it has been suggested that the use of the Index Figure of Retail Prices inadequately reflects the actual rise in prices which has taken place in the group of goods and services predominantly consumed by Africans.

This system of payments in kind raises problems of personal expenditure (personal responsibility and psychological outlook of the African) in an exchange economy and in the adjustment of large numbers of Non-Whites to the environment of a money and financial economy.

Graph 4 shows the changing disbursement of the National Income on a percentage basis between the principal economic

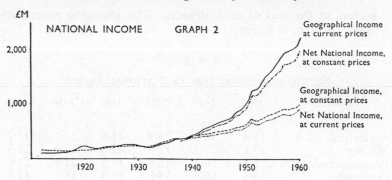

£M

NATIONAL INCOME   GRAPH 2

Geographical Income
at current prices

2,000

Net National Income,
at constant prices

Geographical Income,
at constant prices

1,000

Net National Income,
at current prices

1920   1930   1940   1950   1960

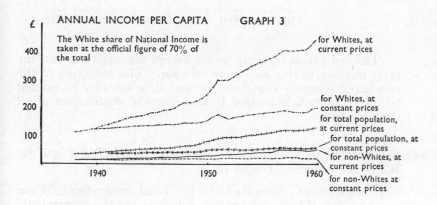

£

ANNUAL INCOME PER CAPITA   GRAPH 3

The White share of National Income is
taken at the official figure of 70% of
the total

400   for Whites, at
                                             current prices

300

200   for Whites, at
                                             constant prices

                                             for total population,
                                             at current prices

100   for total population, at
                                             constant prices
                                             for non-Whites, at
                                             current prices
                                             for non-Whites at
1940   1950   1960   constant prices

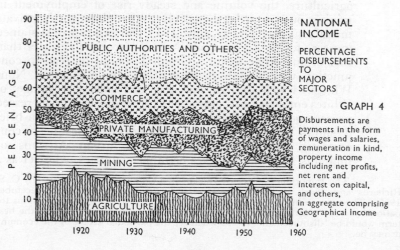

90

80   PUBLIC AUTHORITIES AND OTHERS

70

60

COMMERCE

50

PRIVATE MANUFACTURING

40

30   MINING

20

10

AGRICULTURE

P E R C E N T A G E

1920   1930   1940   1950   1960

NATIONAL
INCOME

PERCENTAGE
DISBURSEMENTS
TO
MAJOR
SECTORS

GRAPH 4

Disbursements are
payments in the form
of wages and salaries,
remuneration in kind,
property income
including net profits,
net rent and
interest on capital,
and others,
in aggregate comprising
Geographical Income

251

sectors at the end of each decade. The changing percentages since 1910 are as follows :

TABLE 2

SECTORIAL DISTRIBUTION OF NATIONAL INCOME

Sector	1912	1920	1930	1940	1950	1960
	%	%	%	%	%	%
Agriculture	17·4	20·9	13·9	11·8	13·1	11·7
Mining	27·1	21·3	17·3	22·8	13·6	13·3
Private manufacture	6·7	10·7	15·4	17·5	22·1	24·6
Commerce	13·5	16·8	14·5	14·3	15·1	11·8
Public authorities ⎱ Other ⎰	35·3	30·3	38·9	33·6	{ 10·3 { 25·8	10·5 28·1
	100·0	100·0	100·0	100·0	100·0	100·0

The reductions in every sector except manufacture, and the great increase in this sector are striking. The reduction in the commerce sector is significant in that it is contrary to normal trends : but care is needed in assessing the significance of all these changes.[1]

(c) *Employment : Graphs 5 and 6. Output : Graphs 7, 8, 9, and 10. Wages and Salaries : Graph 11*

(i) Employment : Graphs 5 and 6. Total employment, White and Non-White in the major sectors, shows the permanently greater number of workers, mainly African, absorbed by agriculture, the volume and steady rise of employment in mining, outstripped only recently by employment in private manufacture which has, since 1933, shown a rate of sustained increase for both White and Non-White, much greater than that of any other sector. Graph 5 should be read in conjunction with Graph 6, percentage employment of Non-Whites, which brings out the increased percentage of Whites employed in a period of depression, and the increased percentage of Non-Whites in times of prosperity. In brief it shows that in the past unemployment has been concentrated on Non-Whites, whether urban Africans or migrants from the reserves or other countries, who act as a

[1] See 'The Importance of Sector Income in a Competitive Economy', by C. S. Richards and Mary V. Piercy, *South African Journal of Economics*, December 1960. The main point of this article is that the use of the term 'contributions to' national income is fundamentally misleading and it is now suggested that the best term would be 'disbursements to' — whatever the particular sector of the economy it may be.

buffer or cushion in employment cycles since not only is this part of government and traditional policy but also largely because many Africans return to the reserves when employment falls off.

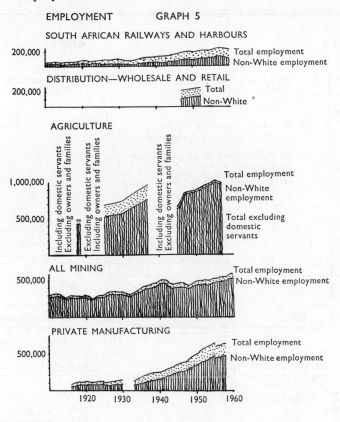

EMPLOYMENT   GRAPH 5

SOUTH AFRICAN RAILWAYS AND HARBOURS

200,000 ⌐ .... Total employment
        Non-White employment

DISTRIBUTION—WHOLESALE AND RETAIL

200,000 ⌐ ⁻⁻⁻ Total
        Non-White

AGRICULTURE

Including domestic servants
Excluding owners and families
Excluding domestic servants
Including owners and families
Including domestic servants
Excluding owners and families

1,000,000

500,000

Total employment
Non-White employment
Total excluding domestic servants

ALL MINING

500,000

Total employment
Non-White employment

PRIVATE MANUFACTURING

500,000

Total employment
Non-White employment

1920 1930 1940 1950 1960

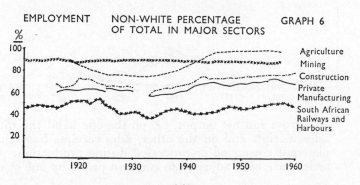

EMPLOYMENT   NON-WHITE PERCENTAGE   GRAPH 6
%   OF TOTAL IN MAJOR SECTORS

100
80
60
40
20

Agriculture
Mining
Construction
Private Manufacturing
South African Railways and Harbours

1920 1930 1940 1950 1960

253

(ii) Output : Graphs 7, 8, 9, and 10. An attempt has been made
to calculate a series for each major sector of the economy for

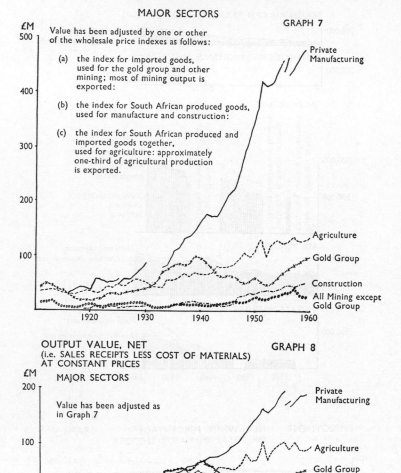

both gross and net output, *i.e.* on the one hand the total of
sales receipts and on the other, sales receipts less value of
materials consumed or processed during production. Both
series have been adjusted to constant prices by one or other

TABLE 3

PRIVATE MANUFACTURING INDUSTRY

Census Year	No. of Establishments	Value of		Employment		Salaries and Wages		Materials Used £1,000	Value of Output	
		Land and Buildings, £1,000	Machinery and Plant, £1,000	Total No.	Whites No.	Total £1,000	Whites £1,000		Gross £1,000	Nett £1,000
1915-16	3,638	9,804	8,413	88,844	35,220	7,691	5,848	21,116	35,699	13,954
1924-5	6,182	18,194	16,561	131,562	51,076	14,524	10,539	35,669	66,295	28,794
1938-9	8,614	33,529	26,103	236,123	93,054	27,848	19,821	73,213	140,587	64,068
1944-5	9,316	50,565	40,814	361,004	112,219	67,353	40,223	160,453	304,083	137,810
1954-5	13,725	216,563	218,254	652,635	184,334	216,416	135,056	628,283 *	1,110,388	482,101
1954-5†	9,685	193,868	210,967	604,633	162,647	199,186	122,107	643,069 *	1,061,498	418,429
1958-9	9,861			632,168		237,989		725,945 *	1,210,631	484,685

* Including fuel, light, and power. † Classification changed to exclude a large number of small industries.

of the price indexes, with the idea of determining the *real value* of the item to the country, *e.g.* the output value of gold has been adjusted by the relatively high import index *as the value of gold production to the country is actually its command over foreign imports whether capital or consumer goods*.

Graph 7 : Gross output value. The principal feature is the rapidly increasing sales value of manufactured products, especially since the war. The graph brings out clearly the fall in the real exchange value of gold due to its fixed price since 1935 in relation to a generally rising price level, despite the great increase in physical production (and in current value from £105·285 m. in

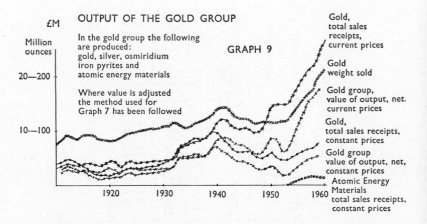

1945 to £268·00 m. in 1960) shown in Graph 9 which, incidentally, indicates various other facets of South Africa's gold problem. A comparison of Graphs 7 and 8 (gross and net output value respectively) again shows, though in a lesser degree, the greatly enhanced position of manufacture. Table 3 gives additional information.

Graph 10 again shows the gross value of output in a block graph on a sector basis for purpose of comparison with the other block graphs of employment (Graph 5) and Wages and Salaries (Graph 11).

(iii) Wages and Salaries : Graph 11. This graph, showing the sector distribution of wages and salaries, should be read in conjunction with Graph 5 (employment) and Graph 10 (the value of output) from which comparison *this fundamental fact emerges : the greater the employment of Non-White labour,*

VALUE OF OUTPUT, PRINCIPAL SECTORS   GRAPH 10

GROSS AND 'NETT' (i.e. SALES RECEIPTS, AND SALES RECEIPTS LESS 'COST OF MATERIALS')

AT CONSTANT PRICES

Adjustment to constant prices has been made
using the Wholesale Price Index:
    (a) manufacturing—the Index for South African produced goods
    (b) mining—the Index for imported goods
    (c) agriculture, distribution, S.A.R.H.—the Index for all groups of goods

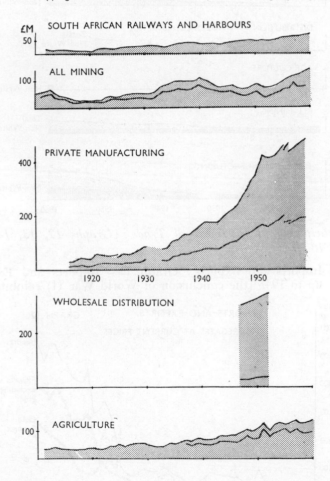

Economic Development for Africa South of the Sahara

e.g. *in agriculture and mining* (i.e. *labour intensive industries*), *the lesser the value of output and the lesser the amount distributed in wages and salaries as compared with the position in manufacturing industries.*

WAGES AND SALARIES, PRINCIPAL SECTORS   GRAPH 11

EXCLUDING PAYMENTS IN KIND

AT CONSTANT PRICES   Value adjusted by Retail Price Index

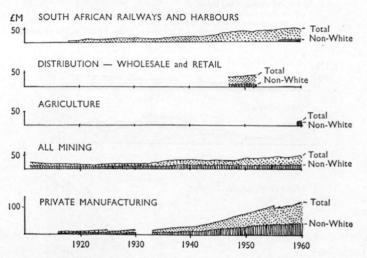

(d) *Participation in International Trade: Graphs 12, 13, 14, 15, and 16*

(i) Imports and Exports : Graph 12. Imports and Exports up to 1945 (the conclusion of World War II) exhibited no

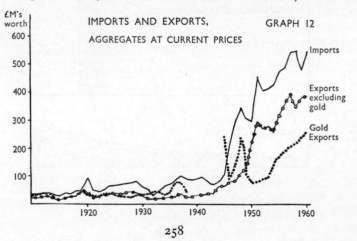

significant changes except for the inevitable decline during the Great Depression. Since 1945, however, the great growth in imports and exports (and since 1953 in gold exports) is clearly shown in the graph, being vitally affected, in the case of gold production and exports, by the currency devaluation of 1949 : the significant fall in imports in 1959 should be noted as also the fall due to import control after 1948.

(ii) Imports : Graphs 13 and 14. The significant features of the import picture are the preponderance of two groups, *i.e.* the

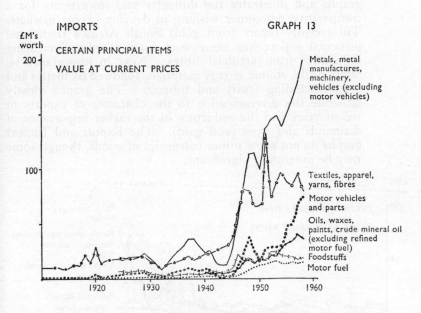

IMPORTS

GRAPH 13

£M's worth

CERTAIN PRINCIPAL ITEMS

VALUE AT CURRENT PRICES

Metals, metal manufactures, machinery, vehicles (excluding motor vehicles)

Textiles, apparel, yarns, fibres

Motor vehicles and parts

Oils, waxes, paints, crude mineral oil (excluding refined motor fuel)

Foodstuffs

Motor fuel

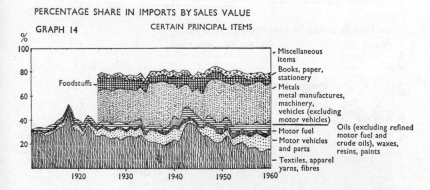

PERCENTAGE SHARE IN IMPORTS BY SALES VALUE

GRAPH 14

CERTAIN PRINCIPAL ITEMS

Miscellaneous items

Books, paper, stationery

Metals metal manufactures, machinery, vehicles (excluding motor vehicles)

Oils (excluding refined motor fuel and crude oils), waxes, resins, paints

Motor fuel

Motor vehicles and parts

Textiles, apparel yarns, fibres

Foodstuffs

capital goods group (machinery, metals, etc.), and the consumer group of textiles (apparel, yarn, etc.). This latter has been falling as a percentage since 1942, owing to the development of domestic industry, whereas, despite the expansion of the domestic iron and steel and engineering industries, the great industrial development of the country has also required a considerable increase in imports.

(iii) Exports : Graphs 15 and 16. The fluctuating and competitive risk character of the export trade is obvious from the graphs and illustrates the difficulty and uncertainty for a comparative newcomer wishing to develop export markets. Till recently (apart from gold) South Africa's traditional principal export has been wool, now meeting increasing difficulties from artificial fibres. Next in importance is, temporarily, atomic energy materials, followed by metals and food (excluding fruit) and tobacco. The graphs clearly illustrate the diversification in the character of exports in recent years and the reduction in the earlier importance of diamonds and wool (and gold). The Export and Import graphs do not show minor categories of goods, though some may be potentially significant.

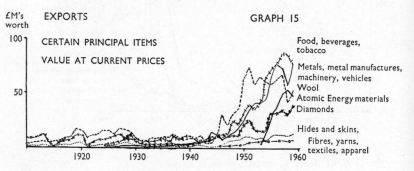

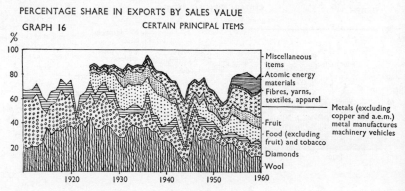

(e) *Prices : Graph 17*

This graph shows the price indexes of retail, wholesale, and imported goods, and exhibits movements similar to those experienced in many other countries. The retail index cannot

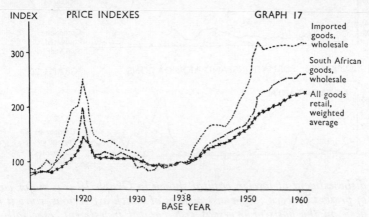

INDEX   PRICE INDEXES   GRAPH 17

Imported goods, wholesale

South African goods, wholesale

All goods retail, weighted average

BASE YEAR

be used as a Cost of Living Index, but since October 1958 a new index, not used here (Consumer Price Index), has been developed (base October 1958) as the result of a detailed survey of White consumer expenditure. The Retail Price Index will not be published after March 1961.

(f) *Savings : Graph 18. Capital Imports : Graph 19. Company Flotations : Graph 20*

These three graphs show the great growth in domestic capital formation and investment (a concomitant of the increasing national income) which, together with foreign risk capital investment since 1945 (no previous statistics are available), have been

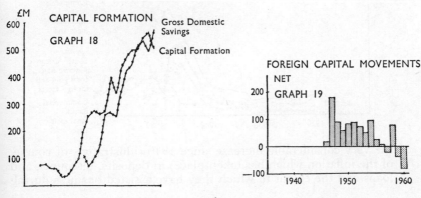

£M   CAPITAL FORMATION   Gross Domestic Savings

GRAPH 18

Capital Formation

FOREIGN CAPITAL MOVEMENTS

NET

GRAPH 19

responsible for the great industrial and economic development
which has taken place and which is also illustrated in Graph 20
showing company flotations over the years. *The increasing current*

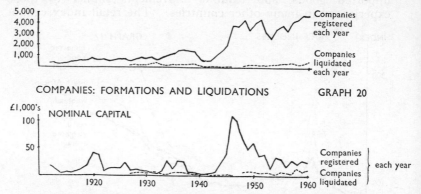

COMPANIES: FORMATIONS AND LIQUIDATIONS   GRAPH 20

*disinvestment of foreign capital shown in Graph 19 is a major cause
of present concern : the consequences of which are serious, since it has
been on the basis of overseas risk capital investment, especially as
regards local offshoots of foreign firms, that domestic investment has
been induced and stimulated, and national income and standards of
living greatly increased.*

(g) The Banking Position : Graphs 21 and 22

The graph of Total Deposits of the eight Commercial Banks
of the Union (mainly Barclays, Standard and Volkskas) shows

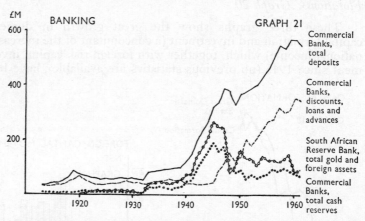

the very considerable increase since 1940 (illustrative, of course,
of the inflation which has taken place) in deposits, discounts, and
loans and the extent to which they have assisted business during

that period. The tendency of the reserves to fall, shown in actual figures and in ratios, both of the Commercial Banks and the

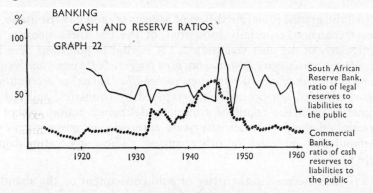

Reserve Bank in recent years is clearly brought out and is another phase of the situation shown in Graph 19 and accounts for the slow reduction in economic activity in the past two years : an indication also of the growing lack of confidence and uncertainty.

(h) *Communications : Graph 23*

This graph requires no comment, the increases in the factors graphed again illustrating another aspect of post-war

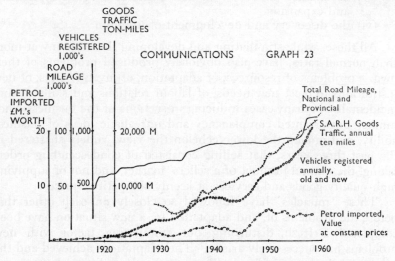

development — and the country is now traversed by a network of first-class tarred trunk roads, constructed by the National Roads Board.

III. SUMMARY

All the graphs illustrate different aspects of, and pay tribute to, the great expansion, especially industrial, of the last three decades and particularly of the post-war period. It is vital to point out here that *this almost continuous expansion has been triggered off by and has been the result of a series of almost fortuitous rocket-like 'bursts' or accelerations, almost miracles,* not normally experienced by countries, and has not primarily been the result of conscious deliberate action, except indirectly, on the part either of private enterprise or government, due to population increases or other causes. These generating factors were :

   (i) the increase in the price of gold consequent on the abandonment of the gold standard at the end of 1932, followed by further subsequent increases and the consequent expansion of the gold-mining industry, and of the economy generally ; [1]
  (ii) war and consequent inflationary expenditure and economic development, 1939–45 ;
 (iii) the post-war boom, especially industrial ;
 (iv) the discovery and exploitation of the Orange Free State and West Rand Gold Fields, and the further stimulus to industrial and other expansion ;
  (v) devaluation in 1949 — a new stimulus to gold exploration and expansion ;
 (vi) the discovery and development of uranium.

All these, while stimulating and developing the economy at more than normal rates, have also obviously produced problems of their own — problems of resources, of adaptation, of inventiveness, of new institutions to meet new needs, of labour relations and skills — and, incidentally, in many cases inducing in sections of the business community unwarranted complacency and unrealistic ideas of business ability, and among the lower echelon the view, rudely shattered in the past three years, that selling consisted of condescending order-taking, the natural product of a sellers' market, and not of supplying high-quality goods and services at keenly competitive prices.

These 'miracles' have followed so closely on each other that before the problems of, and adaptation to, a new situation have been completed a fresh, disturbing but stimulating, factor with new problems has successively arisen. The adaptations achieved and the results produced are alike a tribute to the flexibility and enterprise

---

[1] See (i) 'Whence South Africa's Present Prosperity', by C. S. Richards, *South African Journal of Economics*, September 1935. (ii) 'Economic Revival in South Africa', by C. S. Richards, *Economic Journal*, London, December 1934.

of the free market economy and the mental agility and resource exhibited by the system of entrepreneurial initiative. These new economic complexes and situations have, incidentally, given rise to the inauguration and development by the State (and partly by private enterprise) of new organizations and institutions and by new legislation to cope with developing situations where it has been thought that private interests were not coincident with social interests or where the rapid pace of development required reasonable curbs and restraints. These institutions and legislative enactments are mentioned later.

IV. THE PROBLEMS OF EXPANSION: ADAPTATION AND ADJUSTMENT

The modern development of South Africa dates from the diamond discoveries of 1865 and the gold discoveries of 1886, producing the first halting steps towards industrialization, population concentration, advanced communication, national markets, and participation in world trade and world problems. Prior to that, life was static, simple, mainly agricultural and pastoral, in scattered communities, and racked by intertribal or internecine wars. The influx of highly mixed population elements, attracted by the lure of diamonds and gold, the development of subsidiary activities and small industries, the rapid agglomeration of areas, laid or accentuated the basis of many modern problems. The outstanding fact is, however, that the beginnings of South Africa as a modern state date from the precious metal discoveries.

History repeats itself, and, apart from the effects of World War II, the surge of expansion of the last thirty years again springs from the same source, *i.e.* the expansion of the gold-mining industry, due to the increase in the price of gold at the end of 1932, leading to the expansion of the mining industry generally and the stimulation of secondary industry. Obviously such development of the economy accentuated old problems and produced new ones of adjustment and adaptation — the intensification of race mixture and race problems, of population concentrations, of wage differentiation, of management and administration, of international exchange and finance, and most unfortunate of all, the lack of real co-operation among the two White elements — and all this against a background of great urgency for the evolution of satisfactory solutions to economic and social problems, not only of national importance but also of great international consequence.

Economic Development for Africa South of the Sahara

It would be idle to suggest that permanent 'solutions' to any of the economic and social problems have been found : many partial solutions and temporary *modi vivendi* have been adopted, but in the circumstances problems have tended to become intensified rather than solved, particularly as a result of the multiracial environment. A brief review of the major problems is illuminating. The special problems of South Africa will be stressed : general problems of economic growth met frequently elsewhere will not be dwelt on.

Gold mining has been, and still is, the key to the development, but the expansion of this industry has involved difficult technical and economic adjustments. The limit of mining depths prior to 1945 was about 7,500 ft. ; some mines now run to 10,000 ft., and other mines (*e.g.* Western Deep Levels) will touch 13,000 ft. At these greater depths increased heat conditions and increasing rock pressures have had to be overcome ; water problems and ventilation, especially in the new Free State Gold Mines, have been met by the cementation process ; African labour supplies from foreign and domestic sources (and the supply of White miners) have been stepped up from 301,500 in 1945 (Whites 37,450) to 377,223 in 1960 (Whites 49,518), and African labour utilized more economically and their better training systematically provided for. European training has also been greatly improved. The costs of bringing a gold mine to the production stage have increased from about £3 m. in 1939 to between £12 m. and £15 m. today. Capital for this expansion (which so far has resulted in twenty-eight new gold mines since 1939, plus five in the development stage) has been obtained both from overseas and local sources, to the amount of £375 m., mostly raised after 1945, and more than half of which has come from external sources.[1]

In addition, exploration on an ever-widening scale by geophysical methods has been undertaken and, provided overseas risk capital can still be obtained, for the immediate future there seems no reason to anticipate any reduction in current output despite the number of mines (nine) which have already reached the marginal stage, apart from those which will become marginal in the near future. An increased gold price, though now perhaps seemingly less likely in the near future, would, of course, further transform the scene and a reduction in taxation would greatly assist. Administrative, managerial, and other improvements have been made, and the rise

[1] Capital raised by the gold-mining industry has been as follows : Up to 1909 = £136 m. ; 1910–32 = £36 m. ; 1933–9 = £63 m. ; 1940–5 = £5 m. ; 1946–1959 = £370 m. — a total of £610 m., of which more than half came from external sources. 'In all, the mining industry has raised £610 m. in "new money" and has appropriated out of profits an additional £235 m. for capital purposes.'

in working costs continuously restrained, in the face of an implacably fixed gold price and inflationary price rises generated overseas and domestically.

Moreover, opportunity was taken in conjunction with the Natural Resources Development Council [1] to plan the development of the new mining areas, which are now in many ways models of advanced social and economic conditions and amenities : native hospitals, living conditions, etc., much superior to their counterparts elsewhere and due largely to the progressive attitude of the mining industry. The expansion of the industry has also led to the development of efficient local engineering firms supplying highly specialized plant and equipment, *e.g.* in 1945 the gold-mining industry spent £32·014 m. on stores and equipment : of this £30·671 m. was consumed by the large gold mines, of which £26·143 m. was classified as of South African origin : in 1959 the figures were £140·9 m. (including roads and buildings) of which £126·7 m. approximately was classified as South African in origin and £14.2 m. as imported. The recent international metallurgical congress held in Johannesburg in April-May 1961, focused attention on the problems successfully met and the results obtained. Similar problems have been met and successfully tackled in coal and other mining.

V. THE PROBLEM OF ALTERNATIVE ACTIVITY: MANUFACTURING INDUSTRY AND TERTIARY SERVICES

(i) *The Pattern of Development*

During the last thirty years the economy of South Africa has gradually changed from a primarily agricultural-mining complex to one of mining, manufacturing, and tertiary services. Gold mining is, like all mining, ultimately a wasting asset, and the problem of the substitution of alternative economic activities has engaged the attention of successive governments since 1924. When the continuance of gold mining looked dim (though increases in the price of gold since have postponed for many years its inevitable demise) and when the Carnegie Commission's conclusions on the poor white problem heightened the urgency of finding alternative economic activities, the adoption of the principle of moderate industrial tariff protection, on a selective basis in 1925, by the first Nationalist Government, provided a stimulus to manufacturing industry constantly reinforced since by other factors.

[1] Established by the Natural Resources Development Act, 1947.

Subsequent investigation by two Commissions,[1] the powerful stimulus of the war (when many restrictions were relaxed), the more recent report of the Commission on Protective Policy, 1958,[2] the effect of Import Control, 1948–54, have been followed by the development of manufacturing industry already shown in the graphs.

Great progress has clearly been made. Unit size has increased: in 1924–5 the average value of the fixed capital invested in the 6,009 privately owned factories was £5,133, average number of White employees 6½, total employees 19 ; in 1938–9 the figures were £6,923, 10, and 28 ; and in 1954–5 (latest comparable) £31,680, 13, and 48. But the majority of plants are still small, though an increasing percentage of total production comes from a lesser number of much larger units. Large-scale production is limited primarily by a comparatively small domestic and export market and by distribution costs.

The determination of industrial location has been complicated by socio-economic policy in the past, by the non-homogeneity and relative immobility of labour, and, in the last twelve years, by the innovation of separate 'Group' areas for the different races. Despite these frictions and the declared policy of 'apartheid', or separateness, and the institution of 'influx control', the employment of Non-Whites in industry has greatly increased, especially in the four main industrial areas, as obviously it was bound to if industry was to expand. In the latest phase of separate development, however, the declared policy of future industrial expansion on the borders of native reserves seems unlikely fundamentally to alter the prevailing pattern of racial interdependence. Indeed, the 'unscrambling' of the mixture in race location, built up over many years, seems largely impossible both physically and economically. Neither mining, agriculture, secondary industry, nor virtually any other activity, can eliminate or even greatly reduce dependence on Non-Whites.

Table 4 shows the distribution of Africans between urban, rural, and 'reserved' areas :

As for the Bantustan development (*i.e.* development of Native Reserves), official policy seems to have relegated this to the continuing development of raw material resources started many years

---

[1] (i) Customs Tariff Commission 1934–5, U.G.5/36. (ii) Third Interim Report of the Industrial and Agricultural Requirements Commission U.G.40/41 : critically reviewed by the present writer in 'Fundamentals of Economic Policy in the Union', *South African Journal of Economics*, March 1942, pp. 47-72 ; cf. also the present writer's 'The Task Before Us with Special Reference to Industry', Presidential Address to the Economic Scoiety of South Africa 1943–4, *South African Journal of Economics*, September 1944.   [2] U.G.36/58.

ago, together with the development of any local enterprise dependent on African initiative where considered necessary, under the auspices of the recently established Bantu Investment Corporation.

Both the above projected expansions must obviously involve heavy capital expenditure, either in addition to, or at the expense of, established industry. If, however, Bantustans are to be developed as self-governing areas a huge capital investment over many years

TABLE 4

DISTRIBUTION OF AFRICAN POPULATION

Year	Total Population	In 'Bantu (Reserved) Areas'		Urban		Total African Population	On White, Coloured, or Asiatic Farms	
		No.	% of Total African Population	No.	% of Total African Population		No.	% of Total African Population
	(m.)	(m.)		(m.)		(m.)	(m.)	
1904	5·175			0·361	10·3	3·491		
1911	5·973			0·512	12·7	4·019		
1921	6·927			0·661	14·1	4·697		
1926								
1931								
1936	9·588			1·244	18·9	6·596		
1946	11·416			1·888	24·1	7·831		
1951	12·647	3·307	38·7	2·290	26·8	8·535	2·374	27·8 *
1960	No details available							

* 6·7 per cent of African population elsewhere.

will be necessary, but such investment will carry with it no prospect of immediate returns, or indeed of any adequate return at all. On the contrary, it will definitely involve a reduction in returns from other and more productive avenues in which it would otherwise be invested, involving a reduction in standards of living for the whole economy.

Non-White labour (mainly African) has shown itself adaptable and amenable to training, and it has been increasingly required in operative work. Without this inflow, expansion would have been severely limited, not only because of lack of numbers but also because of the unwillingness of Whites to undertake this work. Expansion has actually been limited by the scarcity of skilled White labour, a serious existing difficulty produced largely by a restrictive immigration policy dating from 1948 for both 'economic' reasons (*e.g.* the policy of employing poor Whites) and other reasons. Official job reservation [1] in the last two or three years has endeavoured, in terms of recommendations by the Industrial Tribunal, to preserve certain jobs to particular work groups, mainly White, directing Whites to low-grade jobs, and has created increased frictions. The conflict of the 'economic' and the 'ideological' aspects of the colour problem finds its sharpest contrasts in industry.

Wages are largely determined by recommendations after investigation by the Wage Board, or by Industrial Council Agreements, but Non-White trade unions are strongly discouraged and still have no place in recognized negotiations. While official and private policy, based on investigations concerning poverty and native wages, has, generally, in the last few years led to an improvement in Non-White wages, recognition of the importance of the local Non-White market has been a coincident factor in this change of policy. Industrial legislation controls working conditions, and industrial 'harmony' is governed by the Industrial Conciliation Act (1924), and there is legislation governing White Unemployment Insurance.

A continuous and serious deficiency in the numbers and quality of executive and managerial skill has been, and will be for long, a permanent problem, but it is being tackled by private organizations and by public institutions such as the universities.

The Public Sector and its legislation has been continuously developed since 1933. Modernization of the Companies Acts (based on the reports of two Commissions, Lansdown, 1936, and Millin, 1947), and other industrial legislation, have been paralleled by the establishment by government of organizations such as the Council for Scientific and Industrial Research (CSIR), the Standards Bureau, the Natural Resources Development Council, the National Council for Social Research, etc., and by many Public Utility Corporations, *e.g.* the Iron and Steel Industrial Corporation (ISCOR), the Electricity Supply Commission (ESCOM), the South African Coal, Oil, and Gas Corporation Ltd. (SASOL), the South African Phosphate Development Corporation (Pty.) Ltd. (FOSKOR), Klipfontein Organic Products (KOP), the Industrial Development Corporation (IDC), etc. : so much so that in view of the innumerable Government Marketing Boards (about twenty) serious doubts are expressed concerning government intrusion, activity, and control, in an economy, ostensibly anyway operating under the aegis of private enterprise.

[1] See 'Statutory Work Reservation I and II in the Union of South Africa', by Mary V. Piercy, *South African Journal of Economics*, June and September 1960.

(ii) *The Finance of Investment*

The supply of the necessary capital for the striking development of recent years has also posed a major problem. Privately it has come largely from three sources :

(*a*) domestic savings, now asserted to be supplying about 90 per cent of total 'requirements' ;

(*b*) reinvestment of profits (the traditional method) ;

(*c*) overseas investment, largely of British and American origin, through the establishment of branch or subsidiary activities, but also from France, Belgium, and Switzerland.

As the relevant graph shows, foreign investment has fluctuated widely over the years, but, in 'bursts' after 1932 and 1945, it has been this foreign investment which has largely supplied the 'risk' capital for the initial exploitation and development of the new gold-mining areas and many of the major industrial ventures. The repatriation of capital in the last two years (between £80 m. and £90 m. in 1960), and the flow of domestic savings to Building Societies, Treasury and Municipal loans, and other 'safe-and-fixed-return' institutions, have not only reduced current activity but embarrass future prospects. Despite occasional statements to the contrary the continued influx of foreign risk capital is essential to South Africa's continued development and increase in the standards of living.

Nor has government policy been blameless as regards the volume and direction of private investment, for, by over budgeting, really over taxing, by frequent savings' levies, by over taxing the gold mines, government has for years skimmed off much of the cream from the private pool for diversion into many of the new public utility corporations previously mentioned, such as SASOL (£48 m.), FOSKOR (£2·5 m.), KOP (£2 m.), etc., either directly or through the medium of the Industrial Development Corporation whose 'capital', in consequence, has swollen from £5 m. to about £70 m. The IDC has fostered other development mainly in textiles, and in recent years has been granted the privilege of starting industries of its own. Overseas 'risk' capital not only supplies the necessary funds but, what is more important, most frequently the technical 'know how'. The Industrial Finance Corporation (an offshoot of the IDC and the South African Reserve Bank) and others, together with many private industrial finance corporations, have also entered the market.

The *money market* has shown parallel development.[1] New

[1] See two articles, 'The Development of the South African Money Market', by G. F. D. Palmer and A. B. Dickman, *South African Journal of Economics*, December 1958 and December 1960, respectively.

commercial banks like Volkskas, the French Bank, and recently the Chase Manhattan Bank (U.S.A.), and the National City Bank (U.S.A.), have challenged the sovereignty of the long-existing Barclays, Standard, and Netherlands complex and introduced a highly competitive element into interest rates and short-term facilities, and in order to compete with the many hire purchase offices and credit corporations, have themselves begun to offer these and other facilities. The National Finance Corporation (1949), in which, under the aegis of the South African Reserve Bank, all the major financial institutions (banks, mining houses, building societies, insurance companies, etc.) have a share, has mobilized hitherto 'idle' resources and formed the sound nucleus of a short-term money market in terms of which five merchant banks and acceptance houses, one discount house, and other similar institutions have since developed.

VI. TRADE AND EXPORT PROBLEMS

One of the principal points made by the present writer in 1942 was that :

if South African manufacturing industry was to take the place of the gold mining industry in the economy as an export sector it would involve a transition *from* the present position where both agriculture and secondary industry can exist only because of the excess sums they receive from the gold mining industry, *through* the position when they receive no such sums, (that is when they can exist without any form of protection or assistance, either direct or indirect), *to* the position when they can compete in world's markets as efficient export industries.[1]

How far has this been realized in the last two decades ? The following figures show the value and percentage composition of the Union's exports for certain years.[2]

It is clear that progress has been made. Manufactured goods now constitute between one-fifth and one-sixth of total exports, and gold, though a highly important 'stabilizer', occupies now less than half its former relative export importance. Nevertheless, it still supplies the exchange for the purchase of imported 'raw materials' and consumer goods : but certain sections of secondary industry would not seem profitably attractive.

[1] See p. 268, footnote 1 (ii).
[2] See Report of The Commission of Enquiry into Policy Relating to the Protection of Industries (U.G.36/58, p. 46).

TABLE 5

VALUE AND PERCENTAGE COMPOSITION OF UNION EXPORTS

Year	Agricultural and Pastoral Products — Fish, Fresh or Frozen, and Wool, unmanufactured	% of Total Exports	Minerals and Metals	% of Total Exports	Gold	% of Total Exports	Manufactured Goods	% of Total Exports
	(£m.)		(£m.)		(£m.)		(£m.)	
936–7	23·9	20·1	8·3	7·0	82·8	69·7	3·8	3·2
952–3	103·5	23·4	105·3	23·8	141·1	31·9	92·4	20·9
954–5	119·7	25·2	96·4	20·3	166·7	35·1	92·1	19·4
956–7	147·5	24·7	143·3	24·0	198·7	33·3	107·5	18·0

It is known,[1] however, that the terms of trade have moved against this country since 1950, particularly in the last year and a recent close study [2] showed that :

(i) the exports of South African products, without gold or uranium, have increased fourfold (at constant prices) between 1938 and 1958 ;

(ii) the best customers of the Union were, in 1958, the United Kingdom (36 per cent), Western European countries (22 per cent), Communist European countries (1 per cent), Africa (principally the Federation of Rhodesia and Nyasaland) (22 per cent), United States of America (9 per cent), other continents (10 per cent) ;

(iii) purchases by Commonwealth countries have increased in the period from one-half to three-fifths of the total exports ;

(iv) about 85 per cent of the Union's African exports went to British or Commonwealth territories ;

(v) there has been a significant shift in export destinations, from industrialized to less developed countries, accompanied by a shift in the type of export goods, from raw materials to manufactured articles, e.g. of a total of £253 m. worth of exports to *industrialized countries* go 65·6 per cent of raw materials and fresh products, 28·6 per cent of products of primary or extractive industry, and 5·8 per cent products of secondary or manufacturing industry, and to *less developed countries* the corresponding figures are 9·9, 17·7, and 72·4 per cent.

As a by-product, increasing industrialization has greatly complicated the problems of race mixture and race relations.

[1] See 'Changes in South Africa's Terms of Trade, 1950–58', by T. van Waasdijk, *South African Journal of Economics*, June 1959.

[2] 'Changes in the Union's Merchandise Exports, 1938–58', by F. F. Winklé, *Finance and Trade Review, Volkskas Bank*, March 1960.

At a time when only a very small footing in export markets for manufacture has been secured, and when certain traditional exports are being challenged by new synthetic materials, it is evident that certain additional factors will increase the competition that South African exports are likely to meet : the larger economic units planned in Europe affecting both the Republic's European and African markets ; the boycotts and trade restrictions imposed by other countries (especially African countries) opposed to our internal racial policies ; and our departure from the Commonwealth. The import control recently reimposed, on financial grounds, and the internal campaign to increase local purchases of South African manufactured articles, together with the continued move to increase the domestic Non-White market should help to increase sales, but there is, of course, a definite danger that import control will adversely affect costs and efficiency. On the selling side the recent export sales 'ship' containing South African products did not apparently meet a great deal of success. The three current trade missions now visiting Europe, the Americas, and the Far East are evidence of the degree of importance rightly attached to the development of the export market.

VII. THE PRESENT POSITION [1]

In the preceding sections I have tried to present a comprehensive picture of the South African economy and its problems, supported by statistics and other evidence and illustrated in the graphs. In what follows all I can do is to put forward my own point of view, well aware that it may not find agreement everywhere even though it is written solely and objectively in the interests of the country as a whole, and because in the present situation economic and political views are so intertwined that in many questions it is impossible to separate the two.

While the word 'crisis', whether applied politically or economically, has, through its indiscriminate use, lost a great deal of its significance, it would be foolish to deny that conditions in South Africa in the last two years, especially the last few months, have shown increasing stress and exhibited serious economic aspects. For this there are three fundamental reasons :

   (i) the general economic and political position in the rest of the African continent caused by the somewhat hasty withdrawal

[1] In June 1961. For a brief but penetrating survey of the present position see the statement (released June 9, 1961) of the Chairman, Mr. H. F. Oppenheimer, to the annual general meeting of the Anglo-American Corporation.

of European powers and the granting of independence, in some cases, to economically and politically immature states, leading to a lack of confidence in the immediate future of *all* states in Africa in the minds of European and American investors and entrepreneurs ;

(ii) the government's racial policy of apartheid or separate development, which, while misunderstood in many parts of the world (not entirely excluding South Africa), has none the less promoted their active opposition as being morally unacceptable ;

(iii) the Union's adoption of a republican status and its withdrawal from the Commonwealth with all that it implies both politically and economically (despite the standstill agreement in Britain for one year).

These have resulted in a great lack of confidence, not only overseas, but also internally, which is reflected in innumerable economic and other factors : the steady withdrawal of overseas capital (£80 m. to £90 m. in 1960) ; the virtual cessation of capital imports ; the difficult banking position, and the steady reduction in reserves ; the suspension by the Reserve Bank (May 16) on forward currency dealings by South Africans, to cover Stock Exchange transactions and the importation of consumer goods ; the unsuccessful attempt to substitute local credit to replace the overseas disinvestment ; the flight of local capital ; the higher bank rates on overdrafts and savings, and higher building society interest rates ; the reduction in amounts for overseas visits ; the reimposition of import control on luxuries and on a wide range of goods made in South Africa which is calculated to cut imports by up to £100 m. ; the visit of the International Monetary Fund officials, in connection with projected loans to pay off maturing government obligations ; the serious fall in Stock Market prices since January 1960, and especially since the Referendum on the Republic on October 5, 1960, which has had adverse effects on domestic investment ; the continued excess of emigration over immigration, especially of intellectual and other leaders (in 1960, 12,613 as opposed to 9,789) ; the shelving of some important plans for industrial expansion ; the fall in property values ; the reduction in or postponement of some mining exploration programmes ; the prospects of reduced mining dividends to provide internal capital for essential mining development ; the restrictions on domestic building loans and the reduction in building plans passed ; and the increase in unemployment. All these are symptomatic of economic malaise and sickness, a condition which stands out in marked contrast to the intensive economic activity currently displayed in Europe, America, and elsewhere throughout the world.

Economic Development for Africa South of the Sahara

Nor is the existing position inherent in the South African *economic* scene. Its physical assets are no less than before: its mineral wealth, both precious and base, is the same, the surface only scratched ; its industrial plants, its agricultural and pastoral wealth and its entrepreneurial skills have not been impaired ; projects for heavy capital expenditure running into hundreds of millions of pounds on some public utilities are to be undertaken. But till confidence is restored the path is certain to be difficult and the problems intractable. And this restoration turns primarily on political as well as on economic factors, which are inextricably combined : on a change in attitudes, both domestically and externally, of South Africa to the World and the World to South Africa, the latter attitude having been influenced partly by the South West Africa position, by Sharpeville, and by two sets of Emergency measures. Never were economic prospects so dependent on a change of political conditions and attitudes. They cannot be separated if 'solutions' to South Africa's problems are to be found.

What are the prospects and what are the future problems ? Their extent and difficulty is such that no simple interpretation of democratic principles can possibly succeed ; prolonged discussion, compromise, the abandonment or at least relaxation of stubbornly fixed objectives, and the willingness to consider varying constitutional adaptations and economic relationships mirror the attitude which, it would seem, can alone produce a workable solution designed to preserve what has been built up, and give opportunity for the fullest development of all its varied population elements and natural assets, in a system of private enterprise and individuality still obviously with White leadership. The alternative is that even the principle of democracy on a limited scale will be challenged in favour of an extension of authoritarian control.

The future of South Africa clearly and irrevocably depends on the acceptance and development of a workable multiracial society, giving opportunity for both Non-White and White contributions and development. Uncompromising extremism by White or Non-White can lead only to greater difficulties — neither can do without the other — and co-operation, particularly economic, is essential.

A great deal has for many years been done in South Africa by government and private enterprise for the Non-White, and more is projected ; but some 'solution', ultimately involving a gradual degree of Non-White political representation, while definitely preserving White leadership, and lying between the ideas of African National domination, which is wholly unacceptable, and current official policy, would seem to be the only line. Human and citizenship rights cannot be denied indefinitely solely on grounds of race and colour, no matter how highly qualified such individuals may be. Particularly does this question arise in the case of the permanent urban African dwellers.

World opinion, which may perhaps be translated into economic action, is primarily opposed to certain aspects of South Africa's official racial policies. The present official interpretation of apartheid means the creation of independent African 'states' or homelands coincident with the existing reserved areas and is advanced as the answer to world criticism and domestic need. Unfortunately, these particular social and political objectives of apartheid are, as shown, entirely dependent upon economic factors such as the adequate internal development of the reserves (Bantustans) to absorb expanding populations, together with the industrialization of White areas bordering on the reserves (which is at present being attempted), the complementary character of production in border areas to products of White areas, the nature and training of the labour available in these areas, the discovery of suitable markets, and the availability of capital. Development along such lines is fraught with many difficulties and would seem to offer little hope of success sufficient to meet both economic and political aspects.

Unfortunately, the recent concatenation of economic and political circumstances has induced in response a siege or 'laager' attitude, a mental and other withdrawal from contacts and environment from which no actual withdrawal is feasible, an attempt to make a virtue of necessity. 'Withdrawal' in a world becoming smaller every day means a curtailment of international exchange when the necessity is that it be rapidly stepped up. It is a serious matter that it is now becoming apparent that the Republic cannot be the industrial leader on the continent. While doing all it can to expand exports it must therefore look increasingly to the expansion of its domestic market, for increased production, lower costs, higher wages, and better living for its Non-Whites. Unfortunately, higher wages in industry, however, may react adversely on mining costs since rising mining wages mean reductions in mining activity. This represents a marked conflict in sectional interests.

Some significant recent changes in policy can be noted. A department of White immigration has been set up to rectify the errors made after 1948, in curtailing immigration, aiming at an influx of 30,000 Europeans per annum, and thus reducing current number disparities. The establishment of Departments of Coloured and Asiatic Affairs show relaxation of former attitudes. But constant consultation is essential : job reservation should be discarded and

Non-White trade unions be permitted official participation in negotiations : Non-Europeans used more and more in higher grades of work, thus providing more supervisory opportunities for Whites for which there must be adequate training : automation and other means to efficiency adopted wherever possible : and export markets explored.

The record of South Africa in the international capital market, public or private, is excellent : no repayment defaults, profits repatriable, and no onerous restrictions on foreign investment.[1] Current returns on equities and government stocks are attractive — in fact, the past investment climate has been much better than that existent in the countries of many of South Africa's critics. And compared with other countries there has been, since Union, great stability in government. Capital imports, it must again be stressed, however, are essential if standards of living are not to be reduced.

The measures just mentioned coupled with real efforts (and not oral urges) towards White unity, the relinquishment of the extremes of current policy, a reduction in unnecessary government economic activity contradictory to the principles of a private competitive economy, would largely restore confidence and the forward march of the economy.

The immediate current and future economic problems of South Africa are primarily racial and political : substitutes for solutions of current difficulties such as deflation, devaluation, import control, and the like are toying with symptoms. While the problems are great and seemingly intractable there is no reason to believe that progress along sound lines will not emerge : the pointers to that, dim and uncertain though they may be, are surely present.

---

[1] Since this was written and completed for the Conference, the record indicated has most unfortunately been broken by the announcement on June 16 that overseas owners of South African shares will not be allowed to repatriate funds from the sale of their shares on the Johannesburg Stock Exchange. This is a most serious event with far-reaching adverse consequences and must be added to the list of items set out on p. 275.

PART II

Chapter 10

POPULATION MOVEMENTS AND PROBLEMS IN SUB-SAHARAN AFRICA

BY

J. J. SPENGLER

Duke University, Durham, N.C., U.S.A.

No estimates of future population or depopulation formed
upon any existing rate of increase or decrease, can be
depended upon.—T. R. MALTHUS, in *Essay* (II, 13).

THIS paper is made up of three parts : (1) a review of some findings
relating to fertility, mortality, and present and prospective natural
increase in Sub-Saharan Africa ; (2) a review of some findings
relating to migratory movements in this region ; (3) a brief indication of the economic implications of current population movements.

I. FERTILITY, MORTALITY, AND NATURAL INCREASE

Natural increase (*i.e.*, excess of births over deaths) is the primary
determinant of population growth in the states under discussion,
with international migration contributing appreciably only to the
expansion of growing or emerging urban centres. Within states, of
course, migration redistributes population and thereby contributes
to the growth of some parts, usually those which are urban in
character, whilst holding down that of others. Migration sometimes
also affects the sex ratio significantly, above all among adults, but
usually plays only a negligible rôle in shaping age composition which
presently depends predominantly upon the level of fertility. Because
data relating to fertility, mortality, migration, changes in population
totals, and age composition, etc. are quite inadequate, conjecture
necessarily enters into the demographer's findings.[1]

[1] See *Problems in African Demography*, issued by the Union Internationale
pour l'Étude Scientifique de la Population, Paris, 1960. Also bibliographical
information in Frank Lorimer, *Demographic Information on Tropical Africa*,
Boston: Boston University Press, 1961. See also K. M. Barbour and R. M.
Prothero, eds., *Essays on African Population*, London: Routledge and Kegan
Paul, 1961, which appeared after this essay was completed.

Population growth has become significant in the indigenous population of Sub-Saharan Africa only in recent decades. Malthus supposed that the positive checks, together with obstacles to the increase of subsistence, were preventing Africa's population from growing much, if at all.[1] This supposition has been endorsed in substance by demographers (some of whom have supposed that numbers may have decreased slightly between 1650 and 1850) who infer that Africa's population did not begin to grow significantly until in the second half of the nineteenth century, rising from a supposed level of 95-100 million in 1850 to about 200 million in 1950 (about two-thirds of whom are situated in tropical and southern Africa). By the 1950's, according to the United Nations, Africa's population numbered between 243 and 257 million and was increasing 1·8-2·3 per cent per year, or at the same rate as Asia's population.[2]

Kuczynski's monumental study of population movements in what was British Africa indicates that the rate of population growth usually was very low until recently, though it varied somewhat by region.[3] The population of British West Africa had 'probably re-

[1] *Essay on the Principle of Population*, New York : Bk. I, chap. 8. 'Tribal peoples lived almost entirely at subsistence level' in the Africa of which David Livingstone reported a half-century after Malthus wrote. See Barbour and Prothero, eds., *op. cit.* p. 193.

[2] United Nations, *The Determinants and Consequences of Population Trends*, New York : United Nations, 1953, pp. 10-11 ; Lord Hailey, *An African Survey Revised 1956*, London : Oxford University Press, 1957, pp. 119-22. R. R. Kuczynski concluded : 'There is not the least doubt that many territories in West Africa had a larger population before the advent of European slave-traders than they have now, but it is doubtful whether British West Africa as a whole had at any time more than 50 inhabitants per square mile'. At the time of writing (1946) the population of British West Africa approximated 50 per square mile 'as compared with about 7 in French and in Portuguese West Africa, and about 11 in Belgian West Africa'. See *Demographic Survey of the British Colonial Empire*, I, London : Oxford University Press, 1948, p. 14. Regarding the demographic position of East Africa (where slave-trading had been much less important than in West Africa) Kuczynski was less certain. He remarked only that one could not say that the total population was larger in 1940 than in 1895, or smaller in 1895 than in 1875. He also noted : 'But with our present, better knowledge of native agriculture and native habits in general we have no reason to assume that population density was at any time higher than in 1900 (or in 1940) and while our knowledge of the demographic effects of the slave-trade and intertribal wars is still more imperfect, we are less inclined to lose all sense of proportion in dealing with these topics which are now no longer "problems"'. *Ibid.* II, 1949, pp. 120-1, 124-5. Density ranged from 5 per square mile in Northern Rhodesia to 45 in Nyasaland and Uganda in the 1930s. *Ibid.* p. 102. According to C. J. Martin in East Africa between 1920 and 1948 the rate of population growth, by area, ranged from ½ to 1½ per cent per year. See Barbour and Prothero, eds., *op. cit.* p. 53. See United Nations, *Demographic Yearbook 1960*, New York, 1961, pp. 7-10, on the quality of demographic data relating to Africa.

[3] Inasmuch as sample studies constitute the source of much information regarding fertility and mortality in Sub-Saharan Africa, the heterogeneity of whose population is suggested by the fact that over 800 separate languages are used, Kuczynski's caution respecting illicit generalization is in order : 'the differences between the customs of the "tribes" in England are smaller than between the various tribes in most East African Dependencies so that a generalization of

mained stationary during the first quarter of this century, but apparently increased somewhat in the course of the following 15 years'.[1] The population of British East Africa, though perhaps stationary for some time before 1895, decreased in 1895–1920 and thereafter apparently increased, though hardly more than 0·5 per cent yearly.[2] High mortality served to hold down natural increase in both regions, though the behaviour of fertility was not the same everywhere. In West Africa there was 'no justification for assuming that the fertility of native women is higher than it was in England 60 years ago, and it may well be lower'. 'It is certain that fertility among the native women in British East Africa is higher than it is in Western Europe, [but] lower than it was in Eastern Europe around 1900. But whether it is higher or lower than in England 60 years ago it is impossible to tell. Since, however, there is no conclusive evidence that fertility is extraordinarily high anywhere, while there is conclusive evidence that fertility is low among some important tribes, it seems unlikely that fertility as a whole is higher than it was in England 60 years ago.'[3] In Basutoland fertility apparently was 'very high' formerly, but declined appreciably after 1921.[4] The data available for Bechuanaland and Swaziland were too sparse to permit inferences respecting their population growth.[5] It is to be presumed that comparable inquiries into the demographic

the results obtained in England is less risky'. See *op. cit.* II, p. 115. I shall not refer to his *The Cameroons and Togoland*, London, 1939, because the data are too poor to permit inferences other than that fertility was both high and low and population growth was not great.

[1] *Op. cit.* I, pp. 14-15. There was 'no evidence' that Gambia's population had increased before or after 1920. That of the Gold Coast and Togoland probably had not increased before 1920, though it had risen 'considerably thereafter, owing in part to natural increase, and in part to immigration'. The population of Northern Nigeria had not decreased much in 1850–1900 or increased in 1900–25, but it had grown perhaps as much as 10 per cent in 1926–40. That of Southern Nigeria increased considerably in the latter part of the nineteenth century through immigration, but it grew only slightly in 1900–40. The population of Sierra Leone had increased through immigration. *Ibid.* p. 15.

[2] *Ibid.* II, pp. 122-4.

[3] *Ibid.* I, pp. 8-12, II, pp. 118-19. Respecting East Africa Kuczynski noted specifically that mortality was high everywhere, much as in the late nineteenth century. *Ibid.* p. 119. Gross reproduction rates approximated 2·3 in England in 1870–80 and 2·8-3·2 in Eastern Europe around 1900. See Kuczynski's essay in L. Hogben, ed., *Political Arithmetic*, New York : Macmillan Co., 1938, pp. 54-60.

[4] *Demographic Survey*, II, pp. 65, 72.

[5] *Ibid.* pp. 81, 87. In the Island of Mauritius (with gross and net reproduction rates of 3·19 and 2·44 in 1952) gross reproduction approximated only 2·38 (as compared with around 2·5-2·7 in 1870–90) in the early 1940's and the yearly rate of increase approached only 'two-thirds of 1 per cent' in 1923–40 (as compared with 0·25 per cent in 1870–1922). *Ibid.* pp. 870, 885. Indians began to immigrate into this island in the 1830's at which time the population was predominantly African ; by 1952 they comprised two-thirds of the population. Recently J. E. Meade described as catastrophic the impact of continuing uncontrolled population growth upon Mauritius. See 'Mauritius : A Case Study in Malthusian Economics', *Economic Journal*, LXXI, 1961, pp. 521-34. See note 2 on p. 285.

TABLE 1

IMPLICATIONS OF VARIOUS GROSS REPRODUCTION RATES

Gross Reproduction Rates	Expectation of Life at Birth = 30 yrs.				Expectation of Life at Birth = 40 yrs.				Expectation of Life at Birth = 50 yrs.			
	Percentage of Stable Population aged 15–59	Births per 1,000 Inhabitants	Deaths per 1,000 Inhabitants	Natural Increases per 1,000 Inhabitants	Percentage of Stable Population aged 15–59	Births per 1,000 Inhabitants	Deaths per 1,000 Inhabitants	Natural Increases per 1,000 Inhabitants	Percentage of Stable Population aged 15–59	Births per 1,000 Inhabitants	Deaths per 1,000 Inhabitants	Natural Increases per 1,000 Inhabitants
4·0	49·2	59·8	35·3	24·5	47·3	57·3	24·1	33·2	45·8	55·7	16·2	39·5
3·0	54·5	47·7	33·7	14·0	52·5	46·0	23·3	22·7	50·9	44·9	15·8	21·9
2·5	57·6	40·6	33·2	7·4	55·6	39·3	23·2	16·1	53·9	38·4	16·0	22·4
2·0	60·9	32·7	33·6	−0·9	58·8	31·7	23·7	8·0	57·2	31·1	16·8	14·3
1·5	63·8	23·8	35·0	−11·2	61·6	23·1	25·6	−2·5	60·0	22·7	18·8	3·9

Source : See footnote 1, p. 285.

history of parts of Sub-Saharan Africa under non-British control would reveal conditions roughly similar to those reported by Kuczynski.

Since each of the regulators of natural increase, natality and mortality, is subject to variation in both the short and the long run, conjecture respecting African population growth in the future must allow for both modes of variation. At present, as will be noted, gross reproduction, though usually very high by Western standards, falls quite short of the theoretical maximum. Whether it will decline or fall in the immediate future depends, therefore, upon whether socio-economic changes re-enforce fertility-favouring or fertility-checking circumstances. Mortality also is very high by Western standards. It may, however, be expected to decline, for while man and his institutions often resist birth control, they seldom wittingly oppose death control, and ever more effective means of death control are being developed outside as well as in Africa.

The variable impact of possible changes in mortality and fertility upon natural increase in Sub-Saharan Africa may be illustrated with the assistance of stable-population models. A limited range of values from such models, deemed applicable to Africa in the near future, is presented in Table 1.[1] The vertical columns indicate how age composition, natality, mortality, and natural increase change as gross reproduction falls, with expectation of life at birth held constant at 30, 40, and 50 years, respectively. The horizontal lines indicate how age-composition, natality, mortality, and natural increase change as expectation of life at birth rises, with gross reproduction held constant at 4·0, 3·0, 2·5, and 1·5 respectively.

In the late 1950s the United Nations experts estimated expectation of life at birth among Africans to be around 30 years in Middle and Northern Africa and around 42·5 years in Southern Africa. They supposed gross reproduction to be 'very high', probably around 3 in all three regions.[2] With gross reproduction around 3, an

---

[1] The models used, together with Table 1, are derived from models elaborated in United Nations, *The Aging of Populations and Its Economic and Social Implications*, New York : United Nations, 1956, pp. 26-7. Inasmuch as mortality and fertility have not changed much in Africa, the structure of its population probably approximates that of a stable population.

[2] United Nations, *The Future Growth of World Population*, New York : United Nations, 1958, pp. 3-5, 53 ff. While Asian (principally Indian) fertility appears to have begun to decline in Tanganyika and South Africa, it has been very high in the past in areas where Asians have settled. Thus their gross reproduction has approximated 2·9 in East Africa and perhaps exceeded this level in South Africa. See C. J. Martin, 'A Demographic Study of an Immigrant Community : The Indian Population of British East Africa', *Population Studies*, VI, March 1953, pp. 233-47 ; L. T. Badenhorst, 'Territorial Differentials in Fertility in the Union of South Africa — 1911-1936', *ibid.* November 1952, pp. 135-62, especially p. 157, and 'The Future Growth of the Population of South Africa and Its Probable

Economic Development for Africa South of the Sahara

expectation of life at birth of 30 permits the population to increase
about 1·4 per cent per year, whereas a life expectancy of 42·5 permits
it to increase about 2·4 per cent yearly.[1] Put more generally, should
gross reproduction remain in the neighbourhood of 3, increasing
control over mortality could easily raise the annual rate of natural
increase to a level of 2 per cent or more.

Although the Sub-Saharan African populations do not often
resort to contraception or abortion in order to regulate their numbers,
their gross reproduction rates, supposedly in the neighbourhood of
3, fall short of maximum levels which lie in the neighbourhood of
4. Socio-economic circumstances thus serve to hold gross reproduction below its physiological limits. These checks vary ; they include
restrictions on sexual activity, among them deferment of marriage,[2]
and a variety of taboos limiting intercourse (e.g. prolonging lactation
for 2-3 years during which period intercourse often is not sanctioned)
to certain periods. Disease (e.g. malaria, malnutrition, venereal
disease, etc.) may occasion sterility, make for involuntary abortion,
or prevent the live birth of children.[3] Polygyny, common in parts

Age Distribution', *ibid.* IV, June 1950, pp. 3-46, especially pp. 10-12, 25 ; J. G. C.
Blacker, 'Fertility Trends of the Asian Population of Tanganyika', *ibid.* XIII,
July 1959, pp. 46-60. In 1952 gross reproduction in the Indo-Mauritian popula-
tion (3·32) was below that in the Chinese population (3·76) but above that in the
rest of the population (2·91). See M. V. M. Herchenroder's paper in United
Nations, *Papers : World Population Conference* (1954), I, New York : United
Nations, 1955, pp. 851-74, especially pp. 870-2 ; this work will be cited as *Papers*
hereafter.

[1] Badenhorst in 1950 estimated that the Bantu population would increase only
about 1·9 per cent per year, whereas the Coloured would grow about 2·3 per cent.
He assumed, however, that whereas expectation of life among the Bantu would
increase from about 40·5 in 1950 to about 53·5 by 1980, gross reproduction would
remain below 3. See 'The Future Growth . . .', *loc. cit.* pp. 13, 15, 25.

[2] The importance of this check is corroborated by the reproductive experience
of Cocos Malay women ; those married by age 16 averaged 9½ live births by age
40, whereas those not married until 20-21 averaged only 6¼ births by age 40. See
T. E. Smith, 'The Cocos-Keeping Islands : A Demographic Laboratory', *Population Studies*, XIV, November 1960, p. 110 ; also A. J. Coale, 'The Significance of
Age-Patterns in High Fertility Populations', *Milbank Memorial Fund Quarterly*
XXXIX, October 1961, pp. 631-46. See also Frank Lorimer, ed., *Culture and
Human Fertility* (Unesco), Paris, 1954, pp. 54-6, where it is estimated that deferment of marriage to age 24 reduced fertility by about one-fourth below the attainable maximum. R. Blanc and G. Théodore emphasize the fertility-restrictive
effect of customary limitations upon relations between spouses. See 'Les Populations d'Afrique Noire et de Madagascar. Enquêtes et résultats récents', *Population*, XV, April–June 1960, p. 421. African women marry early by nineteenth-
century standards, but often quite some time after puberty. See also note 3
below and note 1, p. 287.

[3] On checks of the sort described see L. T. Badenhorst and B. Unterhalter,
'A Study of Fertility in an Urban African Community', *Population Studies*, XV,
July 1961, pp. 76-86 ; Lorimer, *op. cit.* pp. 54-7, 86-8, 93-4, 102-3, 125-7, 248,
265-8, 300-1, 347-8, 367, 379, 390, 393 ; Kuczynski, *op. cit. passim* ; C. S. Ford,
'Fertility Controls in Under-developed Areas', in United Nations, *Papers*, I,
pp. 841-9. Because of the reasons mentioned above as well as others described
by K. Davis and J. Blake (see 'Social Structure and Fertility : An Analytical
Framework', *Economic Development and Cultural Change*, IV, April 1956, pp. 211-

286

of Africa, is somewhat less favourable to fertility than is mono-gamy.[1]

Africans thus live in a world in which some conditions are un-favourable to fertility and some are favourable. Moreover, each set of conditions tends to change as economic development proceeds. Mention has been made of social and physiological conditions un-favourable to fertility. Among the offsetting conditions favourable to high fertility much weight must be given to lack of knowledge of effective contraceptives, to want-restricting illiteracy, to emphasis upon corporate kinship which makes a woman's position depend largely upon her child-bearing capacity, to the presence of an extended family system which facilitates marriage and reproduction, and to what may be described as an 'apathetic acceptance of cir-cumstances'.[2] With the modernization and detraditionalization of life in African communities, some conditions now favourable to fertility will be weakened ; for example, urbanization will be accom-panied by increase in literacy, wants, and capacity to regulate numbers while the regulatory influence of corporate kinship, the extended family, and tribal ties will diminish as social relationships and obligations are monetized. At the same time the impact of factors unfavourable (*e.g.* disease, malnutrition) to fecundity or gestation will diminish as may the influence of taboos and other factors which delay marriage or restrict sexual relations on the part of spouses. Accordingly, while it is certain that in the longer run economic development, urbanization, and decline in child mortality will be accompanied by a decline in gross reproduction, it is by no means absolutely certain that this decline will not be preceded, in some areas, by a temporary rise in fertility. Among the Bantu in South

235), gross reproduction seldom is as high as it might be. According to Lorimer (*op. cit.* p. 56), the number of live births per woman living through the child-bearing period 'rarely rises above an average of 6·0 to 6·6'. In the absence of any sort of restriction upon fertility, P. Vincent concludes, a mother surviving to 45 years might normally bear 8-10 children. See 'Recherches sur la fécondité biologique . . .', *Population*, XVI, January–March 1961, p. 106. According to Lorimer and Karp, the number of children ever born per African woman in the 40's generally averages 5-6 or more. See *Population in Africa*, Boston : Boston University Press, 1960, p. 5.

[1] *E.g.*, see V. R. Dorjahn, 'Fertility, Polygyny, and Their Interrelations in Temne Society', *American Anthropologist*, LX, October 1958, pp. 838-60. C. Tietze estimates that breast-feeding offers 'better protection than "ineffective" con-traception up to about ten months after confinement, but not beyond that point'. (See his 'The Effect of Breast-feeding on the Rate of Conception', prepared for the population conference held in New York in September 1961, by the Inter-national Union for the Scientific Study of Population.) Polygyny is therefore less favourable than monogamy to fertility in that abstention from sexual relations is more likely to be combined with prolonged lactation under conditions of polygyny than under those of monogamy.

[2] *E.g.*, see Lorimer, *op. cit.* pp. 70-2, 78, 81, 83, 90, 93-4, 131-2, 247-8, 266-7 367, 378-80, 388-9, 392.

Africa, however, there is some evidence of a slight decline in fertility.[1]

Gross reproduction appears to be in the neighbourhood of 3 in Sub-Saharan Africa. This statement is not absolutely demonstrable, for data relating to fertility, mortality, and age composition are inadequate ; moreover, it holds only on the average, since fertility varies with region and people and is relatively low in some tribes. Given that expectation of life at birth is in the neighbourhood of 30, or at least not much above it, the data on the age composition of Africans suggest a gross reproduction rate of around 3 and crude natality rates in the 40s in Middle and Southern Africa.[2] Sample studies of African populations suggest that in some states and among some peoples gross reproduction and crude natality are at these levels. For example, a birth rate of around 52, a death rate of around 21, and a gross reproduction rate of about 3 have been reported for samples of the population of Ghana. Corresponding (though not necessarily compatible) figures reported for French Guinea are 62, 40, and 3·5 ; for the Central African Republic, 39, 26, 2 ; for the Ivory Coast, 59, 28, 3·7 ; for Senegal, 48, 24, 3·1 ; for the Sudanese Republic, 53, 41, 3·3 ; for Southern Rhodesia, 42-45, 13-19, 3·7. For the Republic of the Congo a sample birth rate of 54, but a gross reproduction rate of only 3, is reported. For a number of states sample African birth and death rates have been reported : Ghana, 52 and 21 ; Sudan, 52 and 19 ; Union of South Africa, 42 and 25 ; Belgian Congo, 34 and 22 ; Northern Rhodesia, 57 and 32 ; Uganda, 42 and 25 ; Ruanda-Urundi, 50 and 15 ; Tanganyika, 44 and 25 ; Togoland, 73 and 45 ; Madagascar, about 44 and 22 ; for Nigeria, a birth rate of 49. The average number of children ever born to samples of women who were 45 or older and had completed reproduction have been reported for several states : Ivory Coast, 6-6·5 ; Sudan, 4·9 ; Senegal, 4·3-5·3 ; Central African Republic, 4·2 ; Republic of the Congo, 4·6 ; Togo, 6·2 ; French Guinea, 5·5 ; Ghana, 5·1-6·6 ; Uganda, 4·8 ; Kenya, 5·3 ; Tanganyika, 4·4 ;

---

[1] *E.g.*, see *ibid.* pp. 132, 248-51 ; Blanc and Théodore, *op. cit.* p. 421 ; J. E. Goldthorpe, 'Population Trends and Family Size in Uganda', in United Nations, *Papers*, VI, pp. 859-68 ; V. Brebent, 'Tendances de la fécondité au Congo Belge', *ibid.* I, pp. 775-92. Moslem practice could become more favourable to family limitation, however, as economic development proceeds. See M. Seklani, 'La Fécondité dans les pays arabes : données numériques, attitudes et comportements', *Population*, XV, October–December 1960, pp. 831-56. For evidence of a slight but prospectively slow decline in fertility among urban Bantu women see Baden-horst and Unterhalter, *op. cit.*

[2] United Nations, *The Future Growth* . . ., pp. 32-7, 53-4 ; W. F. Wertheim, 'The Forty Percent Test : A Useful Demographic Technique', in United Nations, *Papers*, VI, pp. 215-25. According to the 1960 *Demographic Yearbook* of the United Nations crude natality approximates 47 per 1,000 in Tropical and Southern Africa, and crude mortality, 28 per 1,000.

Spengler — *Population Problems in Africa*

Northern Rhodesia, 5·9 ; Southern Rhodesia, 5·7 ; Angola, 3·6-4·2 ; Mozambique, 3·5-3·8 ; Portuguese Guinea, 3·3 ; Swaziland, 4·5 ; Belgian Congo, 4·2 ; South African urban Bantus, 4·9. The ratio of children under five per 1,000 African women aged 15-49 is estimated and/or reported for a number of states : Angola, 565 ; Basutoland, 711 ; Bechuanaland, 406 ; British Cameroons, 1,064 ; Guinea, 673 ; Mozambique, 564 ; Nigeria, 1,118 ; Portuguese Guinea, 461 ; South West Africa, 550 ; Fernando Po Island, 374 ; Swaziland, 944 ; Tanganyika, 979 ; Uganda, 874 ; Union of South Africa Bantus, 622, and Coloured, 718 ; Zanzibar and Pemba, 564.[1]

Studies made of the reproductive behaviour of particular peoples yield results in keeping with the data presented. They indicate, for example, that fertility and especially natural increase vary greatly, with gross reproduction sometimes around 3 and sometimes below.[2]

[1] The figures reported in this paragraph, the accuracy of which varies, are drawn from various sources : United Nations, *Demographic Yearbook 1959*, Tables 2, 3, 6, 8 ; Lorimer, *op. cit.* pp. 72, 130, 302, 316-17, 345-6, 368 ; Blanc and Théodore, *op. cit.* especially pp. 430-2 ; Badenhorst and Unterhalter, *op. cit.* p. 78 ; J. R. H. Shaul and C. A. L. Myburgh, 'A Sample Survey of the African Population of Southern Rhodesia', *Population Studies*, II, December 1948, pp. 339-353, 'Estimating the Fertility and Mortality of African Population . . .', *ibid.* X, November 1956, pp. 193-206, and 'Vital Statistics of the African Population of Southern Rhodesia in 1948', *ibid.* IV, March 1951, pp. 432-8 ; C. J. Martin, 'Some Estimates of the General Age Distribution, Fertility and Rate of Natural Increase of the African Population of British East Africa', *ibid.* VII, November 1953, pp. 181-99 ; Badenhorst's papers cited in note 2, p. 285 ; J. R. H. Shaul, 'Preliminary Results of the Second Survey of the African Population of Southern Rhodesia', *Central African Journal of Medicine*, I, September 1955, pp. 246-9, and 'Results of the Demographic Sample Survey of the African Population of Northern Rhodesia', *ibid.* November 1955, pp. 307-11 ; C. A. L. Myburgh, 'A Brief Comparison of the Fertility and Mortality Rates of Africans in Various Countries', *ibid.* II, April 1956, pp. 155-9 ; J. L. Sadie, 'Differential Aging in South Africa', in United Nations, *Papers*, III, pp. 527-36 ; G. A. Marzouk, 'Some Data on Fertility and Mortality in the Sudan', *ibid.* I, pp. 483-92 ; V. Brebent, *op. cit.* ; United Nations, *Additional Information on the Population of Tanganyika* (Population Studies, No. 14) and *The Population of Ruanda-Urundi* (Population Studies, No. 15), New York, 1953 ; Louis Chevalier, *Madagascar, populations et ressources*, Paris : Presses Universitaires de France, 1952, pp. 77-82 ; J. L. Boutillier, *Bongounau, Côte d'Ivoire*, Paris : Berger-Levrault, 1960 ; papers by C. J. Martin and J. R. H. Shaul, in Barbour and Prothero, eds., *op. cit.* Shaul reports survey-based estimates of the age structure of the African population in Southern Rhodesia as indicating 45 per cent of the population to be under 15 years of age ; this fraction corresponds to that found in a stable population with gross reproduction at 3·0, life expectancy at 50, and natural increase at 2·9 per cent per year. Shaul's estimates of mortality and natality yield similar results. See *ibid.* pp. 41, 48, also p. 48 for estimates indicating what amounts, under stable-population conditions, to a gross rate of about 3·0 and life expectancy in the low 30's.

The rates reported in the text above are subject to varying degrees of error, which in some of the studies are estimated. It should be noted, however, that bith rates as high as 60 and over are quite possible when child-bearing begins very early as in parts of Africa. See Coale, 'The Significance of Age Patterns', *loc. cit.*

[2] Even when natality is high, it may vary greatly as in Northern Rhodesia and the Sudan. See Shaul, 'Results of the Demographic Sample . . .', *loc. cit.* pp. 308-10 ; F. J. Simoons, 'Problems of the First Sudan Population Census', *Geographical Review*, XLIX, October 1959, p. 574. Regarding high natality see

They indicate that even though a state's aggregate population may be increasing, components of it may not. For example, some Northern Rhodesian tribes appear to be increasing 2-3 or more per cent per year, whereas others are declining in number.[1] Similar situations are encountered in the Congo and in what was French Equatorial Africa.[2] Whether gross reproduction has generally decreased in recent years is not certain, given the quality of the data, though here and there evidence of decrease exists.[3]

It is more difficult to get satisfactory mortality data than fertility data. The United Nations experts state that 'the expectation of life in Middle Africa may approach 30 years, but it is not very likely to rise much above this figure within the near future', whereas that in South Africa may be as high as 42·5 years.[4] In some instances, however, higher values are reported for African populations: Belgian Congo, 37·6 and 40 for males and females; Southern Rhodesia, 48 and 49; Ivory Coast, 35 for both sexes; Guinea, 30·5 and 35·8 for rural and urban (male and female) populations, respectively.[5] Sadie estimates life expectancy among the South

D. J. Stenning's study of the Woodabe Fulani, *Savannah Nomads*, London: Oxford University Press, 1959, pp. 149, 152-5, 162, 164; J. C. Mitchell's estimate of Yao gross reproduction at 2·8-2·9, in an 'Estimate of Fertility in Some Yao Hamlets in Liwonde District of Southern Nyasaland', *Africa*, XIX, October 1949, pp. 293-308; *African Abstracts*, V, 1954, items 594, 596, IX, 1958, items 163, 175, X, 1959, items 217, 284. On low natural increase and factors making for relatively low fertility see *African Abstracts*, IX, 1958, items 73, 182, 321, X, 1959, items 224, 369, 420, 426, XI, 1960, item 364; S. F. Nadel, *The Nuba*, New York: Oxford Press, 1947, pp. 514-16; L. F. Nadler, *A Tribal Survey of Mongalla Province*, London: Oxford University Press, 1937, p. 57; Monique de Lestrange, *Les Coniagui et les Bassari*, Paris: Presses Universitaires de France, 1955, pp. 8-11.

[1] Shaul, 'Results of the Demographic Sample Survey . . .', *loc. cit.* p. 310; C. M. N. White, *A Preliminary Survey of Luvale Rural Economy* (Rhodes-Livingstone Papers, No. 29), Manchester: Manchester University Press, 1959, pp. 54-6. White remarks that the low fertility of the Luvale is not attributable solely to venereal and other infections. Low fertility 'occurs extensively from French Equatorial Africa and the Middle Congo to Angola to link up with the Luvale areas of Northern Rhodesia'. *Ibid.* p. 56.

[2] *E.g.*, see *ibid.*; Marcel Sorel, *Les Kongo Nord-Occidentaux*, Paris: Presses Universitaires, 1960, p. 15. On the Congo and French Equatorial Africa see papers summarized in *African Abstracts*, I, 1950, items 75, 87, 102, 559, 564, II, 1951, item 100, IV, 1953, item 358, V, 1954, items 598, 599, 605, VI, 1955, items 75, 383, 402, VII, 1956, items 359, 380, IX, 1958, items 360, 537.

[3] *E.g.*, see D. F. Roberts and R. E. S. Tanner, 'A Demographic Study in the Area of Low Fertility in North-east Tanganyika', *Population Studies*, XIII, July 1959, pp. 61-80; Badenhorst, 'Territorial Differentials in Fertility . . .', *loc. cit.* pp. 150-61, whose findings indicate that overall Bantu fertility will fall as the fraction of the Bantu population living in cities rises. Badenhorst's reference that urbanization will slowly reduce Bantu fertility is strengthened by his recent findings. See Badenhorst and Unterhalter, *op. cit.* See also *African Abstracts*, X, 1959, items 369, 420.

[4] *The Future Growth . . .*, pp. 3-4, 53-4. Life expectancy for the South African coloured population is estimated at 42·5. See United Nations, *Demographic Yearbook 1960*, p. 602.

[5] United Nations, *Demographic Yearbook 1959*, Table 32, and *Special Study*

African Bantu at only about 36.[1] Myburgh reports a few estimates for females ranging between 34 and 48.[2] Blanc and Théodore report expectancies (presumably) for the two sexes combined ranging from 20 to 38 in what was formerly French Equatorial Africa.[3] Martin's study suggests that death rates in East Africa range between 25 and 35 per 1,000.[4]

Mortality has fallen somewhat in recent years, and it may be expected to fall somewhat in the future. One does not encounter in the literature, however, expectations that mortality will fall as rapidly as it has fallen in parts of Asia and Latin America. Even so, given continuing efforts by national and international agencies to reduce mortality in Africa, it is probable that life expectancy in Africa will rise to the 40's in the near future.

Because of the decline in mortality, the rate of natural increase is higher than it was several decades ago. Inadequacy of the data do not permit one to say with certainty what is the overall annual rate of natural increase, though the United Nations experts put it currently at 1·9 per cent in Tropical and Southern Africa. This is higher than the rate of 1⅛ per cent estimated for 1925–50.[5] Local studies have revealed considerable variation in the rate of natural increase, with estimated rates ranging from around zero to 2·5 per cent and higher.[6] This variation is present also in the rates of population growth reported in Table 2 for the period 1953–9. These rates, of course, are subject to considerable error, as is the rate for Africa as a whole which is estimated to fall within the range 1·8–2·3 per cent per annum.[7]

What happens in the future will turn largely on the rapidity of the decline in mortality. For while gross reproduction could rise here and there, it will decline in the longer run, though probably quite slowly given low literacy rates, lack of knowledge of contraception, low level of urbanization, etc. Moreover, while deferment of marriage and the beginning of childbearing could lengthen

on Social Conditions in Non-Self-Governing Territories, New York : United Nations, 1958, p. 203, where life expectancies of 38-62 are reported (though these seem much too high). [1] *Op. cit.* p. 534.

[2] 'Estimating the Fertility and Mortality . . .', *loc. cit.* p. 206. See also his 'A Brief Comparison . . .', *loc. cit.* p. 155 ff. where mean expectation of life at birth is estimated at 38 for Ghana and 48 for Swaziland.

[3] *Op. cit.* pp. 430-1.   [4] 'Some Estimates . . .', *loc. cit.* pp. 195, 197-9.

[5] United Nations, *The Future Growth . . .*, p. 26.

[6] Martin, 'Some Estimates . . .', *loc. cit.* pp. 197-8 ; Myburgh, 'A Brief Comparison . . .', *loc. cit.* pp. 155-9, and 'Estimating Fertility . . .', *loc. cit.* p. 206 ; Blanc and Théodore, *op. cit.* pp. 430-1 ; L. T. Badenhorst, 'Prospects for Future Population Changes in South Africa', in United Nations, *Papers*, III, pp. 159-71.

[7] The table is taken from United Nations, *Demographic Yearbook 1960*, Table 1 ; see also for estimates, *ibid.* pp. 7-10. In 1950-9 the average annual increment to the whole of Africa's population was 4·0-5·3 million. *Ibid.* p. 9.

TABLE 2

POPULATION DENSITY AND GROWTH IN SUB-SAHARAN AFRICA

Region and State	Area Km.² (000)	Population in 1959 (000,000)	Population per Km.² (1959)	Annual Increase (1953–9) (%)
Tropical, Southern Africa	19,961	159·00	8	1·9
Ghana	238	4·91	21	1·6
Guinea	246	2·72	11	3·4
Liberia	111	1·25	11	—
Sudan	2,506	11·46	5	—
Union of South Africa	1,223	14·67	12	1·8
Belgian Congo	2,345	13·82	6	2·2
Central African Republic	617	1·19	2	1·3
Chad	1,284	2·60	2	—
Republic of the Congo	342	0·795	2	—
Gabon	267	0·42	2	0·2
Dahomey	116	2·00	17	4·4
Ethiopia	1,184	21·80	18	—
Ivory Coast	322	3·10	10	4·9
Mauretania	1,086	0·73	1	5·2
Niger	1,189	2·56	2	2·7
Senegal	197	2·55	13	3·6
Mali	1,204	4·30	4	—
Upper Volta	274	3·54	13	1·5
Madagascar	590	5·24	9	2·4
Angola	1,247	4·55	4	1·1
Mozambique	783	6·31	8	1·1
Portuguese Guinea	36	0·57	16	1·1
Basutoland	30	0·68	22	1·4
Bechuanaland	712	0·34	0	1·0
Kenya	583	6·46	11	1·6
Nigeria	378	33·66	38	1·9
Northern Rhodesia	746	2·36	3	2·7
Nyasaland	117	2·77	24	2·2
Southern Rhodesia	389	3·00	8	2·9
Sierra Leone	72	2·40	33	2·9
Uganda	243	6·52	27	2·5
Zanzibar and Pemba	3	0·30	115	1·3
British Cameroons	88	1·62	18	1·8
Ruanda-Urundi	54	4·79	88	2·4
Tanganyika	937	9·08	10	1·8
Togo	57	1·44	25	5·6
South West Africa	823	0·55	1	3·0

Source : United Nations, *Demographic Yearbook 1960*, pp. 99-104.

the interval between generations and probably also reduce gross reproduction, such deferment is likely to be slow in emerging. mortality, on the other hand, will certainly decline, though slowly. By the year 2000 United Nations experts have indicated that the 13·9 million living in Southern Africa may number 47-52 million, while the 142 million living in Middle Africa could number 323-449 million. The annual rates of increase implied are around 2·5-2·7 per cent in the former case and around 1·75-2·25 per cent in the latter. It is supposed that fertility will show little tendency to decline in either Middle or Southern Africa over the next forty years, but that life expectancy, after remaining stationary, will rise from around 30 to 42·5 years in Middle Africa in 1975–2000 ; in Southern Africa life expectancy is expected to rise from the 30's in the 1950's to around 60 by 2000. It is expected, however, that some of the Middle African populations will grow faster than others.[1] Projections of this sort serve merely to indicate orders of magnitude. We cannot guess what is in store until we have better census, mortality, and natality data. It is doubtful whether gross reproduction will remain little changed for some decades. It is likely, however, that mortality will fall more than the United Nations estimates imply.

II. MIGRATORY MOVEMENTS

The distribution of population in Sub-Saharan Africa may be described as transitional ; it is the product of many past migratory movements, or the former impact of war, slave trading, etc., and of the partial adjustment of numbers to land under conditions of a traditional agricultural technology and subject to unevenly dispersed sources of water and disease. With the exception of the Yoruba 'towns', few towns are of African origin ; the older towns were Arab creations, while the new ones are recent European products which have not long influenced population movements. Only in recent times has the distribution of Africa's population begun to reflect appreciably the influence of European settlers and culture, of modern technology and urbanization, and of associated flows of migrants from the interior to coastal regions and from poorer areas to European-type cities and other areas of greater opportunity. Accordingly, while population density varies greatly (see Table 2),[2]

[1] United Nations, *The Future Growth* . . ., pp. 7-9, 26, 69-70, 72.
[2] The variation is much greater, of course, when density is computed for small areas instead of for states. For maps see G. T. Trewatha and W. Zelinsky, 'Population Patterns in Tropical Africa', *Annals of the Association of American Geographers*, XLIV, June 1954, pp. 135-62, and 'The Population Geography of Belgian Africa', *ibid.* pp. 163-93, also G. H. T. Kimble, *Tropical Africa*, New

the pattern of population distribution is likely to undergo considerable change as modernization proceeds, Africans become dominated by economic incentives, transport improves, and the proportion [1] of the labour force engaged in agriculture diminishes.[2]

Data relating to past or current African migratory movements are incomplete and deficient, even though they do reveal considerable mobility.[3] Inasmuch as political borders did not coincide with ethnic or cultural borders in Sub-Saharan Africa in the past and migration was free, interstate or interterritorial migration resembled internal migration rather than international migration. Such migration will continue if not impeded by the development of political barriers as new states emerge. This migration has been affected by a variety of influences in recent times, among them the emergence and expansion of essentially modern urban centres,[4] the opening

York : Twentieth Century Fund, I, 1960, pp. 87-123, for maps which are based upon work by Trewartha and Zelinsky. On population mapping in Africa see Barbour and Prothero, eds., *op. cit.* chaps. 6-10, 13-15. On towns see *ibid.*, chaps. 13-14. I give no data on arable land *per capita*, by country, because so little is known of the behaviour of African soils.

[1] Less than one-tenth of the population lives in places of 5,000 or more in Sub-Saharan Africa, outside South Africa ; this fraction is exceeded only in the Rhodesias, Ghana, Zanzibar, Eritrea, French Somaliland, and (possibly) Ethiopia. Few places exceed 100,000. See Kimble, *op. cit.* I, p. 97. In 1950, 60 per cent of the African males over 15 years of age were estimated to be engaged in subsistence farming, 27 per cent in commercial farming within indigenous economies, and only 13 per cent in outside wage earning. Between 'two-thirds and three-quarters of the total land area cultivated by Africans was used for subsistence production'. See United Nations, *Economic Survey of Africa since 1950*, New York : United Nations, 1959, p. 99, and *Enlargement of the Tropical Exchange Economy in Tropical Africa*, New York : United Nations, 1954, p. 17. African labour only gradually became highly sensitive to economic incentives.

[2] The probable effect of diminution in the rate of growth of the European population, at least outside of South Africa and the Rhodesias, is hard to assess. In the recent past, European population has been a complement to, not a substitute for, the African population, especially in non-agricultural branches of the economy. The European population has exceeded 100,000, or 1 per cent of the population, however, only in South Africa, the Rhodesias, the Belgian Congo, Kenya, Angola, and Senegal. On the changing response of African labour to economic incentives see J. C. Mitchell's essay in Barbour and Prothero, eds., *op. cit.* especially pp. 199-206.

[3] G. P. Murdock reviews past movements in his *Africa, Its Peoples and Their Culture History*, New York : McGraw-Hill Book Co., 1959, though it is doubtful if many firm conclusions can be reached in the present state of knowledge ; the index lists over 6,000 names (some of which are synonymous) that refer to African tribes or peoples. For mappings of tribal territories and population densities see Barbour and Prothero, eds., *op. cit.* chap. 15. M. J. Herskovits reports over 800 separate languages in use in Sub-Saharan Africa. See his *Africa*, a study prepared at the request of the Committee on Foreign Relations of the United States Senate, 86th Congress, 1st Session, Washington, D.C. : Government Printing Office, 1959, p. 35. Concerning past migration see C. R. Niven, 'Nigeria Past and Present', *African Affairs*, LVI, October 1951, pp. 225, 265-75 ; *African Abstracts*, VI, 1955, items, 96, 552, IX, 1958, item 219, X, 1959, items 28, 61, 79, 145, 166, 206, 207, 256, 258, 266, 581.

[4] Although about three-fifths of the Yoruba live in 'cities' of over 5,000 inhabitants, these Nigerian cities do not, as a rule, answer to the description of modern cities. They are 'large, dense, permanent settlements, based upon farming

up of centres of cash-crop agriculture or mineral exploitation, the increase of population pressure in rural areas, interregional differences in rate of economic development and in local availability of labour, and the subdivision of economically active Africans into traditional agriculturalists, persons permanently separated from the traditional agricultural economy, and persons 'domiciled in rural areas but temporarily employed outside African agriculture either in other sectors of the domestic economy or abroad'.[1] African migration is usually seasonal and short-term in character, especially in dual (*i.e.* European and African) states in which Africans often circulate between their tribal social systems and employment with Europeans ; yet, under favourable circumstances and given opportunity to reside permanently in or near centres of employment, the migrant is likely to become a long-term or permanent settler in the community of immigration. It is rational in form in that potential migrants move when they believe opportunity elsewhere — above all, economic opportunity — to be sufficiently in excess of that available at home to warrant movement.[2] It reflects the operation of both 'push' and 'pull' factors, that is, of deterioration in income and other opportunities available at the migrant's point of provenance, and of improvement in similar opportunities at accessible points of destination. It also reflects the mobility-reducing influence of distance, in that migrants, though they may travel many more miles than did intra-continental migrants in nineteenth-century Europe, tend to move to proximate rather than to remote points.[3]

rather than upon industrialization, the pattern of which is traditional rather than an outgrowth of acculturation'. Handicrafts and trade engage the few not dependent on agriculture. In recent years, however, some of these towns (*e.g.* Ibadan) have become more 'urban'. See William Bascom, 'Urbanization among the Yoruba', *American Journal of Sociology*, LX, March 1955, pp. 446-54 ; *African Abstracts*, XIII, January 1962, item 76. See also on Yoruba towns, Barbour and Prothero, eds., *op. cit.* chap. 14.

[1] United Nations, *Economic Survey of Africa since 1950*, pp. 41-2. See also p. 294, footnote 1 ; D. H. Houghton, 'Men of Two Worlds', *South African Journal of Economics*, XXVIII, September 1960, pp. 177-90. A typical migrant worker in South Africa leaves home at 16, holds 34 jobs over a 31-year period (64 per cent of which is spent away from home), and returns home at 47 to settle there permanently. *Ibid.* pp. 180-1. See also on Central-African migration J. C. Mitchell's essay in Barbour and Prothero, eds., *op. cit.* pp. 199-244.

[2] On rational aspects of migratory behaviour see W. J. Barber, 'Economic Rationality and Behavior Patterns in an Underdeveloped Area : A Case Study of African Economic Behavior in the Rhodesias', *Economic Development and Cultural Change*, VIII, April 1960, pp. 237-51. See also W. O. Jones, 'Economic Man in Africa', *Food Research Institute Studies*, I, May 1960, pp. 107-34.

[3] In his study of Uganda Walter Elkan found that the low wages offered for unskilled work attract mainly migrants who are distant from the market where these wages are to be had ; their labour-supply price is relatively low as they lack comparable opportunities in or outside farming back home. In contrast, people who live close to the main centres of employment have a relatively high labour-supply price ; they can grow food for sale in town or crops for export markets, or find employment in industry or distribution at wages above those paid for

The causes of migration are both economic and non-economic, with the former predominating. Potential male migrants find themselves pushed to move by the increasing pressure of a growing agricultural population upon the limited amount of utilizable land available, given prevailing technological conditions and the widespreadness of fallow farming. The land may not suffice to employ everyone; it may become subject to classical diminishing returns; and it may undergo depletion of soil fertility, should the number of years land is left fallow be unduly reduced.[1] In consequence the land tilled by a family may no longer support it, with the result that adult males emigrate, leaving the women and children to cultivate the land and support those remaining. This tendency is accentuated, of course, by the increasing need of families for money wherewith to pay taxes and buy the products of civilization, and by the fact that money income, though absolutely low, usually is much higher in industry and in urban centres than is the cash value of the produce a traditional-agriculturist family can raise. In general, then, the origin and direction of migration is dominated by the desire for improvement in the migrant's economic circumstances.[2] In fact,

unskilled work. See *Migrants and Proletarians*, London: Oxford University Press, 1960, pp. 5, 33-41. J. C. Mitchell finds that in Rhodesia migrant workers come more largely from close-by than from distant places of origin, and that labour turnover is lower among workers from near by. See Barbour and Prothero, eds., *op. cit.* pp. 223-8.

[1] *E.g.* see International Bank for Reconstruction and Development, *The Economic Development of Nigeria*, Baltimore: Johns Hopkins Press, 1955, pp. 46, 198; L. D. Stamp, *Our Developing World*, London: Faber and Faber, 1960, pp. 103-4, 'Land Utilization and Soil Erosion in Nigeria', *Geographical Review*, XXVIII, January 1938, pp. 32-45, and *Africa*, New York: John Wiley and Sons, 1953, chap. 5. See also International Labour Office, 'Interterritorial Migrations of Africans South of the Sahara', *International Labour Review*, LXXVI, August 1957, p. 294, where a 50 per cent drop in soil fertility is reported; and Paul Bohannan, 'The Migration and Expansion of the Tiv', *Africa*, XXIV, January 1954, pp. 2-16, where it is shown how the spread of the Tiv people has been affected by the growing scarcity of the land at their disposal. On the impact of population growth and pressure upon cultivation and the disposition to migrate see also W. B. Morgan, 'Farming Practice, Settlement Patterns, and Population Density in South-Eastern Nigeria', *Geographical Journal*, CXXI, September 1956, pp. 320-33; R. M. Prothero, 'The Population of Eastern Nigeria', *Scottish Geographical Magazine*, LXXI, No. 3, 1955, pp. 165-70; Meyer Fortes, *The Dynamics of Clanship among the Tallensi*, New York: Oxford University Press, 1945, p. 156; Barbour and Prothero, eds., *op. cit.* chaps. 9-10. *African Abstracts*, II, 1951, items 64, 196, III, 1952, items 15, 429, 555, 598, 660, IV, 1953, items 181, 267, V, 1954, item 644, VII, 1956, items 103, 238, 298, IX, 1958, item 331, X, 1959, items 93, 181.

[2] *E.g.* see preceding note; Barbour and Prothero, eds., *op. cit.* chaps. 11-12; Elkan, *op. cit.* chaps. 4, 10; Barber, *op. cit.*; International Labour Office, 'Inter-Territorial Migrations . . .', *loc. cit.* pp. 293-6, and *African Labour Survey*, Geneva: International Labour Office, 1958, pp. 42-3, 67-8, 128. I. Schapera mentions 'economic necessity', 'growth of new wants', cash for taxes and other obligations, insufficiency of arable land and other agricultural resources, and, in the past, pressure exerted by and through chiefs who needed money. See *Migrant Labour and Tribal Life*, London: Oxford University Press, 1947, chap. 4. W. Watson mentions, among other things, the need of money to pay taxes and obligations and satisfy marriage payments, and the desire for commercially available

migration is the main source of wage earners, the ratio of whom to the male labour force is high only in countries subject to considerable migration.[1] Migration is affected also by non-economic factors, among them the desire to exchange kinship obligations, poverty and fear, and irksome tribal traditions for the entertainment, the freedom (albeit limited), and the prestige and advantages to be had in urban centres. It is difficult, however, to determine how much influence non-economic factors exercise, in part because economic and non-economic ends are mixed and economic means are often required to satisfy non-economic ends.[2]

Migration in Africa differs from migration in much of the world, in that so small a fraction of the migrants settle permanently in the places where they find employment. This impermanence is attributable largely to the fact that such employment often does not provide support enough for both a workman and his family, and that satisfactory familial housing and security in old age are seldom to be found in places of employment; frequently families must depend upon both subsistence farming and urban industry for support.[3]

goods. See *Tribal Cohesion in a Money Economy*, Manchester : Manchester University Press, 1958, pp. 36-47, 70-1. Better remuneration, less onerous work, the need for money to pay off various obligations, escape from feudal obligations, agricultural over-population, the opportunity to earn and accumulate money and satisfy present and future wants are among the factors mentioned in A. I. Richards, ed., *Economic Development and Tribal Change*, Cambridge : W. Heffer and Sons Ltd., n.d., pp. 46, 64-72, 149-51, 212-13, 220-1, 266-7. See also United Nations Committee on Information from Non-Self-Governing Territories, *Some Aspects of Rural Development* (mimeographed), New York, 1961, pp. 10-11, 35, on agricultural population pressure as cause of emigration in East Africa. On the need of money for taxes as a cause of migration see A. H. M. Kirk-Greene, 'Tax and Travel among the Hill Tribes of Northern Adamawa', *Africa*, XXVI, October 1956, pp. 369-79. On economic factors see also *African Abstracts*, VII, 1956, item 496, IX, 1958, item 74.

[1] International Labour Office, *African Labour Survey*, pp. 666-7, and 'The Development of Wage-Earning Employment in Tropical Africa', *International Labour Review*, LXXIV, September 1956, p. 242 ; United Nations, *Economic Survey of Africa*, pp. 42-3.

[2] *E.g.* the Thonga found wages a preferable alternative 'to the struggle to win status through the traditional mechanisms' which was made difficult by ecological considerations. See M. Harris, 'Labour Emigration among the Moçambique Thonga : Cultural and Political Factors', *Africa*, XXIX, January 1959, pp. 55-8. See also Elkan, *op. cit.* pp. 132-4, respecting how economic motives may be dominating non-economic motives. On the influence of non-economic motives (*e.g.* desire for adventure and change, escape from domestic, tribal, and chiefly control, relief from fear of sorcery, etc.) on migration, see Schapera, *op. cit.* pp. 115-21 ; Watson, *op. cit.* pp. 43-7 ; Richards, *op. cit.* pp. 150-151, 213, 221-3 ; International Labour Office, 'Inter-Territorial Migrations . . .', *loc. cit.* p. 295 ; M. P. Banton, 'Economic Development and Social Change in Sierra Leone', *Economic Development and Cultural Change*, II, June 1953, p. 136 ; G. Balandier, *Sociologie des Brazzavilles Noires*, Paris : Librairie Armand Colin, 1955, *passim* ; *African Abstracts*, VII, 1956, item 496, IX, 1958, item 190.

[3] 'Native agriculture cannot support the African population, while the principal alternative source of income, *i.e.* industry, remunerates the African workers on whom its functioning depends at rates that do not support life in the city. African society therefore depends largely on both types of economic activity ; subsistence

297

Economic Development for Africa South of the Sahara

Indeed, the ability of women to carry on agriculture and support themselves has made it easy for men to assume the rôle of migrant workers and enter the wage system temporarily, and sometimes work at very low wages.[1] But it has also accentuated forces making for an excessive supply of unskilled labour in cities, even at very low wage rates,[2] and thus has made for uneconomically high rates of labour turnover ; and it has thereby retarded agricultural improvement, the development of a stable, industrial labour force, and the augmentation of productivity per worker (which remains very low, as a rule).[3] The ratio of wage earners to the able-bodied male population has been increasing markedly in some Sub-Saharan countries, however, with employment expanding rapidly in manufacturing, building, and construction. Moreover, either because of demand for labour is rising in relation to supply, or for other reasons, in some European-governed countries the number of occupations open to Africans is expanding, increases in productivity are taking place, and migrants are settling permanently in communities where their jobs are located.[4] Where wage, housing, and security provisions have not

agriculture at the base and industrial employment to raise income to the vital minimum.' See International Labour Office, 'Inter-Territorial Migration of Africans . . .', p. 295 ; also idem, African Labour Survey, pp. 274-8, 278-89, also pp. 324 ff., 355-6, and chaps. 11-12 on social security and housing. See also J. C. Mitchell's excellent essay on labour movement in Central Africa, in Barbour and Prothero, eds., op. cit. pp. 193-248 ; also FAO, State of Food and Agriculture 1958, Rome, 1958, chap. 3, especially pp. 119-27, on recurrence of food shortages in areas of overall food adequacy.

[1] E.g. see Harris, op. cit. pp. 50, 53, 55-8 ; also International Labour Office, African Labour Survey, pp. 68-70, 354-9, on sexual division of labour and the infrequency (albeit declining) of woman's being employed outside agriculture. On when urban wages are depressed by the African worker's deriving some support from the land see D. H. Houghton, 'Land Reform in the Bantu areas and Its Effects Upon the Urban Labour Market', South African Journal of Economics, XXIX, September 1961, pp. 165-75.

[2] Other factors have had a similar effect. In Nigeria and Ghana, for example, the disposition of younger people to escape unattractive rural situations is accentuated by the spread of primary education, with the result that migration to cities greatly exceeds the number currently employable there. This experience is probably being repeated in other countries. E.g. see African Abstracts, X, 1959, item 9.

[3] 'The number of Africans actually employed at a given time' is between one-fifth and one-third of the number 'who make part of their living out of wages.' International Labour Office, 'Inter-Territorial Migrations . . .', loc. cit. p. 295, also pp. 307-10 on labour supply and low productivity. 'It is general practice in Africa to use several Natives — sometimes as many as six — for a job that would be done by one worker in a more advanced country.' Ibid. p. 296. See also idem, African Labour Survey, chaps. 5-6 ; and Houghton, 'Men of Two Worlds', loc. cit. pp. 181-4 ; also African Abstracts, VIII, 1957, item 439.

[4] See ibid. ; International Labour Office, 'The Development of Wage-Earning Employment in Tropical Africa', International Labour Review, LXXIV, September 1956, pp. 238-58, especially pp. 242, 248-53, and 'Interracial Wage Structure in Certain Parts of Africa', ibid. LXXVIII, July 1958, pp. 20-55, especially pp. 36-48, 54-5. Elkan questions if better housing and better wages alone will suffice to diminish temporary migration ; reform of land tenure is also essential. See op. cit. pp. 133-40.

conduced to the permanent settlement of workers and their families in cities, they have not been able to cut tribal ties completely, and detribalization, so essential to political unity and economic development in multi-tribal national communities, has not been fully carried out.[1]

With the spread of independence the circumstances affecting international migration in Africa will change somewhat. Business firms operated by Whites will be under pressure to open all sorts of occupations to natives ; but not many of the latter will be able to avail themselves of these opportunities until the requisite forms of technological and business education are made widely available at the secondary level (probably through recourse to teacher-saving devices and arrangements). For there is a limit to the number of unskilled persons who can be employed in a country, and a shortage of appropriately trained secondary-level personnel is presently among the constraints on the employment even of unskilled persons in various African countries.[2]

The volume of migration in general, internal and external, will depend largely upon the rate of population growth and of progress in agriculture, while the amount of migration that assumes international form will depend largely upon the extent to which urbanization and non-agricultural employment expand at requisite rates in various countries. If there is little improvement in agriculture and the current agricultural labour force is needed to meet the population's growing food requirements, there will be available for non-agricultural employment only the fraction of the labour force that is

[1] The word 'fully' probably needs to be qualified, since tribal cultures always leave some deposit in the culture to which they give place. On circumstances favouring detribalization see *ibid.* pp. 48-52 ; M. Banton, 'Adaptation and Integration in the Social System of Temne Immigrants in Freetown', *Africa*, XXVI, October 1956, p. 354 ; *African Abstracts*, VIII, 1957, item 258, IX, 1958, items 27, 81, 166. On circumstances which block detribalization see J. Van Velsen, 'Labor Migration as a Factor in the Continuity of Tonga Tribal Society', *Economic Development and Cultural Change*, VIII, April 1960, pp. 265, 272-8 ; A. L. Epstein, *Politics in an Urban African Community*, Manchester : Manchester University Press, 1958, *passim* ; K. Little, 'Structural Change in the Sierra Leone Protectorate', *Africa*, XXV, July 1955, pp. 231-2 ; also *African Abstracts*, X, 1959, items 30, 70, XIII, January 1962, item 79, on the unifying effects of pan-tribalism. J. L. Sadie describes how 'traditional tribal culture' blocks economic development in 'The Social Anthropology of Underdevelopment', *Economic Journal*, LXX, June 1960, pp. 294-303. On the impact of urban living in a Nigerian city (Lagos) see Peter Marris, *Family and Social Change in an African City*, London : Routledge and Kegan Paul, 1961. See also T. T. Poleman, 'The Food Economy of Urban Middle Africa : The Case of Ghana', *Food Research Institute Studies*, II, May 1961, pp. 121-75.

[2] Even in the Union of South Africa, it is estimated, expansion of the demand for native labour, whether from the Union or abroad, depends predominantly upon the expansion of secondary and tertiary employment. See S. P. Viljoen, 'Higher Productivity and Higher Wages of Native Labour in South Africa', *South African Journal of Economics*, XXIX, March 1961, p. 40. Such employment usually presupposes more than primary education. See also Elkan's discussion of education and skill in *op. cit. passim.*

not required in agriculture, together with the natural growth of this labour force. International migration will depend largely upon the extent to which this growing non-agricultural labour force can find employment at home at wages not greatly below those to be had elsewhere. A careful analysis of the prospective values of the determining variables would probably indicate that the volume of both internal and external migration will rise much above present levels for several or more decades.

While every African country is experiencing considerable internal migration, above all those with coastal areas and cities, and while some experience about as much emigration as immigration each year, a few are centres of attraction for temporary or permanent inter-territorial migrants, and a few are important sources of emigrants. The Union of South Africa is the principal such centre ; in 1951 there were in the Union about 650,000 Africans from outside, of whom over 400,000 were migrant workers. In that same year there were 247,000 African workers from the outside in Southern Rhodesia, and by 1956 this number exceeded 300,000. In Ghana, which now experiences an annual seasonal migration estimated as high as 300,000-400,000 workers, there were 175,000 Africans of foreign origin already in 1948. In 1956 the Belgian Congo employed about 77,000 Africans from outside, and Northern Rhodesia, 45,000, or about as many as it supplied elsewhere, principally to Southern Rhodesia. In 1957 Uganda employed about 55,000 outsiders, and Tanganyika about 41,000. Among the main sources were Nyasaland, about 164,000 ; Mozambique and Angola, about 254,000 ; Ruanda-Urundi, about 69,000 ; Bechuanaland, Basutoland, and Swaziland, about 57,000. Over 350,000 move each year, mostly for the season, to Senegal, the Ivory Coast, and Ghana, from the Upper Volta, the French Sudan, Togo, Niger, and the north of Guinea.[1]

[1] The data relate principally to 1956-7. International Labour Office, *African Labour Survey*, pp. 127-37, and 'Inter-Territorial Migrations . . .', *loc. cit.* pp. 300-7 ; United Nations, *Economic Survey of Africa*, pp. 42-4, 49 ; Kimble, *op. cit.* I, pp. 582-6. Nigeria experiences net emigration as well as a great deal of internal migration. *E.g.* in the 1952-3 dry season, of 259,000 migrants (one-sixth of whom came from French territory), mostly from Sokoto Province in Northern Nigeria, one-sixth reported Ghana to be their destination. See R. M. Prothero, 'Migratory Labour from North-Western Nigeria', *Africa*, XXVII, June 1957, pp. 251-61. Jean Rouch estimated at nearly 400,000 immigrant workers from the North (mostly from former French Africa) engaged in agriculture, commerce, and manufacture in Ghana. See 'Migrations au Ghana', *Journal de la Société des Africanistes*, XXVI, 1956, pp. 192-6. See also on seasonal migration to Ghana and the Ivory Coast from former French colonies, *African Abstracts*, XIII, January 1962, items 44 and 55. On Southern Rhodesia see Peter Scott, 'Migrant Labor in Southern Rhodesia', *Geographical Review*, LIV, January 1954, pp. 29-48 ; on South Africa, Houghton, *op. cit.* ; on Uganda, Elkan, *op. cit.* and Richards, *op. cit.* ; on Bechuanaland, Schapera, *op. cit.* ; on Central and East Africa, Barbour and Prothero, eds., *op. cit.* chaps. 11-12.

III. ECONOMIC IMPLICATIONS

The economic implications may be dealt with under three headings: (*a*) optimum size of population versus optimum size of polity and economy ; (*b*) the costs and the benefits of population growth as such ; and (*c*) the impact of migratory movements upon the cultural unity of the population and the rationality of the distribution of economic activities in space.

(*a*) It is essential to distinguish between the concept of optimum size of population and the concept of optimum size of state, or, put briefly, between population optimum and political optimum. For these may differ greatly, particularly in areas such as Sub-Saharan Africa where most of the actually and the potentially sovereign states are of sub-optimum political size. We may say that the population of a state is of optimum size when, given the geographical size of that state, together with its technology, its resource endowment and its external relations, this population is of a size to maximize whatever income or welfare index is chosen for maximization. The magnitude of the optimum thus depends not only upon a state's resource endowment and external relations but also upon the content of the welfare index ; it will be smaller if *per capita* income rather than family size is emphasized ; it will be larger if political rather than economic values are emphasized, since the maximum for political values is considerably larger than the maximum for economic values ; and so on. None the less, howsoever the welfare index is defined, the population optimum resulting for a state of given territorial extent may still be far too small to permit such state to realize the economies of scale and manœuvre which it could realize if its territory as well as its population were greater. In other words, a state is of political optimum size only if, given its international relations, its territorial extent is great enough and its population large enough to permit realization of these economies and make possible maximization of a welfare index that suitably reflects economic, political, and cultural values. This political optimum may increase, as may a population optimum, as technology improves ; but this is not necessarily the case.

Most of the states situated in Sub-Saharan Africa are of sub-optimum political size, given modern technology, international relations, the overhead cost of government, etc. Accordingly, even if their populations should become of optimum size for their present territories, the difficulties associated with being of sub-optimum political size would probably remain. Moreover, they would not prove remediable through population growth as such, since the limitational factor consists primarily in territorial extent. It is not possible here to indicate just what constitutes optimum political size under the circumstances, or even to examine the determinants of political size, for this essay centres on population problems as such. My present concern is merely to indicate the need, on grounds of theory as well as on grounds of policy, to distinguish between the population optimum and the political optimum.[1] It is probable, however, that in most of the African states, an increase in numbers as well as in territorial size is indicated, but not a high rate of increase in population.

(b) Three sorts of cost are occasioned by population growth : absorption of resources ; disadvantages attributable to an unfavourable age composition ; and increase in the pressure of numbers upon a state's endowment of resources. The order of magnitude of the first cost, though hard to put in internationally comparable terms, may be suggested by supposing that in an under-developed country a rate of saving of 4-5 per cent of the national income is required to offset a 1 per cent per year rate of population growth and maintain the wealth-population ratio. Given a population growth rate of 2 per cent, savings of 8-10 per cent of the national income would be diverted from increasing wealth per head to equipping new increments of population, with the further effect that a larger fraction of these savings would assume forms marked by relatively high capital/output ratios. Had the population not been growing, these savings, if invested in increasing capital per head, might have increased income per head by 1-2 per cent. This suggests, as has been implied, that if further population growth is found desirable, it had best take place slowly, particularly since the rate of saving *per capita* also tends to vary inversely with the rate of natural increase.

The second cost flows from the fact that, with a population growing 2-3 per cent per year, the fraction of the population of working age (say, 15-59) will be 10-15 per cent smaller than when the population is growing very little.[2] Under *ceteris paribus* conditions, therefore, potential productivity *per capita* will be 10-15 per cent lower. This potential productivity, if actualized and invested, might increase output per head by 2 per cent or more and so make possible a decidedly higher rate of capital formation. Illustrative of the capital shortage accentuated by unfavourableness in age composition is investment in education *per capita*, apparently one of the most productive forms that capital may assume even though 4-16

[1] Some of the issues involved are dealt with in Austin Robinson, ed., *The Economic Consequences of the Size of Nations*, London : Macmillan and Co., Ltd., 1960.
[2] See the columns headed Percentage of stable population aged 15-59, in Table 1 and read down to ascertain what takes place under stable-population conditions.

years may have to elapse before some of it begins to yield a return.[1] For the ratio of persons of school age to persons of an age to be teachers in high-fertility countries is about double that found in low-fertility countries. It is much more difficult, therefore, even under otherwise similar conditions, to supply education in high-fertility countries.

The third cost of population growth, increase in the pressure of numbers upon resources, is not easy to state in general terms, depending as it does upon concrete conditions and hence varying with the state of the arts, external relations, etc. One manifestation in a predominantly agricultural economy based upon bush-fallow is the reduction in the number of years the land is left fallow, with the result that the soil is depleted, yields fall, and it becomes necessary to introduce crops (*e.g.* manioc) adapted to depleted soils.[2] This outcome may be checked, at least within limits, through improvement in agricultural methods, but such improvement is likely to be more difficult to introduce as a result of population pressure and the resulting capital-absorption which operate in general to reduce the *per capita* output of raw materials to be had in the long run from a nation's endowment of natural resources.[3]

There may exist some offsets to these disadvantages of population growth. Effective habitation of parts of Africa is possible only if population density exceeds some minimum level.[4] When a

[1] For estimates relating to an under-developed country see Carl S. Shoup, *The Fiscal System of Venezuela*, Baltimore : Johns Hopkins Press, 1959, chap. 15 and *passim*. Illustrative of the magnitude of the educational problem is *Investment in Education*, A Report of the Commission on Post-School Certificate and Higher Education in Nigeria, Lagos : Federal Ministry of Education, 1960.

[2] *E.g.* see L. D. Stamp, *Africa*, chap. 5 and *passim*, and *Our Developing World*, chap. 7 ; also Kimble, *op. cit.* I, chaps. 4-5 ; W. O. Jones, ' Food and Agricultural Economies of Tropical Africa ', *Food Research Institute Studies*, II, February 1961, pp. 8-13.

[3] I have not referred to data relating to mineral and other natural resources and their significance since the inventorying of Sub-Saharan Africa's resources has not been completed. This resource endowment tends to be exaggerated. The United Nations reports suggest that iron and coal are abundant only in the South and that the contribution of non-ferrous metals to gross national product is limited. See United Nations, *World Iron Ore Resources and Their Utilization*, 1950, *Survey of World Iron Ore Resources*, 1955, and *Non-Ferrous Metals in Under-Developed Countries*, 1956 ; these studies have been published by the United Nations in New York. See also W. R. Jones, *Minerals in Industry*, Middlesex : Harmondsworth, 1950 ; Kimble, *op. cit.* I, chaps. 4-7, 9 ; Robert McKinney, ed., *Background Materials for Review of the International Atomic Policies and Programs of the United States*, Vol. 4 of Report to the Joint Committee on Atomic Energy, Congress of the United States, Washington : Government Printing Office, 1960. At present mining is quite important only in the Rhodesias, the Union of South Africa, and the Belgian Congo. See United Nations, *Economic Survey of Africa*, pp. 16-17.

[4] *E.g.* R. J. H. Church states that a minimum density of 70 per square mile is essential in regions subject to infestation by the tsetse-fly. See *West Africa*, London : Longmans, Green, 1957, p. 164. This notion of a minimum may be fitted into the general theory of a population minimum. *E.g.* see Jean Sutter and Léon Tabah, ' Les Notions d'isolat et de population minimum ', *Population*, VI, July-September 1951, pp. 491-8 ; A. Sauvy, *Théorie générale de la population*, Paris : Presses Universitaires de France, 1952, chap. 3.

population is large, there is greater scope for division of labour, cultural intensification, etc. When a population is growing, a given degree of economic flexibility is attainable with less difficulty, and it is possible to change the value-composition of a population more rapidly.[1] And so on.

(c) Inasmuch as births and population growth are seldom distributed in space in the proportions required if economic activities are to be distributed optimally in space, considerable internal migration is required to bring about or maintain an optimum distribution of people in space. This requirement may be particularly high when a predominantly agricultural economy begins to undergo transformation and opportunities emerge, especially outside agriculture, for individuals who are under-employed in agriculture, or whose labour is relatively unproductive in agriculture even according to local rural and urban standards. For reasons indicated toward the close of Section II, it is to be expected that a large amount of internal migration will accompany economic development in Sub-Saharan Africa, being essential thereto, and that if development proceeds much more rapidly in some countries than in others, numbers, if free to move, will migrate to the former from the latter countries.

Migration should contribute greatly to the establishment in African countries of a sufficient degree of cultural homogeneity to facilitate political and economic development. The number of tribes and tribal cultures in any one country is very great and constitutes a major hindrance to the achievement of the necessary minimum of cultural unity. Migration will mix tribes in cities, most of which are too small to accommodate tribal ghettos. Under the circumstances, therefore, skilful political, educational and industrial, leadership should be able to bring about this unity.[2]

DISCUSSION OF PROFESSOR SPENGLER'S PAPER

Professor Peacock introduced Professor Spengler's paper under three headings : the facts of population growth and structure ; the causes of

[1] When a population is backward and its transformation depends largely upon change in its value orientation, it is possible, *given the educational personnel to supply instruction,* to increase the *relative* number of persons with lower and (perhaps) secondary education faster when a population is growing (say) 2 per cent per year than when it is growing only 0·5 per cent per year. As a rule, however, the educational personnel are lacking and transformation of the population can be carried out faster with a relatively low rate of population growth.

[2] Concerning the political and related aspects of this problem, see J. S. Coleman's essay in G. A. Almond and J. S. Coleman, *The Politics of the Developing Areas,* Princeton : Princeton Press, 1960, chap. 3.

population growth ; and the economic consequences of population trends in African countries.

Starting with the facts, he commented that obviously data on population were of fundamental importance for the study of economic growth in Africa. The extrapolation of population trends based on demographic data was of great importance in economic planning as, for example, in estimating the future labour force and its age composition and in measuring the effects of population growth on the demand for government services, such as education and health. Professor Spengler had clearly done a splendid job in collating and interpreting population data for a large number of countries combined with the prodigious documentation for which he is justly famous.

Professor Peacock had two comments to make about the facts as presented. It was hardly Professor Spengler's fault that the data varied so much in reliability and in coverage so that useful extrapolations for the task in hand were difficult to make. He felt it would be useful to steer part of the discussion towards the technical problems of calculation under African conditions, for the experiences of census taking and sampling in Africa, involving such difficulties as the lack of skilled enumerators, the sheer physical effort of covering vast areas, and the downright resistance of the subjects of the inquiries, provided an interesting example of the difficulties encountered by scientific investigation in developing countries. His second comment related to population projections. Of necessity, perhaps, Professor Spengler's paper was backward, rather than forward, looking, although brief reference was made to the UN projections; he felt that whatever might be the hazards of projection we should try to take a view of the influences on future population trends in the light of possible changes in mortality and fertility rates, and, in the case of individual countries, possible changes in migration.

Turning to causes, he said that it might seem at first sight that the causes of population growth were not a fit subject of inquiry by economists. Certainly with the falsification of Malthus's forecasts in the case of Western countries, it had been usual for the economist to take population trends as given in any analysis. However, there had been a revival of the general approach of Malthus, with his emphasis on the interaction of economic growth and population growth, although this was not to say that Malthus's assumptions were accepted. He referred to the work of Leibenstein and others, which attempted to embody an economic theory of population in growth models, designed to explain the phenomenon of the 'low-level equilibrium trap'.

It might be interesting, therefore, in the light of Professor Spengler's observations, to consider the general question of the specifically economic influences on population growth in Africa. Mortality rates had a long way to fall in African countries, and their decline might be a function of economic advance. Other things being equal, a large decline in mortality rates caused by economic advance might itself, through its effect on population growth, affect the pace of economic advance. If the UN experts were right, Africa might not experience the rapid decline in mortality rates which occurred in some Asian countries. It was often argued that falling mortality rates might be accompanied by falling fertility rates. The process of urbanization and industrialization might bring a downward shift in fertility rates in two ways : (*a*) through introduction to modern techniques of contraception ; and (*b*) through the declining importance of the family as an economic unit and source of social security. He could not say whether these forces would be at work in African societies, but he noted that Professor Spengler had some doubts about the effects of urbanization on fertility reduction, and that the UN experts discounted the importance of falling fertility rates as an influence on future population trends. So far as individual countries were concerned, migration might be influenced very much by economic conditions. He had nothing much to add to Professor Spengler's discussion of migration and to the contributions of others on the same topic, but he suggested that with more definitive political boundaries and with planning carried out by many separate national units, political factors might be an important influence on migration in the future.

Turning to the consequences of population growth, *Professor Peacock* argued that the basic question at issue was whether the projected rate of increase in population in African countries would help or hinder the growth process. The answer to this question depended on two factors. The first was the target of growth. Obviously the answer would be different if we desired a target rate of growth of, say, 5 per cent per annum increase in *per capita* income than if we desired a 2 per cent *per capita* growth rate. The second factor, put in technical language, was the view we took of the shape and position of the aggregate production function relating population (through labour supply) and output. Malthus assumed, roughly speaking, that all other factors were fixed. In a dynamic setting, it was to be hoped that under African conditions the production function might be moved upward as a result of the growth in the supply of capital, know-how, and enterprise, simultaneously with the growth in population.

Professor Peacock wished to relate this observation to Professor Spengler's discussion of 'optimum' population and the 'costs' of population growth. He had never thought that the concept of an optimum population was a very useful one, except for illustrating the kind of fallacy, perpetrated by natural scientists, which implied that there was an 'optimum' population density which was compatible with the maximization of *per capita* income. As usually stated, the theory of the optimum was a static one. However, if it were possible to influence population trends by policy measures, we should have to have very fine adjustments as the optimum would shift with each change in factor endowments. While governments might influence population trends through influencing mortality rates and migration (but not fertility rates), they could not do so with any precision. He disagreed, therefore, with Professor Spengler about the use of the concept of the optimum, and he also doubted whether a movement towards the optimum (in the sense of an increase in *per capita* incomes) necessarily required an enlargement of the political unit. If this was what was meant by Professor Spengler, the same objective might be achieved by freer international trade and by customs unions, without a change in the size of political units.

So far as the 'costs' of population growth were concerned, *Professor Peacock* suggested that Professor Spengler seemed to argue that if we compared one situation in which population grew, at say 2 per cent, with another in which it did not grow, economically speaking the latter situation was to be preferred because a given rate of saving would increase capital per head at a faster rate than the former situation, and because in the latter situation 'a larger fraction of these savings would assume forms marked by relatively high capital/output ratios'. This argument completely excluded the possibility that the capital/output ratios might be affected by the growth in labour supply as a consequence of population growth. To some extent, Professor Spengler implicitly countered this argument by showing that with a 2–3 per cent growth the fraction of population of working age would become smaller compared with the situation when population was growing very little. However, he would be interested to know whether under African conditions, given present life expectancies and health conditions generally, it was realistic to assume that the working population should be defined as the age-group 15–59.

Professor Leduc doubted the usefulness of discussing the methodology of population measurement thus encroaching on the work of statisticians and demographers. The most that economists could do was to formulate certain desiderata and comment on the usefulness of the available information. The most important fact in relation to population was that there had been a real demographic revolution in recent years, confirmed by studies in many countries, implying a population increase as great as 2 per cent, sometimes 2½ per cent. There had, however, been differences between urban and rural areas in most of the countries concerned. Was this a general movement? He himself did not believe that it was common to the whole of Africa; in some cases rates of population growth were lower or even stationary. He thought one should start with an investigation of the differences of rates of population growth and their causes.

Professor Robinson inquired how far these rapid population growths represented a real change rather than an improvement of census methods. *Professor Leduc* had the impression that, while methods had undoubtedly improved, the increased numbers enumerated were real and not merely the result of better census taking.

Professor Walker commented that the first effective census of East Africa was taken in 1948. The second was in 1958–9. The latter census gave much higher figures than had been expected, both in Uganda and in Tanganyika. Part of this might be due to immigration, particularly into Uganda. But he did not think there had been any significant improvement in enumeration so far as East Africa was concerned. Indeed the 1948 census was probably the more accurate.

Professor Bézy said that a recent 10 per cent sample census in Congo showed the combination of a high mortality and a high population increase (over 2 per cent per annum). The fecundity rate was high, with the additional phenomenon that the urban natality rate was much higher than the rural. This was perhaps due to the fact of the different structure of the urban population : it was younger, but the ratio of women to men was much lower (under 65 women per 100 men). Medical services were much better in the towns. It was evident that town life had not changed the attitude of women with regard to children. The recent increase of the birth rate could perhaps be attributed to the availability of powdered milk ; formerly mothers had suckled their children for 2–3 years during which there were taboos on intercourse. It was evident that urbanization did not reduce birth rates in the Congo.

Professor Dupriez agreed with Professor Bézy that the statistics revealed by the Congo census permitted clear inferences to be drawn from wholly reliable data, though it was not possible to make comparisons with earlier censuses. In certain regions there had been a distinct reduction of population. The reasons were not wholly clear. It was perhaps due to the fact that emigration from some of the least healthy regions was not balanced by immigration. He was not wholly convinced by some of the conclusions drawn by Professor Spengler from data relating to large areas. Global statistics might reveal little change where there had been considerable changes in particular regions.

Dr. Wade agreed with what Professor Leduc had said about revolutionary demographic changes. Census inquiries in Senegal had recently shown a considerable population increase, some of which might be due to better enumeration. He did not believe that even new census methods were wholly reliable. Their experience agreed with what Professor Bézy had said about the relative fecundity in urban and rural areas. He estimated that the black population of Africa was increasing by about 2–3 per cent per annum, largely owing to the disappearance of wars and slave-raiding in the twentieth century as compared with earlier periods.

Professor Frankel emphasized the dangers of excessive population growth. There had been population cycles in earlier periods and he distrusted all attempts to guess long-term trends from short-term changes. The structures of populations were being reconstituted in relation not only to ecological changes, but also to the disappearance of wars, the inroads of tsetse, and similar factors. It had to be remembered that African populations even now were primarily rural and that any interruption of the peaceful development of Africa could very easily throw the continent back into conditions of grave overpopulation with a substantial decline in the standard of living.

Mr. Menon (Economic Commission for Africa) thought that census taking had improved very considerably and that this explained a sub-

Spengler — Population Problems in Africa

stantial part of the apparent burst of population growth. In several countries, including Ghana and the Ivory Coast, the apparent increases of population were considerably larger than could be explained by natural increase, even ifthat were as great as 2–3 per cent per annum. He thought there had been a considerable underestimation of populations in the past. He thought it should be borne in mind that births registered in the towns were not necessarily births to the urban populations.

In reply to a question by *Mr. Moran*, *Professor Spengler* agreed that there had been considerable changes in the rates of population growth and of fertility during the past twenty-five to thirty years. Various cycles had to be taken into account. Full employment and improved economic conditions had effects on marriage and fertility. The present cycles had not yet been fully worked out and it was not yet possible to judge how long present fertility rates would persist. He thought similar considerations would apply to Africa.

Dr. Singer wished to know whether it was possible to discover any relation between education and birth rates in Africa. Would not this throw light on the longer term trends? *Professor Spengler* was unwilling to draw any conclusions regarding differential birth rates on the basis of education. There were not sufficient data. Improved education brought, he thought, improved economic conditions and increased total capacity of a country to support its population. *Professor Williams* said that in Ghana a differential birth rate was developing in the towns. Higher education meant postponement of marriage. Further, in the towns there was a tendency for the extended family to break up, and this increased the problem of bringing up children. Moreover the natural restraint during lactation was still practised. *Mr. Menon* said that Indian experience suggested that education was associated with lower birth rate only when the education reached a fairly high standard.

Professor Robinson was anxious to broaden the discussion. Was Africa over- or under-populated? What was the relation between growth of population and growth of income? Was the growth of income per head being kept down by population growth, or were the increasing returns to transport, public utilities, distribution, and manufacture sufficient, as he believed, to offset the diseconomies of population growth?

Dr. Singer thought that Africa suffered, and was likely to continue to suffer, from poverty rather than either over-population or under-population. Moderate changes of population were not likely to affect living standards in either direction.

Professor Williams argued that everything depended on the assumptions made regarding techniques of production, particularly in agriculture. If one were thinking of 'take-off', that would happen, if it happened at all, in the modern industrial sectors, leaving traditional agriculture behind. One should concentrate attention on the modern sector, and forget the rural sector, unless population there was growing so fast as to have important repercussions on the modern sector.

309

Professor Leduc thought that it was wholly a matter of dynamics. Some areas were over-populated; some were under-populated. The right question to ask was whether the rates of population growth were favourable or unfavourable to increased income per head. He thought there were more cases where population growth was favourable in that sense than unfavourable. He did not share Professor Frankel's fears.

Professor Dupriez shared the view that the answer depended on the techniques assumed. One area in Ruanda Urundi had seemed to be at the limit of its power to absorb population, but when allowance was made for migration the situation appeared very different. There had been significant changes in the ratio of work to leisure, which again affected the issue. He did not think that industrialization would greatly change the situation. In Europe the numbers employed in industry had been very small in the early stages of industrialization.

Professor Bézy also stressed the wide regional differences. The average density of population in Congo was very low, but the main agricultural areas were very densely populated.

Mr. Onitiri also argued that the situation was a dynamic one. So many things were changing, especially in regard to techniques of production, that population was likely to be influenced unpredictably. Africa was not over-populated as a whole, though it might be in small areas. But he thought that it was important to introduce education in birth control even before it actually became essential.

M. Roland Pré agreed that there was no present problem of over- or under-population in Africa as a whole. There were, however, local problems of over-population in the High Volta and the Cameroons. These local problems might change considerably if the political pattern were changed.

Dr. Singer thought it misleading to talk about population growth as a single issue. Population growth was the result of a combination of birth rates and death rates. In Africa what was principally the matter was that both birth rates and death rates were high. Both a high birth rate and a high death rate imposed heavy costs on the community. What was most desirable was to reduce both rates substantially.

Professor Peacock was convinced that there was no one answer. Everything depended on the scarcity of African endowments of skills and materials, and the important demands were exogenous to the African economies.

Dr. Wade said that one could only speak of serious over-population where almost all land was used. In Africa large areas of good land were not cultivated at all. With new techniques there were great possibilities of expanding agricultural production. If one asked whether Africa could feed very much larger populations the answer was clearly in the affirmative.

Dr. Vopicka was impressed by the unlimited possibilities of Africa. The future of Africa depended greatly on the development of economic relations. We should be discussing the possible changes in methods.

Spengler — Population Problems in Africa

He thought that Professor Spengler had neglected this aspect.

Dr. Yudelman warned that appearances were often deceptive in Africa. It gave the impression of an empty continent. But when account was taken of soils and climates the available agricultural areas were limited.

The discussion then turned towards the problems of migration. *Mr. Onitiri* thought that migration and migration patterns could not be effectively considered in isolation from political and racial policies. *Professor Frankel* replied that political factors were less important than the fact that African natural resources were far removed from the normal homes of African populations. *Mr. Cookson* argued that future political decisions would affect the flows of migration. *Mr. Moran* pointed out that labour migrations presented a thorny political problem in many parts of the world : in the U.S.A. in respect of Mexican labour, in Western Europe and the United Kingdom in respect of Italian labour. He thought it would remain a problem equally for Africa. *Dr. Wade* stressed the importance of distinguishing seasonal from more permanent migrations.

Dr. Yudelman drew attention to the economy of migratory labour in respect of house-building, as had been pointed out by Professor Arthur Lewis, in relation to urbanization in Ghana.

Summing up, *Professor Spengler* said that he hoped that the Economic Commission for Africa would work out a model for census taking throughout Africa, including suggestions for more thorough sample surveys. He hoped that attempts would be made to establish the standard errors of such sample censuses. He thought Africa would probably be better off with three times the present population, but would like to see that sort of total approached more slowly — say at 1 per cent per annum rather than 2–3 per cent. He thought African states were too small ; larger units would give more room for movement. He emphasized finally and again the widely ramifying interdependence of population growth and economic growth.

Chapter 11

THE PROBLEMS OF LABOUR
IN AFRICAN DEVELOPMENT

BY

D. HOBART HOUGHTON

Rhodes University, Grahamstown, South Africa

I. ASPECTS OF THE PROBLEM

THIS topic is so vast, the workers so diverse in their skills, work
attitudes, and cultural heritage, economic factors are so heavily over-
laid by political aspirations, and the process of change so rapid, that
it is difficult to make any meaningful generalization about African
labour. It may well be that the driving forces behind current
changes in Africa are more psychological in character than economic,
in that they represent the mass aspiration to assert the African's
equality with other peoples, socially, politically, and culturally, rather
than the more limited desire for a higher standard of material welfare.[1] Nevertheless, if these political and other aspirations are to
succeed they must rest upon a viable economic order, capable of not
only maintaining itself, but also of providing a higher standard of
living. This implies major structural changes in most African
economies.

It is generally accepted that African economic development at
the present time depends primarily on the progressive change from
the traditional low-productivity subsistence economies to a market
exchange economy with its greater opportunities for growth and its
potentialities for raising *per capita* output. This, of course, involves
consideration of entrepreneural abilities, the increased application of
capital, the development of markets, innovations, and improved
techniques, administrative efficiency, political stability, and the
general attitude of the societies towards economic growth as a positive
aim. All these fall outside the scope of this paper, although oblique
reference may be made to some of them.

From the specific aspect of labour the precondition of African
development appears primarily as a progressive disengagement of

[1] For an interesting discussion of some aspects of this problem see Mark Karp,
The Economics of Trusteeship in Somalia (Boston), chap. 1.

312

labour from subsistence farming and its redeployment in a setting where the advantage of division of labour, specialization, and the economies of scale are possible. This process is taking place throughout the continent, but it is much more advanced in some areas than in others. It was estimated in 1954 [1] that in some of the tropical territories as much as 70 per cent of the population was still wholly dependent upon subsistence agriculture. For example, the percentage was 77 for French West Africa and 70 for Kenya, but it was as low as 21 in the Gold Coast. For tropical Africa as a whole 70 per cent of the cultivated land and 60 per cent of the labour was found to be still engaged in subsistence agriculture.[2]

At the other extreme — in the Republic of South Africa — the number wholly supported by subsistence farming is almost nil, because even in the reserves where aspects of the traditional economy still survive the population relies heavily upon remittances from migrant workers in the cities.

The traditional subsistence economies of Africa should not be equated with the static economy of classical theory; but they are social units in which endogenous change is likely to be extremely slow. The forces tending to conserve the present and inhibit innovation are strong, and the stimuli to change are weak. This is partly a matter of size, for in small units when economic and social relationships are limited to only a few hundred people and linguistic intelligibility to only a few thousand [3] the chances are remote that such a society would produce those rare human beings with the ability, energy, and courage to do that which has never been done before. Yet it is upon such people that all progress ultimately depends. Moreover, such social microcosms are closely knit and permit little individual deviation from what is customary.

Change in Africa is today mainly the result of the external impact of the cultural values, the techniques and the economic ideas which have been developed through the centuries in Western Europe and have spread from there through the greater part of the world, including, of course, the Soviet Union.[4]

This external impact has come at different times and in varying intensity to the peoples of Africa. Trading connections between West Africa and Europe date back to the fifteenth century; there has been white settlement in the South for over 300 years; but

---

[1] *Enlargement of the Exchange Economy in Tropical Africa*, UN (1954), p. 17.
[2] *Idem.* p. 3.
[3] Godfrey and Monica Wilson in *Analysis of Social Change*, C.U.P., 1945, describe such social microcosms in Nyasaland, chap. 1.
[4] Karl Marx learned philosophy from Hegel, economics from Ricardo, and he did most of his work in the British Museum.

in the greater part of tropical Africa the impact has been very recent. The Pioneer Column moved into Southern Rhodesia in 1895, Lugard established British rule in Northern Nigeria in 1903, and mining in Katanga and the Copper Belt commenced only in 1911.

These outposts of the world exchange economy, that have been established by traders, missionaries, administrators, or settlers, offer to the African an alternative to subsistence farming — perhaps for the first time in the history of the majority of its peoples.

The transition from subsistence farming to employment in an exchange economy may conveniently be viewed from three aspects which for brevity may be called the propensity to change, the environment in which the change takes place, and the degree of commitment.

The propensity to change is the sum total of those economic, social, and psychological pressures which tend to induce a worker to transfer his labour from the traditional economy to the modern exchange economy. These constitute two sets of forces which may be described as the 'push' and the 'pull' factors.[1]

The push factors are all the inadequacies in the traditional society. Basically these are economic — lack of land, declining productivity as a result of soil erosion, the pressure of increasing population, or the imposition of money taxes which can be paid only by going to work in the money economy. Some of them may be less directly economic, such as a desire to escape from the burdens of tribal or family life.[2] Although life in a subsistence economy may often be 'poor, nasty, brutish and short', and however strong the push may be, there is no escape unless an effective alternative is available.

The pull factors are those associated with opportunity and the positive attractions of the new way of life. These too are generally economic ; and the great mining centres of Kimberley, Johannesburg, Katanga, and the Copper Belt acted as magnets drawing workers from their traditional society. The reasons why particular individuals desire to earn money vary greatly. From traders, settlers, and missionaries, some Africans have learned to know and desire the products of the civilized world. 'In 1899 Sir Harry Johnson was astonished when Ganda chiefs requested him to supply them with gramophones. He found the people of Baganda "greedy for cloth and almost every manufactured article".' [3] But the pull is not always wholly economic, particularly in the case of those who have embraced Christianity and wish to identify themselves fully with the

---

[1] *Why Labour Leaves the Land*, ILO, 1960, p. 17.

[2] In *Migrant Labour and Tribal Life*, chap. 4, Schapera, in addition to economic pressure lists the desire for adventure and change, and escape from domestic and communal problems as reasons for going out to work.

[3] *Economic Development and Tribal Change*, (ed.) A. I. Richards (Heffer), p. 18.

new way of life in the hope that they may become a permanent part of the new order. Whatever the initial motive may have been, Western food, clothing, housing, and the other amenities of civilized living soon become at least conventional necessities.

There are yet others, however, who are attracted by the possibility of earning money, not through any desire to enter the modern economy, except for a specific limited period, but rather from the opposite desire to improve their status within their tribal society. They go to the mines, for example, with the limited objective of earning money so that they may buy cattle for *ukulobola*. Often there is a strong economic pull towards work in town combined with strong resistance to cultural change. P. Mayer has recently made a study of the differences between the conservative pagans or 'Reds' and the Christian or 'School' people among the Xhosa, and draws attention to the cultural incapsulation of 'Red' migrants even in town.[1]

> The people known as *abantu ababomvu*, 'Red people', or less politely as *amaqaba*, 'smeared ones' (from the smearing of their clothes and bodies with red ochre), are the traditionalist Xhosa, the conservatives who still stand by the indigenous way of life, including the pagan Xhosa religion. 'Red' Xhosa are not just a few picturesque survivals : on the contrary, they are a flourishing half of the Xhosa people today, and are particularly strong in the areas nearest to East London. The antithetical type, *abantu basesikolweni*, 'School people', are products of the mission and the school, holding up Christianity, literacy and other Western ways as ideals. . . .
> . . . As an area of actual White settlement this [the Eastern Cape Province] ranks among the oldest in sub-Saharan Africa, White and Black having both claimed it as home since the 1820's. . . . In effect the Red Xhosa are those who have been looking askance at White people and their ways in every successive generation since what would be identified in England as the time of George IV; the School Xhosa are those who have looked and have accepted.

This difference between conservative and progressive has important consequences in the field of labour in relation to incentives, the acquisition of skills, and the degree of commitment.

In different parts of Africa the 'push' and the 'pull' forces differ in their intensity and their relative importance. In South Africa both are particularly strong, because lack of land (due to the alienation of areas formerly occupied by Africans), population growth (stimulated by the cessation of tribal warfare and the benefits of

[1] P. Mayer, *Xhosa in Town*, vol. II, *Townsmen or Tribesmen*, p. 4, O.U.P., 1961.

modern medicine), and bad husbandry, force large numbers to migrate to seek work. At the same time the employment opportunities in mining, construction, manufacturing, and commerce offer an outlet. It is therefore not surprising that the movement out of subsistence farming should be more advanced there than elsewhere on the continent. In countries where subsistence farming offers a reasonable standard of living in the traditional style and employment opportunities are limited, the process of redeployment of labour will be much less marked.

The environment in which redeployment of labour occurs is also important. It may range from the reorganization of the traditional economy by the successful introduction of a cash crop to the wholesale removal of workers from their former environment to plantations, mines, or industrial centres. In the former case the workers remain in close contact with their traditional way of life, whereas the latter involves major problems of personal adaptation. While mining and construction works may perhaps be successfully carried on by migratory workers who circulate between their tribal homes and the industrial centres, employment in factories requires a more permanent labour force and a fuller adjustment to modern industrial and urban life.

The concept of commitment has been defined by Feldman and Moore as follows : [1]

> Commitment involves both performance and acceptance of the behaviours appropriate to an industrial way of life. The concept is thus concerned with overt actions and norms. The fully committed worker, in other words, has internalized the norms of the new productive organization and social system. By implication, therefore, there are degrees of commitment.

In another chapter in the same book[2] Clark Kerr applied the concept to African labour. He sees the worker who goes from his traditional environment to the mines for a specific limited period as the uncommitted worker. The perpetual migrants who circulate between the traditional and the modern economies are semi-committed workers, while the man who has severed his connection with the traditional rural background and become a permanent urban worker is the fully committed worker.

The emigrants from the traditional economy are of three types, which in the Keiskammahoek survey[3] were designated *emigrant*

[1] W. F. Moore and A. S. Feldman, *Labor Commitment & Social Change in Developing Areas*, N.Y., 1960, p. 1.   [2] *Idem*, p. 351.
[3] D. Hobart Houghton and Edith M. Walton, *Keiskammahoek Rural Survey*, vol. II, *The Economy of a Native Reserve*, p. 116 *et seq.*

breadwinners, emigrant families, and *absconders.* The first are those men who are forced by economic pressure to augment their family's income from subsistence farming by working in the industrial areas. Their families remain in their traditional rural setting but rely heavily upon remittances from their absent menfolk, who are thus semi-committed to both the industrial and the subsistence economies. The emigrant family, as the name implies, is the case where the response to economic pressure is for a man to move to town with his family, abandoning for the time at least his stake in the subsistence economy. There people appear to be more fully committed to the industrial economy, but in South Africa some of them are not wholly committed for many send their children back to the tribal areas to be brought up there by relatives, and because of the insecurity in town many try to retain some rights in the rural economy. The absconders (or, as they are called in parts of East Africa, 'The Lost Ones') are individuals for whom the burdens and responsibilities of the extended family prove too heavy or who have offended against their social group. They seek escape by going to town and severing all connections with their relatives. Having broken completely with their past these people are fully committed to the new industrial economy. These absconders and the second generation in town of the emigrant families can both be regarded as having moved completely out of the traditional subsistence economy and as being fully committed to the money economy of the towns.

These three aspects of the problem — the propensity to change, the environment in which the change takes place, and the degree of commitment — must each receive attention in the following discussion of labour in African development. There are, however, many other aspects related to the type of labour required by the modern exchange economy and the essential disciplines it imposes. It is proposed to discuss some of these under the heads of labour in agriculture, in mining and construction, and manufacturing and commerce.

II. THE AGRICULTURAL WORKER

At first sight the easiest transition from a subsistence to a money economy would appear to be through the modification of subsistence farming by the introduction of a cash crop for sale on the world's markets. If the new crop is supplementary to the production of the traditional food supplies, and employs labour not previously fully employed, there need be no reduction in the output of food ; and if it can be produced by methods not fundamentally different from those traditionally employed, the workers will not need to acquire new techniques nor make major adjustments. The new export crop will earn foreign exchange which can finance imports essential for other developments. But it is a fortunate country that can find a suitable crop for which there is a ready world market and which also it can introduce without upsetting the traditional economy. Cotton in Uganda, coffee in Tanganyika, and cocoa in Ghana would seem to be relatively successful introductions of this sort, although the exploitation of a successful export often has adverse effects upon domestic food production.

In countries where there are white settlers, restrictions designed to maintain quality, prevent disease, or improve marketing have made it difficult for Africans initially to conform to the standards laid down by the whites, and although these difficulties have success-fully been overcome in many areas they undoubtedly have an inhibiting effect on the introduction of cash crops into the indigenous economies.

In South Africa the money-earning opportunities offered by employment in mining and industry provide an alternative which has reduced the urgency of a change in farming methods. Although there is poverty and mass migration from the reserves, little advance in farming methods has taken place in the last hundred years, and productivity has even tended to decline. Thus it comes about that, when an African peasant was asked why he did not grow a cash crop on his land in addition to his maize, he replied that Africans grew maize to eat, they did not grow crops for sale. If they wanted money they earned it by going to work in town.[1] There would appear to be some sense in his view, for the marginal revenue product of the African's labour is mining or industry is much greater than in farming *in the traditional manner*. Be this as it may, the fact remains that although there has been a hundred years of contact with a market economy, and in spite of experiments in freehold tenure, and government schemes for soil conservation and education in improved farming methods, little successful cash production takes place in the African areas of the Ciskei or Transkei. These areas are not even self-supporting in food, and the deficiency is met by importation from the white farming areas. Yields per acre on farms owned by whites are three or more times the yields of African peasants in the same area. The only substantial export from these areas is the export of labour.

Another difficulty arises from the rôle of cattle in tribal life. Besides their recognized value in yielding milk and meat and drawing

[1] D. Hobart Houghton and Edith M. Walton, *op. cit.* p. 154.

the plough, they are used in marriage in the normal practice of *ukulobola* for wife, they are the means of keeping on good terms with the ancestors by appropriate sacrifices and thus of avoiding sickness and disaster, and finally the possession of cattle is important for a man's status.[1] These things are facts, and their recognition does not imply acceptance of anthropological theories about a cattle complex. If cattle were valued primarily for their yield of milk and meat the problem would not be so intractable, because the advantages of a smaller number of better quality cattle could easily be demonstrated. The fact that cattle are used as money [2] and that the bride-price is fixed at a certain number of beasts, places the emphasis on quantity and not on quality. The result is continuous over-grazing of the pastures by poor quality animals whose half-starved condition makes them an economic liability rather than an asset. Stock limitation has been persistently urged by the authorities, but in no other aspect of economic adjustment has resistance and conservatism been so tenacious, and all attempts at raising the productivity of the African farmer have been thwarted.

South African experience seems to show that it is often much more difficult to transform a subsistence peasant economy than it might at first appear. If the transformation is to succeed modern techniques must be introduced, but even relatively simple innovations may have a disruptive effect. The comment of an African chief when he had been presented with a plough by one of the early missionaries that 'this thing that the white people have brought into the country is as good as ten wives' [3] reveals his recognition of the technical superiority of the plough over primitive hoe culture. However, it raised difficulties, because traditionally the cultivation of the fields was women's work, and care of cattle the duty of men Oxen were required to draw the plough, and this required a change in traditional work rôles. The more recent introduction of motor tractors necessitates some mechanical training if the machinery is to be satisfactorily maintained. This presupposes some formal education and literacy among agricultural workers.

Land tenure also must undergo change. The traditional small units were suitable for hoe cultivation by women, but are much too small if modern methods are applied. Communal grazing too must go, and something resembling the enclosure movements in England

---

[1] For a fuller account see Monica Hunter, *Reaction to Conquest*, O.U.P., 1936, pp. 68-71.

[2] H. M. Robertson in '150 Years of Economic Contact between Black and White', *South African Journal of Economics*, 1935, refers to the operation of Gresham's Law and to the fact that 'The lean kine have indeed eaten up the fat kine'.   [3] William Shaw, *Story of My Mission*.

in the sixteenth and eighteenth centuries will have to take place. It is sometimes suggested that it should be possible to teach modern farming methods to Africans without destroying their traditional social system. But modern agricultural techniques rest upon chemistry, physics, biology, genetics ; upon teaching in schools and universities ; upon research ; and upon the scientific and experimental approach to man's environment.

The difficulties of transforming the traditional subsistence economies are great. It appears easier for an African to make the change away from his traditional environment by working on the farms of white settlers or in mines or towns, than where he is surrounded by the powerful forces of custom and conservatism. A distinguished American negro speaking to African university students said that his experiences in Africa had convinced him that the shackles of tradition were so great that advance was not possible unless the old social system was destroyed, and he added that his forebears had been detribalized in the slave ships that took them to America. A similar note is struck by C. W. de Kiewiet when he writes

> The degeneration of the tribe was an emancipation for its individuals. . . . Slums in Johannesburg, Durban and Cape Town are the unsightly camping grounds of men who are laboriously migrating to a new environment in which their rags and filthy shacks are not a sign of decline, but evidence of their escape from the hopelessness of their collapsed tribal system.[1]

If the traditional social environment is too inimical to change it may be that the most hopeful method of improving the African agricultural worker's productivity is to transport him into a new environment of commercialized agriculture in place of peasant farming. Such commercial enterprises, plantations, or collective schemes should be large enough to employ modern techniques and first-class advisers, and be able to take advantage of the economies of scale in both production and marketing. Where schemes of this kind have been tried the mistake is sometimes made of creating the new environment as an artificial and imperfect replication of the traditional pattern.[2] Even a perfect replication, if attainable, might not be desirable ; for a jolt and a sharp break with tradition may be necessary to make an effective transition to a new way of life. The aim should not be to perpetuate the old, but to help the African

---

[1] C. W. de Kiewiet, *The Anatomy of South African Misery*, p. 36.
[2] See the account of the failure of the Niger Irrigation Project in 'Management in Economic Transition', by Peter B. Hammond in Moore and Feldman, *Labor Commitment and Social Change in Developing Areas*, p. 109 *et seq.*

to enter into and feel secure within the new. The real problem is not the adaptability of the African, which is much greater than was once believed, but that of stimulating him to make the forward step towards the new. Perhaps under the influence of Indirect Rule, 'allowing the African to develop on his own lines' and some anthropologists' concern with the past, the real fault of the Western impact on Africa has been that — in striking contrast with the revolutionary radicalism of communism — it has not been sufficiently forward-looking and dynamic. The unfortunate failure of the scheme for the mechanized production of groundnuts in East and Central Africa may have somewhat damped enthusiasm for bold enterprises of this sort, but against this should be put the positive achievements of Gezira.

In this paper attention has first been directed to agricultural labour because its importance in Africa at the present time far outweighs that of labour in mining or industry. To certain aspects of these latter we must however now turn.

III. LABOUR IN MINING AND CONSTRUCTION WORKS

Non-agricultural labour can conveniently be divided into two broad classes — labour employed in mining and construction works forms one group, and labour in manufacturing, commerce, and transport is the other group. This division rests upon the fact that in mining and construction works (such as railway and road building) a large part of the labour force consists of relatively unskilled workers. Moreover, both these activities have in the past in Africa relied largely on temporary workers whose families remain in the rural areas, and they appear to be successfully undertaken by a semi-committed labour force of migratory workers. In the former case this is in part due to the historical fact that mining activity in a new area precedes urban development, in the latter case because the rural character and shifting location of construction works precludes permanent settlement. Manufacturing and commercial activities, on the other hand, are usually associated with settled urban communities, and require a higher standard of training, greater technical skill, and a more fully committed labour force. It is of course true that when mining activities are long established in an area urban conditions develop, and as the African worker progressively rises to more highly skilled employment and the industry becomes more mechanized, conditions in mining tend to approximate more closely to those in manufacturing. Thus, unless legislation or custom restricts urbanization, the labour force becomes more permanent and more fully committed to sustained industrial effort.

Consider, however, the more general phenomenon of migrant labour. The temporary migrations of work seekers often over great distances has long been a feature in Africa ; and, since the opening up of mining operations, they have assumed huge proportions. It is, of course, a symptom of imbalance in the rate of economic development necessitating workers to move from areas where the market value of their labour is low to areas where it is higher. The concentration of enterprise, capital, and advanced techniques in areas where mineral deposits have been exploited has attracted workers from the subsistence sector of the African economies. The majority of these leave their families in their traditional rural setting, and they return home periodically between periods of work in the industrial centres. It has been estimated [1] that in South Africa alone there are some two million such workers who circulate between the industrial centres and their rural homes for the whole of their working lives. On the average they spend over 60 per cent of their working life from the age of 16 to 47 years outside their tribal area, and in the aggregate they travel some 370,000,000 man-miles per annum. The labour wastage to South Africa has been estimated at 600,000 man-years per annum.[2] Apart from the obvious waste of time and resources in travel, the intermittent character of their employment has serious effects upon their productivity in both industry and subsistence farming. It condemns them to being undifferentiated units of unskilled labour because no sooner have they acquired a little skill at a particular job than they return home. Next time they go out to work they may have a new job with another firm possibly even in a totally different industry.

There is another aspect of the migratory system which has perhaps even deeper significance. Elsewhere I have described these migratory workers as 'Men of Two Worlds'. This position of only semi-commitment in the industrial system has important bearing upon money wages, incentives, and the supply of labour.[3] The Transvaal Chamber of Mines has long maintained that there is a

[1] D. Hobart Houghton, 'Men of Two Worlds — Aspects of Migratory Labour', *South African Journal of Economics*, September 1960.
[2] Summary of the Report of the Commission for the Socio-economic development of the Bantu areas within the Union of South Africa (Tomlinson Commission), p. 96.
[3] For an interesting analysis of a somewhat similar problem in Somalia see Mark Karp, *Economics of Trusteeship in Somalia*, pp. 11 *et seq.*, and for aspects of the same problem in Uganda see W. Elkan, *Migrants and Proletarians*, O.U.P., 1960, chap. 8.

backward-sloping supply curve of African labour,[1] and have resisted pressure to increase wages on the ground that to do so would reduce the supply of labour because higher earnings would enable African men to spend longer periods at home between stints on the mines. The general proposition upon which this contention rests is that the typical African mine worker is motivated by his requirements in his 'other world' of tribal life in the reserves. There is certainly much truth in this view and it is supported by the correlation between good and bad farming seasons and the outflow of migrants from the reserves. The implicit assumptions (1) that there is no alternative to mining for would-be money earners, and (2) that the standard of living in the reserves remains constant are, however, open to question. It is not our purpose here to attempt an analysis of the labour market of the South African mines, but rather to draw attention to certain features of the situation that have a wider application.

It is too commonly assumed that the incentives appropriate to a fully committed labour force in Europe or America should also apply to a semi-committed African migrant worker. When the African does not respond to higher wages or money incentives in the way that management thinks he should, the African is described as lazy or lacking in ambition. Some of the more efficient industrial firms which employ migrant workers have recognized that incentives offered should be related to the migrants' personal objectives. In a survey of industrial labour in the Eastern Cape Province, we found that one of the largest employers of African labour had a stable labour force and was well satisfied with its productivity. Moreover, this firm was regarded by African workers as the best employer in the area. Ranking high in their esteem was the fact that the firm granted, annually, a month's holiday on full pay, that there was a regular deduction from weekly wages towards a holiday fund, and that good work was rewarded by extra credits to this fund. Thus, when his annual holiday came, the African worker had plenty of money with which to buy presents, and cash to take home to his family. The system of remittances and deferred pay on the mines meets the same desires.

The migratory labour system is a natural temporary adjustment or cushion for the semi-committed worker between the two worlds of subsistence farming and industrial employment, but in South Africa it has persisted for nearly a century and appears to be growing in magnitude. But as the Fagan Commission so aptly pointed out 'a cushion' is not the only appropriate simile. 'The idea has also

[1] Native Affairs Commission 1903–5 Report, para, 278. See also Witwatersrand Mine Natives' Wages Commission, U.G.21, 1944, para 207.

been expressed to us in the form of another simile : that of a bridge. But a bridge is intended to be crossed, not to serve as a permanent abode.' [1] In view of its socially disruptive effects in both the towns and rural areas and its wastefulness of human resources, it cannot be described as giving the African the best of both worlds. Yet it does enable the conservative elements to go on having their two worlds, and to postpone the final abandonment of their traditional past. In countries where migratory labour is a prominent feature of the labour market there is urgent need for detailed studies of the forces — legal, social, and economic — which inhibit the full redeployment of the worker and his family in the industrial economy. The migratory system may be useful as a temporary expedient, and inevitable in the case of railway and road construction gangs, but every effort should be made to prevent it becoming a permanent feature of the labour market.

IV. LABOUR IN MANUFACTURING AND COMMERCE

(i) General Problems

Apart from unskilled operations, such as cleaning, loading, etc., labour in manufacturing and commerce normally demands a higher degree of commitment on the part of the worker than is required in mining and construction. Semi-skilled and skilled operations involve specific training and the development of proficiency on the part of workers. Hence a continuous and stable labour force is almost essential if a reasonable standard of productivity is to be maintained. If it takes three months to train an African to become a competent weaver, and if he leaves after a further three months' service, the effective productivity of the man is halved. Moreover, the cost in training-looms and instructors is more than any commercial textile factory could support.

Throughout the continent there are complaints about the instability of the industrial labour force and its low productivity in comparison with labour in other more industrially developed lands. There is, moreover, a great lack of scientific and documented studies of the efficiency of African factory workers, and generalizations are unlikely to be of much value because labour productivity means little except in a specific factory context. Since Northcott's pioneering effort [2] many more investigations have been undertaken, and bodies like the Inter-African Labour Institute have drawn attention

---

[1] Native Laws Commission 1946–8 (Fagan Commission), U.G.28, 1948, p. 43.
[2] C. H. Northcott, *African Labour Efficiency Survey*, Colonial Office Research Publications, No. 3, 1947, H.M.S.O.

to the problems.[1]   There is still need for many more specific factory studies like that conducted at the Dunlop factory in Durban.[2] Unfortunately, many firms are reluctant to permit publication of the results of research into the productivity of their labour force because, as one manager put it, 'It has cost us headaches, effort, and much money to achieve our present happy position because we have had to learn by mistakes and bitter experience. Why should we present our findings to our competitors ? They, like ourselves, will have to learn the hard way.'

Industrial development has progressed much further in the Republic of South Africa than elsewhere on the continent : and the number of Africans employed in private manufacturing industry exceeds 400,000, and they represent 57 per cent of the industrial labour force.   Admittedly, the majority is in relatively unskilled jobs, but since 1940 there has been a remarkable increase in the number employed in semi-skilled and skilled jobs.   Experience in South Africa may therefore be useful as a guide to other areas where industrialization is taking place.   It must, however, be remembered that in two important respects South Africa differs from most African territories : on the one hand, the presence of a large white industrial labour force has undoubtedly facilitated the transfer of technical skills and appropriate factory attitudes to Africans ; on the other hand, the existence of certain legal and customary barriers to African advancement must certainly have reduced the incentives to excel and to acquire the necessary technical skills to advance to higher jobs.

The most serious labour problems in manufacturing industry in South Africa are undoubtedly those associated with high labour turnover.   In 1948 a study of African labour turnover in large industrial and commercial concerns in Johannesburg revealed an average turnover of 117 per cent per annum, or a complete numerical replacement of the African labour force every ten months.[3]   There was a tendency to discount this as being the temporary result of rapid post-war expansion.   However, two recent surveys confirm the position revealed in Johannesburg.   One of these, in Cape Town in 1956, found the average turnover of African labour to be 138 per cent per annum.[4]   And the other, conducted in the same year in

[1] *The Human Factors in Productivity in Africa* — A preliminary survey.   Inter-African Labour Institute, 1956, C.C.T.A.

[2] *The African Factory Worker*, Department of Economics, University of Natal, O.U.P., 1950.

[3] R. H. Smith, *Native Urban Employment* — A study of Johannesburg employment records.   Industrial Research Section, University of Witwatersrand, 1948.

[4] Sheila v.d. Horst, 'Native Labour Turnover in Cape Town', *South African Journal of Economics*, December 1957.

East London, revealed a turnover of 119 per cent. These overall average figures may, however, give a false impression, because more detailed inquiry in East London [1] revealed that some industrial firms appeared to have a remarkably stable and efficient African labour force. It was found that the labour turnover of the larger firms ranged from 36 per cent per annum to over 600 per cent, and even varied greatly between firms engaged in the same type of production.

The opportunity offered to interrogate a random sample of the whole male African labour force and an alternative approach to the problem was made through the employment histories of the individual workers. It was found that 55 per cent of them had been in their present job for more than one year, and that 29 per cent had been in their present job for four years or more. This would indicate a stable and committed labour force by most standards.

At the other end, however, it was found that although rapid industrial expansion had been taking place and there was alleged to be an acute labour shortage, 10 per cent of the African labour force was unemployed at the time of the survey, and a further 16 per cent had been in their present jobs for less than three months. These two groups together accounted for a little over a quarter of the total workers, and further inquiry revealed that they were constantly changing jobs : one man having had thirty-two jobs (with periods of unemployment between each job) in the space of two years. The reasons the workers gave for the termination of their jobs showed extreme labour instability and a complete lack of industrial commitment — 'tired of riding a bicycle', 'did not like job', 'work starts too early and cold', 'too exacting', 'did not go to work on Monday', 'tired and resigned'. This group presents a major social and industrial problem because many of them appear to be virtually unemployable. They may be regarded as casualties in the process of adjustment from tribal to urban life, and as the by-product of slum conditions and social and family disintegration caused by the migratory labour system. Nevertheless, they should not blind us to the fact that the majority of the workers are stable and responsible members of the industrial society. It is the high turnover of the unstable group which raises the overall average and conceals the stability of the more dependable 55 per cent of the workers.

We expected to find that the stable workers were drawn from

[1] D. Hobart Houghton, ed., *Economic Development in a Plural Society*, O.U.P. 1960, chap. 10. This book is the published report on the economic aspects of the Border Regional Survey (1955–60) which was undertaken by the Institute of Social and Economic Research at Rhodes University, Grahamstown. The observations presented here are based upon information collected in this investigation.

the settled urban population and that the unstable workers were migrants from the reserves. This, however, was not the case ; both migrants and urbanized were represented in the stable and the unstable groups roughly in proportion to their numbers in the total labour force. Some men whose wives and families lived in the reserves were found to have ten years' service or more with the same firm. They returned home only for their annual leave or occasional week-ends. Conversely some of the unstable workers were town-born. The degree of the workers' commitment to the industrial system did not, therefore, seem to be related to the degree of urbanization of their families. The only differences to be discovered between the two groups was that in the stable group the percentage of older and married men was higher than in the unstable group, and the average earnings of the stable group were higher. This latter fact is most probably the effect of their stability rather than its cause, because being dependable they would rise to more responsible positions and would receive any long service bonus there might be.

In the labour market there appeared to have developed a sort of natural affinity between the good workers and the good employers on the one hand, and between the bad workers and the bad employers on the other. The efficient firms with a good reputation among African workers experienced little difficulty in securing labour, and had little complaint about its stability or productivity. The Lancashire-born head of a large textile firm employing an all-African operative labour force of about 2,000, said that African workers compared favourably with rank-and-file workers in many parts of the world. The majority of employers, however, reported adversely upon African labour as compared with white labour. In some firms, particularly those with a very high labour turnover, management reported that African labour was lazy, inefficient, and unstable. Among the African workers certain definite attitudes had developed towards particular firms : employment in certain factories was much sought after, while there were others in which they would only work as a last resort.

The efficiency of the individual worker is only one element in productivity, because capital equipment, factory layout, maintenance, and the general efficiency of management are also of major importance. Even the most efficient workers will have low productivity in a badly run factory. This is, of course, well known ; but it is often overlooked by some who generalize about the productivity of African labour. The same group of workers reacts quite differently in different situations. Although it is probably true that the unstable element is at present proportionally higher among African workers than among white, the fact that some employers have been able to enlist an efficient, productive, and stable African labour force seems to indicate that the general efficiency of the concern and its skill in labour management is more important in determining productivity than the racial group from which the workers are drawn.

It may be of interest to list those factors making for stability and high productivity of African workers revealed in visits to over 300 concerns and interviews with both management and workers.

(ii) *Recruitment and Selection*

A powerful factor in determining productivity of labour in any factory is the care taken in recruitment and selection of its African labour force, yet in the great majority of firms investigated, recruitment was quite haphazard. Many employers who were questioned about this replied that : African labour was not worth taking trouble over ; most labour was bad ; they come and they go, and it is just the luck of the draw if you get a good one. Indeed, it may well be that the worst effect of the migratory system is the demoralizing effect it has upon management. That this most common attitude is founded upon error was clearly demonstrated by the excellent results obtained by firms which took care in the selection of their African workers. The Dunlop factory survey showed that merely by careful selection the productivity of African labour could be raised by 72 per cent.[1] Our own experience in East London would tend to confirm this. At one canning factory the recruitment was by indiscriminate selection from a crowd of African work-seekers at the factory gates. Workers were judged entirely on their performance in the course of work and dismissed instantly if unable to maintain the required output, and were replaced from the head of the queue. Turnover per annum was immeasurable, being as high as 50 per cent on a single day. Another factory whose recruitment policy included individual interviews, medical examination, and the obtaining of full histories of the men's previous employment and home circumstances reported a labour turnover of only 6 per cent per annum over the last two years, and a maximum absenteeism of 3 per cent.

The method of recruitment of new workers adopted by many of the best firms was that of personal introduction by an employee. If a vacancy occurred the management asked its African employees to find a suitable person to fill the vacancy. This method seems well

[1] *The African Worker*, p. 99.

adapted to the African social system and to be beneficial to the management. The African would usually bring a relative or someone from his own home place, but would be unwilling to jeopardize his standing with his firm by bringing in someone whom he did not think would prove satisfactory. This aspect is more fully discussed in a forthcoming book.[1]

Many of the better employers stressed the desirability of personal interviews with African recruits, and the need to explain certain features of factory discipline (particularly who was to be his immediate superior), and to give full details of the system of pay, promotion, holidays, etc. One personnel manager said that Africans like to be treated as *persons*, not as impersonal units of a labour force, and in his factory every effort was made to respect this and to build up the personality of each African worker as far as was possible.

(iii) *Instruction and Training*

J. B. Heigham [2] has drawn attention to the need for adequate training, not only in the skilled trades, but in the basic skills required even of an unskilled worker in, for example, the handling of a pick or shovel. The African's cultural background has often afforded him no opportunity to acquire skill in handling even the simplest of Western tools. This fact is seldom fully appreciated by the instructors, especially if they have recently come from a country with a long history of technical development. The instructors take too much for granted and when the African fails, they attribute this to lack of intelligence. Added to these difficulties there is often the problem of communication. Accepting that linguistic difficulties have been successfully overcome, it is still necessary to give instructions in minute detail, covering the handling of tools and materials. One very successful instructor stated that he treated African men as if they were children of 5, not because he thought they were lacking in intelligence, but because many of them had had less experience of a modern industrial community than a white child of 5 years of age. From the African side this would appear to be appreciated, because the greatest commendation of many African workers was to say that in X factory 'they tell you nicely what you have to do'. This, however, requires a skill in teaching and patience that is seldom found. In a carefully prepared statement by the

---

[1] *Xhosa in Town*, vol. I, *The Black Man's Portion*, by D. H. Reader, O.U.P., 1961, chap. 5.
[2] J. B. Heigham, *Labour Productivity in the Gold Coast*, quoted in *The Human Factors in Productivity in Africa* — Inter-African Labour Institute, Appendix G, p. 129.

management of a large factory employing many Africans, there is this comment :

The proportion of Natives who are able rapidly to develop simple manual dexterity seems very small. In hand-wrapping of products highly paid European girls are far cheaper to employ than the greater number of Natives needed for the same output. *Perhaps it is due to lack of opportunity in childhood, and almost as much due to lack of sympathetic instruction by European supervisors.*[1]

Many firms set great store by in-factory training. A large textile firm which trained its spinners on the job, found it necessary to have a small training school for its weavers. The results were discouraging until the training-looms and instructors were moved into the factory when the trainees immediately became keen and alert. The atmosphere of a well-run factory and the rhythm of the machines seem to have an exhilarating effect upon many African workers, and South African experience would seem to indicate that when the overall management is good they make excellent operatives.

(iv) *Management and Supervision*

The general management of the factory is of prime importance, and productivity of African labour appears to depend largely upon the degree of supervision. The overwhelming majority of African workers appeared not merely to tolerate supervision and strict factory discipline, but to prefer it to a lax atmosphere, and to associate strict discipline in the factory with efficiency. Certainly our findings were that where supervision was effective the firm was successful, but a failure in this respect was almost invariably accompanied by low productivity and a variety of labour problems.

The general attitude of management and of white fellow workers towards Africans was also found to be important. Even where top management was personally sympathetic, the presence of a white foreman or supervisor whose attitude or treatment was disliked soon earned for that firm a bad reputation with the African workers. Strict factory discipline was welcomed, but anything savouring of victimization, unfair treatment, or of personal rudeness, was strongly resented. Although African trade unions have no legal recognition in South Africa, there is a quite remarkable solidarity among African workers. There is a tendency to attribute definite characteristics to a firm, and many employers would be surprised to know the particular connotations their names have among the general body of workers.

[1] Quoted from *Xhosa in Town*, vol. I, *The Black Man's Portion*, by D. H. Reader, O.U.P., 1961, p. 88. Italics are mine.

A 'bad' firm will find it extremely difficult to recruit good workers.

Two-way channels of communication between management and African workers would appear to be highly desirable, especially where the work force is multiracial. This channel should be other than the normal channel of command and instruction, and can best be achieved through a sympathetic welfare officer whom the Africans respect. It has two advantages in that it makes the African workers feel that they are considered by the management, and it enables them to have independent access to the management. There is always the danger that such an arrangement may undermine the authority of foremen and supervisors, and care must be taken to avoid this. On the other hand, these posts are often filled by whites who have the technical knowledge and skill, but who lack sympathetic attitudes towards and understanding of the African workers. The right type of welfare officer for the African workers often makes the difference between a contented, stable, and productive labour force and one in which there is constant tension and discontent.

(v) *Nutrition and Welfare Services*

Adequate nutrition is obviously an important factor affecting the productivity of labour, and, unfortunately, the diet of many urban Africans is deficient, consisting as it often does largely of white bread and mineral waters. Many firms have instituted canteens which supply cheap or free meals to African workers, but almost invariably the workers resent receiving a portion of their wages in kind. It is therefore important that firms make it clear to their workers that free or subsidized canteens are a benefit over and above the workers' basic cash wage. Undoubtedly, this is an additional cost to the firm, but firms providing it assured us that it was worth while, because of the increase in output.

Welfare services for African workers include those things normally included in these concepts in Western countries, but firms should go beyond this and employ welfare officers who have some understanding of the workers' cultural background. Writing of workers in Uganda, Elkan says:

> It is important . . . to realize that much writing about efficiency has little relevance to conditions in Uganda. Before men can work efficiently, at least two conditions must obtain: an employer must know how to evoke the qualities and abilities of his labour force effectively, but this in turn depends on whether the qualities and abilities, and in particular the basic feelings about work, are there to be evoked. In Western countries there exists now a labour force whose attitudes are appropriate to an

331

industrial society. Uganda, however, resembles more the England of Robert Owen than that of the Institute of Personnel Management.[1]

Although these remarks may be relevant to many parts of Africa, in addition to Uganda, they are only of slight relevance to South Africa where many members of the African labour force have behind them three or four generations of contact with Western ways of life, and are, in general, much more fully committed to a modern economy. Nevertheless, there are many matters in which management could benefit from the advice of someone well versed in the African way of life. To give but one example, a large firm established close to African tribal areas and employing only Africans as machine operatives commenced by recruiting African youths of 16 and 17 years of age, on the ground that at this age they would learn more quickly than older men. It was, of course, realized that within a year or two the youths would wish to leave to undergo circumcision and initiation into manhood, but it was confidently expected that when this was over they would return and work for the factory for many years. These hopes were not fulfilled. The youths were trained, left for initiation, but did not return; and the labour turnover of 130 per cent per annum was crippling the factory. Management then discovered that it was contrary to custom for an African man to perform the same job he had done as an uncircumcised lad. The factory switched to recruiting older men and, although they took a little longer to train, it soon had a stable and efficient labour force and labour turnover dropped to about 30 per cent per annum.

(vi) *Wages*

Although there may be some doubt about the importance of the wage rate in evoking a supply of labour from semi-committed migrant workers, the African industrial workers in South Africa are, for the most part, so fully committed to the money economy that the wages offered are the most important single factor in attracting a force of efficient and stable workers. The more progressive industrialists have recently become alive to this fact, and there have been several instances of increases in African wages to a level of about £1 per day. In South African industry the average wage paid to whites has been several times greater than the wage paid to non-white workers. During the period of rapid industrial expansion

[1] W. Elakn, *An African Labour Force*, East African Studies, No. 7, East African Institute of Social Research, Kampala, 1956 (quoted in *Human Factors in Productivity in Africa*, p. 34).

between 1945 and 1950 white labour was in short supply and many firms recruited non-white labour for jobs formerly performed by whites. The success of this operation depended very largely upon the wages offered to the non-white workers. One factory changed from white to non-white labour, paying the latter at the same rate that had been paid to whites. The result, to the astonishment of the management, was a decline in absenteeism and labour turnover and a marked improvement in both volume and quality of output. The wage offered had attracted only the less satisfactory type of white labour, but in relation to prevailing rates was high enough to attract the best of the non-white workers. The general state of the industrial labour market in South Africa at present is very similar to that prevailing in America when Henry Ford pioneered the doctrine of high wages. From the responses of the workers it was clear that for the vast majority the wage offered was the most important consideration in accepting work. In the reasons given for leaving a particular job low wages featured frequently.

(vii) *Incentive Schemes*

Employers were sharply divided in their opinions of the value of incentive or bonus schemes as a means of improving the output of their African workers. Many stated that they found African labour unresponsive to monetary incentives, others that there might be a temporary increase in output, but that there appeared to be a certain level beyond which workers were not prepared to push themselves. There were, on the other hand, a few firms where incentive bonus schemes had proved outstandingly successful. One firm placed its African salesmen on a bonus scheme, and was astonished by an increase in orders of several hundred per cent while the salesmen were able to raise their individual earnings to four times their basic wage. The manager of a textile factory was enthusiastic about an incentive bonus. It worked better with African labour than in Lancashire, because on pay day African workers would wave their pay chits in the air and boast of their week's earnings while friends shouted challenges that they would beat them next week. A factory producing metalware reported that money incentives and organized competitions between shifts had proved most popular with African workers and had led to a 100 per cent increase in output.

Two considerations throw some light on the conflict of opinion about incentive schemes. Firstly, those firms with a highly committed labour force met with a more satisfactory response than firms with semi-committed migrant workers, except where the incentive scheme was related to the social background of the migrant and took the form of relatively long holidays and extra payments when the workers went home for their annual leave. Secondly, in many firms there appeared to be strong resistance to incentive schemes, because workers feared that the management wanted to step up production to establish a new norm of performance, and that having achieved this it would reduce wages to the old level, but seek to enforce the new level of output. Where workers trusted the management this resistance was not encountered.

V. CONCLUSIONS

All generalizations about the productive efficiency of African labour are dangerous and likely to be misleading. Not only do African workers differ greatly in their cultural background, their attitudes towards work, and the degree to which they are committed to a money economy, but the same individuals react differently in different environments. The completely Westernized African worker with fully developed appreciation of time, precision, efficiency, and the causal relationship between productivity and wages, is still comparatively rare in most parts of the continent. The complete traditionalist enclosed within a small-scale subsistence economy is rapidly becoming a thing of the past. Many are today men of two worlds, alternating between membership of the traditional society and membership of a modern industrial proletariat. But the same individual may respond in one way when he is dressed in white overalls in a large power-driven and efficient factory, and in quite another way when he is in traditional dress minding cattle at home and watching his women folk hoe the small fields.

Experience in South Africa would seem to indicate that it is very much easier to make an African into an efficient mine worker or factory machine operator than to convert him into an efficient agricultural producer, except when he leaves his tribal home and goes to work for a white farmer. One might have expected an African with industrial experience, or one who has worked for an efficient white farmer, to return to his own home and, seeing that the traditional methods were antiquated and of low productivity, to purchase a tractor and fertilizers and initiate an agricultural revolution. The number who have attempted this is, however, extremely small. In the traditional setting the pressure of custom, problems of land tenure, and the fact that innovators are looked at askance make it much easier to conform.

Development of mining, manufacturing, and commerce are important in the general development of the African continent, but increase in agricultural productivity far transcends in importance all other sectors, and is in many areas the essential pre-condition to the establishment of a more diversified economy. The productivity of African labour in agriculture is low, and it must be raised, but this is the most difficult of all labour problems. Unless this is done soon, and rapidly, the political aspirations of the independent African states may be reduced to nothing by poverty, discontent, and the pressure of population upon the means of subsistence. Today most of the African states still look to the Western world for inspiration and guidance, but some are turning towards communism. It may well be that it is the radicalism of the communist approach to development problems which attracts them, rather than communist doctrine itself. The Western approach to agricultural problems in Africa has, in general, tended to be conservative and based upon the hope of gradual evolution and progressive improvement in agricultural techniques. On the other hand, it is sobering to remember that of all sectors of the Soviet economy agriculture has persistently proved the most difficult and intractable.

DISCUSSION OF PROFESSOR HOUGHTON'S PAPER

M. Roland Pré, opening the discussion, stressed the explosive ideas that were affecting Africa. Colonialism had tended to maintain the structures of the traditional African societies. The attractions of communism came largely from the fact that it was inspired by wishes to change the traditional society, while the West appeared to wish to maintain it. He thought that it was difficult to make fundamental changes in working conditions without even more fundamental changes in ways of living and in attitudes. It was necessary, in the first place, to consider the inducements to move from the subsistence economy into the modern economy. The wish to move was the important thing. The change implied was more important than Professor Houghton had suggested. It involved a wish to be associated with a new social structure, to adopt the urban way of living and to abandon the tribal environment.

The second main problem was how to adapt the African worker to a modern industrial job — whether in agriculture, industry, or mining. His training as a human being was at least as important as his technical training. It was necessary to transform the African worker rather than train him in a new technology. It entailed adjustment to a whole range of new situations and new psychological factors, and was the main obstacle to the introduction of Africans to modern industrial life. He was himself convinced that adjustments could be made rapidly, but advancing industry was making ever greater claims on workers. He thought that the behaviour of human beings under these stresses deserved much greater study.

Professor Bézy emphasized the wide differences between South Africa and other parts of Africa. In the Union, African agriculture was static and exercised a powerful outward push on population. He was astonished at the existence of 2 million migratory labourers in the Union, spending 60 per cent of their working life outside their traditional homes. While labour turnover in the Union was more than 100 per cent per annum, in the Congo it was about 10 per cent on average, with individual concerns in Katanga as low as 3 per cent.

He attributed the difficulties of the Union in respect of labour turn-over and industrial relations largely to a mistaken policy of cheap labour wastefully employed, partly as a result of racial discrimination. In the Congo wages had been doubled between 1950 and 1952 ; in Léopoldville they had been trebled. Labour productivity had risen fourfold. Costs and prices were lowered. Employment was substantially reduced. He advocated an economy of high African wages, with no racial discrimination. In the Congo, when about half the European supervisory staffs had been lost, production and productivity had not decreased. He thought the causal factor had been the increase of wages, which had led both to economy of labour and to higher efficiency of the African workers concerned.

Mr. Ngcobo thought there was a tendency to relegate South Africa to a special case, whereas he believed that the development that had taken place in the Union could be used as a basis of study for other parts of the continent. It applied, he thought, not only to the Union but also to the Rhodesia-Nyasaland Federation. He thought the value of Professor Houghton's paper was that it put the problems of labour in their general setting, and brought to bear a lot of research which had been done in the Union. Professor Houghton's paper suggested that the number of persons in the Union wholly supported by subsistence agriculture was negligible. He would have liked to have had, for the Union, figures of the proportions in which African incomes came from subsistence agriculture and from the money economy. In Nyasaland 35 per cent of African incomes came from the money economy, and in Northern Rhodesia 55 per cent, while 65 and 45 per cent respectively came from the subsistence economy. He wondered what the comparable figures would be for the Union.

He thought some warning of the special character of the African labour market was necessary. The total labour force was composed of a number of non-competing groups. In connection with the labour turnover, which had so surprised Professor Bézy, it was necessary to have in mind the climate of the prevailing political philosophy and the impact of the policies of recent years. These tended to increase and emphasise the migratory character of African labour.

His own investigations bore out the fact that it was not the settled urban population that provided stable workers, while the unstable workers were migratory workers from the reserves. In fact the opposite was true. In Salisbury it was found that labour that came from within thirty miles was less stable than labour from Nyasaland.

Professor Houghton regretted that he could provide no over-all figures of the proportions in which African incomes were derived from subsistence agriculture and the money economy respectively. But a detailed study of one reserve showed an average cash income of £42 and a value of subsistence agriculture (unfortunately affected by drought) of £7. The Tomlinson Commission had estimated the money incomes accruing to Africans in Bantu areas, calculated to include non-commercial transactions which took place in the subsistence economy, at £87 million, covering a population of about 600,000 families and 3,500,000 persons.

Professor Leduc commented on the reduction of employment implied by Professor Bézy's suggestions. He wondered whether the increase of productivity was not to be ascribed to maintaining output with a reduced labour force. He thought that any division into self-subsistence agriculture and the modern economy was an over-simplification. Also all Africans sold some of their production, either locally or for export. *Professor Bézy* thought that any unemployment that might result would be only for a short period. Unemployment was not a problem in an expanding economy.

Professor Samuels drew attention to the natural affinity, to which Professor Houghton had alluded, between good workers and good employers. Good employers, who use good workers more effectively, could afford to pay them more and suffered less from labour turnover. He stressed the importance of improving managerial skills, both by training and by attracting more from abroad.

Dr. Wade emphasized the importance both of discovering prospective new enterprises likely to succeed and of improving technical skills. With present methods it took 300 days of work to cultivate a hectare of land in Senegal.

Professor Walker stressed the demoralizing effect of low wages on management. Professor Houghton had indicated that the factories that showed the highest productivity were those that went in for careful selection of workers. He had found the same thing in East Africa. In one textile factory, with careful selection of labour, they had reduced turnover to about the levels expected in the United Kingdom. In East Africa poor management was one of the great problems. It was partly, he thought, due to a shortage of managerial talent ; it was partly due to the demoralizing effect of cheap labour which encouraged slackness. But firms were often badly managed by people who had good records in England.

What could be done by public action ? He thought they should try to attract more and better managers from abroad and improve facilities

M   337

for training managers locally. But he thought it equally important to increase wages, even dramatically, and induce managers to realize that they must use labour efficiently. Despite the short-period abundance of labour it was vitally important from a long-period point of view to build up a trained and responsible factory labour force.

Professor Houghton entirely endorsed Professor Samuels' comment on the affinity between good employers and good workers. A great deal of thought had been given in South Africa, especially by organized industry, as to what could best be done to improve conditions. Chambers of industry had tentatively put forward proposals for a dramatic increase of African wages. The Bantu Wages and Productivity Association had been founded by 120 of the largest industrial concerns in South Africa with the object of stimulating education in the management of labour.

He thought that it should be remembered that, within the Bantu population, there existed both progressives and conservatives : there were those Africans who advocated progress by integration of the two races and those Africans who wished to develop along their own lines. In some areas the latter were a majority.

Mr. Ngcobo agreed with Professor Houghton's last remarks. This helped to explain an apparently puzzling feature of Union politics — that there were Africans who found the apartheid policy acceptable.

Political limitations were, however, preventing a large group of skilled labourers from working. Policy was aimed at levelling Africans as an unskilled labour group. It was a mistake to identify groups who preferred the reserve way of life with unskilled labour — many Basutos lived in reserves in the intervals of doing semi-skilled work in the gold mines.

Professor Houghton, in reply to a question from *Dr. Cookson* on the alleged backward-sloping supply curve of labour, said it had been a matter of controversy for over fifty years. He thought it a correct analysis as far as concerned gold mines because they were virtually the only avenue of employment for Africans from subsistence reserves. If wages were raised, they would stay at home longer. But otherwise the evidence did not support it ; firstly, because the standard of living and requirements of Africans in the reserves had risen considerably in the last fifty years, and there had been an unaccountable change in African demands in the 1940s (due, perhaps, to many having served in the forces); secondly, because industrial development provided an alternative field of employment. More were now employed in manufacturing industry than in gold mines. *Professor Bézy*, also replying to Dr. Cookson, said that the labour supply curve was not backward sloping in the Congo, except possibly among women.

Professor Spengler asked whether Africans, when they entered industry, stayed on to their early sixties or withdrew earlier. *Professor Houghton* answered that so far as concerned immigrant workers mutating between the reserves and the mines, they stopped working in their late forties (daughters often took their place as money-earners). There were no firm statistics for the urbanized population, but he thought the norm was around sixty.

Dr. Singer asked Professor Houghton five questions. Was not high turnover good to the extent that it gave a large number of people training in factory work, and so equipped them with modern skills? Could not management find ways to attach African workers more firmly to specific occupations? Was there a case for self-employment? As an individual employer would presumably not find it worthwhile to train workers, was there not a case for government training schemes? Was it true that there was great difficulty in making Africans conscious of the need for maintenance and repair of tools?

Professor Houghton replied to the first question that he thought not. The unstable element was not composed of new workers, but of about 25 per cent of the working population who changed jobs 8-10 times per year. He agreed that management could do something, and there had been outstanding examples. Self-employment might help, but this was difficult with so much commerce and industry run by white traders. Under the policy of separate areas, a class of African entrepreneurs was growing. There were now some 75,000 African car-owners. He thought government training schools would have less chance of success than private training schools. In large industries maintenance and repair work was looked after by management. The familiar saying was, however, all too true in some small industries, and especially agriculture: 'Give us the job and we'll finish the tools'. There was need for supervision and training in maintenance.

Professor Walker stressed the importance of environment in the development of the African farmer. The introduction of new methods brought a new attitude. The same was perhaps true of industry. To this *Professor Houghton* agreed.

Mr. Onitiri thought that Professor Houghton's paper was a good analysis of the South African situation and could have applied to Congo before independence — economic solutions must await political solutions. One must not generalize for the whole of Africa. The shackles were not those of tradition but of politics. Did South Africans fear the effects of high wages?

Professor Houghton agreed that the colour bar might cause barriers in industry, but it did not in agriculture. In South Africa there was possibly an abnormal situation in emphasis on cattle as means of payment — quantity rather than quality. In areas to the north where the tsetse-fly was prevalent the attitude was quite different.

Chapter 12

EDUCATION IN AFRICAN ECONOMIC GROWTH

BY

JOHN VAIZEY

Research Unit in the Economics and Administration of Education,
University of London Institute of Education

I. THE IMPORTANCE OF EDUCATION

IF it is the case, as is sometimes said, that education is 'investment in human capital', then it should logically follow that the accumulation of this human capital should be a factor in economic growth.[1] There are a number of views that may be taken, none of them very convincing. One such view deducts from the total rate of growth the contributions of physical capital and population growth, and finds a very large remaining factor — which Aukrust has named the third factor. American scholars have taken a second view, that the differential incomes earned by educated people over those earned by uneducated people measure the 'return' on education. This implies a series of assumptions about the economy — notably full employment and an acceptable distribution of earned incomes mirroring a perfect labour market — which seems implausible. The third view is less bold in its claims and more orthodox in its ancestry, relying chiefly upon the work of Marshall and Marx. It draws attention to the secondary effects of education, and the supply of skills ; and emphasizes the importance of pragmatic analysis of each case. In a number of countries (India, Pakistan, and the Philippines) there is the phenomenon of 'intellectual unemployment', which shows that education can often be abortive and irrelevant to economic growth. In Africa south of the Sahara intellectual unemployment is not at present a problem, because of the acute shortage of skilled and qualified people. Nevertheless, the Nigerian economists have drawn attention to the 'unemployability' of the semi-educated, who despise manual work ; and in some parts of Africa until recently the colonial societies made it difficult for African university graduates

[1] I have examined the place of education in economic development in *The Economics of Education*, Faber & Faber, London, 1961.

340

to find employment. Intellectual unemployment (even among scientists) marked all Western societies before 1939. Therefore, it follows (as must seem so obvious as to be banal) that education is not the single key to growth ; if it were, some Asian countries would be much richer than they are. It might be argued that this represents an imbalance in the higher education systems of these countries.

But it is not true that a little education spread widely is necessarily more effective than a great deal of education given intensely to a few people. Japan, for example, had mass education and economic growth ; but its economic growth was threatened till recently by an enormous population problem. The classical economists drew attention to the fact that compulsory education raised the cost of rearing a family, especially when it was combined with child labour laws. This can become an important part of the process of population control. The point here is that if mass education were a major source of economic strength *per se*, there would be (by definition) no population problem. (This is the view of the present Chinese government, rendered somewhat implausible by the current famine.)

There is, as one would expect, a clear impression from the preliminary work which has been done on the proportions of national income devoted to education in different countries at different stages of growth, that the proportion of national income devoted to education rises with national income ; and that very few countries (of which Japan and the U.S.S.R. are two) were out of line in this respect. In other words, education — like some personal services — is highly income-elastic. Work within countries, on the distribution of education between socio-economic classes confirms this ; the richer families spend a higher proportion of their incomes on education. Evidence of this kind redoubles my suspicions of the use of the words 'investment in education'.

This suggests a paradox of sorts. The alternative to using education to stimulate growth is to use economic growth to stimulate education.

II. EDUCATION AND THE OVERALL STRATEGY OF DEVELOPMENT

It is pointless to build a school system unless there are jobs for the people to go to, and capital equipment for them to work with. That is to say, an education plan should be conceived of as part of a general economic programme for raising the economic level of a community; both because education has to justify its claims to national resources in competition with social services, like health, and investment in physical capital, and because experience has shown that growth requires an integration of all aspects of economic and social life if individual projects and plans are to come to their full fruition. It is in this context that allusions are made to 'human capital'. It is obvious that the use of the term 'human capital' is, in large part, an emotive use of language designed to carry over the positive association of 'physical capital' to expenditure on education. I have three objections to the use of this phrase. First, the analogy is extremely forced, and, at not too great a distance from the first association, positively misleading. Secondly, it is likely to lead people to expect too much from education, and when they are disappointed (as in my opinion they are certain to be) the reaction may be unfavourable. Thirdly, education is necessary for human dignity. A poor country, just like a rich country, has in my opinion the moral and social duty to educate its people, and this would still be so even if the education made them materially poorer.

The major problem, so far unexamined by those who have analysed the part of education in economic development, is the time horizon involved. If children are educated the yield is obviously long-term; if adults are educated, the horizon may be nearer.

Education is usually given three initial rôles. One is to supply skilled manpower and technicians without whom physical capital would be wasted. This is a very common phenomenon in poor countries and was a well-known part of travellers' reports on the early years of the U.S.S.R., who described tractors rusting in the fields for lack of skilled workers to repair them. The second is to generate 'a climate for growth' by giving the masses a capacity for thinking beyond their immediate needs and troubles. Only some kinds of education are capable of doing this. Most education in most countries is overtly conservative in its ultimate aims, instilling a love of country, religion, and family. These often, but not always, conflict with the characteristics desirable, for example, in an entrepreneur. The third is to teach the cultivators simple and elementary rural skills which will yield a small surplus over subsistence consumption, and which can be the basis for physical accumulation.

None of these three tasks is necessarily implied by any of the others; indeed, rural mass education can be a conservative force (and is intended to be so by the anti-urban apostles of community development). The purpose is to keep the population on the land and to keep them from flooding into the towns. This is often contrary to the view that the industrial sector is likely to lead in many processes of development. A revolutionary ideology can be impractical. Nevertheless, in general they are loosely linked.

III. THE CONTENT OF THE EDUCATIONAL PROGRAMME

The content of the education is quite crucially important to its place in development. A great deal has been written on the content of education, most of it consisting of *obiter dicta* of more or less *a priori* origin. (UNESCO is undertaking a programme of research which will throw light on this problem.) Once literacy is achieved, there seems to be a consensus of opinion that mathematics, scientific method, and a major language (English, French, Spanish, or Russian) should take priority. There is dispute over two other areas of curriculum. The first is literature and history — raising enormous problems of social morality, nationalism, and personal psychology. Hitherto in Africa and Asia there can be little doubt that these studies, English and French literature and history, have been anti-growth, because of their development of attitudes which despised practical affairs. The other major area is vocational training. This is often separated from the ordinary process of education. There appears to be a strong case for a common school which teaches all these subjects, since it tends to reduce the status-differentiation of different subjects, whereby the more clever and socially superior read arts subjects, and the less clever and the socially inferior become engineers. On the other hand, we may be entering a phase of history where administrators are educated in the physical and social sciences and not the humanities. This is not necessarily an improvement.

Clearly, a major point here is whether general education should be given or whether people should be developed in a particular narrow skill; the antithesis being between the American high-school and college, and the Soviet polytechnicum. In a highly planned, centrally directed, fully employed economy, the Soviet model is cheaper and more effective; in a more flexible, less fully-employed economy, the generally educated man has a far greater opportunity. In my view a society with such an education system will be more resilient.[1]

Obviously, what will help to get the economy off the ground is an attempt to train the population in rational modes of thought and in an objective empirical attitude to nature and society. This implies

[1] See Nicholas DeWitt, *Soviet Professional Manpower*, Washington, 2nd edition, 1961.

a radical retraining of existing teachers. International aid is best directed to this end. It also (see below) implies a radical change in the technology of education.

If it be allowed that this is the case, there are two things that can be said straight away about how education can be developed.[1]

The first is that it is possible to export physical capital to overseas countries, or by exporting consumption goods allow them to use local labour and resources to develop their own physical capital. It is extremely difficult to export teachers.

All Western countries have a chronic shortage of teachers, and the number who can be spared from the U.S., Canada, and the other OECD countries for the whole of Africa, Asia, and Latin America is certainly less than 50,000. These people can, of course, play an all-important strategic rôle in the development of education, above all in teacher-training and in developing universities.

Indigenous teachers can be trained in overseas countries. This is a form of aid which requires the most careful planning. 'Wastage rates' among overseas students are sometimes double those of the average university student in Britain and other Western countries. The need for initiation courses, careful student guidance, and courses oriented to the needs of the under-developed countries is great. The Ford Foundation and the Point Four authorities have developed a process of institution building which links American universities and colleges in an organic way with universities and colleges in the under-developed world. These links give confidence and ensure proper care to be taken of overseas students.[2]

Books and other equipment can be sent, but the most important cost of education — teachers — has, by its very nature, to be locally provided. There are language barriers. There are the difficulties of using foreigners to teach children whose cultural assumptions differ so widely from theirs as to present almost insuperable difficulties, except to the very gifted teacher. Increasingly, there are national or racial barriers to what is regarded as cultural imperialism.

Thus, education for this technical reason, has to depend on teachers drawn from the local population. It is precisely this which

---

[1] I have developed the argument in this paper in considerable detail in 'Education in the Strategy of Economic Growth', presented to an OECD Washington Conference, October 1961, published by the OECD early in 1962. Alice Rivlin, *Research in the Economics of Higher Education*, the Brookings Institute, Washington, 1961 (mimeographed), has surveyed some of the existing literature on this problem. In *Tiers-Monde* (vol. I, nos. 1 and 2, janvier-juin 1960) a thorough examination is made by a number of economists, sociologists, and anthropologists, of the problems of education in economic growth in tropical areas.

[2] Roy Manley, of the Council for Education in the Commonwealth, is preparing a report on this subject.

gives it its strength in the competition for the scarce resources for development projects.

In most under-developed countries there is a chronic labour surplus. The degree of under-employment in subsistence agriculture is notorious, in the sense that given the opportunity the people concerned would substitute work for the market, for leisure. Certainly, labour, relative to capital, is cheap. Therefore, the use of people as pupils and teachers is low, in terms of opportunity cost. There are almost inevitable expenditures associated with education — especially social benefits, like scholarships, meals, and boarding costs — which modify this somewhat extreme statement.

Teaching can be in such forms that a very minimum of other resources is required (especially in warm countries where buildings can be very exiguous), and the only drain on reserves of foreign economy is for books and equipment.

IV. THE TECHNOLOGY OF TEACHING

A subject in which the Research Unit in the Economics and Administration of Education, University of London Institute of Education, is at present working, is the change in the technology of teaching, which is associated with different levels and rates of economic growth and factor endowments. It is often not realized that the technology of education has changed frequently and profoundly. The chronic shortage of teachers in the advanced countries points in three directions : first, the use of more capital-intensive methods of teaching (books, machines, television) in countries where capital is freely available ; secondly, to a proposed modification of teaching so that it is more effective — which implies investigation of the learning process, and modification of programmes and curricula to make learning easier ; thirdly, to the use of new techniques which economize both in labour and in capital. Professor Skinner's teaching machines (developed at Harvard) are a sign of what can be done if effort is devoted to this process. Education may well be a case where Africa can develop a new technology which the countries of Europe and North America will be glad to copy.

In principle, therefore, labour for education can play the rôle in an economy which is relatively well endowed with labour, that unlimited fertile land played in American economic growth ; it is there to be developed. The cost of developing it is the use of scarce skills in teaching, and in organizing the education system, and, of course, the capital associated with education. Even in a rich country like

Britain, labour costs form three-quarters of current outlays in education (omitting transfer payments), so that capital costs are, in fact, almost certain to be low, except in the higher education of physicists and other scientists. Initially, at least, these specialists may be trained abroad, where (fortunately), even in the absence of aid, the authorities impose fees which are much lower than marginal costs. These skills depend on investment in physical capital and imported specialists and goods. One problem is to minimize these inputs.

One kind of country has unemployed intellectuals — most of South-East Asia, the Muslim countries of the Middle East, and South America fall into this category. The other kind of country — central and eastern Africa being the most obvious examples — has no such category.

V. THE NEED FOR A MANPOWER PLAN

Now the secret of developing education in those countries with unemployed intellectuals is to bring them into the education system as teachers.

Clearly, it would be preposterous to use intellectuals to train yet more intellectuals to be unemployed in their turn ; unless it takes place in a context of vigorous economic growth, and above all of a manpower plan, the development of education is merely an open invitation to revolution.

Thus, a manpower plan, implicit or explicit, is a necessary basis for the use of education as a means of economic growth. I here state an extreme view, in the context of the planning mechanism which in fact pertains in most under-developed countries. The alternative is a policy designed to promote the full employment of trained talent, which in turn implies a fairly perfect labour market, which means fairly directly the marginal productivity of skilled labour of different types. This seems a situation so far from realization that it can be neglected.

It may well be, too, that in the previous pages I have been a little too emphatic in arguing the grave social disadvantages of intellectual unemployment. In this respect two main *arrières-pensées* are present in my mind : the first is that intellectual unemployment has been widely prevalent in many countries for many years, and a potent source of discontent and unhappiness ; secondly, that the urgency of removing poverty and ignorance from Africa and Asia is overwhelming, and that the failure to use every degree of skill as fully as possible is a major misapplication of resources.

A manpower plan is also often a necessary basis for the development of education. Unemployed intellectuals are often unwilling to teach because teaching has a low social status. Many people have struggled to get a degree, and would be most unwilling to leave the towns to go back to the country and live in the villages ; a rural teacher's life is lonely and isolated ; and if he is to be successful at his job he has often to outrage his children's families. Only some sense of national drive can, in fact, overcome this difficulty at all rapidly.

This raises sociological issues of great complexity. How far people can be 'conscripted' into education, either as pupils or as teachers, is a matter of profound dispute, both on practical and on socio-political grounds. It may be thought that in this passage of my paper I have underestimated the importance of human freedom. This issue is complex. All that I would wish to say at this stage is that the weighing up of terrible poverty and the social duty of educated people to remove that poverty is a matter for the peoples of Africa themselves to decide ; my argument is that if education is to play a part in rapid growth, a condition of that rôle is that the educated people should be used.

An economist should suggest, perhaps, that money would be a helpful way of encouraging new recruits. Raising the pay of teachers is a most effective barrier, however, to the quick development of education. In most cases actually investigated in Europe, the 'shortage' of teachers does not represent a shortage resulting from their salaries being fixed by a monopsonist government below market equilibrium, but a *functional* shortage arising from a scarcity of training places or university places.

I have said that the argument for rapid growth of the education system as a factor in rapid economic development is based in part on the cheapness of the real resources available to be used in the education service, but it would be easy to price these real resources out of the market. One of the difficulties of using teachers from the developed countries is that their salaries have to be very high ; and the almost inevitable consequence of this is a jacking-up of the whole salary structure in the country concerned.

The limit to the growth of education in a non-socialist economy is, in fact, the size of the budget. It is difficult for a government of a poor country to levy enough taxes to pay for a fraction of the services it feels it should provide.

In his paper Professor Peacock has presented some fascinating data on this subject, showing first how far already the countries of Africa are approaching the limit of budgetary resources, and how heavily their public finances are committed to education. Experience has shown that there is no need to convince African governments of the need for education ; what they ask for is guidance as to the methods of financing it, and a strategy which will suggest which parts of education should be developed first.

In other words, if education is to expand rapidly, the government has sometimes to pay salaries to teachers at or near subsistence level. But salaries at this level make teaching such a low-caste occupation that people would sooner remain unemployed than enter it.

I should point out a most important qualification to this argument. Skilled and educated people used full-time in education are diverted from other occupations. In advanced countries up to one-third of the output of higher education is used by the education system itself ; in the case of women in England, two-thirds of the products of the grammar schools (selective schools) enter teaching. Consequently, the *net* contribution of education to the stock of skilled people in the economy is far below the *gross* output of the education system. Consequently, the real costs of the education system where there is full employment of skilled manpower are very high (given prevailing labour-intensive techniques).

The corollary to a manpower plan is in fact a wage and salary plan. This is made easier by the fact that in many developing countries the greater part of educated manpower is (or will be) in the public sector ; that wages and salaries in this sector are administered prices and not market prices ; and that the public sector is dominant in the sense that when it establishes norms of income the private sector will tend to follow.

It is necessary to keep salaries down if some occupations are not to require so much expenditure for so few people that they cannot play any pioneering rôle in development.

It is important here to consider the possibilities of part-time teaching. A high proportion of graduates and skilled people should have the opportunity of acquiring pedagogic skills ; and it may well be that patriotic and social duty will require them to use these pedagogic skills — in training apprentices or teaching adults — free of charge. Mass literacy campaigns often rely upon volunteer members of youth movements, for example ; while in America the development of 'each one, teach one' campaign has been important.

In fact, it seems as though we are inescapably driven to the conclusion that to use education as a major means of accelerated growth — to diffuse the will to grow, to spread simple techniques, and provide cadres of skilled manpower — some measure of control of the economy, and above all of the labour force, is essential. This is a challengeable assertion, but I am reluctantly driven to the view that for the poorer countries it is a virtually inescapable conclusion — given the premise that rapid economic growth (in the absence of world market forces developing such growth) is desired politically.

May I take as an instance the Ashby Report on Nigerian education.[1] This report is based partly on the work of Professor Harbison who (with due qualifications) attempted heroic estimates of the needs of Nigeria in 1970 for trained manpower. His statistics are, of course, open to question ; as was his taking of Egypt as a 'benchmark' for Nigeria's needs. Nevertheless, within broad limits, his major conclusion, that Nigeria needs many more skilled people if growth is to take place, is broadly acceptable. Now what is noteworthy in his work is that the price system is absent from it. It might appear — as Professor Stigler has argued with some force in *The Demand and Supply of Scientific Personnel* — that a true *economic* shortage is only indicated when the price of the scarce labour has risen disproportionately, or (in the case of the poor countries) where the differential between the wages earned by qualified people and unqualified people is so great that it is quite disproportionate to the costs of education and training. It would be expected that people would flock to the schools and colleges, and that ultimately the quasi-rents of the educated will be eliminated. The reason why this aspect of the question is usually omitted from discussions, seems to me clear ; education is (or will be) publicly provided, and the greater part of trained talent will be used in the public sector. Inevitably, therefore, we are dealing with a system which is not responsive — directly, at least — to market forces ; we are dealing with an administered price system.

VI. THE PROBLEM OF BALANCE IN THE EDUCATIONAL PLAN

The balance of education between primary education and higher education, between general education and vocational education, and between full-time and part-time education, is essentially a pragmatic problem, determined to a surprising extent (as I indicate below) by the technical relationships of various parts of the education system. This is so even in the often-discussed question of boys versus girls. It is argued, for example, that education in a poor country should be restricted to boys, because they alone will be 'productive'. Leaving

[1] *Investment in Education*, Lagos, 1960.

aside the somewhat utilitarian picture of education which this implies, there are several objections to this view, which to my mind are overwhelming. First, in some countries (Ghana, for example) women are important in the marketing and enterprise sections of the economy. Secondly, they play quite crucial rôles in some parts of agriculture — in Uganda, for example, the men cultivate the export crops, while the women largely produce the subsistence crops. Thirdly, the effect of women on the home and the general cultural environment is all-important. Lastly — and this point is by no means self-evident — girls make good teachers, nurses, and stenographers, and often their earnings in alternative employments (their 'opportunity costs') are especially low. They therefore provide the major source for the expansion of the education system itself.

It is clear that with a manpower programme the very rapid development of higher education can provide a cadre of teachers who are in turn able to stimulate primary education, which will result (very quickly) in a flow of secondary graduates who will in turn supply the higher education system with students. But in fact a series of compromises can result in graduates with no jobs, and a secondary system which is too small to fill the places in higher education, while primary education does not expand rapidly enough to satisfy the politicians. There is the additional problem that the rich get more education than the poor. In a publicly-financed education system this can mean that the poor are taxed to educate the rich, who in turn are unwilling to educate the poor, because of the loss of status involved in becoming primary teachers.

An analysis of the flows of people in education will frequently dictate a series of places in education at different levels in an almost technical fashion. For example, in order to produce one graduate there may have to be 100 primary pupils and 25 secondary pupils ; because in this case experience has shown that only 1 in 4 primary pupils proceeds to secondary level, and of secondary pupils only 1 in 25 eventually graduates. In a reverse way, if 1 in 3 graduates teaches, and you need 1 graduate for each 50 secondary school pupils, it will obviously be necessary to establish a relationship between university output and the demands of the schools for teachers. In other words, education is a special case of 'manpower planning' and it is possible to work out far more carefully than at present the indirect consequences of any single act of policy. The decision to increase the number of university places by 100, that is to say, can be seen in terms of its demands on other parts of the education system, and its influence on the supply of teachers.

This quite elementary point — so obvious to any businessman, let alone an economist — has been neglected to an extraordinary extent in the United Kingdom and Western Germany where quite autonomous decisions have been taken about higher education and secondary education, with no consideration of the relations between them.

It seems, too, that apart from these 'technical' input-output relationships, there is something to be gained from attempting, however roughly, to calculate the cost of the different kinds of education which are provided, and to try to estimate benefits. For example, the complex problem of deciding whether to stimulate urban or rural education is made easier of solution if costs and benefits can be attributed to different courses of action ; and, particularly, if attention is paid to the expressed demand for trained manpower in different occupations.

I am not, of course, suggesting that only those parts of education that 'pay' should be stimulated, nor am I placing great reliance upon manpower projections. But in a quite pragmatic fashion it is possible to identify actual or potential shortages of particular skills, and to take steps to remedy these shortages ; and France has developed an admirable system of indicating to its young people the skills and occupations which are likely to 'pay' best in the future, with the result that *without direction* they are able to get the balance of students in the different faculties that the planners themselves believe will be most suitable. Of course, if the planners are wrong, the consequences will (presumably) manifest themselves in the incomes of the students, but a fairly rapid reorientation of new recruits to the faculties is then possible. In any case, it is improbable that an uninformed student will make a better judgment than an informed one.

Frequently, it seems to me, the most 'economical' course will not be the most popular. Mass rural education, for example, is extremely expensive in manpower and its effects seem not to last. Mass literacy campaigns fail because the people not only have no books but have no need to read them. The training of a small *élite* is less popular but probably far more potent economically. Yet often, for social and political reasons, mass literacy will have to be chosen. This is not necessarily wrong, it is just far more costly in terms of the possibilities of growth which have to be forgone.

What I have said in this paragraph is shorthand for a more complex argument. Briefly, mass literacy is in itself extremely disappointing unless it is part of a wider scheme for improving agricultural techniques, improving communications, opening up access to markets, developing local political institutions, and promoting local hygiene programmes. In this case the education programme is part of a total programme which can be justified as a whole, but only doubtfully in its particulars. On the other hand, the development of *élite* education is something to which one is, on principle, opposed, and which bears within it the seeds of ultimate social and economic inefficiency, as is now being seen in England. What is here being argued is that the development of mass education depends on the development of cadres of skilled people, and that this is essentially a logistic problem. The time sequence is : first, cadres ; then, mass education ; and a simultaneous development, while inevitable in practice, is (in principle) a slower process.

There is also a problem of finding pupils in poor countries. Those who are likely to reap the greatest benefit from education are the ones most likely to earn a wage to help their families ; or to play an important part on the family farm. It appears, therefore, that forbidding child labour and a tax on juvenile employment are useful ways of helping to support the schools without raising the educational budget. Undoubtedly, this leads to problems of enforcement (in countries short of people who can be inspectors, for example) and may also plunge families into poverty (the number of widows is always very great in countries with high death-rates) ; so that any policy of extending education is almost certain to entail a policy of family support. It is worth noting, in fact, that only when education is seen in this social and economic context are the real problems of its extension seen. For this reason, as well as others, I myself am suspicious of policies which seek to divorce education from the other social services, hoping in this way to serve priority for education over — say — health. The whole policy of social infrastructure provision needs to be kept in balance ; and any attempt to push education too rapidly ahead will, in itself, create an overwhelming and unfulfillable demand for other social services.

To summarize, the closest possible links between the central planning mechanism of a country and its education authorities are necessary if waste and imbalance are to be avoided. In this connection, two problems peculiar to education have to be considered. The first is that in the greater part of British Africa south of the Sahara, missionary activity has provided a substantial proportion of the schools. It is to be doubted whether this activity will continue on its present scale, or whether it will continue to be a high proportion of total provision of schools and colleges, but, nevertheless, it raises a problem of co-ordination and planning which is especially difficult. Secondly, British Africa has inherited an almost theological belief that education should be a locally provided and controlled activity. Increasingly, it is coming to be thought that this method of provision and administration has not been without its faults in England and Wales; it makes little, if any, sense in the context of rapidly developing economies. This is especially relevant to the question of inspiring and changing the technology of teaching; in conditions of local control and initiative this is made a great deal more difficult than in areas where education is centrally directed.

The structure of education in a poor country is a problem to which the methods of economic analysis can be usefully applied. In general, the wastage rates at various levels of education are extremely high. These wastage rates represent a very real misuse of resources. It becomes clear that attempts to reduce these wastage rates are a considerable economy in themselves. They arise from a variety of factors (among which social and pedagogic influences are, of course, supreme); but here it may be said that the uncritical importation of foreign models is almost certainly a major basic fault. Africa south of the Sahara represents the clearest example of this. French and British Africa have inherited complete systems of education from their former imperial governments; and the effects on the culture of the two areas have been profound and, in many cases, beneficial. But it is only now, with independence, that it is realized that the basic problems of tropical agriculture, the social organization of a society still based on the tribe and the extended family, and the cultural traditions of the African nations themselves have been neglected in favour of producing people who could enter the Sorbonne or Oxford without difficulty. In this respect the countries of Asia, with older and more resilient cultures, have been perhaps more fortunate than the African countries. That is to say, the education system is bound to have high wastage rates because it is not attuned to the local social and economic circumstances; and even if there were no 'drop-out' from the system, much of the education would be irrelevant to the needs of the local society.

Again, as I have shown, there is a most serious problem of finding the finance for education. Yet most education goes to the better off. If they had to pay for it there would be more finance for an extension of the education service. The arguments for charging fees are very strong. Education is scarce, and it should be carefully husbanded; while it is free people undoubtedly 'waste' it — attendance is irregular and students do not study hard. The successful students often command high salaries, so that their policy-provided education yields them high individual returns. The poor pay taxes and the rich benefit. On welfare grounds, then, the case for charging fees is strong in many poor countries. Yet as a matter of 'principle' education is supplied free.

Most political and social judgment is, of course, entirely against fees ; and I am wholeheartedly with those who would supply education 'free'. But as a matter of pragmatic judgment I consider that the supply of education without charge is a policy which will limit its growth, until a certain stage of economic development is reached. Fees are not, of course, the only sources of finance. Loans to students are another, though they are notoriously difficult to administer. I have suggested elsewhere a tax on the use of skilled manpower ; or a requirement on the part of large users of labour, or projectors of schemes which will use labour, that they should provide adequate training schemes. After all, a new business makes demands on the social overhead and on the infrastructure which are not negligible, and there is a great deal to be said for identifying these demands and, if possible, pricing them and charging for them.

VII. THE NEED FOR STATISTICS

The statistical analysis of education, save in France, the Netherlands, and Sweden, is not a matter for pride, even in developed countries. An adequate system of statistical control is a necessary prerequisite of adequate planning, and it is to be hoped that early attention will be paid to this problem. Education is far too often left entirely in the hands of pedagogues, and their warm hearts or lofty minds inhabit a non-quantitative world of quite frightening inefficiency and waste. For example, the identification of when drop-out occurs and its causes, is a complex problem, but enormously rewarding, since a student who can be persuaded to stay on to complete a course is a very much cheaper addition to the qualified working population than a new recruit to the student body.

VIII. CONCLUDING REMARKS

It would perhaps be unnecessary to labour these and other points were it not that education is regarded as something outside economic considerations by those who advocate its indiscriminate extension. I should not like it to be thought that I am blind to the importance of education to human dignity and freedom. A meeting of academics may perhaps take this for granted in a way that might be unwise in other contexts. But I feel that education for its own sake has not lacked its advocates ; whereas education for use most definitely has.

Further, whether education is for good or bad purposes, to lay up treasures in heaven or on earth, it still uses resources which might conceivably be used for other purposes no less worthwhile in themselves.

Education thus can be seen as a very potent weapon in the armoury of those who wish to help the economy to grow. But it is so only on certain conditions ; by itself it probably consumes more resources than it produces. Given these conditions, however, it can play a crucial rôle, provided that its objectives are clearly designed and closely related to the other parts of the programme for development, and that it is cheap in its demands on finance as well as in its use of resources.

DISCUSSION OF MR. VAIZEY'S PAPER

Professor Spengler, opening the discussion, said that Mr. Vaizey, having noted that education was expensive and variable as to content, assigned it three rôles : (*a*) to develop skilled manpower ; (*b*) to generate a climate for growth ; and (*c*) to diffuse elementary rural skills. He implied that, should improper content be given to education, it might create an intellectual proletariat, and hence inferred that it must be planned as an integral component of a country's general economic programme and subjected to rigorous control by authority, presumably that of the state. Mr. Vaizey had argued that the educational function should be performed by local teachers, among them unemployed intellectuals, paid at subsistence wages and supplemented by a minimum of auxiliary resources. He also indicated that the training of a small *élite* was preferable to mass education because it was more economical, though often not easy to achieve, both because the people might prefer literacy and because turning out one college graduate might entail enrolling 100 primary and 25 secondary students. Mr. Vaizey's paper posed a number of issues on which the Conference might focus attention :

(1) Did education aid growth ? He suggested that it did this by creating skilled manpower and changing a society's aims. *Professor Spengler* would supplement this by saying that education enabled the individual to receive, store, and transmit that information on the basis of which a developing economy was administered. He would, therefore, attach much more weight to mass education, since it was communication at lower levels that was more important in the aggregate than that at higher levels. Mass education had the additional advantage of dissipating the prestige that attached to education *per se*.

(2) What parts of the educational system should be developed, the

primary, the secondary, or higher education ? Mr. Vaizey attached less weight to the primary and secondary, he believed, than did some of those present at the Conference. They could not really answer the question, however, until they looked at the relevant demand and supply conditions. He suggested, none the less, that one was somewhat bound by the logic or structure of the educational system, since the output of higher education was a function of the input of primary and secondary education.

(3) They came next to the demand for education. Mr. Vaizey implied (and *Professor Spengler* agreed) that they must distinguish between actual and potential demand. Much of contemporary discussion ran in terms of potential demand. Yet it was the actual to which they should look. They needed to treat education as a future-facing input which would not yield returns for 8–16 years. This was a long time to wait in any society in which interest or the cost of waiting probably should be assumed to run to 10–20 per cent per year. The true actual demand would be quite low, therefore, and should be estimated in terms of the number of jobs in whose performance education to some level was essential. Of course, if education was viewed as a consumer good and supplied at a very low price, the quantity demanded would be very high. Acquiescence in such demand would be wasteful, however, since resources were so limited. He would suggest as a means to economy charging fees for secondary and higher education, together with a limited scholarship plan, as in Israel. He also believed that more economy and better orientation could be achieved if there was considerable local responsibility for the programme.

It might be noted, parenthetically, that demand for education was sometimes expressed as some percentage of the national income. W. A. Lewis put this percentage at 3 per cent, Hans Singer, resting on American data, put it at 7–8 per cent. If one looked only at age composition and neglected all other relevant factors, one would say that the percentage should be about twice as high in an under-developed as in a developed country. This would suggest a requirement of 2–6 per cent, or more, of the national income. This was in line with Professor Peacock's observation that labour, being the relatively most abundant factor, was the one we must try hardest to improve.

(4) This brought them to the limiting factor, the present supply of teaching capacity. What this capacity would be depended on how many potential and actual teachers there were who might better be employed teaching than doing something else. It depended on how the population was distributed in space, since this affected the pupil-teacher and the capital-pupil ratios. It also depended on what teacher-time-saving facilities were used, such as radio, television, teaching machines, teaching aids, and so on. It seemed

a foregone conclusion, however, and this was emphasized by Mr. Vaizey, that the capacity of any under-developed country to supply education compatibly with the alternative use-value of the input required was quite low. Moreover, it could not be much supplemented by foreign personnel, though foreign sources could supply teaching aids.

Professor Spengler commented that, in his view, no teaching personnel would be forthcoming if only a subsistence wage were offered, unless the teachers were put into uniform under a military system. The pay surely would have to be high enough to call forth an adequate supply. If one could vest teaching with prestige, this supply price would be lower and salaries could be kept lower. For prestige functioned as a subsidy and might lower the supply function for teachers, as it certainly did for the governmental bureaucracy, which was the reason why it was not necessary to pay very high salaries to any but very high-level civil servants in many under-developed countries.

But to return to the main theme, however one might view it at present, the supply of teaching and educating capacity was quite small. It had, therefore, to be husbanded carefully and all infra-marginal demands had to be rejected. Unlike Mr. Vaizey, he would concentrate heavily upon primary and secondary education, in so far as employment opportunities existed. He would emphasize agricultural and industrial training. He would count on 2–4 years of secondary schooling to supply elementary scientific and mathematical training, book-keeping and accounting, and writing skill. He would taper off most people who wanted more than secondary education with a year or two of junior college. Four-year college could be reserved for but a few.

This approach rested partly on the fact that one did not need to be very educated to be a good entrepreneur in a private, or what was rare, in an intelligently conceived public setting. It rested also on the fact that on-the-job training served to spread technological knowledge. It recognized that the world pool of knowledge could be drawn on. Above all, it recognized that it was uneconomic to hire a man to do a boy's work. Ten to twenty years from now the solution would be different.

Mr. Moran argued the importance, in any reorganization of the African education system, of taking account of the new techniques of education, which could greatly economize scarce teaching skills. Like Professor Spengler, he disagreed with Mr. Vaizey over his suggestion that teachers should be paid no more than a subsistence wage. He thought that much more responsibility should be placed on local authorities, and they should be made much more aware of the heavy costs involved in education. But for all that he believed in the importance of education. Africa's greatest need was for social change and for change of attitudes.

Professor Robinson argued the case for substantial public contribution to education. He thought that Professor Spengler had gone much too far in the direction of suggesting that the amount of education should be limited, apart from a limited number of scholarships, to actual demand, if by that he meant to the power of parents to pay for the education of children. He recalled the earlier discussion of the unspecified factor in economic progress, accounting for over three-quarters of the increase of productivity. Education, directly and indirectly, probably accounted for a large part of this. Moreover, the marginal productivity of capital investment depended in considerable degree on the educated intelligence of the labour using the capital. Absolutely identical equipment had widely different outputs in different countries. From the point of view of an actual employer, it paid him, within limits, to be taxed for the education of his workers.

Professor Dupriez also emphasized the relationship between education and economic development. But he thought that Mr. Vaizey's paper went too far in making economic development the sole objective of education. One had to remember the importance of well-being equally with well-faring. He thought that in this respect Mr. Vaizey's approach was too narrow. It was necessary, moreover, to hold the balance between education and health, which was equally important. But he agreed that one primary necessity was to change African mentalities and outlooks.

Dr. Singer challenged Professor Spengler's 15–20 per cent time discount. Investment in knowledge and intelligence was highly mobile. One must not, therefore, apply to it rates of return which might be appropriate to very specific forms of physical investment. One could reduce the investment in education if one were prepared to limit it to the localities in which development might be assumed to take place. Expenditure on education tended to be relatively less because it was a recurrent rather than a capital expenditure, and thus did not attract foreign aid, which had a bias towards capital projects. If mortality rates fell, as was likely, investment in education would be spread over a long life and thus be more productive.

Professor Bézy argued that one could apply to education the same principles one applied to capital investment generally, in order to judge whether it should be widely distributed or concentrated. He quoted figures from the Congo where the number of students per 1,000 of population was higher than in any other Central African country apart from Ghana. (101 per 1,000 as against 116 in Ghana, 91 in Northern Rhodesia, 73 in Uganda, and 57 in Nigeria.) Education was, however, badly planned. There was too much rural primary education of very low standard. It had been intended to develop a wide primary education before going on to education of higher standards. But time had been insufficient. There was, moreover, a certain level below which education was ineffective. Thus the attempt to widen education in the early stages had proved unproductive. If the same expenditure had been differently distributed, with much less to primary and much more to secondary education, the results would have been incomparably greater.

Mr. Dowuona did not believe that there was any social resistance to education or any lack of demand for it. He stressed the need for general education as well as technical training, including the inculcation of social values. This was even more important for the development of Africa than mere technical knowledge. He agreed on the importance of the development of new teaching aids. He hoped that both primary and secondary education could be widely dispersed.

Dr. Gavrilov also stressed the importance of cultural as well as technical education. Colonial régimes had done little to build up a framework of education. It should be based on the national culture and language. In particular, the training of women was necessary.

Dr. Okigbo gave a brief account of the work and recommendations of the Ashby Commission in Nigeria. Nigeria proposed to devote a very large part of its national resources to education. *Professor Robinson*, in the light of a recent visit to Nigeria, agreed with Dr. Okigbo's comments. A great deal of re-thinking of educational policies was needed in Africa. He thought that inadequate use was being made of very scarce specialist teachers and was surprised and disappointed at the very small classes at the higher levels of some schools and universities.

Professor Leduc gave the Conference some account of a Conference held in Addis Ababa some two months earlier on the problems of African education. Three conclusions, he thought, had emerged. First, education should not be regarded simply as an investment for increased productivity, but should, none the less, be biased towards those forms which might help economic development. Second, general planning of education over a sufficient period of years was indispensable ; the effort had to be distributed over the different levels of education. Third, Africa would not be in a position to finance the desirable expenditures on education, and appeals should therefore be made for foreign aid. It should be recognized that even those expenditures on education which were technically recurrent, in fact represented a capital investment. These expenditures might properly be financed, not only by taxes, but also by grants and loans.

Mr. Beheiry raised the question as to how far an African state could or should, under African conditions, attempt to mould the minds of its future citizens. There had been philosophies underlying education in all countries — in the U.S.S.R., the U.S.A., the United Kingdom, France, and the rest.

M. Rist regretted that Mr. Vaizey's paper, by raising so many controversial issues, had distracted attention from the importance of some of the central issues. The dominant problem was the training of a competent labour force. He thought that the discussion of the balance of cultural and technical education had been somewhat confused. The right distinction was between the training of the mind and training in manual skills. This distinction became more important at the level of secondary education. With the limited number of available educated Africans, it was very important that they should be properly used. *M. Rist* mentioned the existence of an institute within the World Bank for the study of programmes, of other than the strictly normal types, that were worthy of support ; these included education.

Professor Houghton referred to the wastage in education, such as had been described by Professor Bézy. He agreed that if education was not carried to the point at which an African became permanently literate, it was wasted. This point he put at Standard 4 in the South African system, representing about 6 years of education. Literacy was most important. Illiterate workers were only employable on unskilled jobs. The basic objective of mass education should therefore be literacy.

Mr. Vaizey stressed the point that, despite its important rôle in society, someone had to pay for education. He himself was not convinced that the assimilation of education to investment was really more than a rhetorical phrase. Education had no direct yield, and the indirect yields were problematical. Education throughout the world was at present very inefficient and there was need for thorough investigation of it. He himself believed that in any country there were strong grounds for central control. There was, moreover, need for a new technology of education. There had been enormous changes during the past ten years. But there were many new techniques in the teaching of mathematics, for example, which were not yet properly exploited. There were at the same time certain ineluctable technical relationships between different levels of education. Some 35 to 40 per cent of the output of higher education had to go back into education in an African country until a cadre was built up. Thus, the increase of the educated population could only be progressive. He stressed the need for more teachers, particularly at the secondary level. The number of teachers that the developed countries could supply would be no more than a drop in the ocean of need. *Mr. Vaizey* was very critical of the Ashby report for making no suggestion as to how the enormous increase that it visualized might be financed. A Pakistani report had been much more practical and realistic. He agreed with Dr. Gavrilov about the importance of educating women, which could contribute more than anything to changing the attitudes of the whole society — a thing which, he believed, was easier to do in Africa than in some of the Moslem countries outside Africa.

Chapter 13

CREATING INCENTIVES FOR ECONOMIC DEVELOPMENT [1]

BY

STEPHEN ENKE

Duke University, Durham, N. Carolina, U.S.A.
Visiting Professor, University of Cape Town, 1960–61

I. INTRODUCTION

IF any national economy is to increase *per capita* income, more rapidly over time than hitherto, there are certain things that its adult population must do. First, its entrepreneurial managers must innovate better methods and more useful products faster, whether they do so on their own account or as government officials. Secondly, people must work longer and harder, and perhaps some persons now outside the regular labour force must become productively occupied. Thirdly, people must save more, and these savings must somehow be invested economically. Obviously, there are many other things that backward but developing countries must attempt, such as expanding exports to attract foreign capital. But the fundamentals of development are more improved technology, more labour effort, and more invested savings.

Because of population increases, it is often not enough that the people of a country always invest some constant fraction of their income and that some customary fraction of the population always works with traditional intensity. Such conditions, combined with no technological change, are often compatible with economic stagnation. *Per capita* incomes may remain unchanged for decades.

As an illustration, suppose the net market and subsistence output of a country is a function of technology (ϕ), labour (L), and capital (K). Suppose constant returns to scale when natural resources are included. Assume also that the supply elasticity of output for labour and capital are 0·5 and 0·2 respectively : that is, an x per cent change

[1] The title of this paper, as originally prescribed for another writer, was 'Private and Public Initiative in Development Programming'. The present author has interpreted this to mean organizing ways in which government can encourage public officials, and especially private persons, to do some of the things most necessary for a 'typical' African national economy to develop.

in labour will occasion a $0.5x$ per cent increase in gross value added. Now, if a country has a population increasing at 2.5 per cent a year, this will increase output by 1.25 per cent annually. And if 0.05 of national income is saved net, and national income to capital stock has a ratio of 1.25, this additional capital will contribute another 1.25 per cent increase to annual output. This means that *per capita* income will be absolutely stationary without more work, more investment, or more advances in technology.[1]

There are many ways in which government can encourage people to innovate, work, and invest more, and so improve their economic behaviour. But the selection of incentives has to be very different in background from advanced countries. Many indirect methods of persuasion — *e.g.* taxes and subsidies — are useful but less effective in subsistence economies. More direct kinds of government intervention would often be useful if only enough officials of ability could be recruited. And, where private capitalists will not venture, government must try on occasion to provide the enterprise.

However, there is nothing more sterile than doctrinaire controversies regarding public versus private ownership of industry, and it is better to adopt a pragmatic approach and let circumstances decide each issue. It matters more that people work harder than whether they are employed by a public or private concern. It matters more that productive factors be organized by managers who have technical knowledge and an experimental spirit than that these resources be owned by particular individuals or the general population. Because it is the economic attitudes and behaviour of individuals that are most important, and not the relative sizes of the public and private sectors, we shall now consider ways in which government can encourage additional people to do more of the innovating, working, and saving that are necessary for accelerated economic development.

II. ACCELERATING THE TEMPO OF INNOVATION

What constitute innovations? Old products are made in new and better ways, new products are introduced, and perhaps new exploitation of existing natural resources is undertaken.

---

[1] These calculations assume a constant labour force to total population ratio, and a current rate of return on capital of 25 per cent a year. It is noteworthy that incremental capital of 5 per cent of income is associated with extra income of 2.5 per cent of income. A careless observer of this association might assume that the incremental capital to output ratio was 2.0. This would be just double the actual rate of return on investment.

For the United States, over the seven decades since 1870, economists at the National Bureau of Economic Research have estimated that over 80 per cent of the increase in American *per capita* output came not from extra factor supplies but from miscellaneous elements including improvements in the state of the arts.[1] Many of these innovations in the U.S.A. had to wait upon scientific discovery and industrial invention. In this respect, more backward countries are favoured, for at least the technological knowledge already exists overseas.

Unfortunately, these new innovations cannot be adopted without new *kinds* of real capital and new *kinds* of labour, and above all radical changes in institutions and attitudes.

The new kinds of capital can always be imported, if foreign exchange is available, and nowadays it often is. But it is not enough to import tractors, dockside cranes, and shoe machinery. There must also be new kinds of labour, in the sense that workers have to be trained to use them. And, what is far more serious, they have to be trained to maintain them. It takes less skill and training to drive a fork-lift than to repair it. And preventive maintenance — *e.g.* thinking about lubrication before one is reminded by expensive noises — is not an outstanding characteristic of recently primitive people. Regrettably, the advanced countries cannot export repair personnel along with every crate of machinery, and the paucity of such ability among the present native populations is often a real constraint on the rate of innovation that can be useful.

Part of the solution is more education and a drastically re-orientated curriculum. Presumably, most children will continue in time to learn reading, writing, and arithmetic. But the top fifth of the boys — including the few who will go into professions — should probably learn some elementary biology or physics or mathematics. In addition they should have some rather special vocational training, such as machine metal worker, electrician, junior soil analyst, automotive repair mechanic, assistant veterinarian, or book-keeper. Many school subjects that were traditional in colonial times will have to go. And for years to come, because there are so few teachers and facilities, most elementary education may have to be limited to the intelligent and industrious males who can live near present schools. But eventually there will be more skilled and semi-skilled workers who can use modern technology. And from this group a small minority of the most imaginative and enterprising are more likely to introduce the numerous small improvements

[1] M. Abromovitz, *Resource and Output Trends in the U.S. since 1870*. National Bureau of Economic Research, N.Y., 1957, Occasional Paper 53.

here and there that collectively contribute so much to economic development.

The spread of literacy and a few major languages should stimulate government to publish periodicals, priced below cost, to disseminate simple technical information in addition to explanations of new government policies. For villages in remoter areas, where illiteracy continues for lack of schools, the same sort of information might be broadcast by battery-wireless loudspeakers one hour every evening. Political abuse of such mass media is probable, as is strengthening of one party government, so real political liberty and economic development are once again in conflict.

Innovation is of course considerably simpler in industry than in agriculture. If a product has never been made before in a country — as is often the case — there are no customary and local methods to be displaced. Enough money is at stake to justify the temporary use of foreign experts and to organize special training courses. And the number of industrial employees to be instructed is comparatively small. Nevertheless, the cost of training is not inconsequential if a firm is the first producer of some good in a country, especially if there is a real danger that rival and later firms may subsequently hire these recently-trained men away. In this connection, although it smacks a little of indentured labour, there is much to be said for an apprenticeship system.

Agriculture is more of a problem. It is usually harder to teach new methods of raising traditional products than to introduce new products entirely. Actually it is surprising how many foreign crops have spread through Africa, from maize and manioc to coffee and cocoa, but a similar receptivity to alien ideas on animal husbandry and soil cultivation has not been evident. It is unfortunate that cattle have in many places acquired a status and exchange price often quite independent of their value as meat. Communal use of land sometimes precludes a single sub-family from trying a different fertilizer, soil preparation, or crop rotation. Where scientific and technological knowledge are lacking, and a crop failure may mean actual famine, one cannot blame rural families for following 'safe' customs rather than 'outside' advice by experts who do not risk starvation.

Real progress in agriculture is likely to be slow rather than spectacular. It takes time to spread ideas, especially in sparsely populated regions. Government may have to train agricultural specialists who, with government funds, will go into the countryside and start small demonstration farms with local hired labour. After a few years, if some of the new methods come to be accepted, the official can move on to another area and start again. He will leave behind some important social capital in the workers he has taught. These government 'missionaries' of the new agriculture will play a vital rôle and enough 'seminaries' for their training cannot be established too soon. (These agricultural officials may also direct various community projects to be described later.)

Agriculture is so much a way of life, and people who live on the land are so numerous and distributed, that it will take many new 'missionaries' to convert enough of the rural population. Accordingly, government may have to make a determined effort to channel a large fraction of the best young men through agricultural high schools and on into 'field' demonstration work. Every effort must be made, including good pay and allowances, to offset the prevalent idea that ambitious officials can only advance through urban office jobs. It will cost money and resources to counter the stigma that intellectuals have attached to agriculture.

The necessity of an agricultural revolution is stressed here for two reasons. One is simply that in many African countries, if the output of subsistence sub-economies is included, agriculture contributes about half the national product. The other is that increasing output of food is essential if industrialization is to be possible.

When labour migrates from rural agriculture to urban industry, a considerable fraction of its previous share in the home kraal food supply is now eaten by the relatives who remain behind, and so more aggregate food production is required to support a given population that includes more town dwellers. Also, and more significant, the extra industrial output of a closed economy cannot be sold at prices that cover costs unless *per capita* incomes and food intake are rising. Persons who have low fixed incomes are usually not so willing to eat even less in order to buy, say, kitchen stoves and motorized bicycles. But if output per head is rising, this increment will obviously not all be eaten, and a market will develop for all sorts of durable consumer goods.[1] Industrialization requires that fewer people be able to produce more food. Hence innovations in agriculture are a prerequisite. To force industrialization before an increase in agricultural productivity is to misallocate resources.

[1] The above argument is not so strong if 'industry' — including capitalistic and specialized agriculture — can export. Despite complaints about fluctuating prices, fortunate indeed are those countries that can export tea, coffee, sugar, copper, uranium, etc. Few backward countries have any major comparative advantage in making *finished* producer and consumer goods. If new fabricating industry is to improve the trade balance it will usually be through further processing of materials before exporting or importing goods at a lower stage of completion.

However, if agricultural productivity can be increased, an effective demand for less necessary consumer goods will develop. And some of these can be made domestically to advantage. The innovator is then the man who first decides with reason that a factory to make shoes or assemble bicycles would now be profitable. And, if over the years improved processes and increased demand cause him to lower prices, there will be a further increase in real income, which in turn may make a 'place' in the domestic economy for some other novel lines of production.[1]

Each innovating firm with a new product may also occasion other pecuniary economies or diseconomies, for subsequent enterprises, through the forces of joint supply and joint demand. Extractive industries must often construct roads, eliminate mosquitoes, dam rivers to create lakes, and so on. Such activities are not designed to benefit others, but in fact they often do, and at a zero price to the incidental beneficiaries. Alternatively, by constructing blocks of flats, local demand for furniture may be stimulated. Against these effects are those of rival supply and rival demand, which give rise to pecuniary external diseconomies, and so must be set against the 'economies' of joint supply and joint demand. Moreover, there are vertical 'external' economies, as when the establishment of a large fruit cannery increases the prices paid to fruit growers and decreases the prices paid by consumers of tinned fruits.[2]

There seems to be a widespread and optimistic view, among those who write about developing backward countries, that so-called external economies outweigh the diseconomies. This rosy supposition, hard to demonstrate even for a specific investment, has been used as an argument in favour of public as against private enterprise. It is held that private investment, because it cannot 'internalize' these external economies, will be suboptimum. But a government, concerned with social profit rather than financial profit, would presumably invest if total revenue plus unrealized external economies exceeded total costs. Presumably similar results

---

[1] Assuming that the activities of the first enterprise do not increase the cost of productive factors to subsequent firms.

[2] These various kinds of 'pecuniary external economies', as they have been named by Professor Tibor Scitovsky ('Two Concepts of External Economies', *Journal of Political Economy*, April 1954), are really quite distinct from those defined by Alfred Marshall (see *Principles*, 8th edition, pp. 221, 263). Marshall's external economies arose from changes in the output of an industry, and accrued only to firms within that industry, whereas the economies that economic development writers are always examplifying flow from their instigators to others. In reality, the 'external' economies so often cited today are usually either examples of Pigou's second type of divergence between social and private marginal net product (A. C. Pigou, *The Economics of Welfare*, p. 174), or a species of Marshallian buyers' or suppliers' surplus. The old names are being misapplied or forgotten.

would follow if government paid private firms a subsidy based on estimated 'external economies'.[1]

If history is a guide, a great many private innovations outside of agriculture are likely to be made by aliens, and in Africa during the past century this has usually meant Western Europeans and Indian immigrants to whom Africa is often rightfully home. Whether the black majorities will encourage the browns and whites to continue their innovating contribution will be a real test of the maturity of the newly independent régimes. It will be a severe test because many innovations will be rewarded by substantial profits and so the white and brown minorities will still have some of the highest incomes and hence be an object of envy. Professor W. A. Lewis, now back in his native British West Indies, ably expressed the problem when he wrote :

> Many under-developed countries, awakening . . . to a strong desire for economic development, are embarrassed by what it seems to require in terms of inequality of income, whether as between the 'middle' classes and the farmers, as between foreigners and natives, or as between profits and other incomes. For the climate of our day is hostile to income differentials in general, to foreign differentials in particular, and to handsome profits in the extreme. These, however, are part of the cost of development.[2]

III. INCREASING THE AGGREGATE INPUT OF LABOUR

In all countries, including even advanced economies with large capital stocks, labour is by far the most important source of income. And in the immediate future, if an increase in output is paramount, the only physical way to obtain it is usually for more people to work longer hours. A government that wants additional output more than does the public will have to conscript labour directly or indirectly.

There are probably no significant instances in Africa of regions or industries where it would be physically impossible for workers to increase their effective labour. For this would mean that people, although working long hours daily, could only command enough food and shelter to stay alive and labour. In the capitalistic sectors, employees can usually work longer and effectively, even though this may require them to eat more and buy less of other things. And

[1] One argument of those who favour a 'big push', and simultaneous investment in government production of a wide range of goods, is that external economies will thus be mostly 'internalized'. But government projects can be financed from taxes as well as sales receipts. Hence, although a case can be made for subsidy, the 'deduction' that there must be *simultaneous* and broad investment, is an unwarranted additional argument.

[2] W. A. Lewis, *Theory of Economic Growth*, Allen & Unwin, 1955, p. 182.

Economic Development for Africa South of the Sahara

malnutrition in subsistence sectors sometimes results from a preference for leisure to more food. None of this denies that net extra output will be less than gross — because of necessarily higher food intakes — or that incremental hours may have lower productivity. The assertion is rather that extra hours worked, whether or not from the existing labour force, will have a positive marginal net product.

A popular view among occidental economists is that there is a great deal of under-employment in rural subsistence agriculture. From this it is commonly argued that rural labour is a free good without opportunity cost to urban industry. This is supposed to justify the use of incremental capital output ratios for ranking alternative investments in industry. However, even if the marginal product of this labour in subsistence agriculture were zero, opportunity costs would not be zero. There is the difficulty — described in the section preceding — that the minimum national aggregate requirement for food will be increased by such internal migration. And there is the additional requirement of urban amenities — *e.g.* shelter, utilities, and sewage — that are costly and properly a deduction from any extra urban output.

Another fundamental error is the failure to distinguish between the product of an hour of labour and of a worker within the subsistence sector. Paradoxically, as explained below, the ratio of marginal to average product of an hour of work may be very much higher than the ratio of marginal to average product of an agricultural worker. It is very possible that the former ratio might be, say, 0·5 and that the latter might be 0·05 or even zero.[1]

The explanation for this difference is that, when rural labour emigrates, remaining workers may labour more hours a year. This may be because certain agricultural tasks are more or less definite. The cattle have to be taken to water so often, put in a kraal at night for protection, and be periodically dipped. Or custom may dictate that certain lands are always planted in mealies.[2] Another influence

[1] Suppose a small rural community having a labour force of 10 persons. They work collectively 10,000 hours a year, or each about 4 hours a day for 250 days a year, and the total output is 250 'somethings'. Thus the average product of an hour's work is 0·025 'somethings' and we shall suppose that the marginal product of an hour's work is 0·0125 'somethings' or half as much. The average product of a worker is 25 'somethings' a year. However, if a worker migrated to urban industry, there is no reason to suppose that the remaining workers would each continue to earn 1,000 hours a year. Suppose they each instead worked 1,100 hours a year, for a total of 9,900 hours, which would mean an incremental loss of 100 hours or 1·125 'somethings'. For a worker, the ratio of marginal to average product is hence 0·05, or one-tenth the similar ratio for an hour of work.
[2] If there is communal sharing of output, and there are 10 workers, each one's immediate family only gets one-tenth of the marginal product of an extra hour's work. So there is a diminished individual incentive to work more. A collective

is that men in some regions traditionally leave most cultivation of crops to women, and that women seldom seek jobs in towns, so that the departure of a village male may have a very slight effect on the community's crop output.

The policy significance of this distinction between the comparative marginal product of a worker and work is that extra hours of rural labour may have a by no means negligible product. If government wishes a greater national input of effective labour, it may be that many or most of the extra hours worked should initially be in agriculture, and not in industry. The net incremental output of having the rural labour force work a full day most days a week, and yet be able to live economically in the back areas, might be quite considerable.[1]

How can rural labour effort be altogether increased? Incentives might be 'personalized', so that the product of an extra hour of work is not shared among many others at a later date. Where annual tasks are determined by custom, a government propaganda campaign might induce groups to increase the areas they cultivate. Eventually men might be willing to supplement the work of women in the lands. However, where an unproductive culture is the obstacle to economic expansion, it is questionable how 'persuasive' government exhortations are likely to be.

Despite its unpopularity, left over from colonial days, there is much to be said for a substantial and nominal poll tax to compel increased work and output. Initially it might be levied only on adult males. But a lower assessment might be made on women. And as a partial deterrent to high birth rates, assuming the 'ownership' of children could be identified, a poll tax might be levied on them but payable by a 'parent'.[2]

decision on what rural tasks must be done is more likely to be influenced by custom when there is output sharing.

[1] Making the same assumptions as in the footnote before last, taking one worker out of agriculture lost an output of 1·25 'somethings', gained some industrial output, and incurred costs for extra urban amenities. If the worker stays in the rural community, but works the same 8-hour day as he would in industry, say, he would produce an extra 12·5 gross and net 'somethings'. If it could be arranged for the whole community's labour force to work 8 instead of 4 hours there would, under these assumptions, be an output gain of about 125. This extra output might be worth more than the net value addition of having everyone migrate to urban industry.

[2] Most areas of Africa, with the exception of particular areas such as the Nile Valley, are not yet seriously burdened by over-population despite rapid reductions in death rates. But, taking a viewpoint of 25 years or so, the proportion of the population that is too young is sensitive to the birth rate. Very approximately indeed, a country with birth rates of 40 per thousand a year, will have almost 40 per cent of its population under 15 years of age, and one with birth rates of 20 will have somewhat over 20 per cent of the population under 15 years. The effect on output of having almost one-fifth of the population productive rather than non-productive would increase national output.

A special feature of this nominal poll tax would be that payment could be made in money, certain labour services, or particular staple products. Hence the tax can be thought of as a statutory labour requirement commutable at so much per day of work not performed. Or it can be considered a levy on the output of certain staples. The effect is to set a money price and several commodity prices on a certain number of days of work. If these prices are higher than a person can earn, working for others or himself, that person will presumably report to the government for work. This discretionary feature of the nominal poll tax gives everyone an opportunity to follow his or her comparative advantage.

What would the government do with people who present themselves for work? Ideally, government should seek to determine labour intensive projects that are useful and local, do not require many simultaneous workers, and can be completed before enthusiasm flags. In most communities there are useful projects — *e.g.* making water reservoirs, building roads, constructing river fords, sinking bore-holes, draining land, installing cattle dips — that need to be done. But they are not done because the community is unprepared to make the joint effort, lacks capital to buy certain materials and equipment, or cannot organize itself. Government may not always be able to find qualified supervisors, but it can supply materials and draft local labour.[1]

The effect of government setting a labour price on certain staples, such as food grains, cocoa, and tobacco, is to establish price supports for these products. If these prices are expected to remain rather constant, the output of these goods will be encouraged, and by this means export credits may be augmented. The nominal poll tax can thus encroach upon the subsistence economy in several ways.

Economists in advanced countries tend to oppose poll taxes as being income regressive in their incidence. But the alternative of an income tax — progressive or otherwise — has limited meaning in a really backward country. Its assessment, except against the comparatively very rich and few, is too difficult to be justified. Moreover, many backward countries collect a considerable fraction of their revenues from import duties on consumer goods, and these imports are mostly of a kind not purchased by the poorer elements.

---

[1] Obviously government cannot start projects in every community at once. Hence the poll tax in some areas will have to be paid in money or approved staples unless persons are prepared to leave their families while they discharge the tax in work. The government will not be dismayed if people do not in fact report for work because money and staples can be used to purchase necessary materials or finance general expenditures.

It can be argued that citizenship imposes obligations as well as rights and that the concomitant of one man one vote is one man one poll tax.[1]

A great merit of the poll tax is that, being impossible to evade by a change in economic behaviour, it is likely to encourage work and production. If a household finds itself with, say, a fifth less real income because of the tax, the marginal utility of consumption is presumably increased, and there is a strong likelihood that all members of the family will make more effort to earn or produce. This is in marked contrast to taxes on income, and even consumption, which may discourage output. Hence, if output effect is the criterion, even a tax on pure economic rent would seem inferior to the nominal poll tax proposed here.

Enactment of a nominal poll tax would underline the fact that there is no painless way an economy can develop at an unnatural pace. The alternative may be Chinese style communes and forced labour with no ifs and buts. Peoples who have material ambitions that cannot wait may discover they have lost their liberties.

IV. INCENTIVES TO SAVE AND INVEST

Officials of backward countries are prone to bewail the low propensity to save in their economies — usually a propensity of from 5 to 10 per cent of national output — and ascribe this to low *per capita* incomes. But it is often bad government as much as human poverty that is guilty. Fiscal irresponsibility leading to inflation, failure to protect people in their property, and corruption of tax collectors so that long-term investments are avoided, these are all to blame.

The states of Africa, in comparison with those of Latin America and some of South East Asia, have been fortunate as regards inflation during the past. But should the new governments begin financing public projects through bank credits and money, so that price levels rise 20 per cent or more every year, private indirect investment apart from equities will come practically to an end. Assets defined in money will not be attractive to savers, and government will be unable to borrow from the public.

Many families save against bad crops, unemployment, and sickness or death, especially where social insurance schemes are lacking.

---

[1] A poll tax, commutable into, say, 25 days of labour a year, might seem excessive. But the personal income tax in the United Kingdom or the United States, for the average person who pays them, represents probably more days a year of working for the government.

Those who are 'ahead', and not in debt, must have some object as a store of wealth that is invulnerable to inflation and political unrest. Small savings may accordingly be held as coinage. The more prosperous may favour precious jewels and metals. And wealthy sophisticates can discover foreign bank balances in responsible countries. In all these instances *net* national savings do not result in productive national investment. These savings, from the economy's viewpoint, have been wasted for the time being. But this would not occur under conditions of good government.[1]

Corrupt government can result in savings being diverted from long-run investment into quick turnover transactions that are often denigrated as 'speculative'. A successful business that must invest in fixed and durable assets is always subject to a 'shake-down' by officials who want to be 'partners' in the profits without sharing in the risks. Thus the owner of a hotel may be 'squeezed' by the property tax assessor. Under such a régime, it is prudent to offer no permanent assets as hostages to fortune but rather to specialize in buying goods at one place and time, selling them soon in another so that any profit can be taken quickly before officials come 'in' on the transaction.

Indirect equity investment is inhibited by unwillingness of many savers to entrust their money to a strange corporate manager who is not a relative and may be of another tribe or religion or race. Government might be able to reassure indirect equity investors by inspecting all joint stock companies, and so protecting the saver from management in part, but confidence is slow abuilding. Government might somewhat increase the liquidity of company stocks by operating or subsidizing a local stock exchange.

Investment by government in the public sector is a common reaction to 'inadequate' private saving and investment. The invested funds may come from taxes, profits on other government enterprises, or new bank credits. Borrowing from the public is usually of not much importance if inflation is well under way.

Although some governments make considerable profits from public sector production or marketing — *e.g.* India from railways and Ghana from cocoa respectively — it should not be overlooked that possibly important 'pecuniary external economies' are being sacrificed. Government operated utilities and companies should presumably follow marginal cost pricing and not seek maximum profits. And a public marketing board that buys from local growers

---

[1] This does not mean that savings used to buy land are wasted. It is what the seller of the land does with the proceeds that matter. He may invest them (*e.g.* in trading stores), consume them (*e.g.* take a trip to Europe), or expatriate them (*e.g.* buy Swiss securities).

and sells abroad should presumably attempt to maximize the algebraic total of its profits and sellers' surplus.[1]

It is often suggested that government should increase tax rates, and thereby accumulate a budget surplus on current account, which it would invest. But an examination of the public finances of a number of central governments in backward countries indicates that, during the past decade at least, the ratio of extra public investment to extra tax receipts is about one-fifth. The rest has been spent on an enlarged bureaucracy, upon police and military, and a variety of current social services. In other words, the marginal propensity of government to save is not very high either, and it may be lower than the marginal saving propensities of those who contribute extra tax proceeds. In such cases, which are quite likely to arise when it is the 'rich' who are 'soaked' for extra tax monies, net investment of the country may decline despite extra tax recipts and government services.[2]

If a government does have a budget surplus of 5 monetary units (*e.g.* millions of pounds), with which it wishes to stimulate investment, it has a choice of investing itself or subsidizing private investment.

Suppose the supply and demand of loanable funds within the country is now 200 monetary units at an interest rate of 10 per cent. Perhaps the supply of loanable funds would be 300 units at 13 per cent and the demand 300 units at 8 per cent. If the government was prepared to subsidize the difference, and *if* it could discriminate so as to subsidize only the increment, 5 monetary units spent in this way would indirectly evoke extra national savings and investment by 100 units. And, as 100 units is 20 times 5 units, the indirect subsidization of investment would occasion a greater investment increment in the first twenty years (ignoring reinvestment of returns on investment) than would repeated annual investments directly of the government's budget surplus.

---

[1] In this latter case, if the government is 'between' a positively inclined domestic supply schedule and a horizontal or negatively inclined foreign demand curve, what should its marketing board do ? It should not adjust its buying price so that marginal purchase cost equals marginal revenue from selling. It should set a buying price that will be equal to marginal revenue. If the country's exports have no effect on the commodity's international price, suppliers' surplus is at a maximum when government profit is zero, and the official marketing scheme must be justified on some other grounds.

[2] Some people would argue that all expenditures for education — teachers' salaries as well as school buildings — should be considered 'investment'. But educating a people is like dredging a river mouth. A great deal of education is to replace educated people who have died, just as a great deal of dredging is to maintain rather than deepen a navigable channel. Only expenditures that increase the number of educated people alive in the country is a net investment — and a very important one it is too — but this is only a fraction of the total bill for education.

However, in the longer run this is not necessarily so, because 5 units a year on subsidy simply *maintains* a constant investment increment of 100 units. The indirect method is more effective over long periods only under rather special conditions. Specifically, even assuming government can discriminate between those who were previously intra- and extra-marginal lenders and borrowers, it is necessary that (1) saving and investment increase markedly for each percentile point of 'spread' between the two subsidized interest rates, (2) the subsequent marginal rate of return on investment is still at a high (though lower) level afterwards, and (3) the reinvestment of income from investments is at a high rate. A consideration of the interactions concerned would suggest that indirect subsidization of investment is not likely to prove as effective as direct government investment over long periods.[1]

The rather pessimistic conclusion is that government can do more to stimulate savings and investment by acts of omission than commission. If it would not depreciate the currency, if it would not contribute to political unrest and harassment, and if it would not permit corruption of tax officials to deter certain long-term investments, the productive use of capital would probably be greater in many countries than it is today. The records of some Latin American countries, and of some newly independent nations in Asia, are a sombre warning to the new African states.

V. CONCLUSION

The point of this paper is that the incentives that matter are those that encourage more innovation, more work, and more useful saving. These have always been the requirements of development. Backward countries differ from advanced ones in that the specific

---

[1] Suppose a government has an annual surplus Q. It can invest this each and every year. Or it can use Q to subsidize extra lending and borrowing of A. That is to say, Q equals $A(i_s - i_d)$, where i_s is the subsidized supply interest rate, i_d is the subsidized demand interest rate, and government does not subsidize previously intramarginal lenders and borrowers. There is no question but that during the first year A will be greater than Q. But Q summed over a number of years, plus the return of this investment that is re-invested, might come to exceed A plus reinvested returns on that investment. The two series will neither converge nor diverge when $rs^1 A$ equals Q, and r is the rate of return and s^1 is the proportion of income from investments that is re-invested. And A equals $Q/(i_s - i_d)$. Algebraic manipulation then leads to the conclusion that the indirect stimulation of investment through subsidization is more effective in the long run as well as the short run when

$$\frac{rs^1}{i_s - i_d} > 1$$

We can suppose that r approximates i_d. Thus, if i_s is $0 \cdot 13$ and i_d is $0 \cdot 08$, the critical value for s^1 is $0 \cdot 625$.

incentives that encourage people most are likely to be different. Use of the nominal poll tax is an example. And, to avoid sectoral imbalance, it is especially necessary that everything possible be done to increase productivity per hour and hours per worker in the subsistence economy.

It will be noted that 'capital' has not been given pride of place but has been listed after innovation and work. This is not to deny the importance of saving. But the current identification of development with capital — often an alias for grants in aid from abroad — is too easy a way out. Of course, by emphasizing loans, 'responsibility' for non-development can be placed on others. But a far greater need is for the extra innovation and extra work that can only flow from broad cultural changes. It is up to the native populations to relinquish custom and superstition, open their minds to more successful ideas, and accept other attitudes and values.

Meanwhile, because these truths are unwelcome, people will continue to turn to panaceas. As Professor J. K. Galbraith has stated :

> Development will not occur if it is believed to come automatically with escape from colonialism ; if it is identified as a matter of course with faith in free enterprise or socialism ; if it is regarded as the special magic that will be provided by a particular political personality, or if it is to be accomplished by some single stroke of genius such as the building of a particular road, the settling of a particular jungle, or the watering of a particular desert. In all instances, the result, not long deferred, will be serious disappointment.[1]

What he is implying, and it is a view to which surely we can all subscribe, is that the subject of economic development is presently in need of more analysis and less 'escapism'.

DISCUSSION OF PROFESSOR ENKE'S PAPER

In opening the discussion of Professor Enke's paper, *Professor Williams*, at the request of the Chairman, deliberately extended the field of consideration to cover the subject of entrepreneurship ; the author of a paper on that subject which had been planned for the Conference had unfortunately not been able to complete it or to attend the Conference. *Professor Williams* described entrepreneurship as the driving force in any economy, attempting continually to change its pattern. The entrepreneur

[1] Galbraith, J. K., 'A Positive Approach to Economic Aid', *Foreign Affairs*, April 1961.

everywhere lived in a world of resistance to change and had to overcome it. The stronger was the resistance to change, the stronger had entrepreneurship to be. The entrepreneur was born rather than made. His chief characteristics had to be originality and adaptability. The qualities of an entrepreneur could be developed and strengthened by education, but education was not a necessary condition of success. He needed also technical skill and understanding, and the technical innovator clearly needed to have technical insight. But again a high level of academic technical training was not a *sine qua non*. It was a mistake to suppose that because a man had technical skill he would also have entrepreneurial ability. There were many weavers in Africa who had the skills but were lacking in any entrepreneurial capacity to exploit them. The entrepreneur needed to have capital at his disposal and to have opportunity to draw on loans, though the latter would not, probably, be sufficient in themselves. Moreover, too generous advances, given before there was real need for them, might lead to failure at a later stage.

There were various handicaps against which an entrepreneur in Africa had to contend. First, there was the extended family system ; this led to a tendency to look inward, with one's loyalties directed to a narrow group ; it led to difficulties in the individual accumulation of capital. Second, the family pressure to spend on prestige symbols, such as over-elaborate houses, was a further drain on the collective accumulation of capital. Third, there was a lack of trust, which made it difficult for businesses to grow beyond a certain size. The formation of partnerships and limited companies was as a consequence of this more difficult. Finally there was a general lack of respect for business success. More often business was regarded as a stepping-stone to a political career, and the entrepreneurs who might have done much to develop the resources of the country withdrew from economic activities. Those who remained often adopted a too narrow concept of their functions, stressing the making of money rather than the creation of a large business.

Professor Williams went on to quote examples of successful entrepreneuring. There were in Ghana African entrepreneurs (many of them women) running small stores, and sometimes large stores, owning canoes and trading in fish, acting as importers and distributors of foreign goods (there were 50-100 larger businesses of this kind in Ghana, doing a trade of £20,000-£30,000 per annum). Most of the road transport and almost all the taxis were in African hands. On a larger scale, almost all the growing of cocoa was African. Even before 1930, there were several quite large African firms buying cocoa in the Kumasi area. But in recent years he felt that the force of entrepreneuring had declined. Either resistance to change had grown or the driving spirit had become less powerful.

Professor Leduc emphasized that, if African countries south of the Sahara wished to develop their economies on the principle of free enterprise, entrepreneurial ability was extremely important. Any progressive economy needed people to assume risks and carry responsibility. Entrepreneurial ability could, he believed, be developed. About this he felt less pessimistic than Professor Williams. If this could not be done, there were only two alternative solutions. Firstly, the economy could be 'functionalized'. The State would have to take over the strategic direction of the economy and the main tasks of entrepreneuring — this was not to be recommended. Secondly, entrepreneurs could be found elsewhere, in Europe, America, or Asia. A number of these were operating already, and most of the African governments showed no sign of aiming to get rid of the entrepreneurs established under colonial rule. He saw no unbridgeable gulf between the capacities of Africans and the requirements of entrepreneurship. In West Africa women traders were active. Africans played a large part in transport. The remaining sectors were largely covered by Lebanese, Syrians, and Greeks, who could be emulated and copied by Africans.

Dr. Wade emphasized the difficulties of training entrepreneurs, given their present milieu and family environments. Even where they were ambitious to engage in entrepreneuring, there were the difficulties of capital and credit. It was necessary to change the existing agricultural systems and to diversify them if new techniques and new products were to be introduced. Africans had no knowledge of accounting and there was no emphasis on saving. At present he thought that the typical African preferred to work for a Lebanese rather than try to overcome all the obstacles to setting up in business himself.

Dr. Okigbo stressed the difficulties that arose in West Africa from the close identification of political and commercial power. In Nigeria in the late nineteenth century and early twentieth century one of the big trading concerns was itself the Government. Some of the rising entrepreneurs of that time were ruthlessly destroyed by the use of political power. This experience had a gravely discouraging effect on small entrepreneurs. For the small business man the model to be copied was not the large trading company but the medium or small enterprise, usually Lebanese; these had been effectively copied. One of the difficulties of business expansion was that, in the absence of accounting experience, personal and business affairs tended to get inextricably mixed. Capital was consumed without awareness of the fact. The extended family, as had been said by others, complicated the problems of savings and capital, and with better public health, more rapidly growing population, and falling death rates, savings went down as the expectation of life went up.

Professor Bézy drew attention to some of the wider problems of the training of skilled staff in Africa. The problems of training had been much more difficult during the colonial period by racialism. Those who were engaged in training and advising the companies as to what responsibilities could be carried by Africans were the very people who would be displaced if great responsibility were given to Africans. In Congo, and particularly the Léopoldville area, after the hurried departure of a third to a half of the higher staffs of firms, it was necessary to hand over jobs to Africans. After a very short period of decline, production and even productivity, per head recovered to the original figure and even exceeded it. Because African staffs, even after considerable salary increase, were paid less and the share of higher management in the total salary bill had previously been high (often 50 per cent as compared with about 20 per cent for the same grades in Belgium) unit costs generally fell. They had been faced with new problems of training. These had been solved partly by training on the job, but the greatest success had been with technical training outside the actual firm, conducted by foreign specialists recruited for this specific purpose. He suggested that, in addition, there ought to be a change in the wage-policy adopted by some African countries. There had been too much emphasis on narrowing the differentials between skilled and unskilled. He had no hesitation in advising a wider differential in favour of technical skills as against clerical and unskilled work.

Mr. Moran did not think that general education contributed much to the development of the entrepreneur. He recommended more practical help in the form of strictly technical training. The idea of entrepreneurship was associated with the word 'private'. Africans were not, he thought, greatly interested in private enterprise.

Mr. Vaizey stressed the ephemeral character of the business man in so many under-developed countries. Most businesses in developing countries were very short lived. He thought the greatest contribution to the development of a business enterprise was to expand its potential markets. With regard to African agriculture, he believed that it was more important to get efficient entrepreneurs into the marketing of the products. Without that, community development of agriculture or any industrialization of agriculture, such as Professor Enke had suggested, was a waste of resources.

Professor Houghton commented that, while the working life of some African entrepreneurs was short, a new generation of more solid and persistent entrepreneurs was growing up. A large number of the best educated and most intelligent entered government service, thus depriving industry of their possible contribution. In South Africa, many Africans preferred themselves to deal with the white man, because they feared exploitation. That attitude needed to be changed.

Dr. Singer was doubtful whether one could create entrepreneurs. But much could be done to economize the need for them to possess large capital as a condition of setting up. The government itself might take over the responsibility of providing the economic infrastructure, and provide services cheaply rather than at the full marginal cost in present conditions.

Professor Williams agreed with what Dr. Okigbo had said regarding the inextricable confusions between business and personal income. African traders did not appear to think in terms of this distinction at all. He suggested that the will to survive in competition was as important as

378

knowledge of how to survive. Some of the large firms had been taking in trainees and trying to give them entrepreneurial experience. He was by no means sure that this was a practical way of teaching people how to make decisions. In Ghana the private entrepreneur was finding the scope for his services rather limited. The chief desire was to find means of replacing existing foreign by local entrepreneurs rather than to create new opportunities.

Dr. Vopicka regretted that the Conference had not had a paper dealing with the issue of the relative advantages of public and private enterprise. He thought that the problem of the intervention of the state in the economic activities of under-developed countries was the key problem both of economic and of political development. The state itself was the only tool that these countries possessed to bring about change and reach their revolutionary aims. It was his belief that, if they wished to develop a truly independent national economy, they must diversify agriculture, change the international division of labour, and broaden the basis of education. In his view this could not be achieved in a society wholly governed by the profit motive and in which foreign monopolies were free to follow their own objectives. Only the state could concentrate financial resources and at the same time use foreign capital in accordance with the nation's own criteria of development. The state could use all the necessary weapons — the budget, the central banking system, the monopoly of foreign trade, and the planning of its own capital investment. And it was only the state which could subordinate the activity of the private sector to the overall interests of the African population. Without state-ownership of the means of production and without state intervention in the planning of development, it was impossible to realize the essential plans for development. He realized that many of those present would not share his views, but believed that African history would in due course prove them to be right.

Professor Robinson was anxious to assure Dr. Vopicka that many economists who might not wholly agree with him did not wish to recommend the pursuit of profit because they wished to see profits, as a form of income, maximized. Rather they regarded the making of profits as a test that inputs were being minimized — that costs were being reduced to an absolute minimum by good organization and the right choice of technical methods. Profits were only an incentive to efficiency. Through competition it was hoped that profits were continually under pressure and reduced to a minimum.

Dr. Yudelman reminded the Conference that in agriculture the largest input was labour. The problem was to provide incentives to increase the input of labour. In planned economies there was a tendency to make agriculture pay for development. By taxing agriculture, or diverting part of the price of agricultural products, governments were robbing agriculture of the necessary incentives.

Professor Stanley argued that the frontier between the public and the private sectors should depend on which could make best use of resources. There were different criteria in the two. In the public sector the authorities were concerned with giving people what they supposed to be good for them. In a mixed economy, the private sector took more account of what people wanted, and provided a safety valve. The conference recently held in Addis Ababa on education had established the value of education as an investment in an under-developed country. But not all education was valuable to the exclusion of everything else. One had to achieve a balance in all these forms of development.

Dr. Gavrilov emphasized the different approach of economists in the Socialist Republics. New African governments were facing new problems. But many of these had previously been faced by the Socialist Republics and Africa might usually learn from their experience. He thought that their method of developing the public sector had special attractions for African states. At present they were too weak to create the full basis of a national economy. To make up ground fast they needed to expand the public sector.

Professor Robinson said that the frontier between the public and the private sector could be discussed either on ideological or pragmatic grounds. He preferred to be pragmatic. In Europe it was very broadly true to say that manufacturing and distribution were left to private enterprise. Public utilities — transport, energy supply, posts, telegraphs, and telephones — were in the public sector, largely because they were inevitable monopolies that needed to be controlled. Certain semi-monopolistic key industries — like steel — were in the public sector in some countries, in the private sector in others. He thought that Africa might learn from this experience. But there were special problems in Africa. There was shortage of the sort of entrepreneuring ability that could control the biggest concerns. In some ways it was easier for a very large public concern to hire foreign experts for so long as they were needed and to dispense with them when Africans became available, than for individual African entrepreneurs to do the same thing.

Mr. Vaizey raised the point that there were considerable differences of opinion with regard to the frontiers of private and public enterprise within the countries of the West, as well as differences between them and the Socialist Republics of Eastern Europe. This was relevant to the problems of Africa where the issues were not exclusively whether public or private enterprise was more efficient, but were also concerned with the objective of the two. The two sectors that he thought should remain in private hands were distribution and agriculture. He thought that heavy industries should be in the public sector in Africa.

M. Roland Pré emphasized the dangers of introducing ideological concepts into the discussion of economic development. Mistakes had been made in both directions. He thought that each case should be decided without prejudice on its own merits.

Professor Spengler disagreed with Mr. Vaizey's division between the public and private sectors. It was most important that African industries should be organized and run so as to pay their way.

Professor Enke, concluding, said that one outstanding advantage of Africa had been that expenditure on defence had hitherto remained very small. He feared that there was danger that this might not continue during the next decade. Defence expenditure could be a heavy drain on development.

Chapter 14

PRICES AND PRICE FORMATION
IN AFRICAN ECONOMIES

BY

GASTON LEDUC
Faculté de Droit et des Sciences Économiques,
Université de Paris

I. THE SCOPE OF THIS PAPER

THERE are, of course, prices in the (independent and dependent) economies of Africa south of the Sahara, just as there are prices in all the countries of the world which have left the barter economy behind them and use some monetary instrument in their payments.

In each of these countries, the price system has some sort of structure, in the sense that the price pattern is certainly not purely fortuitous and that one price conditions another in some degree. This is true of product prices (for goods and services) no less than of factor prices, wholesale and retail prices, and of the prices of imported and domestically produced goods, whether the latter are destined for domestic sale or for export to other countries of Africa or overseas. It is true also of the prices of goods and services produced by private enterprise or under the direct or indirect auspices of public authorities (the price of public services).

But this is not a statement which has in any way special relevance to Africa. In all countries of the world, including, so far as we can tell, the communist countries, the price problem is the hub of the economy and the general price structure always reflects the overall situation of the country or group of countries under consideration, both at any given moment and over time.

If my observation, therefore, is somewhat lacking in originality, it does set me on the right road for my analysis. Let me be clear, first, on what this paper is *not* intended to do. It does not set out to describe the general conditions of price formation in the type of economic system which is closest to that of the various African countries south of the Sahara — namely, a market and free-enterprise economy tempered by more or less far-reaching and co-ordinated government intervention.[1] Nor shall I try to interpret massive statistical material with a view to making comparisons in time or space ; to do this, I would need access to information and research facilities I do not possess. I did attempt this kind of work [2] some time ago on a more limited scale and in a political and social context which has since been overtaken by events, so that the earlier study cannot now even serve as a point of departure for my present purposes.

My aim here is more limited. It seems to me best to look for whatever may be peculiar to Africa in the formation and behaviour of prices. This may help towards a better understanding of conditions which, in many aspects, are still very different from those in economically more advanced countries, especially Western Europe and the United States. It may help, also, to define more closely what precise part the price mechanism, as it functions at the moment, can play in an economic policy designed to strengthen the economic independence of the young African nations and to promote balanced and rapid economic growth.

I must acknowledge also a geographical limitation to my ambitions. Even within the terms of reference 'south of the Sahara' I would have to consider a group of very heterogeneous countries differing greatly with respect to the nature and the degree of development of their economy, as well as to the structure of their relationships — especially their commercial and financial relationships — with the outside world, to say nothing of political status. Generally speaking, I have concentrated mainly on the problem of French-speaking Africa, and even there, more particularly on those of the 'countries and territories having special relations with France', to use a phrase now current in the texts of international agreements (*e.g.* the Rome Treaty of March 1957, which established the European Economic Community and associated with it a certain number of African countries).

In this group of countries I include also the island of Madagascar, even though it is in many respects very different from its mainland neighbour. On the other hand, I am very much aware that I would have to modify my subsequent discussion quite considerably if it were to be extended, especially, to the Union of South Africa, a country with a rather advanced economy in which peoples of European origin play an important part. My horizon is comprised within the

[1] Government intervention and co-ordination is no doubt at the back of what certain leaders of French-speaking Africa call 'African socialism'. But so far the fundamental aspects of the economic systems have not changed. Guinea may well be an exception, but I confess to being regrettably ill-informed about developments there.

[2] Gaston Leduc, *Les Hauts Prix en Afrique Noire — essai d'analyse comparative*, Industries et travaux d'Outre-Mer, Paris, 1953–4.

two Tropics, and even in this central strip of the continent does not go beyond the French-speaking parts of Africa.

II. THE GROWING SIGNIFICANCE OF PRICES IN AFRICA

Prices are expressed in terms of money, and the conditions of price formation cannot, therefore, be usefully discussed without precise reference to the monetary system of the country or countries considered.

The first point to note is that in Africa a greater or lesser part of economic activity gets along without recourse to money at all. I have in mind the so-called subsistence sector, where goods and even services are produced for consumption either by the producers themselves or by the members of their social group, without exchange on the market. Although this sector is considered stationary, it does leave room for some sort of saving and investment in kind and may, therefore, make some economic progress. There may also be exchange on a barter basis, but this need not concern us here, except to note in passing that its extent is generally underestimated and is, indeed, difficult to assess.[1] Generally speaking, its importance varies from country to country and tends to be greater in 'national' production and consumption when the country is poor than when it is rich in exportable mining and agricultural resources. Barter plays a greater rôle, for example, in Nigeria than in Ghana, in Mali than in Senegal, on the Upper Volta than on the Ivory Coast, and so on. All in all, barter is probably on the decline. The economic development of Africa has, among many other effects, also that of enlarging the rôle of money in the economy, as the sphere of exchange based on prices spreads to more and larger occupational and geographical sectors (especially to primary activities and in the countryside). In these circumstances the phenomenon of prices as such is bound to gain in significance.

The monetary system of the African countries south of the Sahara generally evolved together with their political status. Many new currencies have been created in recent years. Public issuing institutes have come to replace the old currency boards or private banks of issue operating under concession. Bank money in turn is

[1] A United Nations publication, *Enlargement of the Exchange Economy in Tropical Africa*, 1954, estimated (on the basis of information relating generally to the years 1948 to 1950) that on the average some 65 to 75 per cent of cultivated land in tropical Africa is devoted to subsistence agriculture, and that, in 1950, 60 per cent of the adult (over 15 years old) male population was occupied in it. Of the 40 per cent working for wages, about one-third was employed outside the indigenous agricultural economy.

gaining in importance with the spread of the use of cheques among the native populations and with improved banking facilities.[1]

Many of the new currencies, however, still keep their links with outside currency systems, such as the sterling area, or the franc, or the escudo area.

This is a special and important aspect of African prices. In effect, the general price level in any of the countries here considered is largely determined by the official rate of exchange between the local currency and the respective leader currency. For instance, with the sole exception of French Somaliland, whose Djibouti franc has been linked to the dollar since 1949 for special reasons connected with the territory's position in relation to its hinterland, all the African countries (including Madagascar) belonging to the franc area have a currency unit called franc and worth two old French francs. The reasons and historical origins of this state of affairs do not concern us here. We simply take note that these countries would not have the prices they do if they had never belonged to the franc area or had left it, or yet if the parities and exchange conditions with other currencies both in tropical Africa and elsewhere were different from what they are.[2]

In now turning more specifically to the conditions of price formation in the market sectors of the African economies, it may be useful to recall some of the latter's structural characteristics.

(1) Whatever is produced for sale is largely exported. It is, however, an exaggeration to say, as is sometimes done, that everything that is not 'self-consumed' is exported and, by implication, that everything that is bought for consumption is imported. To quote again the United Nations study on the *Enlargement of the Exchange Economy in Tropical Africa* (Table 4, p. 14, figures mostly referring to the years 1947–50), 'areas mainly under crops for market', which amounted to 31 per cent of all cultivated land, were

---

[1] This development was accompanied by progressive — and now all but total — disappearance of primitive money tokens, such as cowrie shells, manilla, and the like, which have become collectors' items. I did, personally, still find cowries in use on rural markets of Uganda in 1959.

[2] It would be interesting to know the effects of Guinea's withdrawal from the franc area on her domestic prices. I have reason to believe that these effects cannot be determined precisely now, when most prices are controlled and therefore deprived of their full economic significance.

Mali, it will be recalled, decided to introduce exchange control for all currency transfers abroad, including the franc area. This decision does, no doubt, not amount to withdrawal from the franc area on the Guinean model, but it must have had some repercussions on domestic prices, if only by reducing the outflow of capital (and so increasing domestic money supply) as well as the import of goods (by cutting down import licences). But in interpreting the facts the observer would always have to allow for the stray effects of official controls and also of smuggling, which is rife along a frontier hard to watch.

about evenly divided between crops for domestic markets (16 per cent of the total) and crops for export (15 per cent). Export crops can be supposed to be more valuable and their share in the national product is therefore certainly in excess of 15/31ths of the product of market crops and even more so of 15/100ths of the product of market and subsistence crops together (the latter, in any case, remain to be valued).[1] And all this refers only to crops. If these estimates were extended, for example, to cattle raising, we would no doubt observe, like the same UN study (p. 16), that the 'relationship between the commercial and subsistence activities of labour engaged in pastoral production is still more difficult to measure'. All that can be said is that, with the exception of hides and skins, animal products are exported only to countries within the African continent, and that 'in view of the relatively under-developed state of [the domestic] market and in view also of the considerable social significance which many pastoral tribes attach to cattle, it seems probable that in terms of labour input, the proportion of labour devoted to subsistence production may be on the average higher for pastoral activities than for agriculture'.[2]

(2) By contrast, a large part of the consumer goods bought are of non-African origin. All told, the non-African proportion is certainly higher in purchases than in sales, because a certain portion of both private and public spending income originates in financial transfers from outside. At least, this is true of the 'countries and territories' of the franc area, which receive large remittances from the French government for civil (technical assistance and budget aid) and military expenditure as well as under the heading of grants for economic and social development; it may not be so universally true of other African countries. Where marketing boards and other similar institutions exist, there may even be a net transfer of funds abroad, especially to London, whenever surpluses are allocated to reserve in the form of British Treasury Bills.

(3) In spite of all their diversity and heterogeneity, it does seem

[1] The United Nations *Economic Survey of Africa since 1950* (Table 4, I, p. 204) estimates the share of goods and services in gross domestic product as follows:

	%
Belgian Congo (1957)	41·9
Ethiopia (1957)	12·0
Ghana (1958)	30·0
Federation of Rhodesia and Nyasaland (1957)	45·6
Tanganyika (1954)	23·4
Union of South Africa (1956)	15·5

The high percentages of the former Belgian Congo and of the Federation are attributable to mining, the whole output of which is exported.

[2] *Ibid.* p. 16.

that all these countries have this in common that a sizeable proportion of local production is marketed either locally, or domestically within the producing country, or within the African continent. Examples of such inter-African trade currents are West African exports of cola nuts towards the north, and the return flow, in the opposite direction, of dried fish and a certain amount of livestock products.

The importance of these inter-regional exchanges has rightly been underlined by Marcel Capet in his *Traité d'économie tropicale.*[1] He points out that this trade goes far back in African history and rests on geographical conditions : exchange between the desert and the savannah, between the savannah and the forest. The arrival of the Europeans naturally upset these trade currents, but they survived. Most often trade became triangular, with the insertion of imported products and the spread of the use of money. Thus European or Asian textiles go from Nigeria to the Republic of Chad, where they are used as money in the exchange for livestock. In general, Capet notes, 'the interior regions of the savannah today send more products to the desert, the forest and the coastal areas than they receive in return. Equilibrium comes about through a trade surplus (that is, with the help of foreign trade). The forest areas, for instance, export more to metropolitan France than they import from it ; the proceeds of the surplus are used to buy foodstuffs from the Sudan.' Whenever these circuits involve currencies belonging to different currency areas, such as trade between Nigeria and the Republic of Chad, the exchange rate is in part determined by prevailing local rates. (For many years, sterling currencies commanded a distinct and sometimes considerable premium over franc currencies.)

Leaving exports apart, local and national markets are beginning to attract a growing range of products. Originally, the products involved were mostly foodstuffs, the flow of which from the countryside into the towns has, incidentally, often been underrated in the past, as is shown by a number of recent surveys (especially so far as the Ivory Coast is concerned). Now there are additional and in part complementary currents of manufactured goods and services from the towns or suburban areas to markets in the bush country.

(4) To solve the distribution problem created by these different trade currents, a very complex commercial organization gradually developed. We shall here merely recall its great diversity and the changes which result from its continuous evolution. The most

[1] Marcel Capet, *Traité d'économie tropicale: les économies d'A.O.F.*, Librarie générale du droit, Paris, 1960, p. 121.

authoritative study in this matter is still P. T. Bauer's *West African Trade : A Study of Competition, Oligopoly and Monopoly in a Changing Economy* (1954). Bauer brings out very well the important rôle played in the past by the great import-export companies and their restrictionist tendency to keep out newcomers. We cannot here examine in detail all the changes which happened during the last few years and which forced these companies to concentrate on wholesale trade, to close many of their bush agencies, to cede certain markets to special representatives of the producer firms and to resign themselves to the growing development of African and Asian trade, which tends progressively to spread from the retail to the semi-wholesale and eventually to the wholesale field.[1]

It stands to reason that the manner in which this trade is organized and functions cannot fail to have a strong influence on the determination of the sales price of the products involved. In the past, monopolistic — or at least oligopolistic — tendencies often widened trading margins unduly and so pushed up the price to the local consumer, while the African producer got little. This fact has often been denounced and represented as one of the defects of a 'colonial-type' situation. This is another subject which might well repay close study. The companies concerned generally pleaded in defence that they often had to work in very hard conditions and that the time had gone when the mere fact of having got there first and being well established could procure generous profits without causing a rush of newcomers.

(5) Next to the commercial sector, which is so important in economies wide open to the outside world, we have to consider transportation as such. This occupies a paramount place in a continent like Africa, which can be reached from outside only by sea and which cannot easily be penetrated by waterways, partly because most of the rivers are blocked by rapids near the mouth. To circumvent these difficulties, roads and railways have had to be built. Both are costly to run and keep in good repair, mainly because of weather conditions, but also because there are often considerable differences in the freight to be carried in the two directions. Only the Union of South Africa escapes these difficulties to some extent, though on the other hand distances are very great and differences in altitude complicate railway traffic.

In these circumstances, it is clear that transport cost is an important determinant of prices on African markets. We really need

---

[1] Cf. Henri Didier, 'L'Évolution de la structure commerciale en A.O.F. depuis la dernière guerre', *Marchés tropicaux du monde*, March 22, 1958, and M. Capet, *op. cit.* Part I, chap. II, §2.

a comparative study of costs and operating conditions for the various types of transport (road, railway, waterways, air transport) ; but this cannot be done in a few lines and we have to rely on other published work. The analysis of the particular conditions of interior African trade should, furthermore, be extended to price determination for sea freight to or from African ports. Maritime freight rates are also an important ingredient of African prices, both the retail prices of imported consumer goods and the prices the African producer gets for export goods.

The local producer has to sustain the double burden of transport cost to a port of exit and from a port of arrival. Moreover, transport cost as such is swelled by a great number of extras for unloading, lighterage, storage, forwarding, etc., not to speak of frequent reloading during the journey itself (from board ship on to a truck, then maybe on to a railway, a barge, a truck again, etc.).

As a result the terms of trade, in gross real terms, of certain African products in relation to foreign goods are severely affected. This reduction in the local real value becomes very considerable, especially in the exchange of heavy and bulky goods, say, unshelled groundnuts against cement. It has been calculated that, according as the exchange takes place in a British port or at Sokoto in Northern Nigeria, the purchasing power of groundnuts in terms of cement is reduced by something like nine-tenths.

Similar calculations for Madagascar show even worse results for the local producer, because of the high maritime freight rates.[1]

(6) The last major element in African price determination is the rôle of government, or rather the combined effect of public intervention in the economy.

The most important single factor here is taxation. As in all countries at the same level of economic development, the bulk of ordinary revenue comes from indirect taxes on the movement of merchandise, that is, import and export taxes.

The incidence of these fiscal levies is not difficult to assess. Import taxes, whether in the form of an effective tax or customs duties, are fully borne by the sales price of the good in question, because neither the foreign seller nor the shipper nor the intermediary merchant is likely to shoulder any part of them. It is just conceivable that, in exceptional cases, some producer or merchant, or even the shipper, might accept a temporary reduction in his receipts so as not to lose traditional clients who might be in passing difficulties. But generally speaking, the African market is not of

[1] Cf. René Gendarme, *L'Économie de Madagascar*, Éditions Cujas, Paris, 1960, p. 91.

such importance to foreign suppliers that they are likely to accept particular sacrifices just because local taxation is so high.

Export taxes have the opposite incidence, in that they fall entirely on the local producer, who has no means of imposing his wishes on the foreign markets. For the local producer, foreign markets are competitive, in so far as Africa's share in the world supply of the products in question is too small to carry any real market power. Diamonds are no doubt an exception, Africa being to all intents and purposes the sole producer. But as regards gold, to the world output of which Africa contributes 50 to 60 per cent, it is common knowledge that its price on the international market is largely determined by official parities and especially the dollar parity, which has not changed since 1934 (35 dollars per troy ounce of fine gold). The producers can do nothing about it. Other commodities of which Africa produces more than half of total world output are palm and palm kernel oil (more than 80 per cent on the average), sisal (about 65 per cent), cocoa (more than 60 per cent), and cobalt (about 70 per cent). For the record, we might mention also uranium. Although variations in African output certainly do influence the market position of these products, it is hard to see how the isolated action of one country or of one country's organized producers can have any strong and durable effect on export prices. A case in point is cocoa.

We have to conclude that whatever the fisc collects in export taxes will mean that much less for the local producer. There is some justification for querying whether taxes of this kind deserve the name of 'indirect taxes'; they are really just a form of taxation on agricultural incomes, in proportion with gross receipts.

Apart from fiscal levies, there are also those collected with a view to the accumulation of reserves designed to cushion the impact of price fluctuations on the producer and his income. I have in mind stabilization funds, price-control schemes, marketing boards, and such like. The effect of such arrangements is that the producer gets less when prices are high and more when prices are low on export markets. This certainly has a stabilizing effect, but from the point of view of our analysis we have to add that the sums put aside by these institutions in periods of high prices reduce, by the same amount, the local producers' total disposable income and tend to have a general deflationary effect on the domestic economy — unless, of course, the government were to use these reserves to finance other expenditure. In practice, however, these reserves are normally invested abroad and serve at the same time as a foreign exchange reserve. The opposite effect comes into play when the stabilization funds draw on their reserves to pay more to the producers than a market price regarded as too low.

These remarks on the effects of such stabilization measures on local prices are not, of course, all that is to be said about the question of whether or not intervention of this kind on balance serves the general interests of the national economies concerned. This is a controversial question, and the marketing boards, for example, do not come in only for praise. In effect, their operation amounts to imposing a sort of forced saving on producers when prices are high and to substituting collective administration of the savings for such arrangements as the producers might make for themselves if they had sufficient foresight. Furthermore, stabilization of this kind does not go beyond the country's own frontier. The question of price stabilization for commodities or base products assumes far greater importance but also raises formidable difficulties when it is posed, as it should be, on the international plane.[1]

Fiscal and parafiscal measures are, of course, not the only ones by which the government can influence price formation, in Africa as elsewhere. There are many others. Those which we believe to be of particular relevance south of the Sahara include public works for the installation or improvement of a general economic infrastructure, which is a necessary, though not necessarily sufficient, condition for a reduction of transport cost and various handling charges, as well as of the price of energy, especially electricity. On the whole kilowatt prices are very high in the French-speaking countries of Africa and, for a number of reasons which would require another special study, much higher than in most other countries.

Price formation also frequently feels the impact of political factors, especially in foreign relations. There is no need to dwell at length on the fact that tariff or monetary links with foreign countries necessarily have an effect on the price level. When these links were still of a colonial type, the domestic price level in African countries was largely determined by prices in the respective mother country. It was a one-way and assymetric arrangement, typical of what François Perroux calls a 'domination effect'. The result was, and in most cases still is, that price disparities as between different countries were, or are, merely a reflection in Africa of the price disparities existing between the metropolitan countries themselves. For instance, during the post-war period until very recently the African countries linked to France had a markedly higher price level than their neighbours. In large part, this was an extension to Africa of the franc area's high relative prices at the official exchange

[1] See especially the *Symposium* organized by the late Ragnar Nurkse and published in *Kyklos*, 1958, No. 2, and 1959, No. 3.

rate. Today, this basic divergence has largely or wholly disappeared, thanks to the measures France took in December 1958 to realign and strengthen her own currency and eventually also the African currencies of the franc area (CFA franc).

There are, furthermore, particular factors which may attenuate or acerbate the local effects of such inter-metropolitan disparities. For example, indirect taxation on imports was generally heavier in French territories than in countries belonging to the sterling area. In the former, a more rigid commercial structure led to distinctly higher trade margins, and money wages, pushed up by the French policy of adapting local civil service rates to those current in France, were distinctly higher than in neighbouring countries, especially in the public sector. All these things help to explain why the price level in the African countries of the franc area was higher than elsewhere, and they are all, in turn, explicable in terms of political decisions.

This political framework of the economy has changed since the countries concerned became independent. To the extent that external relations still influence price formation in Africa, they are no longer the result of imposed decisions, but of commitments freely contracted by the African authorities themselves. I have in mind, so far as most of the French-speaking countries are concerned, the formation of a free trade area between the new nations and the former metropolitan power, their continued adherence to the franc area and their acceptance of association with the European Economic Community on the conditions laid down in the Rome Treaty — subject, of course, to adjustments which can be expected in the near future and certainly not later than at the expiry of the five-year period envisaged in the special protocol applying to the 'associated territories'.[1]

III. PRICE FORMATION IN DIFFERENT SECTORS

I am now in a position to attack more directly the real subject of this paper. To this end I distinguish two categories of prices : the prices of import and export goods, and the prices of goods and services entering domestic, or at most, inter-African, trade.

(i) *Prices of import and export goods.* In neither case, as we have already noted, is the weight of African supply or demand as a rule sufficient to justify the conclusion that prices are determined by factors proper to Africa.

[1] Cf. G. Leduc, 'La Communauté économique européene et les pays sous-développés', *Revue Économique*, November 1960.

In imports, c.i.f. prices must be considered as given and to all intents and purposes not subject to any influences emanating from African markets, whose bargaining power is too weak, at least so long as there are no local substitutes. The same goes for the determination of f.o.b. prices and of freight rates to and from Africa. Several Shipping Conferences encompass the African continent in their network of agreed rates, and although the Liberian flag flies freely on the high seas everywhere, this is of no particular advantage either to Liberia herself or to her neighbours. I confess to some perplexity on this score and think that this is a question worth special study.

But the c.i.f. price is only the beginning. There are all the marketing margins in the widest sense, from unloading and transit charges, transport and storage costs, to taxes, and finally wholesale and retail trade margins. In the bush, there are in addition also the innumerable middlemen and pedlars who, in tropical Africa, account for so large a proportion of the tertiary sector. According to M. Le Héragat, the total marketing margin of imports for the whole of former French West Africa amounted in 1956 to 58,154 million CFA francs, compared with a c.i.f. value of 66,730 million.[1]

Taking all imports together, the total marketing margin breaks down as follows : 36 per cent import taxes or duties, 13 per cent forwarding costs (handling and transport), and 51 per cent miscellaneous expenses (insurance, commission losses) and net trading profit. The average mark-up was 87 per cent on the c.i.f. price, somewhat less for foodstuffs and certain industrial products, but much more for petroleum products (274 on each 100 of import value). However, in the interpretation of these results we should not forget the author's warning : [2] 'In spite of the considerable work which went into calculating these results, they should be taken with a grain of salt. In theory, it should be possible to try and decompose prices into a series of prices according as payment is made in cash or later. But for many reasons prices are not known exactly, and on many small markets there is price discrimination according to customers ; the average price which comes about is unstable and follows demand variations very closely. This makes the valuation of the differentials represented by marketing margins even more difficult. The size of demand, available stocks, and the policy of large firms all play a part in the determination of the global margin on imported goods. Furthermore, the preponderance

[1] This wide differential has been the subject matter of an excellent specialist study : *Sur les marges de commercialisation*, by M. Le Héragat, Rapport No. IV des comptes économiques de l'Afrique occidentale française pour 1956 (Dakar, March 1959). [2] *Op. cit.* p. 43.

of the large import-export houses links the margins on imports and exports, since the companies' fixed cost is common to both and the purchasing power of the population depends in large part on trading results.'

Thus the problem of exports is, as it were, inversely symmetrical to that of imports. Here, it is the f.o.b. price at the African port which is determined by the outside markets (or by international arrangements for certain products, such as oil seeds and nuts within the franc area). To work backwards from this price to what the producer himself actually gets, we must deduct all the marketing margins, such as the margins of local buyers, transport cost to the port, handling charges, and export taxes.

M. Le Héragat has worked out that the difference between export prices f.o.b. and the price to the producer is, on the average, 37 per cent of the f.o.b. price, and always within the range of 10 to 50 per cent of it. In terms of percentages of the price to the producer the figures are nearly 100 per cent for oil seeds and nuts, 66 per cent for vegetable oils, 65 per cent for minerals, and between 40 and 50 per cent for other major export products, including coffee, cocoa, timber, and oil-cake.

There remains the question whether the residual which goes to the producer is enough to cover his cost. But the concept of cost in this context is exceedingly vague and can hardly ever be determined. With the exception, no doubt, of plantations of a capitalistic type and of mining, cost for the African producer is not expressed in money terms but with reference to psychological attitudes and, secondarily, in terms of opportunity cost. There is another aspect of our subject which needs examination and analysis.

(ii) *Local price formation for products not for export but for local trade.* These may be either products from the countryside traded with the towns in the case of foodstuffs, or in the case of local manufactures, goods mostly made by artisans, moving from the towns to the country.

Normally this kind of trade does not cross national frontiers, though sometimes it is international within the African continent. I have already mentioned some important trade flows involving African products, especially as among West African countries and between countries of different climate : savannah and forest, mountain and plain, coastal and interior regions.

Generally, the consumers of African products are the African peoples themselves. But here again I must not exaggerate. These products are also bought by non-Africans, certainly by Asians and sometimes by Europeans, in spite of a form of snobbery which makes people prefer to serve wilted apples just imported from Europe by air when the banana and mango trees outside the window are heavy with fruit (I speak from personal experience). Conversely, it is obvious that imported products are not consumed solely by non-Africans. Indeed, the native populations increasingly tend to buy foreign goods, even basic foodstuffs such as wheat flour, which in most towns is beginning to replace rice and secondary cereals like millet and sorghum.

Should we, in these circumstances, conclude that there is a certain dualism in the general price structure, the sector of export and import prices being determined from outside and the other by purely local conditions ?

There is some truth in this statement. It is, after all, only the application to prices of the more general thesis of the dualism of under-developed economies. The prices of local produce or domestic manufactures are necessarily lower than those of similar goods imported from Europe or elsewhere. The saving in transport cost and in any number of marketing margins and fiscal and other levies is bound to find expression in the price. On the other hand, the geographical market range of many of these products is fairly limited and prices often reflect purely local conditions, which may not be the same in other parts of the same country or elsewhere in Africa. Hence a certain tendency towards price diversity and, as a rule, instability.

Marketing margins still exist, of course, but it is very difficult to determine them. As M. Le Héragat pertinently remarks,[1] the marketing channels of African products consumed in Africa are difficult to trace : 'If the local product under consideration is an industrial product, its origin can almost certainly be established and the statistician will wisely refrain from parading the information he may have found ; if it is an agricultural food product, very little is known about the price to the producer and at various intermediary stages, because of the way in which these products are marketed (direct grower-to-consumer sale, barter, etc.). The basic distinction between market and non-market production is then difficult to establish in the present state of our knowledge and is in any case entirely artificial.' On the other hand, the number of intermediaries inserted into the marketing channels of local products is generally exceedingly high.

M. Le Héragat's own calculations led him to conclude that by and large the overall marketing margin of local products in former French West Africa amounted in 1956 to about 50 per cent of the

[1] *Op. cit.* p. 53.

price received by the producer. For textiles and hides it was as high as 100 per cent, which means in effect that the consumer paid twice as much as the producer got.

However, the formation of these local prices does not entirely escape outside influence. The division between the two sectors is not watertight. Both producers and consumers have certain possibilities of substitution, which open up an alternative between selling or buying on the local market and selling for export or buying imported goods. There are even examples of a choice between production for subsistence or the market (millet and groundnuts in Senegal, cassava and coffee or cocoa on the Ivory Coast).

These considerations are not altogether academic. They may be important in practice for economic policy and may help in guiding the decisions of the policy makers.

For example, it has always been our personal view that a modification of official exchange rates — in the particular case, a devaluation of the CFA franc — would have immediate and mathematically certain effects on the prices of all import and export goods and would eventually, through the more or less rapid diffusion of these effects by virtue of the more or less dominant position of the externally-conditioned sector in each country, affect all local prices. To say this means in effect to deny the existence of structural dualism, at any rate in any absolute sense which does not correspond to the facts.

IV. SOME GENERAL CONCLUSIONS

In his investigation of the general characteristics of prices in the economies of the countries which used to make up French West Africa, Marcel Capet concluded that these prices were *discriminatory, unstable, and high.*[1]

They are *discriminatory* in various degrees, according to the nature of the product and of marketing practices. Discrimination is due to absence of any sort of book-keeping by most producers and middlemen, the narrowness of the market, and the attitude of the trade.

They are *unstable* both because supply is unstable and because demand fluctuates greatly, together with the general trade situation.

They are *high*, because everything that is not produced locally

[1] Marcel Capet, *op. cit.* p. 232. Bauer, *op. cit.*, also stressed the strong seasonal instability and the extreme diversity of African prices, and attributed both to lack of transport facilities and to the numerous deficiencies in the organization and functioning of the markets (bad storage facilities, etc.).

necessarily costs more than elsewhere.

I believe that these adjectives describe the situation well enough, although they do not tell the whole story and need some qualification.

Taken as a whole, the present price structure reflects the present situation of Africa both as regards the exploitation of her productive resources and the pattern of her external relations.

The price structure is also determined to some extent by the current low levels of economic development in Africa, or more precisely, by the kind of development achieved so far by the different countries concerned. What price movements are we to expect once economic development gathers the momentum which we must all hope for ?

Prophecy is always a delicate matter. Nevertheless, it is probably safe to say that technological progress in production and transport as well as an improvement of the infrastructure should cause a general downward movement of prices, at least in the form of a reduction of the marketing margin in the widest sense. Taxation is perhaps the only exception, unless the under-developed countries' customary indirect taxes are gradually replaced by direct ones which do not affect prices.

Furthermore, the rapid demographic growth in most African countries shown by recent inquiries (no less than by the surprising results of the last population census in Ghana), together with the spread of a certain degree of economic ease to wider classes of the population, should expand the demand for local foodstuffs and tend to raise their prices. I am in agreement, on this point, with Marcel Capet, who foresees opposite movements in the long-term price trends for imported goods and domestic manufactures and services, on the one hand, and for the farm prices of agricultural export commodities and foodstuffs.[1]

The former prices should tend to fall and the latter to rise, more for foodstuffs than for export commodities. All this sounds fairly promising for the future of the African peasant. It would mean an end to his indigence, wherever he has not already left it behind. But I must repeat that in a field where so many factors come into play, these forecasts are very hazardous.[2]

If, indeed, conditions of life can be improved in the future by a greater stability of real prices (neglecting purely monetary fluctuations) and by their progressive reduction under the combined influence of technical progress and better organization of distribution

[1] Marcel Capet, *op. cit.* pp. 246-7 and 287.
[2] Remember, for example, what Colin Clark said ten or twelve years ago about the trend of the terms of trade for primary producers.

channels, this will be a reward of collective effort, both on the private and on the public plane. The main thing is to raise productivity, in the public sector no less than in private production, in whatever field and on whatever scale. Another thing of paramount importance is to make sure that in the new political context of Africa, where so many young nations are striving to create a sound economic base for their independence, the growth of the various sectors which contribute to general economic progress should be as balanced as possible, and that the new potentialities conferred upon individuals and government alike are used to intensify efforts and not to reduce them.

DISCUSSION OF PROFESSOR LEDUC'S PAPER

Professor Walker, introducing the discussion of Professor Leduc's paper, said that he wished to refer first to some of the points made by Professor Leduc in his paper and would then like to mention a few additional points which seemed to him relevant in connection with the general subject matter of the paper.

He believed that Professor Leduc drew too sharp a distinction between the subsistence sector and the monetary economy. On the one hand, there were now few families in Africa which had no cash income, and, on the other hand, almost every African farming family grew its own food. He would make here two additional points : first, that the price of food and other crops in the market economy affected the extent and composition of production in the subsistence sector ; second, that very often money was used as a unit of account, though not as a medium of exchange, in connection with transactions within the subsistence sector : such transactions seemed to him, then, to be much more transactions of the money economy than the subsistence economy.

Professor Leduc drew their attention to the effects of the monetary arrangements between African countries and the metropolitan powers, both on the general level of prices and on relative prices. Two aspects of this might be discussed. To what extent was it the trading relationships that were important rather than the monetary arrangements ? To what extent were these monetary links, and in particular the present rates of exchange, completely adequate and suitable for the African countries ?

In the main section of his paper Professor Leduc emphasized six main points that were important when considering prices in Africa. The first two related to the importance of foreign or external influences. In most African countries imports and exports constituted a high proportion of domestic expenditure and output and these prices were, in the last resort, strongly influenced by external factors. A point for discussion might be the extent to which African countries singly or in groups might be able to influence the prices reserved for their products. Increased trade with the Soviet Bloc or with Japan and the signing of long-term contracts were the sort of measures he had in mind. There was also the possibility of joint action with respect to shipping freight rates and insurance.

In considering the prices of goods produced and consumed locally Professor Leduc seemed to take the view that there was nothing very special to notice concerning the process of price formation. He would return to that later in his remarks.

Professor Leduc then considered the effects on prices in African countries of the operation of commercial firms and the transport undertakings. Concerning the large import/export expatriate trading companies he would like to say how important was their rôle as providers of credit and how such credit often flowed many hundreds of miles up-country. In his view, however, the commercial and distributive system in many African countries was somewhat inefficient, in the sense that margins were high. An association of high margins and low turnover seemed to be the pattern maintained by a rather oligopolistic set up.

Finally, Professor Leduc discussed the importance of government action through taxation, the operation of Marketing Boards, and the price policies of public utilities. He would have welcomed Professor Leduc's comments on the extent to which the establishment of Marketing Boards could reduce the real costs of marketing and thus enable growers to receive a higher price.

Professor Walker said that he would like, finally, to refer to a couple of topics which Professor Leduc did not directly touch upon. First, and most important, was the question whether in most African countries there existed a price *system* in the sense that one normally understands by that term, *i.e.* a system of prices which reflected scarcities and cost of production and which acted as effective indicators for the movement and allocation of factors of production. For his part he was doubtful of this. To a substantial extent it seemed to him that there were many localized markets rather than a coherent single market system ; costs of transport and the size of the effective market limited the development of a national market and thus a national price system. There was also a considerable inelasticity of supply, with respect, particularly, to non-agricultural commodities, reflecting the lack of enterprise, capital, and know-how ; and this greatly limited the effectiveness of price as a regulator and co-ordinator of economic activity, as did the absence of a strong commercial spirit, of people eager to make profits and to prevent their competitors from making profits. Government policy had often not been particularly encouraging towards the development of the commercial spirit. Finally, he felt that many African businessmen were often ignorant of their costs of production through failure to consider their capital costs and their opportunity cost as salary earners. This again limited the effectiveness of price. If he was right in questioning the existence of an effective price *system*, there arose the question as to whether any action was required to improve or to supplement its operation.

The other point he would mention was with respect to levels of wages. If there was to be an effective price system, relative factor incomes should reflect relative factor scarcities and productivities. In his view this was not so in many parts of Africa. In the first place, the wages of unskilled workers in the towns were usually in excess — because of trade-union pressures, minimum wage legislation, etc. — of the true economic wage and considerably in excess of the average productivity, let alone the marginal productivity, of workers in the agricultural sector. And, secondly, the wage structure was distorted at the upper end by the tendency to establish graduate and other top people's salary scales at levels linked to the salary scales of expatriate workers, whose salaries were in turn linked to the levels of incomes in the metropolitan countries which reflected average levels of productivity many times that of the African countries.

Professor Robinson, as Chairman, suggested that the discussion might profitably be directed to four main issues : first, the relative importance of the subsistence sector and the inter-relations between the availability of goods in the market and the activities in the subsistence sector ; second, the dominance of external factors in determining prices in Africa ; third, the degree of monopoly in trade in Africa; fourth, the extent to which a price system could and did work in African conditions.

He went on to elaborate some of the questions that seemed to him relevant to the issue as to whether a price system did in fact exist and operate. How far was there a response to price changes ? How far, that is to say, were there elasticities of supply ? How far were there responses to changes of other related prices ? Were entrepreneurs sufficiently aware of their true costs of production (he had doubts whether all road transport operators knew their costs) ? Was production animated by a zeal to earn profits rather than by a zeal to placate government officials or even missionaries ? Did factor prices truly reflect the relative scarcities and productivities of the various factors (he very much doubted it) ?

Mr. Ngcobo commented on the relative importance of the subsistence sector and the monetary economy as revealed by the figures for Nyasaland. In the northern part of the territory it represented 17 per cent and in the southern part 10 per cent of the total income. He wished that similar figures were available for more African countries.

Professor Williams urged the importance of care in discussing the subsistence sector. It was better to think in terms of the monetary and the non-monetary sectors. A great deal of trade in African products took place in Ghana through itinerant women traders. There were close links between small local markets. There was a great deal of trade not only in such products as salt, but also in the regional products of different parts of the country. Money was increasingly used for trade of this kind and the subsistence economy was changing slowly into a partly monetary and partly exchange economy.

Dr. Yudelman agreed that any division into subsistence and market economies was greatly over-simplified. He suggested (and the Conference repeatedly returned to his analysis) that agricultural producers in Africa fell into four groups : those who produced exclusively for their own consumption (of these he thought there were few) ; those who produced mostly for consumption by the family unit, but sold small quantities in the market (these he thought were numerous) ; those who produced mostly for the market, but also produced a little for the consumption of the family unit (these were becoming more numerous) ; those who engaged solely in specialist production for the market (these included the majority of European settlers).

Mr. Beheiry said that in the Sudan there were considerable regional differences in respect of the importance of subsistence agriculture. In the cotton-growing areas the amount of cotton grown in any year reflected the price of cotton in the previous year. If cotton prices had been low, less cotton was grown and more millet was produced for the local market. In the South of the Sudan they had organized an experimental project in connection with a dam and irrigation scheme. It had been intended to develop an integrated project of cotton growing and cotton manufacture. But the scheme had not worked out as they had originally hoped. The prices paid for cotton were to be related to world prices. But other commodities, including coffee and citrus fruit, could also be grown. In practice cotton had not been very popular and there had been, from time to time, significant shifts towards and from both cotton and other products. It was observable that there was considerable sensitivity to prices.

Dr. Singer wished to emphasize two dynamic aspects. He thought that the use of money was rapidly developing. This had one consequence of great importance for economic planning. If the monetary economy was small, the volume of saving tended to be small. If the monetary economy tended to grow, the demand for money itself would also grow, and the potentially available savings from this source could be used for development without causing inflation. Secondly, he argued that self-sufficiency was not merely a matter of feeding the family unit. It could be extended to the creation of capital for a self-contained economic group by communal effort to build schools, to build houses, to make local feeder roads, and to promote local development generally.

Professor Frankel found himself in strong agreement with Mr. Beheiry. In his experience Africans had shown great capacity for the allocation of their resources. The Nilotics had grazed cattle and game together long before scientists had explained the benefits of their symbiotic relations. What characterized the subsistence economy was not the attachment to it of the African but the limitations of scale which did not permit the achievement of economies through exchange. The new factor was not the introduction of trade, but the improvement of techniques to the point where exchange brought further advantages. A self-subsistence economy was one in which the absence of sufficient scale meant the limitation of incomes and a narrowly limited range of consumption. Where new opportunities had been created by railways, Africans had been quick to seize them. Railway construction in Tanganyika had brought an unexpected increase in maize cultivation, so that a railway built primarily for the carriage of minerals derived a major part of its revenues from maize. *Professor Frankel* felt obliged to disagree with Dr. Singer. The surplus resources created could not be taxed away and used to create capital. They were the product of the Africans, and the desire to increase consumption was the motive that led to their creation.

Professor Williams thought that, if people wished to hold money, this represented real savings. They had, in Ghana, the problem of the missing millions of pounds which had disappeared into African holdings. Some of this was possibly buried in hoards. In fact these additional holdings were not used and formed a source of savings.

Mr. Moran returned to the problem of the dimensions of the subsistence economy. He thought that there was a large and significant move from Dr. Yudelman's first group to the second group, and thus, in effect, a shift into the modern monetary economy.

Dr. Gavrilov argued that there were no really free markets in Africa. The big corporations exercised a powerful influence on all prices. The greater part of the receipts from the ultimate sales of produce went to excessively high cost transportation and to excessive middlemen's margins, so that in some cases as little as 15-20 per cent of the ultimate price was received by the original producers. Thus prices were distorted. The producer could not afford, out of his receipts, to save and modernize techniques. Some method had to be found to bring this to an end by correcting the price structures. It was desirable to replace the private trade by state or co-operative enterprises.

Dr. Okigbo stressed the relations between the availability of goods in the market and the decline of self-subsistence. He could only attach meaning to self-subsistence in relation to the increase of available goods. He expected to see a progressive decline in self-subsistence. But these changes bedevilled any attempts to measure changes in real standard of consumption; it was almost impossible to be certain whether some changes were real additions or merely a shift from self-subsistence to exchange.

Dr. Wade said that pure self-subsistence had disappeared from West Africa. There was no West African territory which did not make large use of money. For purposes of analysis one should distinguish the pricing of imported goods in the local market, which was partly affected by competition and substitution and partly by demand in the European and snob markets, from the pricing of local products and the output of local industries. In Senegal and the Sudan, for instance, cotton goods received effective protection because of the transport costs of imported substitutes. Thus prices of these goods were determined *a posteriori* by the degree of monopoly.

Mr. Beheiry wished to emphasize that isolation was the major factor in maintaining the existence of isolated pockets of self-subsistence.

The discussion then turned to the extent of the dependence of African prices on factors external to Africa itself. *Mr. Onitiri* argued that the more general economic dependence of African countries was largely the consequence of the currency-board systems that prevailed. But apart from that there was a considerable degree of monopoly in both the import and export trades. The question was how to reduce this dependence. There was a need to increase the elasticity of the monetary systems. Central banks had, it was true, been created, but as yet the elasticity had not been significantly increased. He was interested by Dr. Gavrilov's suggestion of the possibility of using co-operatives to break the monopoly of the import trading houses and to take over the monopoly exercised by exporting firms. It had been suggested that one of the important issues for Africa was the division of the gains of international trade between the countries that engaged in the trade ; in the case of Africa the gain to the African countries from trade was remarkably small. It was most desirable to get more of the gains of foreign trade into African hands so that they might be ploughed back and used for development.

Professor Dupriez emphasized the influence of import and export taxes on prices. In the African environment it was necessary to use these to replace the yields of sales and turnover taxes in European countries. Where commodities, such as copper, were sold almost exclusively in the export market, he was tempted to regard any export taxes as neutral in their effects. The situation was different where commodities were sold both in export and domestic markets ; here there might be distortions which could be very considerably to the detriment of African agriculture. Some taxes, again, were purely fiscal, and contributed, through the expenditures they permitted, to economic welfare.

Dr. Cookson pointed out that in any competitive market price dominates the producer, in the sense that it must be accepted by the producer. If African exporters were selling in perfectly competitive world markets, it was inevitable that they should be dependent on the prices in those markets. The real issue was the division of the market price between the middlemen and the original producers.

Dr. Okigbo developed the same argument. Import prices, measured c.i.f., were externally determined. Any attempt to modify this must take the form of pressure on distributive margins within Africa and on a re-direction of import trade towards external suppliers who could provide the necessary goods at lower cost. The pattern of African trade had in the past been politically determined. A complicating factor was the level of taxation determined for revenue purposes. On the export side f.o.b. prices were, it was true, externally determined. But they could be influenced in many cases by groups of African countries acting together. He thought it was important to secure prices that were high enough to stimulate production. While he felt critical of some of the detailed price policies of marketing boards, he believed that they were valuable instruments and that African experience had shown their benefit. He would himself emphasize, to a greater degree than Professor Leduc had done, the importance of increased food production, together with a switch from consumption of imported European foods, largely for fashion and ostentation, to domestically produced foods.

Professor Williams commented on the efficiency of distribution in West Africa. Measured by the size of the actual margins, he did not think that distribution could be said to be costly and inefficient. For textiles, for example, the margins were not more than 4-5 per cent. Measured by the number of persons engaged, partly or wholly, in this activity it appeared very wasteful. Something like 10 per cent of the population were engaged in selling things of one kind or another in the various markets. Professor Bauer, in his book on the subject, had emphasized the extent to which monopoly and imperfect competition pervaded the import markets. It was true that there were big middlemen : there were about 10 large importers and about 100 medium-sized importers. But there was an enormously greater number of potential importers knocking at the door and ready to enter if profits seemed sufficiently attractive. He himself doubted whether the trade was really very monopolistic. He was equally doubtful about the advantages of the governments attempting themselves to embark on marketing. In Ghana there had been a period of co-operative activity, but this had declined in recent years. In transport the West African governments were taking steps to mitigate the effects of the international monopolies. The Ghana airlines were government owned but within the system of international regulation of fares. Similarly, the government-controlled Black Star Shipping Line was inside the shipping conference. When these were started the purpose was to protect Ghana against monopolistic exploitation. When it came to the point it was easy for the government to slip into the position of expressing pride in their capacity to show good profits. One must not hope too much to secure substantial price reductions through governmental or co-operative activities.

Professor Peacock wished to know more about the way that the price system worked in Africa. Was it a question of minor imperfections ? Was the whole working of the price mechanism of a different order from that assumed in advanced countries ? Were motivations similar or different ? While in the full sense one might not find pure profit maximization, was it more than a matter of degree ? One would expect to find more emphasis on uncertainty, not only regarding costs but also about yields and out-turn, and about the dimensions of the internal markets. He thought that in many ways Africa resembled eighteenth-century Scotland. It was made up of a set of local economies with localized and scarcely interconnected markets — a situation in which the concept of the dual economy was not really helpful. In Scotland of the eighteenth century the very similar situation was transformed by the building, by the English under General Wade, of military roads. He thought that in Africa governments failed to appreciate the value of markets and communications. There was over-strict transport licensing. Intervention should stimulate rather than restrict marketing and communications. *Professor Peacock* also wished to know more about the way that governments operated in the economic field. Their own expenditures represented a large part of total activities in the monetary sector. They were large buyers and could exercise a big influence on the market. Not enough was known about the systems of tendering and their general methods of operation.

Dr. Yudelman stressed the imperfection of the market forces in agriculture. He had found that most producers were more concerned about the adequacy of their food supplies than about the fluctuations of the prices of cash crops. It could not be assumed that they operated like the supposed economic man in a completely monetary and exchange economy.

Professor Frankel agreed that the principal fear was of famine. Limitations were imposed on specialization and production for the world market through fear of crop failure and inability to buy. Kenya, for example, had refused to permit the large-scale import of food, because of uncertainty about the possibility of storing stocks of foodstuffs. This held up the industrialization and diversification of African economies.

Dr. Cookson asked whether there was reason to think that in African countries there were backward-rising supply curves of labour, so that the response to rising prices of products was less effort and greater leisure. There seemed, in the United States, to be rather steeply rising marginal cost curves in agriculture. Was the same true in Africa? He also wished to know whether any study had been made of the real cost of providing the necessary information to guide economic decisions. A perfect market assumed perfect information. There were high costs in securing and making sufficiently widely available the knowledge of prices in a large number of separated local markets. But if monopoly was to be prevented and if the entry of new competition was to be facilitated, it was important to make market information available as widely as possible. He thought measures to ease the entry of competition preferable to government intervention.

Professor Robinson was anxious to know whether prices in African markets now reflected market forces. When he first knew Africa, some thirty years ago, he understood that for many African foodstuffs and similar products there were traditional prices which, in any given district, hardly varied. Was that still the case? Did market prices now reflect scarcities? *Dr. Yudelman* thought that maize prices certainly varied widely from season to season and were much more truly market prices. *Professor Williams* said that in Ghana, in the actual markets in which African foodstuffs were sold, the prices charged by dealers varied quite considerably according to the conditions of supply. On the other hand, the prices paid by the dealers to the original producers tended to be much more stable. There was a considerable lag in the response of cocoa production to prices — possibly as great as six years — largely because it was a tree crop. In studying the response of cocoa production to price one must not be misled by the relatively small change in aggregate production. There had been a substantial increase in some areas balanced by reductions in others.

Professor Dupriez gave some account of a study that had been made in Ruanda as to the extent to which the various markets for primary products succeeded in equalizing demand and supply. There were markets of various types : those in which producers and traders came together locally ; those in which traders moving from place to place traded in temporary markets with the local producers and traders; and the permanent markets of the big towns. Prices fluctuated according to the conditions of demand. There were considerable imperfections in the markets. It sometimes happened that peasants would sell and repurchase the same product three months later at double the price. These peripatetic and permanent trading centres tended to eliminate the wide differences between one place and another and between one time and another, and to equalize and stabilize prices.

Professor Leduc, replying to the discussion, said that there were many complex interrelations between the monetary and subsistence economies. As regards capital formation, he thought that there was substantial capital formation in the subsistence sector that was not included in national income estimates. So far as concerned the dependence of African prices on factors outside Africa, there was no question of its past importance. But he thought that this domination would be progressively reduced as domestic consumption developed and the dependence on foreign trade became less. As regards the extent of monopoly, he had relied principally on the studies by Professor Bauer. He had little doubt himself that there were considerable imperfections in the competition. As regards the extent to which there could be said to be an effective price system, he thought that there had been great advances in the past ten years. While it could not be said that there was a completely integrated price structure, such as one found in the United States and Great Britain, it was now a matter merely of imperfection. It could no longer be said that the African system was invertebrate.

Chapter 15

CAPITAL AND CAPITAL SUPPLY IN RELATION TO THE DEVELOPMENT OF AFRICA

BY

S. HERBERT FRANKEL
University of Oxford

I. INTRODUCTION : CAPITAL AND DEVELOPMENT

WHEN I received the invitation to contribute a paper for this Conference I was reminded that a quarter of a century had passed since I wrote the first draft for Lord Hailey's African survey of my subsequent book on *Capital Investment in Africa*.[1] It is, therefore, perhaps natural that I should be led to take this opportunity of reflecting on some of its conclusions in the light of the political, social, and economic changes which have taken place since it appeared, in order to elucidate some of the continuing problems with which Africa is faced.

In looking at some previously unpublished parts of the book, I was interested to find the following passage : 'The Leitmotiv which runs through this study is the importance of the realization that the supply of capital itself is only one of the many factors which determine economic development. Capital itself can only play a relatively inefficient rôle unless the co-operative factors of supply (labour, natural resources, raw materials, skill, organization, etc.) with which it is to be combined are available in suitable forms and at suitable prices. Capital cannot be applied *in vacuo* and much confusion has resulted from the fallacious belief that the supply of capital alone can solve the economic problems of development.'

During the last two decades a vast literature has poured forth on economic growth and on models intending to portray and elucidate its nature and process ; many of these models take it almost for granted that capital investment is its prime cause. I have always

[1] S. Herbert Frankel, *Capital Investment in Africa. Its Course and Effects*, Oxford University Press, 1938.

doubted the wisdom of formulating the rôle of capital in these mechanistic terms or of regarding the consequences of investment as in any way automatic. Thus I wrote some ten years ago : [1]

> To regard the investment of capital as leading automatically to that net increase in the value of the capital which increase can be detached as 'income', is a common fallacy. The symbolism of accounting is a device to assist the making of choices ; but no amount of calculation guarantees the result.
>
> The accumulation of capital was never regarded in the nineteenth century, as it now frequently is, as the necessary consequence merely of an 'investment' decision . . . [or] as necessarily consequent upon, and automatically resulting from the exercise of individual or social *will*. On the contrary, as the common tongue of enterprise clearly shows, the success of 'venture' capital was regarded, and rightly regarded, as having much to do with 'good fortune', 'wise-choices', the correct 'embarking' of capital in the 'right' directions, at the 'right' time. It was seen to be a matter of 'patience', 'waiting', 'flexibility', 'adaptability', 'experience', 'growth', and as dependent upon the 'character' of the entrepreneur, his 'intuition' and 'experience', his 'connexions', 'goodwill', his courage in meeting 'unforeseen circumstances', and his 'foresight' in being able to ally himself with the new opportunities, innovations and resources which would yield the 'quasi-rents' of new endeavours.
>
> Much confusion has resulted from the fact that the large volume of fixed-interest bearing securities issued by modern governments (mainly for purposes of war finance) led to the belief that investment was something which automatically yielded income. Thus it became fashionable to speak as if (and for some apparently even to believe that) capital *necessarily generates* income of itself ; both 'capital' and 'income' came to be regarded as 'abstract', functionally related entities.

The essence of economic progress is to be found in the change of traditional methods, occupations, and forms of economic activity. Without change, both the creation and the utilization of additional capital are not possible. In the last resort, society remoulds itself by the process of action, for what is really involved is the evolution of a different art of living and working.

I make no apology for referring to these basic factors : although the language of economics changes in attempts to elucidate its problems, the economic problems themselves do not necessarily change with it. Happily there are some indications that the tide is

[1] S. Herbert Frankel, *The Economic Impact on Underdeveloped Societies — Essays on International Investment and Social Change*, Basil Blackwell, Oxford, 1953.

turning from excessively mechanistic formulations : as Mr. Colin Clark has recently written :

Economic theories and 'models' of growth formulated during the post-war period of capital shortage which threatened growth and investment are now out-of-date. It is more correct to say that capital is created during growth than that growth is a creation of capital. [He concluded] : The principal factors in economic growth are not physical but human . . . [and] Human factors develop steadily but slowly.[1]

II. TIME AND CIRCUMSTANCE

The title of this paper is, I fear, misleadingly neat and concise. For to speak of capital investment as a whole in Africa south of the Sahara is to endeavour to bridge a vast diversity of geographical, ecological, institutional, racial, political, and economic conditions : and it can easily cause the most important factor of all to be over-looked — the factor of time. The populations of large areas of the continent have only recently begun to be incorporated into a money economy, and linked together through market-orientated activities, and a considerable proportion of them are still not part of modern economy. It is often forgotten that 91 per cent of the area and 91 per cent of the population south of the Sahara lie within the tropics ; only the remaining 9 per cent of the area is in the temperate zones, which, broadly speaking, includes the Union of South Africa, South West Africa, Basutoland, and Swaziland. The temperate zone contains only 9 per cent of the population.

Tropical Africa, for the most part, remained isolated from the outside world until very recent times. For all practical purposes its penetration by the economic forces of the modern world did not commence before the beginning of this century — whereas, at the tip of the continent, it had begun three centuries before. Man has nowhere in the world succeeded in grappling as successfully with the ecological and economic problems of the tropics as he has been able, or forced, to do in its temperate zones. Broadly speaking, the tropical areas of the world are areas not only of general under-development, of poverty, of low income per head, of malnutrition and disease, but of ignorance concerning the natural environment and of how to cope with it. In Tropical Africa all these disadvantages and disabilities are intensified by the fact that its overall population

---

[1] 'Growthmanship', by Colin Clark. Hobart Paper 10. Published for Institute of Economic Affairs by Barrie and Rockliffe, 1961.

density is very low, and the distances which have to be spanned in order to establish trade between its large land mass and the outside world are extremely large. A further general factor which has affected Africa's rate of economic development has been the relatively small permanent immigration from abroad. Whereas, in the years from 1886 to 1929, there was a gross emigration from twelve countries in Europe of just over 28 million people (which figure probably accounts for three-quarters of the whole of the gross emigration from Europe in that period), only 1·7 million (6 per cent) went to Africa while the *net* emigration to Africa was only 300,000 (1·6 per cent).[1] Contrast with this the experience of only one country in Latin America — Argentina — which during the forty years from 1870 to 1910 received a net immigration of over 2 million.

The dominating feature of economic activity of the past in Africa was that it was based on subsistence agriculture, primitive pastoral production, food gathering, and hunting. If a modern statistician were to be transported back in time to the beginning of this century to apply the technique of national accounting to Africa by imaginary computations of money values, he would have found a large number of isolated societies, with very low levels of income, fluctuating according to the alternating bounty or niggardliness of nature, and with a man-made capital stock composed mainly of a minimum of consumer durables, primitive weapons of war and of the hunt, meagre investment in housing, negligible investment in roads and even less in permanent improvements to the land. Its 'inventory capital' would have consisted largely of relatively small seasonal stocks of surplus food (owing to lack of permanent storage facilities) and herds of cattle whose size fluctuated with the human population in accordance with the niggardliness or bounty of nature, the toll of drought or disease, and the ravages of tribal war.

The African populations had, until very recently, to concentrate all their efforts on the day-to-day task of survival through minimum standards of consumption. High infantile death rates and high adult morbidity rates regulated population growth. The size of any population unable to benefit from economies of production for wider regional, national, and international markets, necessarily depends on the food supplies which can be obtained locally. Generally speaking, African ecological conditions — particularly the lack of reliable rainfall over vast areas — are unlike those which enable the production of enough food, under traditional systems of husbandry, to meet

---

[1] Cf. *The Balance Sheets of Imperialism : Facts and Figures of Colonies,* by Grover Clark, published for the Carnegie Endowment for International Peace. Columbia University Press, 1936, p. 49.

minimum basic subsistence requirements of dense populations as in parts of Asia.

III. THE EVOLUTION OF EXCHANGE ECONOMY

Capital investment in Africa south of the Sahara during the last hundred years (the first sustained large-scale investment took place as a result of the diamond discoveries in the Cape Colony in the sixties of the last century) can in the main be regarded as having laid the foundation of modern exchange economy. As is shown in Table 1 which gives figures of the value of trade of each African territory as a percentage of the total value of the trade of Africa

TABLE 1

VALUE OF TRADE OF EACH AFRICAN TERRITORY
AS PERCENTAGE OF TOTAL VALUE OF TRADE OF
AFRICA FOR SELECTED YEARS, 1907–56

	1907	1929	1935	1956
Total West Africa	11·71	16·14	12·43	15·80
Total East Africa	3·97	7·22	5·98	7·90
Central African Federation	3·45	5·42	7·17	11·00
(Northern Rhodesia, Southern Rhodesia and Nyasaland)				
Belgian Congo and Ruanda-Urundi	2·85	5·61	4·33	10·80
Total French Community	9·06	7·95	8·34	12·90
Total Portuguese territories	4·37	3·99	2·57	4·20
Sudan	1·76	3·82	3·12	3·60
Total 'Tropical' Africa	37·17	50·15	43·94	66·20
Union of South Africa, South West Africa, and Protectorates	62·42	49·65	55·93	33·40

Notes.—Percentages of trade for Italian Somalia and British Somaliland have been excluded ; these would have brought the total for each year to 100 per cent.
East Africa : 1907, 1929, and 1935 comprises Kenya, Uganda, Tanganyika, and Zanzibar ; 1956 comprises Kenya, Uganda, and Tanganyika only.
Belgian Congo : 1907 excludes Ruanda-Urundi.
Percentages are taken from *The Tyranny of Economic Paternalism in Africa*, by S. Herbert Frankel (Supplement to OPTIMA, December 1960), p. 46.
Sources : 1907, 1929, 1935 : S. H. Frankel — *Capital Investment in Africa*, Table 47.
1956 : Colonial Office Annual Reports :
UN *Economic Survey of Africa since 1950*.
UN *Economic Developments in Africa 1956–1957*.
East Africa High Commission *Quarterly Economic and Statistical Bulletin*.
Federation of Rhodesia and Nyasaland *Annual Statement of External Trade*.
Union of South Africa *Monthly Bulletin of Statistics*.
Mémentos économiques et statistiques des principaux pays et territoires d'outre-mer associés à la Communauté Économique Européenne (Bruxelles, 1958).

Economic Development for Africa South of the Sahara

for selected years from 1907 to 1956 this process, though increasingly rapid throughout Africa in recent decades, is (except in the Union of South Africa) still in its infancy; and as I write, its further development is being gravely threatened, or even reversed, by political uncertainties and civil war over large areas of the continent. It is in the Union of South Africa that by far the largest proportion of the population of any state in Africa has been drawn directly or indirectly into modern economic activities. Broadly speaking, it gives employment to as many wage and salary earners in non-agricultural occupations as all the rest of the countries of Africa south of the Sahara taken together.

Table 2 shows the percentage which the gross domestic product

TABLE 2

GROSS PRODUCT PER HEAD IN AFRICAN TERRITORIES
AS PERCENTAGES OF LEVEL IN UNION OF SOUTH AFRICA

	Gross Domestic Product in Money Economy (excl. Subsistence) per Head		Gross Domestic Product (incl. Subsistence) per Head	
	£	%	£	%
Union of South Africa (1956)	128·5	100·0	128·5 [1]	100·0
The Gambia (1956)	—	—	20·0 [2]	15·6
Ghana (1956)	—	—	55·6 [3]	43·3
Nigeria (1956)	—	—	25·3 [3]	19·7
Sierra Leone (1956)	—	—	15·0 [2]	11·7
Kenya (1956)	23·6 [4]	18·4	31·4 [4]	24·4
Uganda (1956)	15·5 [4]	12·1	20·9 [4]	16·3
Tanganyika (1956)	10·6 [4]	8·2	18·0 [4]	14·0
Central African Federation (1956)	52·7 [5]	41·0	61·8 [5]	48·9
Mauritius (1956)	—	—	79·8 [6]	62·1
Belgian Congo (1958)	34·6	26·9	38·5	30·0

Note.—Union of South Africa statistics do not distinguish the Subsistence Product from the Total Domestic Product. The proportion of Subsistence to the Total is relatively so small as to enable it to be ignored in comparison with other countries listed in this table.

Sources :
[1] South African Reserve Bank *Quarterly Bulletin of Statistics.*
[2] D. T. Jack, *Economic Survey of Sierra Leone* (1958).
[3] UN *Statistical Yearbook* (1958).
[4] East Africa High Commission *Quarterly Economic and Statistical Bulletin.*
[5] Federation of Rhodesia and Nyasaland *Monthly Digest of Statistics.*
[6] Colonial Office Report.

N.B.—[2] is the only source that gives direct figures *per head* ; all other sources give the *total* Gross Domestic Product, and the figure per head has been calculated with reference to Total Population.

per head in various territories is, of the corresponding figure for the Union. It will be noted that no single country in Africa has reached the Union's average *per capita* income, although by international standards the latter itself is low. The statistics of the gross domestic money product (excluding subsistence production) per head of the *total* population show the relative importance of money-producing activities, and the relative extent to which the average inhabitant could have shared in the money-income produced, if it had been divided equally between all the inhabitants, notwithstanding that many of them, of course, made little or no contribution to modern economic activities. For example, Tanganyika reached only 8·2 per cent, while the Federation of Rhodesia and Nyasaland, with its important mineral production, attained to 52·7 per cent of the Union's money-income per head. However, whether comparisons are made on the basis of income calculations, or on the basis of exports (see Table 3), or other indices, the diversities are too great to be subsumed under any single series of averages. It must be remembered that even the national averages conceal vast differences. What really emerges finally from these comparisons is the extraordinary economic backwardness of the continent as a whole, the effects of which are being intensified by a rapid growth of population. Population has been estimated to have increased by 60 per cent in South Africa, 47 per cent in North Africa and 30 per cent in the rest of Africa from 1925 to 1950 and that between 1950 and 1975 the corresponding percentage increases will be 62-76, 65-70, and 42-62.[1] Moreover, modern economic activity has developed only spasmodically and patchily in Africa mainly in areas with exploitable mineral or other valuable resources. The intervening spaces are largely devoid of it. The inhabitants of the latter have made contact with the modern economy mainly as migrant workers.

IV. THE CHALLENGE OF ENVIRONMENT

But even this is an over-simplified picture, for the challenge of Africa's environment is as diverse as its peoples. Over vast areas it is inhospitable to man, in others only considerable investments of capital could enable an appreciable population to engage in agricultural pursuits with certainty. In still others, given modern techniques, enterprise, and organization, relatively small amounts of capital could greatly increase agricultural productivity and incomes per head.

[1] *The Future Growth of World Population*, United Nations Department of Economic and Social Affairs. New York, 1958.

TABLE 3

AFRICA 1956

	Population (million)	Total Domestic Exports (£ million)	Exports per Head (£)	Gross Domestic Product, incl. Subsistence Economy (£ million)	Gross Domestic Product per Head (£)	Total Exports as % of Total Domestic Product
British Cameroons	1.5 [1]	4.2 [1]	2.7	—	—	—
The Gambia	0.2 [1]	2.2 [1]	8.9	6.0 [2]	20.0 [2]	36.7
Ghana	4.7 [3]	85.9 [4]	18.3	261.0 [5]	55.6	32.9
Nigeria	31.8 [3]	132.3 [6]	4.2	806.9 [5]	25.3	16.4
Sierra Leone	2.1 [7]	12.2 [1]	5.8	31.5 [2]	15.0 [2]	38.7
Total West Africa	40.4	236.8	5.9	1,105.4	28.4	21.4
Kenya	6.2 [8]	29.0 [8]	4.1	193.4 [8]	31.4	15.0
Uganda	5.6 [8]	40.4 [8]	7.2	117.1 [8]	20.9	34.5
Tanganyika	8.5 [8]	44.9 [8]	5.3	152.4 [8]	18.0	29.5
Zanzibar and Pemba	0.3 [1]	5.9 [9]	19.7	—	—	—
Total East Africa	20.5	120.2	5.9	462.9	21.8	26.0
Central African Federation	7.3 [10]	185.4 [11]	25.5	448.7 [12]	61.8	41.3
British Somaliland	0.7 [3]	1.3 [1]	2.0	—	—	—
Mauritius	0.6 [1]	20.8 [1]	35.9	46.2 [1]	79.8	45.0
Belgian Congo and Ruanda-Urundi	17.5 [13]	191.1 [3]	11.0	353.6 [14]	20.3	54.0
A.E.F.	4.9 [3]	28.2 [14]	5.8	204.3 [7]	41.9	13.8
A.O.F. (excluding Guinea)	16.5 [7]	112.1 [15]	6.8	865.3 [7]	52.4	13.0
French Cameroon	3.2 [3]	26.8 [3]	8.4	—	—	—
French Somaliland	0.1 [3]	0.8 [15]	11.9	—	—	—
French Togoland	1.1 [3]	9.5 [16]	8.8	—	—	—
Madagascar	4.9 [3]	33.2 [3]	6.8	183.2 [7]	(1953) 37.3	18.2
Total French Community	30.6	210.6	6.9	1,252.8	47.6	16.8

Moçambique	6·0 [3][15]	(1955) 18·9 [3]	3·1	—	—	—
Portuguese Guinea	(1950) 0·5 [15]	1·9 [15]	3·7	—	—	—
San Tomé and Principe	(1950) 0·1 [15]	2·2 [15]	36·7	—	—	—
Total Portuguese territories	11·0	63·7	5·8	—	—	—
Spanish Guinea and Fernando Po	(1957) 0·2 [15]	2·5 [15]	11·7	—	—	—
Italian Somaliland	1·3 [3]	3·3 [16]	2·5	—	—	—
Ethiopia and Eritrea	18·0 [15]	(1955/6) 22·3 [15]	1·2	—	—	—
Guinea	2·5 [7]	10·4 [15]	4·2	109·8 [7]	43·9	9·5
Liberia	1·0 [15]	15·9 [15]	15·9	—	—	—
Sudan	10·3 [3]	68·6 [3]	6·7	—	—	—
Total 'Tropical' Africa	161·9	1,152·9	7·1	—	—	—
Union of South Africa, South West Africa, Basutoland, Bechuanaland, Swaziland	15·6 [3]	558·9 [17]	35·8	(1955/6) 1,788·3 [18]	128·5	31·3
GRAND TOTAL	177·5	1,711·8	9·6	—	—	—

Note.—'Domestic Exports' includes gold bullion, but excludes specie and re-exports.

Sources:
1 Colonial Office Reports.
2 D. T. Jack, Economic Survey of Sierra Leone (1958).
3 UN Economic Survey of Africa since 1950 (New York, 1959).
4 Ghana, Office of the Government Statistician, Digest of Statistics.
5 UN Statistical Yearbook (1958).
6 Federation of Nigeria Digest of Statistics (January 1959).
7 Service des Statistiques d'Outre-mer, Outre-mer 1958 (Presses Universitaires de France, 1960).
8 East Africa High Commission Quarterly Economic and Statistical Bulletin.
9 Digest of Colonial Statistics, No. 35 (H.M.S.O., 1957).
10 UN Structure and Growth of Selected African Economies (New York, 1958).
11 Federation of Rhodesia and Nyasaland Annual Statement of External Trade.
12 Federation of Rhodesia and Nyasaland Monthly Digest of Statistics (June 1959, Supplement).
13 Royaume de Belgique, Ministère des Colonies, La Situation économique du Congo Belge et du Ruanda-Urundi.
14 UN Economic Developments in Africa 1956–1957 (New York, 1958).
15 Statesman's Year-Book (1959).
16 Mémentos économiques et statistiques des principaux pays et territoires d'outre-mer associés à la Communauté Économique Européenne (Bruxelles, 1958).
17 Union of South Africa Monthly Bulletin of Statistics (April 1957).
18 South African Reserve Bank Quarterly Bulletin of Statistics.

Finally, in many regions land is 'overcrowded' in the sense that it cannot under customary systems of production continue to yield even the 'subsistence' livelihood which the population hitherto was content to accept as its lot. In such areas man has by deleterious agricultural and pastoral practices (such as 'overstocking') destroyed fauna and flora and exhausted the resources given by nature. The land can now only be regenerated by moving the population elsewhere.

Even the growth of money incomes can easily be deceptive and give rise to misleading impressions concerning the real net productivity on the land. Thus, for example, Dr. Hugh Fearn in his valuable and well-documented study of the Nyanza Province of Kenya Colony [1] concluded :

Although it can be claimed that the Nyanza economy has developed over the last fifty years, the development has not been as large as might have been expected from the increased opportunity for marketing and the technical aid and assistance given by government . . . [the] increase in the tonnage of marketed produce . . . has to some extent been made possible by an uneconomic use of natural resources : unless there is a more scientific use and conservation of these resources production will probably decline in future years. The available produce for marketing will be limited by the growing subsistence needs of the population and the African families of Nyanza will have to make a choice between marketing for a cash income or using the produce for food requirements.

The answer to the question : Why has the African farmer failed to respond to the need of scientific farming ? [he finds] is related to the African preoccupation with the problems of the present, and not those of the future, so that in the more favourable regions of the province there has been a tendency to grow crops for present subsistence and cash needs, without any concern about the harm over-cultivation will do to the land. In the more densely populated areas of the Province, the farmer has not been over-worried about productivity of his land because he has been able to obtain an income from alternative employment to meet his cash requirements and supplement any deficiency in subsistence crops. But the major factor which has hindered the introduction of scientific farming has been the continuance of traditional land tenure systems and customary methods of cultivation.

This situation can be paralleled by documented examples from many other regions throughout Africa.[2]

[1] *An African Economy : A Study of the Economic Development of Nyanza Province of Kenya 1903–1953*, Oxford University Press, 1961, pp. 231-2.
[2] Cf., for example, the analysis of the problem conducted by the East Africa Royal Commission, Cmd. 9475, 1955. A fundamental factor in preventing proper

The fact is that not only do saving and investment require a surplus from which they can be made, but also institutional arrangements and incentives to individuals and communities to make them. Similarly, unless the benefits of land conservation or improvement accrue to those who have to make them they are not likely to be made voluntarily, and cannot be made at all if population presses so heavily on available resources that there are no surpluses from which to replace what is being consumed at the expense of the future. Particularly in Africa — where *Raubwirtschaft* in many forms has been and still remains so prevalent — it is easy to confuse capital and income, and even easier to fall into the common error of confusing what is the using up of an asset with the creation of a new one.

Thus, Africa, standing as it does on the threshold of the modern world, is nevertheless still enveloped in the mists and twilight of the past. It is a situation as fraught with challenge as it is with the dangers which spring from ignorance and superstition, be they national, tribal, or racial — old or new.

Capital and the Heritage of Improvement

In this situation an understanding of the rôle of capital investment is crucial. As Edwin Cannan pointed out long ago, capital (as measured against the measuring rod of money) forms a most important, perhaps the most important, part of 'the heritage of improvement'. But capital is not the whole heritage. There are other ways of adding to the heritage of improvement besides saving and addition to capital. Such other additions to, or changes in, the heritage often call for no increase in capital. Indeed, they may wipe capital out and are all the more beneficent for thus enabling us to discard the tools, machinery, and stock rendered unnecessary 'owing to newer methods of technique and production which no longer require them'.

An interesting statistical example of this process in Africa, which is worth mentioning in passing, is provided in the excellent paper by D. G. Franzen and J. J. D. Willers on 'Capital Accumulation and Economic Growth in South Africa',[1] which shows (in an analysis

allocation of resources has been the discouragement of economic cash crops by a mistaken administrative policy of regional self-sufficiency. African producers have not been permitted to respond to market prices. See also the excellent paper of W. O. Jones, 'Economic Man in Africa', Food Research Institute Studies, vol. 1, no. 2, May 1960. Stanford University.

[1] Cf. International Association for Research in Income and Wealth, Series VIII, edited by Raymond Goldsmith and Christopher Saunders. Cambridge, Bowes and Bowes, 1959.

of the capital co-efficients of individual industries between 1919 and 1945), a greater decline in the capital co-efficient for agriculture than in other industries with the exception of railways and harbours. The authors ascribe this to the relative decline of 'inventories' — particularly livestock — in the agricultural field. The interpretation of the meaning of changes in capital co-efficients is as yet, with our limited knowledge and experience in this field, a very hazardous business, and the use of these, as also of other national income and expenditure aggregates, is strewn with pitfalls — as Mr. L. Samuels stressed in this city of Addis Ababa, in his excellent paper to the International Conference on Income and Wealth last year.[1] Nevertheless, this particular example is of special interest because over very large parts of Africa much land is utilized by the indigenous peoples for grazing of cattle of poor quality and little economic value which by proper modern pastoral techniques and improved management could be reduced in numbers and transformed into valuable sources of money income. In addition to the relatively small capital investments for fencing and bore-holes for water, what is most required is a new attitude towards, and new methods of, stock improvement and the provision of modern channels of distribution.

The Unspecified Factor

However, just as, on the one hand, improvements in the social and economic heritage can reduce the need for capital, so, on the other hand, can the effectiveness of capital be negatived if necessary complementary improvements in the social and economic structure do not take place. The capital investment may then be only a wasteful expenditure of scarce resources. For the use of capital provides an opportunity for 'setting free' labour for other tasks than those to which it had previously been devoted. But if improvements to the general social and economic heritage and structure lag behind advantage cannot be taken of such opportunities.

Mr. Colin Clark, in the study to which I have already referred, quoted the findings of Dr. Odd Aukrust in an investigation into the contribution of the different factors to the real national production Norway between 1900 and 1955 to the effect that, 'With no additions to capital at all and no change in the labour force "human factors", *i.e.* better knowledge, organization, skill, effort, education, enterprise, etc., sufficed to raise productivity at the rate of 1·8 per cent per year. A one per cent addition to the labour force, all other things being equal, would only raise national product by $\frac{3}{4}$ per cent;

[1] L. Samuels, 'Some Reflections on the Uses and Limitations of National Accounting with Special Reference to South Africa'.

and a one per cent addition to capital stock by only 0·2 per cent.'

Mr. Colin Clark and his associates found 'A higher marginal return to capital, and a lower but still substantial return to "human factors"' when they made an analysis for all countries for which they had information. They concluded : 'The unspecified factor is found to raise productivity on the average of 1·3 per cent'.[1] But what, after all, I would ask, is this 'unspecified factor'? It is surely nothing but the non-material but all-important heritage of social and economic improvement. Mr. Clark is surely right to remind us that : 'We must not neglect the wisdom of the classical economists who saw that the agents of production are land, labour, capital, and enterprise ; neither economic theory nor recent experience provides support for the view that one factor takes absolute precedence over all others'.

Indeed, I would venture to suggest that what is most significant in the experience of the more developed economies is that they have developed the aptitudes and social mechanizing for rapidly and successfully combining and re-combining all the factors of production in suitable economic proportions in response to the signals of highly specialized markets ; and their success has varied with the extent to which markets were permitted to function freely. The 'unspecified factor' which I quoted above, as an example of current thought, is not something autonomous or extraneous by which the other factors of production, land, labour, capital are somehow multiplied. Rather it reflects the very success or failure of the community to engage upon those individual and social processes and those correct economic choices between alternative opportunities on which its well-being depends.

It is precisely in regard to these subtle bonds of modern economic co-operation through highly developed systems of commercial intercourse, law, and public administration, that the economic and social heritage of under-developed societies is deficient, and in most of Africa the deficiencies are greater than elsewhere. In this connection it is only necessary to mention that Africa has the highest rate of illiteracy — 80-85 per cent — of any of the continents, equalled only in South Central Asia.[2]

---

[1] They state that 'these are combined results for countries in a very wide range of stages of economic development. For the wealthier countries, in more recent times, a higher rate of return to labour and a lower rate on capital would probably be found.'

In quoting these calculations I do not want to subscribe to the view that it is meaningful to attempt to separate out the contributions of the different factors to the real national product in this way.

[2] *International Statistics Relating to Education, Culture and Mass Communication*, UNESCO, Paris, 1959.

TABLE 4

WAGE EMPLOYMENT IN AFRICA

	Population (all Races) ('000)	Gross Domestic Product in Money Economy (£ million)	Gross Domestic Product in Money Economy per Head (£)	African Wage Earners ('000)	African Wage Earners as % of Total Population
Kenya (1959)	6,450	163	25	537	8·3
Tanganyika (1959)	9,000	106	12	433	4·8
Uganda (1959)	6,500	89	14	224	3·4
Nyasaland (1959)	2,800	26	9	181	6·5
Northern Rhodesia (1959)	2,400	164	68	265	11·0
Southern Rhodesia (1959)	3,000	239	80	630	21·0
Central African Federation (1959)	8,130	429	53	1,076	13·2
Nigeria (1956/7)	31,000	n.a.	—	475 *	1·5
Ghana (1958)	4,800	n.a.	—	313	6·5
Belgian Congo (1958)	13,600	470	35	1,100	8·1
Union of South Africa (1957)	14,167	1,945	137	—	—
,, ,, ,, (1951)	12,672	—	—	3,608	28·5

Sources:
East Africa High Commission *Quarterly Economic and Statistical Bulletin.*
   The Gross Domestic Product of Tanganyika 1954–57 (Dar-es-Salaam, 1959).
   Tanganyika Statistical Abstract (1960).
   The Geographical Income of Uganda 1950–56.
   Domestic Income and Product in Kenya (Nairobi, 1959).
Uganda Protectorate *Enumeration of Employees* (June 1958).
   National Accounts of the Federation of Rhodesia and Nyasaland 1954–1959 (Salisbury, 1960).
Advisory Commission on the *Review of the Constitution of the Federation of Rhodesia and Nyasaland,* Appendix VI, Cmnd.
   Bulletin de la Banque Centrale du Congo Belge et du Ruanda-Urundi (November 1959).
   La Situation économique du Congo Belge et du Ruanda-Urundi en 1959 (Brussels, 1960).
   Economic Survey of Nigeria 1959.
   Ghana Quarterly Digest of Statistics (December 1960).
   Reported Employment and Earnings in Kenya 1959 (Nairobi, 1960).
P. Ady and M. Courcier, *Systems of National Accounts in Africa* (OEEC, 1960).
Union of South Africa *Union Statistics for Fifty Years* (Pretoria, 1960).

Hardly anywhere in Africa, for example, are the indigenous customs and laws which govern the division, ownership and use of land and natural resources, suited to modern enterprise. Even the modern economy in South Africa is retarded by severe legal fetters on the free mobility of the factors of production. In most of Tropical Africa indigenous customs of the past still inhibit the full use of the human factors, with the consequence that the resources of vast areas remain completely outside the scope of world commerce. In this connection it is worth stressing that not only does the absence of suitable modern systems of land tenure and ownership inhibit land under cultivation from being farmed more productively but, as, for example, in Nigeria, it prevents additional land — which is in many areas readily available — from being utilized for commercial purposes. It thus prevents the further development of food production and cash crops for local and export markets and of agricultural credit necessary therefore. Even building in, and development of, urban and industrial areas is prevented by the absence of appropriate financial machinery which cannot be developed under the existing laws and customs affecting land ownership and land tenure.

Relative Expansion in Wage Employment

Nevertheless, in spite of the fact that large areas of Africa have for so long remained remote and untouched by, or were mistakenly excluded from, the directing forces of the market mechanism, the last thirty years have witnessed such important changes that a dominant factor in Africa today is the rapid growth of a wage-earning population whose economic security is directly dependent on the modern economy.

Table 4 gives some statistics of the numbers of African wage earners and the percentage they are of the populations of selected territories in relation to gross domestic product per head, and illustrates the striking differences between the tropical and non-tropical areas of Africa, and also the contribution of mining to employment opportunities. Of course, statistics of wage employment are a better index of modern industrial, commercial, and mining activity than they are of the advance of modern economy in the agricultural sector, because statistics of wage employment in agriculture are very defective ; they also generally do not reflect adequately the growth of modern commercial production by peasant proprietors (as, for example, in Ghana and Nigeria) employing little or no paid labour or not registering such labour officially.

The relative backwardness of Tropical Africa is also illustrated by the fact that less than 10 per cent of its people live in communities of 5,000 or more, even though a great many of these communities are more rural than urban in form and function.[1]

V. CAPITAL ACCUMULATION AND INVESTMENT IN THE UNION

The disparity in the economic development of tropical compared with the non-tropical regions of Africa south of the Sahara, is necessarily reflected in the amount of capital accumulation in them. For capital is both partial cause and partial effect of the process of development. Over the continent as a whole the most striking factor is the low capital stock per head. Statistics to illustrate this are as difficult to come by as to interpret, but it is significant that even in the Union of South Africa the amount of the total capital stock *per capita* at 1938 prices (as calculated by Franzen and Willers) was on the average for the decade 1944–53 only £133. The comparable figure for 1909–18 was £94. This can be very roughly compared with Australia £A386 (reproducible tangible wealth 1955–6) and Canada $3,106.

After nearly one hundred years of modern economic development the Union of South Africa is still heavily dependent on capital investment from abroad. As shown by Franzen and Willers, about one-fifth of the amount of gross domestic capital formation (£3,640 million) for the decade 1946–55 was financed directly or indirectly from abroad through a negative balance on current account (£880 million).

Although the statistics involved are not strictly comparable, it seems to me not far-fetched to conclude from the calculations of

[1] By contrast, in the Union of South Africa the percentage of urban population of all races has risen from about 25 per cent in 1911 to 43 per cent in 1951. 'The territories where the percentage of urban population exceeds 10 are Eritrea, French Somaliland, Ghana, the two Rhodesias, Zanzibar, and, possibly, Ethiopia. By way of comparison, in the Philippines the corresponding percentage is about 25, and in Brazil, also a tropical country, about 33. In the United States it is about 60, and in the United Kingdom about 80. Not only is the urban population small, but the bulk of it is found in small cities. According to figures compiled by Trewartha and Zelinsky in 1955, out of an estimated total of 455 places with a population of 5,000 or more, only 41 had more than 50,000, 16 more than 100,000, and 5 more than 200,000. (George H. T. Kimble, *Tropical Africa* (The Twentieth Century Fund, New York, 1960), vol. I, p. 97.) It is often very difficult to know where to draw the line between towns and villages in tropical Africa. To take an extreme example, in Bechuanaland there is at least one purely rural village of 20,000 inhabitants, and several posts of a strictly urban character with no more than 100 inhabitants. In the absence of detailed knowledge of the social and occupational structure of all the communities involved, about the only kind of line that can be drawn is an arbitrary numerical one. (*Ibid.* vol. I, p. 97, footnote (16).)

D. G. Franzen and J. J. D. Willers and from the figures published by
the S.A. Reserve Bank based on the 1956 Census of the Union's
foreign assets and liabilities,[1] that, as at 1955, capital from abroad
accounted for broadly one-half of the depreciated capital stock of
the Union in 1938 prices. Twenty years earlier it would appear,
from my own calculations of the foreign capital invested up to 1935,
that the ratio was then about the same. But there have been
significant changes in the direction of this foreign investment. Up
to 1935 my own calculations (though on a different basis from the
Census figures) indicated that roughly two-thirds of the private
capital listed on the Stock Exchange or in the financial press had
found its way into mining, and by far the largest part into gold
mining. According to the 1956 Census figures published by the
Reserve Bank, mining was still responsible for 37 per cent of foreign
investment (£454 million out of £1,215 million for the private
sector). It is significant, however, that manufacturing industry
accounted for 25 per cent, and foreign investment in it was of almost
the same magnitude as that in gold mining. However, the foreign
liabilities of the public sector have greatly declined in relative importance. The Census figures show that the 'official' sector in
1956 accounted for only 13 per cent of total foreign investment in
the Union, while my own calculations of all capital invested up to
1935 showed a ratio of 43 per cent. This figure is only roughly
comparable with the 1956 Census figures but it illustrates an important trend. As domestic incomes and savings increase it is
easier to finance public works from local sources — whereas, for
private capital, particularly for new or risky enterprises, access to
world capital markets is still necessary. It is, moreover, noteworthy
that when the terms of trade or other circumstances were favourable
to the expansion of export activity (including gold mining) this
required (and stimulated) investment from abroad. The Union's
domestic saving was insufficient to finance development notwithstanding the rise in incomes and savings per head made possible
by the rapid rate of economic growth in the last twenty-five
years.

It is probable that if hampering institutional factors and restrictive paternalistic patterns of law and custom had been modified
there might well have resulted a greater rate of investment from
abroad, more employment in modern economy, and an increase in
the absolute amount and rate of domestic saving. But the supply
of capital, labour, and the state of employment were generally

[1] Cf. S.A. Reserve Bank. Supplement to *Quarterly Bulletin of Statistics*
December 1958, 'The Foreign Liabilities and Assets of the Union of South Africa'

regarded as independent of each other.[1] However, under-employment and under-utilization of resources in the Union were by no means only the consequence of institutional arrangements. From 1895 onwards, with the exception of a short period between the World Wars, the continuing depreciation in the value of money led to rising costs of gold mining, and less favourable 'terms of trade' of gold in relation to the imported goods it was able to command. For long periods, the Union has been hard pressed to maintain or expand export income. This has undoubtedly affected its ability to cope with the burden of financing the development of its large economically backward population. The rise in the gold price in 1931, for the first time in thirty years, released the Union temporarily from the depressing effect of an unfavourable trend in the terms of trade of its main export — gold — and gave real opportunity for a rapid expansion of its export income, for investment from abroad, and consequently for increased domestic saving, and gave opportunity at long last for a rapid expansion of secondary industry.

The Union's experience highlights the fundamental and far more acute problems of Tropical Africa, which consist in the two-fold task of refashioning the institutional structure of the past and earning the foreign exchange to pay for the imports of goods and services complementary to the process.

VI. CAPITAL FORMATION IN TROPICAL AFRICA

Statistics in regard to capital investment in Tropical Africa on a comparable basis with those to which I have referred in regard to the Union of South Africa are not available. The following very approximate figures compiled from various sources indicate roughly the relative magnitudes of the resources being devoted to capital formation in the various territories. For 1956 expenditure on gross fixed capital formation as a percentage of gross domestic product was estimated to have been approximately 19 per cent for the Commonwealth West Africa territories (£3·3 per head), 27 per cent for British East Africa (£5·4 per head), and 28 per cent for the Belgian Congo (£9·1 per head). For the Federation of Rhodesia and Nyasaland the percentage of gross domestic capital formation to gross domestic product at factor cost was 32 per cent (£20 per head), and for the Union of South Africa the average annual percentage of gross domestic capital formation to gross national product was 35 per cent (£28 per head). As the Report of the Mission of the

---

[1] Cf. 'The Tyranny of Economic Paternalism in Africa : A Study of Frontier Mentality, 1860–1960', supplement to OPTIMA, December 1960.

Bank of Reconstruction and Development to Tanganyika has suggested, the high ratios for African countries like Tanganyika with very low *per capita* incomes can, apart from the fact that much of the capital formation was financed from abroad, be explained partly by the fact that much of the basic demand for food is satisfied in the subsistence sector. As a consequence, a higher proportion of monetary income can be devoted to capital formation than in an economy where monetary income covers the bulk of consumption needs. The Mission rightly drew attention to the fact that to understand the vital rôle of public expenditures in the promotion of economic development in Tanganyika, it is necessary to take into account not only capital expenditures, but also many of the current expenditures of central and local government :

... in relation to the centrally important sectors of agriculture and animal husbandry, government current expenditures have been considerably larger than government capital expenditures (including irrigation works and development of rural water supplies). Certain current government expenditures, those on agricultural research and extension work being a leading example, appear likely to have a greater impact, pound for pound, on the growth of production than do many government capital expenditures. It would be highly misleading to equate 'developmental' with capital expenditures and 'non-developmental' with current expenditures.

In the territories with proportionately larger export incomes it has been possible to push such developmental[1] expenditures much further than in Tanganyika. In the Union of South Africa, for over fifty years, very large expenditures on the development of the infrastructure, and particularly of agriculture, have been financed from government revenues received directly and indirectly from taxation or a share in the profits of mining and mineral exports.

In the Belgian Congo a large proportion of the capital investment in the public sector in the past was financed in a similar manner. The very great importance of exports (and of fluctuations in the terms of trade) was recently again demonstrated by Mr. A. G. Irvine's important analysis of *The Balance of Payments of Rhodesia and Nyasaland 1945–1954.*[2] Between 1949 and 1954 the percentage of the gross national product generated by exports and the export multiplier varied between 70 and 75 per cent ; and the percentage generated from investment and the investment multiplier varied

[1] All such 'development' expenditures were, or are, not necessarily justified. Some were a waste of economic resources.
[2] Oxford University Press, 1959.

425

between 25 and 29 per cent. A high proportion of the incomes generated by the latter was attributable to capital exports. Over 80 per cent of the gross national product was generated either directly or indirectly by current or capital receipts from abroad.

VII. IMPORTANCE OF MINERAL EXPORTS

I have already had occasion to refer to the importance of mineral exports ; their dominating rôle in the economically more advanced territories of Africa is further illustrated in Table 5. I found, in my calculations up to 1936, that of the capital invested from abroad in Africa, no less than 66 per cent found its way into the group of territories whose development was greatly influenced by mining activities, comprising the Union of South Africa, South West Africa, Southern Rhodesia, Northern Rhodesia, and the Belgian Congo. In 1935 their trade formed 67 per cent of the trade of Africa, and minerals accounted for 78 per cent of their domestic exports. In 1956 the figures were respectively 55 and 53 per cent.

The special group of mineral territories accounts for a large proportion of the capital made available for private enterprise in Africa, which up to 1935 amounted to £675 million, and of this 71 per cent was invested in these mineral territories. The further expansion in mining and mineral exploration in them has been very important in the last twenty-five years — but comparable figures of the total capital invested are not available.

Mining has continued to attract a large proportion of capital investment from abroad and I think it not unlikely that in the private sector, taking an overall view, a large proportion of the dividends paid from abroad by the mining industry has been again reinvested in Africa in mining and activities associated with it.

The financial resources devoted to mining in Tropical Africa have not been drawn only from overseas. It is significant that in 1956 there was, for example, about £94·8 million of direct investment from the Union of South Africa in the Federation of Rhodesia and Nyasaland, of which £24·3 million was direct investment [1] in mining — not including considerable further investment in associated financial companies. Mining investment from the Union has also taken place in East and West Africa.

Overseas investment in the exploitation of other natural resources (*e.g.* edible oils, coffee, timber, rubber) has also been important.

---

[1] Direct investment refers to foreign undertakings 'controlled' from the Union.

TABLE 5

EXPORTS OF AFRICA SOUTH OF THE SAHARA

	Total Domestic Exports (£ million)	Mineral Exports as % of Total for each Territory	Mineral Exports	
			(£ million)	As % of Total for all Territories
Central African Federation (1959)	190·0	68·9	131·0	23·2
Belgian Congo and Ruanda-Urundi (1959)	177·0	56·5	100·0	17·7
Nigeria (1959)	160·0	3·8	6·0	1·1
French West Africa (1956) *	122·5	4·1	5·0	0·9
Ghana (1959)	113·0	23·0	26·0	4·6
Tanganyika (1959)	45·0	17·8	8·0	1·4
Uganda (1959)	42·0	7·1	3·0	0·5
Madagascar (1956) *	33·2	6·0	2·0	0·4
Kenya (1959)	33·0	6·1	2·0	0·4
French Equatorial Africa (1956) *	28·2	8·5	2·4	0·4
French Cameroon (1956) *	26·8	0·7	0·2	negligible
Total Tropical Africa	970·7	29·4	285·6	50·6
Union of South Africa (1958)	579·0	48·2	279·0	49·4
GRAND TOTAL	1549·7	36·4	564·6	100·0

* Mineral exports are for 1957.

Note.—' Exports ' in all cases includes gold bullion but excludes specie.

427

What distinguishes extractive activity, however, is that it is not so dependent on institutional and social changes. The combination of the factors of production is concentrated, and capital and enterprise, management and skill, can be (and have been) brought together from all parts of the world and combined with available African labour resources causing a rapid rise in incomes. It thus provides a natural opportunity for the first stages of industrialization without the need to await the growth of local markets (and purchasing power) in the rural areas for its products. It gives rise to associated manufacturing industries and is a valuable forcing ground for the acquisition of industrial skills and disciplines which can gradually spill over into the backward regions through the investment of savings accumulated through the higher incomes to which mining gives rise — provided that the whole process, including the natural development of urban areas (which in turn give opportunities for the increased sale in them of food and raw material products from the backward regions), is not held up by restrictionist practices or outworn institutional restraints which curtail the economic mobility of all the factors of production. Plantation enterprises have, of course, had similar effects in attracting capital and raising cash incomes, and, as in the case of mining, the communications and general infrastructure built up in connection with their development have assisted also the expansion of cash crops by peasant producers, which I believe could provide very great scope, and are indeed essential for further economic advance in Tropical Africa. Peasant production of this kind is particularly valuable as, where basic rail or river communications have been developed, it is not dependent on large investments from abroad.

No adequate statistics of private investment in Africa from abroad are available for the post-World War II period. It has been suggested that gross private foreign investment in Tropical Africa, *i.e.* excluding the Union, S.W. Africa, and the Protectorate, reached a peak of about $800 million per year some time between 1950 and 1957. Since then the total rate of gross private investment appears to have been appreciably reduced due to political developments in Africa. Net flow of private foreign investment into Africa has been substantially less than the flow indicated by these investments. Reinvested earnings have formed an important part of European investment in Africa since 1950.[1]

Relatively large capital expenditure for developmental purposes and the provision of a suitable economic infrastructure has, as in other under-developed countries, always been inescapable in African

---

[1] Cf. the excellent Staff Paper by Guy Benveniste and William E. Moran, Jr., Stanford Research Institute, International Industrial Development Center.

territories. Of the foreign capital entering Tropical Africa from 1870 to 1936 my calculations showed that about 45 per cent was public and 55 per cent private capital : the respective regional figures were Commonwealth West Africa 44 and 56 per cent ; British East Africa 64 and 36 per cent ; French territories 61 and 39 per cent ; and Belgian Congo and Ruanda-Urundi 25 and 75 per cent. But much development expenditure of a public nature was in fact financed directly by governments or as part of the 'private' capital investment of particular industries, *e.g.* by mining, exploration, plantation, or other agricultural undertakings which had frequently to find the capital for roads, railways, housing, and other 'public' works or facilities without which their purely commercial operations could not have been conducted.

A major development since World War II has been the financial assistance in the form of loans, grants, aid, and technical assistance through international governmental co-operation and through international agencies. Although estimates of expenditures are available in various forms and accounts (see an excellent compilation in the Staff Paper of the Stanford Research Institute) it is very difficult to discover what the amount of capital investment as distinct from current aid or financial rescue operations of one kind or another has really been.

Notwithstanding their considerable help from public international sources, one cannot escape the tentative conclusion that the total private and public investment in Tropical Africa since World War II has lagged behind the needs of the territories (*e.g.* in terms of population growth) and the opportunities which could have been developed in them prior to the political events which have now so greatly disturbed international financial confidence in Africa.

VIII. THE EFFECTS OF INDEPENDENCE

It may now be useful to consider briefly, in the light of past experience, some of the fundamental problems affecting the supply of capital in the light of the constitutional advances to political independence which have occurred in Africa in recent years. The rate and direction of development in African territories has, in the past, often been greatly affected by capital expenditure by foreign powers for political, military, strategic, or other 'non-economic' purposes. Such windfalls result from accidental historical circumstances which may be of great importance but cannot be relied upon. The demand for capital or other assistance in the form of free gifts by foreign powers or through international agencies (with no strings attached) must presumably be considered as almost infinitely elastic, but the same cannot be said of the supply of such capital.

The grants-in-aid by the governments of the colonial powers were not pure windfalls in this sense, but resulted from their legal responsibilities for the defence and good government of their dominions. The extent to which international assistance will be forthcoming for an independent country will depend on its ability to utilize it as successfully as, and to attract it in competition with, other countries — unless we are to assume that the allocation of scarce capital rescources by the donors or lenders is made by lot. Thus, the attainment of political independence from an ex-metropolitan country which recognized, or was compelled by circumstances to undertake, certain definite obligations to the colony or dependency under its jurisdiction, now involves the latter in dependence on others who have no such clear-cut responsibilities. Whether or not colonial powers in any particular case did or did not exercise their responsibilities as they could or should have done in Africa, it is clear that those responsibilities now fall on the governments and people of the newly independent countries and that the great social, institutional, and economic changes which modern economy requires have now to be initiated mainly by them and not by foreign powers or agencies. In this task the newly independent territories are all faced with the basic problem that their modern activities still form a very small part of their economies. The challenge of independent statehood can release much latent energy and talent and the willingness to shoulder the burdens of change with new-found zest. It may also bring advantages in attracting capital enterprise, skill, and assistance from countries previously unable to trade freely with, or obtain access to opportunities which could be developed in the dependent territory owing to customary or other barriers erected by the metropolitan country. But there are offsetting costs which cannot be overlooked. The cost of pacifying the continent and establishing the rule of law and ordered government was borne mainly by the ex-metropolitan powers, with the result that the colonial territories in Africa were in considerable measure spared the burden of maintaining peace within Africa and defence against enemies outside it ; they were spared also the cost of a large range of scientific, administrative, diplomatic, and commercial services directly or indirectly borne by the metropolitan countries — all of these burdens taken together will be very difficult for some newly independent states to meet without endangering their economic development or independence itself.

Moreover, since capital investment and immigrant skill and enterprise from abroad have been mainly responsible for establishing the economic framework of modern economy in the advanced territories, it will be apparent what difficult tasks, in providing a dependable monetary, fiscal, legal, and administrative framework, face territories which have suddenly attained independence or have had it thrust upon them. They are at that early stage of development in which political independence can hardly prove beneficial unless it is conspicuously and consistently devoted to providing a climate of political and economic security which will attract from abroad the capital and enterprise, and the skilled technicians, to develop their economies.

If, however, independence were to lead to conditions of insecurity, the economic life of these territories would be most gravely threatened, and a large proportion of those of their peoples who have entered the modern economy, and particularly those working in the newly developed urban areas, would be thrown back into subsistence economic activity; an eventuality which, particularly in view of the rapid rate of population growth in recent times, would have the direst consequences. In this connection it should be borne in mind that most of the large towns in the less developed regions of Africa are either mainly administrative centres or are based, not on a prosperous integrated hinterland, but on export, import, and allied activities. Their populations are thus very vulnerable to factors which might in any way interrupt the specialized production on which their livelihood is directly or indirectly based.

Such dangers now threaten the ex-Belgian Congo. The striking economic advances in that country have been due to highly specialized financial, commercial, and technical links with world markets. The Congo has also established a rapidly expanding urban African population directly or indirectly dependent on these economic activities. Any interruption of the world economic network on which they are based is likely to endanger the livelihood of most of the urban and the relatively skilled rural population, and to force down their standards of living to those of rural subsistence economy.

A recent staff paper of the International Industrial Development Center of the Stanford Research Institute,[1] after surveying the development of private foreign investment in Africa, concluded that :

. . . independence has not stopped important foreign investments, but there is also some indication that large undertakings are being

---

[1] Cf. the same Staff Paper by Guy Benveniste and William E. Moran, Jr., Stanford Research Institute, International Industrial Development Center.

delayed or postponed. Although some large investments have continued to take place, small and medium investments have diminished and, in some cases, have been curtailed. There have been considerable differences in this respect from country to country. In the more 'promising' countries, for example, Nigeria, there has been an influx of new capital, but in the less 'promising' countries, for example, the Congo, there has been a serious incidence of disinvestment. Disinvestment, which occurred in Morocco just prior to and after independence, created an economic vacuum at a time when economic growth was most necessary. Ever since, French capital has been finding its way out of Morocco. A similar process took place in the Congo; Belgian statistics on the flight of Belgian and other foreign capital from the Congo prior to independence illustrate this process. These statistics indicate how, a year prior to independence, private capital flowed from the Congo in considerable amounts. It was not until exchange controls were imposed by the Belgian government that this flight was brought to at least a temporary halt in early 1960. . . . The flow of private capital from the Congo was larger in 1959 than the net influx of private capital during the nine preceding years. With independence and chaos, the flight of capital was limited only by monetary transfer problems.

The same report, after commenting on the outflow of capital, recently recorded also from Southern, Central, and East Africa, remarked :

While disinvestment is taking place in parts of Africa where substantial capital investments were made in the past, lack of new private foreign investment is also of concern in other countries, particularly in what used to be French Tropical Africa where French capital is definitely reluctant to go unless the investment is large enough to warrant special concessions and guarantees.

There is no need for me to comment further on the disastrous effects both for the newly independent African states, and indeed for advanced Southern Africa, of a cessation or decline of private foreign investment. It is, however, I think, worth pointing out that the very conditions which deter private foreign investment would also eventually gravely retard assistance from international public agencies in the supply of capital for an expansion of the framework of government communications and public works — which task was previously fulfilled by 'public' capital made available through or under the guarantees of the governments of the metropolitan countries. Nor do I believe that in circumstances of political uncertainty or economic disintegration the gap could be filled in Africa by the alternative of state initiative — not only for the reason that the modern state economic apparatus necessary for it, and indeed, the conditions under which it could operate economically, do not yet exist in most of Africa, but because the resources it could tap have not been developed.

IX. BASIC BARRIERS TO ECONOMIC GROWTH

For the real economic task in Africa under the new political dispensation is no different from the old : it is to find and create the most suitable institutional arrangements for utilizing those natural resources which will yield new and additional net income to the inhabitants — and increase their low productivity. In this search generalized theories such as those of the 'take-off' or the 'big push' have very little relevance. In this connection the remarks of Celso Furtado of the Economic Commission for Latin America, at the conference of the International Economic Association held at Rio de Janeiro four years ago, are of particular interest.[1] With the experience of Brazil particularly in mind, and one should bear in mind that Brazil is far more economically advanced than most territories in Tropical Africa, he said :

> The theory of the big push, by suggesting that investment must be effected on a given scale if it is to be economic, places too much emphasis on the problem of the indivisibility of processes, both on the supply and on the demand sides. It therefore overlooks the broader aspects of social reform that are necessary if a stationary economy is to begin to develop on the basis of its own resources and incentives. The recognition and identification of these necessary reforms is of fundamental practical importance, both for countries which are anxious to emerge from stagnation and for those desirous of intensifying their development. . . .

He went on to say :

> Capital formation, although it has been the main vehicle of the assimilation of new techniques, is in itself responsible for only a relatively small fraction of the increase in the productivity of labour. . . . The replacement of horses by tractors is useful when land taken up for the maintenance of the horses can be utilized with greater economic efficiency. The mechanization of the textile industry is advantageous when there is a growing demand for manpower. But if there is no alternative means of employing the factors released by the progress of technique, the assimilation of new technical processes may have little or no effect on the average productivity of the labour force. In other words, the

[1] *Economic Development for Latin America*, edited by Ellis and Wallich. London, Macmillan, 1961.

P   433

marginal physical productivity of specific sectors, such as manufacturing, may substantially increase without any improvement in the average productivity of the system as a whole. This phenomenon was very well described by Kindleberger as 'structural disequilibrium at the factor level'.

This is not a phenomenon that can be presented out of its historical context. Its essence may be summed up in the following proposition : in the historical context of today the effect of the assimilation of a technical innovation on the rate of growth is a function of the degree of development. The more highly developed an economy is, the greater is the positive effect of the assimilation of a technical innovation. In other words, development depends increasingly upon technique and less on direct capital formation in the productive processes.

As I expressed the point in a different context :[1] 'The belief in the miracles to be wrought by "capital investment" *per se* is an illusion. In particular, it overlooks the fact that the essence of capital itself is that it wears out rapidly unless continually renewed, replaced, or maintained. The poorer a country in skilled labour and in natural resources the less capital it is likely to have, and the less *it can afford to have until the whole social and economic complex of its activities has gradually evolved patterns of economic behaviour suited to its use, reproduction, and further accumulation.*'

Given political stability and order, and the maintenance and development of sound international economic relations, it seems to me that African countries have great opportunities for renewed economic advance. Although the issues have not yet been put to the test, the newly independent countries may, as I pointed out recently,[2] be able to succeed more rapidly in sweeping away those outworn customary and social obstacles to change which the metropolitan powers were not in a position to remove or mistakenly supported. Political and economic democracy in these newly developing countries may find common ground in meeting the pent-up demands for education and economic opportunity among their people.

The African States are entering upon a stage of world economic development in which the great technical and transport developments of our time are so rapidly reducing the barriers to communication of every kind that almost any country or region which has something to contribute by way of labour or natural resources can, given even a modicum of reliability in the conduct of its affairs,

---

[1] *Economic Development for Latin America*, edited by Ellis and Wallich, London, Macmillan, 1960, p. 100. 'Economic Impact on Under-developed Societies.'
[2] *International Affairs*, p. 446.

attract to it those able to assist it to commence the development of potential assets. The barriers to economic growth are more likely to be found in the field of administration and political institutions than in the lack of resources or of individuals, at home or from abroad, to undertake their development. Probably at no previous time in history has there been available such an expanding network of private and public international agencies seeking to assist in the exploitation of the natural resources of the world and experimenting in the problems of training and technique in order to do so. It is the paradox of our times that while science and technique stand poised for major advances in easing the burden of man's labour and in multiplying his powers over the hitherto unopened, uncultivated, or under-utilized regions of the world, the forces of unbridled nationalism and outworn tribalism still bar the way to that private and collective international co-operation without which these advances cannot be made.

In a technically shrinking world there is little room for absolute political or economic independence. If this is realized the problems of Africa will be seen as little different in kind from those elsewhere : as problems arising from the relative rates of change of economic and political institutions.

DISCUSSION OF PROFESSOR FRANKEL'S PAPER

Dr. Yudelman, introducing the discussion of Professor Frankel's paper, stressed the major issues brought out by the paper. Professor Frankel's main thesis was that capital did not in itself create income. Rather it increased the efficiency of other factors in creating income. It had to be asked what kind of expenditure would best contribute to superseding traditional methods by better methods which would extend the African's control of his economic environment. Thus, investment in creating capital had to be balanced against expenditures in other forms — in controlling soil erosion, in agricultural extension work, and so on. Capital investment could explain only a fraction of economic progress. What was it that constituted the unspecified factor ? Was it primarily investment in human resources ? A study of the Mexican economy, conducted in Chicago, had shown a very great increase of production associated with a very small increase in the capital stock. One of the chief problems of Africa was to discover and improve the unspecified factors which most contributed to growth.

He found himself in general agreement with Professor Frankel in his attempts to identify the basic barriers to growth. He did not think that over-all economic concepts such as the capital/output ratio had much value in an African context. Nor did he think that it was profitable at this stage to attempt to think in terms of the 'big push', or even to consider trying to create the preconditions in which an ultimate 'take-off' might be achieved. The greater part of Africa had not yet reached that stage. There was a danger that, if Africa were inundated with capital, it would not be able to make effective use of it. *Dr. Yudelman* suggested that one of the issues on which the discussion should be concentrated was whether capital was or was not a uniting factor in African development. He himself was inclined to put more emphasis on the limitations of capacity to absorb capital and use it effectively.

The first stages of the discussion were devoted to the 'unspecified factor', its constituents and importance. *Professor Dupriez* felt that it could not be interpreted clearly enough to throw light on its rôle in economic development. It was a fallacy to regard capital as something that was always durable and that needed to be replaced. The thesis that economic development was wholly the result of capital investment was economically indefensible and politically dangerous. Capital did not automatically create incomes. Where did increases of real incomes come from? Professor Schumpeter had said from a better combination of all factors of production, including capital. It was fruitless to attempt to argue what was the contribution of capital and what was that of other factors. The issue was the determination of the best combinations. Intellectually it was impossible to dissociate the contributions of various factors. The rôle of capital was essentially complementary to other factors. The important practical issue was the provision of capital at the lowest possible rate. This raised the problems of the best general social and economic conditions to facilitate the flow of capital and also the respective rôles of the state and of private enterprise.

Professor Robinson found himself in close agreement with Professor Frankel in regard to the importance of the unspecified factor. Experience in the United Kingdom, analysed in two quite different ways, first by Cairncross and more recently by Reddaway and Smith, seemed to show that only about a quarter of the increase in output per head could be attributed to a return on increased capital per head, and something like three-quarters had to be explained in terms of what was being described as the unspecified factor. But he thought that care was necessary in making inferences from that fact. He was not at all sure that it could safely be argued that three-quarters of the increase could have been achieved without any capital investment at all. Capital investment, including, of course, reinvestment of depreciation funds, acted as a catalyst in enabling new knowledge and research to be used and new skills and better management to be fully exploited. But, more important, if one believed that these unspecified factors accounted for three-quarters of progress, could one identify them and operate on them? He believed one could. He did not agree with those who argued that there was a natural rate of increase of output per head — identified by Colin Clark, he believed, as 1·3 per cent per annum — which was incapable of being improved. Scientific research and development, general and technical education, training for management, agricultural extension work, were probably the most important elements. He thought that in Africa as well as in Europe investment in human capital formation was fully as important as investment in fixed capital, possibly more important. He was sceptical of arguments which implied that money should to the greatest possible extent be left to fructify in the hands of entrepreneurs, if that was interpreted to mean less taxation and less education. He regarded the absorptive capacity of Africa in respect of capital as needing to be increased.

Dr. Singer thought that it was almost impossible to interpret the relevant statistics with certainty. It was normal to assume decreasing returns to added quantities of any factor. But in practice there were constantly evolving new complementarities, so that the efficiency of capital kept on increasing. He was doubtful whether statistics could be used to prove the point. The rôle of physical capital formation was more evident if one thought in terms of net rather than gross investment. Keynes had argued that if net investment could be maintained at a high level, the marginal efficiency of capital would fall to zero. If net investment stopped, progress did not necessarily stop. The stationary state in that sense was not necessarily a bad thing. The replacement of capital permitted the embodiment of improved knowledge, which in turn could be stimulated by expenditures on research and training.

Professor Houghton quoted a discussion with a leading American banker who was convinced that the parts of the world which gave the highest returns to capital investment were Canada, parts of the United States, and parts of Europe. From the bankers' points of view there was little to be said for investment in Africa, outside of a few places. Investment in Africa was a missionary and not a commercial activity. If Africa were less fragmented it would make investment much more profitable.

Professor Spengler argued that the concept of capital normally employed was inadequate. One needed a more aggregative concept. Growth at any time had to be related to various expenditures incurred earlier. Future-facing expenditures required to be distinguished from present-facing expenditures. The former included a great deal that was normally treated as current expenditure. It was important to balance the various alternative forms of future-facing expenditure so as to secure the highest return.

Professor Frankel intervened to express his agreement that expenditures in the right directions could influence the unspecified factor. A great deal depended on a country's social heritage, its government, and on attitudes generally. While the cost of remedying past soil erosion, for example, might be prohibitively large, something could be done in that and other fields by dissemination of capital-saving knowledge.

As regards the unspecified factor itself, he thought that no one could separate the contributions of the different factors. That was well known to the classical economists. In the whole productive process we made the most arbitrary distinctions, and it was difficult to be sure of the meanings we attributed to the different factors. If one took the factors separately one could not explain the total.

Turning to Professor Robinson's points, *Professor Frankel* commented that it was surely a *sine qua non* that capital enabled other factors to make contributions to progress. Capital creation was a tool-making process. One could either improve the tools or improve the man himself. Capital investment consisted in doing something over a period of time which involved increasing the final product. Education, on the other hand, represented a diversion of resources. There was no certainty that people would be better off because of education. It was wrong to assume that improvement was an automatic consequence of education. Investment might lead to income generation, or it might not if it were wasted. The amount that we could afford to waste depended on how much we had. When societies were poor they could not afford to make investments with no return.

Was progress natural? We were all fallible, whether we were operating as governments or private enterprise. In some cases governments operated competently, in others badly. The same was true of private enterprise. When we spoke of using capital we were using scarce resources : capital was scarce in the sense that it was not a free good. Thus, if expenditure on human capital formation did not yield a net income there was no point in directing resources into it. Capital investment was a flow of resources to generate a flow of incomes.

Professor Robinson asked whether Professor Frankel was arguing that education had no marginal product. Was it not a matter of holding a balance between human capital formation and fixed capital formation? *Professor Frankel* said that if resources were employed in human capital formation the proper criterion was the rate of return. *Professor Robinson* thought that in saying that, Professor Frankel was agreeing that a balance should be held between the two.

The discussion then turned to wider issues of the part played by capital in economic development. *Professor Peacock* wished to return to a point made by Dr. Singer. If the marginal net product of capital were defined in the usual way, how did one make allowance for economies of scale? In Africa these were important. And if one assumed a constant capital/output ratio was there not a danger of error involved? He also reminded the conference that we were not discussing a situation in which any resources employed for one purpose were necessarily withdrawn from other purposes within the same country. A large part of the resources, both for fixed capital formation and for human capital formation, came from outside, in the form of aid, and a reduction of one did not automatically result in an increase of the other. But countries could, and did, have the problems of seeking aid and in that sense there was something of an allocation problem.

Dr. Skorov wished to be allowed to speak as an academic economist rather than as an international official. It was not by capital alone, he argued, that development was achieved. Social reforms were equally necessary, involving a recombining of factors. It was not the reforms but the consequences of the reforms that were important. There had been a great deal of disagreement over the interpretation of the investment that had taken place in post-war Africa. Professor Frankel still remained of the same opinions that he had held in 1938 : that, despite all the changes that had taken place in the world meanwhile, the only solution was private capital investment, provided that the necessary climate of security had been ensured. Private capital investment, *Dr. Skorov* thought, could never solve any of the problems of Africa except in the form of foreign investment. But the purpose of foreign private enterprise was to obtain, in profits, more than it gave. In the process of diversification, however, investment of a non-profitable character had to be made. Could private enterprise fill this rôle ? South Africa had already reached the point where repayment equalled or exceeded the inflow of capital. The problem, he argued, could only be solved by international public investment, which, in the absence of disarmament, did not seem to be practicable. What was needed was the Africanization of all foreign assets. This could give tangible results in combination with other measures.

Professor Bézy said that it was certainly true that political independence had led to a flight of some of the financial capital that had been made available to under-developed countries. This was possibly a short-term phenomenon. These funds were safeguarded during the period while the new governments demonstrated their stability. It was not improbable that they would again become available after this period of probation. Secondly, he drew attention to the fact that the setting up of exchange controls might result in the retention in certain countries of funds which, before independence, were invested abroad. Thus, in the sterling area there were centripetal forces which sometimes worked to the detriment of the backward countries of the area. The London capital market acted rather like a reciprocating pump ; it sucked in funds from the less developed parts of the area and pumped them out to the more profitable areas, which were not always the most backward — Australia, New Zealand, Southern Rhodesia, for example. Sometimes these funds found their way outside the area, to Canada, for instance, or the Middle East. Independent African countries might attract less foreign capital, but at the same time be more certain of retaining the benefits of their own savings. In the Congo, for example, a year after independence, the efficiency of the exchange control had been such that by retaining part of the profits that had previously been expatriated, a new source of capital had been tapped. If investment was not actually taking place, it was largely the consequence of the current political difficulties and the secession of Katanga and other provinces.

Political independence, *Professor Bézy* argued, on balance increased the import of capital, because it increased the opportunities for investment. This had previously been hindered by preference for metropolitan products, even when the local investment was justified by the size of the local market. At the same time, independence would encourage the inflow of foreign capital which had hesitated to come in hitherto because the market was regarded as the private preserve of the metropolitan country, in which it enjoyed, formally or informally, special advantages. Insecurity, which is disastrous to capital inflows, was perhaps no more than temporary, and even now capital was coming in from some large investors who took either a long economic view or a very short political view. There were undoubtedly governments which were prepared to pay court to offers of foreign investment. After independence the criteria of investment would be different. Investment to meet the needs of the home market would take precedence over investment to expand exports. Investment in autochthonous enterprises would be preferred to the expansion of the foreign enclave. This new orientation would again be favourable to development.

Professor Stanley thought that development expenditure might often be more productive than expenditure on fixed capital. One ought, however, to look at the question rather differently. One could have investment either in human beings or in institutions. The question was to discover which was the more productive expenditure and which were the most advantageous objectives of capital expenditure. This could be directed either to serve as an end in itself or as a means of improving the qualities of other factors. He could see no sense in dogmatic distinction. All expenditures should be measured on a scale of profitability. No one kind of expenditure was uniquely useful. One should try to discover their relative degrees of profitability.

Dr. Yudelman commented that the World Bank inquiries had shown the needs for circulatory as well as fixed capital.

Dr. Okigbo thought that discussion could be conducted at two different levels : the level of fact, involving a very detailed knowledge of local needs and conditions ; and the level of the choice of analytical tools — the merits of linear, non-linear, and homogenous production functions and the like. He had the impression that Professor Frankel disapproved of any refined analysis of the problems of economic development.

Professor Leduc said that in the African countries until recently administered by France, economic development had been extremely rapid. This had been due partly to the efforts that had been made to increase capital investment and partly to intensive studies of local development problems made by French experts. The first impulse for development came from the public funds made available without charge. These in turn led on to a multiplier effect, through local public and private investment. Thus, there was a simple and fairly predictable relation between the initial public investment and the ultimate total investment and increase of income. So far as concerned the question raised by Professor Bézy, fear of independence had provoked a flight of capital to the metropolitan country, but one had to distinguish between movements of financial and non-financial capital. The loss was entirely of financial capital. He did not feel certain about the net effects of long-term systematic control of currency on capital formation.

The discussion then turned to the question as to whether capital supply was the chief limiting factor in African development. *Professor Walker* thought the problem was more than a merely semantic one. There was the difficulty as to what one included in capital. Much of current expenditure was income-creating in the future rather than in the present. One could substitute capital, if it were freely available, for other factors involving the use of current resources. In East Africa it was important to distinguish between the public and the private sector. In the private sector investment opportunities almost directly stimulated, and created, savings, and increased investment in the private sector was almost self-financing. In the public sector, however, there was a great shortage of capital. Moreover, though investment in improving transport and the like was extremely important, it was at the same time extremely expensive. Where were funds to come from? There were obvious limits to taxation. External loans carried high rates of interest and investment in long-term development was not fully productive in the short-term. The financing of such investment could, he thought, only be possible through international aid.

M. Roland Pré argued that it was necessary to distinguish between two kinds of capital investment. The first was primarily international in character, designed to meet the needs of world development. Such investment might have very limited effects on the local population. In Mauretania, for example, there had been mining investment of this kind, which involved a very large foreign investment but a very small local employment of labour. On the other hand, there was very important investment in creating the capital infrastructure of a country, which opened up opportunities for changing the local conditions of production and of living standards and had important long-term repercussions.

Mr. Beheiry suggested that there was need for realism in discussing the rôle of private enterprise in African economic development. From a pragmatic point of view the important question was whether there was enterprising in the real sense of the word. Private enterprise showed a remarkable tendency to avoid risk at any cost. African countries should make room for private enterprise, whether local or foreign. Political stability was capable of a number of definitions. African countries would take time to work out their institutions and their political philosophies. This was a sign of African awakening. The present view of African political stability held by the outside world was an obstacle to foreign investment.

Economic Development for Africa South of the Sahara

Dr. Singer emphasized that the essential preconditions for investment did not exist in Africa. It was, necessary, as a first stage, to provide more detailed knowledge and information about the opportunities for African investment. There was abnormal ignorance of possibilities in Africa. Action to remove this and to throw light on investment opportunities was neither tremendously difficult nor tremendously expensive. Feasibility studies required to be made, through either national or international agencies. As of the present, he did not believe that capital supply was the limiting factor. But if African investment opportunities were better analysed and if African absorptive capacity were increased, in ten or fifteen years' time, capital supply might well become the limiting factor. He thought that Professor Frankel had made the mistake of under-estimating the extent to which public aid and development planning had increased the total resources of African countries.

Dr. Gavrilov returned to the conditions governing economic development. Capital was only one of many factors. European immigration into Africa did not create the conditions for African economic development. The settlers had developed export industries only. That was why national capital was insufficient. For capital hardly existed in Africa outside of a few industries, such as mining. The profits of mining were largely reinvested in further mining projects. This led to an increase in the value of the property of the mines but made little contribution to African development. A very large part of the profits were expatriated. There was little or no development of processing industries. The economy of Africa had been allowed to develop only in directions that suited the interests of the metropolitan countries. What was now needed was action by the new African governments.

Dr. Yudelman pointed out that the metropolitan powers had resisted rather than encouraged settlement in some parts of Africa, and *Professor Robinson* said that some of the published statistics of capital formation omitted the very substantial direct capital investment of Africans in agricultural improvement and in community development.

Professor Frankel, replying to the discussion, emphasized that it had been the burden of his paper to stress that it had taken a long time for Tropical Africa to progress as far as it had. With the best goodwill in the world and with all possible aid and technical assistance it would take the more backward areas of Africa a long time to reach even modest standards of living. Despite all its advantages as compared with the rest of Africa, the Union of South Africa was still very poor. Public investment had been, and would continue to be, essential. It provided the majority of the investment in infrastructure. The problem was not that of securing capital, which would be attracted by any country where there was economic activity ; the problem was rather that of re-creating human associations in a new way. Much depended on political stability. The history of South American revolutions and of their effects on economic development should be a warning to Africa. The number of African countries which could

442

immediately provide the conditions for rapid economic development was, he thought, small. He agreed with Dr. Skorov that private investment was not the only source of progress. He disagreed with Dr. Singer, if he was suggesting that capital had no marginal product in Africa. He did not think that Keynes's picture of a superfluity of saving was applicable to Africa. In general, he thought that economists should confine themselves to things as they were and not dream about the things they would like to see.

Chapter 16

CAPITAL AND CAPITAL SUPPLY IN RELATION TO THE DEVELOPMENT OF AFRICA [1]

BY

LEONARD RIST

Special Representative for Africa
of the International Bank for Reconstruction and Development

I. INTRODUCTION

THE major part of this paper is devoted to an analysis of the magnitude and forms of external economic assistance that has been flowing in recent years to Africa south of the Sahara. I have preferred to concentrate on this aspect of capital supply for two major reasons. In the first place, a stocktaking of the types and amounts of external financial resources available for the economic development of the countries in this area, seems to me to be particularly useful to African officials concerned with developmental problems. In the second place, we have only little detailed knowledge of domestic capital formation in many countries of the area. I have, however, brought together in the second part of this paper a number of considerations that are relevant to an analysis of future capital requirements of Tropical Africa.[2]

II. RECENT MAGNITUDES AND PATTERNS OF EXTERNAL ASSISTANCE

Need for Improvement of Information

At the outset I would like to stress that there are numerous difficulties in measuring the volume of external economic assistance

[1] The author wishes to acknowledge here the valuable assistance he received in preparing this paper from Mr. Marinus van der Mel and Mr. Badri Rao, both of the Economic Staff of the International Bank for Reconstruction and Development.
[2] Tropical Africa refers throughout to countries south of the Sahara (i.e. excluding Sahara) and north of the Union of South Africa (but including the United Kingdom High Commission Territories in South Africa, Ethiopia, and the Sudan).

flowing to Africa south of the Sahara ; they arise at several levels. Information provided by capital exporting countries is most commonly given in aggregates ; where the data are shown in some detail they usually refer to currency or political groups, such as 'Territoires d'Outre-Mer' or 'Rest of the Sterling Area', which cut across continental boundaries. Another major difficulty arises from conceptual differences : in some instances the data relate to investment assistance *per se* ; in others they include all kinds of expenditures, such as budgetary support and direct expenditures for current purposes. On a different level are difficulties caused by differences in accounting years, in the time periods covered by the data, and in the meaning of the figures themselves : sometimes they refer to actual expenditures and in other instances they might relate to 'commitments' or 'authorizations'. Again, where data on loans are concerned, they may be 'gross' or 'net' of repayments ; seldom, however, do the net data include other capital movements in the opposite direction.

I would, therefore, like to take this opportunity to stress the imperative need for a uniform system of periodic and detailed reporting on the international flow of economic assistance to underdeveloped countries.

Total Recent Flow of External Public Assistance

The figures given in Table 1 are based on data published by the United Nations. The major advantage of these data over those available from other sources is that they provide information in respect of several individual countries south of the Sahara. However, they are subject to the important qualification that they have a considerable downward bias because of limited coverage ; for instance, they are exclusive of certain amounts of assistance which are quite large but cannot be broken down by countries.[1]

The figures in Table 1 represent identifiable receipts of foreign public economic assistance by the countries specified. They take into account grants and loans with a maturity of at least five years, and generally refer to actual disbursements net of repayments. Some aid to cover current expenditures is, presumably, also included but only to a very limited extent.

[1] The OEEC has recently published an important study entitled *The Flow of Financial Resources to Countries in Course of Economic Development 1956–59*. In this study also an effort has been made to collect data on foreign economic assistance on a uniform basis. A number of references will be made to the study in this paper later. Unfortunately, the study is of only limited usefulness to assess the amounts of external public assistance to Tropical Africa, since it does not provide detailed data for that area.

TABLE 1

EXTERNAL PUBLIC ECONOMIC ASSISTANCE TO AFRICAN COUNTRIES AND TERRITORIES SOUTH OF THE SAHARA, 1954–8 AND 1957–9

(Cumulative ; U.S. $ million equivalent)

	Bilateral Aid		Multilateral Aid		Total	Total Per Year
	Grants	Loans	Grants	Loans		
Angola { 1954–8	—	0·2	0·2	—	0·4	0·1
{ 1957–9	—	0·1	0·1	—	0·2	—
British East Africa † { 1954–8	83·3	53·6	2·1	15·6	154·6	31·0
{ 1957–9	40·5	11·1	1·7	—	53·3	26·6
British Somaliland { 1954–8	9·6	—	—	—	9·6	1·9
{ 1957–9 ‡	—	—	—	—	—	—
British High Commis- { 1954–8	9·4	12·9	0·4	—	22·7	4·5
sion Territories § { 1957–9	7·5	1·6	0·1	—	9·2	4·6
British West Africa ‖ { 1954–8	49·2	3·6	2·1	—	54·9	11·0
{ 1957–9	26·1	0·4	1·0	—	27·5	5·5
Cameroun { 1954–8	76·8	16·3	—	—	93·1	18·6
{ 1957–9	28·7	– 3·4	0·2	—	25·5	12·8
Congo (Léopoldville) { 1954–8 *	—	36·8	0·2	29·7	66·7	13·5
{ 1957–9	—	—	—	9·4	9·4	4·7
Ethiopia { 1954–8	17·3	4·6	2·7	3·1	27·7	5·5
{ 1957–9	13·1	0·5	1·5	1·8	16·9	8·5
Former French Equa- { 1954–8	97·1	13·2	0·5	—	110·8	22·2
torial Africa { 1957–9	30·3	8·5	0·3	—	39·1	19·5
Former French West { 1954–8 ¶	191·2	63·8	3·1	5·6	263·7	52·7
Africa { 1957–9	80·1	3·4	1·0	– 0·6	83·9	41·9
Ghana { 1954–8	8·7	1·6	0·7	—	11·0	2·2
{ 1957–9	3·8	—	0·8	—	4·6	2·3
Guinea { 1954–8	—	—	—	—	—	—
{ 1957–9	4·2	0·6	0·2	—	5·0	2·5
Liberia { 1954–8	8·2	5·8	1·4	—	15·4	3·1
{ 1957–9	4·7	10·6	0·8	—	16·1	8·0
Malagasy Republic ** { 1954–8	62·5	21·4	—	—	83·9	16·8
{ 1957–9	27·9	2·0	—	—	29·9	15·0
Mozambique { 1954–8	—	12·5	—	—	12·5	2·5
{ 1957–9	—	—	—	—	—	—
Rhodesia and Nyasaland { 1954–8	15·8	51·6	0·2	38·9	106·5	21·3
{ 1957–9	4·2	– 12·1	0·1	18·8	11·0	5·5
Ruanda-Urundi { 1954–8	—	—	—	—	—	—
{ 1957–9	—	12·0	—	—	12·0	6·0
Somalia { 1954–8	29·2	—	0·6	—	29·8	6·0
{ 1957–9	16·6	—	0·8	—	17·4	8·7
Sudan { 1954–8	0·3	—	1·5	—	1·8	0·4
{ 1957–9	5·8	5·0	1·2	14·5	26·5	13·3
Total { 1954–8	658·6	297·9	15·7	92·9	1065·1	215·0
{ 1957–9	293·5	40·3	9·8	43·9	387·5	193·8

Notes.—The figures are for fiscal years which in several cases correspond to th calendar year ; they cover grants and loans net of repayments and generally cover fiv years in the period 1954–8 and two years in the period 1957–9 commencing July 1, 195 and ending June 30, 1959. Data for the years 1957–9 are, in many cases, incomplete.

* Including data for Ruanda-Urundi.
† Kenya, Uganda, Tanganyika, Zanzibar, and Pemba.
‡ 1957–9 data for British Somaliland are included in the figures shown for British Eas Africa for those years.
§ Basutoland, Bechuanaland, and Swaziland.   ‖ Gambia, Nigeria, and Sierra Leon
¶ Including data for Guinea.   ** Including Comoro Islands.

Sources : For 1954–8, Table 159 of the *UN Statistical Yearbook 1959*. For 1957–ᵀ Table of the UN's *International Economic Assistance to the Less Developed Countries*, 196

On the basis of these figures one might draw the following conclusions. First, external assistance to African countries south of the Sahara in the period 1953/4 to 1958/9 has averaged, on a net basis, some $205 million equivalent annually ; total public external assistance to Tropical Africa appears not to have changed a great deal during this period.[1] Secondly, bilateral assistance has been preponderant during this period, amounting to roughly nine-tenths of the total. Bilateral assistance went mostly to countries which historically have had close ties with France and Britain respectively, the former in total receiving roughly twice as much as the latter. In the third place it would appear that the share of multilateral assistance in total public external assistance flowing to the area has increased slightly during the period considered, the annual average of identifiable multilateral assistance rising from some $22 million in 1953/4–1957/8 to around $26·5 million in 1957/8–1958/9.

It must, however, be emphasized that the data underlying these conclusions are tenuous and are based on the specific concept of foreign economic assistance underlying Table 1. Quite frequently, the concept as used by donor countries has a much wider coverage. French data, for example, include items such as current administrative expenditures and advances for balancing the budget, most of which apparently have not been taken into account in the UN computations. The UN has included only territorial expenditures of the Fonds d'Investissement pour le Développement Économique et Social des Territoires d'Outre-Mer (FIDES), to be referred to later. But Metropolitan France is known to have undertaken large expenditures both under the so-called general section of FIDES and outside FIDES in these countries. The non-inclusion of such assistance greatly understates the French contribution ; indeed, roughly one-third of French public economic assistance in 1954–8 consisted of either current expenditures, which cannot be readily broken down on a country-by-country basis, or expenditures on general programmes benefitting both North and Tropical Africa.

The data developed by the UN, therefore, need to be set against those that emerge from a study of the bilateral contributions as reported by the major capital exporting countries. Accordingly, the following sections of Part I are devoted to a rather detailed analysis of foreign economic assistance contributed by major countries and international agencies. The treatment is largely in terms of the

[1] At least on the basis of the limited coverage of data for external public economic assistance underlying the UN computations. As we shall see later, individual country sources (notably those of France) would seem to indicate an increase in the total flow of aid in the course of this period. Part of this increase, presumably, also benefited Tropical Africa.

447

institutional machinery through which such assistance is channelled.

On the basis of data supplied by contributors, it would appear that countries in Tropical Africa received external economic assistance in 1957 and 1958 in the order of some $450–500 million annually. Although data based on contributions are seldom strictly comparable, either between countries or with data based on receipts (because of lags in reporting), the estimated figure of $450–500 million is very much out of line with the $205 million per annum shown to have been received by Tropical African countries in the seven years prior to 1960, according to Table 1. I suggest that this only underlines the need for better reporting on this subject.

III. BILATERAL PUBLIC ASSISTANCE

France

France has been by far the most important contributor to the external financing and economic development of African countries. The French approach to its financial responsibilities, in respect to these countries, historically implied a close solidarity between metropolitan and overseas finances.

Metropolitan assistance took a variety of forms, such as straightforward grants to cover current public expenditures, advances for balancing the budgets, grants and loans for investment purposes, direct participation in the capital of enterprises financed out of public funds, technical assistance, and the provision of administrative and other personnel whose costs were borne by the *French Treasury*.

According to a recent OEEC study,[1] covering the period 1956–9, the net amount of the French contribution to economic development in the Overseas Franc Area, including the Overseas Departments (DOM [2]), was at an annual average rate of about $775 million equivalent (see Table 2). This represents a substantial increase over previous years ; it has been estimated that the total French contribution in the four years 1952 through 1956 was at around $550 million per annum.[3]

Somewhat more than 60 per cent, corresponding at an average annual rate of about $490 million equivalent, of French public expenditures in the Overseas Franc Area has been in respect of the

[1] See (footnote 1, p. 445.)
[2] Départements d'Outre-Mer.
[3] On the basis of the Annual Reports of the Fonds de Développement Économique et Social. Part of the increase may be due to differences in coverage ; but there appears to be no doubt that the rise was a real one.

financing of investment; almost 40 per cent (about $285 million equivalent on average) was for current purposes (*vide* Table 2).

TABLE 2

TOTAL NET PUBLIC DIRECT EXPENDITURES, GRANTS, AND LOANS
IN THE OVERSEAS FRANC AREA, 1956–9

(U.S. $ million equivalent)

	1956	1957	1958	1959
	Disbursements			
Direct expenditures and grants for current purposes	203	274	510	302
Tax receipts from overseas departments	[38]	38	36	33
Net current expenditures	[165]	236	474	269
Direct expenditures and grants for investment purposes	285	344	310	393
Loans for investment purposes	223	257	116	176
Amortization receipts	[40]	23	41	42
Net investment loans *	[183]	234	75	134
Total net official contribution	[633]	814	859	796

[ ] Figures in brackets are estimates.

* No allowance has been made for French public long-term borrowing in the rest of the franc area, *e.g.* through the sales of government bonds and two-year treasury bills.

Note.—For the conversion of the original French franc figures into United States dollars the following exchange rates have been used : 1 U.S. dollar = 3·50 N.F. in 1956, 3·75 N.F. in 1957, 4·20 N.F. in 1958, and 4·94 N.F. in 1959.

Source : OEEC, *The Flow of Financial Resources* . . . op. cit. p. 51.

It should be emphasized that the figures cited above refer to assistance by Metropolitan France to the Overseas Franc Area as a whole. Unfortunately, it is not possible to give data on the same conceptual basis for Africa south of the Sahara alone. A rough estimate would be that Franc Area countries in Africa south of Sahara (*i.e.* excluding Algeria-Sahara, Morocco, and Tunisia) annually received in the period 1956–8 an average of $350 million equivalent (gross), for current as well as investment purposes, from Metropolitan France. This would roughly correspond to 40 per cent of French overall expenditures for current and investment purposes in the Overseas Franc Area (Table 3).

As was remarked already, the French public contribution to economic development in Africa has been much larger than that of any other country. This is not only true in absolute terms, but also in relation to gross national product. On the basis of the data on external assistance provided in the recent OEEC study, it can be calculated that bilateral public external economic assistance provided

449

TABLE 3

Gross Public Direct Expenditures, Grants, and Loans
in the Overseas Franc Area, 1956–8

(U.S. $ million equivalent)

	1956		1957		1958		1959	
	Total Overseas Franc Area	Community Countries and Overseas Territories excl. Algeria-Sahara	Total Overseas Franc Area	Community Countries and Overseas Territories excl. Algeria-Sahara	Total Overseas Franc Area	Community Countries and Overseas Territories excl. Algeria-Sahara	Total Overseas Franc Area	Community Countries and Overseas Territories excl. Algeria-Sahara
Direct expenditures and grants for current purposes	203	61	274	109	510	221	302	135
Direct expenditures and grants for investment purposes	285	183	344	194	310	137	393	106
Loans for investment purposes	223	53	257	77	116	38	n.a.	n.a.
Total	711	297	875	380	936	396	n.a.	n.a.

n.a.: not available.

N.B.—The Overseas Franc Area includes the French Overseas Departments (DOM), Algeria and the Sahara, Tunisia and Morocco and Vietnam, Laos, and Cambodia in addition to the French Overseas Territories, independent members of the French Community, and Guinea.

Sources: Comité Monétaire de la zone franc, *La Zone franc en 1958*, and OEEC, *The Flow of Financial Resources* . . . op. cit. p. 52.

to the entire outside world by France during the two years 1958 and 1959 was around 2 per cent of GNP at factor cost, whereas the corresponding percentages for the U.S. and the U.K. during these years were roughly 0·6 per cent.[1] Even if the contribution to Algeria and the Sahara, amounting to roughly a third of the total in 1958, is excluded, the French effort would still appear larger than that of the others.

French public external assistance in the form of current expenditures has been provided directly by the French Treasury. The various kinds of expenditures for investment purposes have been channelled through special institutions. The institutional framework for the financing of investment expenditures in Overseas France, which has shown a gradual evolution since the end of the Second World War, will be discussed briefly in the following pages.

In 1946, pursuant to the law of April 30, 1946, relative to the French public investment programme, the Fonds d'Investissement pour le Développement Économique et Social des Territoires d'Outre-Mer (FIDES) was established; its operations were linked with those of the Caisse Centrale de la France d'Outre-Mer (CCFOM), an agency established in 1941 for note issue and for making advances to local treasuries in the French Overseas Territories (TOM). CCFOM became the executing agency for FIDES.

FIDES' operations have consisted of two parts — general and local — and have been financed by grants from the Metropolitan Treasury and to a small extent by contributions made by the TOM out of their local budgets ; in addition, FIDES has drawn on loans extended to it by CCFOM.

The operations of FIDES have covered a wide field of both interregional projects and projects of direct interest to individual TOM. Projects of interest to the Metropole and to groups of 'Territoires', such as general projects of agricultural, mining, and hydro-electric research, came under the purview of the so-called 'general section' of FIDES. All such expenditures were financed wholly by the Metropole through grants ; because of their regional significance it is difficult to allocate these expenditures to individual 'Territoires' on the basis of benefits received by them.

Investment expenditures on agreed programmes of special interest to the TOM and falling within the scope of the 'local sections' of

[1] The percentages given here are, of course, affected by the coverage of the concept 'public external economic assistance'. There is no doubt, however, that on the basis of a more narrow concept than that adopted in the OEEC study, the contribution of France would also be the highest. For instance, in a recent official U.S. publication (U.S. Senate Executive Report No. 1 of March 8, 1961) French public assistance to low-income countries in the period 1956–9 is estimated at 1·6 per cent of GNP, against 0·5 per cent for the U.S. and 0·4 per cent for the U.K.

FIDES were financed jointly by the Metropole and by the TOM. The latter's share of the programmed costs was initially fixed at 45 per cent ; however, to the extent that the TOM could not meet their share of the contribution, they could borrow from the CCFOM. The TOM contribution having progressively been reduced to 10 per cent, virtually the whole amount of programmed public development expenditures in the TOM was met from Metropolitan public funds, as the CCFOM itself drew its resources from the French Treasury.

The magnitude of FIDES operations can be demonstrated by the fact that total disbursements since its inception in the former TOM, Togo, and Cameroon, under the 'general' and 'local' sections, have amounted to Fr. 526·8 billion [1] as of the end of 1958. Disbursements in 1957 and 1958 alone amounted to Fr. 113·1 billion. In dollar terms, 1957–8 expenditures corresponded to some $290 million equivalent ; of this, approximately $70 million equivalent were incurred on 'general section' projects and the remainder on projects of direct interest to the TOM.

In addition to directly financing the costs of 'general section' projects, the Metropole has also participated in the capital of numerous 'sociétés d'économie mixte' which operate in a wide variety of fields of activity, *e.g.*, food production, mining, and electric power. The capital of these institutions consists of public capital, contributed by both the Metropole and the TOM, as well as private capital. Precise data on such capital assistance are not readily available.

CCFOM also has made loans on its own account besides operating as the FIDES channel for long-term developmental loans and assisting in the establishment of development banks in the rest of the Franc Zone. These operations were financed from loans and advances out of a special fund of the French Treasury, and were made for investment purposes to public agencies as well as to public, semi-public, and private enterprises in the TOM. As of the end of 1958 the cumulative total of disbursements on loans made by CCFOM on its own account to the former TOM, Togo, and Cameroon was some Fr. 120 billion; in 1958 alone, and in dollar terms, the amount was some $60 million. The terms and conditions of CCFOM loans vary from case to case. Generally loans to public authorities are of longer maturity (10 to 20 years) and carry lower interest (about $2\frac{1}{2}$ per cent) than for private borrowers (7 to 10 years at about $5\frac{1}{2}$ per cent).

In March 1959, following the independence of most of the French

---

[1] Because of the several changes in the exchange rate for the franc, conversion into dollar terms of cumulative totals is not meaningful. All figures shown in local currency here are in terms of the old franc. Where the figures have been converted, conversion factors have been applied as indicated in table 2.

Overseas Territories in Africa within the political framework of the 'Communauté', special agreements within France including the following changes in the institutional machinery for foreign aid were effected. In the first place, FIDES was replaced by the Fonds d'Aide et de Coopération (FAC), but only in so far as operations relative to the newly independent countries Cameroon and Togo were concerned. A special office was established with the French Under-Secretary ('Secrétaire d'État') concerned with the affairs of the States of the 'Communauté' as head of the organization.[1]

Unlike FIDES, its predecessor, which had concerned itself only with investment programming and financing, FAC covers all forms of external aid and the provision of experts and technical assistance by France; the extension of budgetary subsidies when necessary also lies within the scope of FAC activities. Requests for aid have to emanate from the countries concerned on their own initiative and have to be related to an overall programme of development showing clearly how the programme is to be financed. FAC aid is then granted from purely Metropolitan sources on the basis of bilateral treaties between France and the member country concerned.

The total amount of investment assistance authorized by FAC to the members of the French Community and Cameroon and Togo in 1959 was the equivalent of $70 million; of this, about 60 per cent was for infrastructure investments, some 10 per cent for agricultural development, and the remainder for general research and social projects. The $70 million of FAC assistance does not, however, reveal the whole amount of economic and social investment assistance received by these countries in 1959, since an additional $60 million had been extended to them in that year through FIDES prior to the cessation of its operations; nevertheless, the level of the French contribution to these countries in 1959 was substantially below that of 1958.

Along with the changes in the structure of the aid programme, the CCFOM was transformed into the ' Caisse Centrale de Coopération Économique' (CCCE), and the execution of the FAC programme was entrusted to it. Like its predecessor, CCCE also may extend, out of its own resources, medium and long-term loans for the economic development of the States of the Community; only rarely, however, will it assist through direct participation in the capital of enterprises.[2]

---

[1] In June 1961 this special office was changed into a 'Ministry of Cooperation', concerned with all economic and financial matters relating to independent countries which had previously been Overseas Territories. Political matters have been transferred to the Ministry of Foreign Affairs.

[2] CCCE loan commitments in 1959 to Tropical Africa (including Madagascar) were approximately $41 million equivalent.

One other form of assistance that deserves mentioning is the guarantee given by the Metropole to loans issued on the French capital market or abroad. In the past it was extended to members of the French Union, but subsequent to the changes in its structure, it is now limited to obligations raised by dependent territories.

United Kingdom

The United Kingdom has traditionally followed the policy of assisting the economic development of its colonies and other countries dependent on it for external financing, through opening the London capital market to overseas issues and through direct private investment. Public grant assistance has historically been of minor significance.

The U.K. has, over the years, developed an extensive institutional framework for public assistance to its colonies and to Commonwealth independent countries ; public bilateral assistance to all areas combined has risen from an average of $140 million equivalent in fiscal years 1952/3 to 1955/6 to an estimated $330 million in 1959/60.

Recognizing its special responsibilities in regard to its colonies, and the need for a special stimulus to the colonies for undertaking capital projects which private enterprise could not be expected to finance, the U.K. enacted in 1929 the *Colonial Development and Welfare Act* whereunder both grant and loan assistance were to be provided for public developmental programmes undertaken by the colonies. The scope of the Act, modest in the beginning, was subsequently enlarged through a series of amendments.

In 1945, for the first time, the U.K.'s commitments were put on a relatively long-term basis through the provision of a total of £120 million (including £20 million unexpended from the 1940 allocations) for the period 1945–56. This figure was subsequently revised and the operative life of the Act was extended. Altogether £220 million had been earmarked for Colonial Developmental Assistance through 1960, by which time a number of colonies were expected to have attained independence within the Commonwealth ; of this amount £45·5 million had been unexpended as of March 31, 1959.

The actual flow of assistance under the CD&W Acts has risen sharply over the years ; expenditures in the period 1951/2–1955/6 were 75 per cent above those in the period 1946/7–1951/2, and the annual rate in the three years 1956/7 through 1958/9 was again some 25 per cent above that in the preceding five years.

The total amount of funds committed under the CD&W Acts, as of March 31, 1959, was £207 million, almost all of which was in grants. Of this amount, assistance flowing into countries south of the Sahara amounted to some £117 million ; Nigeria alone received about one-third of this total. About one-quarter of the assistance going to countries south of the Sahara has been for communications, — primarily roads — and a like amount for agriculture, including related services. The remaining half was for social services with education and health accounting for the largest share.

In April 1959 the operative life of the Act was further extended to March 31, 1964, and a further sum of £95 million was provided. The annual limit on funds expendable in any single year (£20 million) was cancelled and provision was made for £100 million in *Exchequer loans* (not more than £25 million in any one year) for approved colonial development programmes.

The £100 million of Exchequer loans was provided under the amended Act to enable colonial governments to be assured of a minimum of loan finance 'at the appropriate time' ; they are not intended to be a substitute for loans on the London capital market.[1] Indeed, it is implicit that a colonial government will first seek accommodation from the market on reasonable terms. Exchequer loans carry an interest rate $\frac{1}{4}$ per cent higher than that on loans to public corporations, and the terms are determined by individual circumstances ; normally they will not exceed thirty years. In 1960/1, for example, loans to Nigeria and Kenya were for twenty-five years at $6\frac{1}{2}$ and $5\frac{7}{8}$ per cent respectively. Altogether, loans totalling £17·5 million were made to the colonies during fiscal 1959/60 ; in addition, a loan of £3 million had been made to Nigeria in September 1960, before it became independent.

On attaining independence within the Commonwealth, colonies cease to be entitled to CD&W assistance, but to the extent that there are unspent balances from previous allocations, they may continue to draw on them.

To supplement colonial assistance channelled through CD&W, the U.K. established in 1948 the Colonial Development Corporation (CDC). CDC was authorized to borrow £150 million at long-term (of which £130 million was in government funds) and £10 million at short-term. It operates on a commercial basis in association with private interests or colonial governments in a variety of fields, particularly in utilities and agriculture, mining, and forestry which altogether absorbed some 90 per cent of CDC's commitments outstanding at the end of 1959.

As of December 31, 1959, £96 million in all had been committed

[1] Between 1954/5 and 1959/60 a total of some £60 million was raised on the London market by the colonies.

towards loans and equity participation in 88 projects. This may be compared with a total of £48 million for 56 projects at the end of 1954. Commitments in respect of projects in countries south of the Sahara were at £63·5 million as of the end of 1959 (two-thirds of the total) ; actual disbursements amounted to £37·7 million.[1]

In addition to these various kinds of assistance to colonies, the U.K. provides budgetary assistance, under the *Colonial Services Vote*, for meeting current expenditures, as well as for emergency relief. This type of assistance has averaged some £20 million in recent years ; almost all of it is in grants-in-aid.

For independent countries within the Commonwealth, the U.K. provides grant aid and technical assistance under the *Commonwealth Services Vote* as well as long-term developmental loans provided from Consolidated Fund sources under the authority of the act setting up the Export Credit Guarantees Department. The decision to make these loans for 'programmes of sound economic development which cannot be financed in other ways' was taken at the 1959 Common-wealth Economic Conference.[2] Terms vary from seven to twenty years and the interest rate is governed by that which the U.K. government would itself have to pay for similar loans. As of March 1961, a total of £125 million in loans had been made ; the only country in Africa to receive such assistance was Nigeria (£12 million).

In the field of technical assistance, the U.K. provides a wide range of services ; where the colonies are concerned these are pro-vided through the Colonial Office.

Belgium

Belgium's interest in the development of low-income countries has centred primarily on the Congo and the trust territory of Ruanda-Urundi. Belgian economic assistance on public account to the Congo till very recently consisted largely of its guarantee in respect of issues on foreign capital markets by the Congo and Ruanda-Urundi. According to the Banque Centrale du Congo et du Ruanda-Urundi, the total of such issues as of the end of 1959 was the equivalent of some $160 million, of which $104·8 million was from the World Bank.

In addition, Belgium has provided assistance in support of over-seas budgets, consisting of grants and interest-free loans and advances with no fixed repayment terms. During most of the 1950s the amounts involved were rather small. Since 1959 the outflow of Belgian public capital rose rather sharply, as a result of financial

[1] Colonial Development Corporation, Report and Accounts for the Year 1959.
[2] Assistance from the United Kingdom for Overseas Development, Cmnd. 974, March 1960.

difficulties in the Congo. During the period 1956–9 the total of such assistance to the Congo and Ruanda-Urundi amounted to about $65 million equivalent. For 1960, $50 million were authorized in respect of the Congo alone, although it is not known to what extent this amount has been utilized.

Portugal and Italy

Among the other metropolitan countries which have provided public external assistance to African territories are Portugal and Italy ; their contributions have been relatively modest. Portuguese economic assistance consists almost wholly of long-term loans for financing the development plans of Angola and Mozambique. The total of loans and grants provided during 1956–9 was about $6 million net per annum. Italy has provided grants of some $32 million equivalent in 1956–9 to Italian Somaliland.

United States

Despite the large contributions that the U.S. has made to economic development abroad, it is only relatively recently that its assistance to African countries has begun to assume importance. For example, whereas the total amount of public economic assistance to Africa in the post-war years through June 30, 1954 amounted only to $96 million, it was $669 million in the six years ending June 30, 1960.

Somewhat more than one-third of the total in respect of Africa ($272 million) has gone to countries and territories south of the Sahara in roughly equal proportions of grants ($145·7 million) and loans ($126·7 million).

U.S. foreign aid has heretofore been based on a series of legislative measures undertaken at different times and for different purposes. The Mutual Security Act, the Agricultural Trade Development and Assistance Act (PL 480), and the Export-Import Bank Act, cover different programmes and their administration is diffused. A bill has recently been placed before the U.S. Congress with a view to centralizing the foreign aid activities of the U.S. government in a single agency and to putting them on a five-year basis. Emphasis will be on long-term development loans (fifty years), at low or no rates of interest, repayable in dollars as the primary instrument of external assistance.

The *Mutual Security Act* covered economic as well as military assistance. Appropriations to carry out the programme of activities envisaged in the Mutual Security Act are made annually. Except for developmental loans which are administered by the Development Loan Fund (DLF), the International Cooperation Administration (ICA) is responsible for the bulk of foreign economic assistance, including technical co-operation, under the Mutual Security Act. In addition, ICA, with some exceptions, administers loans and grants made out of the local currency proceeds from sales of surplus U.S. agricultural commodities under PL 480.

The *PL 480 programme* consists of three types of activity. Under Title I, U.S. agricultural surplus commodities held by the Commodity Credit Corporation are sold against local currencies to friendly foreign countries. A small part of these local currencies is reserved for the use of the U.S. in the country concerned ; the rest is used for loans and grants. These loans and grants are, as mentioned above, administered by ICA, but the actual sales of the surplus commodities are outside the scope of the Mutual Security Programme ; such sales could occasionally be made under barter agreements whereby the U.S. accepts in payment commodities which are in short supply in the United States.

Titles II and III of PL 480 relate exclusively to free gifts of surplus agricultural commodities for emergency relief, economic development, and donations to voluntary relief agencies.

So far PL 480 has been only of limited importance to African countries south of the Sahara ; as of June 30, 1960, total PL 480 assistance to this area amounted to about $12 million, mostly for emergency relief.

The *Development Loan Fund (DLF)* was established in 1957 with its capital made available by the Congress without fiscal year limitation ; repayments and earnings become part of its capital structure. DLF is concerned solely with under-developed countries and is intended to assist them through loans that can be repaid in 'local' currency under appropriate circumstances. The Development Loan Fund is the official channel for loans under the Mutual Security Programme.

As of December 31, 1960, DLF loans to countries south of the Sahara amounted to $23·4 million (of which: Ethiopia $2·5 ; Liberia $3·2 ; Nigeria $3·8 ; Somalia $2·0 ; Sudan $10·0 ; and Tanganyika $1·9 million). Typical projects financed are textile mills in Ethiopia and Sudan, telecommunications and a sawmill in Liberia, warehouse construction in Nigeria, and agricultural and industrial development in Somalia.

The DLF is required under its statute to finance specific projects and programmes which contribute to the economic growth of 'less-developed free countries', and where countries 'demonstrate a clear willingness to take sound self-help measures'. It is authorized to lend to foreign governments, public and private enterprises, as well as to financial institutions. Until recently, its loan proceeds were freely disposable, but lately they have been tied to U.S. exports. The terms and conditions of DLF loans are individually determined. Ordinarily, loans financing economic overhead type of projects bear a lower rate (about $3\frac{1}{2}$ per cent) than those financing productive ventures ; in the latter case, the rate corresponds to that charged by the Export-Import Bank of Washington (about $5\frac{3}{4}$ to $6\frac{3}{4}$ per cent).

The *Export-Import Bank* was established in 1934 with the primary purpose of fostering U.S. foreign trade ; its loans are for the financing of purchases of U.S. products by foreigners. These loans are repayable in dollars. The Bank gives short-term credits to finance commodity purchases, balance of payments loans, longer term loans ranging from five to ten years for specific projects and up to twenty-five years for infrastructure projects and development loans. The terms of Export-Import Bank loans are individually determined ; the interest rate charged depends on what it would have to pay the U.S. Treasury for similar accommodation and generally is lower for loans to governments and government entities than on loans to private borrowers.

The Export-Import Bank had extended $80 million in loans with a maturity of five years or more for developmental projects in regions south of the Sahara as of June 30, 1960. Of this amount $40·1 million went to Liberia for a variety of projects, *e.g.* highway construction, electric power, iron-ore mining, etc., $27·4 million to Ethiopia for aviation, and $12·5 million to Mozambique for railway construction.

Germany

Among the leading industrialized countries Germany is potentially an important source of external capital for countries in course of development. Heretofore, the scale of its operations in countries south of the Sahara has been negligible, although the gross outflow of public capital to other under-developed countries in the period 1956–9 averaged some $195 million equivalent annually. This was composed of $75 million in reparations and indemnifications, about an equal amount of consolidation credits, $35 million in new credits, and the rest in grants. The *Kreditanstalt für Wiederaufbau* has been the principal channel through which public loans are extended ; it derives its funds both from the counterpart funds accrued under the European Recovery Programme and from the capital market. The terms of KW

459

loans vary from four to twenty years ; interest rates on recent loans have varied between $5\frac{1}{4}$ and 7 per cent, depending on loan maturity.

The emphasis in the German foreign assistance programme has hitherto been on private capital and commercial type of financing, with the government extending guarantees and refinancing facilities. Recently, however, the Federal Parliament approved a two-year programme of public foreign economic assistance covering 1961 and 1962. Of a total of some $1·25 billion equivalent, 85 per cent has been earmarked for bilateral aid. Seventy per cent of the expenditure will be financed out of Federal and State budgets.

Sino-Soviet Bloc

Since 1954, when the U.S.S.R. embarked on its programme for assisting countries outside the Communist Bloc, there has been a very sharp increase in the flow of assistance from the Sino-Soviet Bloc to under-developed countries in other parts of the world. The total volume of credits and grants for economic purposes alone is estimated to have amounted to the equivalent of some $3·2 billion as of June 30, 1960.[1] Some 75 per cent of this total is accounted for by the U.S.S.R. Although only about 20 per cent of the aid committed has actually been used, indications are that the rate of disbursement will rise sharply.

The duration of credits made by the U.S.S.R. in most cases is twelve years ; interest rate charged is uniformly $2\frac{1}{2}$ per cent.[2] The credits cover both the cost of prospecting and research, which are invariably done by Soviet technicians, and the cost of capital equipment supplied by the U.S.S.R.

The share of African countries south of the Sahara in the total to date is relatively insignificant. So far only three countries have obtained credits and grants from the Bloc — Ethiopia $114 million, Guinea $42 million, and Ghana $3 million — making a total of $159 million, of which some $150 million was in credits. It must, however, be noted that Soviet interest in African countries south of the Sahara is of very recent origin ; indeed, the whole amount of $159 million was extended in the fiscal year ending June 30, 1960. It may therefore be expected that the flow of assistance will continue in future. For example, China (Peking) is reported [3] to be considering an interest-free loan of some $25 million to Guinea ; Ghana con-

[1] *Report to Congress on the Mutual Security Program for fiscal 1960*, U.S. Department of State.
[2] 'L'Aide soviétique aux pays sous-développés', *Notes et études documentaires, La Documentation française*, No. 2760, March 13, 1961.
[3] *Barclay's Bank Review*, February 1961.

cluded a trade pact with the U.S.S.R. in August 1960, under which it will receive long-term credits of some $40 million.

Other Bilateral Assistance

The above-mentioned instances of bilateral assistance all relate to financing of Africa by countries situated outside the continent. Over the recent months there have been some cases where countries geographically located in Africa have granted credits and loans to other African countries. Details of these operations are not always available. One loan, however, which has quite recently been announced, seems to deserve special mention. In June 1961 the U.A.R. granted to the Republic of Mali a loan for the equivalent of US$17 million, repayable in seven years at $2\frac{1}{2}$ per cent interest. The Republic of Mali is also reported this year to have received short-term accommodation in the amount of some $11 million equivalent from Ghana.

IV. MULTILATERAL ASSISTANCE

In addition to the major sources of bilateral assistance mentioned above, several international organizations exist for providing financial and technical assistance to under-developed countries.

UN Technical Assistance

The UN provides technical assistance through a network of agencies such as the United Nations Educational, Social, and Cultural Organization, the United Nations Children's Fund, the World Health Organization, and the Food and Agricultural Organization. The UN also provides experts under the programme for the 'Provision of Operational Executive and Administrative Personnel' (OPEX). Experts assigned to member countries under this programme function as employees of the requesting government over the period of their assignment, which is normally one year. The technical assistance activities of the UN are under the overall supervision of the Technical Assistance Board, and are financed out of member contributions to the UN. The number of African countries which have received assistance in this form is quite considerable.

Special Fund of the UN

The scope of the technical assistance programme of the UN was further expanded through the establishment of the Special Fund.

The Fund commenced operations on January 1, 1959, and participates in the financing of various activities, such as resource survey and advanced technical training. In performing its functions it draws on the services of other UN specialized agencies including the World Bank, and works in close collaboration with the UN Technical Assistance Board. The Fund is not a loan-making agency ; it merely shares in the cost of pre-investment surveys out of funds contributed by member governments. As of the end of 1960, it had participated in eleven projects in African countries, costing an aggregate of some $7·7 million, as follows (figures in millions of dollars) : Ethiopia (1·4), Ghana (0·4), Guinea (0·4), Liberia (1·0), Nigeria (1·8), Somalia (0·9), Sudan (0·8), Togo (0·7), and Uganda (0·3).

International Bank for Reconstruction and Development (World Bank)

The International Bank for Reconstruction and Development (World Bank) is a specialized agency established in 1946 with the objective of assisting in the long-range balanced economic growth of its member countries. As of December 31, 1960, it had 66 members contributing a total of $19·9 billion in capital subscriptions. Of this, however, only $1·99 billion constitutes a cash subscription. The remainder represents a guarantee fund and serves as a backing for the bond issues that the Bank periodically floats to replenish its loanable funds ; the amount of its funded debt outstanding, as of December 31, 1960, was $2·16 billion. A third major financial source consists of funds put up by other investors who may either directly participate in a loan at the time it is made or buy out of the Bank's portfolio of loans ; by so doing not only does the Bank increase its lendable resources but it also encourages the flow of private foreign investments in the form of loans as required under its charter.

Indeed, the Bank tries to stimulate private foreign investment in several ways ; apart from the participations already mentioned, it undertakes under appropriate circumstances a joint operation whereby a Bank loan is linked with a bond issue by the borrowing government.

The Bank lends to member governments and their agencies ; it may also lend to private entities in member countries with the guarantee of the government of the country concerned.

The World Bank operates as a banker of last resort ; it has to be satisfied that the borrower is unable otherwise to obtain the needed finance on reasonable terms. It finances only part of the total costs of a project, *i.e.* usually the foreign exchange component of such costs. The Bank normally finances only specific projects; the selection of projects is based on a careful study of priorities within the framework of development programmes, where such programmes exist.

The bulk of its financing is in respect of infrastructure projects. Of some $5·5 billion in loans through December 31, 1960, over 30 per cent was for electric power. Loans for transportation accounted for roughly another 30 per cent. About 15 per cent has gone to finance industrial projects. Most of the loans have been made to governments and public entities, but in the field of manufacturing and mining the Bank has lent only to private enterprise in the belief that these activities had best be left to private initative and management. All these loans must be government guaranteed.

As of December 31, 1960, the Bank had lent a total of $515·1 million to countries in Africa south of the Sahara. By far the largest amounts were to Rhodesia and Nyasaland ($146·6 million) and the Belgian Congo ($120·0 million). Actual disbursements on total loans to Africa south of the Sahara amounted to $333·8 million. The largest single loan made in Africa is the $80 million credit to the Federal Power Board of Rhodesia and Nyasaland in 1956, for the Kariba hydro-electric project. Last year another large loan of $66 million was made to the Société Anonyme des Mines de Fer de Mauritanie. The loan is to finance the purchase of mining equipment and services, construction of a 420-mile railway, and building of a new port at Port Etienne; total cost of the completed project is estimated at $190 million.

In 1960 the Bank made a loan of $5·6 million to the British Colony and Protectorate of Kenya for agriculture. Despite its modest size, it is one of the most interesting of the Bank's recent operations. The loan is not linked to any particular project but is intended to finance a government programme (The Swynnerton Plan) to develop African agriculture and thus to raise the living standards of African farmers. The programme calls for the improvement of an extensive system of roads linking farms with marketing centres, the provision of agricultural extension services, education, and water supply, co-operatives for farming, etc.

A similar loan of $5·6 million equivalent was made to the Federation of Rhodesia and Nyasaland in April 1960 for the development of African farming in Southern Rhodesia.

An important aspect of Bank lending is the technical assistance associated with its normal loan operations. In order that its loans may make a maximum contribution to the economy of the borrowing country, the initial careful assessment of the merits of a project is followed up by periodic checks on the progress of the project.

In addition, the Bank arranges for, and partly finances, general survey missions to help member countries, at their request, draw up development programmes. The countries in Africa south of the Sahara which so far have availed themselves of the Bank's help in connection with their general development programmes are : Nigeria, Tanganyika, and Uganda. A similar survey will be undertaken in 1961 for Kenya. The Bank also provides for training of senior officials of member governments in development techniques through its Economic Development Institute, and arranges for a somewhat similar programme for junior officials in its trainee programme.

International Development Association (IDA)

In the field of international long-term finance, the need for an agency which could assist in the long-term development of under-developed countries on more flexible terms than those of existing agencies became more and more apparent as years went by. Many countries, through no fault of their own, have only a limited or virtually no capacity to service external debt on conventional or commercial terms. If these countries are to develop at an adequate pace, they need help from an institution that can lend on relatively 'easy' terms. To fill this need, the International Development Association, an affiliate of the World Bank, was established in 1960. It had 46 members with initial subscriptions amounting to $868 million as of June 21, 1961. The larger part was contributed by industrialized countries which do not intend to have recourse to its financing facilities. The balance is contributed by countries in the process of development, which may expect at one time or another to seek assistance from the organization.

The IDA has great flexibility in determining the terms on which it makes assistance available. In general it will make loans repayable in foreign exchange but with a long period of grace and subsequent maturities spread over an extended number of years. Moreover, it may not insist on interest payments but only on a small service charge to meet administrative expenses. Thus, the servicing of such loans will bear much less heavily than conventional loans on the balance of payments and budgets of under-developed countries.

The organization did not start operations until 1961. The first developmental credit made by IDA on May 12, 1961, was for financing part of a highway development and maintenance programme in Honduras. The credit was a fifty-year interest-free credit for $9 million repayable in foreign exchange. After the initial ten-year period of grace, repayments will commence at the rate of 1 per cent in the second ten-year period, and 3 per cent in the remaining thirty years. Honduras will pay IDA a service charge of three-quarters of 1 per cent annually on amounts withdrawn and outstanding, to meet IDA's administrative expenses. Two more credits extended by IDA so far are $13 million to the Sudan for financing the Roseires dam, and $60 million to India for highway development; they carry the same repayment conditions as the credit to Honduras. IDA is presently studying a variety of projects such as industrial estates, municipal improvements, and technical training, besides road development, port facilities, and irrigation works.

The criteria for IDA assistance will be based on the same standards of project preparation and execution normally applied by the Bank in its loan operations. Indeed, the same country may well be the recipient of both normal Bank loans and IDA credits; and in some cases the Bank and IDA may participate in financing the same project as, was the case for, the Roseires project in the Sudan.

International Finance Corporation (IFC)

According to the statutory requirements of the World Bank, private institutions in member countries seeking financial assistance must obtain the guarantee of their government. As the growth of private entrepreneurial investment (foreign or national) became more impressive over the last decade, the need was felt for an agency that would deal directly with private borrowers in member countries. Consequently, the International Finance Corporation was established in 1956 as an affiliate of the World Bank. As of December 31, 1960, it had a membership of 58 countries and a subscribed capital of $96·2 million.

IFC's rôle in economic development is essentially that of a catalyst; it uses its rather limited funds to mobilize private capital for investment in private enterprise in the developing countries. Its investment partakes of some of the characteristics of both loan and equity. Thus, quite often part of its interest charges is fixed and part is contingent on profits. It also takes options on shares which, however, it can exercise only for the purpose of selling its participation in any investment. The IFC itself is precluded by statute from owning shares, but an amendment enabling it to do so is now in the course of ratification by its members.

IFC has, as of the end of 1960, made only one commitment in

Africa south of the Sahara. The investment, amounting in all to $6·4 million, was in respect of the Kilombero Sugar Company, and was made in association with the U.K. Colonial Development Corporation, the Netherlands Overseas Finance Company, and Vereenigde Klattensche Cultuur Maatschappij ; IFC's share in the investment was $2·8 million.

International Monetary Fund (IMF)

A discussion of international agencies in the development field should include a reference to the International Monetary Fund (IMF). IMF operational activities relate to short-term financial assistance for balance of payments purposes and not to assistance for development, but it does confer on its member countries a degree of stability in import capacity. Its very activity, therefore, tends to avoid undesirable repercussions of temporary disequilibria on investment activities of its member countries. In addition, a very considerable amount of consultative and advisory work is associated with its normal operations. This should properly be regarded as technical assistance ; in addition, the IMF has a training programme similar to the World Bank but with more emphasis on financial and balance of payments problems.

Fonds de Développement pour les Pays et les Territoires d'Outre-Mer (FEDOM)

FEDOM is an agency of the European Economic Community established under the Rome Treaty. A supplementary convention to the Treaty stipulates that the six members of the Community contribute to FEDOM a total of $581·25 million over the five years 1958–62 for assisting in the economic and social development of their associated territories and countries, most of which are in Africa. These resources are to be allocated by 1962 as follows : $511·25 million to associated territories and countries linked to France ; $35 million for those linked with the Netherlands ; $30 million for those associated with Belgium ; and $5 million for Italian overseas territories.

FEDOM operates exclusively through a system of grants for developmental programmes normally undertaken by public authorities ; it does not finance current expenditures but finances investments. As of May 31, 1961, it had approved total assistance of $158 million ; $92 million for economic projects and $66 million for social programmes. The distribution of the approved investments as between associated territories and countries linked with France, the Netherlands, Belgium, and Italy, was $131·7 million, $12·5 million, $11·7 million, and $2·2 million respectively. Most of the assistance is expected to benefit African countries.

V. FLOW OF PRIVATE CAPITAL

It is difficult to estimate the flow of private capital in recent years that went into countries south of the Sahara, since most of these countries are either in the Franc Zone or the Sterling Area and capital movements within these currency areas are not subject to exchange control. Even data for the United States, which are the most detailed that are available, only show figures for direct investments in these countries. In the following paragraphs private capital flows from France, the United Kingdom, Belgium, the United States, and Germany to Tropical Africa will be discussed in so far as available information allows.

The outflow of direct investment capital from *France* to the Overseas Franc Area is estimated to have amounted to some $350 million equivalent in recent years ; the figure includes reinvestments out of retained earnings. No data are available on how much Overseas residents invested in France. Nor is it known how much of the gross flows was to countries south of the Sahara ; presumably the amounts were small since traditionally North African countries have absorbed the bulk of such flows and by far the major part of investment expenditure in other French Territories or French speaking countries was on public account.

United Kingdom official sources indicate that in the seven years prior to 1960 gross private investment overseas has averaged some £300 million annually. Included in this are loans raised on the London market by independent Commonwealth countries and the Colonies, averaging £55 million annually. The figure of £300 million does not, however, include commercial credits extended by the Export Credits Guarantee Department. Two-thirds of these investments are estimated to have gone to the more developed Commonwealth countries and about £100 million annually into the less developed areas. British dependencies in West and East Africa (including Aden) received about £233 million in the period 1957–9, *i.e.* about £77 million or $216 million annually.

In the three years 1957–9 the overall inflow of long-term private capital from *Belgium–Luxembourg* (BLEU) into the Congo and Ruanda-Urundi was the equivalent of $156 million, but since there was a return flow of capital larger than this, BLEU's net capital contribution to the Congo and Ruanda-Urundi was on private account negative in the amount of $74 million. While the bulk of this decline took place in 1959, and could be attributed to the unsettled political conditions in the Congo, it might be noted that in the nine years (1950–8) prior thereto, the *net* outflow of private capital from BLEU to the Congo and Ruanda-Urundi was only about $37 million in all. This only suggests that the bulk of private investments that did take place during these years was financed out of retained earnings ; indeed, according to data published by the Banque Centrale du Congo Belge et du Ruanda-Urundi, self-financing accounted for not less than 96 per cent of private investments in the period 1950–7.

The *United States* encourages private foreign investment through guarantees of investments abroad. The ICA Investment Guarantee Programme covers risks arising from currency inconvertibility, expropriation or confiscation, and losses incurred by war. Guarantees are accorded to approved investments which further the purposes of the Mutual Security Programme up to a maximum of twenty years ; there is a small fee of one-half of 1 per cent per annum of the amount guaranteed in respect of each type of risk. The Development Loan Fund has also a programme for investment guarantee ; its coverage is broader and excludes only normal business losses. So far, however, there has not been much demand for the DLF's guarantee.

Over the decade 1950–9, the book value of U.S. direct investments in Tropical Africa rose from some $90 million to $370 million. In the three years 1957–9 alone, the total amount of U.S. direct investments financed by net new capital as well as retained earnings was about $150 million ; of this $70 million was in new capital and the remainder was out of retained earnings.

West Germany, like the United States, has a programme for guaranteeing private capital seeking investment abroad. Besides the risks of expropriation, transfer restrictions, and war, the programme covers such other risks as losses through moratoria and currency depreciation. The guarantee is limited to new investments of mutual benefit to the recipient country and to West Germany. Normally the term is fifteen years (in exceptional cases twenty years) ; maximum coverage is limited to 80 per cent of the principal amount and to 24 per cent of returns on the investment.

Direct investments of West Germany in Africa, according to the Information Bulletin of the Federal Government have amounted in all to some $43 million equivalent between February 1952 and December 31, 1960. This corresponds to some 6·1 per cent of the

$695 million of direct investments of West Germany in all parts of the world.

One general observation may perhaps be in order here. One could, of course, presume that recent internal political developments in various parts of Tropical and Equatorial Africa, particularly in the Congo (Léopoldville), should have acted as a deterrent to a further inflow of private capital. In some other countries there may presumably have been a net outflow rather than a net inflow. It is all the more remarkable that new plans for further agricultural, industrial, and, of course, mining investments should come to light so often. Gabon, Nigeria, Ghana, Liberia, Mauretania are the most conspicuous instances. But there are others.

VI. SOME GENERAL CONSIDERATIONS

The preceding analysis of capital inflow in the recent past may now be supplemented by some general comments bearing on the future needs for external assistance of Tropical Africa.

(a) *Mobilizing Domestic Financial Resources*

A first problem which appears relevant in connection with the future requirements for public external assistance, is that of the ability of the various countries concerned to mobilize financial resources themselves, *i.e.* domestically, without resorting to inflationary financing. A complete analysis of this problem would require a detailed examination of financial conditions in individual countries and is outside the scope of this paper. We believe, however, that some general factors can be mentioned which have an important bearing on the subject and affect to a larger or smaller extent the public finances of many of the countries in the area.

In many African countries the possibilities for the accumulation of public savings (*i.e.* the difference between current government revenue and current government expenditure) appear to be small or even non-existent, for the time being.

On the revenue side, a basic fact is that the scope for increasing the tax burden is very limited in many parts of the area, due to the very low *per capita* income levels which still prevail. There are differences in this respect, of course. European settlers, who, apart from the Union of South Africa, are relatively most numerous in the Rhodesias and in Kenya, are a class apart from the standpoint of income and ability to save. Sizeable differences also exist among

African living standards. Overall, however, income levels in many areas south of the Sahara are still among the lowest in the world. Another factor limiting taxable capacity, partly related to the one just mentioned, is the still very important rôle of subsistence agriculture in many areas. There are only a few countries in the area where large amounts of public revenue can be derived from mining, large-scale plantation agriculture, or smallholders' agricultural production for export markets.

On the other hand, current public expenditures are bound to be high in many countries due to a variety of circumstances. In many areas of Tropical Africa there is a particular need for basic infrastructure recurrent activities, such as topographical mapping and soil, water, and geological surveys. Also, there is a pressing need for the development of skills and education generally. The fact that in many areas agriculture is the main source of income now, and is bound to stay so in the foreseeable future, means that relatively high priority will have to be accorded to such items as agricultural research and extension schemes (besides soil and water surveys, already mentioned). Yet another problem is that many countries in the area have small populations, which tends to make the provision of some basic services relatively expensive (a good example is representation abroad).

Due to these reasons a considerable number of African countries will presumably not be in a position to make an important contribution to the financing of public investment expenditures through budgetary surpluses.[1] In fact, a number of countries and territories have been in deficit on their current expenditure budget in the past.

It is, moreover, obvious that the possibilities of mobilizing financial resources for the public sector by means of domestic borrowing other than from the central or commercial banks (*i.e.* without additional money creation) are very small in most cases. Consequently, if expenditure on development is to be increased in the years to come, shortages of financial resources may well give rise to problems of management of domestic finances ; there will be a need to prevent harmful inflationary pressures.

In two respects the general picture of the public finances of African countries presented in the preceding paragraphs is too pessimistic.

In the first place, in a number of countries the assistance provided for current budgetary purposes by the former metropolitan

---

[1] Some countries in the area (such as Ghana, Nigeria, and Uganda) have been in a position to accumulate considerable public surpluses in the course of the 1950s, when prices for their major export products were high. In these cases the financial position is stronger for the time being.

territory is not likely to disappear overnight. It is most unlikely, for instance, that France will suddenly withdraw its traditional support to the budgets of several French-speaking countries, or cease to pay for a number of civil servants whose salaries are now contributed by France under its technical assistance programme.

In the second place, the view can rightly be held that a number of current expenditures, in effect, constitute a contribution to development. Sanitation, communications, maintenance, and, of course, education, entail recurring expenditures which are properly not included in an investment account. They do represent an important factor not only in the welfare but also in the progress of any country.

(b) *Prospects for External Financial Assistance*

We may now add a few general comments about the external financial assistance that will be required by Tropical Africa, and the conditions under which these requirements might be met.

Efforts are sometimes made to approximate the amounts of foreign assistance that will be required by under-developed countries by starting out with a desired rate of growth in income (taking into account the expected rate of increase of population), and calculating the amounts of investment required to achieve this growth in income on the basis of capital output ratios. Required foreign assistance is then found as the difference between calculated investment and estimated domestic savings. Although estimates of this kind may be revealing to show the relationship between a desired rate of growth in income and the amounts of foreign assistance needed to realize this growth, they are of little value and may even be misleading in assessing the amounts of aid that individual countries will be able to absorb for programmes and projects of high priority in the context of economic development. An assessment of this 'absorptive capacity' can only be based on a detailed study of programmes and projects in individual countries, including the feasibility of executing these programmes in the light of available managerial and technical skills. Some areas of Tropical Africa have already made progress along these lines, but in many other cases only very little has been done so far. Under these circumstances estimates of the absorptive capacity for external assistance for Tropical Africa as a whole, when related to a somewhat longer period, are bound to be very uncertain. This simply underlines the need for technical assistance in a great number of fields.

As far as the most desirable distribution of development expenditures by sectors is concerned, generalizations for the area as a whole are just as hazardous. As follows from previous remarks, many areas presumably share the need for considerable expenditures for current development purposes. In the field of investment expenditures proper it is noteworthy that in some parts of Tropical Africa substantial amounts have already been spent on basic facilities like roads, railways, and public utilities ; but this is by no means universally true.

With respect to conditions of future external public assistance, there would in many cases appear to be a clear need for relatively lenient terms. Creditworthiness for the servicing of foreign exchange loans on conventional terms is low in a number of cases. Partly related to this is the probability that the rate at which returns, on a good many programmes and projects, will be realized will turn out to be rather slow. For instance, in the case of projects designed to raise agricultural yields, limited experience suggests that benefits may well be uncertain and delayed. The problems of African agriculture are in many areas complicated by difficult natural conditions and land deterioration, giving rise to a need for investments designed primarily to stop a decline in production rather than to promote an increase in output.

While a substantial and continuous flow of external public funds will be essential to the economic development of Africa, the contribution that private capital could make to development should not be ignored. Political changes and disturbances have not been conducive to the flow of private capital in large parts of Africa in recent years. One may hope that with more stable conditions the tide will turn. Guarantee programmes like those of the United States and Germany may help to increase the flow of private capital, although they are no more than incentives. On the part of host countries, assurances that foreign capital will not be expropriated without reasonable compensation, that facilities for the transfer of profits and dividend will be made available, and that, generally, foreign capital will not be treated less well than local capital, will be of help. But unlike public capital, private capital movements are motivated by strictly financial considerations so that many factors other than the ones mentioned, such as tax levels and the availability of basic infrastructure activities, technicians, administrators, and a skilled working force, may influence ultimate decisions of private investors.

We have seen that the supply of public foreign capital available to African countries in the recent past was predominantly bilateral in nature. An important problem is raised here by the progressive loosening of political ties between the two major aid-giving European countries — France and the United Kingdom — and their dependent

African territories and colonies. It would be unfortunate if this phenomenon were to affect both the total flow of bilateral aid available from these countries and the assurance that aid will be available on a longer term basis (which is important in connection with long-term planning). One may hope that ways will be found that will enable these European countries to continue their assistance to Tropical Africa on at least the same scale as that prevailing in the recent past. As far as United States aid is concerned, it seems fair to assume that this will increase. The growing importance of Germany as a potential source of aid was mentioned earlier. The U.S.S.R. remains an uncertain factor.

In the field of multilateral aid we have seen that the European Development Fund, the Special Fund of the UN, and the International Development Association have been the most important recent additions to the group of international agencies that are able to provide assistance to African countries. Although one may hope for an increase in aid from these sources in the years to come, there are clear limitations on what they can do, stemming primarily from their limited resources.

Given these limitations, the prospects for external economic assistance largely depend on the recipient's capacity to utilize it effectively, if possible, in association with domestically available resources. This assumed to an extent the prior existence of a sound developmental programme, or projects within the general framework of such a programme, and, more importantly, a demonstrated capacity to implement and execute a plan of development. Countries with an efficient planning organization and a trained cadre of administrators capable of drawing up and implementing an investment programme with due regard to the relative priority of its component projects, will clearly find it easier to obtain external economic assistance. Bilateral or multilateral aid can be expected to be motivated by economic as well as financial consideration. The easier it is to demonstrate the economic benefit deriving from an investment programme or a set of projects, the easier it is to convince official assistance that its contribution will materially enhance the well-being of Africa.

Economic Development for Africa South of the Sahara

ANNEX

Sources

OEEC : *The Flow of Financial Resources to Countries in Course of Development, 1956–59*, April 1961.

Report of the European Economic Community (*Direction Générale de Développement de l'Outre-Mer*) *relating to the operations of the European Development Fund,* May 1961.

UN : *Economic Survey of Africa since 1950.*

UN : *Statistical Yearbook 1959.*

UN : *International Economic Assistance to the Less Developed Countries*, 1961.

UN : Reports of the Economic Commission for Africa.

UN Special Fund : *Status of Projects approved by the Governing Council as of December 31, 1960.*

Stanford Research Institute : *African Development, A Test for International Co-operation.*

Banque Centrale du Congo et du Ruanda-Urundi : *Bulletin Mensuel,* November 1959.

Banque du Congo Belge : *Bulletin Mensuel,* June 1960.

France : Reports of the Comité Monétaire de la zone franc : *La Zone franc,* 1957, 1958, and 1959.

Reports of the Fonds de Développement Économique et Social, Second and Fifth Reports.

Caisse Centrale de Coopération Économique : *L'Aide accordé par la France en 1959 pour le developpement des états d'Afrique Noire et de Madagascar, des territoires et départements d'outre-mer,* May 1960.

La Documentation Française : *Notes et études documentaires,* February 8, 1960 and March 13, 1961.

Germany : *Bulletin des Presse- und Informationsamtes der Bundesregierung,* April 6, 1961.

United Kingdom : *Assistance from the United Kingdom for Overseas Development,* Cmnd. 974, March 1960.

The United Kingdom's Role in Commonwealth Development, Cmnd. 237, July 1957.

Return of Schemes made and of Loans approved under the Colonial Development and Welfare Act, March 31, 1960.

Colonial Development Corporation : *Annual Report and Accounts for the Year 1959.*

Colonial Office : Annual Reports on 'The Colonial Territories'.

United States : International Co-operation Administration : *U.S. Foreign Assistance and Assistance from International Organizations, Obligations and Other Commitments,* July 1, 1945, through June 30, 1960.

Development Loan Fund : *Annual Report 1959.*

Development Loan Fund : *Fiscal Year 1961 Estimates.*

Reports to the Congress on the Mutual Security Program, various dates.

Department of State : unpublished memorandum on 'Economic Assistance as a Co-operative Effort of the Free World', 1960.

IBRD-IDA : Annual Reports, Financial Statements, Press Releases, etc.

Chapter 17

TROPICAL AFRICA AND THE WORLD ECONOMY

BY

W. E. MORAN, JR.
International Industrial Development Center,
Stanford Research Institute,
Menlo Park, California

I. INTRODUCTORY

TROPICAL Africa, a late starter, is now inextricably bound up in the world economy. Colonialism characterized its entry. Politically, independence is now replacing colonialism in the area, and economic change follows. How that transition takes place will be of importance to Tropical Africa and the world. In the brief compass of this paper, an attempt will be made to describe the relationships which Tropical Africa has developed with the world economy, the way in which they are changing, and some of the main questions posed in this transition period.

The basic factor in this transition is the assumption by Africans, at their insistent demand, of responsibility for their own affairs. Tropical Africa's participation in the world economy until 1950 was determined by Europeans for their own benefit or for what they felt to be in the best interests of the African population. Until World War II the countries making up this area were parts of large colonial economic units. Their development was conceived in terms of those large units of which they were a part, rather than in terms of the individual country in the world economy. The availability of economically exploitable resources was important but not deter- mining. The extent to which such resources were discovered and exploited, even the extent to which they might be considered eco- nomic, depended on conditions in the larger unit as a whole and on the wealth and economic aggressiveness of the ruling partner in that unit. In the post-war period, increasing attention was given to development and trade from the standpoint of meeting the needs and desires of the peoples of Tropical Africa. Since 1950, with the growth of nationalism in Africa, this has reflected itself in the preparation of development programmes for most of the countries of the area, and in increasing participation in development by others than the ruling colonial partner. Now that African leaders have assumed independent responsibility in most of these countries, it can be expected that the trend toward looking at participation in the world economy from the standpoint of African well-being, possibly the well-being of individual African countries, will be strengthened.

In considering how Tropical Africa may adapt itself to the world economy, it is important to bear in mind that until the twentieth century its people lived in subsistence economies in which trade was largely limited to barter within limited groups. Although its participation in a world market economy has developed greatly over a short space of time, three-quarters or more of its people still live in subsistence economies and have only limited and occasional participation in the market economy. Thus, Tropical Africa's participation in the world market economy is not only recent, but directly affects only a small part of its population.

The way in which Tropical Africa adapts itself to the world economy, and participates in it, will differ greatly from country to country, since they differ considerably in size, composition, and the extent to which their natural and human resources have been developed. However, all of them are interested in improving the well-being of their peoples and the strength of their states, which requires expanded economic growth. Therefore, despite their differences, their participation in the world economy will depend on the way in which they find it possible to achieve the development they seek. This will involve external aid and private investment to finance development, and trade to provide the means of paying for it.

II. THE CLIMATE OF DEVELOPMENT

Traders and investors from Europe, many of whose activities preceded the establishment of colonies, started Tropical Africa's participation in the world economy. In the colonies they maintained the initiative, even the responsibility, for developing the production of marketable export goods. Nationals from the metropole ordinarily maintained a predominant place in its colonies. Until the last war the colonial powers responsible for Tropical Africa were satisfied to let this situation prevail. They acted to keep the peace and maintain their spheres of influence. There was no thought of developing the colonies as independent economic units. The planning of development was not practised. No special funds for development were available and capital investment was limited to that level which current earnings or borrowing capacity made possible. (The Colonial Development Fund of the United Kingdom, under which grants were made, was a limited exception.) Public investment was largely in those fields which would open up new productive capacity for increasing exports. Investment in social infrastructure, health, and education, was limited. Little was done by governments to interfere with or change traditional structures, save as that was necessary to secure the peace and make effective administration possible. An exception was in measures, direct or indirect, to force or induce the local peoples sufficiently into the market economy, to assure minimum revenues required and a reasonable availability of labour. European colonists, where physical conditions made it possible, were welcomed, except in the Congo, although Asian colonists were not.

In these conditions, there was considerable economic growth, particularly where mineral resources or favourable agricultural conditions prevailed. In east and central Africa, colonists opened up large areas to new crops. Traders collected African production of export crops and provided the economic basis for the expansion of such production. Large companies opened up important mineral deposits on the heels of the prospectors. In all of this development, a limited number of Africans participated, and almost exclusively at a fairly low level as labourers or small traders. As a result, local markets were not highly developed and there was little incentive for investment in facilities to produce for the local market, and little development of inter-African trade. Continued growth was dependent almost completely on export expansion.

The war brought some changes into this picture. Cut off from foreign sources of supply, it was necessary to develop production to meet local requirements, which gave birth to some industry in a number of the Tropical African countries. The war economies required raw materials in expanded quantities and gave rise to a considerable expansion of African mineral and agricultural production. This expansion of production at a time when imports were curtailed or limited gave rise to an excess of exports over imports and the creation of substantial financial reserves by many of the countries.

Starting about 1948, a whole new approach manifested itself. The idea of a planned expansion of the countries of Tropical Africa was adopted to one degree or another by all the colonial governments. Old policies of leaving development to the private entrepreneur were modified or dropped. Development planning was still undertaken for the countries of Tropical Africa as parts of larger economic units, but it was aimed at improving the well-being of the local peoples. This in no way precluded the foreign investor, but rather was based on the hope of an increase in private investment, and aimed in part at improving opportunities for such investment. In these new plans, considerable attention was given to the local population. Efforts were made to improve indigenous agriculture and expand production for the purpose of improving local diets and meeting the growing local needs arising from urbanization, as well as for export. The colonial governments assumed a new responsibility for education and training, which in the past many of them had looked to the missionaries to provide in return for limited subsidies. Attempts were made to increase local responsibility for improved well-being through the strengthening of local authorities and through community development programmes.

With the movement toward independence since 1950 there has been an increasing participation of Africans in the planning of development. Even in those countries which may maintain some ties with the former metropole, this has begun to change the focus of such efforts and will continue to do so. That focus will now be first and foremost on development from the standpoint of its contribution to the well-being and prestige of the individual countries. It will be aimed at increasing the capacity of their inhabitants to run their own affairs, both from the standpoint of expanded education and training and from the standpoint of financial and management participation in economic matters — public and private. Expenditures on social overheads are expanding and will continue to do so. Demands for rapid industrialization are increasing. These countries will be unwilling to see the development of their resources held back because world market demand cannot accommodate increased supplies. Traditional investors unwilling to meet these new demands will find themselves pushed aside in favour of more adventurous or less scrupulous investors willing to meet the demand. Eastern sources of money, men, and ideas will be accepted where Western sources are unavailable, unimaginative, or slow in forthcoming. Public companies will be established to achieve what private investors are unwilling to do. New efforts will be made to develop communal or co-operative endeavours. New trade patterns can be expected to emerge. Some expansion of trade with the Sino-Soviet bloc will result. Efforts will continue to be made to develop regional African economic groupings. These seem to be the directions indicated from the limited experience thus far with independence in Africa.

III. THE IMPACT OF DEVELOPMENT PLANNING

In pre-war conditions, when expenditures on development were limited to the funds available or which could be borrowed under normal terms, the colonial economies were reasonably stable. Development was at a low level and seriously cut back in periods of international recession, but revenues were ordinarily adequate to meet requirements of ordinary budgets. Private investment exceeded public investment (see Table 1). Since a large part of investment was of an equity nature and required payments only against earnings, slacking off of trade did not ordinarily result in serious balance of payments difficulties because of the need to meet fixed obligations in foreign currencies.

TABLE 1

FOREIGN CAPITAL ENTERING AFRICA, 1870–1936

	Public	Private
	%	%
Commonwealth West Africa	44	56
British East Africa	64	36
French Territories	61	39
Belgian Congo and Ruanda-Urundi	25	75
	45	55

Source : S. H. Frankel, *Capital Investment in Africa*, London, 1938. Table 28, as quoted in *The Importance of Private Capital Movements in Economic Development with Special Reference to Africa*, by Derek T. Healey, Institute of Commonwealth Studies, Oxford University, No. 24, Oxford, 1959.

The attempt to catch up under-planned development programmes over the past decade has created quite a different situation. Heavy investments have been made in physical overheads, power, and in transportation. In many cases these have not been followed quickly enough by productive investment to earn the wherewithal to amortize and maintain such investments, and they have become a charge on ordinary budgets without an adequate compensation in revenues. Heavy investments in social overhead have done much to improve health and well-being, to expand populations, and to increase the number of literate and educated persons, but have also created economic problems. The increase in population requires an increased rate of economic growth just to stand still. Even where these investments have been made on the basis of grants they have created large annual recurrent costs which are a charge on ordinary budgets ; these charges are accentuated and include foreign exchange obligations where such investments have been made on the basis of foreign loans. Finally, the increase in the number of healthy and better-qualified people increases the demand for suitable employment, particularly in the urban areas to which the educated tend to gravitate, and thus increase the need for employment producing investment.

The Republic of the Congo (Léopoldville) represents this situation in a rather aggravated fashion because of the rapid rate of development attempted, although the trend is fairly generally applicable. The Congo undertook a major development effort under the Ten-Year Plan covering the period from 1950–60. For the 1950 budget year, the Congo government had receipts in excess of ordinary expenditures equivalent to $22,420,000, which made it possible for it to contribute substantially to the first year of development under the plan out of current surplus. In addition, the Congo had substantial reserves as the result of previous budgetary surpluses. Its total public debt at the end of 1949 was $73,800,000. It had a surplus in its balance of payments equivalent to $61,740,000 on current account, or $117,240,000 taking into account capital movements, and had substantial foreign exchange and gold reserves. By the end of the plan period, in 1959, during which the public debt was increased by an amount equivalent to $800,000,000, the Congo had reached the point at which revenues had consistently failed by increasing amounts to meet current obligations since 1957. The deficit for 1959 was equivalent to $61,520,000. It had run a deficit in its balance of payments regularly since 1956 and the deficit in 1959 was the equivalent of $66,080,000 on current account, but $112,800,000 taking capital movements into account. Reserves in foreign exchange and gold had declined to a very low point. The public debt at the end of 1959 was the equivalent of $874,400,000, representing a charge of 17 per cent of its budget, and the equivalent of $490,840,000 of this amount was foreign debt. Thus, after ten years of expanded, planned expenditure of the equivalent of $1,140,000,000 on development during a period of rising economic activity, the Congo had reached a point where it was unable to meet its ordinary annual requirements from ordinary revenues, and was hardly a suitable candidate for further large loans. A review of the second Ten-Year Plan, which was in preparation at the time of independence, shows that there was a requirement for further heavy development expenditures with no early promise that expansion of revenues would begin to meet requirements. This was accompanied by an expansion of unemployment in urban centres resulting from improved productivity but accentuated by the continued movement of people from the rural to the urban areas.

This is not to suggest that in the Congo money was wasted nor that expenditures were not made on good and worthwhile projects. It is to suggest that the countries of Tropical Africa need very substantial increases in investment in order to bring about quickly the change they seek, and that many of these investments will not produce revenue quickly. The attempt in the Congo to provide the whole of such investment on normal loan terms has not proven to be an adequate response. It is doubtful that the attempt would be any more successful in any other Tropical African country. The conclusion of the survey mission of the International Bank for Reconstruction and Development, after its study of the economy of Tanganyika, is illustrative. That Mission came to the conclusion, concerning current development plans of that country, that the returns from the proposed government activities, if they are well planned and executed, will be sufficient to justify the government of Tanganyika in borrowing the limited sums required, provided that they are available on reasonably favourable terms. The report stressed that development in Tanganyika could be greatly assisted by continued and expanded inflow of grants and technical assistance and by the availability of loans at low rates of interest, and with long amortization terms or periods of grace.

Experience to date leads to the conclusion that new approaches to the provision of external financial assistance may have to be contemplated if development efforts in Tropical Africa are to be successful. It also suggests that existing knowledge of the development process as it applies to that area may not be adequate and some new methods may have to be devised.

Some means of passing a large part of the responsibility for social overhead to local communities with some support from central governments for initial investment, but assumption by the local authority for recurrent expenditure, would be a great help with this sector of the economy which is causing so much trouble to so many of the countries of Tropical Africa.

An expansion of productive facilities to produce jobs and revenues and an expansion of internal markets and African participation in the market economy are important to economic growth in an acceptable political framework. The lack of indigenous entrepreneurs and local savings available for investment stands in the way of these developments at an acceptable pace under traditional private enterprise methods. Some of the countries of Tropical Africa are experimenting with new approaches to these problems. Some of them, such as Guinea and Ghana, are trying to find means of direct investment of labour. Ghana is also trying to develop productive investment on the basis of co-operatives with state support. There is a tendency to assume an ideological basis for such efforts, and they have at times been compared to the commune experiment of Communist China. In the absence of much greater Western support than these efforts have thus far received, they might take on an ideological context or follow the Chinese pattern for lack of an alternative. New approaches are necessary and all of the countries giving aid to Tropical Africa would do well to search their experience for useful models, and take a positive and imaginative approach to these problems.

IV. EXTERNAL ASSISTANCE

The dependence of the countries of Tropical Africa on substantial amounts of external technical assistance in men and money characterizes the relationship of the area with the world economy. The need for and the way in which such assistance has been and may continue to be provided will have much to do with the way in which that relationship develops.

There is no precise measure available of the extent of Tropical Africa's requirement for external assistance. However, some idea may be gained from consideration of individual problems and the extent to which they are being met. Despite the great effort over the decade of the fifties, many of the basic problems remain largely unsolved.

According to the *Economic Survey of Africa since 1950*, published by the United Nations in 1959, the *per capita* national product in 1956–7 at 1954 prices exceeded $150 in only one of the countries in the area and for a group of countries making up more than half of the area's population was under $100. This is one measure of the extent to which local savings or local government revenue can be expected to be available for development purposes.

The great mass of the population, ranging from 70 to 85 per cent, is engaged primarily in subsistence agriculture, and thus is in a poor position to contribute in the way of monetary investment or taxes to the improvement of their own lot. But this group is becoming aware of the change which is taking place and will increasingly demand improvements from the new governments. The demand for schools is already an important political force, and the demand for other amenities will not be far behind. The demand will be for the very kind of investment which only pays off in economic terms over a long period of time. In the absence of any substantial growth of the idea of local responsibility, this will be a demand for central government expenditure. Thus, these new governments are faced with a large part of their population in a poor position to make any immediate contribution to economic growth, but in a position to make demands on the limited resources available.

The human resources available to these governments are not adequate in number or kind to begin to meet the tasks faced. Illiteracy is in the neighbourhood of 85 per cent. In only a few of these countries has any substantial percentage of the school-age population received post-primary education. Advanced education was primarily in the professions. The local entrepreneur ready to invest in and manage modern farms, trading facilities, or industries, is exceedingly rare. Indigenous peoples with experience above the level of petty trader, labourer, or clerk, from whom an entrepreneur class might be drawn, are also scarce. Shortages of skilled or qualified people are great. The demand for personnel in government and teaching, both of which have status, is heavy. There is no substantial entrepreneurial tradition. In the circumstances, it can be expected that for some time to come there will be few people in these countries who can step forward and initiate the activities necessary to produce the new jobs and wealth so badly needed.

According to figures prepared by the Economic Commission for Africa, the countries of this area received external aid in an amount substantially in excess of the equivalent of one billion dollars over the period from 1954 to 1958, and nearly two-thirds of this was in the form of grants. This is at best a very rough presentation, because the amounts available differed greatly from one country to another. For example, the amount available annually during this period ranged from $0·14 *per capita* in Angola to $21·05 in Somaliland, and the sum available to the then Belgian Congo was over 95 per cent loan, while that available to Somaliland was all grant. It should be noted that these funds were made available during a period when practically all of the countries in question were still colonies, and the largest part of this assistance was provided by the colonial powers. Now that African countries have emerged into independence, the question arises whether, how, and in what amounts, external assistance may continue to be available to them. The discussions in the Development Assistance Group suggest that the Western powers recognize the need for a continuation, even an expansion, of such assistance. There is, however, as yet no assurance that the division of responsibility for continuing such assistance will be easily arrived at, nor that sufficient attention will be given to the kinds of financial assistance required. All recent moves suggest that funds will be more readily available as loans than as grants, even though a casual study of the financial situation of most of these countries and the character of the development in which they must of necessity engage, shows how limited will be their capacity to service loans on the scale required. The new American administration, in its proposals for foreign aid, has suggested that loans should be made available at low interest rates for a long period of years and with long grace periods. It is doubtful that the development required can even be carried out with loans on this basis. Loans on such terms may simply be a means of putting off the evil day on which it must be accepted that some substantial portion of the development of Tropical Africa will almost certainly have to be financed by grants. In this connection, it should be noted that financial aid thus far proffered by the Sino-Soviet bloc had not paid much more attention to this problem ; most such assistance has been in the form of loans which had relatively low interest rates but were relatively short term.

The difficulties of the Western countries in facing the problem of external financial assistance for Tropical Africa have been compounded by the fact that many of the newly independent countries of that area fear, for political reasons, the very help they so badly require. They fear economic dependence or involvement in the Cold War may result from bilateral aid. There is, however, no agreement among African leaders that they feel multilateral aid is the answer. Some of these leaders have suggested that there should be some kind of an organization of African states to deal with external aid.

Even if financial resources are provided in an acceptable fashion, and on terms commensurate with the need, the effort required in the public sector to promote sustained economic growth will be difficult to attain unless manpower resources are available. During the colonial period, the upper and middle level professional and administrative personnel needs were largely met by personnel from the colonial power working in a colonial civil service. The heavy pressures for Africanization upon independence may lead to the appearance of a declining need for foreign personnel. However, if these countries are to carry out the ambitious development plans some of them have drawn up and the expanded education facilities they all desire, the requirement for foreign personnel to bridge the gap while local personnel are being trained will increase sub-substantially. The kinds of personnel required are different than they were under colonial administration. The countries which furnished the colonial civil servants are already having difficulties in inducing that group of personnel to stay on, even where they are wanted, and even greater difficulty in securing for these newly independent countries many of the categories of personnel required. Some of the new countries of Tropical Africa are finding it politically distasteful to rely too heavily on personnel from one country, and particularly from the former colonial power, but thus far no alternative source of qualified personnel in adequate numbers and on an economic basis has presented itself. The securing of personnel services in an acceptable fashion will be a difficult and expensive aspect of Tropical Africa's relations with the world economy for some years to come. New ways of recruiting qualified personnel in adequate numbers and providing them to these countries on acceptable terms will have to be found.

The education and training of Africans to provide the local personnel required for expanded economic growth is still another aspect of Tropical Africa's place in the world economy. Education and training may not ordinarily be thought of in these terms, but surely must be when the massive programmes anticipated depend so largely on external financial assistance for investment and perhaps even maintenance, foreign personnel for operations over the early years, and access to foreign facilities for thousands of people for some years to come.

V. FOREIGN PRIVATE INVESTMENT

The participation of Tropical Africa in the world economy has been the result of the actions of the foreign trader and investor. Except for the limited trans-Saharan trade in gold, ivory, and slaves, Africa had no contact with the outside world and no indigenous trade or manufacture on which external trade might have been built, as it was in Asia. The foreign trader established the market which led to new production for export, and the foreign investor opened up the plantations and mines.

Not only did the foreign trader and investor open up Africa's relations with the world economy, but they have continued to dominate these relations, as well as a substantial part of the internal market economy. Except for a few countries where African producers dominate the production of export crops, such as Ghana, African participation has been limited, and primarily at low levels. For the most part, the African has not risen above the position of petty trader, labourer, or clerk until recent years, when some effort has been made in a few countries to meet the demand for Africanization by special programmes of training and promotion. There are few African entrepreneurs who have succeeded in developing modern agricultural or industrial production or trade on any substantial scale. Apart from this limited African participation and the Asian participation in trade in East Africa, the modern economic apparatus of Tropical Africa was, until independence, in the hands of European and a few American groups.

The foreign investor continued to invest willingly and in increasing amounts in Tropical Africa through 1958. By that year the available statistics suggest that French private investment in the Community, including Madagascar, was over $300 million annually, Belgian in the Congo over $150 million, the United Kingdom somewhere in the $50 to $100 million range annually, and the United States about $30 million. This includes re-investment as well as new funds.

The picture since independence in Ghana in 1957 is not too clear or consistent, and it is difficult to foresee with any precision what the future trend may be. Ghana has attempted to create state-owned industries, using its own considerable reserves, and has issued conflicting statements concerning the place of private investment. These actions seem to have made potential investors cautious. There was considerable slowness in arriving at a decision on the Volta River project in Ghana, which was attendant on the difficulties of raising the capital for the private investment in the aluminium refinery.

In Guinea, major investments in alumina processing and aluminium refining, which had been under serious study before independence, have not as yet materialized. In some areas where difficulties have occurred or threatened, such as the Congo, Kenya, and the Federation of the Rhodesias and Nyasaland, there has been disinvestment and flight of capital.

On the other hand, a number of major mining projects are going ahead apparently on schedule in Liberia and the French-speaking states other than Guinea. In Nigeria, in addition to investment in oil production, a number of rather large industrial investments have been or are being made.

In the United States certainly, and to some extent generally in capital-exporting countries, there is a demand for some kind of guarantee of private foreign investments against political risk in the developing countries. The way in which these demands have increased of recent years suggests, at least, that the willingness of the foreign private investor to continue to invest at anything like the past level in Tropical Africa and other developing areas may depend on the extent to which governments or international bodies find it possible to provide acceptable guarantees.

The countries of Tropical Africa as they achieved independence have shown a decided interest in a continuation or even an expansion of foreign private investment. With the exception of Guinea, none of them have engaged in expropriation, although it should be noted that the experience of independent governments in this area is very limited. This expressed, and undoubtedly sincere, interest in attracting foreign private investment is not, however, the whole story. The desire for real independence is great, and there is undoubtedly a resentment at the control of such a large sector of the economy by foreigners and the limited possibility of any early change in the situation through the emergence of African entrepreneurs. There is also a distaste for the character of much of the privately controlled development, which, with the exception of a few fairly recent investments in industries to meet local requirements, has been largely concerned with the export of raw materials and the import of finished goods. There is a general demand for a greater amount of processing of raw materials for export and for industrialization. Finally, these new countries want a great expansion of private foreign investment to bring about the increase in production, employment, and revenues they so badly need. Some attention is being paid to the first of these problems ; copper, lead, and zinc are processed to metal in the copper belt, bauxite to alumina in Guinea, and aluminium will be produced at Volta. Exporters are aware that their continued participation in Tropical African markets may depend on some local processing or manufacture, and this has begun in countries with reasonably large markets, such as Nigeria and the Federation of the Rhodesias and Nyasaland, but the smallness of many of the African countries and their limited markets in the absence of any as yet realized regional economic groupings is a limiting factor on such developments. The rapid expansion of private investment so desired by these countries has not materialized.

If some means is not found to bring about the desired level and character of private foreign investment, more of these countries may, as Ghana has, attempt to develop publicly owned industries. This will present problems of staffing and management because of the shortage of qualified local personnel. For those countries without large financial reserves, which is the case for most of them, such development will depend on foreign loans. Even if adequate funds are available, this will mean a further extension of fixed annual obligations in foreign exchange. This need not mean the end of opportunity for private enterprise, as witness India, but might have that effect if the foreign private investor reacted adversely and became even less interested in investing in Africa than he is now.

VI. FOREIGN TRADE

The ability of Tropical Africa to achieve the expanded economic growth it seeks depends on its continued capacity to import capital equipment, goods, and services. Short of grants, this capacity depends on the ability of the countries of this area to produce and sell in international markets. Because these countries have as yet no local production of capital goods or of many of the other necessary or desired manufactured goods, and are so short of qualified personnel, this dependence on imports for growth is quite high and will probably continue to be so for some time.

Quite apart from the importance of exports to maintenance of imports, export trade is an unusually important factor in the national income of Tropical African countries. The large part of their populations involved in subsistence agriculture and the limited development of local consumption in these countries, which have been developed largely as suppliers of raw materials, makes this inevitable. According to the United Nations publication, *Economic Survey of Africa since 1950*, exports represented 48 per cent of the national income of the Congo (Léopoldville), 45 per cent of that of the Federation of the Rhodesias and Nyasaland, and 25 per cent of that of Ghana in the 1956-7 period. Thus, the maintenance of a high level of export trade is essential to the maintenance of existing levels of economic activity.

A start on development has been made through anticipation of future earnings of foreign exchange as a result of foreign public loans and foreign private investment. As payments come due on the foreign public loans and remittance of earning on foreign private investment increases, the continued ability of these countries to base development on the anticipation of earnings may come into question. It will only continue to be possible if income from foreign sources can be maintained at a level substantially in excess of payments to such sources. At some point this may become impossible; that point seems to be close in some of these countries already.

Ultimately, Tropical Africa's capacity to maintain the necessary level of imports depends on its ability to export in such a fashion as to cover the cost of imports, repay foreign loans, and remit earnings on foreign private investment. For this reason, it is important to examine Tropical Africa's export trade from the standpoint of the effect of short-term fluctuations in world markets and from the standpoint of long-term prospects.

All of the countries of Tropical Africa depend on a few crops or minerals for a large portion of their total exports. In most of them one or two products constitute half to three-quarters of their total exports. In only four of them were minerals in this list of products in 1957. The narrow range of these products for the whole area is also noteworthy. A half-dozen agricultural crops representative of tropical produce and two minerals make up the list of products constituting the bulk of the exports of the area (Table 2).

TABLE 2

PRINCIPAL EXPORTS OF SELECTED AFRICAN COUNTRIES
AS PERCENTAGE OF TOTAL EXPORTS, 1957

Country	Exports	Percentage of Total Exports
Angola	Coffee	42·0
Congo (Brazzaville)	Wood	49·0
Congo (Léopoldville) and Ruanda-Urundi	Copper and coffee	45·0
Ivory Coast	Coffee and cacao	79·0
Dahomey	Palm and palm oil	67·0
Ethiopia	Coffee	67·5
Ubangi-Shari	Cotton and coffee	78·0
Gabon	Wood	72·0
Gambia	Peanuts and oil	93·0
Ghana	Cocoa	56·0
Kenya, Uganda, and Tanganyika	Cotton and coffee	57·3
Liberia	Rubber and iron ore	86·2
Mauritania, Senegal, and Soudan	Peanuts and oil	83·0
Nigeria	Cocoa, groundnuts, and palm kernels	54·7
Sierra Leone	Palm nuts and iron ore	53·7
Rhodesia and Nyasaland	Copper and tobacco	66·8
Sudan	Cotton	46·0
Tchad	Cotton	81·0
Niger	Peanuts and oil	85·0

Sources : 'Quelques Données statistiques sur les états africains et malgache de la communauté', Paris, December 1959 ; and *Economic Survey of Africa since 1950*, United Nations, E/CN/14/28, 1959, pp. 167-70.

New mineral products such as bauxite, manganese, and petroleum are assuming some importance in a few of these countries. However, there is no early promise of new agricultural products of importance ; all too often diversification in a given country means new production in that country of one of the standard half-dozen tropical products, most of which are already in surplus world supply.

In these conditions, the export prospects of the area are precarious. They are dependent on a few products, most of which are chronically in surplus world supply. They react quickly to any slacking off of world markets, as they have over the past two years. Those who plan economic development are seriously hampered by these severe and abrupt fluctuations which reflect themselves in restricted availability of foreign exchange and government revenues. This becomes increasingly important as these new governments have assumed increased responsibility for the maintenance of expanded facilities resulting from investment of the recent past, and are faced with heavier fixed annual charges in foreign exchange for the servicing of foreign loans.

There has been much talk in recent years of finding a means of stabilizing prices of primary commodities of the sort on which Tropical Africa depends. Ultimately, such schemes must depend on bringing production and consumption into balance at least over time. The needs of Tropical Africa for expanded income and foreign exchange would not be met if stabilization meant cut-backs or restraints on production ; such action might result in a better assurance of regular prices, but at the price of the expansion needed. Therefore, it would seem that stabilization schemes would only be acceptable to these countries if they took place in the framework of a level of growth in world consumption which would assure expansion as well as guarantees of prices, or if the African countries had acceptable alternatives in the way of marketable products to which they could turn. Recent studies by GATT question whether consumption of the usual tropical commodities in the important traditional markets of Western Europe or North America can be expected to provide the necessary expansion in markets. There has been little done to determine what products capable of being produced in these countries might be expected to have real opportunities over the next ten or fifteen years, either from the standpoint of projections of world requirements or from the standpoint of developing new production in the area.

The long-term outlook for the growth of existing African exports to traditional markets does not lead to the hope that consumption in these markets will be adequate to absorb the increases in tropical agricultural production which can be foreseen. It appears that the surplus position of such products in the world picture is chronic and will remain so unless new markets are developed or production is restrained. Tropical Africa has traditionally exported the bulk of its production to the industrialized countries of Europe and North America. The substantial economic growth of these countries since the war has not resulted in a concomitant expansion of consumption of tropical products, nor can it be expected to. When a certain point is reached in such societies, the addition of income does not result in an expansion of consumption of articles such as coffee or cocoa, or even of fibres and oils. Further change takes place with the introduction of synthetics and the improved use of raw materials in manufacturing processes. Imports from Tropical Africa are not growing as rapidly as the growth of gross national product in the industrialized countries. At the same time, the Tropical African countries are increasing their imports and expanding their production of foods and fibres in the hopes of paying for these imports, only to see prices fall and their hopes dashed. GATT and others noted this development in recent studies. (Table 3.)

TABLE 3

COMMERCIAL BALANCES OF PAYMENT OF NEWLY DEVELOPING
COUNTRIES, 1953–5 AND 1973–5

($ billions)

	1953–5	1973–5
	$	$
Exports toward industrialized nations	19·9	31·8
Imports from industrialized nations	19·5	43·0
	0·4	– 11·2

Source : Jean Royer, 'Is the Economic Structure of Industrialised Countries Compatible with the Development Needs of New Economies ?' *Économie Appliquée*, vol. XII, No. 4, Oct.-Dec. 1959, Table F, p. 515.

The picture in Tropical Africa is clouded by special trade relationships between some of the countries of the area with European countries, as a result of which they have been able to do rather better than the developing countries generally. But it would appear that the problem of the developing countries as a whole will eventually be felt by all of Tropical Africa.

An absurd situation now prevails. In the same book or meeting concerned with the developing countries, economists say, 'Two-thirds of the world goes to bed each night badly fed and ill-clothed', and 'We don't see how we can accommodate substantial increases in food and fibre production in Africa (or in the tropical countries)'. Here lies the dilemma. It is in this context that the long-term problem must be resolved. A way must be found to integrate the developing countries into a changing and expanding world economy.

Over-populated countries needing raw materials and food, such as Japan and India, must somehow be helped into the position of meeting these needs on an economic basis through trade with those countries which are in a position to produce the products they need. Such an adjustment will require very substantial changes in world trading patterns, but there does not seem to be any alternative.

VII. CONCLUSION

The attainment of self-sustaining, economic growth adequate to meet the needs and desires of the people of Tropical Africa will require a long-term effort including substantial investment of a social nature, which cannot be financed altogether on a loan basis. Major socio-economic change, probably along lines somewhat different from traditional Western private enterprise practices, will be required to move the mass of the people into the market economy and establish the production and distribution facilities necessary for the expansion of local economies. This change need not be of such an ideological nature as to interfere with economic relations with Western countries if those countries are sympathetic to the need for such change and are prepared to help bring it about. Present approaches by Western countries do not indicate an adequate appreciation of this situation.

External financial assistance for the public sector will continue to be required for a long period of time. The amount needed in the immediate future will probably be greater than the level established over the past five years. The level and character of external debt already assumed limits the capacity of these countries to meet their further requirements fully on a loan basis ; there are great differences among the countries and individual consideration of this problem will be necessary. The large requirements for social investment which cannot be expected to result in early increase in revenue is not susceptible to financing on a loan basis. Unless there is a reconsideration of this problem and an adaptation of financing to local requirements, which will mean frequently an increase in grants and long-term, low interest loans, a number of these countries will be in difficulties soon. If a critical approach is taken to loans, they will not receive adequate assistance. If an uncritical approach continues, they will be in default with all the attendant difficulties. Not nearly enough attention is being paid to this problem.

The ability of these countries to use their own resources and large amounts of external assistance effectively depends on their securing personnel from abroad in large numbers over a period of years while adequate numbers of their own people are being educated and trained. The provision of such personnel in an acceptable fashion and meeting the demands of the area for education and training, locally and abroad, is a problem of the first importance. It is not being adequately met, nor do prospects look good for its being met at an early date.

A substantial expansion of private foreign investment is needed, not alone in raw materials production for export but particularly in new industries for the local market and export. Many of the countries of the area do not present great opportunity for the latter type of investment because of the limited nature of the market. There is some evidence that existing and potential investors are hesitant to expand their activities because of political risk; problems of re-patriation of capital in the non-export industries may also play a part. Regional economic groupings, particularly of the smaller countries, some form of international guarantee for investments, better local planning and presentation of prospects, and greater interest and understanding on the part of the investing community are all needed if these problems are to be met. The outlook for this is not bright.

Almost all of the major agricultural export crops of Tropical Africa are in or coming to be in a chronic surplus position of world supply. For only a few countries do minerals constitute an important part of exports or give promise of doing so at an early date. Wide fluctuations in the prices of the primary export commodities on which these countries rely so heavily have made meeting of fixed obligations and planning of development difficult. Existing projec-tions of consumption of these commodities in traditional markets do not suggest the kind of growth which would accommodate the potential increases in production and correct the current surplus situation and attendant price and earnings fluctuation. No important possibilities of new marketable crops which might be produced in these countries have appeared, and only a few of them have any early prospects of significant diversification through new or expanded mineral production. The immediate and medium-term prospects for Tropical Africa to earn the increased amounts of foreign exchange required to repay debt and maintain a higher level of imports are not good. Some major changes in the character of development and in world trading patterns will probably be required for any real improvement.

Tropical Africa has entered a new transition phase in its relations with the world economy. Unless its traditional trading partners

493

work hard with the new African authorities, it promises to be a very difficult period of transition.

DISCUSSION OF MR. MORAN'S PAPER

Professor Samuels, opening the discussion, remarked that there had been repeated allusions in the course of the discussions to speakers as being too optimistic or pessimistic in their assessments of the potentialities of the territories in Africa for future development. He thought these terms were not really very helpful. Anybody living in Africa, anxious to play a part in raising the still miserable standards of consumption of the people of that continent (at least as seen through Western eyes), had necessarily to be optimistic. But this ought not to blind them to the complicated character of the processes involved in raising living standards, such as the lack of real capital and skill, the still primitive methods of organization, of techniques, and so forth. The problems of improving the productive powers of the population, improving their real income-creating capacity, was not simply a matter, as some speakers had suggested, of substituting Western techniques for traditional methods. This was in reality an aspect of the larger problem of changing mental attitudes, creating appropriate incentives, and inducing new sets of values. As the Chairman had rightly reminded us in his paper, in the developed parts of the world these processes had occupied a long period of time.

Mr. Moran dealt at length with the obstacles in the way of developing modern economic organizations in Tropical Africa so as to make it capable of rapid economic growth — obstacles such as the absence of a literate, trained, and educated population, the unwillingness of private foreign investors to invest unless there were some guarantee against political risks in these economies, the distaste in at any rate some of the countries of Africa for the kind of investments which had been traditionally made by foreign investors, the fear of foreign control and so on. We had heard about some of these difficulties that morning.

He would refer to only one aspect Mr. Moran had posed in a very challenging manner. The very attempts made in Tropical Africa and elsewhere to hasten planned development were creating serious budgetary and foreign exchange difficulties, which might inhibit the further inflow of foreign funds for development. The heavy investment expenditures in the field of utilities, social overheads, and other productive devices had not, in many cases, produced sufficient incomes to amortize and maintain such investments, thereby becoming a growing charge on ordinary budgets. On the other hand, these investment expenditures had succeeded admirably in improving health, educational, and other standards, accelerating in the process the influx of people to the towns and thereby increasing the need for still further investment.

Mr. Moran had illustrated the dilemma involved by referring to the experiences of the Republic of the Congo (Léopoldville), which embarked on a Ten-Year Development Programme covering the period 1950–60. The Congo government was in an extremely healthy financial shape when it started the plan in 1950. By the end of the plan period in 1959 its public debt had risen substantially, imposing a high charge of 17 per cent on the budget ; the public expenditures had since 1957 consistently outstripped revenue, while the chronic deficits in its balance of payments since 1956 had drawn down the gold and other foreign exchange assets to a low level, although external liabilities had in the meantime risen very sharply. After ten years of rapidly expanding planned expenditure, the the Congo, Mr. Moran pertinently notes, 'was hardly a suitable candidate for further loans'.

The Congo story was extremely interesting but more information was required to assess the meaning of Mr. Moran's statistics. What happened to export incomes during the ten-year period ? Were the Congo's external financial difficulties significantly due to the outflow of foreign funds, or was this confined to the period since 1959 ? It would be useful to fill in the picture during the discussion of his paper. The lessons of the experience of the Congo seemed to indicate the need for large-scale expansion of export earnings and/or capital imports, to sustain for any lengthy period large and growing expenditures, connected with a rapid process of urbanization and industrial growth, especially when expenditures promised at best distant returns.

Mr. Moran was conscious about the problem raised by large-scale public expenditures on social and other activities with no early promise of a substantial expansion in incomes. He believed that the way out of the difficulty would be the provision of grants or long-term loans at low rates of interest. He also made the interesting suggestion that a large part of the financial responsibility for social overheads should, where possible, be passed over to local communities with some financial assistance from central governments. This was being done in some countries in Africa, for example South Africa where gold-mining companies had developed townships and the whole infrastructure for population attracted to the new gold field, and were in process of handing over such townships to local authorities under agreed conditions.

Professor Samuels wondered whether we were not to some extent inventing problems for ourselves by imagining that all economies on the eve of their development should first equip themselves with an elaborate outfit of capital goods for the development of an infrastructure before economic expansion and improved living standards could take place. This was not his experience of how development had in fact taken place in the more advanced economies of Africa. Development of communication, educational institutions, power resources, and so on had taken place as part of the whole process of expansion — not for economy as a whole but piecemeal as new market opportunities appeared as a result of the removal of market obstacles to expansion. It was worth noting that expenditures for development had freqeuntly been undertaken not merely by governments, but by privately operated enterprises — the gold mines, for example, sugar companies, and other large employers of labour in South Africa, the copper producers in Northern Rhodesia and Katanga, and the large-scale producers of agricultural and other products in other parts of Africa.

Professor Samuels turned next to the importance of African export trade. Mr. Moran had rightly stressed the fundamental importance of achieving a high volume of exports if the capital equipment and other imports were to be obtained to sustain a rising scale of economic activity. There was nothing particularly regrettable about a country's dependence on foreign trade. It was true that in engaging in trade a country put itself at the mercy of external events. This was the price paid within a domestic market as well as where there was any international division of labour. If a country seeks development, it needs foreign influence if it is to succeed. It requires foreign equipment, foreign capital, and foreign ideas. How could countries with a limited range of resources hope to pay for their equipment and other needs except by exporting ? Again, how could one expect an economy to be permeated with ideas that are a seed-bed of true development if one deprived it of the kind of contacts with foreigners that trade automatically produced ? Trade was no mere exchange of goods, particularly where countries were at different stages of development. Trade was a source of the desire for development, of the knowledge and of the experience that made development possible.

Professor Samuels concluded with a discussion of the question whether exports were likely to be an engine of growth in Africa as they had been in Europe in the nineteenth century. Foreign trade, he argued, posed serious problems. Some of these problems affect especially the tropical countries whose domestic income depends on a narrow range of exports. As regards the expected surplus of tropical products, he wondered whether the present situation provided a reliable base for pessimistic forecasts in this respect — whether in fact the market for the exports of these territories was really as inelastic as appeared. This was a serious problem which affected particularly the countries of Tropical Africa. In part the countries which lay in the tropical latitudes were partly screened from competition with advanced countries (apart from the competition of new synthetics), but were not screened from competition with one another. Other tropical countries were likely to be alternative sources of supply. They were almost equally well placed, after a lag, to do as well or not much worse than their neighbours. Implicit in this was of course the possibility of gains as well as of losses, once new producers had had time to come into production in particular territories or other countries. This raised the whole problem of the growth of world consumptions for such products which Dr. Moran had discussed.

Professor Fauvel emphasized Africa's dependence on exports of a very small number of products. He thought, none the less, that the prospects for the future were bright. There were the great possibilities presented by the opening up of markets in the U.S.S.R. Soviet economic policies had started by giving great priority to heavy industry. The U.S.S.R. had now a surplus of productive capacity in several branches of the heavy industries. On the other hand, Soviet agriculture was lagging. There were opportunities for profitable exchanges of African agricultural and tropical products for Soviet capital goods. He hoped that we might be told more about the probable Soviet demands for cocoa from Ghana and Nigeria, for bananas from Guinea. If these and other exports could be developed, could it be hoped that the African producers would secure better terms of trade and be less exploited in future ?

Professor Leduc felt rather critical of Mr. Moran's paper. It was composed of two elements : an account of what had happened in the past ; an expression of views as to what might happen in the future. He found himself in disagreement with both. The colonial period of history was a fact and could not be ignored. But had it always been bad ? It was far too early to prepare an objective assessment of the whole of the colonial epoch. Mr. Moran had thought fit to reproach those nations which had permitted the present situation to have developed. But in the years 1900–20 there could not have been economic planning in the modern sense. In practice a considerable measure of economic development was achieved through the ordinary economic processes. Africans had, for example, greatly expanded the production of ground-nuts in Senegal. There had been considerable investment in Guinea. He was sorry that Mr. Moran had made no mention of the effects of monetary areas which had in turn promoted economic areas. The full effects of these needed to be brought into the picture. He thought that Mr. Moran had been too negative and too pessimistic and that he had shown no real appreciation of the rôle of the more advanced metropolitan countries in assisting the economic development of their associated African territories. There had been very substantial assistance from France to the African territories in her economic area during the past ten or fifteen years. In the same way the European Economic Community was continuing to assist their development.

Mr. Onitiri thought that the prospects for primary products were not bright. Even if they had been, he did not think that was an argument against considerable diversification of African economies. There was obvious advance in increasing the elasticity of one's supply of exportables and of one's demand for importables, even if one hoped that the ratio of exports to national income would remain at its present level. It was absolutely essential to have it clearly in mind that Africa was entering a new political phase. A new approach to old problems was needed. If private enterprise was prepared to spend money, as Professor Samuels had said, on creating an economic infrastructure, that was not an act of generosity ; it was because it helped to raise African productivity. He thought that conditions in South Africa were fundamentally different from those in other parts of self-governing Africa. In those parts they were seeking new solutions, which might be very different from the solutions found in Western countries, with less emphasis on the test of profit and with new methods of financing development. He was convinced that there still remained much scope for private investment. It was the concern of governments to facilitate its inflow. Private investment could secure in Africa a return at least as favourable as in the advanced countries ; in practice the handicaps under which it might operate were negligible and the guarantees given were valuable. He thought that the economic relations between African countries and the advanced countries were improving all the time. He was, however, disappointed that more had not been done to create and improve the working of the financial institutions needed for development. He regarded the European Common Market as potentially an intensification of the earlier schemes of monetary and economic areas. He hoped that ultimately there would be unification in a wider common market.

Mr. Beheiry was concerned, firstly, about the increases in current expenditures which resulted from capital expenditures designed to improve education, health, and the like. It had become a real issue how to allocate resources over a period of years among these competing services. In the Sudan they were concerned also with the question of how to hold the balance between expenditure on revenue generating schemes and on social developments which did not directly generate income. He was interested, secondly, in Professor Samuels' suggestion that more financial responsibility should be devolved from the central government on to local governments. He agreed that there was too much dependence of the latter on the central governments.

Professor Dupriez said that there had been a profound change in the attitudes of metropolitan powers to African economic problems. Down to about 1949, they had believed in natural economic development in response to market forces. From then onwards the concept of development had been assessed in terms of the welfare approach. There were thus two widely different sets of historical circumstances.

Professor Robinson was puzzled by the second paragraph of Mr. Moran's paper. He seemed to argue that because investment decisions in regard to Africa had been made in the past to benefit the nationals of other countries, they must have been to the detriment of Africa. That implication had appeared several times before during the Conference. It was surely fallacious. He had been brought up on the writings of Mr. Moran's great fellow-countryman — Professor Taussig. Surely Professor Taussig had argued, following a long tradition, that international trade normally benefited both parties and not only one : if both countries could specialize in the activities in which they had a comparative advantage, both would gain. What was at issue was the division of the gain, and the proper balance of long-term gain against short-term gain. *Professor Robinson* was not so certain that the division of the gains of African trade had always been as equitable as it might have been, or that the infant industry argument had always been accepted and applied when it should have been. He himself believed that trade had in fact been an important channel of technological development in Africa. He took Mr. Onitiri's arguments to be for the development of new channels of trade and new types of long-term exports in addition to the traditional exports of African products : that he intended that these traditional exports should be maximized, but was sceptical whether the price- and income-elasticities were such that the traditional exports would grow *pari passu* with national incomes. *Professor Robinson* thought that was a tenable view, but he was not sure that it was not over-pessimistic. It was true that a large proportion of African exports went into foodstuffs and suffered from the low income-elasticity for food in general. But some tropical foodstuffs enjoyed, he thought, the rather higher income-elasticity associated with more luxury foods. And though the raw-material content of manufacture was declining, manufacturing was growing faster than national incomes and there were great potential demands for manufacturing raw materials, if the balance of payments problems of the rapidly growing under-developed countries could be solved. He thought that African countries had to develop more flexibility than they had yet shown, and to put more emphasis on discovering new export products in agriculture as well as in manufacture. Great Britain had been forced to change progressively the character of her exports. African countries must be prepared to do the same. For all that, he thought that in the present context of slowly growing earnings from traditional exports, African countries were right to explore the possibilities of import-saving and the means of concentrating their export-earnings on those imports which might most contribute to growth.

M. Roland Pré was concerned about the basis on which it was possible to envisage African export trade and its entry into the world economy. The first need, he thought, was to find ways in which the elucated African could be brought into touch with the advanced technologies of the outside world. It was through these contacts that the young Africans could be stimulated to move into activities that would result in African development. He was concerned also about the equitable division of the gains from African trade. A considerable part of the profits made from investments in Africa had been diverted to new investment in other countries. He thought it was most important that educated Africans should play a large part in all discussions of the problems of development in Africa.

Dr. Cookson argued that it was generally accepted that there was a downward bias in the estimation of elasticities, so that these tended away to be underestimated. The important thing was that African countries must expand exports. He suggested that private foreign investment in developing African trade was inhibited, firstly by uncertainties of profitability, secondly by the risks represented by the uncertainties of the development of demand, thirdly by political uncertainties and the banker mentality as regards risks. He thought the real danger was presented by subtle indirect expropriation. He believed that there was a large unexplored market for African products in the Soviet bloc and was anxious to know whether any attempt had been made to project the potential demand.

Dr. Singer returned to Professor Robinson's worries as to whether the gains of African trade had been equitably divided. If the division was to be fair, trade should be free of all restrictions. That had not invariably been true. There was, he suggested, no connection between pessimism about the prospects of demand for traditional African export commodities and emphasis on improving particular exports. The United Nations had been engaged in producing a spate of projections of particular exports. For some of these there appeared to be very bright prospects — for meat, for example. Exports of primary products should not be considered in isolation from manufactures. In India, for example, it was being sought to expand manufactured exports to under-developed countries in order to be able to import more primary products. It was in the interest of Africa to develop closer trade links with over-populated under-developed countries. As regards trade with the U.S.S.R. he was less confident about the long-run possibilities. The present opportunities for primary product exports to the U.S.S.R. arose from the fact that agricultural had lagged behind industrial development. That situation might very probably be reversed. *Dr. Singer* commented also on the interrelations between technology and research. He thought it was a weakness of the world economy that there was a bias in the nature of technological change. The nature and direction of research was largely guided by the requirements of one or two advanced countries.

Dr. Okigbo thought the prospects for primary products were rather gloomy. There were two choices open to countries which wanted to increase their export earnings : they could try to find new markets for their existing exports or they could try to find new commodities to export. He himself believed that under-developed countries in Africa were well advised to attempt deliberate industrialization in the hope first of saving imports and ultimately of building up exports. If they all attempted to sell their traditional exports more energetically in the present markets, the most likely outcome would be that they would collectively sell a larger volume to earn about the same amount of foreign exchange. He believed that they should be framing more ambitious programmes of industrialization than those of the past, and they should look for the financing of public expenditure programmes to foreign loans and foreign aid. They were in the paradoxical situation of being penalized today for their prudence in the past.

Professor Walker wanted to see more intra-African co-operation. In the case of the large under-developed countries of Asia there was a fairly large domestic market. But in the smaller African countries there was much less scope for building up an industrial structure based on import substitution. In Uganda, for example, the total trade was of the order of £25 million, of which only £8-£9 million at best was capable of import substitution. Allowing for variety, there were few products which could support a single reasonably efficient plant. The only way out of this dilemma was the formation of customs unions, involving deliberate agreements about the distribution of the benefits.

Dr. Skorov reminded the Conference that there were 1·2 billion people living in the Socialist world and representing a great potential market. He outlined the possibilities of developing that market and the conditions which would have to be achieved. He thought that the first factor to be borne in mind was the very rapid increase of the industrial production of the Socialist countries. They would have available many of the types of capital goods which under-developed countries needed. Secondly, he emphasized that there were possibilities of new plans for the use of the cultivated areas of the Socialist countries. He illustrated this by reference to the Socialist production of cotton and sugar. If long-term agreements could be made with the Sudan and Egypt for cotton, or with Cuba and other cane-sugar producing countries for sugar, the U.S.S.R. would reduce domestic production of cotton and beet-sugar, to the benefit of both parties. It was, of course, essential that any supplies of food and materials should be reliable and planned on a long-term basis. Thirdly, he thought that loans from the U.S.S.R. could be negotiated on a favourable basis and repayment could be made in the traditional export commodities. On these bases he thought that a new pattern of international division of labour could be worked out between the Socialist countries and the under-developed countries. At present only about 5 per cent of U.S.S.R. imports came from under-developed countries. It had been asked whether there were dangers in State-trading. Finland did 40 per cent of its trade with the U.S.S.R. If this were disadvantageous, Finland could long ago have found other markets and sources of supply. It had been asked what were the desirable patterns of African trades. Should they concentrate on primary products or diversify? He was convinced that they should diversify. Diversification should not mean that every country should produce all of a wide range of items. It should aim at providing countries with a satisfactory diet of locally produced foods and at meeting the principal needs of the domestic markets.

Dr. Yudelman reminded the Conference that export earnings were going to be the main source of the foreign finance available for development. If in the emphasis on diversification the effects on costs of production were ignored it would be a tragedy. He thought it was much more advantageous to substitute low-cost for high-cost products on the basis of international agreement to expand trade. The basic foodstuffs of the densely populated advanced countries of the temperate zones came principally from other countries of the temperate zones. Some of these products were becoming relatively scarce. The tropical countries should examine the possibilities of producing substitutes which would enable them to compete in those markets. This might reduce the intense competition of tropical countries in the limited markets for their present limited range of products.

Dr. Gavrilov was glad that the possibilities of trade with the U.S.S.R. had been raised. He thought it was difficult to discuss the problems of African development without reference to potential trade with the Socialist countries. The U.S.S.R. was prepared to work out suitable terms for expanding trade. He was convinced that African countries must create their own national economies. The monopoly of the Western countries in the supply of machinery had now been broken by the U.S.S.R. and the scope for trade had consequently been widened.

Mr. Moran, replying to the discussion, was convinced that the rest of the world must recognize the great changes that were taking place in Africa and face the full implications. He thought the next ten to fifteen years would be the most difficult. He reminded the Conference of the current discussion of the problems of guaranteeing prices of tropical products. These were difficulties in diversification. If costs of tropical products were raised in consequence or through monopoly action, the competition of synthetic products was to be feared; this had been seen in the case of textile materials, rubber, diamonds, coffee, to quote a few very different examples. He was convinced that Africa had a hard job. The only way to do a hard job was to do it well.

Chapter 18

COMMODITY AND TRADE POLICY IN AFRICA: THE TERMS OF TRADE OF AFRICAN PRODUCERS

BY

LÉON H. DUPRIEZ

Université de Louvain

I. INTRODUCTION

THE development of productive processes in the different regions of Africa entails, necessarily, effort directed in two directions : on the one hand, a local development of a variety of activities which, employing European techniques, may be achieved gradually, as the abilities of the populations to make use of them progressively develop ; in every economic society there is a wide range of such activities ; on the other hand, a development of activities directed toward the exterior world and subject to the requirements of the international division of labour, operating through the system of international pricing ; the level at which this necessary contact can be established dominates the general formation of prices and of money incomes in each region, as well as the techniques to be used and the possible volumes of production.

My purpose is to examine the conditions under which this contact tends to be established in Africa and to define certain problems which require solution. I shall not tackle the problem of the political methods of intervention, such as the commodity boards.

II. DEFINITION OF THE PROBLEM

The problem of the terms of trade is generally examined at the level of relations between nations ; it is conceived as an examination of the trends of comparative advantages, at the immediate level of the barter conditions of the products that cross the frontiers. The point of view is clearly mercantilist ; merchandise must therefore

503

be statistically observed at the point where costs cease to be incurred in one economy and begin to be incurred in the other. To give an example, it is in this spirit that British terms of trade, established at London prices (thus imports f.o.b., exports c.i.f.) have been corrected in order to take into account the fact that transport was usually assured on British bottoms and that insurance was contracted in Britain ; thus imports f.o.b. are properly related to exports c.i.f.[1]

The controversy which opposed R. Prebisch to J. Viner, in the early fifties, has been dominated by this way of looking at the problem. It is not meant to shed light on the more fundamental problems of equilibrium of production between industrialized regions and African regions, which it is our purpose to discuss.

In the perspective of secular expansion, the question one should ask is this : As they progressively leave the subsistence economy and become capable of producing export products with increased technical efficiency, do producers obtain a better reward for their labour ? Does financial productivity follow physical output ? Or is it offset by the lower technical efficiency of the whole population, by the pressure of a labour market that is always redundant, by an excessive elasticity of supply in the face of every price increase ? In other words, do the populations producing export goods encounter, in their effort to get out of the Malthusian state, difficulties analogous to those which European populations encountered prior to 1848 ? Or can they, under certain circumstances (as example, by the creation of developmental blocks), greatly better their condition ?

As the problem is stated, its solution through secular development is clearly dominated by local progress in technical efficiency and by the relations of power which play on the market. Production equilibrium is thus at stake, especially the capacity of populations not to create an overwhelming supply as soon as real receipts increase beyond customary levels.

Mercantilist discussions insist, in this respect, on the difficulties which assail the producers of staple foods as regards the increase of their sales, on account of the action of Engel's law among the consumer groups — in other words, on account of an income elasticity below 1. If we accept that the purpose of production is the consumption desired by individuals, this is an obstacle which can only be overcome by modifying the type of production. The gravity of the problem resides in the action of King's law, which asserts that in the short period price variations will be more than proportional

---

[1] E. Quevrin, *Terms of Trade and Economic Development*, Doctorial Thesis, Princeton.

to the changes in quantities produced : it is the price inelasticity of demand which de-stabilizes the income of producers in case of dis-equilibrium between production and consumption.

The measurement of the terms of trade, so regarded, must clearly be made on the spot, at the level of each region of production. Such terms of trade may differ very distinctly from those measured for the same products at European ports. The difference will be greater, the further one moves into the interior of the African continent — the distance from the sea being measured in costs of trade and transport.

In order to establish as good a measure as possible of the conditions which govern the share of African labour in the equilibrium of exchange and of production, it is necessary to distinguish two cases :

(i) When the African participates in the processes of production of export produce by hiring his labour, the most direct measure of the variations in the fundamental equilibrium of production is to compare his 'double factoral terms of trade' ; in such a case an additional computation in terms of import merchandise is required, in order to measure the change in his purchasing power for such goods (see (ii) below).

(ii) When the African produces himself the export produce and sells it on the market, measurement becomes more difficult : prices obtained at the central market of the region should be compared to prices paid for the import produce ; but in the long period, one should take into account the average progress achieved in output per head. By combining these two series one obtains something like single factoral terms of trade. It is practically impossible to reason further.

These single factoral terms of trade reflect concurrently progress realized in Africa, progress realized in Europe, and progress resulting from better means of communication. It is by these terms that changes in the capacity of the African producer to participate in the goods produced outside of his region can best be appreciated ; but such a measure does not only reflect progress realized in the techniques of these producers and changes in their relations of power. It is decisively affected by progress realized throughout the world. This is not the case for the double factoral terms of trade, which reflect, rather, the changes obtained in the productive qualities and in the power relations on the market.

The study of the single factoral terms of trade in Africa entails a special difficulty. While exports toward industrialized countries bear almost exclusively on a small number of staple goods, whose prices can be established with some safety at the point of departure (or at least their variations), the contents of imports is a wide variety of finished industrial products. The prices of these cannot be observed in time ; but if one considers only unfinished industrial products, a bias is clearly introduced : in the twentieth century, technical progress in Europe has taken the form more and more of increasing elaboration of products. Their relative prices have thus been lowered. Improvement obtained by substitution of new products for old products is also not subject to estimation.

Another difficulty arises especially in the study of the double factoral terms of trade. In order to be completely valid, such a study should have regard to the several factors of production and not to one only. Nevertheless, in our present case, this objection should not be sustained. In most regions here considered, capital has been in the hands of Europeans or, at least, of social groups other than the regional groups. Its reward is not directly at stake in our argument. Land rents, very different from case to case, when natural resources are exploited, are sovereignty receipts, under various forms.

Finally, in many cases, the reward of higher management, which has moved differently from that of wage earners, is also a factor exterior to the local community. It is therefore acceptable to think only in terms of the rewards of labour.

III. THE ECONOMIC SIGNIFICANCE OF PRODUCERS' TERMS OF TRADE

If we consider the problem of the terms of trade at the level of the factors and of their real reward, it is possible to disentangle our interpretation from its usual mercantilistic context and to make it bear on the secular distribution of the produce. The following points must, however, be borne in mind :

First, one must remember that the single factoral terms of trade should be measured in the European industrial centres for the Europeans, and in the African centres of production for the Africans. It is hardly to be expected that the two observations should diverge seriously as a consequence of 'conjunctural' variations in the short period : except where regulatory powers intervene, such as those exercised by commodity boards, any sudden impacts are transmitted. But important causes of divergence can and should occur, when long-term changes are involved.

It is thus not impossible that the single-factoral terms of trade should be improved for both parties — this being the case where Adam Smith's principle applies, that the opening of means of communication and the extension of trade should be profitable to all parties. The following facts render this mutual improvement highly probable in the case of economic progress. It remains thus to measure to what extent progress accrues to each.

The fundamental fact which allows barter terms to change favourably for all groups of producers intervening in trade is the opening of means of communications. At a first stage, this consists in eliminating the obstacles which make any communication almost impossible and keep the various markets separate; in Africa, it implies that the pure subsistence economies are supplanted by economies having their antennae of growth abroad; trade begins with the introduction of new products, possessing no clear connexion with local products. The comparative advantage of this introduction is not measurable. It is nevertheless at the origin of every such transformation.

The maritime regions of the world were progressively favoured with lines of communication from the fifteenth century onwards. For the continental regions, it was the work of the nineteenth and twentieth centuries. The most central regions have acquired only real means of communication very recently : for example Ruanda-Urundi since 1920 and the Tchad only with the progress of aviation. In an African continent hardly favoured with inland water transportation, the most important example of breaking such a bottleneck was the opening of the Matadi–Léopoldville railway in 1898 : this opened the whole Congo basin and its affluents to commerce with Europe.

The commercial contacts thus established remain at first very 'thin', especially where land transport is involved ; the capacity of this land transport is often limited and its very cost restricts possible contacts to products whose value per ton is high ; the economic link with industrial regions is at first imperfect and requires progressive improvement.

Along the coast, commerce has certainly benefited from a progressive decrease in the relative prices of freight rates and from a still more important decrease in maritime insurance costs, as well as from increased port facilities. But right from the beginning, these costs represent only a small part of the price of most imported and exported products. Things are different inside the continent : land transport is expensive : the cost per ton-km. by rail or by road may become prohibitive for many types of merchandise at the distances involved for reaching the interior of the continent. Moreover, transport breaking points imposed by changes in the type of transport add greatly to cost and increase the risks of deterioration of the product. These breaking points may be as many as four or five for regions such as Kivu and Ruanda-Urundi.

It should thererefore be recognized that commercial openings for industrial Europe are, today, relatively easy around coastal ports, but that they are more difficult and 'thinner' as one enters more deeply the centre of the African continent. As produce has to be delivered at the same export price, whatever its origin, the terms of trade of the African producer are a direct function of the 'economic' distance from the sea.

This proposition attributes a vital importance to the decrease of transport costs on the great axes of communication going from the sea to the central regions of the African continent. The economies realized on transport go to local populations, both as increased price for the produce and as diminished price for articles bought. An example of the extent of what can be realized in this respect is given by the Matadi–Léo railway, which is vital for the whole Congo basin : at the opening, in 1898, the average receipt per ton-km. was 1·32 fr. (gold) ; in 1907 it was still 0·87 ft. ; in 1954 it had fallen to 0·86 present-day francs. Taking monetary depreciation into account, this means a decrease of real costs of the order of 50 to 1.[1]

Decreases of costs of such magnitude are only possible on transport lines with a considerable traffic. These may only lead to navigable rivers or to lakes, which permit the easy assembly of produce, or to dense centres of production (which hardly exist in agriculture) or again, to mining regions of high metallic content. Wide areas, with a low demographic density and with scanty resources, remain outside exchange possibilities, except for a few articles of the carrying trade.

It is therefore obvious that the possibilities of increasing the single factoral terms of trade may not be extended uniformly to a vast continental territory, thinly populated ; to its centre, only a limited number of means of communication are economical and acceptable. The improvements in terms of trade are thus conducive to some sort of polarization. The sites of polarization become necessary centres of demographic concentration — otherwise, the cost of transfer of the advantages of international commerce become prohibitive. Examples of such regrouping are easy to find. Thus the movement of populations southward, all along the coast from Sénégal to Nigeria, answers such an urge. The constitution of poles of development in the previously little populated regions of Katanga and Northern Rhodesia answers another requirement of economic concentration. The localization of palm-oil plants, in Congo, which are placed

[1] A. Huybrechts, 'La Formation des prix du chemin de fer de Matadi à Léopold-ville, 1898–1954', *Bull. Inst. Rech. Econ. et Soc.*, 1955, p. 550.

almost exclusively near river communications, entails local re-groupings.

On the other hand, efforts to decentralize production entail social costs, which must be kept within reasonable limits : thus the development of the *paysannats indigènes* in the oriental province of Congo for cotton production has been extended into an area which increases internal transport seriously ; the average cost of the crop is likely to be affected if means of transport are not rapidly improved.

Before examining some of the statistical data it is appropriate to assess a fundamental principle governing the secular implementation of the process of distribution of the produce between factors, and at the same time to show its bearing on our present problem.

In accordance with principles brilliantly expounded by J. Schumpeter, the product of newer and better combinations of factors is distributed, at the end of every period of conjunctural strain between the elementary factors of production ; in consequence of this process, sales prices tend to come into equilibrium with production costs. Within a given community, redistribution operates partly through a better direct reward for factors ; partly, also, by a more diffuse transmission to consumers. This latter process affects mostly products submitted to great technical progress.

As regards changes in relations between regions of a different nature, secular redistribution operates in two ways :

(i) a possible modification in the double factoral terms of trade, especially for manual labour ; this implies changes in the average efficiency of workers of the regions involved and other changes, probably more limited, in the relations of power ;

(ii) a transmission, very important at the secular scale, of the fruits of technical progress to consumers, whoever they may be.

This latter proposition implies that, with increasing flows of trade, African populations should enjoy an important share in the progress realized in Europe ; and European populations of an important share in the progress realized in the methods of production of produce exported from Africa. The principles of economic distribution thus require that benefits shall be partaken in common.

The truth of this proposition is confirmed by certain historical events. The clearest among them is the trend of the British terms of trade from 1694 to 1854, *i.e.* during the first industrial revolution, which primarily developed long-distance trade in textiles. According to W. Schlote [1] the price of imported staple foods and materials

---

[1] W. Schlote, *Entwicklung und Strukturwandlungen des englischen Aussenhandels von 1700 bis zur Gegenwart*, Jena, 1938, pp. 119-23.

reached index 169, that of exports index 47 ; as measured in London, the terms of exchange fell from 100 to 28 in a century and a half. This does not correspond to a period of commercial disadvantages for Great Britain, but to a period of flourishing trade : the registered difference is really a gross measure of the result of technical progress which Britain had to concede to its clients.

Since 1870, the rapid geographical extension of crops has reversed the tendency : Europe has benefited by it under the form of lower prices, but these entailed difficulties to sell ; the sudden glut of the markets for agricultural products after 1928 created the same result and provoked adjustments in agricultural technique to meet the changed barter terms of trade. From recent figures (cf. *infra*), it can be seen that certain types of produce can be sold at decreasing prices without diminishing the local reward of labour (wool, palm oil), while others cannot.

It is therefore clear that the problem is the distribution of the accrued fruits of efforts made by both parties and that the principle of economic distribution, at the level of world relations, determines the shares, just as it does at the national level.

IV. ANALYSIS OF THE TERMS OF TRADE OF THE PRODUCERS OF SOME AFRICAN STAPLE PRODUCTS

I shall now try to illustrate the working of some of the principles discussed above by a few historical examples. These are only a first approach to a statistical study, which would have to be greatly expanded, if it were to be used to help to select the most effective methods of economic development. Circumstances have obliged me to assemble rapidly obtainable data, rather than to make a rational choice of interesting cases. Moreover, it is often difficult to secure data at the point which is theoretically most appropriate. But certain general conclusions can be drawn from the adjoining graphs.

(i) *Cocoa*

Cocoa is mostly a 'half picking' crop or a product of native farming, cultivated predominantly in regions having easy access to the sea ; grown in regions with exuberant vegetation, its supply can be very elastic to incentives playing on numerous producers : as the bean grows on small trees, increases in production capacity are reflected in supply with a minimum lag of four to five years.

Facts have been studied, according to three different sources, on three graphs (I, II, III), relating to Ghana and Nigeria. The

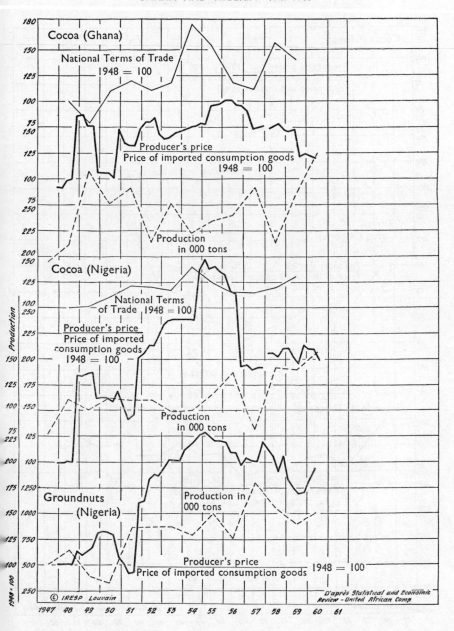

COCOA AND GROUNDNUTS

GHANA AND NIGERIA 1939-1951

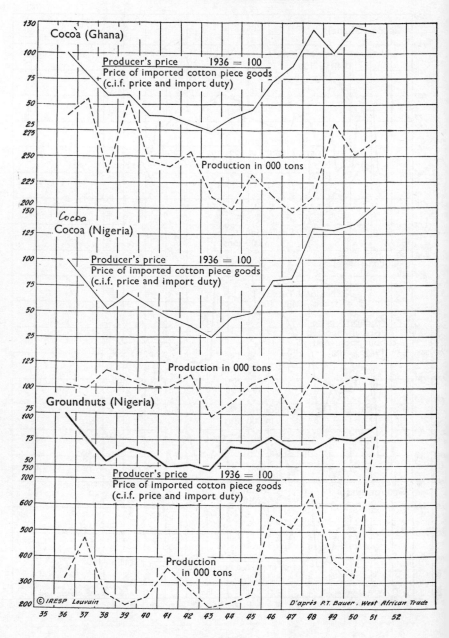

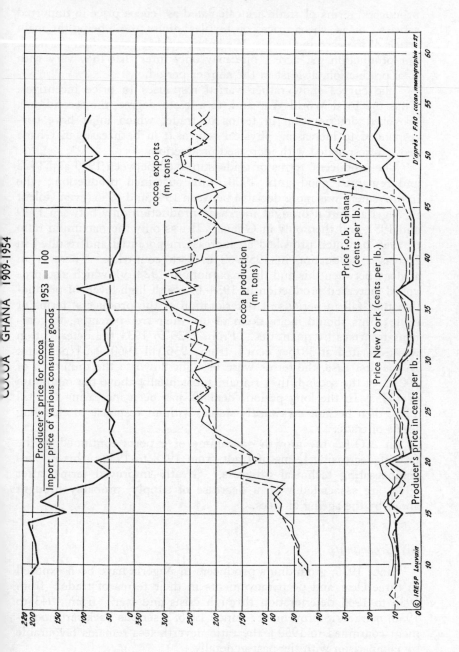

COCOA GHANA 1909-1954

Producer's price for cocoa
Import price of various consumer goods } 1953 = 100

cocoa exports (m. tons)

cocoa production (m. tons)

Price f.o.b. Ghana (cents per lb.)

Price New York (cents per lb.)

Producer's price in cents per lb.

© IRESP Louvain

D'après : FAO , cocoa. monographie n: 27

producers' terms of trade are calculated as 'cocoa price in imported articles', or as 'cocoa prices on textiles' alone, these being the main article of the carrying trade. We know, neither production per head, nor production per acre ; one may only infer that they vary with total production, at least in the shorter period.

The curves show rather varied responses to price incentives. Thus the First World War and, to a lesser degree, the second one, provoked deterioration in terms of trade, which must have corresponded to increasing physical returns ; in both cases in Ghana growers responded with increased production.

The producers' terms of trade improved between 1919 and 1928 and remained good until 1930, with sustained production ; the improvement was more decisive between 1945 and 1956 (even violent in Nigeria), but it brought increased production only between 1949 and 1951, and then only in Ghana. It was only the maximum ratio of 1955–6, which provoked an increase in potential and resulted in increased production in 1959–60 in both countries. There is an analogy between this and the maximum of 1928–30, which also provoked increased production in 1934–6. Both high levels of production thus fall in periods of deterioration of the producers' terms of trade ; this should incite them to use their tree-potential, to compensate prices by quantities. From 1928 to 1934 the deterioration was estimated at 38 per cent ; from 1956 till 1960 at 31 per cent. In the first case, the terms were brought down to the minimum of 1921 ; in the second, they remain substantially above the minimum of 1945. In the long period, demand has been increasing fast till 1924, then became awkwardly stable, without response to changing terms of trade.

In A.O.F., the growth of volume of exports continued in the face of decreasing terms of trade from 1928 to 1936 ; this implies compensating technical progress. Greatly improved terms, after 1948, are associated with a decrease of supply, probably brought about by the ageing of trees.

(ii) *Groundnuts*

Since 1936, groundnuts producers in Nigeria have been exposed to three clear and deep movements in their terms of trade : from 1936 to 1943 deterioration through crisis and war ; from 1943 to 1956, marked improvement ; since 1956, a serious backward movement continued to 1959 ; the ratio nevertheless remains favourable by comparison with the past generally.

Production is in structural expansion, which should mean that it

PALM OIL   A O F   1922-1939

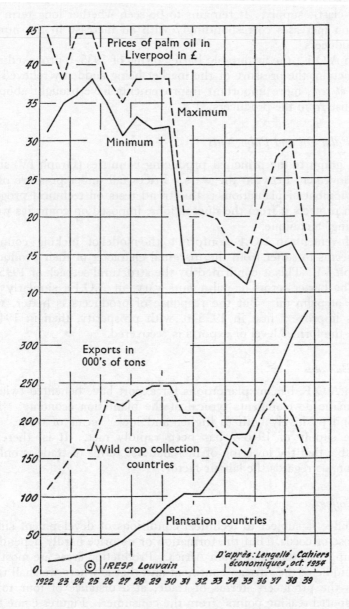

Prices of palm oil in Liverpool in £

Maximum

Minimum

Exports in 000's of tons

Wild crop collection countries

Plantation countries

© IRESP Louvain

D'après: Lengellé, Cahiers économiques, oct. 1954

1922 23 24 25 26 27 28 29 30 31 32 33 34 35 36 37 38 39

competes well with possible products of substitution. In the shorter period, it is very 'conjunctural', with upper points often corresponding to feeble decreases in the terms of trade. These should be attributed to an elastic supply. It remains to be seen whether long-term production increases correspondingly with an increase in the number of producers.

In A.O.F., the favourable barter terms of 1935-6 provoked a big production, the pressure of the market being suddenly relieved ; in 1949 *et seq.*, more important improvements have brought about no response from the producers.

(iii) *Palm Oil and Palm Nuts*

A graph to the principal producing countries (Graph IV) shows the movement between the wars. Prices fall under pressure of the development of plantations ; this trend rests on technical progress, which protects it from the fluctuations, imposed on countries with a 'picking' technique.

Movements in A.O.F. conform to the model of 'picking' countries and seems to suffer from the marginal character of their production (Graph V). This is confirmed by the structural setback of 1945.

The barter terms of palm nuts vary, in A.O.F., similarly with those of palm oil. But the response of producers is better, when terms improve : first in 1935-6, with prosperity, then in 1947-8, when the former level of exports is recovered.

(iv) *Bananas*

In A.O.F. banana plantations for export have benefited twice by systematic developments typical of the plantation economy. They respond positively both to higher and lower terms of trade. The scarce supply of 1946-7 has been rapidly met. It is, therefore, probable that the lowering of merchandise terms of trade is only an illusion, as regards the labour factor.

(v) *Coffee*

Coffee is subject to technical conditions of development similar to those of cocoa. But the formation of its price hardly depends on the supply forthcoming from Africa. Production areas are mostly in the middle of the African continent and that is where we shall try to assess the producers' terms of trade, at a distance of four to five 'transport breaking points' from the consumer. Figures come from Ruanda-Urundi, where producers are natives.

PALM OIL, PALM KERNELS AND GROUNDNUTS
A O F 1925-1952

Indices 1938 = 100

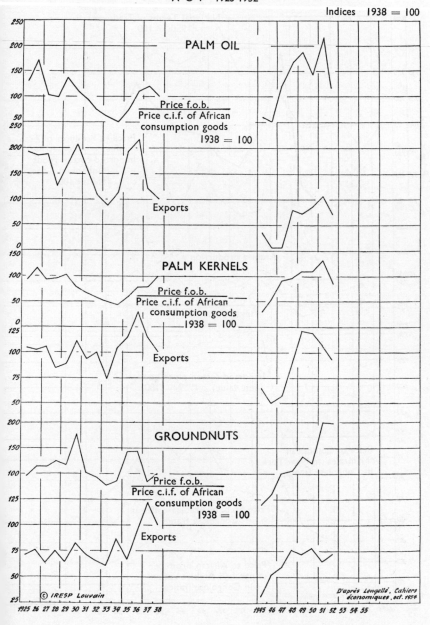

PALM OIL

Price f.o.b.
Price c.i.f. of African
consumption goods
1938 = 100

Exports

PALM KERNELS

Price f.o.b.
Price c.i.f. of African
consumption goods
1938 = 100

Exports

GROUNDNUTS

Price f.o.b.
Price c.i.f. of African
consumption goods
1938 = 100

Exports

© IRESP Louvain

D'après Lengellé, Cahiers
économiques, oct. 1954

1925 26 27 28 29 30 31 32 33 34 35 36 37 38   1945 46 47 48 49 50 51 52 53 54 55

517

COFFEE RUANDA URUNDI 1945-1960

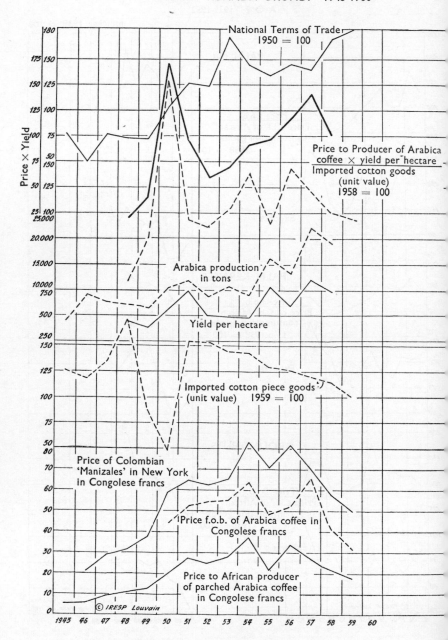

COFFEE, COCOA, AND BANANAS

A O F 1925-1952

Indices 1938 = 100

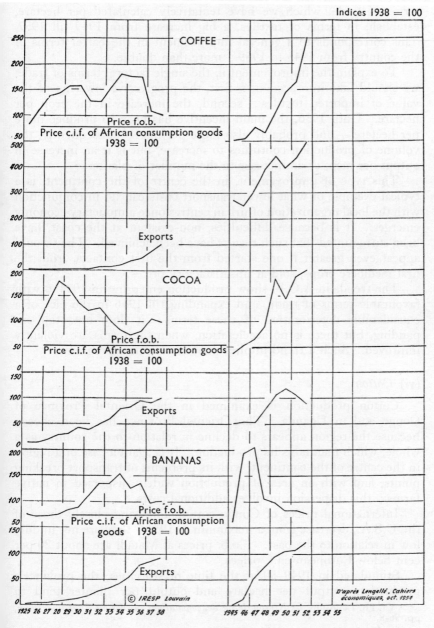

COFFEE

Price f.o.b.
Price c.i.f. of African consumption goods
1938 = 100

Exports

COCOA

Price f.o.b.
Price c.i.f. of African consumption goods
1938 = 100

Exports

BANANAS

Price f.o.b.
Price c.i.f. of African consumption
goods 1938 = 100

Exports

© *IRESP Louvain*

D'après Lengellé, Cahiers économiques, oct. 1954

1925 26 27 28 29 30 31 32 33 34 35 36 37 38   1945 46 47 48 49 50 51 52 53 54 55

The movement is dominated, as for most products, by a big increase in prices and in merchandise terms of trade until 1956 ; there is a subsequent deterioration. Nevertheless, the single factoral terms of trade, which we have tentatively calculated per hectare, establish, in terms of textiles, a big increase from 1949 till 1957. This corresponds to a general improvement in the barter terms of the country from 1945 to 1959 : more than double.

To explain the improvement in the single factoral terms of trade, we should take into account : first, the progressive lowering of the value of imported textiles ; second, the increase in the crop per hectare. Until 1956, the main incentive has been to produce more per hectare — and probably also more per man ; subsequently, the volume of production continues to increase, but is it an increase in output per man, or an increase in the number of planters ?

This type of improvement, in the centre of the continent, is a typical example of what lower transport costs can do in conjunction with the local organization of urban centres once a monetary economy emerges. It is because difficulties, non-existent at the coast, have been surmounted that such results have been achieved. They would appear even greater if one started from the first contacts, from the first mediocre crops, sold at unsatisfactory prices.[1]

The trends in A.O.F. show production emerging in 1934–6 with favourable terms of trade, and expanding till 1946 in the face of a considerable deterioration of these terms ; it does not stop expanding, but there is no acceleration, when the terms are violently improved. Such a trend implies marked technical progress.

(vi) *Cotton*

Cotton production is examined in the Oriental Province of Congo and in Uganda. The Oriental Province has been chosen because the region appears to decline in relation to the country as a whole, which maintains its production. It is again a case of a region in the centre of the continent, with its problems of transport breaking points, and with an area of production widely dispersed in native farms ; this dispersion involves additional costs.

International prices of Congo cotton, following closely those of the U.S.A., decrease from a maximum in 1951 ; they are not unduly low in relation to the past. F.o.b. prices at Matadi are about 20 per cent below European c.i.f. prices.

Stimulated in 1949–50 at the time of scarcities, the province's production, output per hectare and output per planter tend to

[1] Cf. Ph. Leurquin, *Le Niveau de vie des populations rurales du Ruanda-Urundi*, pp. 96-8.

COTTON CONGO

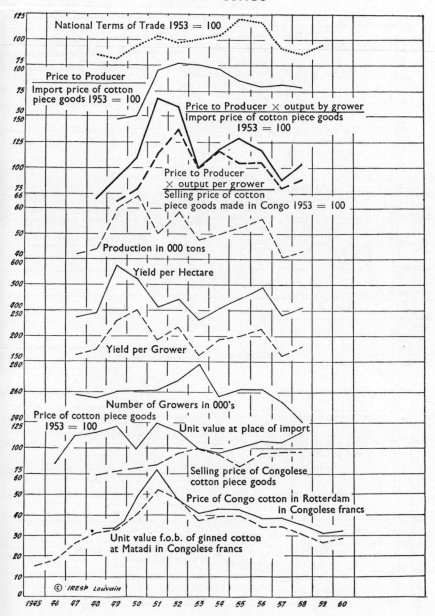

National Terms of Trade 1953 = 100

Price to Producer
Import price of cotton
piece goods 1953 = 100

Price to Producer × output by grower
Import price of cotton piece goods
1953 = 100

Price to Producer
× output per grower
Selling price of cotton
piece goods made in Congo 1953 = 100

Production in 000 tons

Yield per Hectare

Yield per Grower

Number of Growers in 000's

Price of cotton piece goods
1953 = 100

Unit value at place of import

Selling price of Congolese
cotton piece goods

Price of Congo cotton in Rotterdam
in Congolese francs

Unit value f.o.b. of ginned cotton
at Matadi in Congolese francs

© *IRESP Louvain*

1945 46 47 48 49 50 51 52 53 54 55 56 57 58 59 60

COTTON UGANDA

Indices 1953-1954 = 100

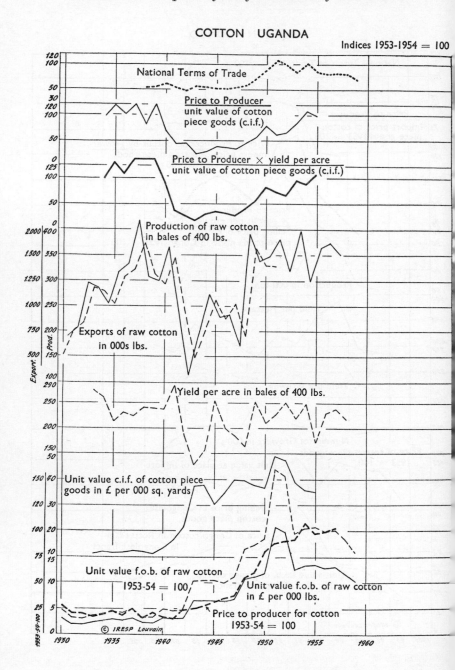

National Terms of Trade

Price to Producer
unit value of cotton
piece goods (c.i.f.)

Price to Producer × yield per acre
unit value of cotton piece goods (c.i.f.)

Production of raw cotton
in bales of 400 lbs.

Exports of raw cotton
in 000s lbs.

Yield per acre in bales of 400 lbs.

Unit value c.i.f. of cotton piece
goods in £ per 000 sq. yards

Unit value f.o.b. of raw cotton
1953-54 = 100

Unit value f.o.b. of raw cotton
in £ per 000 lbs.

Price to producer for cotton
1953-54 = 100

© IRESP Louvain

diminish thereafter. Nevertheless, they are all stimulated in 1955–6 by better terms of exchange. Since 1957, lower prices are acting as a brake.

Terms of exchange expressed in textiles have been calculated both on cloth coming from Léopoldville and cloth coming from Europe. Both series show deterioration after 1951–2. The downward movement of the curves is exaggerated, as cloth produced in Leopoldville has improved in quality. This interpretation is confirmed by the general terms of exchange of the country. On the whole, there has been a pressure of the barter terms since 1951 with conjunctural fluctuations.

In Uganda, the general barter terms of the country reach a very favourable level in 1952, corresponding to the high international prices of cotton ; thereafter they decline, but remain favourable in comparison with the period prior to 1947. Prices paid to producers exceed the maximum of 1951–2 and improve slowly till 1957. Thus the producers' barter terms improve progressively from 1947 at least to 1955, with a probable fall after 1957. Reorganized in 1948 at a level hardly above the pre-war level, production remains more or less constant with climatic variations ; output per acre does not improve ; the methods of production do not seem to respond to the terms of trade.

(vii) *Wool*

Wool has been studied here for comparison, as it is not an African export product north of the Zambesi. How does a produce behave which comes from a 'new' and distant country, where production is organized in big farms ?

The price of wool and the terms of trade of Australia move similarly to the price of cotton and the terms of trade of Uganda, with a sharp highpoint in 1951 and a regular deterioration after that. The conjunctural fluctuation appears a year after price quotations both in production and in export prices.

The number of sheep and the production of wool have increased progressively by about 55 to 60 per cent since 1946. A 30 per cent deterioration in terms of trade from 1954 till 1959 has not checked this trend. The trend of the figures implies an increase of productivity.

(viii) *Copper*

In this industry the problem of the terms of trade for the African producer takes a different form for one is concerned to measure

WOOL AUSTRALIA

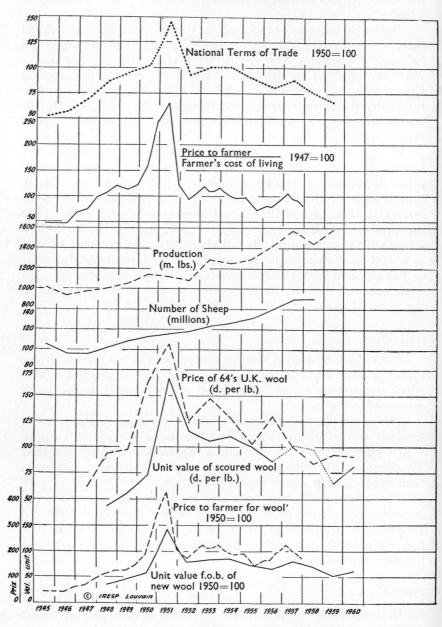

National Terms of Trade   1950=100

Price to farmer
Farmer's cost of living   1947=100

Production
(m. lbs.)

Number of Sheep
(millions)

Price of 64's U.K. wool
(d. per lb.)

Unit value of scoured wool
(d. per lb.)

Price to farmer for wool'
1950=100

Unit value f.o.b. of
new wool 1950=100

© IRESP Louvain

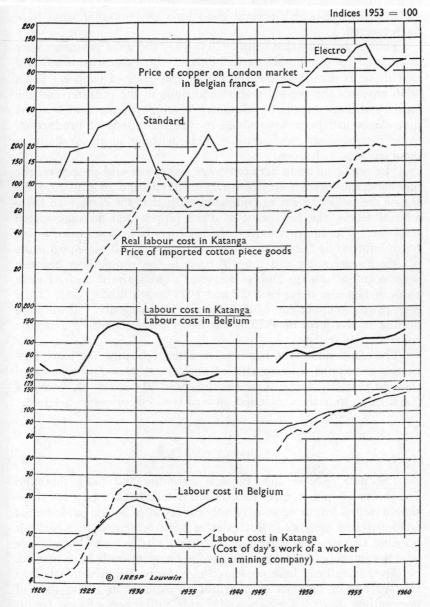

COPPER   CONGO   1922-1960

Indices 1953 = 100

directly the terms of trade between wage payments. I have available to me only the figures for Katanga copper, a region that is continental in the fullest sense, but with a concentration of actual production in an area towards which several good lines of communication have been created.

The figures show that from 1920 to 1939 the wage payments were dominated by the working conditions of the enterprise itself, and that these in turn were determined by the price of copper. From 1946 onwards the general world conditions in the industry and the local conditions were both relevant. Wage payments, which in the first stages had been determined by the conditions of production, came progressively to determine them without doing so quite as completely as in Europe.

The terms of trade between wage payments and money on the one hand, and textiles on the other, reflected from 1930 to 1935 the lag in the fall of wages as compared with that for cloth. In more general terms, the low point of 1932 represented an exaggerated response. The improvement since 1947 has been due to real forces but reinforced by the progressive monetization of all wage payments.

More interesting and more precise is the comparison between wage costs in Katanga and in Belgium. The upward push of wage costs in Katanga between 1927 and 1929 was a direct result of the high price of copper and of the consequent prosperity. Equally the decline to the level of 1925 is the cruel consequence of a serious restriction of activity.

The trend since 1946 has been steadier, reflecting the more continuing conditions of integration of world markets. Over a period of thirteen years the terms improved by some 60 per cent in favour of Katanga, despite the continued upward trend of prices in Belgium.

V. CONCLUSIONS

The data here set out require a further and more thorough examination based on more precise and detailed statistics ; and these should represent more closely the concepts of single and double factoral terms of trade. But even as here presented they make it possible to trace the direction of certain changes and to indicate how the impacts of the variations in the terms of trade have worked.

They have been here presented in a form designed to facilitate the analysis of regional equilibrium of production rather than of mercantilist issues ; they show the wide differences of local conditions and of the responses of producers ; differences in localization, in area covered by production, in types of production methods, in technical requirements, in means of transport and methods of trading. Producers must take into account advantages and disadvantages in all these respects when organizing production for sale in an international market whose elasticity is obviously limited.

The way in which producers react, both structurally and in response to conjunctural fluctuations, helps to show where the problems of economic *progress* arise which have to be solved in a world where progress is both competitive and general.

———

DISCUSSION OF PROFESSOR DUPRIEZ'S PAPER

Mr. Onitiri, in opening the discussion of Professor Dupriez's paper, argued that in studying African trade the most important issues were two : first, how the gains from the trade were divided between the two nations that were trading ; second, how the gains accruing from trade in particular commodities were distributed between different parties within the separate countries concerned. Simple calculations of the commodity terms of trade took no account either of changes in productivity in the two countries or of changes in the quality of the traded products. The long-term terms of trade had moved favourably to the manufacturing countries and adversely to primary producers. There were, moreover, a number of market imperfections. Trade was often bilateral rather than multilateral ; thus, market imperfections arose from political factors. One had to ask whether, in a world of wider and freer trade, the terms of trade would have been so adverse to primary producers — he thought they would not. The terms of trade were considerably influenced by the degree of monopoly and the market structure on both sides. On the African side it was clear that trade union organizations or other organizations to strengthen African bargaining power had been restricted. This had accounted for the larger ratio of profits in foreign enterprises in Africa.

Looking ahead, *Mr. Onitiri* expected a further deterioration in long-term terms of trade between primary products and manufactures. Any short-term improvements of the past decade — as during the Korean war — he regarded as due to accidental factors. In the light of these trends he thought that African countries were well advised to seek to diversify their production and to increase their flexibility. He thought that if manufacturing countries adopted a too rigid attitude towards African desires to diversify and develop industrial production, this might in the end reduce the volume of world trade. In the past a large contribution to development had come from export taxes and from the profits of commodity boards. He foresaw a diminution of this source of funds and a further need for international assistance to fill the gap.

Turning to the problems of the stabilization of the terms of trade, *Mr. Onitiri* argued that what Africa needed was not a stabilization of existing terms but a reversal of the trends of recent years. This could be achieved, he thought, only if the advanced countries were prepared to give sympathetic consideration to the development problems of the backward countries, to the extent of welcoming terms of trade which would add to the resources which these countries could earn for their own development. A great deal of thought had already been given, and was currently being given in the United Nations, the International Monetary Fund, and elsewhere, to the problem of compensatory financing and the provision of some sort of insurance against falling primary product prices. Ghana, Nigeria, and other West African territories had suffered severely from contracting markets and falling prices for their products. They had to take speedy measures to find new markets and to diversify their exports as well as their total production.

Professor Robinson, as Chairman, suggested that the subsequent discussion might profitably be directed to three main issues:

(1) the problems of measuring the terms of trade;
(2) the factors that influenced the terms of trade of African territories — including monopoly and marked imperfections;
(3) the desirability and practicability of influencing long- and short-term trends of the terms of trade.

The further discussion followed this general pattern.

Professor Baldwin wished to comment upon the usefulness of the various concepts of the terms of trade for measuring the long-run benefits from trade for either developed or under-developed countries. Professor Dupriez very rightly stressed that the single factorial terms of trade were the most useful for this purpose. The much more frequently used 'commodity terms of trade' were quite unsatisfactory for making long-run analyses. Whether they went up or down did not definitely tell one whether the economy, in any sense, was better or worse off than before. About the only statement one could make was that if everything else had remained unchanged, and the commodity terms of trade had improved, the economy would have been better off. But this was an empty statement to make for long-run analysis, since the terms of trade were influenced by these other factors and might have changed because of changes in them. The single factorial trading terms took into account changes in one of the most important of these other elements, namely the average productivity, in some sense, of the factors of production. But even movements in these terms of trade were difficult to interpret: an improvement told one that the real income of the productive factors employed in the export industry had increased, but the total real income earned by exporting might have been greater if the single factorial terms had worsened rather than improved. One other connection that was sometimes suggested to deal with this point was to include an index of the volume of trade. The difficulty with the terms of trade concept when it got thus complicated was that a given percentage change in the terms of trade could have many different implications in welfare terms. But at least it improved the chance of assessing the direction of real income change for the country.

Professor Baldwin also agreed with Professor Dupriez in the importance he attached to the income terms of trade. For long-run purposes they suffered from many of the same drawbacks as the commodity terms of trade, but for short-run purposes they were extremely useful, for they concentrated upon the two factors that were likely to change most on the short-run — namely price and output. The other factors, such as productivity, changed also, but their change was likely to be swamped by variations in the components making up the income terms of trade and thus would not falsify one's estimate of the direction of real income change.

The double factorial terms of trade, which attempted to measure the distribution of the gains from trade were, he thought, a less useful concept. Besides some of the drawbacks he had already mentioned, use of this concept invariably led to rather emotional discussions — devoid of much analytical content — about what might have happened if some factors had changed differently while others had remained the same. One trouble with discussions concerning the distribution of trading gains was the lack of a generally accepted goal of international policy. Sometimes discussion was carried on under the assumption that the goal was to maximize the real income of a particular country ; at other times under the assumption that world income was to be maximized. In the first case, monopolistic actions such as tariffs and quotas were quite acceptable, since a country could increase its real income by these devices. However, as far as world income was concerned these measures reduced income. It was quite proper, therefore, to attempt to show the adverse effect of these measures on other countries. But the double factorial terms of trade were not very useful for this purpose. Firstly, they indicated only the relative distribution of gains and took no account of the effect of restrictive measure on the total trading gains. Secondly, they were affected by so many other real factors besides monopoly action that it was impossible to isolate this latter factor. There were better, more direct ways of dealing with the effect of restrictions than by using a terms of trade concept.

Dr. Singer argued that one needed to consider the total rôle of foreign trade in the economic development of a backward country before one chose the best measurement of changes in the terms of trade. If one chose the single factorial terms of trade, that had the virtue of isolating the trade effect, which was relevant if the chief cause of increase of productivity had been the development of export trade through contact with foreigners. If, however, the volume of production of export goods was such as to create a surplus, the social cost to the country of the marginal exports was nil and any price represented a gain. As regards monopolies and imperfections of the market, he thought this was an emotional subject in the history of economic thought. But there was no implication that there had been a world conspiracy to harm the primary producing countries. There were two ways in which the world could share out the gains from increased productivity : through higher incomes to producers, and through lower prices to consumers. Inside a single country, the two alternatives, though affecting incomes of particular groups, made no net difference in total. But as between countries there was a considerable difference. If, in the case of primary producers, there was a tendency to pass on the gain of productivity to consumers, this meant that the gain was largely passed outside the country itself.

Professor Leduc stressed the important effects on terms of trade of changes in transport costs, both as they affected exports and as they affected imports.

Professor Bézy thought that Mr. Onitiri had been right in stressing the market domination of the main consumer manufacturing countries. The economies of the primary producing countries were dominated by the prices of their products. He illustrated this by reference to the effects of copper prices in Katanga and Northern Rhodesia. He argued that the fact of market domination always operated to the detriment of primary producing countries.

Dr. Yudelman thought that Professor Bézy's point was an over-simplification. There were many instances in which under-developed countries had succeeded in squeezing out the producers of advanced countries. He quoted the success of Mexico in capturing markets in Japan from United States producers.

Professor Walker urged the necessity for greater care in making inferences from changes in terms of trade as to changes in the benefits from trade. Mr. Onitiri had been stressing the unfavourable movements in the terms of trade in recent years. But in East Africa in 1959 they had only got back to the same terms of trade as in 1949. He thought it could be questioned whether there really was evidence for a persistent long-term decline in the terms of trade. He thought Professor Dupriez was right in stressing the desirability of calculating the terms of trade at the level of the actual primary producer. He had himself been impressed by the sensitivity of primary producers to price changes. In the case of Uganda there had been considerable local changes of production between cotton and coffee when the latter proved more profitable.

Professor Baldwin wished to return to some earlier remarks by Dr. Singer concerning the commodity versus the single factorial trading terms. He agreed with him that if one would use the single factorial terms of trade, and if productivity were not influenced at all by factors in the exporting industry, one might perhaps want to use the commodity terms of trade. He would think, in fact, that in most under-developed countries the greatest changes in export productivity had been caused by factors relating to the export sector. However, surely in practice both domestic and export factors entirely affected productivity in the export sector. By taking only the commodity terms, one introduced a bias in the direction of minimizing the gains from trade. Moreover, if factors entirely unrelated to the exporting sector affected productivity, they still would affect real income earned in the export sector. And this after all was what one wanted. If we included import prices in the terms of trade measure, and if we really followed Dr. Singer's reasoning, then we should exclude these since they are affected by factors entirely outside the country.

The reason why the prices of the products of developed countries had not decreased despite larger increases in productivity was not, he thought, unrelated to real factors on the demand side. If it had been entirely due to monopolistic action it would have had the effect of reducing employment in the export sector and causing an adverse balance of payments. Since there was little evidence that this had happened, he would suggest that the high income elasticity for these products had compensated for the increase in productivity. This was entirely consistent with classical, free trade analysis. Incidentally, concerning the terms of trade of primary versus manufactured commodities, he thought Professor Kindleberger had established once and for all that this was not the case. The under-developed countries, he concluded, had suffered a deterioration, but this was a different matter.

Professor Robinson was not wholly persuaded by the arguments that the terms of trade were likely to move persistently to the detriment of African primary producers. There was rapid growth of populations, particularly in Asia. If the over-populated Asiatic countries could adjust their economic structures to their longer-term needs, they would surely tend to become large buyers of primary products in the less-populated parts of the world. On the other hand, as had earlier been said, there were already signs of shortages of many temperate zone primary products. Was there not opportunity for African producers if they could develop substitutes for some of the temperate zone primary products, such as paper, cellulose, timber, and the like? Was not the chief problem the inflexibility and conservatism of African primary producers?

Dr. Singer thought that during the previous few years prices of industrial materials had been firm. If there were industrial expansion in Europe and America he thought that terms of trade might well improve.

Chapter 19

ISSUES IN COMMODITY STABILIZATION IN AFRICA[1]

BY

P. T. BAUER

London School of Economics and Political Science

I SHALL discuss some major topics of commodity stabilization in under-developed countries, especially Africa, principally by setting out issues rather than by reviewing past policies or advocating courses of action, though these will also figure, albeit incidentally. This distribution of emphasis seems appropriate to the functions of the economist, especially in a conference paper designed to introduce and promote discussion. My major, but not exclusive, concerns will be in the national, territorial context, rather than with international aspects, as governments of under-developed countries and their technical advisers are more directly concerned with the former. Moreover, major problems and dilemmas in this sphere are thrown into clearer relief when examined on a local level.

I. THE CAUSES OF FLUCTUATION

The inelasticity of supply and demand, especially of short-period supply, together with changes in the conditions of supply and demand, are the principal reasons for the wide price fluctuations of primary products, especially of agricultural products. However, according to a recent study by the International Monetary Fund, variations in volume also often cause significant fluctuations in the export proceeds of primary producing countries, and in the last few decades, and especially in recent years, their importance has grown relatively to that of the instability of prices.[2] Fluctuations in volume as a

[1] I have had much help from Professor B. S. Yamey in the preparation of this paper.
[2] 'Fund Policies and Procedures in Relation to the Compensatory Financing of Commodity Fluctuations', International Monetary Fund, *Staff Papers*, November 1960. This study also shows that the fluctuations in the export earnings of industrial countries are often also very wide, much wider than usually assumed, and not much less wide than those of primary producing countries.

factor in variations in export proceeds and in incomes has been rather neglected in the literature which has tended to stress price fluctuations ; moreover, unless they are due to major natural disasters, variations in incomes caused by crop fluctuations rarely induce governments to intervene. This asymmetry of treatment is unfortunate. First, it leads to neglect of the possibility of smoothing fluctuations in proceeds and incomes, as distinct from prices. Second, by inducing the authorities to prescribe producer prices regardless of the size of the crop, it has on occasions led to a destabilization of producer incomes by removing the compensating factor provided by price changes varying inversely with the size of the crop.

Wide fluctuations in the prices of primary products are confined neither to internationally traded commodities nor to the present or recent past. The prices of kola nuts, and of local foodstuffs in West Africa and elsewhere, often fluctuate very widely within and between seasons, and so did the prices of foodstuffs in Europe before the nineteenth century. Some of these fluctuations are far wider than those in the prices of the staples of international trade. This accords with expectations, because the narrowness of local markets in space and time (reflecting the poorly developed transport and storage facilities, and the absence of forward markets) enhances the inelasticity of supply and demand. This reminds us that measures which serve to narrow the markets for primary products enhance the price fluctuations in some markets, whatever their other results may be. Measures for raising or stabilizing the prices or incomes received by particular producers, or groups of producers, by reserving for them part of the market, are likely to enhance the price fluctuations in the unsheltered markets.

Wide fluctuations in the prices of crops which are an important source of cash incomes, of foreign exchange, and of government revenue, are obviously more far-reaching and significant than are the even wider fluctuations in local markets, even though these latter may reflect distress conditions. And at first their persistence may seem surprising with the development of wider markets, of more numerous sources of supply and of end uses, which might have been expected to reduce the inelasticity of supply and demand considerably. Lord Keynes, who greatly interested himself in these matters, stressed in this context the reluctance of private interests to carry large stocks, and the very sharp fluctuations in prices associated with relatively small deviations in the volume of stocks from conventional levels. Greater readiness to carry stocks would increase the elasticity of the short-period demand confronting the producers, and the short-period elasticity of supply confronting the users, and thus reduce price fluctuations. Keynes and others have drawn attention to the heavy carrying costs as a factor in this situation. But there is also another reason well recognized by those operating in the markets. This is the impossibility of forecasting confidently the future movement of prices, and the very high and possibly crippling cost of mistakes which accounts for the reluctance of private traders to enter into large uncovered commitments notably to hold large stocks. The difficulties of forecasting prices reflect the uncertainties of future supply and demand conditions. The uncertainties are often enhanced by government intervention, the timing, magnitude, and outcome of which cannot be predicted by private participants in the market, though they are often capable of discounting certain short-period changes such as a prospective bumper harvest or short crop.

II. SOME FUNDAMENTAL DIFFICULTIES

In this section I shall discuss certain simple fundamentals to be noted before there can be any worthwhile examination of the merits and methods of a stabilization scheme. They are: the impossibility of confident correct forecasting of future prices, and of distinguishing in advance between a fluctuation about a given trend and a change in the trend; the vagueness of undefined stabilization and its consequent uselessness as a guide to policy; the importance of distinguishing stabilization in some clearly defined sense from other objectives of policy; and I shall also consider, though more briefly, the inherent difficulty of assessing the effects of a scheme smoothing prices or proceeds on the decisions of producers.

The practical impossibility, save in exceptional circumstances,[1] of distinguishing with any degree of certainty between a fluctuation about a given trend and a change in the trend is a corollary of the practical impossibility of forecasting the future course of relative prices, that is the prices of particular commodities. This is obscured by the habitual references to rising and falling prices. In fact at any given time the price of a commodity is not rising or falling. It may have risen (or fallen), and for specific reasons it may be expected to rise (or fall). References to rising and falling prices suggest analogies with natural phenomena, such as a constant or predictable velocity or acceleration of a moving body in defined conditions. Yet as Pigou has reminded us, the virtual absence of constants is an important and fundamental difference between economics and the

---

[1] Such as the announcement by a public authority to purchase or sell a specific quantity at a set price over a limited period.

physical sciences. We can hardly ever say whether a price change will be followed by a further movement in the same direction or will be reversed, and we cannot normally forecast the extent and duration of price movements. This also suggests the danger of references to high and low prices. These are necessarily relative to some norm or base, past or future, which is usually left unspecified. And, of course, high and low and rising and falling are not synonymous, though in this context they are often used interchangeably. And what is perhaps most important, not only is it impossible to forecast turning points of prices, but it is also impossible to forecast the long-term supply and demand prices, which would appear to be the primary relevant data for successful *long-period* price stabilization.

Professor Sir Isaiah Berlin said of liberty that it is a concept so vague and porous that there is practically no interpretation which it is capable of resisting. Much the same can be said about stabilization in its common use. I can mention only a few of the many different interpretations of this concept, some of which are not only different from others but are indeed their diametrical opposites. Thus, stabilization may refer to prices or incomes, in money or in real terms ; to the establishment of a floor or to the imposition of a ceiling on prices or incomes ; to the constancy of the share of the producers in the national income ; and so on. These different and conflicting interpretations make possible the plausible advocacy, pursuit, or justification of different and possibly contradictory policies. Recently these ambiguities have come to be recognized at least in the technical literature, and stabilization has come to be defined and interpreted as the smoothing over a specified period of fluctuations around a trend of prices or incomes.

The impossibility of forecasting the movement of prices, combined with the vagueness of the concept of stabilization when left undefined, are partly responsible for the frequent confusion of objectives in so-called stabilization policies, notably the failure to distinguish stabilization in one or other of its various interpretations from other objectives of policy. Though some of its most important and spectacular instances have emerged since the Second World War, this is no new phenomenon. For instance, in the 1920s and 1930s primary producers often solicited government support for restriction schemes with the plea that they were required for stabilization of prices or incomes. These were, however, generally measures designed to raise prices and incomes by means of monopolistic restrictions of entry, capacity, production, and exports. Vestiges of this particular discrepancy of objectives remain in some contemporary commodity schemes, including the sugar scheme. But since the Second World War the development of stabilization into sustained and severe taxation of producers has been the more characteristic and significant divergence between the ostensible aim and actual results of stabilization in under-developed countries.[1] This has been the development in West Africa, Uganda, and Burma, of which the first is the most important, as well as the best documented example.[2]

The process has often been described by which the statutory export monopolies of West Africa, established to serve the producers by withholding part of the sales proceeds of high prices and paying out their surpluses in periods of low prices, have developed into instruments of extremely severe taxation. Although various political factors have played a major part in this, failure to ask certain relevant questions when these measures were introduced certainly also played a part. In particular, no one seems to have specified or even asked what was meant by high and low prices which, as just noted, are meaningless unless explicitly related to a base or norm. This led those in charge of these organizations to take the easiest course, which was to strengthen the organizations themselves either simply by accumulating funds or using them in spectacular or politically popular directions, at the expense of their ineffective, unorganized, and illiterate constituents. This process came to be rationalized as necessary for disinflation or for compulsory saving. Whatever the merits of these objectives in the particular context, it is usually agreed that their costs are appropriately borne by the community as a whole by means of fiscal or monetary measures, and not by an arbitrarily selected group, namely the producers of export crops subject to stabilization policies.

Though it is not yet generally appreciated that without clear definition stabilization cannot serve as a worthwhile guide to policy, the difference and distinct nature of stabilization, disinflation, and compulsory saving are now widely recognized within these territories. But the policy which has in part led up to this confusion of objectives and in part issued from it has left lasting effects on their political and social landscape.

Confusion of objectives is apt to issue in policies which do not promote either stabilization or other generally accepted objectives of social policy, or at least do not do so effectively. Consider, for

---

[1] This is not to deny that a particular policy measure may serve both to raise (or lower) the average level of producer prices and also to stabilize them in the sense of reducing fluctuations around the higher (lower) average level. But it is necessary for clear thinking to disentangle the different effects which may be the intended or unintended results of a particular measure.

[2] Similar policies were also pursued in the Argentine in the 1940s and early 1950s but without invoking stabilization for their justification.

instance, the confusion of stabilization with disinflation or compulsory saving. This has permitted the imposition or continuation of very heavy taxation of the producers subject to stabilization policies. This taxation was not integrated with the rest of the fiscal structure and ignored both the ability to pay or its repercussions (desired or undesired) on output, investment, and the supply of productive resources generally.

In West Africa the accumulation of vast surpluses by the export monopolies has made politically possible sharp increases in the rates of export duty on these products, because increases merely diminished the surpluses of the Boards without affecting producer prices directly. The taxes levied on these producers thus came to be much higher than those on the rest of the community, including the producers of the few commodities not subject to such monopolies, or people with much higher incomes.

Consider the Nigerian experience. In that country oil-palm produce is derived from naturally occurring trees, so that the establishment of capacity is not affected by the net returns of producers. Cocoa is a highly profitable cash crop grown on a relatively accessible area, where most of its producers enjoy incomes higher than obtainable in alternative agricultural pursuits. Groundnuts and cotton are annual crops grown in relatively outlying areas on the margin of the exchange economy by much poorer producers. Yet for much or most of the period since the establishment of export monopolies the taxation on the producers of cotton and groundnuts was very heavy, appreciably heavier than on the producers of cocoa or oil-palm produce.[1]

In Ghana a large part of the incomes of cocoa producers has been simply confiscated by fixing producer prices far below market prices and diverting the difference to general governmental purposes, contrary to the most specific guarantees when the export monopolies were established. Meanwhile taxation on the rest of the population, including relatively highly paid salary earners, has been generally comparatively light.

The development described in the foregoing paragraphs is of some general interest because it is not accidental. A territorial stabilization scheme in an under-developed country, especially one covering crops produced by smallholders, is far more likely to become an instrument of taxation than a device for sustained raising of producers' returns. This is so for several reasons. First, the possibility of monopolistic price raising is virtually absent or very weak. Second,

[1] This in spite of the fact that the high elasticity of supply of cotton and the importance of encouraging its cultivation used to be recognized in its exemption from a then modest export duty, until it came under a statutory monopoly.

sustained subsidization of producers is impracticable because of the absence of other substantial sources of public revenues. Third, the producers are likely to be politically ineffective. Thus, if there is any prolonged difference between market prices and producer prices, that is a deviation of the actual from the ostensible aim of stabilization, it will take the form of taxation of producers and not of subsidization.

Finally, we must note a problem presented by the difficulty of assessing producer responses to different patterns of prices or proceeds through time (as distinct from responses to differences in the average level of prices through time). Different time patterns may affect producers' expectations of future prices, their ability and readiness to add to capacity, and their assessment of risk. In principle, different time patterns could elicit different responses, and there is no universal or even widely applicable generalization enabling one to predict the particular responses to a postulated stabilization scheme affecting the time pattern of prices or proceeds. In the discussion which follows this limitation needs to be remembered, although the major themes are not affected substantially. It will be observed, however, that in a few places (which will be clear from the context) specific kinds of response are assumed in accordance with statistical and other observations in Africa and elsewhere in the under-developed world.

III. THE ESSENTIALS OF A STABILIZATION POLICY

Stabilization policies for agricultural products (as distinct from the monopolistic international schemes), attempted since the Second World War in under-developed countries in Africa and elsewhere, have covered almost wholly crops produced by smallholders ; and my concern will be largely with schemes affecting such crops. But most of the subsequent argument applies more generally, regardless of the type of producer affected.

As noted, an effective stabilization policy, in the sense of the smoothing of fluctuations, requires that this should be kept distinct from other aims of policy. Moreover, the period over which incomes and prices are to be smoothed (that is reserves accumulated and fully distributed by the stabilization authority) also needs to be specified, as otherwise almost any policy can be spuriously justified by reference to some postulated price changes in the distant or undefined future. In particular, the sustained withholding from producers of part of the sales proceeds can be justified on this ground with superficial plausibility. Moreover, even if this does not happen, failure to define the period of smoothing is still likely to involve serious disadvantages.

First, it may necessitate periodic discontinuous price changes to regain contact with market prices. Second, it may lead to paradoxical results, especially when prices have risen over a number of years. This is because the higher are prices, the larger are the absolute amounts required to maintain them at a given level over a stated period, and therefore a given sum is more likely to appear insufficient as a stabilization reserve. Surpluses accumulated over a number of years of relatively low prices, and representing large percentages of producer prices at the time of their accumulation, may be held to constitute an insufficient reserve at a subsequent date (by which time prices have risen greatly), even though the fear of a decline had been adduced as a reason for their accumulation. When prices have risen over a number of years it is therefore quite likely (in the absence of a clear definition of the period of accumulation) that the producers who received low prices in the early part of the period are called upon to surrender a proportionately large part of their incomes for the creation of reserves which may either be accumulated indefinitely, or used to subsidize much higher producer prices in face of a possible decline. This decline may represent a much smaller proportion of the higher prices than the proportion which the producers have to surrender at a time of much lower prices. And, of course, the beneficiaries of this process may be a group of persons greatly different from those who have had to make the sacrifice. This has been in evidence under several post-war schemes and has happened on a large scale in Nigeria and Ghana.

And there is at least one important reason for keeping the smoothing period relatively short. The composition of the body of producers changes through time, so that in any compulsory comprehensive stabilization scheme there is always some lack of correspondence between those from whom part of the sales proceeds are withheld and those to whom they are subsequently paid out. If the period is long then instead of smoothing fluctuations the scheme simply taxes one group of producers and subsidises another quite different group.[1]

From the point of view of a national scheme it is immaterial whether the external (market) price is determined essentially by unhampered market forces or affected materially by international inter-governmental schemes. Such schemes may reduce the range of price fluctuations over a period, but may be followed by sharp

---

[1] Other practical aspects of stabilization discussed in Sections 5 and 6 below reinforce the case for keeping the smoothing period relatively short.

discontinuous changes brought about, for instance, by the establishment or collapse of a restriction scheme, or a change in its administration, or by the exhaustion of the stocks held by a buffer stock authority. Thus the presence or absence of an international scheme does not affect the case for a national scheme either way.

I shall review later, after outlining a possible scheme, the major arguments for and against a clearly defined and circumscribed national scheme, especially in Africa. But there is one specific objection which is best considered now, namely that national schemes enhance the fluctuations in external market prices, since they tend to encourage production in times of comparative over-supply and discourage it in times of relative scarcity by subsidising producers in a slump and taxing them in a boom. The analytical validity of this objection cannot be disputed, but its practical significance is likely to be small. It is unimportant when exports from the country operating the national scheme are a relatively small proportion of world production of the particular commodity and of its close substitutes.[1] And where the products are bush or tree crops a temporary tax or subsidy cannot affect current supply (as distinct from the establishment of capacity) until several years later, by which time market conditions are likely to have altered greatly. The destabilizing effect might be significant if the scheme affected an annual crop in a country or group of countries which accounted for a large part of world supplies, and where producers responded quickly and substantially to small changes in current prices and also ignored the temporary nature of the difference between market and producer prices. But there is in any case no strong argument for a smoothing scheme in such a situation where the short-period elasticity of supply is very high. In all other conditions a national scheme would not materially affect current world market prices.[2] It is also not out of place to note that any such effect would be small compared to those induced by changes in export duties and other taxes levied in the producing countries.

IV. SHOULD A SCHEME BE VOLUNTARY OR COMPULSORY?

In principle, a smoothing scheme can be voluntary or compulsory, that is, participation may be left to the discretion of individual pro-

[1] This applies to all major African agricultural exports with the exception of cocoa and sisal.

[2] It may induce the type of instability in prices and outputs discussed in the familiar cobweb theorem. But since this can manifest itself also under unregulated market conditions this contingency cannot be said to induce additional destabilizing effects attributable to a smoothing scheme as such.

ducers or it may be comprehensive and compulsory. Producers often smooth fluctuations in their expenditure by saving more in times of prosperity and saving less (or even dis-saving) in times of adversity.[1] They may wish to remain outside an official scheme, or, alternatively, they may welcome the opportunity of improving their own smoothing arrangements by participation in an organized scheme.

The difficulty of an organized voluntary scheme is the prevention of abuse through claims for subsidy by non-members, and the avoidance of levies by members. However, a smoothing scheme could still be provided for producers requesting it. The abuse could be prevented by basing levies and subsidies on specified quantities of the product from each member, quantities which need not be the same for all members. A smoothed producer price could be calculated by those in charge of the scheme, designed to smooth fluctuations in prices or in proceeds.[2] This price is periodically compared with the market price to establish the appropriate rate of levy or subsidy which participants pay or receive on the quantities for which they contracted. A participant would in effect have a savings account with the smoothing scheme, with the special characteristic that the amounts of periodic contributions or withdrawals would be determined by the administrators of the scheme in accordance with a smoothing formula. Such a scheme could be operated by official, co-operative, or private organizations. Indeed, more than one scheme could operate in the same area offering different smoothing methods and formulae. The scheme need not handle the purchase and sale of the commodity in question ; its concern need be only with the provision of smoothing facilities.

The administration of such a scheme is practicable wherever individuals can be made to honour their contractual obligations ; in practice this would include at least all those who are direct tax-payers, own real property with registered titles, or who have prolonged commercial contacts with banks, insurance companies, or the larger merchant firms. This applies widely to smallholders in under-developed countries including Africa, and applies particularly to the more substantial smallholders who might wish to participate in such

[1] The readiness of many smallholders to take long views in their production decisions, as, for instance, by planting tree crops, is direct evidence, if any is needed, that they do not live entirely in the present.

[2] Although each participant's claim on subsidy or liability to levy is calculated on his fixed quantity, smoothing of proceeds simply requires an adjustment in the amount of subsidy or levy per unit of output. The organizers of the scheme determine the total amount receivable or payable in any season on the basis of a chosen formula designed to even out fluctuations in prices or in proceeds. The quantities contracted for by participants determine the division among the participating producers of the total amounts receivable or payable by the organization.

a scheme. Even this minimal requirement would be unnecessary if new participants were admitted to the scheme only at times when levies were payable.

Variants of this scheme suggest themselves readily. For example, a government could subsidize such a scheme to encourage participation. I do not propose to pursue these matters further. My purpose has been to show that contrary to what is generally taken for granted,[1] a voluntary smoothing scheme is practicable in conditions of small-holder crops in under-developed countries.

Despite their attractions, the adoption of voluntary smoothing schemes in under-developed countries is, for political reasons, un-likely in the foreseeable future. Accordingly, the rest of the paper is concerned essentially with compulsory schemes.

A compulsory and comprehensive stabilization scheme can be administered either through statutory export monopolies (monopoly schemes) or by means of special export duties and subsidies super-imposed on revenue duties, if any (duty-subsidy schemes). Under the former the authority prescribes the price payable to producers by its agents ; and as these are reimbursed on the basis of the pre-scribed prices and their costs, these prices are maxima as well as minima, except in so far as the agents themselves are prepared to absorb some of the costs. Under a duty-subsidy scheme the rates of duty can be adjusted to smooth the year-to-year fluctuations in prices paid to producers in local markets. The former method ensures a fixed price throughout the season. The latter retains fluctuations within the season but (if successful) reduces the discontinuous adjustments between them. It sacrifices the fixed intra-seasonal price which is often said to conduce to political stability and adminis-trative convenience, besides looking neat on the diagrams of annual reports. The political importance of this advantage is unlikely to be great when year-to-year fluctuations are in any case smoothed. Moreover, the duty-subsidy method avoids the withholding or rush-ing of supplies to buying stations by producers and dealers trying to secure windfall profits or avoid windfall losses in anticipation of the discontinuous price changes.

There are other much more significant advantages in a duty-subsidy scheme compared to a monopoly scheme, which are impor-tant in under-developed countries, notably in Africa.

The establishment of export monopolies greatly reduces the external contacts of the local population. Local producers and

---

[1] Also in my own earlier writings. It is Professor B. S. Yamey who has out-lined to me the practical requirements of a feasible voluntary scheme. He and I discuss the implications of voluntary smoothing schemes in a forthcoming article.

traders are prevented from seeking external buyers, and foreign merchants are discouraged or prevented from establishing themselves locally. This is apt materially to retard economic progress by restricting the transmission of new ideas, methods, crops, and wants, which in turn are potent factors in breaking down traditional customs and attitudes, including those most detrimental to economic progress. Professor Cairncross has recently reminded us [1] that foreign trade is much more than the exchange of physical commodities, and that a major part of its rôle as an engine of economic progress derives from those far-reaching effects in attitudes, outlook, customs, and methods which it engenders. For obvious reasons this consideration is specially important in Africa. The restriction or severance of crucially important external contacts is a major disadvantage of any scheme which requires a statutory export monopoly.

The second major disadvantage is the practical political improbability, or even impossibility, of preventing the statutory monopoly from extending its function far beyond the passive administration of a scheme for smoothing fluctuations according to a formula. The familiar discrepancy of interest between administrators and their constituents is only too likely to appear in under-developed countries, especially in Africa, since not only do the administrators of such a scheme enjoy statutory monopoly powers, but they are also politically influential, literate, and often vocal, while the producers are dispersed, uninformed, illiterate, and politically ineffective. This is likely to result in an early change in arrangements, notably in the replacement of smoothing according to a definite formula by discretionary price fixing, which does not amount to stabilization in a definite or even definable sense ; and the system is likely soon to develop into severe taxation of producers in a form not conducive to economic progress nor in accordance with the usual canons of fiscal equity. Moreover, the concentration of power inherent in statutory monopoly over the crops providing the major source of cash income to producers is bound to have far-reaching political repercussions, especially in Africa. It is not to be expected that governments will not use this powerful instrument to strengthen their own political position.

Third, the establishment of statutory export monopolies aggravates the difficulties of local processors of the controlled crops, especially processors for export.[2] This problem does not arise in a

---

[1] 'International Trade and Economic Development', *Economica*, August 1961.
[2] This, of course, does not apply when the scheme uses accumulated funds to subsidize their operations. But this is unlikely except for officially established or operated processing facilities.

duty-subsidy scheme as the levies or subsidies of the unprocessed product can easily be offset by corresponding duties and drawbacks on the export of the processed products.

Fourth, a monopoly system gives powers of patronage to those operating it in such matters as the appointment of buying agents and the selection of personnel, quite apart from the vast powers over the control of accumulated funds if these are not distributed to the producers. This is a significant implication of this method, especially in Africa, because of the great difference in effectiveness between the administrators of the scheme and their constituents, the claims of the extended family and the clash of loyalties it often entails, and the attraction of power and patronage for ambitious men.

Thus there are major disadvantages to statutory monopoly schemes compared to duty-subsidy schemes, even if the former are required to work with a clearly defined formula for stabilization.

A smoothing scheme could be applied either to prices or to incomes (used here as synonymous with proceeds), that is, it could be made to compensate for crop fluctuations as well as price fluctuations. A scheme designed to smooth proceeds would destabilize the incomes of those individual producers whose output fluctuates in a direction opposite to that of the total crop. Further, the real value of the price of the commodity, rather than the real value of the proceeds of producers, may be deemed the more appropriate object of smoothing. However, if there is a general case for smoothing, it would seem on balance to apply more strongly to proceeds than to prices. Fluctuations in the volume of the crop are just as much outside the control of producers as price fluctuations, and can cause as much or greater hardship. Similarly, they can cause wide short-period fluctuations in the demand for merchandise, in public revenues, and in the balance of payments. Lastly, discontinuous increases in producer income, resulting from temporary increase in output, set up social obligations which are difficult to reverse in much the same way as does temporary prosperity resulting from higher prices. These considerations suggest that if there is a case for a compulsory smoothing scheme, it applies more strongly to proceeds than to prices.

V. THE CHARACTERISTICS OF A SATISFACTORY SCHEME

Some years ago Professor Paish and I proposed in two articles in the *Economic Journal* a scheme for the smoothing of the fluctuations in the incomes of primary producers.[1]

I shall outline our proposals only briefly both because they are easily accessible and because my main purpose on this occasion is to set out issues rather than to propose policies.

The scheme was designed to smooth the proceeds accruing to producers under a monopoly scheme, but it could be applied equally to a duty-subsidy scheme, and in a slightly modified form to the smoothing of producer prices as distinct from proceeds. The method could also be applied to the calculation of the levy or subsidy in a voluntary smoothing scheme such as that outlined in section 4 above.

Under the scheme, producer prices are determined by a formula calculated as the sum of two components. The first would be a fraction of the estimated market price for the forthcoming year, the second, which is designed to provide the smoothing element, would be derived from the difference between the realized proceeds per ton in past years and the amounts paid out in those years on account of the first component. It is obtained by subtracting from the total proceeds over a given number of past years the amounts paid out on account of the first price component, that is the aggregate of the first component of the price, multiplied by the number of tons exported in each year. This difference is averaged over the given number of past years, which yields the aggregate amount to be distributed in the forthcoming year on account of the second component. This amount is then divided by the estimated volume of the forthcoming crop which gives the second component of the price to be paid. The number of years refers to the period over which proceeds are to be smoothed. Under the monopoly scheme the price is that prescribed by the authorities ; under the duty-subsidy scheme it is the average local market price for the forthcoming season to be aimed at when the rate of duty or subsidy is determined.

The formula proposed in our article is set out in a note at the end of this paper, together with a shorter version suggested privately by Professor Harry G. Johnson.

The following are the principal advantages of this scheme. Errors in the estimate of the prospective price and output are self-liquidating over the smoothing period. There is little possibility of sustained loss of contact with the trend of prices ; and any temporary divergence from the trend is corrected by a smooth change over the next year or two, and not by means of large discontinuous changes characteristic of so-called stabilization schemes. The scheme is

[1] 'The Reduction of Fluctuations in the Incomes of Primary Producers', *Economic Journal*, December 1952.
'The Reduction of Fluctuations in the Incomes of Primary Producers Further Considered', *Economic Journal*, December 1954.

designed at smoothing fluctuations in incomes and not at stabilizing prices. It clearly defines stabilization as the smoothing of proceeds over a specified period, and thereby provides a specific meaning to the concept and also distinguishes it from other objectives, and thus safeguards against a confusion of aims. This in turn promotes effective pursuit of stabilization, and also enables a ready comparison to be made between policies actually pursued and those postulated by this defined objective. Further, the scheme makes possible a fairly close and reliable estimate for some years ahead of the future level of money incomes. This is because under this scheme producer incomes in any one year depend substantially on sums retained out of previous years' incomes which are exactly known. The smoothing of fluctuations and the more accurate forecasts in the remaining movements in the flow of incomes would have important social and political advantages.

The relative importance to be attached to the two components in the formula is a policy decision. The larger is the first term, that is, the greater weight is given to the forthcoming year in the calculation of the average, the less is the smoothing of producer incomes. If it is desired to effect a large measure of smoothing over a number of years then the first term will be small relative to the second. This has the advantage of smaller year-to-year variations in incomes, but at the cost and risk of some delay in transmitting to producers a change in the trend of prices.

So much for the main advantages of the smoothing scheme outlined in this section. But attention must be drawn to a particular limitation of smoothing schemes involving elements of estimate, including the scheme under discussion. Errors in the estimates of prospective market prices and volume of crop imply a higher (or lower) producer price in the present season, and, conversely, lower (or higher) producer prices in the remainder of the smoothing period, though the errors are self-liquidating over this period. Thus there may at times be greater loss of contact with the market than is implied in the scheme as such. This particular source of loss of contact could be avoided (that is, that deriving from errors in estimates) only by basing the formula solely on past proceeds, that is, by introducing a lag. But this itself would be a source of loss of contact with the market. These possibilities of loss of contact with the market are inherent in smoothing schemes. This may be held to be a disadvantage in any smoothing scheme, and one which may be thought to strengthen the case against a compulsory scheme which forces producers to assume this particular risk.[1] In a voluntary

[1] Such a loss of contact can have particularly adverse effects where short-period responsiveness of producers to price changes is high.

scheme each producer can decide whether to accept these risks rather than the risks of short-period fluctuations in market prices.

VI. THE MERITS OF COMPULSORY SMOOTHING

I shall now examine more generally the merits of compulsory smoothing which are still left open by the foregoing discussion.

The following seem to be the principal arguments in favour of compulsory smoothing of fluctuations in proceeds or prices. This case of paternalism can be regarded as an educative restraint, to apply Professor Hutt's vivid phrase. The sharp and discontinuous fluctuations in the prices and output of primary commodities often affect producers who have only comparatively recently joined the money economy, and although there is much evidence of their ability to take a long view, such producers cannot be expected generally to envisage the temporary nature of their prosperity and to set aside part of their proceeds in good times. Thus, this educative restraint may ease the gradual progress of the money economy. Second, in conditions of many under-developed countries, especially in Africa, a spell of exceptional prosperity may force producers to accept onerous social obligations, often (though not necessarily) by incurring debts which enhance the difficulty of saving from exceptional incomes. For this reason producers may in fact welcome compulsory smoothing. Third, the smoothing of fluctuations has familiar advantages in the sphere of public finance, including public investment. Fourth, it may serve to reduce the extent of windfall profits and losses of dealers in imported manufactures, the supplies of which are often inelastic in the short period, windfalls which in various ways may set up considerable tension. Fifth, in many under-developed countries the ratchet economy has made its appearance, in that major cost elements are flexible upwards in prosperity but resistant to reduction in subsequent adversity.[1] Sixth, wide fluctuations are likely to provoke or even compel extensive government intervention, and it is preferable to have this carefully designed to achieve a definite purpose by specific means, instead of relying on *ad hoc* measures which are only too likely to result in a confusion of objectives. Last, a considerable measure of predictability of cash incomes under a scheme such as that outlined above would have important advantages of its own.

---

[1] These costs are not necessarily or primarily those incurred by producers; they may be those of other sectors of the economy affected by variations in the expenditures of producers.

Most of these points reduce to the argument that a successful smoothing scheme can reduce the strains of adjustment to rapid and possibly discontinuous changes in money incomes, and it may be held that even if the desirability of a voluntary scheme is recognized, the response to it would be insufficient to achieve this aim.

Some of these objectives cannot be secured effectively by general budgetary or monetary measures. For example, they cannot secure the measure of predictability of incomes provided under the type of scheme just outlined. Moreover, when there are two or more major export products in an economy (for instance, coffee and cotton in Uganda, or cocoa and oil-palm products in Southern Nigeria) the fortunes of the producers of the one may move in directions opposite to those of the other, so that overall measures would be inappropriate.

There are also very important arguments against the adoption of compulsory smoothing. First, this act of paternalism may retard the emergence of self-reliance ; and throughout Africa the social and political effects of paternalism have often been severely adverse or even disastrous.[1] Second, there is always the danger that, even if categoric and formal assurances are given that the scheme is intended for smoothing only, it will soon develop into a method of taxation or even into an instrument of political tyranny. This is relevant mainly to smoothing by a monopoly scheme rather than to an export duty-subsidy scheme, since the government in any case has comprehensive taxation powers. Third, it may be argued that in the absence of specific controls, especially over imports, the tensions and disadvantages of price and income fluctuations are exaggerated and that these are readily accepted by the population unless accompanied by wide changes in the price of purchased supplies or by monopsonistic price rigging on the part of buyers. It may be held, therefore, that the costs and risks of a smoothing scheme are unwarranted, including the disadvantages even of those temporary and foreseeable differences between producer prices and market prices which are inherent in a perfectly operated smoothing scheme ; this applies more strongly in view of the practically inevitable errors.

The next disadvantage may be sufficiently important to warrant discussion at greater length. There are at times important advantages in exceptionally high prices, even if these are relatively short-lived, especially for planted tree crops (as distinct from the products of naturally-occurring trees). Such exceptional prices may be required to induce or make possible the establishment of capacity along and outside the external margin of the cash economy, which then serves

---

[1] This, of course, would not apply to a voluntary smoothing scheme.

to push outward the money economy. Once the capacity is established it is often operated even when prices are much lower ; this is an instance of the familiar irreversible supply curve. Such a development presents a case of a big push in development, but without the tensions and stresses usually associated with it. This form of development, although it results in the establishment and extension of capacity outside the previous margin of the exchange economy, does not require a major break with traditional pursuits. Indeed, at times it has proceeded with so little strain that for many years the establishment and spread of new cash crops remained unnoticed or were greatly under-estimated. Examples include the kola-nut industry of Nigeria and the smallholder rubber industry of Sumatra and Borneo. The removal of the exceptional prices for tree crops implied in smoothing would obstruct or greatly retard such a development, which is important when large parts of the economy are still in the subsistence stage, and when the extension of the money economy encounters severe physical and institutional obstacles.[1]

VII. CONCLUSIONS

Thus, even if stabilization is strictly interpreted, clearly defined, and kept distinct from other objectives, the case for a national stabilization scheme depends on the assessment of the relative importance of conflicting considerations. For reasons indicated, chiefly the severance of valuable external contacts and the likelihood of departure from the objectives of the scheme, I think that if stabilization is thought to require a monopoly scheme the balance of the argument is against it. In that case it would be preferable to rely on budgetary surpluses in prosperous times to increase the flexibility and augment the reserves of the economy and to accumulate funds for the alleviation of distress.

Ultimately, the choice between different courses of action, including that between various forms of scheme or non-intervention, will depend in part on technical economic reasoning ; in part on the assessment of various local factors, including market structure, various institutional and social factors, the play of political forces, and the factors affecting the progress of the exchange economy ;

[1] If the inducement to expand capacity were dependent solely on an erroneous belief in the persistence of the high price, it could be argued that the expansion of capacity was wasteful (which would strengthen the case for a smoothing scheme). But this is not the only way in which an exceptionally high price may bring about an expansion of capacity. The possibility of subsequent periods of high prices may add to the attractiveness of the investment ; and the high prices, even if only temporary, may provide the necessary finance.

and in part also on value judgments. Thus, there is clearly no simple answer. But in this respect at any rate commodity stabilization does not differ from other major problems of economic policy.

NOTE

Formulae for the Smoothing of Producer Incomes

The following is the general formula for the scheme proposed in the article in *Economic Journal*, December 1952.

$$S_t = \frac{\bar{P}_t}{X} + \frac{1}{n}\left(\frac{P_{t-1}Q_{t-1} + P_{t-2}Q_{t-2} + \ldots P_{t-n}Q_{t-n} - \dfrac{(\bar{P}_{t-1}Q_{t-1} + \bar{P}_{t-2}Q_{t-2} + \ldots \bar{P}_{t-n}Q_t}{X}}{\bar{Q}_t} \right)$$

S_t = producer price ;
P = market price (net proceeds per ton) ;
$\bar{P}$ = expected market price (net proceeds per ton) ;
Q = volume of crop ;
$\bar{Q}$ = expected volume of crop ;
$\dfrac{1}{X}$ = fraction of expected proceeds of current year paid out, *i.e.* included in calculation of producer price ;
n = number of years over which proceeds are averaged for smoothing fluctuations.

Professor Harry G. Johnson has suggested that the formula could be written more briefly as follows :

$$S_t = \frac{\bar{P}_t}{X} + \frac{F}{n\bar{Q}_t}.$$

The notation is the same as in the other formulation except for F which refers to total reserves, *i.e.* the difference between total net proceeds and the amounts paid out over the previous n years.

Professor Johnson's formulation is simpler and briefer. The original formulation has the advantage of showing more clearly the underlying variables.

DISCUSSION OF PROFESSOR BAUER'S PAPER [1]

Professor Robinson (Chairman) suggested that in discussing this paper it might be helpful to distinguish attempts to 'stabilize' on a world scale from attempts by any one country (or a group of countries) to stabilize

[1] The discussion of Professor Bauer's paper had to be conducted in the absence of the author, who, to the regret of the Conference, found himself unable to come to Addis Ababa.

the incomes or prices received by its own producers. Any one country could, if it wished, accept the world price but pass on to its own producers a more 'stabilized' buying price.

On the world scale, as he saw it, there were broadly two types of scheme possible : the buffer stock schemes, which involved almost inevitably some degree of co-operation of consumers, if only because of the very high cost of carrying large buffer stocks ; the quota schemes for the regulation of production, which involved the close collaboration of all major producers in what was essentially a monopolistic policy. Both types of scheme involved difficulties of different kinds. The buffer stock scheme gave rise to considerable difficulties in distinguishing short-term fluctuations from long-term trends, both in demand and in costs. The quota scheme gave rise to all the difficulties of holding together a mono-polistic organization, since the most profitable position was always to accept the advantages of higher prices consequent on the scheme while standing outside the system of regulation. Rubber schemes had provided repeated examples of this ; almost all quota schemes presented serious conflicts of interest between high-cost and low-cost producers. The history of international schemes did not suggest that they would provide an easy solution of African problems unless co-operation could be very close and friendly and unless such schemes were backed by the goodwill of importing countries. It was almost impossible to draw a line between stabilization and monopolization.

Mr. Moran commented that if stabilization schemes, through mono-polization, raised prices out of line with other prices, they might well lead to more rapid substitutions of synthetic products for natural products. In answer to *Mr. Onitiri* he said that he thought that, while with proper care their expansion could be accommodated in the market, synthetic products were in fact an inevitable consequence of technical progress, and in fact were the consequence of strategic considerations.

Dr. Singer thought that the long-term cost of natural products was normally below that of synthetics. The problem was essentially a short-term one. Both *Dr. Singer* and *Professor Spengler* argued that the com-petition of synthetics was in some degree irreversible. They required high capital investment, which would not be undertaken unless at some moment the market prospects justified, but once undertaken the sub-sequent marginal costs were low.

Dr. Yudelman stressed the tendency to surplus production for such a product as coffee in tropical countries. It was very necessary to weigh the advantages and disadvantages of some attempt to regulate output.

Dr. Wade reminded the Conference that African countries sometimes benefited from the invention of substitute products. He instanced the case of margarine. He thought that there should be co-operation of African primary producing countries to work out an international system of regulation.

M. Roland Pré thought it was difficult to define the frontier between economies and politics in all these issues. There was a wide field of intervention of public authorities between African producers and European. The whole concept of terms of trade was obscured by the existence of taxes and subsidies. For example, the prices of European textiles to Africans were deliberately raised as a means of taxing the present generation of Africans to speed up economic development in the interests of the Africans of the future. Moreover, technological changes were constantly taking place, and could completely alter the situation. For example, the rising prices of high-grade iron ores had led to developments in the techniques of using low-grade ores.

Professor Bézy agreed that competition came not only from synthetic products but also from new ways of using lower-grade products. The same thing had happened in the case of cotton, where the relative values of long- and short-staple cottons had been changed by improvements in manufacturing methods. The competitive capacity of individual primary products was largely determined by efficiency in manufacture. It was necessary that African producers should become more flexible and better able to switch over to varieties in greater demand. What was needed was an aggressive sales policy. He thought that attempts at monopoly would evoke retaliation and a long and bitter struggle. It was too early for Africa to get involved in such struggles.

Professor Leduc thought that a policy of international stabilization in the short-term was likely to be dangerous. It was dangerous to advise African countries to embark on it. He thought they would be better advised to embark on diversification and industrialization.

The Chairman suggested that the remainder of the discussion should be primarily addressed to the operation and desirability of national schemes, accepting a world price and regulating buying prices or output within the national economy.

Dr. Okigbo drew attention to the frequency with which such national stabilization schemes neglected to define what it was that was to be stabilized — the price, the sales, or the incomes of producers. He thought that the argument as to whether regulation schemes should be voluntary or compulsory was irrelevant. Schemes had to be accepted as a fact. The suggestion that unorganized and illiterate producers should be left to enter into a voluntary scheme made little sense. The practical effect of a stabilization scheme was a larger measure of taxation on producers of the commodities concerned. The main problem was to devise a formula that would best secure the objectives that the national schemes set out to achieve.

Professor Peacock argued that both voluntary and statutory schemes were expected to increase the returns to producers. The choice between schemes was comparable with the problem of equity in taxation — the equitable distribution of a tax burden. If sacrifices were properly related to benefits received, it was justifiable to make a scheme compulsory. There were, however, very obvious difficulties in accounting.

Professor Walker said that in discussing these schemes it was necessary to put their past history behind us. In the early years, unquestionably, the marketing boards had taken away too much. But if one was to be forward-looking there were two kinds of justification : first, the elimination of risk and uncertainty, and the improvement of power to foresee the long-term outlook ; second, the effects on the economy as a whole, including the reduction of marketing costs and the exploration of new markets. He thought that justification was possible along these lines.

Chapter 20

SOME ASPECTS OF AFRICAN
AGRICULTURAL DEVELOPMENT [1]

BY

M. YUDELMAN

Visiting Lecturer and Research Associate at the Center for
International Affairs, Harvard University

I. THE ECONOMIC DOMINANCE OF AGRICULTURE

ALTHOUGH statistics pertaining to agriculture in Africa have to be
treated with great caution, the following data amply demonstrate
the significance of agriculture in the overall economic setting (see
Table 1). Available evidence based on national output estimates,
derived within recent years, confirms the overwhelming importance
of agriculture in the economies of almost all countries that fall in
this region. In fact, the agricultural component is estimated to make
up more than half the value of the gross domestic product of all
West Africa and most of East Africa ; it constitutes around one-fifth
of the value of the gross domestic product of the former Belgian
Congo and the Central African Federation, both of which have large
mining sectors in their national income. Agricultural exports
dominate foreign trade of all these economies except the two mineral-
producing areas. In other countries agricultural exports range from
99 per cent of the value of all exports in the Sudan, 90 per cent from
Nigeria and former French West Africa, more than 90 per cent
from British East Africa, and 46 per cent from former French
Equatorial Africa.[2]

The agricultural sectors of the economies of Sub-Saharan Africa
are important not only for their contribution to production for
export and for domestic markets but also for their production for
direct 'farm' consumption. A very high proportion of all agricultural
production does not reach the market — it is estimated that 28 per

[1] The writer is indebted to Dr. Franz Lutolf and Dr. A. Kamarck, colleagues
in the Mission to Uganda organized by the World Bank, for many helpful comments.
[2] The Union of South Africa falls out of this general category though its
agricultural component comprised 11 per cent of its national income and agricultural exports comprise about 30 per cent of all exports.

cent of all agricultural production in Ghana, 31 per cent in former French West Africa, and 69 per cent in Kenya falls in this category. These estimates testify to the low level of monetization of large parts of the economy which are predominantly subsistence with a more or less significant cash sector superimposed on production for self-subsistence.[1]

In circumstances such as these it is evident that a very high proportion of the population must be concerned with agricultural production. The total size of the labour force in most of these countries is unknown but the numbers of 'wage earning' labourers represents a very small proportion of the total populations ; it is close to 3 per cent in Ghana and as low as 1·8 per cent in the former British Cameroons (see Table 2).[2] Virtually all of the non-wage-earning labour force in most areas is self-employed in agriculture and — as is shown in Table 1 — a very high proportion of males over 15 is self-employed in subsistence production. Furthermore, agricultural production in much of Africa is essentially a family affair (with the women attending to food crops, the men to cash crops, and the children herding cattle). In addition, many men are migratory labourers who divide their time between wage employment and self-employment in agriculture so that the numbers of self-employed in agriculture represent a significantly larger proportion of the population than would be indicated by the usually accepted definition of the labour force. Within the wage-earning labour force itself there are more persons engaged in agricultural production than in any other form of wage-employment (see Table 3). All in all, it might

[1] While national accounting precedences refer to subsistence incomes and the subsistence sector there is seldom any clear segregation of subsistence and non-subsistence production, particularly where output can be sold or consumed by the household (*e.g.* maize, groundnuts, etc.). It is suggested that the organization of production in tropical Africa passes through four stages :
    (i) purely subsistence production or production for direct consumption ;
    (ii) primarily subsistence production with a small production for the market ;
    (iii) mostly for the market with some production for direct consumption ;
    (iv) specialized production for the market.
Very few African producers are in Stage 1, except for those who rely entirely on the sale of their labour for money incomes or are completely isolated, *e.g.* Bushmen in the Kalahari. There are a small number of producers in the fourth stage, primarily cocoa producers on the West Coast. The great bulk of African producers in East and Central Africa are in Stage 2, while those in West Africa are in Stage 3 — the problem in each of these areas is to encourage the sale of change from 2 to 3 and 3 to 4 respectively.
[2] The figures in Table 2 are compiled from various sources and there is a wide discrepancy as to definition of 'wage earning' and 'labour force'. The 'wage earning' labour force in Ghana is closer to 3 per cent of the total population than 30 per cent as shown in the table. However, for the sake of consistency between Tables 2 and 3 the higher figures have been included in the tables so that the labour force is considered to be 1·3 million, including 900,000 people in agriculture, all of whom are not wage earners although they are included in this occupational category. The same applies to Mozambique.

TABLE 1

AFRICA : SELECTED DATA RELATING TO AGRICULTURE

	Ghana		Nigeria	
	1950	*1957*	*1950*	*1956/7*
1. Gross domestic product	223 m.	325 £	597 m.	812 £
Agricultural sector * (%)	58·7	51·3	68	62
2 (*a*) Subsistence prod. as % of GDP	—		—	
(*b*) Subsistence agric. as % of agr. prod.	27	28	—	
3. African (indigenous) contribution to monetized agric. prod. (%)	*1950* 100		*1950* 100	
4. Population	*1958*		*1952/3*	
Total (millions)	4·8		31·2	
Rural African % of total			95	
% of econ. active in agric.			74 †	
% males over 15 in subsist. agric. (1950)	21		57	
5. Exports : av. 1956–58				
Total value	237 m. $ US		366 m. $ US	
% Agricultural	66·7		91·3	
6. Imports : av. 1956–8				
Total value	252 m. $ US		437 m. $ US	
% Agricultural	20·5		14·7	
7. Food :				
% of total value	16·9		11·1	
8. Expenditure : Current	*1957/8*		*1957/8*	
Total	47·2 m.£		30·5 m.£ ‡	
Agricultural §	5·7 m.		0·3 m.	
% of total	12·1		1·0	
Capital	*1951–9*			
Total	136 m.£		37·4 ‖	
Agricultural	7 m.		1·8 m.£	
% of total	0·8		4·8	

m = million

* Includes forestry and fishing. † Males only. ‡ Federal only.
§ Includes irrigation, livestock, etc. ‖ Federal and local (regional)

Former French West Africa	Togo	Former French East Africa	Cameroun
1958 478 b. CFA 55·6	*1958* 25 b. CFA 60	*1956* 200 b. F. 50	*1956* 79 b. CFA 58·2
— 31·3	28 —	38·5 —	— 41·3
1957 19·8 95 77	*1959* 1·2 95 —	*1957* 4·9 95 62	*1958* 3·2 94 —
64·6 b. CFA 96·6	3·2 b. CFA 93·8	16·5 b. CFA 46	*1956* 13·1 b. CFA 77·9
77·4 b. CFA 18·5	4·2 b. CFA 33·3	25·4 b. CFA 13·4	16·9 b. CFA 17·2
Av. 1955–7 23·3	*Av. 1955–7* 19·3	*Av. 1955–7* 18·7	*Av. 1955–7* 19
	1958 2,449 m. CFA 108 0·4		
	193 m. CFA 1 m. 0·5		

m = million   b = billion

[*Continued on next page*

TABLE 1—*continued*

AFRICA : SELECTED DATA RELATING TO AGRICULTURE

	Former Belgian Congo	Rhodesian Federation	
1. Gross domestic product	*1957* 64 b.F.	*1954* 332 m.	*1959* 169
Agricultural sector * (%)	26·7	22·1	20·2
2 (*a*) Subsistence prod. as % of GDP	11	43·6	40·1
(*b*) Subsistence agric. as % of agr. prod.	—	—	
3. African (indigenous) contribution to	*1952*	*1952* †	
monetized agric. prod. (%)	45	11	
4. Population	*1957*	*1958*	
Total (millions)	13·2	7·8	
Rural African % of Total		91	
% of econ. active in agric.	82		
% males over 15 in subsist. agric. (1950)	42	51 †	
5. Exports : av. 1956–58	*Av. 1957/8*		
Total value	22·3 b.F.	442 m. $ US	
% Agricultural	33·6	24·3	
6. Imports : av. 1956–8			
Total value	19·4 b. F.	461 m. $ US	
% Agricultural	10·9	13	
7. Food :	*Av. 1956–8*	*Av. 1955–7*	
% of total value	9·7	9	
8. Expenditure : Current	*1958*	*1958/9* ‡	
Total	11,325 m.F.	89·9 m.£	
Agricultural ¶	3,130 §	6·3 m.	
% of total		7·0	
Capital		*1957–61* ‖	
Total	5,953 m.F.	121·7 m.£	
Agricultural	478	1·1	
% of total	7·2	0·9	

m = million   b = billion

*Includes forestry and fishing.   † Southern Rhodesia.   ‡ Federal and local.

§ All economic services, of which agriculture is one.   ‖ Federal only, proposed.

¶ Includes irrigation, livestock, etc.

Tanganyika	Kenya	Uganda	Sudan
1954 *1958* 142 m. 169 £ 61·9 59·1	*1954* *1958* 160 m. 207 £ 46 42	*1952* *1958* 99 m.* 115 £	*1955/6* 284 £ 62
— 60·2 61·6	— — 59·7	26·2 26·9 —	— —
	1952 18	*1950* 94	
1958 8·8 96	*1958* 6·4 94 (1948)	*1958* 5·8 98 (1948)	*1956* 10·3
63	70	59	40 —
119·7 m. $ US 84·5	84·4 m. $ US 81	124·8 m. $ US 95·2	52·6 m. f. Egypt 99
101·5 m. $ US 8·3	189·2 m. $ US 9·1	78·4 m. $ US 5	58·7 m. f. Egypt 23·8
Av. 1957–9 6·3	*Av. 1957–9* 7·2	*Av. 1958–9* 3·5	

1958/9
 19·5 m.£
 1·1 m.
 5·6
	1957/8
	 38·5 m.£
	 2·6 m.
	 6·8
		1957/8
		 18·8 m.£
		 1·4 m.
		 7·5
			1955/6
			 0·8 m.£ ⎫
			         ⎬ 6% all
			         ⎭ expenditure

5·2 m.£ 0·3 m. 5·3	6·0 m.£ 2·0 m. 33·3	6·7 m.£ 0·4 6·0	1·3 m.£

* Net domestic product.   m = million

Economic Development for Africa South of the Sahara

be said that between 80 and 90 per cent of the population of Sub-Saharan Africa is rural and as such depends directly on agriculture for its livelihood.

TABLE 2

LABOUR FORCE OF SELECTED AFRICAN COUNTRIES
SOUTH OF THE SAHARA
(In thousands) *

Countries	Total Population as of 1950 (estimated)	Labour Force † (dates noted)	Per Cent of Total Populations
West Africa			
Ghana (1954)	4,300·0	1,300·0	30·2
Liberia (1950)	1,300·0 ‡	30·0	2·3
Nigeria and British Cameroons (1952)	27,800·0	500·0	1·8
Sierra Leone (1951)	1,900·0	100·0	5·3
French West Africa (1950)	17,100·0	392·0	2·3
Central Africa			
Angola (1951)	4,100·0	800·0	19·5
Belgian Congo (1951)	11,300·0	1,267·5	11·2
French Equatorial Africa (1951)	4,400·0	216·5	4·9
Federation of the Rhodesias and Nyasaland (1952)	6,200·0	1,176·1	19·0
East Africa			
Kenya (1952)	5,600·0	434·5	7·8
Madagascar (1951)	4,300·0	—	—
Mozambique (1952)	5,700·0	1,633·5	28·6
Ruanda-Urundi (1951)	3,900·0	128·0	3·3
Tanganyika (1954)	7,700·0	440·2	5·7
Uganda (1952)	5,100·0	321·0	6·3
Southern Africa			
Union of South Africa	12,400·0	2,250·0	18·1

* Compiled from United Nations, *Statistical Yearbook, 1957*. Official reports and surveys of various governments.
† See footnote 2, p. 555.
‡ Population estimate as of 1955.

Despite the high degree of subsistence production, agricultural production in Sub-Saharan Africa has increased rapidly since the war years. According to FAO, the estimated average annual rate of increase of about 3 per cent exceeds growth in all other major regions except the Near East. In spite of an acceleration in population growth, *per capita* production appears to be about 20 per cent higher than before the war, though the evidence indicates that it has levelled off since 1955/6. However, while production has increased, the level of *per capita* output is still very low and is estimated to be only

TABLE 3

LABOUR FORCE OF SELECTED AFRICAN COUNTRIES
BY OCCUPATIONAL CATEGORIES
(In thousands) *

Occupations	French Cameroons (1952)	Ghana (1952)	Fed. of Rho-desias (1952)	Kenya (1952)	Tan-gan-yika (1952)	Union of South Africa (1946)
Labour Force (numbers)						
Agriculture	1,081·8	902·7	709·8	202·7	203·5	2,250·0
Mining	4·8	50·0	106·8	5·9	24·9	446·0
Manufacturing	12·0	73·2	67·7	41·9	18·1	229·0
Construction	21·6	50·4	74·9	15·6	18·2	103·0
Communications and transportation	8·2	35·8	27·3	7·9	34·3	84·0
Commerce	15·3	112·5	—	17·8	13·0	110·0
Services	38·4	70·6	123·4	141·5	82·7	831·0
Gas and electricity	—	4·8	6·6	1·3	—	7·0
Miscellaneous	13·5	—	59·5	—	45·4	208·0
Total	1,195·6	1,300·0	1,176·0	434·6	440·1	4,268·0
Labour Force (percentages)						
Agriculture	90·5	69·4	60·4	46·7	46·2	52·7
Mining	0·4	3·8	9·1	1·4	5·7	10·4
Manufacturing	1·0	5·6	5·7	9·6	4·1	5·4
Construction	1·8	3·9	6·4	3·6	4·2	2·4
Communications and transportation	0·7	2·8	2·3	1·8	7·8	2·0
Commerce	1·3	8·7	—	4·1	2·9	2·6
Services	3·2	5·4	10·5	32·6	18·8	19·4
Gas and electricity	—	0·4	0·5	0·2	—	0·2
Miscellaneous	1·1	—	5·1	—	10·3	4·9
Total	100·0	100·0	100·0	100·0	100·0	100·0

* Compiled from United Nations, *Statistical Yearbook, 1957.* See footnote 2, p. 555.

about one-third more than that of the Far East. In addition to low output per man, the average yield per acre for most crops is considerably below world averages. In circumstances such as these both real incomes and *per capita* money incomes are bound to be extremely low.[1]

[1] *Per capita* money incomes have, of course, been influenced by the changes in terms of trade. I presume this will be discussed elsewhere.

TABLE 4

POPULATION SIZE AND DENSITY IN COUNTRIES OF AFRICA
SOUTH OF THE SAHARA, BY TOTAL LAND AREA AND USABLE LAND *

Countries	Total Estimated Population 1955 (Millions)	Total Land Area (1955) (Sq. Miles)	Total Density per Square Mile	Total Usable Land (1948)	Density per Square Mile, Usable Land
West Africa	63·3	2,539,918	25·0	1,045,321†	60·6†
British Cameroons	1·5	34,081	4·4	n.a.	n.a.
French Cameroons	3·1	166,489	18·6	n.a.	n.a.
Ghana	4·6	91,843	50·1	44,437	103·5
Liberia	1·3	43,000	30·2	33,484	38·8
Nigeria	31·3	338,919	92·3	160,716	194·8
Sierra Leone	2·0	27,925	71·6	n.a.	n.a.
French Togoland	1·1	21,893	50·2	n.a.	n.a.
French West Africa	18·7	1,815,768	10·3	803,268	23·3
Central Africa	28·9	2,830,311	10·2	764,036	37·8
Angola	4·3	481,351	8·9	35,700	120·4
Belgian Congo	12·6	904,756	13·9	625,069	20·2
French Equatorial Africa	4·7	968,860	4·8	846,985	5·5
Federation of Rhodesia and Nyasaland	7·1	475,344	14·9	256,282	27·7
East Africa	35·1	1,227,294	28·6	377,889	92·9
Kenya	6·0	224,960	26·7	57,968	103·5
Madagascar	4·8	227,799	21·1	42,768	112·2
Mozambique	6·0	297,654	20·2	72,480	82·8
Ruanda-Urundi	4·3	20,900	205·7	15,675	274·3
Tanganyika	8·3	362,000	22·9	126,344	65·7
Uganda	5·5	93,981	58·5	62,654	87·8
Southern Africa					
Union of South Africa	13·7	472,491	29·0	361,198	37·9

* Compiled from United Nations, *World Resources Survey*, 1948; United Nations, *Statistic Yearbook*, 1957.
† Excluding British and French Cameroons, Sierra Leone, and French Togoland.

II. THE FUTURE RÓLE IN AGRICULTURE

It is apparent that agriculture will have to maintain its dominant position as a source of savings and provider of employment in these economies for the foreseeable future. While some industrialization is proceeding, rapid and massive industrialization does not appear to be feasible : there is a widespread lack of managerial and technical skills and the lack of monetization of the economy and the low level of *per capita* money incomes limit the size of the domestic market for industrial products;[1] furthermore, it seems unlikely that African industrial exports could compete effectively with those of the industrialized nations in the African market let alone in overseas markets. Until there are alternative exports most countries will have to depend on the agricultural sectors to provide the greater part of the savings and revenues needed to create the infrastructure for development.[2]

However, the volume of world trade in agricultural products is increasing at a slow rate.[3] Domestic food output in the industrialized countries is expanding, substitutes are increasingly replacing agricultural raw materials, and the income elasticity of demand for most foodstuffs is low. Consequently the short-run prospects for substantial increased export earnings from African agricultural products are anything but favourable. Projections derived from estimates of future world market prices for the major products and from an assessment of likely trends in the main consumption and import centres, along with a rough estimate of Africa's future share of total world supply, indicate that export earnings for such important commodities as sugar and tobacco are unlikely to rise. Proceeds from palm oil, cocoa, and coffee may actually decline, while cotton, groundnuts, and rubber exports offer some hope for modest increases. Naturally, the margin of error related to such exercises is great, but it seems hard to escape the general conclusion that export prospects for agricultural products from Africa south of the Sahara cannot be relied upon to improve materially over, say, the next 10–15 years.[4]

[1] Conditions differ from country to country, but the case of Uganda presents an illustration of the limitations of industrialization arising from the size of the market even where there is an aggressive and well managed State Development Corporation. The Uganda Development Corporation has made the most of every opportunity; it has capital, good management, and technical competence, but its activities are restricted by the size of the market; the same is true of general conditions in Southern Rhodesia.

[2] I am disregarding the mineral sector but I am, of course, aware of its importance in many parts of Sub-Saharan Africa. No doubt this sector offers potentiality; however, more has to be known of the available desposits and the opportunities for exploiting those deposits.

[3] Between 1950–8 the continent as a whole produced more than 80 per cent of the world's output of palm kernel and palm oil, and more than 60 per cent of sisal and cocoa beans, around half of the cassava, sweet potatoes, between one-third and one-half of the world's supply of groundnuts, millet, and sorghum. During this same period Africa provided more than 90 per cent of the world's export in groundnuts and palm kernels, between one-half and two-thirds of the world's cocoa beans, palm oil, groundnut oil, sisal, and palm kernel oil.

[4] These projections are based on GATT, OEEC, and ECE analyses. One should not overlook the possibilities of expanded trade between Africa and the Sino-Soviet bloc countries. In addition it is not inconceivable that Africa, as a low-cost producer, may displace some of the higher-cost traditional suppliers of agricultural products as they embark on industrialization programmes (Latin America and certain Asian countries). Furthermore, natural calamities in any one region of the world can change the pattern of trade substantially in the short run, *vide* the effects of the current Chinese drought on the disposal of 'surplus' Canadian and Australian wheat.

Within the continent, domestic demand is increasing slowly, though where there has been urbanization, as in the former Belgian Congo, the rate of output for the market has increased at a much faster rate than has subsistence production. There are also limited possibilities for increasing import substitution ; though food imports are not of great significance in most countries (see Table 1). There are opportunities for increasing production of certain commodities such as sugar in East Africa or Ghana and other specialized crops both for domestic and non-African consumption, *e.g.* tea and livestock products. However, in the main, the overall prospects for an increasing rate of demand for foodstuffs and agricultural products is not favourable.

In the long run, therefore, levels of income in these areas will only be raised by a transfer of human resources out of agriculture and a shift, within the agricultural sector, from subsistence production to specialization of production for the market. There will have to be a reallocation of those land resources now being used for production for direct consumption to production for the market as well as a general rise in levels of productivity so as to increase food supplies as urbanized populations increase.

However, while the long-run goals are fairly self-evident there are peculiar problems of the re-deployment of resources in the short run. For instance, while conditions vary, productivity could probably be raised by population moving out of agriculture or being shifted out of agriculture. However, since there are limited employment opportunities elsewhere — and even the most ambitious industrialization programmes are likely to absorb no more than a marginal proportion of the available labour force — the marginal product of the transferees will be zero and the agricultural sector will have to bear the cost of transferring the population and feeding them, as well as providing the savings that will be required for the high level of capital formation needed for housing and infrastructure for the population moved into industry.[1] Consequently, while it is essential that resources in agriculture be used as effectively as possible, it appears equally important that this should be done in such a manner that people are not displaced from agriculture at a rate at which they cannot be absorbed by the non-agricultural sector.

In these circumstances under-employment in a tribal agriculture with some production for self-subsistence and for sale may be more

[1] The estimated average cost of creating one industrial employment opportunity in the Central African Federation in 1958 was £1,250. See unpublished manuscript on 'African Development Problems' by M. Yudelman to be published by Harvard University Press.

advantageous than specialized production that leads to unemployment in urban areas ; [1] because of the costs involved there is little to be gained by displacing the rural population until added employment opportunities are created in the non-agricultural sector.

The economic development of Sub-Saharan Africa will depend to a great extent on the rate of non-agricultural development ; however, there is still much that can be done to develop the agricultural sectors of these economies so as to expand the size of the internal market as a concomitant for industrialization. In many areas the marginal productivity of small-scale investments in African agriculture can be very high, though as I will point out the needed investments have to be of a different type than those usually considered by international lending agencies. Furthermore, because of the costs of transferring populations out of agriculture the nature of the problem is such that there has to be development without the type of radical reform that will displace too large a proportion of the rural population too rapidly. I would like to touch on these and other aspects of the development problem in the remainder of this paper.

III. AGRICULTURAL PRODUCTION SYSTEMS

The nature of agricultural production in any area depends on physical, social, economic, and cultural factors. In this regard Sub-Saharan Africa does not form a cultural or agro-economic unit and the organization of production varies considerably. There are large-scale capital-intensive farming and cattle-raising systems in the dual economies where there is European settlement (South Africa, Rhodesia, Kenya) ; and there are enclaves of highly organized vertically integrated plantations in countries such as the Congo (oil palms) and Tanganyika (sisal). In these areas, modern agricultural production methods have been introduced, and production and growth compare favourably with most other agricultural regions in the world ; in fact in Southern Rhodesia it has been one of the highest in the world.[2] Nevertheless, although European settlement and

---

[1] The advantage of joint production of self-subsistence and cash crops in a period of extremely low prices was demonstrated in Uganda in the 1920's. The sharp fall in commodity prices ruined many plantation owners who had to pay wages for labour; however, small-scale African producers who employed family labour were able to maintain and increase output despite falling prices. See *Crops and Wealth in Uganda*, by C. C. Wrigley, East African Studies No. 12, East African Institute of Social Research, Kampala, Uganda, 1959, p. 82.

[2] Agricultural output in Southern Rhodesia increased at a rate of 10 per cent per annum between 1948–58 ; 48 per cent of the country is allocated to European producers and 42 per cent to Africans. Most of the increase in output came from

modern enclaves form a most important part of the agricultural picture in many countries and have contributed much to the increased rate of output of the area as a whole, our concern is with the indigenous producer.

Naturally there are a wide range of production systems in much of Africa, but generally African agriculture is responding slowly to a changing set of conditions which existed when the greater part of the continent was integrated into the world economy. At that time, which is still in living memory in many parts of Central, East, and West Africa, the organization of the African economy was a simple one centred largely around a plentiful supply of land. This applied to both pastoral and agricultural producers and was most pronounced in areas of uncertain and sparse rainfall. The pastoralists required land for extensive grazing, moving their livestock as the occasion demanded, whenever grazing areas were over-grazed or water supplies diminished. The agriculturists, and in the southern and eastern region of Africa many of these were also cattle owners, required extensive supplies of land to practise shifting cultivation and bush fallow. Generally this system of agriculture involved a form of land rotation whereby land was used as long as it was fertile, possibly up to three or four years, then once its fertility was diminished it was left to revert to bush until it was restored. The producers, in the interim, moved to another patch of land. On some occasions and in some areas, as long as twenty years would elapse from the initial abandonment of land to its regeneration : frequently, too, entire African villages would move as the need arose for new lands.

Shifting cultivation and land rotation made both agronomic and economic sense in the circumstances in which it was operated. Agronomically it was a concession to the nature of the soil and a relatively sparse population was in ecological balance with its environment. Economically the peasant producer was rational in his production methods : land was plentiful, labour was relatively scarce, and 'capital' virtually non-existent. The plentiful and free land

the European area as African output only increased at 3 per cent per annum. The differences in organization of production are illustrated by the fact that there were 6,651 European holdings with an average size of 4,000 acres, of which 140 were cultivated ; there were 312,000 African holdings with an average size of 100 acres of which 9 were cultivated. Aggregate labour inputs in both areas were approximately the same but there was a vast difference in capital inputs ; for example, there were close to 10,000 tractors in the European areas and less than 20 in the African areas ; £18,000,000 of credit was used in one year by European producers compared with £66,000 by Africans. On the output side, yields of maize in European areas were 10+ bags per acre while those in the African areas were 2 bags per acre ; total output was valued at £68 million in 1959 but £41 million came from the European area — this included 88 per cent of all marketed output.

supply was substituted for any intensive labour effort that might have required extra energy-inputs.

In circumstances such as these the African producer was, and in many ways still is, a product of a closed subsistence economy characterized by strong tribal ties ; he was non-acquisitive and status was determined by factors other than material wealth. There was a timelessness about society and production was considered in terms of immediate wants ; there was little saving and production for consumption was a seasonal exercise. Within this system agricultural production required relatively little sustained effort, and there was little division of labour other than by sex, with the women doing the field work ; there were very few household industries ; some basket weaving, some working on iron and a little weaving of cloth. The digging-stick, hoe, and axe were the basic production implements. The producer in this traditional economy was not inventive and he was not one to stir himself to innovations or change ; his system was adequate to provide for his needs. Non-economic activities (or non-productive activities) occupied much of the time of the typical tribesman. These activities were undeniably an important element in traditional man's system of values ; the market place, as understood by economic man, was virtually non-existent.

Traditional man had minimal subsistence goals, and low production targets in terms of physical output. Once there was an adequate food supply it became a matter of indifference to him whether output was increased or not, though it seems fair to assume that it was a matter of some concern if increased output could only be 'bought' at a price of increased economic activity, *i.e.* loss of leisure. However, in the words of Professor Myint, discussing a similar situation elsewhere, 'while the people might have lived near the minimum subsistence level that standard, according to their own lights, did not appear too wretched or inadequate. Thus in spite of low productivity and lack of economic progress there was no problem of economic discontent and frustration ; wants and activities are on the whole adapted to each other and the people were in equilibrium with their environment.'[1]

The extension of the exchange economy disturbed the internal equilibrium of this closed economy as it raised the levels of wants of the producers ; the appearance of new goods and services introduced new desires. The spread of education and the influence of the Church widened horizons. The indigenous producer found his earlier non-money traditional system in conflict with a system that required him to produce taxation to meet cash obligations such as

[1] Myint, 'Economic Backwardness', *Oxford Economic Papers.*

taxes or sell his labour to satisfy his needs.[1] At the same time the land available for practising shifting cultivation was diminished by population pressure and by the extension of the European settlers' frontier where institutional and political arrangements restricted the amount of land available to African producers.[2]

IV. LAND USE

Traditionally, increased output in African agriculture has come from added inputs of land and labour rather than from higher productivity per unit of land or labour ; in recent years this expansion has not been a 'frontier movement' but rather unused land has been taken up in the vicinity of settled villages as population has increased. As the subcontinent is still sparsely populated — with an average population density of 15 per square mile, a very low figure for a predominantly agricultural community — there would appear to be considerable leeway for increasing output in the traditional manner. However, the limits of this type of expansion are curtailed by the quality of physical resources and the methods of land use.[3] In the first instance, while precise land classification is

[1] In a survey conducted among 297 males in Bechuanaland in 1947 close to 40 per cent of the producers reported they left 'home' to seek employment in the Union of South Africa because of the need for money to pay taxes. See *The Economic Causes of Labour Migration from Bechuanaland in Migrant Labour and Tribal Life*, by I. Schapera, Oxford University Press, 1947. Also see Gulliver, P. H., *Labour Migration in a Rural Economy : a Study of the Ngoni and Ndendeuli of Southern Tanganyika*, Kampala, Uganda, East African Institute of Social Research, 1955, pp. 19-21.

[2] I refer to the 'reserve' system in Kenya, Southern Rhodesia, and Union of South Africa — in South Africa 13 per cent of the land is reserved for Africans, in Southern Rhodesia 42 per cent is African, and in Kenya all but 1 per cent is African. The shortage of land together with the imposition of cash taxes and a desire for goods and services that can be bought by money has contributed much to the male migratory labour system — one of the phenomena of Sub-Saharan Africa.

[3] Africa south of the Sahara does not form any kind of agricultural unit and the subcontinent encompasses a wide range of climatological and physical conditions though most of it falls in the tropics. However, in the most general terms, it can be classified as falling into two broad climatological zones. About a quarter of the area around the Guinea Coast and of the western edge of the continent down to the Congo falls into the region of high, wet tropical climate. Rainfall is heavy and regular in this area. It is suitable for forest crops but the soils tend to be deficient in phosphates. The remaining 75 per cent of the subcontinent that includes the eastern and southern portions of Africa, and the belt close to the Sahara, has the monsoon-type climate. The characteristics of this area are short rainy seasons so that quick-maturing crops have to be grown. While the soils of this area are more fertile than those of the forest area, irregular rainfall limits agricultural possibilities. Thus in a very broad sense the areas of good soil have poor rainfall, and the areas with poor soils have good rainfall ; compensation for these disparities requires a higher level of management than in the great farming areas of South America where the climatic and physical conditions are much more favourable for low-cost production.

unavailable, the figures on population densities are deceptive, for much of the area is 'unusable' for agricultural purposes. This is indicated in Table 2, and in the most general terms it might be said that not more than half of West Africa and one-third of East Africa and a little more than a quarter of Central Africa can be classified as agriculturally 'useful' land.[1] Consequently, while the overall average density of the population is less than 15 persons a square mile, so giving the appearance of a very favourable relationship between land and population, the high proportion of unusable land alters this relationship to one that is much less favourable. In addition, of course, the increasing population is changing this ratio with each passing year.

Despite these features there is still no overall shortage of land in Africa though there is an apparent shortage in many areas ; if present methods of land utilization could be changed the 'effective' supply of land could be increased considerably so as to absorb larger numbers in agriculture. The methods of farming now employed vary from area to area but almost all of the farming systems still rely on the traditional system of 'resting' periods to maintain or restore the fertility of the soil ; during the resting period a large proportion of the available land supply is immobilized. The amount of land out of production varies considerably and depends on the quality of the soils and the ecology and environment and the needs of the crops grown in the area. Thus in West Africa where there are rich soils over igneous rocks and where there are primary materials rich in nutrients, it is possible to maintain an equal division of land under cropping and land where it is fallow. However, for most of the soils of West Africa, especially those that are deep-weathered and leached in the high rainfall areas such as southeast Nigeria and Sierra Leone and those developed from sedimentary rocks consisting largely of inert quartz sand, such as in coastal Nigeria, a year of cropping may require up to ten years of resting to restore fertility.[2]

Theoretically, the effective supply of land could be increased by substituting capital and management for a resting period. However, it is at this point that the link between economics and agricultural science breaks down, for the agricultural scientists simply do not know enough about the effects of disturbing the ecological balance

[1] Unusable land would include tsetse-infested land, mountains, swamps, rocky outcrops, and desert. See *Population Pressures in Africa South of the Sahara*, by Richard W. Stephens, Population Research Project, George Washington University, 55 pp.
[2] *Some Prospects for Subsistence Agriculture in West Africa*, by P. H. Nye, West Africa Science Association, April 1956.

to suggest the most suitable substitute for resting land. A good part of this lack of knowledge can be attributed to the fact that the great backlog of information derived from research over the past hundred years has been based on findings related to conditions in the temperate zones of the world and much of it is inapplicable to the tropics. In this regard tropical Africa is very much a late-comer, and being a late-comer is not advantageous to agriculture as it is to industry as the opportunities of technological leap-frogging are limited.[1] Furthermore, the introduction of new systems of production can be hazardous in the extreme if there is a lack of detailed knowledge of the resource base of an area. Some very expensive mistakes have been made in the past where untested hypotheses have been substituted for knowledge.[2]

The situation varies considerably from country to country ; in some countries such as Uganda there is still ample scope for increasing output by land extensive methods. In neighbouring Tanganyika, however, the problems are those of maldistribution of resources — large areas of potentially usable land are immobilized because of lack of investment in water supplies. The same situation appears to apply to Northern Ghana and parts of Nigeria. However, it is clear that the problem of intensifying land use and the raising of productivity of land and labour is one that will become more and more significant. In some areas the limitations on acreage without compensating changes in production techniques are already leading to soil depletion and large investments are being made to restore soil fertility by mechanical means ; these investments, however, are producing very low returns because while they are substituting capital for land they are not leading to increased outputs ; in fact the capital output ratio from many of these investments is close to infinity because of a neglect of complementary investment in improving the quality of labour to utilize these improved lands.

Elsewhere, even though there may or may not be immediate pressure on land, it is very difficult to justify high-cost land clearance by mechanical means or tsetse eradication because of the low returns from the cleared areas.[3] The effective supply of land in African

---

[1] However, this would not preclude such novel approaches as aerial spraying of crops or 'sowing' missing chemicals such as phosphates by air.

[2] Perhaps there has been no more tragic example of this than the failure of the East African groundnut scheme — this scheme, which was to have been the largest mechanized operation in the world, cost the British taxpayers £27 million. Many factors contributed to its failure but among the principal factors responsible for failure were the lack of research and knowledge about the amount and distribution of rainfall and the compacting of the soils shortly after the cessation of the rains. See *Agriculture and Ecology in Africa*, by John Phillips, Faber & Faber, London, 1960, 344 pp.

[3] Tsetse eradication is estimated to cost £250 per square mile in Uganda.

agriculture can be increased by changing techniques of production and by investments in reclamation, tsetse clearance, and bush clearance. However, the root of the land-use problem is essentially a problem of improving levels of management, and as such is part of the problem of education, research, labour, and incentives to improve farming practices. It is obvious that if there is to be any programme to raise agricultural incomes without displacing labour then priority must be given to research into methods of expanding the land supply by changing techniques of production, *i.e.* improving productivity of labour.

V. LABOUR AND INCENTIVES

There is no doubt that there can be an increase in output in many areas without displacing labour if producers would increase inputs of labour, but there is still a great deal of under-employment in African agriculture. Part of this is seasonal and part of it is related to the poor combination of factors of production ; however, much of it is voluntary in the sense that producers still have high leisure preferences based on traditional value systems whereby they choose to limit their inputs of labour rather than to maximize their money returns by forgoing non-economic activities.

There have been very few detailed studies as to why this occurs and how producers can be encouraged to increase labour inputs. One study indicated that many producers in Southern Rhodesia still visualize security in terms of visible food supplies irrespective of 'price', and once their immediate wants are satisfied, together with an adequate 'famine' reserve, then the marginal cost of self-employed labour rose very rapidly. It is only at this stage that the price factor assumed importance ; if prices were high then there were increased labour inputs for harvesting ; if they were low then the returns were not considered adequate to offset the costs of forgoing leisure.[1]

Another study in Northern Rhodesia indicated that producers were apathetic about responding to price differentials for 'improved' farming. Substantial inducements and price differentials were offered to farmers to follow improved farming practices but only 4 per cent of the farmers in the area responded to money incentives to improve their production methods by adding labour inputs.[2] In contrast to this, experience in Uganda and Nigeria has indicated

[1] *A Note on the Economics of African Development in Southern Rhodesia with special reference to Agriculture*, by M. Yudelman and S. Makings, February 1960, 67 pp. mimeograph by S. Rhodesia Government.
[2] *African Farming Improvement in the Plateau Tonga Maize Areas of Northern Rhodesia*, by C. E. Johnson, Dept. of Agriculture, N. Rhodesia, 62 pp.

that producers do respond to price changes and increase production for the market by added labour inputs.

There is a widespread belief that producers have fixed income goals set at a low level partly because of limited horizons. Consequently the problem of increasing labour inputs is viewed as one of raising income goals through consumer demonstration effects, making consumer goods available, and so forth, so that producers will be motivated to expand production.[1] This upward shift in demand for money incomes is considered to be slow in maturing, so it is argued that if prices were to rise output would be reduced and a smaller quantity of output would suffice to satisfy target incomes and vice versa. This view provides part of the logic behind the backward-bending supply curve and is used to justify the supply aspect of those marketing board price policies that contend that a low fixed price does not discourage increased output.

It is debatable whether violent fluctuations in prices do more to bring producers into the money economy than do stable prices. Large increases in prices — through violent shifts in the terms of trade — frequently 'pull' producers into the money economy. Once in the economy and once they have acquired a taste for certain goods and services it is unlikely that they will revert entirely to subsistence production. They will then continue to produce for the market and it is at this stage that low prices may lead to increased output. There is also the obverse : producers' wants may well move in 'plateaus' and it may well depend on which 'level of wants' they are on as to whether they will increase output for the market or not, *e.g.* the producer whose wants are at a bicycle plateau may have a different outlook from one who has moved to the stage where he wants a corrugated roof. However, in many parts of East Africa the ascendancy in the scale of 'acquired wants' is determined by the chief who sets the pattern ; individual want may be constrained because of conformance which requires that no one surpass the leader in conspicuous consumption. Thus in many areas a 'progressive' chief who is materialistically inclined can be a powerful catalyst for increasing production.

The evidence, such as it is, is fragmentary ; however, several

[1] The availability of consumer 'incentive' goods is a factor in changing attitudes; however, investigations in East Africa indicated that there is a problem of having a sustained supply of goods available — demand has to be created and the cost of creating demand by demonstrating goods through holding them in ready supply is more than many traders can afford. Thus the range of goods available tends to be modest and so much of the 'incentive' effect is dissipated. Where there is a sustained programme of making consumer goods available the effects have been remarkable — classical examples are the Coca-cola and Pepsi-cola programmes in East Africa.

conclusions appear to be warranted. The first is that there are many interdependent factors at work and frequently what appears to be voluntary under-employment is in reality a distrust of the marketing system. Thus in Uganda and Nyasaland cotton and tobacco remain unpicked, not because of high leisure preferences but because of a clash in labour requirements between cotton picking and harvesting food crops ; as security is still conceived to be in terms of visible food supplies producers do not use their labour to maximize their money incomes but rather to reduce uncertainty.[1] Furthermore, in many areas there is a rationality about not expanding acreage because of the shortage of labour for labour-intensive harvesting. This is one reason why mechanization of cultivation of cotton has been a failure to Uganda, and it highlights the difficulties of partial mechanization of production (and explains the reason for so much favour being given to the introduction of animal-drawn power).[2]

It is difficult to generalize about the rôle of incentives in reducing under-employment and increasing output ; however, the whole problem must be viewed in a dynamic rather than in a static context and as part of the transitional process whereby producers are becoming money-orientated. There is no doubt that attitudes are changing and the best augury for the future is the rapid increase in numbers passing through the school system, so adding to forces already at work in creating money conscientiousness and a desire for higher levels of income. However, there is very little that can be done in

---

[1] Professor Raeburn has expressed this view succinctly : 'The conditions of production impose even more obvious limitations on the economic commercialisation of agriculture — specialisation in accordance with comparative advantages. Consider the position, for instance, of the typical Kikuyu farmer with say $4\frac{1}{4}$ acres of land in South Nyeri District. On paper, single-value estimates of costs and returns from his range of possible products clearly suggest that to use his limited land for coffee would be by far his most profitable alternative. But capital would be required both to establish the coffee and to make up for the food crops he would lose while waiting for the coffee to bear. His risk and uncertainty bearing would increase both because of the pests of coffee — not all of which are completely and cheaply controllable — and because he would become much more dependent on the widely fluctuating price ratio — in his own locality — of coffee to foodstuffs.' 'Now with lack of capital, short lives, high risks and, often, disruption of old social organisations, this rate of interest can be quite high — even more than 20 per cent. Also farmers' ideas of the effects of present outputs on future outputs, and more particularly of present inputs, especially new types of input, on future outputs and savings of future inputs, may be far more pessimistic than those of the experts who, *nota bene*, may be assuming very low or even zero rates of interest.' 'Some Economic Aspects of African Agriculture', by John R. Raeburn, *The East African Economics Review*, Vol. 5, No. 2, pp. 45, 47.

[2] Seasonal labour requirements for labour intensive crops present difficulties in many parts of Africa — it is doubtful if the Gezira scheme would have been a success if the annual pilgrimages to Mecca did not bring thousands of itinerant pilgrims from West Africa into the area at a time when they were able to earn their passage by helping with the harvest of the crop.

the interim and while facilities can be provided to encourage increased labour inputs and to ease drudgery, there is still no process whereby capital can substitute for time.[1]

Nevertheless, if resources are to be used more fully, then enterprise must be encouraged and there must be an acceleration in the transition of tribal values to economic values — the apex of this problem is in land tenure or rights to use land, and the problem of improvement of agriculture without displacing labour centres around the institutions that govern land use.

VI. LAND TENURE

Perhaps there is no area where the conflict between traditional values and economic concepts is more difficult to reconcile than the issue of rights to land use. The tribal system of land holding, which still predominates in much of Africa, and land rights is part of the woof and warp of tribal society, and it tends to discourage enterprise though it encourages social stability. Briefly, the major facets of African tenurial systems are : the tribal chief is the custodian of the land and all land is held on a kinship basis. Individuals within the group do not have absolute ownership but have specified rights qualified by membership of the group. Thus individual rights exist concurrently with those of the clan or local group. Once land is allocated to a family it remains the 'property' of the family in the sense that they have the right to use the land, but there is no concept of absolute ownership. The period of the use of land may be limited and, if necessary, it can be reallocated by the tribal authorities to accommodate other members of the clan. Land may be reallocated to make sure that it is used ; however, land may not be disposed of outside the extended family group nor may it be sold though it can be pledged. Pledged land is redeemable at any time as a safeguard against it being permanently lost to its user. There is no collective ownership of land or rights to land but there are individual rights within a system of communal ownership. Where there are livestock these are kept on a communal or common grazing land.[2]

---

[1] There are several 'coercive' methods that can be used to increase labour inputs — taxing leisure is a popular device but in many areas this has accelerated the rate of migration out of agriculture. The other method used is to penalize producers who do not follow a set pattern of farming, involving fixed inputs of labour. This system is used in the Gezira scheme.

[2] There are many variations of tenurial systems ; in some areas there are rights of inheritance, in others there are not ; conditions of tenure also vary according to whether tree crops or annual crops are produced. See *Land Law and Custom in the Colonies*, by C. K. Meek, Oxford University Press, 1949.

In many areas traditional systems of tenure have evolved to meet changing conditions. Nevertheless, the communal character of land ownership and the obligations that go with it tend to be a drawback to the emergence of progressive farmers. As the tribal system is based on distribution of land according to subsistence needs and is interwoven with concepts of mutual self-help and reciprocal labour arrangements, these group obligations limit the freedom of operation and choice of producers.[1] Where producers wish to break out of the tribal mould by employing labour or machinery — and so moving in the direction of having a division of labour — they engender group hostility and, as the rights of land use are governed by personal relations rather than contract, opportunities for expansion are restricted.

Initiative, ambition, and enterprise are thus penalized and can only be encouraged by modifying or breaking down the tribal system of tenure. Creation of an impersonal land market has been suggested as a means of resolving this problem. A further argument in favour of private ownership is that the security of ownership will encourage growers to increase the rate of capital formation as they would know they could reap the returns from their investments ; in addition, if land could be sold producers would be encouraged to invest as they could capitalize on the sale of land. However, in several countries where there has been a survey, demarcation of holdings, and adjudication of rights, and the subsequent creation of a land market, some unexpected problems have come to light. There are the problems of determining whether society should be egalitarian and whether all holdings should be the same size, or whether holdings should be based on the *de facto* situation, whether the size of holdings should be adjusted to fit the concept of an economic unit based on an income concept or on an employment concept. There is also a peculiar set of problems related to dividing up communal grazing areas. However, focusing on problems of land reform should not override socio-economic considerations.

In Southern Rhodesia where there has been allocation of individual holdings it has reduced the elasticity of the tribal system. It has succeeded in the primary goal of making land a factor of production with a 'cost' to it rather than a 'free good', but in so doing a considerable amount of rural, under-employed labour has been displaced. The adjudication of lands rights, together with safeguards against fragmentation, have weakened the communal obligation to

[1] Contrary to popular belief there is a wide range in the size of holdings in many areas. Frequently the relatives of those who have allocative authority have large holdings, *e.g.* in one area of Southern Rhodesia it was found that holdings ranged from 43 acres to $\frac{1}{2}$ acre.

provide land for kinsmen. Subsequently, these persons have been forced to seek employment out of agriculture and so have swelled the ranks of the unemployed in urban areas. A similar process is occurring in Kenya where the allocation of land has caused repercussions in Uganda where displaced persons have moved into grazing formerly held by certain nomadic tribes ; the result has been that pressure has been generated on communal grazing lands, so creating problems in those areas.

A further result of creating a land market has been that the concept of communal obligation for the care of the aged, by providing them with a subsistence holding, is being discontinued and it is no longer possible for any tribesman who retires from employment to return to his tribal area where he can automatically secure a subsistence holding to provide his food needs. Thus, the cost of social security formerly borne by the group will now have to be borne by the state.[1]

VII. AGRARIAN REFORM

There is need for 'agrarian reform' in African agriculture ; however, the concept of agrarian reform is not necessarily one conceived in terms of social justice where there are inequitable landlord tenant relationships that give a high return to land and a low return to labour, but rather it is a reform that aims at raising the productivity of both land and labour. This is all the more necessary to raise the level of rural incomes so as to prevent outward migration and urban unemployment.

[1] The following comment by a well-known student of labour problems in East Africa points up some of the problems in connection with land 'ownership' and social security. 'If the future income of a farm, however small, cannot be capitalized, the farm must exercise a strong pull. So long as a man cannot obtain compensation for vacating his land and, on the other hand, cannot normally maintain his right to it unless he or his family are in actual occupation, he has no inducement to vacate it and he is therefore bound to regard employment as in some sense temporary. It is sometimes argued that the compensation for abandoning the land comes in the form of higher wages which a long period in employment is bound to bring him, that low wages are the consequence of low productivity, and that low productivity is caused by the fact that men have not committed themselves to employment. Such reasoning is naïve. An individual's wage is not determined in such simple ways, and Africans who work for wages are less easily deluded by such comfortable moral theories than their employers or their governments. It is one of those hypotheses which are true in general and in the long run ; it is not a consideration which could influence very potently an individual about to make a choice. At present, if a man were to withdraw permanently from the countryside, he would be giving up both a part of his income *and also a form of insurance against unemployment or ill health.*' 'Migrant Labor in Africa : An Economist's Approach', by Walter Elkan, Makerere College, *American Economic Review*, Vol. XLIX, No. 2, May 1959, p. 195.

While the situation varies from country to country, low-yielding land-extensive systems now used will have to give place to more intensive system productions. This will have to be done by modifying the present systems of production rather than by introducing radical reforms which will destroy the tribal system without providing compensating benefits that exceed the costs of its destruction. Consequently, the grant of individual title will have to be approached with caution and selectivity. The problem of reconciling traditional values and market concepts is one of the unresolved dilemmas of African agriculture and one which requires investigation and flexibility. There are possibilities of co-operative land ownership, individual land ownership, and tribal land ownership. Circumstances vary and the methods applied will have to be devised to meet particular requirements and, if necessary, there can be a combination of all three systems of tenure. However, it is plain that there can be no blanket acceptance of the notion that private ownership resolves more problems in the development in African agriculture than it creates.

There is much that can be done to raise the levels of productivity of agriculture within the present framework of production. The weakest aspect of production is the low level of technical proficiency of most producers ; in many areas this arises from lack of knowledge and shortage of working capital. In some instances these problems have been resolved through partnership schemes where external groups have provided the management and other services while African farmers participated as individual producers within the general framework of the joint venture. This approach was most successful in the Gezira scheme and may succeed in the projected tea plantation schemes in Kenya and Uganda and the sugar-producing plantations in Tanganyika. In each instance management, capital, and supervision have been provided under centralized operation while African outgrowers produced the commodities mentioned above.

However, it appears that in the main the basic production unit in African agriculture will be the small-scale producer. Thus, either the state or some parastatal body will have to provide the services needed to raise productivity. These services include research and the diffusion of the information derived from research, and while this aspect of development has been neglected in the past, some of the results of recent research work indicate that higher yields can be obtained through simple procedures of pest control and in the dissemination of higher yielding varieties of seeds. The Food Crop Division of INAEC at Yangambi had developed varieties of rice capable of yielding 2,500 kgs. per hectare as an upland crop

577

compared with 500-700 kgs. obtainable from local varieties, and in similar fashion manioc yields have been increased from 10 to 48 tons per hectare, and yields of groundnuts from some 800 kgs. to 2 tons per hectare for improved varieties cultivated under favourable conditions.[1] And there seems no reason to doubt the view that maize yields in much of West Africa can be doubled by the introduction of improved varieties and without use of fertilizers. Research into pest control for coffee, cotton, and maize has produced insecticides which can reduce losses without requiring fundamental changes in production methods.

The virtue of technological change of this kind is that it can be introduced by modifying rather than transforming agricultural production systems. In other words, there can be increased output without any radical change in production methods or the displacement of labour.

In the short and long run the key to improving African agriculture must lie in the improvement of the quality of human resources in agriculture. At present there is an absolute and relative shortage of skilled personnel both to provide needed services and to operate holdings ; [2] thus, one of the first requirements for any modification or transformation of agriculture is the provision of training facilities to provide a vast increase in the supply of trained personnel.[3]

A further aspect of this reform is that there has to be a far greater infusion of capital into the agricultural system. In the past, capital formation has been largely through bush clearance and the direct application of labour to land. However, more intensive farming operations will require 'working capital', the nature of which will depend on the requirements of each area, but in many areas simple implements are required to replace the axe, knife, or hoe which are still the major instruments of production. At present the opportunities for increasing output are restricted by the drudgery and the sheer limits imposed by the extent of physical strength of producers.

[1] See *The Staple Food Economies of Western Tropical Africa*, Stanford Food Research Institute, by B. F. Johnston, Stanford University Press, 1958.

[2] This is graphically illustrated by the fact that in Southern Rhodesia the one independent variable that appeared to distinguish producers with high yields from those with low yields was the training received by producers. (Yet the budget for African agriculture included millions for soil conservation and hundreds for training.)

[3] There can be any number of illustrations of the shortage of skilled personnel — one of the most striking, however, is that there are at present only 1 veterinary officer for each 100,000 head of cattle in East Africa compared with 1 for each 3,500 in the U.K. and 6,000 in the U.S.A. At present East African professional agriculturists are trained at Makerere College (Uganda), the college has a capacity for training 24 agricultural scientists (pop. 20 million), however there are only 10 students studying agriculture.

Similarly, there is a need for simple mechanical aids to reduce the very high labour inputs required for such items as food processing and carrying water ; perhaps there is no area where small-scale mechanical equipment could be more effective in raising productivity than in the post-harvesting process.[1] In some regions simple changes in techniques of production have created technological revolutions.[2]

However, in most areas the approach to providing working capital has been based on orthodox lending policies that are wholly unsuited to most of African agriculture. Land is still considered to be the major form of collateral in a society where most people are not land owners. What is required is a programme which will both provide instruments of production and at the same time induce producers to use them. A novel approach to this could be to utilize external aid funds to provide subsidies and grants whereby producers would receive equipment which would be heavily discounted with the remainder being 'written off' if it is effectively used.[3] This is partly the method recommended by a recent Bank Mission to Uganda.

VIII. CONCLUSION

It has only been possible to touch on several factors relating to agricultural production in sub-Saharan Africa. It is clear that the short-run outlook for increased export earnings from agriculture is not too favourable so that the conversion from subsistence production to that for the market will have to depend to a large extent on urbanization and industrialization. Where this is occurring there has been a noticeable shift towards commercial production, *e.g.* in the former Belgian Congo production for the market increased far more rapidly than subsistence production as employment increased in the mineral areas ; in addition, producers have diversified their output to include milk and vegetables to satisfy the higher income elasticity of demand of urban dwellers. However, as we have seen, the prospects for rapid industrialization are not very promising, consequently, it may be advantageous to retain labour in agriculture by avoiding drastic reforms which would force labour out of the

---

[1] Food preparation by hand occupied as much as 30 per cent of the total family labour input in certain areas of Central Africa.

[2] The introduction of the plough in Southern Rhodesia enabled a considerable expansion of production to take place by shifting the burden of work from women to oxen ; it increased the productivity of labour and at the same time converted oxen from non-productive capital used for dowries to productive capital.

[3] 'Supervised credit' is usually considered to be an effective means of maximizing returns from a credit system, but this imposes a drain on scarce manpower, *e.g.* in Brazil, where cultivators have an average of 10 acres, it was found that 1 agricultural expert was needed to supervise every 30 farmers.

rural areas into urban areas where there would be limited employment opportunities. Thus, it is suggested that in the short run, production systems be modified while at the same time the basis be laid for transforming agriculture from tribal subsistence production to one better suited to exploit existing resources.

The transition to commercial, specialized production will depend on many interdependent factors. Road building, market outlets, provision of transportation are all relevant and important and in this regard many of the statutory marketing boards have performed valuable services. Part of the problem in this connection has been to synchronize the provision of these facilities with the willingness of producers to expand production for the market. In some areas the absence of infrastructure is a drawback to increased output — in others infrastructure yields very low returns because it has been created too far ahead of its need. Thus, the problem of this type of development requires a nice balance between judgment of desire for change and the interest rate !

On the production side the problems are not so much those of increasing physical capacity for production through large-scale investments where capital is substituted for land, but rather ones where investments are made in increasing the capacity of producers to be more productive. It is partly for this reason that so few large-scale investments have been made in African agriculture. The biggest need, both in the short and long runs, is to raise the levels of skills of producers ; in the short run this can be done by modifying production techniques through relatively simple changes such as superimposing pest control and disease control on present systems of production, and by introducing higher yielding varieties of seeds and simple equipment.[1] In the longer run, however, improved management will depend on educating a new generation of producers — in both instances returns from investments of these kinds might well be slow in maturing as most African producers are illiterate, conservative, and still rooted in traditional systems of production. This type of investment would have to be recurrent in nature — funds for education training and research. Thus far, however, they represent a very small proportion of the total public expenditures made by

[1] An important point in this connection relates to 'timelessness' and group 'co-operation'. Cotton output in Uganda can be doubled if producers would plant earlier (but nobody has studied why they do not plant earlier). Some increases in output can only come through group discipline, *e.g.* cattle dipping for tick control. Dipping programmes can raise livestock yields considerably, but it is essential that *all* producers dip regularly ; programmes for dipping have succeeded in European areas in South Africa and Kenya, but have failed in Tanganyika because of the absence of group co-operation and group discipline. The problem of imposing discipline is going to become more important as more countries become independent.

various governments (see Table 1). Nevertheless, they are essentially developmental expenditures, a fact which most governments and lending agencies do not appear to appreciate. In this regard I would like to conclude by suggesting that the international and bilateral agencies cease frowning on making loans or grants for this type of development expenditure and that they should reconsider their lending policies in light of current needs in African agriculture.[1]

DISCUSSION OF DR. YUDELMAN'S PAPER

Professor Houghton congratulated Dr. Yudelman on a very interesting paper. For most people in Africa agriculture was not an economic activity but a way of life, and it could be changed only slowly.

Professor Fauvel emphasized the vast scale and complexity of the task of agricultural reform in Africa. One had to start with the problems of land tenure, the system of tribes and tribal chiefs, with all the rights to land belonging to the tribe rather than to the individual, and the necessity to modify land tenures. One had to start with the problems of the replacement of self-subsistence by a flexible market economy. There was, moreover, need for a closer study of the events of the recent past ; in many respects Africa still showed survivals of the earlier colonial policies. If one was to secure modernization of the subsistence sector, how far was it possible to reproduce in Africa the improvements that had taken place in other parts of the world ? It seemed to him vitally necessary to develop the whole quality and capacity and technical skills of the African populations. This was a task for the governments of Africa. He thought that Dr. Yudelman had been too modest in his analysis. It was not sufficient merely to ask how existing types of agricultural organization might be developed, though remarkable progress had in fact been made both in relation to colonial export crops, where Senegal, for example, sent a third of her groundnuts to France, and in relation to the modernization of traditional agriculture, where Senegal again had made remarkable strides. One had also to learn from the community development schemes of the United States, from the experience of the U.S.S.R., of Israel, of the more advanced agricultural countries of Europe, and of more advanced African countries like Ghana. He would have liked to have seen a discussion of the applicability of such experience to African conditions. He thought that there was still immense scope for research in agronomy in Africa.

[1] The World Bank has shown interest in this direction as exemplified by loans to Southern Rhodesia and Kenya, as illustrated in the paper by Mr. Rist ; however, there is still much that must be done in this direction and the problem of incorporating recurrent expenditures as part of a 'development budget' that is acceptable to lending agencies presents many problems, particularly in regard to 'cost-benefit' ratios. This whole area of development would appear to be a fruitful field for research.

Economic Development for Africa South of the Sahara

The Chairman suggested that the further discussion might be divided between two main themes : first, African agricultural systems ; second, agrarian reform, including such issues as the introduction of capital and changes of land tenure.

Mr. Moran agreed with what had been said by Professor Fauvel about the value of comparative international studies. He thought that there was much to be learned for Africa from successes and failures in other continents. *Dr. Singer* emphasized the importance of research and experimental farms. The importance of pre-investment studies of this kind was being increasingly recognized. Direct loans for agricultural development were not very practical, however.

Professor Baldwin wished to begin by suggesting that Dr. Yudelman was over-emphasizing the non-acquisitiveness of the African in the subsistence environment. He stated that a person's status was determined by factors other than material wealth, as far as Northern Rhodesia was concerned he did not think this was entirely true. As one famous study put it 'wealth makes the chief' and this point had been confirmed by several other studies. Those who acquired material wealth were the ones who could break away and form new villages with themselves as chiefs. The status of the ordinary man was also greatly influenced by his wealth position in terms of the number of cattle he owned, or his ability to distribute goods to others. This point was important not only for understanding the past but for appraising policy for the present. He thought Dr. Yudelman also underestimated the ability of the African to respond to price incentive at the present time. For Southern Rhodesia he had found a good positive correlation between price and the share of total production marketed by Africans. Similarly, there seemed to be a very good response to higher prices in the form of increased production as far as such commodities as tobacco, groundnuts, and cotton were concerned. The Northern Rhodesian study by Johnson, that he quoted, did not indicate very much concerning the response of the African to prices. The reasons why so few joined the African Farming Improvement Scheme were, he thought, more connected with the administrative control exercised over those who do join and the complicated method of farming required under the scheme than by a lack of price incentive. The great increase in maize output among the ordinary farmers along the line of rail as maize prices rose was, he thought, a more characteristic response.

This led to the question of how best to stimulate greater productivity in the rural sector. He wished to suggest that in Northern Rhodesia there had been too much emphasis on attempting to provide more capital, improved European techniques, better education and health conditions, and not enough attempt at the same time to improve profit opportunities under existing methods of production. In line with Professor Frankel's paper, there had been a much too mechanistic attitude about these factors. The African had been presented with the opportunity of raising his income if he would take a big step and adopt European practices. For the average, uneducated African this step was much too big. The risks he saw were too great. Consequently, only the already efficient, better-educated Africans joined these schemes and they turned out to be a costly way of raising the income of a small group. Instead, more attention should be paid, through creating improvements in transport, marketing facilities, and if necessary through a subsidy programme, to improving profit prospects under existing practices. By doing this, he thought that the African would see that he could raise his income still more by gradually adopting European practices. As it was now, the price incentive was not sufficiently used, and yet manipulation of the price system was still one of the cheapest and most effective means of development.

Professor Walker contrasted the achievements in Uganda and Kenya. In Uganda development had been slow but, in the long run, very considerable. In Kenya the spectacular changes in African agriculture had been concentrated in a comparatively short period of time. He thought that much more research was needed to determine where capital could best be employed. There was notable lack of research into subsistence crops. It was very important to ensure that there were sufficient markets for crops that were developed. The development of markets and marketing arrangements must go side by side with the expansion of an existing crop or the introduction of a new crop.

Dr. Okigbo stressed the fact that in Africa today industry absorbed a very small proportion of the total African labour force. Productivity could be raised by shifting people from agriculture into industry and commerce. But the limit to expansion of other sectors was set ultimately by progress on the food front. On this front progress could be hastened by research, extension services, and the like. But since these did not involve foreign exchange, the international aiding agencies were not inclined to finance them.

Dr. Wade argued that development in Africa should start with agriculture and that it was from the proceeds of agriculture that industrialization could be financed. There was a continuing problem of how to make use of the natural resources of African countries. Foreign capital was hesitant in the absence of infrastructure. How was one to find the capital to provide the necessary underlying conditions to attract capital? There were a number of worrying technical problems : firstly, the forms of land tenure ; secondly, the problems of agricultural education and training ; thirdly, the problems of soil erosion. Was there a possibility that some of the big advanced countries could assist in financing the solutions of these problems?

Mr. Bridger (Economic Commission for Africa) suggested that agricultural extension schemes should form the spearhead of African economic development. One way of encouraging production was by subsidizing some of the inputs into agriculture. But he thought there were dangers in this. He believed that both governments and those that advised them had been too much concerned with material incentives. If one expanded subsidies and material incentives, there was a recurrent charge on the budget to finance them, and the disincentives might become almost as great as the incentives. He thought there was too little liaison between planners and social anthropologists. Three-quarters of the problems of development were human and social.

Dr. Gavrilov thought that Dr. Yudelman had exaggerated the difficulties of developing industries in Africa, mainly because of the limitations of skilled labour and of markets. He believed this view was mistaken. One had to bear in mind that all these sectors of an economy were inter-dependent. If African countries did not industrialize, the road to economic development would be very long. The solution of the problems of Africa would, however, involve a very great capital investment. In agriculture he thought that development should take the form of farmers' co-operatives.

Professor Stanley argued that there was no considerable surplus of usable land in Africa. A great deal of investment would be necessary before any unused areas could be made cultivable. He believed that industrialization was the ultimate answer to African development, but it was not a simple answer. If one tried to explain the differences in output between the agriculture of Southern Rhodesia and of other African countries, he would like to know how much was due to better land (had not the early European settlers chosen the best land ?) and how much was due to more capital and better organization of farming ? *Dr. Yudelman* thought that organization and capital inputs, together with a better use of the land and better choice of crops, were the chief explanations.

M. Roland Pré regarded research as the key factor. A number of the technical problems of African agriculture were, he thought, capable of solution by means of research. To quote one example, a main food crop in the African countries of intermediate rainfall was millet. It was very delicate and sensitive to variations of rainfall. If it were possible to develop a millet with a different life cycle, capable of withstanding a 2-3 week variation of rainfall, a great deal of hunger could be eliminated. The great problem of African agriculture was to evoke a better effort, resulting both from increased efficiency and from increased energy. The change from colonialism to independence had provoked a great change in African attitudes. It was necessary now to think in terms of the mobilization of the masses of Africa. The source of inspiration was different, but the underlying nature was the same.

Dr. Yudelman commented that the basic problem was how to get people to produce more — what was the best organization to that end ? In the United States there was an immense volume of agricultural research. When agricultural expansion was required, there was a vast background of research which could be exploited. The problem of Africa was different. Agricultural resources were poor ; systems of agricultural production were poor ; there were factors antagonistic to improvement. There was a commercial organization based on the tribal system. Reciprocal labour obligations inhibited the efficient working of progressive farms and tied the African farmer to a system which would not allow him to operate up to the limit of efficiency. What was achieved was a high degree of security at the expense of a low level of production. How to raise production while retaining security had no simple answer. If one asked what should be done, he thought that part of the answer was small-scale holdings. In tropical Africa, one major difficulty was that the farmer was both labourer and entrepreneur. He suffered from lack of knowledge. There was not sufficient machinery for passing on the best knowledge and experience from the best farmers. In a country like the U.S.A., the best farming practice was demonstrated to others. Centralized operations in Africa raised wholly different problems — centralized management and control, such as had been encountered in the running of plantations. Here, he thought, the main problem was the establishment of material under-standing and sympathy between the central management and the culti-vator. In this type of agriculture, the important thing was, he thought, to let people own their land, but at the same time bring to them the advantages of the type that plantations offered — the full compliance of all concerned in the basic plans of the organization as a whole, discipline in respect of methods of cultivation and of the timing of operations. As regards the possibilities of collective or state-owned farms, he thought the chief problems were not only those of the optimum size of the estate but also the returns to the actual producers. He thought that there were almost inevitably conflicts of interest about getting the right equipment to get the right thing done at the right time. Finally, as regards co-operative systems of farming he thought that both the Yugo-Slav system and that of the People's Republic of China deserved study. The advantage of the Chinese system lay largely in its ability to free large quantities of labour at certain seasons for labour-intensive capital works. In shaping their future policies, African leaders would do well to study these systems.

Mr. Ngcobo said that in South Africa before white settlement there had been a rough balance between population and natural resources. The system of agricultural production was based on some division of labour and on some knowledge of climatic factors — of soil and of other environmental conditions. Economic motives had operated. There was a tendency to respond to opportunities for making profits. Why, then, had there been no development? With the introduction of controlled marketing, Africans had been pushed aside. The methods of encouraging better land use had, he thought, failed to secure their objectives. Mis-takes had been made in encouraging individual land titles. Allotments were too small to be economic. The arable allotments were to be held individually, while stock was to be pastured communally. Little scope was left for response to market stimuli or for substitution of capital for labour. Wherever peasant agriculture was geared to domestic consump-tion, he thought, agriculture tended to be unproductive.

Professor Williams saw no reason for pessimism regarding the re-sponsiveness of peasants to economic incentives in West Africa. Cocoa, for example, had been developed solely as a result of individual initiative. We should not underestimate the ability of peasants in Africa to act as responsive members of economic systems. A much more serious problem was that of getting back on to the land those who had had some education. It was necessary to restore the social prestige of agricultural occupations.

Professor Dupriez shared the general concern to see a transformation of African agriculture. He wondered whether there was not the possibility of seeing a considerable increase in consumption and a high income-elasticity of demand for agricultural products. Additional supplies were needed to improve health. In Ruanda-Urundi, for example, there was an unbalanced diet and malnutrition associated with it. Correction of this would have the two-fold effect of creating new markets and of increasing individual productivity. *Professor Robinson* shared Professor Dupriez's belief that there was a comparatively high income-elasticity of demand for food in Africa and scope for increasing productivity by means of additional inputs of food.

Mr. Beheiry was persuaded to give the Conference a short account of the workings of the Gezira Scheme, as an example of a large-scale collective agricultural organization actually operating in Africa. It was, he stressed, an act of partnership : the government building the dam and the main canals and providing the engineering services for the irrigation schemes ; the Board providing the skilled management, the general supervision of the operation, and the marketing facilities ; the tenants providing the actual cultivation. Some expenses were debited to a joint account. The net proceeds were divided, 40 per cent to the government, 42 per cent to the tenants, 10 per cent to the Board, and the remainder was spent on social services for tenants and contributions to the tenants' reserve fund, to reduce fluctuations in tenants' money incomes. In times of low cotton prices, this reserve is drawn upon. No fixed price was offered. The world price was accepted. In ordinary times the tenants' reserve fund was a form of compulsory saving. Formerly this fund was invested in the United Kingdom and earnings were credited to it. Now the investment had been diversified. By and large, this close relationship had worked well. While there were certain individual responsibilities devolving on the tenants, there was also collaborative endeavour in respect of tractors and various other activities. The return depended on the tenants' own individual efforts ; the quality of the cotton grown was one factor affecting it. Through the scheme a nomadic or semi-nomadic people had been settled and subjected to a certain amount of necessary discipline. There remained certain problems. There was first the human problem — how to make the tenant feel that it was his own show ? Second, there was the need to resist a tendency for the tenant to function as a labour contractor, and become a kind of country gentleman. Third, there was a problem of seasonal labour supply for cotton-picking ; this was creating certain difficulties. Fourth, it had to be remembered that the Gezira Scheme was not nationalized as a whole ; it was only the use of land that was nationalized. Fifth, certain problems had arisen from the fact that, in the interest of security, the tenant had originally been given a certain amount of irrigated land to grow his own food ; that had been sensible twenty-five years ago but was not an economic proposition today ; it was probably better to encourage an alternative cash crop, such as groundnuts. Finally, there was the perpetual problem of assuring continually increasing efficiency, to meet higher operative expenses and higher expectations of earnings.

Chapter 21

PROBLEMS OF THE AFRICAN MINING ECONOMY

BY

ROLAND PRÉ

Bureau Géologique et Minier Français

I. INTRODUCTION

No matter what the development problem — and mining is no exception to this rule, especially in young, newly-independent countries — the basic factors governing the conditions under which progress can take place are always the same, namely :

men, with their qualities and faults, their knowledge and their education ;

nature, *i.e.* the soil, with its climatic and geographical conditions, and the sub-soil ;

capital accumulated in its two possible forms — the material and equipment already on the spot and the financial means available, representing the potential resources in reserve.

If these factors are to be assessed at their true worth, a few more details are necessary.

The value of the human element in a country cannot be gauged merely by the amount of technical or scientific knowledge possessed by its inhabitants, nor even by their moral or social code ; it has to be evaluated as much as a function of the behavioural reactions they have acquired and which condition the way in which they practise any contemporary activity. This implies not only a certain conception of the outside world involving subservience to intellectual disciplines, a regard for organization, and a rejection of the irrational in one's attitude to life, but also an instinctive grasping of the concepts which have permitted the development of modern civilization, such as the straight line, the plane surface, exact time, and the expression of the duration of time ; in other words, it is a question of the ability of a people to integrate itself into a measurable universe and into events which can be broken down into a relationship of cause and effect.

Nature itself cannot be considered as a plain, ungarnished fact. It has links with Man : to a certain extent the soil has been shaped or affected by Man, and although the same cannot be said of the sub-soil, nevertheless, the value of the latter to human beings depends entirely on how much they know about it ; here again, its usefulness as a factor in development stems from the part played by Man.

The concept of accumulated capital should also be understood in a very wide sense ; although the idea is clear as far as financial means are concerned, it is more complex when we are dealing with material means and when it includes all the forms of constructive intervention known to Man, comprising not only all the installations required for production and investigation, but also the entire range of amenities constituting the general infrastructure, such as means of transport, housing, telecommunications, health, education, and other public services.

These brief explanations emphasize the way in which all the different factors complement each other and interlock, especially in sectors of development where complex activities are taking place. And their effect becomes increasingly vital in any venture which aims at exploiting the wealth of the sub-soil.

In this sector, particularly in recent years, technical progress has enabled vaster and more difficult geological and mining problems to be tackled. Under these circumstances it is not surprising that the development of mining should need human resources of a higher and higher quality and increasingly substantial amounts of capital, thus creating a number of delicate legal, financial, and political problems. We shall see this again and again in the present study as we examine the way in which this development of the sub-soil is being achieved from the specifically African standpoint. In point of fact, these circumstances have altered more rapidly in the last fifteen years than throughout the entire previous period, and the changes have by no means come to an end ; they will certainly go on in the future along lines which can already be discerned.

II. THE MEANING OF THE TERMS ORE AND DEPOSIT

Before analyzing the conditions for the development of a mining economy, the concepts on which this economy is based should first be clearly specified. What do we understand by the terms 'ore' and 'deposit'? This is not only a question of vocabulary, it is a question of essentials, as we shall see by the purely relative nature of the conceptions behind these words which is revealed when an attempt is made to analyse their real significance in practice.

We end up, in fact, with definitions more or less along the following lines :

ore : a constituent of natural rock which can be used directly or after concentration as raw material in the metallurgical or chemical industries ;
deposit : an area from which ore can be extracted as an economic proposition.

It can be seen at once that these two ideas are essentially contingent, as they are linked to contemporary industrial conditions ; they do not, therefore, depend on any intrinsic features, determined once and for all, but on economic and technical factors which by their very nature vary in space as much as in time.

What, then, are the determining factors ?

They are, firstly, the techniques applied and the requirements of the consumer industries on which the possibility of using ore and the nature of the demand are dependent, and, secondly, the economic and technical conditions prevailing at the different operating stages involved in supplying the ore, as these govern the cost price and the economic feasibility of the mine working.

Despite this purely relative nature of the concepts of 'ore' and 'deposits', there is a clearly discernible trend in the way these terms are being used.

Generally speaking, their field of application is tending to expand, that is to say, they are being ascribed to increasingly numerous categories of rocks ; this is quite natural since industrial activity tends to break down into different branches as its means of action and its requirements multiply.

In the first instance the progress made in dressing techniques enables the term 'ore' to be used of rocks to which it was never applied in the past. The most typical example is that of the minette of Lorraine which has become the basic feature of the steel industry in that area since the discovery of the Bessemer process. At more or less the same time, the use of electrolysis on an industrial scale for treating alumina, which made aluminium an economic proposition, transformed bauxite — the raw material of alumina — from a valueless rock into an 'ore'.

The opening-up of entirely new sectors of technical activity can also result in the use of substances which were formerly of no worth and which remained unnoticed. This is true of most of the materials which are bound up with the development of the atomic energy industry, and the best illustration of this type of change is the sudden transformation of the waste from South African gold mines, which had been abandoned for years on the dirt-tips, into ore which is now very much sought after because of the traces of uranium it contains, but which could not previously be used in any way.

Lastly, it has now become possible to manufacture ores artificially by means of concentration techniques in so far as the latter permit the conversion and treatment of poor and barely extractable minerals as an economic proposition. This is true, for instance, of a great many impregnated rocks or magmatic rocks which originally could not be processed but which can be concentrated today in economically acceptable conditions, as modern techniques can be used to convert low mineral-content rocks into rich concentrates at very reasonable prices. Hence, after being treated on the site, the taconite found in Labrador turns into a high-content iron ore which can compete quite easily with rich natural ores ; similarly, at the Djelida mine, high-yield concentrates of the same quality as the best conventional lead and zinc ores have been obtained from impregnated rock.

On the other hand, the demand for a given mineral species seldom dries up completely, although its sale price may tend to fall and requirements as to its ore-content and quality may become severe. To a certain extent, it can therefore be said that some rocks formerly listed as ores and some production areas listed as deposits no longer merit these names since they are no longer used as such.

Their eclipse may be temporary and bound up with a special set of political or economic circumstances. It only becomes permanent if it corresponds to more far-reaching technical developments. An example of a temporary eclipse is provided by the low-content tungsten deposits, the market for which has been considerably reduced in recent years after the period of tension during the war in Korea, although a rise in price might make these marginal mines a good economic proposition again. However, the low-content iron ores, which are incapable of being concentrated and are now hardly ever mined either in Europe or in America, fall into the second category where a reversal in trend is no longer possible.

On the whole, the relative nature of the term 'deposit' is probably even more apparent than that of the term 'ore'. The latter, in fact, essentially depends on the development of the user industries down the line, whereas the idea of the deposit is subject to the same conditions, but is also influenced by all the technical and economic factors governing the profit-making potential of mining itself. There are a great many of these factors, as the working of a deposit entails a whole series of activities ranging from the discovery and extraction of the ore to its transport by land and sea, not to mention the concentration and primary dressing operations in the field before it is carried away, and which are often indispensable as an adjunct to extraction. The cost of these activities varies continually with time and space and, of course, the concept of what forms a deposit varies with the cost. In particular, it depends on innumerable local conditions which are often much more important as far as the economic feasibility of the working, and hence the practical existence of a deposit, is concerned than the intrinsic value of the ore and the amount available. In the under-developed regions of Africa, these factors play a decisive rôle.

Firstly, in respect of the investigation of mineral traces, it should be noted that the progress made in geophysics and geochemistry enables internal geological structures to be examined and can reveal, under the surface layers, deep-lying deposits which could previously only be brought to light by extremely expensive direct investigations using for instance, drill-holes and shafts. It has thus proved possible to investigate a deposit successfully without burdening any subsequent workings by incurring disproportionate prospection costs which, in some cases, might jeopardize the economic value of the whole undertaking. For instance, the investigations conducted into the iron deposits of the Kursk magnetic anomaly would not have been economically possible without the recent progress made in geophysics and, in fact, it was not until such progress had been made that new methods enabled the magnetic traces to be established as a definite deposit. An even more striking example is provided by oil, where prospection for new fields has been extended to areas which it was formerly considered impossible to investigate. All this is not due to geophysics alone, however ; the progress of research technology covers a vast range and we need only recall the example of uranium prospection which has been made so easy and inexpensive by the Geiger counter.

This is why, particularly in Africa where direct geological investigations are often difficult and expensive, either because of the forest cover or because the lateritic or sandy overburden — not to mention transport difficulties — these methods, sometimes enhanced by aircraft, have almost completely transformed research conditions. Their cost, and hence their influence on the cost price of the ore, have been reduced, thus enabling research, which once would have been considered too expensive to be carried out, on a far greater number of deposits.

At the same time, similar progress has been made in extracting ore. The development, chiefly owing to wartime requirements, of large-scale earth-moving equipment which can perform the stripping operations required for open-cast extraction at low cost, or can remove large quantities of material economically, has undeniably lowered the cost prices of the enormous material handling operations seen on some mine workings and has thus made them economically feasible. A typical example is that of German lignite which could never have been used without these cheap working methods. Another example is that of phosphate mines in general, where developments were bound up with the progress made in designing large-scale equipment.

Above all, however, the economic prospects of workings can be completely transformed by high-capacity, heavy transport equipment. The introduction of new techniques, such as heavy-load trucks, heavy trains on reinforced tracks — like the 14,000 ton train used at the Labrador mines — giant ore-carriers, oil-tankers of 60,000 and even 100,000 ton, pipelines for both liquids and solids, and even cargo aircraft, is at the origin of the far-reaching changes in the structure of the ore market ; materials which once could not be mined because they were handicapped by the prohibitive costs involved in transporting them to their places of use are now more and more able — due to these transport developments — either to compete with the output from older, nearer, but poorer deposits or, at least, to increase the overall supply. This fact has had a considerable effect on the mining industry, and mines where extraction is expensive and the ore poor are no longer profitable, however well-located, while large deposits with high-ore contents have suddenly assumed a pre-eminent rôle even if they are in formerly inaccessible areas. At times, the user industries themselves have given up their installations near the older deposits and have now set up in the deep-water ports which supply the large consumer areas and where huge ore-carriers can deliver cheap high-content ore from remote deposits. Hence, the old arguments about the impossibility of working ores in the middle of the African continent or in the Far North of America have completely disappeared. What used to be called the mineral fringe of Africa is continuously being extended into the heart of the continent as means of transport improve. At the same time, a coastal steel industry is progressively replacing the old steel centres in the midst of the mining areas, because the cost of sea transport is losing its relative importance. On the other hand, in places where cheap transport is still not possible, the mineral discoveries are useless and the term deposit has no practical significance ; this is true, for instance, of the greater part of the coalfields in the Siberian Arctic.

Naturally, the geographical conditions and the extent to which a given area has been developed have a great influence on the cost of transport, and this gives a doubly relative character to the term deposit.

It is only natural that the cost price of ore should vary according to whether it can or cannot be evacuated through an already existing infrastructure or not and according to whether or not the cost of the latter's amortization should be included in the cost price. Similarly, the cost of sea transport may vary and the sale price of the ore on arrival at its destination may be more or less competitive depending on whether the mineral railway terminates at a deep-water port where heavy ore-carriers can come alongside — thereby giving rise to low freight costs — or whether the loading point can only take small-draught vessels. The existence or absence of a deposit will depend on an assessment of these different factors.

These various considerations illustrate the fact that technical progress, geographical conditions, the stage of infrastructure development, and the general state of the world market all have a bearing at all times and in all places on the momentary value of an ore or of a deposit. Their influence is reflected not only by price fluctuations, but also by variations in the volume and nature of the demand ; the concept of a commercial ore can therefore have only a temporary significance and the same applies to the idea of a workable deposit. This has produced a category — the volume of which increases or decreases according to circumstances — containing all those mines which are temporarily at the limit of their profit-making activity and which, for this reason, are called marginal mines.

The idea of the relative nature of the situation emerging from all these considerations must, however, be completed by acknowledging a definite trend in developments. The future lies with the vast deposits which can supply, either directly or after concentration, high-content ores able to be evacuated by heavy-load transport. On the other hand, the typical advantages of the old-style deposits, such as their accessibility, easy working conditions, and easily recognizable mineral nature, are losing their importance. Mining prospection and extraction will, therefore, turn increasingly towards the new countries with their vast areas and lack of traditional infrastructures.

These are the problems that we shall now examine.

III. PROBLEMS OF DISCOVERING DEPOSITS

The entire future of the mining economy of a country depends on the initial stage in the development of its mineral wealth. This stage comprises the various and very different aspects of geological and mining investigations. These investigations will clearly assume even greater importance in the new countries which, unlike their older counterparts, have not been subject to numerous and detailed studies, supplemented by results, from a great number of actual workings. This is particularly true of Africa, except for a few privileged areas.

In order to understand the problems involved in the discovery of deposits, we shall first briefly describe the origin of the latter.

The earth's crust is made up of different rocks which can be classified into a number of types according to their origin :

Magmatic rocks, which are the original rocks from the depths of the earth and which, on solidifying, created the first continental shelves as well as the intrusions which later slipped or were driven through the cracks and fractures of the earth's crust during subsequent erogenic movements.

Sedimentary rocks, which represent the accumulation of detrital features in the bottom of river basins or valleys and which usually stem from marine or lacustrian deposits that piled up during the different geological ages.

Metamorphic rocks, which arose from the structural transformation of the rocks already in place under the effects of chemical and physical factors such as pressure and heat.

Lastly, *lode-bearing rocks* created by the filling of cracks and fractures in the crust by gaseous or liquid agents rising from the depths.

The way in which these different rocks came to occupy their present positions is bound up with the geological history of the earth.

The old continental shelves, forming the original base of the first land to emerge, are related to the magmatic rocks.

The great geological basins, the remains of former marine or lacustrian transgressions, are obviously related to the sedimentary rocks.

The fractures are often filled with magmatic or lode-bearing features.

The alluvium and eluvium, which were created by the removal of *in situ* rock by run-off water, and then its subsequent transportation and deposition by rivers after grading of its particles, are obviously related to their original formations.

The existence of deposits of a given type is clearly bound up with these different geological formations as well as with the nature of the ground constituting the formation. Several types of deposit can be distinguished, namely :

Depositions (lode or sedimentary) resulting from the transportation, at a given moment, of mineral particles into cracks or folds, the accumulation of such particles forming a deposit.

Altered deposits corresponding to the transformation of some rocks *in situ*, under the effects of external physical agents which cause a concentration of a given mineral element. This alteration may be caused by superficial altered deposits usually arising from the action of atmospheric agents such as washing-out by rainfall, solar radiation, electric currents, or micro-organisms ; a typical example is provided by bauxite deposits. On the other hand, alteration may occur at depth, for example, by the contact of intrusions with the enclosing rock, this being the case with some primary deposits of wolfram and cassiterite.

Impregnated deposits which are created by the impregnation of a layer by migratory particles from the vicinity. The lead and zinc deposits at Djelida already mentioned and the oil-fields in general are good examples.

Lastly, *disturbed deposits*, especially those of alluvial and eluvial origin, which are created by a kind of natural grading and enrichment process effected by atmospheric agents, rivers, or marine movements, on the detrital fragments of *in situ* rock carried away by these agents.

Generally speaking, altered deposits are found on old shelves, impregnated deposits in sedimentary basins, lode deposits in fractures and disturbed deposits in river basins or on former river-banks.

These different types of deposit have not usually been worked at the same period, as rather different economic and technical conditions are needed for their development. The vein deposits were usually the first to be mined because they consisted of high-ore concentrations and could easily be distinguished, while the volume of materials to be handled was not very great. In the same way, the disturbed deposits, which are usually of recent date and readily accessible, and therefore easy to mine and to uncover, usually gave rise to the first mine workings in young countries where the means available were very limited. Now that large-scale working can be undertaken, concentration methods can make rich ores out of poor ones, and prospection techniques can reveal deposits in depth — even if their traces are not immediately apparent — there is an increasingly marked tendency for mining research to turn towards the altered or impregnated deposits while the increased demand would have dictated this trend in any case. It can, in fact, be said that reserves of this type are usually estimated in millions of tons whereas those of conventional lode or alluvial deposits are assessed rather in hundreds of thousands of tons. The effects of both technical progress and economics have therefore combined to encourage the tackling of more and more of these mineral formations which were formerly considered unworkable or incapable of being treated, but which usually contain very considerable volumes of materials.

This development has been particularly favourable to a large part of the African continent where the old massive shelves and the huge sedimentary basins have not suffered the same geological upheavals as the more troubled areas of the earth's crust, and have been more easily subjected to the continuous action of external surface or deep agents over millions of years.

Discovering the Deposits

Whatever the nature of these deposits, the problem of investigating the mining potentialities of an area is always the same, namely, how to discover signs of ore and how to localize such signs in the best possible conditions.

These exploration operations obviously cannot be carried out haphazardly without some guiding idea behind the research; we might just as well look for a needle in a haystack. It is necessary to grasp the guiding threads that geologists have gradually unravelled from their observations and knowledge of the earth's history. These threads are usually of two kinds, namely, the nature of the rocks classified by geological series and the structures in which these rocks appear. Comparison with similar cases about which information is available can supply general data on the nature of the deposits likely to be found and the type of sign that prospectors should look for. The great value of preliminary geological investigations of a purely scientific nature can therefore be appreciated; their purpose is not to culminate in a strike, but to obtain information about the overall geology of an area. In these preliminary studies, investigation of the geological series and of tectonic accidents will be particularly valuable in determining the subsequent trend to be followed by the explorations.

It can therefore be seen that *general geological studies* are of fundamental importance in the young countries, and that geological prospection and, above all, the preparation of maps should normally precede the mining investigations proper.

Once this basic information has been obtained, it can be used to direct, if not with complete certainty, at least with an acceptable proportion of success, what we call prospection, *i.e.* the *actual search for signs*. This second stage consists of attempting to find in the field a certain number of mineralization 'signposts' which the preliminary geological studies suggest may be present. These signs may vary considerably; they range from the visible presence of

597

mineralized features on the ground surface to the indirect study of deep-lying formations and structures. What has to be borne in mind, however, is that these investigations are extremely difficult in countries where prospection is only incipient, especially when there are additional natural obstacles due to transport difficulties and the surface cover of the ground. In any case, they would probably only result in the skimming off of a few particularly obvious surface features, or even in completely negative conclusions, if the work is not guided and concentrated on areas shown to be favourable by the preliminary basic studies. This is particularly true of Africa where, more than anywhere else, the first and fundamental basis for research is more thorough geological knowledge.

The finding of the signs is not in itself enough, however ; we still have to decide whether the discovery is a true deposit or whether it merely consists of a few isolated and unworkable mineral features. The third stage, therefore, consists of *studying possible deposits* ; what has to be determined is the exact structure of the mineralized zone and how far it extends beyond the traces distinguished visually, its behaviour in depth, its ore-content, possible concentration and dressing methods, and, lastly, its possible yield. In this third stage research obviously moves away from pure science to technology, and from there to economics, all three factors being closely interrelated, as it is pointless to start a working if there is no deposit or if the ore cannot be used after enrichment, or, again, if it cannot be marketed at competitive prices.

It should also be noted that the respective importance of the three stages varies according to the age of the mining development of an area, the value of geological studies being in directly inverse proportion to this age ; unfortunately, the leaders of new countries sometimes tend to underestimate the importance of geological research proper and prefer to devote most of their efforts to everything that they feel will lead to immediate mining development ; nor do private investors feel naturally inclined to carry out research of general interest, the value of which can only be indirect. That is why it is important to provide the leaders and public opinion of these countries with correct and detailed information on mining development.

The means that have to be used to put these principles into practice bring into play an extraordinarily varied range of scientific and technical activities calling for a considerable wealth of manpower and equipment. First on the list comes geology, with its numerous scientific and technical branches, requiring all kinds of experts, laboratory research undertaken in close conjunction with investigations in the field, discussions, and publications. It is a science which knows no frontiers and which operates on a very wide international scale. Its features must be respected ; if the geological campaign in Africa were to be broken down into a host of small, hermetic organizations, this would completely destroy the working conditions which are becoming increasingly imperative for this type of study.

The other two stages, namely the search for signs and the study of the deposits proper, use applied techniques of growing complexity. This is not the place to describe them, but the scale and varied nature of the means they involve should be stressed. In the field of indirect exploration, for instance, geophysics has witnessed the birth over the last forty years of its different branches, which now include magnetism, gravimetry, seismic surveys, and electromagnetism, and the list is certainly not closed. New geochemical methods have been added to those already existing and a very complex observation is gradually being perfected, particularly in the U.S.S.R. ; this should eventually give much more accurate results from indirect exploration.

Direct exploration methods, on the other hand, are aimed, as their name suggests, at acquiring direct knowledge of *in situ* features. In addition to such conventional methods as pits and cross-cuts, more recent methods of taking specimens by drilling and core-sampling or of measuring the physical characteristics of rock by electric sampling, occupy an increasingly important place and are continually being perfected. Here again, just as the development of preliminary indirect exploration methods can set narrower limits to the less rapid and more expensive direct exploration programmes, so the more efficient use of drilling techniques can reduce the rôle of mining exploration works which, for the same reasons, should only be used as a last resort.

However, this concern with constantly improving the efficiency of research does not depend solely on the use of the most effective and cheapest methods at the various stages of mining investigation. It also presupposes that a constant effort should be made to find the most profitable signs and deposits, *i.e.* those that are the least expensive and are likely to give the best results cannot be estimated accurately, and in order to make a choice possible and to direct all efforts towards the best possible solutions the people in charge of the investigations must always be in a position to assess the prospects from the factors already known, and thus be able to gauge the effectiveness of the capital and the means already devoted to the investigations as well as those that would have to be used to carry on with further exploration. But these comparative calculations themselves are only possible if a large number of signs or deposits are being worked on, so that the rules of probability can be applied. The rôle of such statistical assessment bureaux can be very useful in increasing the productivity of the investigations, but they can only be used effectively, *i.e.* as concentralizing and dispatching offices, if there are sufficient investigations to be co-ordinated.

This survey of the different exploration stages and of the methods used demonstrates that powerful organizations are becoming increasingly necessary in order to ensure that means are sufficiently varied and that studies are properly co-ordinated. This is particularly true of the under-developed countries where a large number of investigations all have to be undertaken at the same time. We have really come to the end of the 'amateur' period of exploration as practised in the past; in this field it is now more and more imperative to operate on vast groups of countries and to devote a considerable proportion of the efforts made not only to exploration proper but also to the study of methods, that is to say, to the study of technology.

IV. WORKING OF THE DEPOSITS AFTER EXPLORATION

We have now reached the final stage of mining development : the working of the deposits once they have been discovered. Let us recall once again that if the authorities of the young countries often tend to concentrate the greater part of their efforts on this final stage because of their desire for an immediate and profitable yield, and correspondingly tend to reduce work on general studies, the price of their error is usually either mining under-development or an irrational organization of the development programme. In countries where most of the infrastructure, ranging from evacuation routes to urban agglomerations and the introduction of services, has to be created from scratch, it is very important to make a systematic study of all development problems, including the mining potentialities of the great geological areas, and in this way to investigate the whole question of the rational organization of a mining basin in its entirety instead of merely skimming the cream off a few privileged points, as it were ; in general, the opposite method only results in the creation of infrastructures which later prove inadequate for future development.

When we speak of deposits in the African countries, we are using the term in its widest sense and therefore mean the mining basin rather than the individual mine ; the problem of working the deposit is thus naturally affected by the whole question of the economic development of the area. Conversely, if the deposit does not fit in with the wider aspects of economic development in most cases it will be incapable of bearing the cost of the infrastructure and hence will not be covered by the definition we have already given, namely : 'an area from which ore can be extracted as an economic proposition'.

Once the problem of development has been understood in this way, it gives rise both to technical questions relating to the choice of working methods and to questions of economic strategy relating to the function and size of the mining venture to be undertaken.

(i) *The Choice of Technical Working Methods*

This choice involves a series of problems which, once solved, will determine the technical features of the mining proper.

First of all, the *working rate* must be chosen ; this will depend on several factors, the most important being the extent of the workable reserves. But even this notion is relative because it can vary not only with the quantity and quality of the ore in place, but also with the mining costs and, possibly, with concentration conditions. The other factors are transport available for evacuating the ore, the cost price of this transport, and, lastly, the situation on the market absorbing the output, *i.e.* the volume and quality of demand. The choice made according to these factors will govern the overall volume of investments, which will be more or less great depending on the production rate decided upon. Finally, the personality of the country's leaders or of the people responsible for financing will play an important part since the choice usually lies between the immobilization of funds with prospects of a profitable yield if an optimistic view is taken of the marketing potentialities, and more modest — and hence more accessible — investment based on a less ambitious view of the future.

The actual mining and dressing also give rise to equally important problems of alternatives. Here, however, technical facts play a more important part than in the previous case. The problem of the actual mining is very often one of deciding what part should be worked in the open air and what part underground, as underground working, which is more expensive, can usually only be seriously considered as from a certain depth and when certain capital costs have already been amortized. Obviously there is always a limit below which underground mining alone is possible.

As a general rule, a choice has also to be made between extensive mechanization and the use of manual labour to varying degrees. The choice is not always a free one, as the considerations which influence the final decision cannot be strictly technical when the problem of human under-employment arises, and this problem does arise in new countries, particularly in Africa where, as compared with highly industrialized countries, any labour which is not directly used in primary activities has difficulty in finding employment in secondary or tertiary activities.

The *problems of concentration* also tend to assume increasing importance as attempts are made to work deposits where the ore-content is low but the conditions easy. Preparation of the ore in the field in such cases becomes a determining factor in the mining development proper. The technical features and the cost of the methods adopted are of very great importance, as an assessment of the reserves and the economic feasibility of the working are finally largely dependent on them.

We should emphasize in this connection that there is a tendency to link up the problems of ore processing with those of its structural preparation. We shall subsequently see the effects of this connection in the relationship between mining activity and the user industries down the line.

Other problems of technical choice also arise in connection with the transportation of the ore ; they are usually related to selecting the most reliable and efficient means of transport. In fact, in the under-developed countries this problem raises quite different issues from those which arise in countries with an existing infrastructure to which all solutions must usually conform for economic reasons. In places where mines provide the opportunity of creating a trading circuit with the outside world for the first time, not only the infrastructure of land transport (roads, railways, cableways, pipelines, etc.) but also the infrastructure of sea transport has to be designed from scratch. Now, with regard to this question of ore transportation, and provided, of course, that the deposits contain sufficient reserves, heavy-load bulk traffic solutions are usually the most advantageous from the standpoint of cost prices, although they are the most expensive from the point of view of investment. Generally speaking, it costs less to carry material on a heavy railway than on a conventional line, ore-carriers of 60,000 ton are better propositions than those of 30,000 ton which, in turn, are more suitable than those of 10,000 ton and so on, provided that this equipment is kept working at full capacity, which presupposes a high rate of output. Once more we come up against the issues in the argument between the daring and the cautious, the conservatives, and the innovators.

In addition to these transport problems, there is often a problem of storage. As a rule, the rôle of the latter is to absorb the temporary differences between the rates of activity of the mine, land transport, and sea transport. This problem can be solved in several ways as the stock of material may be kept either at the mine, or at the port of embarkation, or else at the main port of disembarkation. The problem may even disappear entirely if the different elements in the line from the *in situ* ore to the user factory work at strictly cor-related rates. Making allowance for present-day technical methods which enable this co-ordination to be achieved — if it is desired — it can be said that the future trend will be to reduce stocks, or at least fixed stocks, and this will release the capital once required for creating storage installations or producing the ore stock ; such a policy, however, presupposes very extensive co-ordination and a certain integration of the entire line of activity ranging from the production of the ore to its use in industry.

Lastly, the ore has to be sold. The choice of a sales system is a delicate problem, and solutions are usually based on one of two formulae involving the use of either the cost price of the ore or current world prices as the standard by which the sale price is deter-mined. The first system mainly affects mines which work in close collaboration with the consumer industries and are hence sometimes disparagingly called 'captive mines' ; the second is the system used by mines which are concerned with obtaining maximum direct profits for their shareholders. In the past, governments of producer countries have tended to prefer the second sales method which appears to give them more than a sale at cost price when profits vanish, but this is very often a false problem as the great mine workings are usually bound, as we shall see further on, to the authori-ties of the countries where they are located by long-term agreements which, regardless of the more or less artificial market prices, specify the proportion to be given over to the state either through taxation or through participation in the actual profits, but in any case on a less arbitrary basis.

We have just examined a whole series of technical problems which are closely interconnected, the solution of each of them having a bearing on the solution of the others. Setting aside, as far as possible, the boldness or timidity of the country's leaders — since these subjective factors cannot affect a rational choice — the general problem of launching a mine can be put forward as a series of equations with several variables. As a rule, it can be solved by the techniques of operational research and it can be said that the greater the number of equations, and hence the number of variables, the more this analytical method becomes essential. This is particularly true when the deposit is found in a country which has no basic infrastructure, since the latter is then not one of the fundamental elements of the problem but one of the new factors in the mining schemes whose characteristics have to be determined.

(ii) *The Function, Size, and Structure of the Mining Venture*

When examining the exploration conditions, we constantly noted that systematic studies have an increasingly important part to play as compared with the sporadic search for traces of minerals. Similarly, in examining the technical conditions required to work the deposits, we have just emphasized the growing importance of the problems of infrastructure, especially in the young countries. As a result of these findings we are gradually led to contemplate the problem of opening up a mine within the wider context of the development of a mining area. In other words, in the structural development of the mining industry, we notice more and more distinctly the transformation of the conventional idea of a mine into that of a mining complex.

This development obviously completely changes the function and size of a mining venture in the economy as a whole in comparison with the traditional picture. But this alteration in the conditions of activity is also demonstrated on another level, that of foreign relations. The mining venture tends to become part of a production line feeding the metallurgical and chemical industries downstream as it were ; consequently stronger and stronger practical and sometimes even organic links are forged from one end of this series of activities to the other. In addition to this vertical functional integration, there is frequently a horizontal integration of an international character. When large mining units are promoted to the rank of mining complexes, they require financial, technical, and, above all, commercial aid, far beyond the scope of a single, isolated country. When it is proposed to work iron deposits located 600 to 700 kilometres from the coast in countries where the infrastructure has yet to be created, such undertakings are not possible except with heavy equipment corresponding to production on a scale which can only be financed by investment on an international level. That is why mining ventures of this type are always integrated with other undertakings both on the vertical plane and on the international or horizontal plane, the latter being reflected by the acceptance of financial assistance and the signing of long-term delivery contracts. The two links are often complementary, with the purchaser providing direct financial support and guaranteeing that he will make regular purchases for long enough to ensure that the equipment and the undertaking can work at full rate and pay its way. The second guarantee has now become so necessary that the international finance organizations have made it one of the essential conditions for the financial support they grant to mining development projects.

The consequences of this dual development, towards the formula of the mining complex on the one hand and the integration of the mining industry on the functional and international planes on the other, should obviously be very closely scrutinized in the underdeveloped countries, because it may have serious repercussions on economic and social, as well as on political, levels. The danger lies in the fact that when such mining complexes are set up in an underdeveloped country, they rapidly take on the shape of a foreign body developing like a malignant growth in the traditional economy with all the social and economic traumatisms that a change of this nature may involve, including the uprooting of younger members of the population during the construction period because they are temporarily drawn towards jobs which they can seldom hold for long when the actual mining stage begins, the inevitable monetary inflation and the upheaval of local markets. At times, the effects spread far beyond the immediate area of the mining complex because of the influence exerted on the incipient and precariously balanced national economies whose trading means are relatively slight.

On the credit side, these complexes normally ensure a steady and large source of income for the young countries which enables them to make great strides in their development programmes ; in addition, the new infrastructure required by the complexes enables an entire region to be equipped at the expense of the mining venture. Provided suitable measures are taken to rectify or even avoid the economic and social traumatic effects of the running-in period — and solutions to these problems are now known — it can be said that, in most cases, the advantages largely outweigh the drawbacks.

Obviously mining complexes with the features we have just described are going to create all kinds of delicate problems. In respect of financing in the first place, the acquisition of capital to make investments on such a scale, and often of an international character, is an operation calling for a very complicated gamut of resources in which public and private funds and long-medium and even short-term direct loans and participations all have a part to play. Countries which are only just developing are seldom in a position to provide their share of the capital, any more than they can lay down the sureties usually insisted upon by those lending the money and foreign authorities are therefore called upon to supply the means and the guarantees required. These authorities may be international or national or, more often than not, they may be both ; we need only recall here the part played by organizations like the World Bank on the international scene or by national development funds such as the French FAC.

This field of loans and guarantees must be considered in relation to the whole subject of foreign aid for the industrialization of the under-developed countries. This is obviously not the place to dwell on the different features of this subject, but it is important to insist on one aspect which is of particular importance to the mining industry. I refer to the use, for financing purposes, of the long-term sales contracts which the mining companies make increased endeavours to obtain when they are set up. Credit must go to the American insurance companies for originating a method by which these contracts, lodged as securities, can be used as guarantees for loans and especially for those of a medium-term nature. This system, which has tended to grow up along with the development of this type of contract, has undeniably provided the mining industry with very great facilities by mobilizing capital that could hitherto not be used for the purpose on its behalf.

The problem of the legal and administrative status of these mining complexes is also affected by new considerations. In the first instance, the national authorities are obliged to concern themselves more and more closely with the conditions under which undertakings of this size can be set up and operate, as well as with the considerable influence they can exert on the life of a region or even an entire country. It is no less obvious that the suppliers of public and private capital which ensure the financing, and the user industries which determine their activities and sometimes their development prospects by the interests they take up or the long-term delivery contracts they sign are all, for various reasons, concerned with safeguarding the arrangements which permitted or led to their colloboration. The status of the mining complex should therefore be adapted to these different requirements. A problem which is raised in such broad terms and which, moreover, must be solved in the often highly unstable political and economic climate of many young countries, cannot find a conventional answer in the commercial law of the older industrial countries. New and original formulae have to be sought to enable the undertakings to operate properly and to respect all the interests at stake, those of the country possessing the mines as much as those of their foreign companies which have linked their fate to these mines. This raises a host of questions, such as the control of the undertaking's management, the distribution of profits among the various interested parties, and the respective shares in the capital held by those supplying the natural wealth and the others carrying out its development. Satisfactory answers are hardly possible unless there is a fundamental willingness to cooperate on both sides.

The most effective solution found so far is that of long-term agreements by which the country and the mining companies decide on their reciprocal relations over a given period. Usually in these agreements, the country's government undertakes not to alter the operating conditions decided upon by the two parties for the duration of the agreement. These arrangements apply in particular to questions of taxation, the transfer of funds to repay loans and distribute profits, and the exporting of the material produced. They attempt to guarantee that the conditions on which the financing plans, or the production schedules corresponding to the long-term delivery contracts, are based will not be radically altered.

Obviously such agreements are of value only if they are respected by both parties, a fact which brings up the problem of guarantees and, more generally, all the tenets on which the great international mining complexes have been founded from the outset, including the financial stipulations for the capital invested and the regular supply of ore under the conditions specified for the long-term delivery contracts. In short, the question is one of assuring customers and financial partners that the agreements which have been made will not be broken off unilaterally. This problem is delicate because any solution to it must ensure respect for the newly acquired national sovereignty of these young countries and at the same time devise means of bringing pressure to bear which will not jeopardize that sovereignty and yet will vouch for respect of the agreements. At the present time, several possible solutions are being contemplated, some of which make provision for recourse to international arbitration and others of which recommend an international convention binding all the signatory countries, *i.e.* all the under-developed countries and their customers, the industrial countries. This solution would enable disputes about the implementation of reciprocal agreements concluded between the sovereign states and the mining companies to be brought before the courts of all the third-party signatory countries.

The problem is clearly very complicated and we are still at the stage of searching for an answer. For the sake of the future of mining in the under-developed countries, however, it is to be hoped that a solution will be found without further delay.

V. CONCLUSIONS

We have now covered the different problems raised by the discovery and exploitation of mineral deposits in countries undergoing development and the general impression left by this rapid survey seems to me to be that possible solutions involve the increasing use of high-grade techniques, the availability of considerable capital, close links with the industrialized areas of the world, and a willingness to co-operate internationally on a basis of mutual trust and assistance in order to produce the best possible conditions for development.

We should not think that these factors are restricted purely to the mining industry in under-developed countries. The mining complexes of Africa and elsewhere must be considered simply as examples of the way in which production concerns on an international scale can be set up and operate today. We are moving towards an increasingly complex economic and technical organization of the world based on large, integrated units. In these developments, the industrial countries have made technical and human advances which have set them in an advantageous position as compared with the under-developed countries. There is a great risk of the latter only being able to participate in these trends by supplying their natural wealth and of consequently finding themselves falling still further behind, even if they can insist on financial advantages in compensation.

Every possible effort must therefore be made to enable them to grasp the opportunities for technical and human development provided for them by the creation of these complex undertakings and thus to catch up with the modern world. This will depend as much on themselves, on their ability to overcome their hesitations and their ancestral reactions, as on the spirit of co-operation and the sense of historical responsibility displayed by the rich and developed peoples. All the good will in the world will not be too much if success is to be achieved.

DISCUSSION OF M. ROLAND PRÉ'S PAPER

Dr. Cookson, in opening the discussion, said that he did not propose to deal with technical issues, though the topic was essentially a technical one. Rather he proposed to ask questions relevant to the economist.

First, M. Roland Pré had stressed the great importance of careful surveys of the mineral base of the continent. This was an expensive proposition and M. Roland Pré seemed to suggest that the African countries themselves should bear the cost. But *Dr. Cookson* believed that a substantial portion of such survey work represented a legitimate cost that should be borne by the proceeds of actual exploitation of ores. Therefore, no matter who was responsible for the conduct of the survey work, this should not affect their share of the profits — that is, if the African nation is gaining part of the proceeds by taxation the top rates should be sufficiently above the top rates for other foreign enterprises to cover the cost of exploitation. Or if the profits are being shared, then if the African country has done the basic survey work, it should receive a suitably larger share.

M. Roland Pré had then made an interesting point : he said (if it were permitted to paraphrase him in the jargon of the economist) that there were considerable economies of scale in the task of conducting a thorough geological exploration of Africa and consequently there should be some kind of international co-operation. *Dr. Cookson* believed that here one had an indication of the sort of thing which made extensive regional economic co-operation in Africa so important. There 'non-industrial' economies of scale could be exploited only if the new African countries did not set about developing their own organizations which would then be somewhat difficult to absorb into a wider African organization. The industrial economies of scale seemed to him not so urgent to exploit, but the organizational ones might be practical only in the near future.

M. Roland Pré had then moved on to some of the points relevant to the development of a mine. He wanted to ask some of the same questions that M. Roland Pré had asked from a standpoint directly concerned with the economies of the problem.

First, what kind of production function should be selected? The economist usually answered this question by looking at the long-run average cost curve and the long-run demand curve and finding what kind of production function maximized profits. However, in the interests of speeding economic development there were other considerations. Should one go towards labour-intensive methods of production in order to get as many Africans as possible disciplined to industrial society? This, however, reduced the average rate and might lower aggregate demand for consumer goods by the labour force, thereby reducing the profitability of the small trading and industrial organizations which might in principle grow up around a large mining complex. Should one go towards capital-intensive methods in order to raise the aggregate demand for consumer goods by paying out higher wages to a smaller labour force, thereby creating incentives, etc.? Or finally, was the profit maximization criterion itself the best since it provided the maximum revenue for the governments?

Second, how fast should the mines be worked? Technical aspects aside, this he believed could only be answered within the framework of the national economic development plan and the long-run demand for the mineral. Ideally, receipts from exploitation of the mine should be tuned with the needs of the government for revenue for development. If the receipts came too early, then they were held in reserves which might depreciate through a rising world price level, or they might be spent on current government expenditures thereby preventing the development of a tax system which reached everyone and which was helpful in the modernization of the country, and purely because excessive wealth in the hands of politicians had a strong urge to move towards the provision of extensive social services which might be a drag on the development of the country. Once committed to such social services they became a source of recurrent expenditures and drew off money that might better be used for investments which created income streams.

On the other hand, many minerals had to be sold in tightly controlled markets. The virtual integration between the mine operators and the consumers of the mineral reduced the bargaining power of the African country in achieving the desired rates of exploitation.

Third, before turning to the demand side, *Dr. Cookson* wished to comment on the problem of organization of the mining company. Here the basic problems were ownership and sharing of profits. He thought in the future that three rules should be observed : ownership must be in African hands ; the profit share going to the African countries must *increase* over time ; the upper levels of management must incorporate Africans at agreed-upon schedules. These were very controversial points upon which he would make a few very short comments.

As regards the first of these rules, he would like to mention the structure of the ownership of the National Iron Ore Co. Ltd. which was setting out to develop the Mano river area iron deposits in Liberia. Fifty per cent of the company was owned by the Liberian government. Fifteen per cent was owned by the Liberia Mining Company, which was in turn principally owned by the Republic Steel Corporation and Mr. Christie. The remaining 35 per cent was owned by Liberian Enterprises Ltd., which was a holding company, the majority of the stock of which was owned by Liberians. The Liberian stock-owners paid 20 per cent of the stock's par value and the remaining 80 per cent would be paid out of future dividends, but with at least 50 per cent of the dividend going to the owner. One should notice that not only was Liberian ownership firmly established, but as the loans were paid off an increasing share of the profits would go to Liberians.

The division of the profit was of course a major issue between a foreign company developing a mining area and the government of the country in which the area was located. He believed that the African country ought to receive an increasingly large share. The feasibility of this would seem to rest on the long-run market situation.

That Africanization was necessary was self-evident. The main reason for trying to write out in advance a rate of Africanization was that he believed that if management was forced to train suitable Africans, it would do so. If management agreed to accept qualified Africans but without time schedules, opportunities for foot-dragging were immense.

Turning next to the demand side, *Dr. Cookson* commented that in relation to agriculture the Conference had observed that the future earnings of foreign exchanges through African exports would not change very much. They had further discussed briefly the stabilization problems in commodity markets. Three factors, he thought, had led to the present situation in mining, where many minerals were in over-supply.

First, the rapid growth of technology which had made — in M. Roland Pré's excellent distinction — many more ores deposits, the known deposits thus grew rapidly under both increased exploration and new processing techniques, which now made economic the exploitation of previously known sources of the mineral. Incidentally, comparisons of future needs against present known deposits were hazardous because of this technological growth.

Second, the tendency in oligopolistic industries when faced with rising demands was to try to get capacity established first before competitors did. In industrial countries, especially the United States, this tended to sharp investment booms. For international oligopolies dealing with minerals this had led to intensive exploration and sometimes development of capacity. Even if projected demand was accurate, this had a tendency to create excess capacity as companies tried to hold their market shares.

Third, if projected demands were less than actual demands, then over-capacity existed. Sometimes this miscalculation of demand rested upon development of substitutes. Sometimes it rested upon a reversal of a government's policy, *e.g.* the demand for uranium had fallen off because of the U.S. government's decreasing needs. Again, stockpiling policies of the U.S. government in the early 1950s created demand which had now dropped off.

All in all there was for most minerals a plentiful supply. Because of a highly integrated world market there was not the problem that existed in the agricultural commodity markets. However, in agricultural products African production could expand — and profitably if there was a comparative advantage in such production — so long as there was no commodity agreement stabilizing market shares. In the mining industry the market was organized to prevent over-production, sometimes by integration, but also by more or less successful buffer stock stabilization arrangements. Thus African production could not steal a greater market share of existing receipts — as it might in agriculture — unless there was more or less explicit agreement with the consuming industries.

Expansion of foreign exchange earnings must rest on increasing world demands. Thus there was more room for optimism — one did not have Engel's law as a source of discouragement. The future demand for minerals was clearly an important topic for discussion.

Turning next to the mining complex as a centre of development, *Dr. Cookson* said that M. Roland Pré had pointed out that the development of a mining complex in Africa had important secondary consequences for economic development, by the creation of improved transportation facilities, the development of an industrial labour force, the creation of opportunities for secondary industry supplying the mines and the labour force. If the mining complex was to play its full rôle in development, the authorities in the mining company and in the government must give considerable attention to how these secondary consequences were best handled. For example, even at somewhat greater expense, could railroads designed for the mines pass through other areas where transportation availability might expand the mining economy and increase production levels ? Could the mining company give preferred treatment to local small industry for various jobs of a specialized nature ? Could the government and the mining company together provide credit and technical assistance to help the development of local industry ? Could the mining company provide easy consumer credit to allow Africans to purchase durable goods and thereby provide additional sources of demand for local small industry ? Here the important point for discussion was how the mining complex could become a real centre of development for the African and not an enclave economy ?

The Chairman suggested that the subsequent discussion should be focused successively on : the prospects and limitation of future mining activities in Africa ; the influence of mining in African economic development ; the forms of organization in which mining should be developed.

Professor Spengler thought that the economic prospects and limitations would be determined almost wholly by technological considerations, among which he thought that labour- or capital-intensive methods should be included.

Mr. Moran emphasized that the knowledge of mineral deposits was meagre. In planning development, one important asset would be increased knowledge of African resources. Technical progress was making such knowledge cheaper to acquire. He thought that the first need was a complete geological mapping of Africa. *Professor Robinson* wanted to know whether geological explorations had yet gone far enough to enable one to judge the probable upper limits of African resources. The limits were likely to be set partly by the richness or poverty of ores and partly by distances from markets. A study of the problems of handling lower-grade ores made in the United Kingdom suggested that the problems to be solved were chiefly those of cheap handling of very large tonnages of material. This was a field in which much progress had been made and further progress seemed probable.

M. Roland Pré agreed that increased knowledge about mineral deposits was very important. At present knowledge was very scanty. In their 20 m. square kilometres the U.S.S.R. Ministry of Geology employed some 60,000 geologists. In the West as a whole there were not more than 30,000 and in the total of Africa not more than 4,000–5,000. The cost of mining and preparation of ores was the most important factor ; at a price ores could be enriched. But if transport cost was great, even rich ores were uneconomic. The whole problem of mining and transportation to seaboard had to be regarded as one. The experience of Liberia was not typical. There was need for clear agreement between the using industries and the African governments concerned.

Dr. Gavrilov congratulated M. Roland Pré on a most valuable study. He drew attention to two practical problems. First, African countries could not afford the heavy cost of the conduct and finance of geological exploration. This had to be done with great care if potential supplies were not to be missed. He illustrated this from attempts to find oil in India. A concern that already possessed available supplies elsewhere might not be enthusiastic about large expenditure to discover local resources. As regards M. Roland Pré's point that it was necessary to think in terms of the cost at the seaboard, African countries might be able to exploit and use resources inland. But there were shortages of qualified staff. This was the central problem that had to be overcome.

Professor Robinson commented that, apart from a certain volume of iron ore, minerals were increasingly being exported in processed forms. *Professor Enke* confirmed that very few ores were being exported as ores, and that the value of African exports in that form was negligible. The advances of technology were increasing the depths also at which minerals could be worked. He thought that an exploration policy would pay for itself.

Dr. Singer said that there were broadly two methods of exploration : intensive local, including feasibility studies ; the establishment of long-term geological survey departments. He favoured the latter. But these were expensive. A UN study suggested that $1–2 billion were required to be spent on exploration of Africa. When it came to exploitation, he thought there should be labour-intensive techniques. Expenditure on capital was foreign expenditure. Expenditure on labour was domestic expenditure. *Professor Robinson* reminded him that labour-intensive methods applied to mining required a great deal of responsible supervision and this often involved foreign expenditure, or, if not, used a very scarce resource. *Dr. Yudelman* also recalled that the foreign earnings and available capital supplies were very largely derived from the exploitation of minerals by international companies.

Dr. Wade thought that the obstacles to the discovery of Africa's mineral wealth were only partly scientific. They lay partly in the nature of international enterprises. Some of these accumulated stocks of minerals or exploited mines to suit their own international interests. He could see great advantages if the U.S.S.R. could assist African countries with exploration for minerals. But there would still be problems of their subsequent exploitation.

Mr. Dowuona thought that advances of technology could bring harm as well as help. In Ghana, when mines had been closed down, the government, faced by unemployment, had been forced to reopen them and work them uneconomically. He thought that an international geological service, with staff drawn from the U.S.S.R. as well as other countries, should be set up.

Professor Dupriez asked M. Roland Pré regarding the relative mineralizations of central and coastal regions of Africa. Were there likely to be advantages in searching for minerals in some of the more remote areas ? The limitations of present knowledge was some safeguard for the supplies of future generations. *M. Roland Pré* thought that there could be considerable development of the minerals of the central regions when transport problems were overcome. He thought that minerals should be worked wherever they were competitive. If working was postponed, the demand might disappear. With regard to exploration, in a world already fully supplied with minerals, it was more and more necessary to find the best deposits. The fact that Africa was broken up into thirty territories made it impossible to concentrate research into the most desirable areas. It was very necessary to have co-operative research centrally directed, as in the U.S.S.R.

The discussion was then turned to the subject of the influence of mining on general economic development. *Professor Leduc* stressed the contrast between agriculture and mining. In mining, resources could not be replaced, while in agriculture they were. Thus it was important that a country should use these capital resources for capital development. The large capital investment associated with mining had great repercussions on the local economy. It could lead on to processing industries and thus influenced the whole location of development in the country.

Dr. Yudelman and *Professor Robinson* stressed the part played by mining in the economic development and in the contribution of tax revenue in the Union of South Africa and the Rhodesias. Mining had led to the building of railways. The railways in turn had stimulated other development. *Professor Dupriez* described the similar multiplier effects in Katanga. Where there had been no minerals, there had been little development, and with sparse population, industry had been handicapped. *Professor Houghton* similarly described the multiplier effects, through availability of coal, iron-stone and limestone, in the building up first of a steel industry, which became subsequently the basis of an engineering industry, and led finally to the creation of manufactures of import-saving consumer goods. *M. Roland Pré* emphasized the similar effects of the big mining complexes in the former French territories, and the creation of an industrial infrastructure. Ultimately, however, the multiplier effect tapered off.

Professor Spengler thought that one should differentiate between different channels of improvement. Some industries were based on raw materials. Others grew through ability to share in profitable markets that were created. While the raw material was a necessary constituent of the exports it formed only a small fraction of the value of the final product. He thought that African countries ought to specialize more and exchange between themselves. He suggested the need for customs unions. He did not believe in conservation policies. In view of rapid changes of technology it was better to exploit resources quickly.

M. Rist was concerned about the large movements from rural to urban areas and the financial effects of mining development. What did governments propose to do with the large revenues that they acquired during the relatively short periods of the lives of mines ?

M. Roland Pré, in replying, said that African countries should be most careful to secure the best receipts from mining activities, and should be cautious in making agreements. From the investors' point of view the most important thing was regularity in supplies. They should seek to have both a satisfactory international tribunal and an international agreement about the methods of determining shares.

Chapter 22

PROBLEMS OF LARGE-SCALE INDUSTRY IN AFRICA

BY

D. J. VILJOEN

Potchefstroom University

I. INTRODUCTION

AFRICA, with an area of 11,700,000 square miles, is the second largest continent and its population is the third largest in the world, viz. 236,000,000, or 8 per cent of the total world population, the sub-Saharan population being approximately one-half of this. Within its boundaries it has more peoples, tribes, languages, and cultures than any other continent. Apart from the European languages 812 African languages are known.[1] All these peoples are grouped in sixty territories, of which some are self-governing and others are not. Tremendous topographical, climatic, and economic variation and contrast exist within Africa. These differences must be borne in mind if any generalizations are made. An intimate knowledge of the circumstances in each territory is necessary before any reliable recommendation for the economic improvement of the territory can be made.

This continent is experiencing a transformation both politically, culturally, and economically, and much attention is paid and assistance rendered to the several territories in Africa. Although there has been much economic progress during the past few years Africa is still an under-developed area where the standard of living of by far the greatest proportion of the population is very low, the national income *per capita* ranging in most cases from £10 to £50. From a humanitarian and economic point of view the all-important problem today is to devise ways and means to enhance the standard of living in Africa as soon as possible. Moreover, Africa can be an increasingly important source of raw materials and a market for exportable manufactured goods of other countries ; no wonder that so much attention is paid by the governments of the African states and foreign institutions to the rapid economic development of Africa.

[1] *Tegniek*, January and March 1961.

616

Usually a policy of industrialization is considered the most expedient way to obtain the required economic development rapidly. Several questions arise in this connection, namely whether industrialization is not emphasized too much ; and further whether the African countries should concentrate on the establishment of large-scale or small-scale industry and what problems large-scale industries are likely to encounter.[1] These questions will be dealt with in the rest of the paper.

It should be pointed out that the discussion in this paper refers only to large-scale manufacturing industries, although some reference has also been made to power supply industries. By the phrase 'large-scale industries' must be understood manufacturing plants which employ a large number of workers and/or require an enormous capital investment.

II. THE DESIRABILITY OF INDUSTRIALIZATION

As pointed out, some people hold the belief that economic development and industrialization are synonymous, that industrialization is the only way to achieve economic development. Apparently that is the belief of most of the leaders in Africa. It may be that this belief is to some extent a result of the fact that the most advanced and leading countries today are also highly industrialized countries. For this reason developing countries in Asia and the Far East like Afghanistan, Burma, China, Malaya, India, Indonesia, Japan, Nepal, Pakistan, Philippines, and South-Vietnam, all have industrialization as the main element of their schemes for economic development.[2]

Other important reasons for this urge to industrialize are that manufacturing industries provide the unemployed and underemployed with work, thereby causing incomes to rise. This will create a larger market for the products of the several agricultural, extractive, and manufacturing industries. This is especially important in the Far East where a population pressure is experienced. Industrialization is also believed to be the principal means by which the diversification of an under-developed economy can be achieved. This point is especially emphasized by several African countries whose economies are largely dependent upon a very narrow range of export products.

It may, however, be asserted that industrialization cannot be concentrated upon in isolation, because it depends on all the other growth factors. There is, for instance, according to W. Arthur

---

[1] Small industry is dealt with in another paper.
[2] 'Economic Development and Industrialisation', in *Cartel*, April 1959, p. 64.

Lewis,[1] a close relationship between industrialization and agriculture. If manufacturing develops, a demand is created for foodstuffs, labour, raw materials, and capital for the industry while a market for the manufactured consumers' goods is needed. Agriculture must satisfy these requirements, but this can only be done if its productivity has also been raised accordingly.

This higher productivity will provide the greater volume of foodstuffs and raw materials, the higher income for the farmers to absorb the increased production of manufacturing and the necessary saving for investment. But if farming remains stagnant, the shortage of agricultural products will cause an inflation of the prices of these products. This will make it difficult to dispose of the manufactured products. On the other hand, if the income of the farmers remains low, they will be unable to buy the manufacturer's products.

The retarding influence of a stagnant agriculture may to some extent be overcome if the manufactured products substitute the farmers' imports — thereby saving foreign exchange — or if an export market is developed and foreign exchange earned which can be used to pay for the imports of manufacturers. The extent of industrial growth is therefore limited by the export and internal markets. Japan, for instance, found that the increase in the productivity of its agriculture greatly facilitated the growth of its manufacturing industry.

When planning programmes for the African economies it should be kept in mind that the problem is not one of choosing between primary and secondary activities, but rather to ensure a balanced expansion of all the relevant sectors of their economies. An over-rapid and unbalanced growth of the industrial sector, if it is not accompanied by appropriate changes, for instance in the agricultural sector, may cause balance of payments difficulties, inflation, excessive urbanization, and disruption of accepted social patterns which in the long run may hamper economic development.[2] It can be accepted that it will be impossible for low income agricultural countries to advance within a short period to industrialized countries ; but the process need not take so long as in the case of the old industrialized countries, because the under-developed countries now have the advantage of the lessons of the past.

The rate of industrial growth of each country depends to a large extent on its natural resources and the activity of its human element. Under-developed countries experience many problems in this process

---

[1] *The Theory of Economic Growth* (1955), p. 283.
[2] United Nations : *Processes and Problems of Industrialization in Under-developed Countries* (1955), p. 3.

of industrialization which hamper the rapidity of the growth. An outline of some of these problems will give an idea of the possibilities of industrializing the sub-Saharan countries and especially of establishing large-scale industries. It is not intended to deal with each country individually, as this procedure requires an intimate knowledge of the economic and social circumstances in each country. The general problems of under-developed countries correspond, however, to a very large extent.

III. RAW MATERIALS

The problems of large-scale industry in Africa are generally similar to those of small-scale industries applying factory techniques ; they only differ in degree, the requirements of the large-scale industries being more exacting. These problems will be dealt with under the headings of the most important factors of plant location, because these are the factors which an entrepreneur usually closely considers in order to determine the probable size and profitability of his proposed enterprise.

A large factory needs a sufficient and constant supply of raw materials of correct quality at competitive prices. A large and mechanized plant consumes not only a large quantity of raw materials but also requires a constant supply. A shortage of supplies may cause a serious loss in a large concern not only on account of the smaller production but also because of the increase in production costs.

The range, quantity, and quality of raw materials, agricultural or extractive, greatly differ from one country to another. Some sub-Saharan countries are richly endowed with raw materials and therefore have the potentiality to advance more rapidly and to a greater extent than some other countries, which unfortunately are very poor in this respect. Some regions of Africa suffer from an excessive rainfall and are thickly forested, while other parts are arid or have an insufficient or unreliable precipitation, making it unsuitable for cultivation. Large portions consist of grasslands or bushveld, which are more suitable for pastoral production. However, the tsetse fly excludes large portions of the tropical rain forest and savanna areas from cattle farming. These unfavourable climatic conditions, animal diseases, and primitive farming methods in many regions are great obstacles to increased agricultural production, and hence a large and constant supply of foodstuffs and raw materials of a high and standard quality.

But many industrialized countries also have or had climatic problems, and although those of the African countries may be special, it is quite possible that many of them will afterwards be solved. What is urgently needed in Africa is intensive research work on a large scale. Splendid work has already been done by research workers to improve the quality and quantity of the existing crops, substituting for old crops new ones more consistent with climatic conditions and even adding new crops. The research work done at the several agricultural institutions in South Africa has succeeded in putting farming in South Africa on a more scientific basis and in enabling agriculture to keep pace with the growing needs of industry.

One of the most important measures to gain some control over the amount and irregularity of rainfall is the erection of irrigation and in some cases drainage schemes. These schemes are very expensive, but if soundly planned, they will greatly increase agricultural output. Several big schemes have already been completed and now contribute to the stability of the supply and quality of agricultural produce.

Another problem is that many of the African farmers are not used to the system of producing exchangeable surpluses, which is one of the main essentials of modern exchange economy. This attitude necessarily limits supply of raw materials and foodstuffs as well as the purchasing power of the farmers.

It should not be concluded from the above that all sub-Saharan countries are very poor in agricultural raw materials. Already a great variety of products is produced, some of which are exported on a large scale, *e.g.* cocoa, palm produce, cotton, wool, sisal, tobacco, coffee, tea, groundnuts, sugar, citrus and deciduous fruit, and meat. Assuming other conditions to be favourable it appears that there is a sufficient supply of raw materials for a few large-scale manufacturing industries. The fact that these plants have, with a few exceptions, not been established, proves that there are other problems which must still be solved.

As regards mining, some important developments have already taken place. In some countries mining has, however, only made a small contribution to the economic development, but this is not necessarily an indication that these countries have only small mineral potentialities.[1] More private and governmental geological surveys and prospecting are required. The exploitation of mineral resources has always given a great impetus to economic development. Some countries are rich in minerals and a great variety and sometimes

---

[1] H.M.S.O., *Report of the East Africa Royal Commission, 1953–1955*, p. 113.

large quantities are produced, mostly for export to the industrial countries.

Taken as a whole, it would appear that Africa has sufficient raw materials to support large-scale industry. It is of course also possible to import raw materials to supplement local supplies or even to substitute them if local prices are too high. It is, however, not advisable to be wholly dependent upon foreign supplies, because their flow is often irregular, and they are a drain on the importing country's foreign exchange. If financial difficulties should necessitate a limitation of foreign payments, such an industry would be unfavourably affected. It is therefore preferable that local raw materials should be used where possible.

Usually the extent of dependence on local and imported raw materials varies during the process of industrialization.[1] The first stage is characterized by industries processing the raw materials previously exported in their natural state or by manufacturing for domestic consumption, in which case very little raw materials are imported. Although the size of these processing and manufacturing units is predominantly small during this phase, a few large units exist especially in the processing of some of the metallic ores. During the second stage new industries devoted to the finishing or assembling of products are added. These industries are of a more complex nature and require semi-manufactured raw materials which are usually not available locally and must be imported. This stage lasts a long time. In the third stage the tendency is towards manufacturing these imported products locally from indigenous raw materials if available. South Africa is, for instance, considering the production of most of the components for its motor vehicle industry. This will cause some saving of foreign exchange, which can be utilized for other urgent purposes. Obviously the rate of growth through all these stages depends to a large extent not only on the availability of the country's natural resources but also on the exploitation thereof at a low cost.

IV. TRANSPORT

The economic development of a country can be seriously hampered by a deficient transportation and communication system. It affects industries, whether large-scale or small-scale, in several respects, especially in so far as the provision of their supplies and the distribution of their products are concerned. Inadequate transport

[1] United Nations, *Processes and Problems of Industrialization in Under-developed Countries*, p. 47.

facilities may at busy times result in a congestion of traffic, thereby causing the delivery of raw materials to be delayed a long time. This necessitates the keeping of extra stocks. The absence of suitable transport equipment or good roads increases the risk of damage and even makes the conveyance of some goods impossible. Transportation costs might be so high that the establishment of a plant would be an unprofitable venture.

If the industry uses imported materials it is usually established near the ports. This reduces the transport problem in so far as the raw materials are concerned, but increases the distribution problem. An inefficient transportation system not only limits the range of industries but also the scale of production on account of the fact that it also limits the market. This might cause small-scale plants serving a limited market to be established in different areas. On the other hand, a well-developed transport system enables the entrepreneur to locate his plant more conveniently for the distribution of his goods over a wide area and thereby avail himself of the economies of scale.

The transport problem is one of the most important problems which Africa has to face.[1] Large areas have no regular service, and in some parts animal transportation is still found. Although some countries have a fairly well-developed transportation and communication system it cannot be said that they are adequately served. Vast sums of money are being spent to improve transportation facilities which in due course will create the social and economic environments which are more favourable for the establishment of large-scale industry.

V. POWER AND WATER SUPPLY

The supply of power constitutes one of the elements of the infrastructure which is indispensable for economic growth. With the increasing mechanization of manufacturing, the supply of sufficient, regular, and cheap power becomes an important problem. The adequacy and the dependability of power supply are usually more important than the cost of the power, because a failure of power may cause heavy losses especially in the case of large plants. Partly due to this fact some industries have their own power plants. But this procedure has its own technical problems apart from the additional capital investment required. The practicability and advisability of private power generation depend on the adequacy and cost of the oil, coal, or wood used as fuel as well as the supply of water.

---

[1] W. A. Hance, *African Economic Development* (1958), p. 85.

In many regions in Africa this will present a grave problem to the concern and conditions are certainly not favourable for the establishment of large-scale industry.

The capacity of the generating plants of most local authorities is at present too small to meet the demands of large-scale industry. But the governments of the several countries realize the necessity of supplying industry with more power ; several schemes have been planned or put into effect. Although tropical Africa, with the exception perhaps of Southern Rhodesia, is poor in coal, it has a large potential of hydro-electric power. The reasons why the progress in the exploitation of this source of power is slower than one would expect are the high capital investment required by hydro-electric plants, and that in many cases electricity must be transmitted over long distances to the bigger towns or cities. On account of the high capital investment hydro-electric power can only be supplied cheaply if there is a big existing demand for power. Although the capacity installed must be large enough to provide also for the foreseeable future demand, an exaggeration of the potential demand and excessive investment in power projects will not only increase the cost of power but will also divert capital which can be used more beneficially elsewhere in the economy.

Co-operation among the several countries on the African continent in respect of power supply may be a solution to the problem of inadequate demand for the big existing and proposed power schemes. The supply of electricity from the Owen Falls Scheme to Kenya is an example of such co-operation. But apart from the view that strategically it may be advisable to be independent of other countries for power supply, the question of optimum size of hydro-electric plants arises. It may be that smaller plants more evenly spread over the country can supply power more cheaply, if such potential power resources exist in different parts of the country. This is, however, a technical problem which cannot be further dealt with here.

It should be mentioned that the power-generating industry today constitutes one of the largest industries in Africa. The Kariba scheme, for instance, cost approximately £120 million. Production of hydro-electric power started in January 1960, and power is supplied at a tariff of 0·8d. and even less in some cases. The demand for coal from the Wankie Collieries will probably be reduced to such an extent that new sources of demand will have to be found, for instance the erection of an oil-from-coal plant, which may afterwards cause the establishment of large-scale chemical industries, as is at present happening in South Africa.

As regards water, it should be pointed out that some types of large-scale industries use a tremendous amount of water, and a shortage of water supply in many regions in Africa discourages the establishment of such industries.

VI. LABOUR

In Africa, where such a large proportion of the population is rural and farming methods mostly primitive, the recruiting of factory workers presents many problems. The kind of work and rigorous labour discipline of the large factory differ radically from that of the peasant. It is obvious that the process of adjustment is difficult and may be one of the main reasons for the high rate of absenteeism and labour turnover of the African worker. In labour-intensive industries the problem will be aggravated. Notwithstanding the high rate of labour turnover secondary industry usually does not experience a serious shortage of unskilled labour. The high labour turnover, however, not only increases the firm's recruiting costs but also retards a rise in labour productivity. Thus although the wages of the African workers are usually low the firm's labour costs may be high. These costs can, however, be reduced in some instances by a suitable selection and training programme. Experience showed that workers who were quite unfamiliar with machine technology could become reasonably proficient at repetitive tasks within a not too long period of training and practice.[1] Modern large-scale industry usually has many opportunities for employing semi-skilled workers as machine operators. Therefore the more the work in a factory can be subdivided and processes simplified, the more will it be possible to overcome the problem of the low educational standard and lack of skilled labour, so characteristic of under-developed countries. In other cases, however, the demand for highly trained technicians has increased, because the construction and even operation of some industries have become very complicated. This aggravates the problem of shortage of skilled labour.

The lack of skilled personnel is, however, seriously felt in the technical and managerial fields. Large-scale industry requires all kinds of personnel, such as skilled mechanics, maintenance engineers, purchase and sales experts, designers, research workers, cost and accounting personnel, production engineers, and all the other administrative and operative executives who are responsible for the

---

[1] United Nations, *Processes and Problems of Industrialization in Under-developed Countries*, p. 41.

planning, organizing, and controlling of the activities of the enterprise. Without properly qualified personnel to perform these tasks serious inefficiencies may result in the management of the enterprise, *e.g.* bad labour relations ; inadequate maintenance of machinery and equipment ; faulty production and sales planning ; loss of raw materials and manufactured goods. The shortage of these types of personnel is one of the major hindrances to the industrial growth of African countries.

The usual way to cope with this problem is to use, where necessary, expatriate personnel on a permanent or temporary basis for these higher and more responsible posts, while the indigenous personnel receive within-plant training or are sent to industrialized countries to receive the requisite training. It is obvious that the process of qualifying for these higher posts necessarily takes a long time, especially if educational facilities are meagre and large numbers of people must be trained. This will place a heavy burden on the enterprise if it has to provide all the facilities. Large sums are being spent for expanding facilities for a general basic education and for vocational education, which will surely bring improvement.

The shortage of skilled labour has caused a competition between employers for this kind of labour. The result is that these workers must be paid a very attractive salary. This places the enterprise in Africa in a less favourable position in comparison with similar enterprises in industrial countries.

VII. CAPITAL

The capital requirements of the manufacturer are larger than that of the merchant. He has the financial problems of the wholesale merchant plus those incidental to manufacturing activities. A large investment in buildings, machinery and other equipment is necessary, and in the case of a large-scale mechanized concern the capital requirements may reach tremendous proportions. For instance, the South African Iron and Steel Corporation started with a share capital of £6 million, which now amounts to more than £25 million. Approximately £50 million has been invested in the oil-from-coal plant in South Africa. Similarly the amount of fixed capital invested in the several plants of South Africa's Electric Supply Commission up to 1958 was £209 million.

The capital requirements of a manufacturing concern in an underdeveloped country are larger than that of a similar concern in an industrialized country for several reasons. It must import all its equipment and sometimes employ overseas experts to install the plant. It is often necessary to have a stock of duplicate parts in order to avoid delays in case any of the parts become defective. A larger stock of raw materials must be kept, because the stocks cannot be replenished quickly. Moreover, it may be necessary to integrate the ancillary services which in industrialized countries are provided, and usually more cheaply on account of the scale, by independent concerns or public authorities. It often happens that the firm has to provide its own facilities for transport, power, water, housing, and other social services. Salaries of the scarce types of personnel will be higher. Although the wages of unskilled and semi-skilled personnel are usually lower, it is doubtful whether the saving is significant. There may be some saving in regard to land.

The acquisition of capital presents another problem. The investment of capital in a manufacturing concern depends in the first place on the profitability of the enterprise. According to some manufacturers in the United States the return on capital invested is usually higher in foreign investments than it is at home in spite of the difficulties of foreign exchange, language, national feelings, and even revolutions.[1] This is, however, not always true. There are many instances of business failures due to lack of experience, poor management, inadequate working capital, insufficient information and research. Such failures discourage capital investment.

Capital investment is affected to a large extent by the risk factor. Every investor wants his investment to be safe, and this is of particular concern to those enterprises with large capital investments. Instability of political conditions, frequent, sudden, and discretionary changes of the government's economic policy, incompetency and dishonesty in the public administration, and lack of information services, police protection, and facilities for insurance and credit increase the extent of uncertainty and risk and deter investment. A study made by the U.S. Department of Commerce of the impediments to investing American capital in Africa concluded that the lack of publicity in the United States of investment opportunities was one of the important reasons of America's small investment in Africa. Another reason is the absence of a clear-cut statement of government policy outlining the conditions under which American private investments may be made.[2] For instance, the American investor wants to know whether and to what extent the foreign government applies the participation principle to foreign enterprises ; whether there is any restriction on American management and

---

[1] D. H. Fenn (ed.), *Management Guide to Overseas Operations* (1957), p. 106.
[2] C. Grove Haines (ed.), *Africa Today* (1955), p. 462.

technical labour to operate the enterprise ; and whether the government can give definite assurance that the enterprise will not be nationalized or the remittance of earnings and repatriation of capital restricted.[1] Unfortunately conditions in some African countries today are such that satisfactory answers to some of these questions cannot be given.

Closely related to the principle of safety is that of liquidity of investment. The investor not only prefers that his liability be limited, but also that he can liquidate his investment at any time. This will stimulate investment. These conditions are usually found where the company form of enterprise is used and a stock exchange exists, but a very large proportion of the African population is absolutely unfamiliar with these institutions, so that the marketability of shares is very limited. A properly organized capital market exists only in one or two African countries.

Apart from the lack of confidence, the low income and the low rate of saving of such a large proportion of the inhabitants are factors accounting for the shortage of industrial capital.

This fact is aggravated by the absence of an aptitude for industrial pursuits. The farmers and business men are used to investing only in commercial businesses, land, cattle, and even hoard the money or buy imported consumption goods.

Although shortage of capital is an important impediment to industrial growth, it is rather the small enterprise in Africa which suffers most. The large-scale concerns on the contrary usually have more access to the capital markets at home or abroad, and the capital problem is therefore not their most important problem.

VIII. MARKETS

The scope of the market for the manufactured goods is undoubtedly one of the most important factors which determine the desirability of establishing a proposed plant and what its size should be. A narrow market restricts the size of the plant, and this generally implies that an optimum factory unit cannot be established, or if it is established the installed capacity will not be fully utilized and overhead costs will be inadequately spread. The unit cost of production will in both cases increase and this will reduce the competitive power of the firm.

The scope of the local market depends on the size of the population and its effective demand. The populations of the several countries in Africa greatly differ in size, and some are so small that

[1] C. Grove Haines (ed.), *Africa Today* (1955), p. 464.

any possibility of establishing large-scale industries which depend on local markets is excluded. With the exception of one or two countries the national income *per capita* of African countries is very low, which implies that consumption is generally confined to the lower quality and low-priced goods, usually consisting of foodstuffs and clothing. Consequently little scope is left for selling other manufactured products of higher quality, and this restricts industrialization. It must, however, be noted that these low-priced manufactured products are usually standardized products and can therefore be mass-produced locally, if the market is large enough, otherwise it is cheaper to import them.

An analysis of the income distribution in Africa will give a better idea of the structure of the market. The European population falls within the higher income bracket and can afford to buy more luxuries. In many countries they are, however, such a small percentage of the total population that the market for these consumption goods is limited.

Then there is the urban African, whose income is usually much lower than that of the European but higher than that of the rural African. The buying habits of this middle class tend to become Westernized. Many of them now buy some of the higher quality manufactured goods previously purchased only by the Europeans. This enlarges the market considerably, but it is doubtful whether larger than medium-size manufacturing units are necessary to provide the needs.

The income of the farming population, who constitute by far the largest proportion of the population, is usually very low, and the market consequently limited.

The market is also limited by the long distances and inadequate transport and communication facilities. This fact tends to divide a territory into separate small market entities, which favour small-scale rather than large-scale enterprises. In regard to communication it must be mentioned that the creation of a new demand by the usual methods of advertising is limited by the illiteracy and also wide dispersion of a large proportion of the population. Circumstances are, however, changing and the circulation of newspapers among the urban population is increasing.

The demand for local products can be created by substituting imports or exploiting foreign markets. Import substitution has the advantage that a particular market already exists. All that is required is that the local manufacturer must convince the consumers that he can supply goods of equal or better quality at competitive prices. But this is not so easily accomplished, because production costs of the local concern are usually high in the initial stages, the quality of the product poor, and the consumers' preference for the imported product strong. If the local product constitutes a threat to the foreign exporter, as in the case of large-scale production, the local manufacturer may in addition expect severe competition, especially where the market is easily accessible, so that it may be necessary for the government to grant him some protection. During the Second World War the supply of many goods from the industrialized countries was cut off. This greatly stimulated the industrial growth in those countries which already had some industrial climate. But after the war many of these new industries disappeared due to the revival of foreign competition. High transportation costs afford, however, a natural protection to some African countries.

Despite all the above-mentioned obstacles import substitution is an important factor in the process of industrialization. In many cases this is effected by the foreign exporter establishing a branch factory in the importing country or co-operating with a local manufacturer.

If the home market is too small to justify large-scale production an attempt must be made to find export markets. If the African countries with their rather limited internal markets want to establish large-scale industries they will have to seek external markets within or outside Africa. But again it is most probable that competition by old industrialized countries with their established world market will be encountered, and nowadays this competition is severe. As far as export markets are concerned most African countries will probably for some time have to confine their industrial activities to the processing of those primary products for which they have an export market. As indicated previously, some of these processing activities can be on a large scale, such as the primary smelting and refining of metals, sugar refining, cattle slaughtering and preparation, fruit and fish canning, and pulp and timber industry.

Even the processing industries sometimes also meet with competition by similar industries overseas. Nigeria has, for instance, been slow in encouraging the extraction of oil and the processing of oil-cake from groundnuts, partly because of the competition of extracting mills in the United Kingdom. Senegal in French West Africa has developed such a groundnut processing industry, but competition with the metropolitan seed crushers for the French market has since the Second World War resulted in various forms of protection for the metropolitan industry.[1]

[1] United Nations, *Economic Survey of Africa since 1950*, p. 166.

Competition is therefore an important factor in the determination of the size of the market and thus of industrial plants. If internal and external competition is eliminated to a great extent, more large-scale industries might result, which would be the case if the government actively participates in industry. But even this presupposes that the country's economic activities have created a market large enough to sustain some large-scale industries. For instance, South Africa's large-scale iron and steel, engineering, motor assembly, fertilizer and other chemical industries, oil refineries, paper and pulp, textiles, brick-making, cement and ceramic industries, would have been impossible without the existence of a large internal market, only about 5·8 per cent of South Africa's industrial production being exported. Some of these industries have also been established in other African countries but on a smaller scale to suit the narrower market. Fortunately many industries have small minimum sizes which enable them to grow as the market extends.

IX. ENTREPRENEURSHIP

Without the entrepreneurial class whose function is to organize the production factors efficiently, there cannot be any significant economic development. Entrepreneurial and managerial abilities of highest quality are essential for the successful launching of modern large-scale undertakings, and the scarcity of men with these abilities in Africa must be regarded as a most important impediment to a more rapid industrialization of Africa.

The task of the entrepreneur in Africa is made difficult on account of the above-mentioned absence of an appropriate social, psychological, economic, and industrial atmosphere. He must perform many functions which in more advanced countries are done by specialized institutions. This increases the risk factor, and makes a proposed project less attractive, especially in the case of large-scale manufacturing enterprises, which represent one of the least liquid and flexible types of investment and one of the most difficult to manage.[1]

It must be pointed out that entrepreneurial ability and management skill develop as the industrialization and the general economy progress. This apparently explains why the African has so far revealed very little of these abilities. So far the white population and the government have been the sole entrepreneurs of large-scale

[1] United Nations, *Processes and Problems of Industrialisation in Under-developed Countries*, p. 31.

industry. If the industrialization process is to be accelerated the African countries will have to take active steps to attract private entrepreneurs or industrial consultants from industrial countries. In addition the governments will have to participate to some extent more directly in the establishment of manufacturing and other industries.

X. CONCLUSION

In general the problems which large-scale industry have to face in Africa are similar to those usually encountered in under-developed countries, namely irregularity and inadequate supply of raw materials of the right quality, lack of requisite skilled personnel and a capital market, a limited commodity market, and a deficiency of the basic facilities, viz. water, power, and transport, and also a shortage of entrepreneurial and managerial ability.

But it must not be concluded from this that large-scale industries are absolutely precluded from being established in Africa. On the contrary there are several examples of such large enterprises especially in the industrially most advanced countries, and it is doubtful whether all possibilities for the establishment of large enterprises have already been exploited. But the mere fact that they have not yet been founded proves the existence of some obstacle or other, as, for instance, the lack of a thorough knowledge of the industrial possibilities of the territories, and therefore the absence of interested entrepreneurs. Circumstances are, however, changing as a result of a more active policy of industrialization and economic development in general by the public authorities and the activities of financially strong government-sponsored and also private development corporations. The existence of many of South Africa's largest enterprises must be ascribed to the direct participation of these finance corporations.

Large-scale industries have a significant influence on the economy of a country and its establishment should be encouraged where possible. In view, however, of the many requirements of large-scale enterprises, which usually cannot be properly met in under-developed countries, some writers recommend that small-scale industries should receive more attention than at present.[1] This will also stimulate decentralization of industry, and serve as a basis for the development of large-scale industry afterwards as the economy progresses.

[1] W. Arthur Lewis, *op. cit.* p. 78; W. Brand, *Het streven van de economisch onontwikkelde landen naar een hogerealevensstandsard* (1954), pp. 40-3; H. Belshaw, 'Observations on Industrialisation', in *The Economic Journal*, September 1947, pp. 379-87.

Vast areas of Africa are, however, very thinly populated, the inhabitants so poor, and the towns so small that no industry can exist. The position will change if new mineral discoveries are made or the traditional farming methods substituted by modern methods. This will provide the food and raw materials for local consumption and some of the foreign exchange needed for the payment of capital goods imported. The increased activities of the primary and tertiary industries provide the market for the products of secondary industry ; and the development of secondary industry again stimulates the other sectors of the economy, and so a cumulative action is put in motion. It is because of this interdependence of the different economic sectors that it is maintained that large-scale industries and industrialization in general are not the only or most important way of solving the problem of a low national income *per capita*. All sectors should be developed more or less simultaneously, which in Africa certainly cannot be accomplished soon and without extensive planning and hard work.

DISCUSSION OF PROFESSOR VILJOEN'S PAPER

Dr. Singer, opening the discussion, suggested that though the definition of large-scale industry was not very precise, the meaning was sufficiently clear for purposes of the present discussion. Professor Viljoen had raised the question of whether industrialization was a condition of, and synonymous with, economic development. He believed there was a limited element of truth in this. There were countries, such as New Zealand and Denmark, which had become prosperous and had developed through agricultural specialization and export. They had developed a quite different employment structure from that of an under-developed country which had not been through a development process, but different also from that of a developed industrialized country. Professor Spengler had argued that industrialization represented the dynamic factor in economic development. This might be true in some cases, but was not universally true. So regarded, the raising of agricultural productivity would not be an end itself but rather a means to growing industrialization. The argument for industrialization in many under-developed countries was not, as Professor Viljoen had suggested, that it provided a market, nor that it created employment, but that it was a means of raising productivity while reducing the pressure on the limited supplies of land. On the other hand, lags in the agricultural sector, Professor Viljoen argued, were a cause of inflation in many under-developed countries at the time that they were trying to industrialize ; thus the objective should be a balanced expansion. But he thought that, in arguing this, Professor Viljoen had assumed away the basic problem of possible scarce resources. Any doctrinaire prescription, *Dr. Singer* argued, was unhelpful. One could not assume, moreover, that one was starting from a position of equilibrium ; it was more likely to be a position of basic unbalance, with all kinds of inherent bottlenecks. The problem of economic development, moreover, was essentially one of creating a disequilibrium.

Professor Viljoen had said that in his view Africa had sufficient raw materials to support large-scale industry. This raised the question of how far local raw material supplies were a condition of industrial development. *Dr. Singer* was not convinced that they were. Switzerland, for example, had developed without local raw materials. We did not know enough about these linkage effects. In his own view, backward linkage was much more important than forward linkage.

Turning to the problems of transport, *Dr. Singer* suggested that the natural transport systems of Africa cut across regional frontiers. This gave rise to a need for the joint development of intra-African trade. He thought this had not been sufficiently stressed by Professor Viljoen. Regional co-operation in industrialization should be considered as well as the possible impacts of the various market groupings in Europe.

Turning to capital supplies, *Dr. Singer* was not surprised to be told that the expected return on American foreign investment was higher than that on domestic investment, though the evidence was somewhat uncertain. If it were not so, the foreign investment, having regard to the risks involved, would not be undertaken. What was more important was that the foreign investment was very small in volume compared with the domestic investment and probably did not exceed 0·25 per cent of national income. In an under-developed country the domestic investor had to face the same difficulties as the foreign investor and in some respects greater ones. There was a preference in many cases — possibly an irrational preference — for the foreign product on supposed grounds of quality. He suggested that this might justify some element of protection.

Finally, *Dr. Singer* emphasized the rôle that development corporations had played in economic development, providing a mixed African and foreign system of organization. In a number of under-developed countries these development corporations had proved very useful instruments of development.

The Chairman suggested that the subsequent discussion should be concerned in turn with the following questions :

1. Was industrialization the only way of achieving economic development ? What place was there for concepts of balanced growth ? Were there identifiable stages of growth ?
2. Was industrialization dependent on local supplies of raw materials ?
3. What influence were transport facilities and costs likely to have on

intra-African trade ? The possible place for customs unions and joint planning of industrial development ?

4. The rôle of the development corporation.

Dr. Yudelman thought that generalizations as to whether industry or agriculture should come first were not helpful. Much depended on the resource base. There was a great deal of potential elasticity within the agricultural sector. The market was the key problem. He did not think there was any universal policy prescription. *Professor Enke* agreed. It was fruitless to discuss priorities in such broad categories. There were all kinds and stages both of agriculture and of industry. There was a tendency in under-developed countries to regard industrialization as a panacea for increasing income per head. It was also a prestige symbol. Agriculture was despised. Industry was regarded as synonymous with living in the twentieth century. Was there really a negative marginal net product in agriculture ? He thought that most under-developed countries had a strong comparative disadvantage in producing final producer goods and final consumer goods. They might never succeed in building up export markets in these.

Professor Houghton argued that it was important to concentrate on the market for the product at all stages. He did not think it very useful to think in terms of backward and forward linkages or to emphasise distinctions between large- and small-scale industry, but rather between consumer and producer goods. South Africa had started as an agricultural country. Urban centres had produced markets for agricultural products and consumer goods. But most of the latter had at first to be imported. But progressively the market had grown and first increasing proportions of consumer goods and finally a proportion of capital goods had begun to be made in South Africa.

Professor Bézy said that it had been argued that the transfer of manpower from agriculture to industry, and an increase of demand for food and agricultural raw materials arising from industrialization, might cause bottlenecks and an inflation of the agricultural sector. Though this had been true of other under-developed countries, there had been no sign of it in the Congo, largely in consequence of the traditional structure of African agriculture. During the previous thirty-five years, 40 per cent of the male adult population had left the tribal areas to enter the modern industrial sector. This had had little effect on agricultural output, mainly because 80 per cent of the work was done by women who either remained in the tribal areas or continued to produce food on the outskirts of the towns. The main problem was not the volume of agricultural production but the increasing distance between production and consumption. The present solution might be only temporary but it had prevented difficulties of food production acting as a brake on development. Was Professor Viljoen right in saying that differences between large- and small-scale industries were differences only of degree ? The large-scale enterprises

permitted the achievement of internal and external economies of scale.
A ten-times larger enterprise was not merely a ten-times multiplication of
the same factors employed in a small enterprise. It was fundamentally
different and its powers of self-finance were fundamentally different.

Mr. Onitiri found himself in strong disagreement with Professor Enke.
Changes in the whole pattern of production and trade were likely. The
changes in political relations were bound to lead to changes in economic
relations and to structural changes in the economies of the former colonial
territories. He was not convinced that under-developed countries should
concentrate on agriculture because of some inherent and permanent lack
of comparative advantage for the production of competitive goods in
industry. This was a static view. Industrialization was necessary for
economic growth as well as for economic stability. He remained convinced that the terms of trade would move against agricultural products
in the longer term.

M. Roland Pré argued that one must distinguish between two kinds
of industrialization. First, local industrialization designed to meet the
needs of the local population and to process local products. This seemed
likely to have a rapid effect in transforming the activities of the population.
It needed relatively little capital, but some help by way of protection of
infant industries. Second, the introduction of large-scale industry which
could use local material resources. This created quite different problems,
including all the technical problems of a large industrial complex, the
discovery of markets, and the like. The two types raised very different
problems. The second type involved problems of transport and finance,
and often of foreign investment. There was need for a world policy to
assist it. Finally *M. Roland Pré* emphasized the need of education and
training for industry, even at a low standard, in order to produce a
sufficient number of technicians.

Mr. Krishna said that industry and agriculture were not alternatives.
In the African context the question was whether potentialities for industry
existed, and if so how to proceed to industrialize. He was convinced
that in considerable areas of Africa it was true to say that marginal net
products in agriculture were zero or negative because of excessive population pressure. Increases of production were possible only by removing
substantial numbers of men and introducing improved techniques. The
re-employment of those withdrawn was only possible if there was industrialization. He thought that fears of African countries embarking on
heavy industry as prestige symbols were often exaggerated. Industry
need not be export-orientated. There were much greater opportunities
in import-saving industries. Technological advance was no prerogative
of particular nations. Historically it had spread. A much more dynamic
view of African policies of industrialization was needed.

Professor Robinson thought that much of the argument regarding the
rival virtues of agricultural and industrial development was misdirected.
It was, as he saw it, no part of the duty of anyone who was planning the

development of an African territory to take sides about such an issue on purely doctrinaire grounds. As it seemed to him the function of a planner was to foresee the normal trends, to assume the most perfect operation of a perfectly competitive system, and to try to help things to happen more smoothly and more quickly by using any powers possessed by a government to remove obstacles and bottlenecks. One could, he thought, sufficiently foresee the probable pattern of growth to make it possible to develop skills and experience in advance. And one could help to establish progressively a pattern of foreign trade in accordance with the true developing long-term comparative advantages. While markets were for the moment very limited, the income elasticities of demand for industrial goods were high and with growing populations, growing incomes per head, and some element of import-saving, individual markets for many goods were capable of doubling in a decade. In making a longer-term policy one must not assume that present conditions would remain static.

Professor Spengler remained of the opinion that the major source of dynamism lay in the industrial sector. But this was not a complete argument for pushing industrialization. This should keep in step with potential comparative advantages.

Professor Williams suggested that import-substitution proceeded by stages. Value added was small at first and increased gradually. He believed that a certain amount of industrialization was necessary. How far should a planner take into account the deficiencies of those who were supposed to implement the plan? One could both over-estimate and under-estimate abilities. Should one build into a plan one's estimate of what was practicable?

Mr. Beheiry said that the practical issue in the Sudan was not the rival merits of agriculture and industry, but what and how much to do with a given industry in certain circumstances. One had to work in the dark. There were, moreover, other considerations besides the purely economic. Regarding Dr. Singer's advocacy of protection on the basis of the irrationality of consumers, he did not think the African consumer was basically irrational. While there was a case for protecting infant industries, the problem was how much protection to give. Imports should be taxed, but not abolished, in order to avoid the creation of local monopolies.

Dr. Okigbo said that the real issue in many African territories, including Nigeria, was not whether there should be industrialization or not. That issue had already been decided, partly on political grounds. The question was what products could be produced efficiently and how far one should aim at balanced industrialization. In practice the ideal conditions for balanced growth did not exist.

Professor Stanley argued that one should distinguish various stages of industrialization.

Professor Enke regarded Professor Robinson's concept of planning as idealistic. In Latin America, planners seemed to regard industrialization as an end in itself. In Africa, a dichotomy between agriculture and industry was not fruitful. He agreed with Dr. Okigbo that what mattered was the choice of particular industries or particular types of agriculture. As income per head increased, demand grew, and it was a question of which goods could economically be produced locally. If the agricultural population was to become an effective market, agriculture must be more productive and more specialized. In African stores the variety of goods bought was small. Many of these would be able to be produced locally when the market reached a certain size. He hoped there would not be industrialization just for the sake of industrialization.

Professor Dupriez reminded the Conference of the importance of energy supplies. Africa was well supplied with hydro-electricity, but not, as yet, with nuclear energy. Transport and distance were the major problems. He pleaded, as others had done, for a balance between agricultural and industrial development.

Chapter 23

SMALL-SCALE INDUSTRY IN AFRICAN ECONOMIC DEVELOPMENT

BY

H. W. SINGER
United Nations Organization,
New York

I. THE CASE FOR DEVELOPING SMALL-CASE INDUSTRY

THIS question can be considered at two levels : the general or the particular. At the general level, one can discuss the pros and cons of emphasis on small-scale industries in development plans and investment patterns, perhaps with some special emphasis on societies at very early stages of economic development as African countries usually are (in Rostow's terminology, 'traditional societies', or societies in the early phases of the 'pre-condition' stage). At the particular level, one should pay special attention to special features peculiar to African economies, which would not necessarily be displayed by Asian, Middle Eastern, or Latin American economies at the same income level, nor would they be found in earlier European history. The particular approach is more meritorious, but suffers from the difficulty that it may not be possible to generalize too much and the matter had really best be discussed for individual countries ; for this, however, the present author lacks time, space, and competence.

All the same, an attempt will be made along the lines of the particular approach since it seems to me that in the special African circumstances, a specially strong case can be made in favour of small-scale industries. Let me briefly try to list what I considered to be the main points in this specific case.

(1) In Africa, more than anywhere else, the map of development is still *tabula rasa*. This means that there is still a greater chance than elsewhere to develop an element of autonomous technology, *i.e.* technology adjusted to the resource endowment of the African countries. In general, under-developed countries have to rely on the technology of more advanced countries which naturally reflect

their own resource endowment, *i.e.* a relative abundance of capital skills and a relative scarcity of labour. In spite of the best efforts made to adapt subsequently this alien technology to the different circumstances of under-developed countries, the result is not ideal. To cope with this situation, it has been suggested that technology should be based not on market prices, but on 'shadow prices', or 'accounting prices', of capital and labour and other factors of production. This, however, introduces an element of arbitrariness and in any case does not solve the fundamental dilemma that the best adapted technology simply may not be there (or not known to those preparing investment projects). The adaptation of a mechanized technology in the direction of smaller-scale and 'de-mechanization' is as difficult as it is to unscramble scrambled eggs.

There is no doubt that an autonomous technology for African countries would result in typically smaller-scale units of production than in Europe or North America. If, therefore, the development of small-scale industry could be based also on the development of an autonomous technology for Africa — admittedly this is a very big if — the resulting smaller-scale industries could also be high productivity industries in the African context. In this way, something new in economic development could still happen in Africa. Admittedly the chances seem to be against it since the development of an autonomous technology for Africa is a difficult and revolutionary undertaking. The line of least resistance is to transfer technology and adapt it rather than to create it. However, in the present context, the chance of a new departure at least exists and deserves to be mentioned.

(2) One of the great problems in African development will be to make it as fully African as possible from the very beginning. The more we can avoid the creation of enclave economies, the more we avoid transferring to the economic field the frictions arising from 'colonialism' (I am using this unhappy shorthand expression with all due apology), the happier we shall all be. The efficient management of large-scale industries, both in the sense of business management and in the sense of technical responsibility for large machinery complexes, is not at present accessible to large enough numbers of Africans. On the other hand, Africans have already shown and had the opportunity to develop skill in the running of small-scale business, and in the types of mechanical skills applied to individual pieces of machinery and personal forms of organization rather than big complexes and corporate organizations. Therefore, the choice is not an entirely economic choice between small-scale industries and large-scale industries but between African, or largely African, small-scale

industries and foreign, or largely foreign, large-scale industries. I think this situation should tip the balance, in many cases, towards the small-scale developments.

(3) The development of small-scale enterprises of all kinds can be a stepping-stone to larger-scale enterprises, a part of the 'learning process'. I realize that economists differ on this point. I am particularly sorry to disagree on this point with Hirschman, to whose insight we owe so much. I suppose Hirschman would argue that the best way to learn is to plunge into large-scale organization and learn by trial and error. I must disagree with this prescription. I do believe that in these matters there is such a thing as an organic link between small-scale, medium-scale, and large-scale forms of organization. On the whole, it is more productive to move, wherever one can, from the lower end of the range to the upper end rather than jump directly to the top. For one thing, with small-scale organization the learning process can be spread over much larger numbers ; in the second place, the number of different arrangements and situations in which learning can take place with small-scale organization is a multiple of what it is with large-scale organization ; and thirdly (coming back to the earlier point), with small-scale units the learning would be largely by Africans, but with large-scale units largely by outside enterprise.

When it is presumed that small-scale industries are 'inefficient' by comparison with larger-scale industries, such findings or presumptions are often based on the economist's narrow concept of 'output' or capital formation. Part of the 'output' of small-scale industries consists of the creation of skills — 'human capital formation' — which, although it does not enter the economist's figures, is of extreme importance in the development of under-developed countries. But even in terms of physical productivity, smaller industries (less than 100 employees) produced about 90 per cent of the average industrial output per person in the U.S.A. and Puerto Rico and about 85 per cent in the United Kingdom (but only about 65 per cent in Japan).

(4) The development of Africa has so far largely proceeded by forming a large number of 'islands'. Broadly speaking, there seems a choice of either widening the islands or of deepening the islands. By this I mean that development might take the form either of creating more and more islands of development until ultimately they link up with each other, or, alternatively, push forward industrial development inside the islands which have already been created. I would venture the proposition that in so far as there is a policy choice in these matters, it would be better to multiply the islands

rather than to deepen them. This proposition is based on a number of reasons, particularly on the desirability of avoiding excessive migration with its resultant social friction and economic difficulties, and also on the kind of experience (so striking in contemporary Brazil, Italy, and elsewhere) of how difficult it is to revive a region subsequently once it is allowed to become 'backward'. The creation of new islands of development will naturally shift emphasis to smaller-scale forms of organization, both because of the greater scattering of investment that is involved and because islands typically start with smaller-scale units, unless they are based upon a big mining complex. Outside the islands, in any case, population is often sparse and transport is so poorly developed that only local markets exist. This is true both for products and factors of production, and creates a setting for small-scale, and mainly rural, enterprise.

(5) The African savings potential is typically localized or tribalized, and, in any case, highly specific. Small-scale industries can make use of such localized and specific forms of saving which it would not be easy to mobilize on an institutional basis. The most tangible expression of such an unutilized local savings potential is in the available spare time of people — in many parts of Africa particularly among men rather than women — and in the savings potential now going into the building up of economically useless assets, such as unproductive cattle and other status symbols. The conversion of this unutilized potential into small-scale industries seems feasible ; its conversion into large-scale units does not. The importance of status symbols also points in the same direction. It is conceivable to translate the attitude to cattle-counting heads as a status symbol — to the running of a small firm or business. This would mean that the owner of such a firm ploughs back any profits actively into the firm to see it grow as a tangible expression of his social worth and success ; thus, a high marginal rate of savings and re-investment would be achieved. True enough, as, for instance, experience in North-East Brazil shows, at later stages this attitude may become an obstacle to development since it sets limits to the growth of the firm ; owners who are willing to plough back their own earnings up to the hilt are unwilling to adopt non-personal forms of organization, accept partners (at least outside the family), or even utilize bank credit. Thus, while firms grow surprisingly rapidly up to a certain point, the difficulties of growing beyond that point are quite formidable. But in Africa this kind of problem lies more in the future, to be dealt with when it arises. For the moment the problem is not how to remove such obstacles, but to promote

growth up to the point where the obstacle arises. At this stage, the advantages of personal ownership and the smaller scale which this implies seem quite strong.

(6) It is also relevant to point out that in the case of Africa the homogeneous ethnic and linguistic units are often quite small, and in particular may be limited to the village or tribal level. This means that any large-scale unit of production will have to assemble its labour forces from different ethnic, linguistic, or religious groups, which may produce labour friction, difficulties of communications, and lower labour efficiency. For the same reason, in larger-scale units management and workers may be drawn from different groups, which adds a further complication. It may be argued that the linguistic and tribal differences must eventually be overcome in any case if the African countries are to acquire a reasonable degree of economic integration and development. Of course, this is true, but the argument here is that there is no point in meeting these difficulties unnecessarily, or unnecessarily early in development. It is difficult to see how the development of small-scale units, based upon more homogeneous groupings and providing a nursery for larger-scale development, could be other than helpful with respect also to the following stage of national integration.

(7) Given the African desire for independence, personal identification, and the strength and present weakness of business talents, it seems true to say that in many cases the real alternative to the development of small-scale industries would not be the development of large-scale industries, but rather the development of trade and more speculative activities. To that extent, productivity comparisons between investments in large-scale and small-scale industries seem to be somewhat irrelevant. The true comparison should be between development of small-scale industry on the one hand and trading and speculative activities on the other. Although some economists have attributed very high development value to trading — and it is certainly valuable in transforming subsistence economies into money economies, in creating a demand for merchandise and in forming capital — this consideration is also bound to shift the balance towards smaller-scale industries.

(8) In small-scale industries, especially of the more rural type (cottage industries), there is an element of self-employment in the same sense that employment of the owner and of his helping family members will be carried up to the point where marginal productivity of labour falls to zero — on the assumption that the alternative to this type of self-employment is non-voluntary unemployment. By contrast, wage employment in larger-scale units is only carried to

the point where the productivity of labour is equal to the current wage. This means that with large-scale organization and wage employment, and with excess labour supply, part of the labour force will remain unemployed unless there are adequate self-employment opportunities. Hence, where there is a state of prevailing under-employment and lack of employment opportunities — this is particularly true of Africa in its present state of development — the principle of self-employment is better designed to maximize total production than the principle of wage employment. This seems to me a good argument to promote small-scale industries, with an element of self-employment as distinct from wage employment, until employment opportunities have increased in the course of general economic development. The strength of this argument is, of course, diminished where there is ample land and no restrictions on land ownership so that those not accepted in wage employment can employ themselves on the land ; but this situation is by no means universal in Africa.

(9) The development of small-scale industries in African countries has the advantage of building on something that already exists. The extent to which under-developed countries produce their own manufactures is often considerably underrated. This is also true of Africa. In nearly all African countries plants will be found to be fairly widespread-producing on a small scale, whether as urban or rural industry, such things as tiles, flour, pots and pans, brushes, pictures, pottery, paper, matches, glass, soap, beer, shoes, brass work, leather goods, boxes, trunks, furniture, trinkets, and many other consumer goods, as well as simple capital goods, such as spades, hoes, ploughs, harness, hand tools, etc. To develop something that already exists is easier than to build up something entirely new. Among the existing small-scale industries there are already a number of successful producers who have proved their ability and who can be encouraged to expand, and a number of skilled persons who can be encouraged and aided to set up on their own. There is also a great deal of experience to be drawn upon as to the situations, incentives, and obstacles to the enlargement of the scale of existing units. This would make major mistakes and loss of investment less likely if large-scale units are developed out of smaller-scale units. The development of existing units, within limits, also has notoriously more favourable capital/output ratios than the establishment of new units.

(10) One of the great needs of Africa is the formation of new common market and trading areas. The present orientation of African economic relations is based more on history than on economic

rationale. The present political boundaries are also very often drawn without regard to economic requirements. It is clear that any rational development of African countries will have to cope with these two problems. However, this will take some time — very complex and difficult policies and economic readjustments are involved. The main focus of the problem will be the establishment of larger-scale industries serving markets larger than — or at any rate different from — the present country boundaries. A race by African countries towards large-scale industrialization, based on present national markets, could conceivably do great harm and turn out to be very wasteful in the light of the subsequent development of new and more rational economic areas. There is, therefore, a case for delaying such irrevocable decisions — at least in doubtful cases — until the underlying problem of rational trading areas has become clearer. This is all the more reason to push ahead as much as possible with the development of smaller-scale industries in which the question of reorientation of trade and redrawing of economic areas does not arise to the same extent.

(11) This last consideration leads us to a more general consideration. The shorter gestation period of investment in smaller-scale industries will frequently have a particular advantage, in the special circumstances of most African countries. Countries recently acceding to independence or countries awaiting early independence will be faced with much greater than normal uncertainties concerning their resources and requirements over the immediate future. Faced with such a situation, a rational technique of development planning is to allocate present resources with a minimum of prejudice to future decisions, *i.e.* retaining the greatest possible degree of freedom. There is no doubt that a number of smaller-scale units freezes future decisions to a lesser degree than the establishment of a large-scale unit. A large-scale unit will involve the growing up of subsidiary economic complexes and overhead investment around it and will require heavy investment in urbanization of a fixed pattern. The establishment of smaller-scale units keeps the situation much more fluid. Where the peculiar circumstances of African countries put a special premium on fluidity in development planning — and this seems to me the present situation — the balance should to that extent shift in favour of smaller-scale industries.

There is no doubt that an industrial pattern based on large-scale industries and industrial complexes involves more irreversible decisions than does a widening of the development islands with emphasis on small-scale industries.

(12) African countries are faced with specific shortages of in-

digeneous administrators, especially technicians and economists. Yet on the other hand there is no doubt that the chosen route of development cannot be by freewheeling growth but must be by development planning. More than anywhere else the requirements for economic and social overhead capital — transport, power, housing, health facilities, educational assistance — will have to figure very largely. Hence, both with respect to the desperate shortage of capital and with respect to the great shortage of trained people to give attention to different sectors, there is a strong case for concentrating available resources in capital and trained manpower to these overhead sectors. This makes it all the more important to concentrate directly productive investment in those sectors where capital requirements are least and where results are least delayed.

Of the three sectors, agriculture, small-scale industry, and large-scale industry, generally speaking it is smaller-scale industry which seems to satisfy these two key requirements most frequently. An expansion in agricultural production is notoriously difficult, beset as it is not only with economic but also with social and institutional difficulties of all kinds. Moreover, in many sparsely populated areas of Africa it may have to be partly capital-intensive. The development of large-scale industry is mainly capital-intensive, particularly where machinery may have to substitute for skill as well as for simple labour. Besides, the gestation period is long and the danger of major mistakes in African conditions is considerable. Compared with the two alternatives of agriculture or large-scale industry, therefore, investment in smaller-scale industry seems to have much to recommend it.

(13) Perhaps the greatest individual obstacle to the improvement of economic efficiency in small-scale industries is the fear of unemployment. Although this fear may be more imaginary than real (in fact improved efficiency in small-scale industries may lead to added employment rather than unemployment) this does not make it any less real as an obstacle to the development of efficient small-scale industries. It is probably for this reason that small-scale industries have become associated with suggestions of work-making, traditional craftsmanship, and Ghandi philosophy rather than with efficient production. In those countries of Africa which are not over-populated, this fear of unemployment is less marked than it is, shall we say, in India. Moreover, a generally vigorous development policy will also serve to hold fears of unemployment at bay.

The general conclusion would be that *efficient* small-scale industries are best developed as part of a generally vigorous and forward-moving economy.

II. METHODS OF DEVELOPING SMALL-SCALE INDUSTRY

So far this paper has mentioned some of the reasons why the development of smaller-scale industries in Africa holds out some very special attractions and deserves for this reason probably higher priority in our thinking than it has received so far. A few thoughts may be added about the ways of achieving this desired end.

One thought leads us back to the more political problems of the relationship of foreign capital and African capital ; of foreign enterprise and African enterprise, which, beyond doubt, will be such an important determinant of African economic development. Large-scale investments will have to be very often foreign, and the establishment of a mutually satisfactory relationship between foreign investors and African governments and peoples will be a crucial problem. The best way in which such a harmonious relationship can be achieved would be if the larger-scale foreign firms not only were to make a contribution to the development of domestic enterprise and domestic capital, but were also very obviously seen to make such a contribution.

This directs attention to the possibilities of organizing within the African countries a system of sub-contracting and ordering, by which the foreign firms could produce their requirements and components as much as possible within the country in which they are located. There will be limits to this process, particularly at the beginning, but it seems to be a good line of general policy to hew to in everybody's interest. The kind of system one would like to see develop in African countries is that the larger-scale foreign firms (which might also themselves enter into some kind of partnership with local governments and local businessmen) would range around them and nurse along with them smaller-scale African firms. The techniques of doing this will be in need of further study and will need adaption to special African conditions, but it seems a problem to which students of African development problems might well devote attention.

A second thought is suggested by Japanese economic history. In Japan, the economic 'take-off' was not based on displacing small-scale or rural industries. On the contrary, it was accompanied by development of sub-contracting by the larger firms and of a system based on village specialization. These experiences also might provide valuable guide posts for African development.

In the case of Japan, the geographic compactness of the country made it easier to diffuse new ideas and skills through the countryside and thus draw small-scale industries quickly into the production system.[1] This situation of compactness is not frequent in Africa now. It seems a little paradoxical to find compactness put forward as an argument in favour of small-scale industries since generally it is exactly the sparseness of population, isolation of local markets, and high transport costs which are considered to be the best breeding ground for small-scale industry. The fact of the matter is probably that if other prerequisites for the development of small-scale industries are available (in terms of skills, finance, etc.), small-scale industries will draw strength from, and will adapt themselves to, diverse economic conditions.

Indonesia also provides interesting examples of village specialization on such things as ceramics, furniture, umbrellas, etc., where in given villages there are small workshops producing these articles, or parts of them in many homes or in central workshops.[2]

A third method for the development of efficient smaller-scale industries is through the establishment of trading estates. On these trading estates smaller-scale industries can be given the kind of services — power, transport, maintenance, etc. — as well as general technical assistance and such aids to business management as training in accounting, etc. Perhaps even more important, by providing buildings and equipment on a hire-purchase basis or on a rental basis, the overhead costs of starting smaller industries can be reduced and converted into running costs. Such trading estates could be deliberately used as a nursery for smaller-scale industries. New firms would be encouraged to set up on their own, to make room, as soon as they have extended beyond a certain size and proved their economic viability, for new growth on the trading estate, and not only the successes but also the failures should be moved out from the estate in good time. The financing of such trading estates *cum* pilot projects *cum* training facilities would also be the kind of project which might attract aid from abroad.

Another method of small-scale industry development of interest to Africa should be the tradition of the central workshops (The Dutch Centraals or the Indonesian Induks), as developed in Indonesia first by the Dutch government and then by the Indonesian government. These central workshops provide a good focus in which to bring together government promotion, finance, and co-operative elements. The central workshops carry out those operations which are more efficiently carried out on a somewhat larger scale, and provide financial and advisory services of all kinds, while grouping

[1] See W. W. Lockwood, The Economic Development of Japan, Princeton University Press, 1954, pp. 213-14.
[2] See K. N. Rao, 'Small-scale Industry and Economic Development in Indonesia', *Journal of Economic Development and Cultural Change*, January 1956.

around them clusters of small-scale or home industries drawing their supplies or turning in their products to the Centraal or Induk.[1]

DISCUSSION OF DR. SINGER'S PAPER

In opening the discussion *Mr. Moran* said that Dr. Singer's paper provided many useful arguments in favour of the development of small-scale industry in Tropical Africa. There seemed to him, however, too much defensiveness concerning small-scale industry. He also thought that Dr. Singer made too much of the necessity of a choice between large- and small-scale industry. He himself felt that a sufficient economic justification for small-scale industry had been made where the industry in question in its country setting was conducive to effective and economic operation. Such industries had proved profitable and useful in many countries where they had met this test. He did not see any need to consider small-scale industry in the context of competition with large-scale industry, except in the general context of the allocation of scarce resources.

There were industries, such as steel, cement, nitrogenous fertilizers, which were of necessity of medium or large scale. There were other industries which often lent themselves readily to small-scale operations — hand tools, light agricultural implements, clothing, batteries, furniture. The term small-scale industry was not altogether clear and *Mr. Moran* felt it might be appropriate to suggest some definitions which had been made. A review of the efforts of seventy-eight countries to promote the growth of small-scale industry disclosed something of the range. The United States ordinarily considered a business as small if it had less than five hundred employees. Japan classified an industry as small if it had less than three hundred employees and a capitalization of less than $28,000. India used a criterion of fifty employees with power or one hundred without power and a capitalization of less than approximately $100,000. The Stanford Research Institute, in its work on small-scale industry, felt that certain criteria other than numbers of employees were necessary to the classification of an industry as small-scale. These included : extent of specialization in management ; personal contact of the manager with workers ; suppliers and customers ; lack of access to capital through the organized security market. Subsequently, it was found that these conditions were ordinarily met by industries employing less than one hundred people.

Small-scale industry had a definite rôle in a balanced industrial economy. In his paper Dr. Singer cited the contribution which small-scale industry made to industrial production in a number of developed

[1] See K. N. Rao, 'Small-scale Industry and Economic Development in Indonesia', *Journal of Economic Development and Cultural Change*, January 1956.

countries. What that rôle might be in the individual country would depend on the optimum size of various industries as determined in the light of industry characteristics and of circumstances in the individual country, such as nature and size of market, geographical distribution of resources, level of transportation costs, and types of skills available. A note of caution was also in order. What had not been possible, in a given industry in the past might have now become possible, or might some day become possible, as a result of technological change. Countries starting activity in such an industry might find it possible to start at a smaller scale than countries which started earlier.

Returning to Dr. Singer's paper, *Mr. Moran* wished to make the following specific comments :

On point 1 (p. 638-9), he was not so pessimistic about technological information on small-scale industry adaptable to African conditions. Not all industry in the developed countries was unduly capital intensive, and there had already been considerable experience in adapting existing knowledge successfully to the requirements of other under-developed countries, for example, in India. He was satisfied that the research community was able and willing to assist African countries to determine the feasibility of small-scale industry adapted to local conditions. It had not been done widely in Africa because there had not been a market for such research ; but it had been done in such countries as India and Pakistan. In those countries it had been found that such research was most effectively realized where a qualified local institution has been established to determine research needs and seek assistance from public or private bodies, locally or abroad.

Regarding point 4 (p. 640-1), he would like to add to Dr. Singer's point the idea that small-scale industry located in rural areas might contribute to the effort to move people into the market economy by providing wage employment and a commercial market.

Regarding point 5 (p. 641), he was not anthropologist enough to deal with the question of inducing people to use the small factory as a status symbol in lieu of cattle. He would like to suggest that one of the most difficult problems in Africa might well be that of locating the entrepreneur, ready and able to break with tradition and to accumulate the necessary savings.

Regarding point 7 (p. 642), he was not sure that the argument presented here would hold up under investigation. Ordinarily the interest in establishing a large industry would, he expected, be governmental in Africa rather than individual.

Regarding point 9 (p. 643), he did not know the extent or character of small-scale industry in Africa. However, there was interest in it and a number of African governments were doing, or planning to do, something about promoting such industry through the provision of technical assistance and finance. These included Ethiopia, Ghana, Kenya, Liberia, Nigeria, the Federation of the Rhodesias and Nyasaland, Tanganyika, and

Uganda. Such assistance was most important. Experience in many countries had demonstrated that training of craftsmen was not enough to lead to the creation of small industries or businesses with any frequency. Experience had also shown that provision of finance for small industry, even on easy terms, was not ordinarily enough. The entrepreneur needed training and help with problems of book-keeping, costing, inventory practice, and other business practices. The most successful small-industry programmes were those which included training facilities, some form of industrial extension service, research and experimental work, and supervized credit.

Regarding para. 3 (p. 646), Dr. Singer's suggestion seemed to him excellent. ARAMCO has tried something along these lines for some years in Saudi Arabia. Consideration might also be given to inducing the large trading firms and the government to direct their purchases to small local industries to the greatest extent possible.

Regarding para. 3 (p. 647), industrial extension services could do much to provide necessary information to entrepreneurs.

Finally, he wished to point out that it was important for a government embarking on a programme of promoting the growth of small-scale industry to secure the services of experienced personnel to assist in a survey of industrial possibilities and with the design of a programme to meet its own special characteristics.

The Chairman (Professor Robinson) suggested that the subsequent discussion might be devoted, first, to the meaning of small-scale industry in relation to the problems of technology ; second, to the opportunities in Africa for developing small-scale industries, and the contributions they might make to African development ; third, to the difficulties of setting up small-scale industries, and the problems of making them competitive.

Professor Houghton was anxious to know whether it was intended to include rural craftsmen and their problems in relation to agricultural reform, including the provision of a cash income. Both *M. Roland Pré* and *Dr. Okigbo* thought that, to analyse the social impact on the African economy, all small-scale industry, including simple handicrafts, had to be considered. *The Chairman* expressed reluctance to extend the discussion into this wider issue.

Professor Robinson thought that it might help the discussion if one started from very broad principles and tried to see the circumstances in which industries tended to be organized in large or small units. In certain industries in which massive units of capital were inescapably necessary, such as steel smelting and rolling, heavy forging, shipbuilding, units were almost invariably large, and the minimum scale of reasonably efficient organization was large. But even in steel smelting the very large scale of plants in Europe and North America was not a *sine qua non*. Relatively small electrical furnaces were practicable and in some circumstances economic.

But most manufacturing, even in the countries of advanced technology

— leaving out the very exceptional automated equipment of the automobile industries — were in effect large aggregations of small-scale units of equipment. The textile and clothing industries, boots and shoes, printing, pottery, furniture and wood-working, and building, were of this character; while large units were marginally more efficient in such industries, they were not a necessary condition of any production and there were numerous examples of small units competing effectively with large ones. Very much of the most efficient equipment was technically capable of being fully used in quite small firms. In most of these industries new entrants were frequent and began on a small scale with relatively few machines, and grew to large size as their markets expanded and required it. Many of the small firms began as specialized firms, serving the needs of other firms. He thought there were many industries in which regional markets in Africa were sufficient to enable a firm to be set up with a minimum of efficient equipment, provided that entrepreneuring and technical skills could be made available.

Professor Frankel thought that Africa's chief handicap was the absence of any sufficient discipline of industrial experience. The African himself had little chance of entering the market economy. He lacked the background needed for modern industrial organization and found difficulty in adopting the tempo of modern industrial activity.

Professor Leduc emphasized that the choice between large-scale and small-scale industries was largely a matter of the type of industries concerned and the nature of the activity involved.

Dr. Wade thought that small-scale and large-scale industries were not alternatives. The definition itself was bound up with a number of factors — the character of the market, the degree of mechanization, the relative costs at different levels of output. In some parts of Africa there was hostility, not only to the development of large-scale private capitalism, but also to the development of small industries under private ownership. There were many who preferred to see the development of co-operative enterprise.

Professor Peacock suggested that one of the ways in which small-scale industry developed was through trading activities, progressively supplemented by small-scale manufacturing.

Dr. Okigbo argued that, where under-employment was normal, any additional employment represented a social gain. Private saving was too small and the need of an owner to invest in expanding small-scale industry was a means of evoking it. The objective, he thought, should be to organize large-scale, medium-scale, and small-scale industries so that they were complementary. Small-scale industry led to a wider dispersal of technical knowledge as well as a widening of the base of capital-ownership. Mere financial assistance was not enough. The provision of technical assistance was equally necessary. But it was an undoubted help if new small-scale industries could be based on existing crafts. Small-scale industry had the further advantage that it was capable of wider regional diffusion, so that more equal expansion of the national economy was possible.

Professor Williams thought that one should distinguish between the firm which considered the market and the craftsman who thought in terms of his product. The need was to encourage the former kind of enterprise. He thought that one should bravely develop industry first and let skills develop to meet the needs for them.

Mr. Beheiry suggested that while experience elsewhere showed that large-scale and small-scale industry could co-exist, it was not so clear that that was the case in Africa. Their attempts to develop hand-weaving in the Sudan had not been successful and they had found it more profitable to export the raw cotton. It was largely a matter of the size of the market and of the levels of transport costs, inward and outward. African rural communities were small in numbers and poor in incomes. He thought that large-scale industries, by creating incomes and demands, would give better opportunities for improving skills.

Dr. Vopicka emphasized the potential value of small-scale co-operative enterprises. In his view successful development of small-scale industry depended on two things. First, it had to be based on a form of ownership which would provide sufficient incentive under the specific conditions of small-scale industry. Second, the small-scale industry had to be based on a form of ownership which would permit the continuous adoption of progressive technologies — in some cases capital intensive. He thought that these conditions could best be met by the co-operative form of ownership.

Dr. Vopicka illustrated his argument from his experience of the Czechoslovakian Socialist Republic where there were, at present, some eight hundred producer co-operatives, employing 120,000 people, and achieving successful economic results. And however important small-scale industry might be, there was also the need for large-scale industry as a basis for the rapid growth of any modern economy. He agreed with Dr. Singer that large- and small-scale industries had to be developed in parallel in African countries. He did not, however, agree that the choice was between foreign large-scale industries and African small-scale industries. Such development would be contrary to the political independence of Africa ; it would be a kind of neo-colonialism. The problem was to give financial and technical assistance in full accordance with independence. He thought that state enterprises with foreign loans and foreign technical assistance provided the best solution.

Professor Stanley argued that aggressive salesmanship was necessary to enlarge the market. Crafts had a very limited market, transport costs, moreover, introduced an element of imperfection in a country where population was very sparse. The location of industries was very important and should be determined by the market and not by political or sentimental considerations.

Professor Bézy believed that economic progress in Africa must depend predominantly on a transformation of the attitudes of Africans to the modern industrial society. He thought that large-scale industry did much more than small-scale to bring about this transformation. If many workers were employed in a few large centralized concerns they were much more influenced. In regard to location of industry, he thought that the importance of external economies must be remembered. Both in Katanga and in the Léopoldville area the costs of setting up new industrial undertakings were significantly reduced by the existence of service industries. This also had the effect of facilitating closer integration of the economy.

Dr. Cookson insisted that the chief characteristic of economic development was chaos and brutality. History had shown the truth of this. Whatever the strains involved, one should be prepared to bring labour into cities as an aid to development. Small-scale industry helped the creation of entrepreneurship. He thought that extensive credit facilities would be necessary.

Professor Fauvel underlined the possible contribution of co-operative forms of organization. Both workers' co-operatives and state-organized co-operatives had a part to play. *Dr. Gavrilov* elaborated the possible forms of co-operative undertakings.

Dr. Yudelman reminded the Conference of the extent to which the distributive system was in the hands of small traders. It was very difficult for the small-scale industry to provide incentives to the small trader to handle and stock the goods. There was the impression that small-scale industry was preferred because the agricultural sector would have difficulty in maintaining itself in competition with large-scale production. He did not believe that this was the case.

Mr. Moran argued that the rôle of small-scale industry depended on the state of the economy, and recalled Eugene Staley's definition. The functional characteristics of small-scale industry required us to give them special attention. The research programme with which he had been associated aimed at evolving a well-balanced programme of industrial development — with a balance of urban and rural, of traditional and modern.

Dr. Singer agreed with Dr. Okigbo regarding the desirability of ensuring a share for different regions of a country in its industrial development, both on grounds of welfare and of equity. In many countries (he instanced Turkey as one) there were problems of seasonal peaks and troughs in employment, associated with the concentration of labour in harvesting. Small-scale industries could better adapt themselves to these. In trying to see the part to be played by small-scale industries he had not been primarily concerned with the immediate present, but rather with their possible contribution to long-term self-sustaining growth, given the development of local institutions. He believed that, as had been shown by the experience of such countries as Czechoslovakia, small-scale industry could supply the key to industrial development.

Chapter 24

MONETARY AND FISCAL POLICY IN RELATION TO AFRICAN DEVELOPMENT [1]

BY

ALAN T. PEACOCK
University of Edinburgh

I. INTRODUCTION : THE SCOPE OF THIS PAPER

THE purpose of this paper is to review the structure of the fiscal systems of certain African economies, to consider how far a 'successful' fiscal policy is possible under African conditions, and to examine how far the existing fiscal structures might have to adapt themselves in order to make fiscal policy more effective.

The term 'fiscal policy' is used in a fairly wide sense. Following recent discussion of fiscal problems in a dynamic setting it is taken to cover budgetary measures designed to promote and, if possible, to accelerate the rate of economic growth in individual economies, while at the same time seeking to prevent wide fluctuations in incomes. As we shall argue later, it is difficult to separate these two objectives in practice, and it is a moot point whether they are always compatible with each other.

Africa South of the Sahara contains economies of differing degrees of economic and political development, and each economy has distinct problems of its own. Further, they differ in the extent to which documentation of economic trends is available. This paper concentrates on the type of conditions and problems found in British colonial and ex-colonial territories. This means that South Africa is excluded, as are the Portuguese colonial territories. South Africa's economic conditions and problems are difficult to discuss in the context of the paper, and lack of data accounts for the omission of the Portuguese territories. Incidental reference is made to the Belgian Congo.

[1] I am much indebted to Mrs. S. Andic for assistance in preparing the tables, and to Mr. I. G. Stewart for comments and criticism.

II. FISCAL STRUCTURE

As I propose to build a simple model designed to illustrate the problems of fiscal policy under African conditions, it is necessary to found it on certain general features of the structure of the economies considered. In any attempt to describe these features allowance must be made for the lack of relevant information, particularly data in social accounting form.[1]

In Table 1 a rough measure is provided of the extent of government intervention by fiscal means. Government expenditure is expressed as a percentage of Gross Domestic Product.

TABLE 1

GOVERNMENT EXPENDITURES AS PERCENTAGE OF GROSS DOMESTIC PRODUCT AT FACTOR COST, 1950–8

(Percentages)

Country or Territory	1950	1951	1952	1953	1954	1955	1956	1957	1958
Federation of Rhodesia and Nyasaland	21·7	21·0	22·0	26·8	25·4	24·9	27·0	31·1	n.a.
Kenya	n.a.	n.a.	n.a.	n.a.	28·2	25·8	24·1	22·0	21·8
Tanganyika	n.a.	n.a.	n.a.	n.a.	18·1	19·4	18·6	17·4	17·2
Uganda	11·2	12·8	14·9	17·5	17·3	18·5	19·2	20·3	n.a.
Mauritius	14·4	15·4	17·6	17·9	20·1	21·3	20·6	22·8	n.a.
Ghana	n.a.	n.a.	n.a.	n.a.	14·7	17·5	17·1	16·9	16·7
Nigeria	5·3	n.a.	6·1	n.a.	n.a.	n.a.	11·3	n.a.	n.a.
Belgian Congo	14·6	16·6	18·2	20·4	22·1	23·0	25·0	28·6	n.a.

Note: n.a. = not available.

Three features in this table deserve notice. The first is that, speaking very generally, the proportion of government expenditure to GDP has increased quite considerably over the last decade. The second is that there have been fluctuations in the size, from year to year, around the upward trend. The third feature is that, with the

[1] The main sources used are : United Nations, *Economic Survey of Africa since 1950* (1960) ; UN, *Yearbook of National Accounts Statistics* (1957 and 1958) ; P. Ady and M. Courcier, *Systems of National Accounts in Africa*, OEEC (1960) ; *Annual Financial Reports and Estimates* for the Central African Federation, Kenya, Uganda, Tanganyika, Ghana, and Nigeria ; *Annual Estimates of Gross Domestic Product* for Kenya, Tanganyika, and Uganda ; *Economic Surveys* for Ghana and Nigeria ; Federation of Rhodesia and Nyasaland, *Monthly Digest of Statistics Supplement, National Income of the Federation, 1954–58*. The paper was completed before the appearance of the *Economic Commission for Africa Bulletin*, No. 2, 1961, which contains an extensive study of the structure of government revenues and expenditures in African countries.

important exception of Nigeria, the public sector is in some cases considerably larger (as measured by our ratio) in these African countries today than it is in a number of important less-developed countries in South America and Asia. For example, government expenditure as percentage of domestic product was 14·1 per cent in India (1956), 14·9 per cent in Pakistan (1956), 15·5 per cent in Argentina (1956), 12·5 per cent in Brazil (1957), and 14·3 per cent in Chile (1957).

It would be tempting to discuss the origins of these features in detail, but only a few general remarks can be made in this context. The first feature reflects the increasing emphasis on intervention, designed to increase economic growth in colonial and ex-colonial territories, in common with other developing countries. The second feature is more difficult to explain, and probably a general explanation covering all countries would be implausible. In some cases it reflects the dependence of the size of the public sector on fluctuating sources of income, coupled with the fact that it may be difficult to offset concomitant fluctuations in expenditure by government action because of the institutional and political barriers to a deficit spending policy. Even in cases where countries have had considerable reserves in sterling securities, they may have been unwilling to realize them because of the fear of capital losses. On the other hand, a fall (rise) in the size of the public sector relative to GDP may simply reflect the rise (fall) in the relative share of non-monetary output in GDP which will not bring with it a concomitant expansion (contraction) in revenue to finance expenditure. The third feature may perhaps be explained by the relatively short history of these countries as political units as compared to South American and Asian countries. In consequence, we would expect that a much greater effort is necessary to produce a minimum provision of social overhead capital. These efforts have been helped, of course, by the strong support given by loans and grants from the British government and by the existence of considerable sterling reserves available for the finance of government services as a result of war-time prosperity.

A functional breakdown of these figures of government expenditure is also of interest, and an attempt is made to produce the relevant data in Table 2.

At first sight it might be thought that the relatively small amount of expenditure necessary for defence purposes (although this may only be a temporary phenomenon) gives these African countries an advantage over other developing countries. Nevertheless, in countries of vast size and difficult terrain, such as Tanganyika and Nigeria, the costs of administration are bound to be high and, what is important

TABLE 2

AVERAGE DISTRIBUTION OF GOVERNMENT EXPENDITURE
BY FUNCTIONAL CATEGORIES FOR SELECTED AFRICAN ECONOMIES
(Percentages)

	Uganda (1950–8)	Mauritius (1950–8)	Fed. of Rhodesia and Nyasaland (1954–8)	Ghana (1949–54)	Kenya (1951–9)	Nigeria (1949–59)	Tanganyika (1950–9)
Administration and other	19·2	24·8	25·7	23·3	19·8	25·2	25·5
Law and order	7·5	8·2	1·6	5·9	12·3	6·4	10·1
Defence	2·8	1·7	8·4	2·9	3·9	4·7	3·0
Economic services	12·3	15·7	28·3	24·9	16·7	16·0	17·9
Social services	22·3	32·5	24·0	20·2	17·9	4·0	23·9
Education	13·2	13·4	11·2	12·1	11·3	1·1	14·2
Health	7·2	10·7	12·5	6·6	5·5	2·3	8·6
Other	1·9	8·4	0·3	1·5	1·1	0·6	1·1
Public works	19·9	8·6	5·9	13·7	5·1	11·3	8·3
Miscellaneous	15·9	8·5	6·1	9·1	3·4	32·4	11·3
Other*	—	—	—	—	20·8	—	—
Total	100·0	100·0	100·0	100·0	100·0	100·0	100·0

* Emergency Fund Contribution in Kenya.

for our later argument, are fairly inflexible in character. The most important feature of this table, relevant to our investigation, is its manifestation of a philosophy of development which includes other goals than economic advancement. While a case can easily be made for health and education expenditure on economic grounds, the justification for the relatively large expenditures on these services is not made solely in terms of their economic contribution. Obviously, education is viewed as a means for promoting political development and health in terms of its effects on morbidity and mortality rates. In considering fiscal policy, with its emphasis upon variations in expenditures, as a means of mitigating fluctuations in incomes, the existence of other policy objectives reflected in social expenditures is ignored by the economist at his peril, although he is likely to be more aware than other technical experts — doctors, and educationists — of the inconsistencies in policy which are likely to arise if the claims on resources used for these services are not subject to the opportunity cost rule.

The composition of government revenue is also important in any review of stabilization measures. The revenue side of the account is summarized in Table 3. There are basic similarities in the tax structure of all the countries considered. The first is the heavy reliance on import duties as a source of revenue, which is, of course, a common feature in developing countries. While the income tax varies considerably as a percentage of revenue in different cases, it is important in all of them. It must be remembered in this connection that a very considerable part of the receipts from income tax comes from companies. For example, in 1958, the percentages of income tax payable by companies in Uganda was 57 per cent, in Tanganyika 46 per cent, and in Kenya 44 per cent. There is also one important apparent difference and that is the part played by export duties in financing government. However, it is to be noted that the export duty is, in effect, a substitute for the income tax in those countries in which a large part of monetary income is earned by peasant producers.

A great deal more information is required if a full-scale assessment is to be made of the fiscal policy problems of these countries. It would be useful to be able to provide a satisfactory breakdown of government expenditure as between current and capital expenditure, and a breakdown according to the sectoral source of purchases as would be found in an input-output table, and one according to the type of asset purchased. It would be useful also to be able to have a flow-of-funds system in order to examine the financial private and government capital formation in detail. For few countries is it

TABLE 3

COMPARATIVE STRUCTURE OF GOVERNMENT REVENUE
IN SELECTED AFRICAN COUNTRIES
(Percentages)

	Ghana	Fed. of Rhodesia and Nyasaland	Nigeria	Uganda	Kenya	Mauritius	Tanganyika
Income tax	13·4	47·5	11·5	10·6	25·8	27·6	20·8
Other taxes on income	2·7	—	0·3	3·8	5·6	3·1	13·1
Estate duty	—	†	—	0·2	0·9*	0·9	0·3
Export duties	33·0	21·0	21·9	34·0	1·2	0·2	2·9
Import duties	29·3	5·9	39·8	20·3	24·6	23·2	29·0
Taxes on expenditure	3·1	11·0	6·3	9·5	13·9	23·6	13·2
Fees, etc.	5·9	0·9	5·3	4·5	6·2	12·9	5·5
Income from government property	5·2		6·2	3·7	4·5	3·3	9·4
Grants	4·6	0·2	3·4	1·7	9·2	3·1	0·2
Other	2·8	13·5	5·3	11·7	8·1	2·1	5·5
Total	100·0	100·0	100·0	100·0	100·0	100·0	100·0

* Includes Taxes on Land.   † Included under Taxes on expenditure.

Notes : Ghana—Averages of 1949/50–1958/9.
Federation of Rhodesia and Nyasaland—Averages of 1954/6–1958/9.
Nigeria—Averages of 1949/50–1958/9.
Uganda—Averages of 1949–1958/9.
Kenya—Averages of 1951–1958/9.
Mauritius—Averages of 1949/50–1956/7.
Tanganyika—Averages of 1947–1957/8.

659

possible to obtain satisfactory information on these matters, and comparisons in satisfactory form are almost impossible to make.

However, one or two general points about fiscal structure can be added to those already made and may be useful to bear in mind in the later discussion. The first is that capital expenditure as a percentage of total public expenditure is relatively high, being generally as much as 25 per cent and in the Central African Federation it has been well over 30 per cent. The second point is that gross fixed investment by government may be as much as 40 per cent of the total and in some countries for some years it appears to have been considerably more. The third is that a good deal of government capital expenditure has been financed from sources other than the surplus on current account. In East African countries heavy reliance has been placed in recent years on loan issues in the London market, while in Ghana and Nigeria the marketing board surpluses have made substantial contributions. In Ghana alone, the marketing boards over the period 1954–8 provided something like 20 per cent of the finance for government capital formation. A fourth point is that the predominant form of government capital formation is building and constructional work which the government 'produces' itself. A final point is that, as a large producer of capital goods, the government automatically becomes a major buyer of imports of materials for constructional purposes.

III. FISCAL POLICY AND ECONOMIC GROWTH

The practitioner in public finance in search of suitable models of economic growth to demonstrate the influence of government budgets on a developing economy will find a bewildering variety of wares. He will also find that these models can be used to support policies ranging from *laissez-faire* to the most extensive planning. What is he to do ? If the theorists and the econometricians disagree, what guidance should the mere applied economist follow ?

Perhaps the situation is not quite so bad as it looks. There is fairly general agreement about the forces which can be selected as likely to be important in determining those rates of growth. Disagreement centres in the relative strength of these forces at different stages of development. Output, it may be agreed, is a function of the quality and quantity of labour, the amount and composition of capital (including land as capital for our purpose), and technical progress. In developing economies, 'exogenous' forces, such as the terms of trade and the weather, play a vital part. The sources of disagreement are of relative importance of one factor of production, or more technically, the value of the exponents in the production functions, and the structure of the production functions themselves.

A very simple model of growth, including certain transactions of the public sector, will be employed in this contribution. It is based on a Domar-type model, but it is designed as much to show the limitations of this form of model building as to utilize it as a guide to fiscal action. The model initially assumes that there is no difficulty in reaching full capacity of resources caused by insufficiency of demand, and that the economy can call forth available resources without causing such a degree of inflation that the general expectation of it leads to price speculation and to the export of capital.

In the simple Domar model, the rate of change in real national product is a linear function of the rate of change in the capital stock. It may be assumed that the size of the capital stock can be influenced by the public sector in two ways : (i) by the investment undertaken by the government itself ; and (ii) by the influences operating through the tax system which affect investment decisions, as, for example, the taxation of companies. This does not rule out of account other methods by which the government may influence production functions in the economy, but these other methods cannot easily be made explicit in the Domar case.

The model embodying the relevant transactions of the public sector can be set out as follows :

$$\lambda(Y_n^R - Y_{n-1}^R) = I_{n-1}^R$$

where $\quad\quad Y^R$ = real national product
$\quad\quad\quad\quad I^R$ = real investment (net)
$\quad\quad\quad\quad \lambda$ = incremental capital/output ratio.

Let us assume that the level of investment in real terms consists of government investment which is a fixed proportion of real national product and of private investment which is equal to undistributed profits after the deduction of taxation at a proportional rate. Then

$$I_{n-1} = b Y_{n-1}^R(1 - t) + g_i Y_{n-1}^R$$

where $\quad\quad b$ = proportion of undistributed real national income
$\quad\quad\quad\quad t$ = proportional tax rate
$\quad\quad\quad\quad g_i$ = proportion of real national product devoted to government investment (net).
$\quad\quad\quad\quad b, t,$ and $g_i < 1$.

By substitution we got a first order homogeneous difference equation with constant coefficients. The general solution is

$$Y_n^R = \left(1 + \frac{1}{\lambda}[b(1 - t) + g_i]\right)^n \cdot Y_o \quad . \quad\quad . \quad\quad . \quad (1)$$

which may be written in the form

$$\frac{\Delta Y}{Y} = \frac{1}{\lambda}[b(1-t) + g_i].$$

As it stands, the model is an advertisement for the 'big push' method of increasing growth. Raising the level of investment causes a proportional increase in the rate of growth of real output and this can be done by fiscal means either by increasing g_i or by lowering t.[1]

This model is, of course, far too simple, although it suggests a mode of approach which can be explored further with fruitful results. Even simple modifications of this model throw doubts on the popular philosophy of 'big push' if African countries are to rely largely on themselves to raise their rate of economic growth.

The first modification in the model is designed to take account of the fact that real domestic and real national product may differ considerably in African countries. At this degree of aggregation it seems reasonable enough to make both private and government investment a function of real national product and to assume that real national product is a constant proportion of real domestic product (D^r). Put in another way, the net incomes paid abroad, such as profits repatriated by foreign companies, rises in proportion to real domestic product, or the distribution of income between foreign and domestic income receivers is constant. This assumption can easily be modified and linearity is only assumed for the sake of simplicity.

Defining D^r as a real domestic product, then

$$Y^r = zD^r \text{ where } z < 1 \quad . \quad . \quad . \quad . \quad (2)$$

In order to introduce subsequent modifications, something needs to be said about the incremental capital/output ratio. This ratio may differ widely for countries with the same share of gross fixed capital formation in gross domestic product.[2] Allowing for possible statistical errors, this suggests that close attention should be paid to other factors of production.

The usual way of taking account of these other factors is to employ a more sophisticated type of production function, for example, one of the Cobb-Douglas type which explicitly introduces labour and

---

[1] This is something of a caricature, because 'big push' theories which emphasize the external economies produced by government investment also imply the lowering of the value of λ through changes in the composition of investment.

[2] On this point, see *World Economic Survey 1959*, United Nations : Department of Economic and Social Affairs, 1960, pp. 73-5. I have no comparisons as between African countries, but the *Survey* instances Ghana and Turkey. The proportion of gross fixed capital formation to gross domestic product for the period 1950-8 was about 12 per cent in both cases, but the annual rate of growth of output was 4 per cent in the case of Ghana and 8 per cent in the case of Turkey.

a 'trend factor' to allow for innovations and technical progress :

$$P_n = a \, . \, L\alpha \, . \, K\beta \, . \, (1+\gamma)^n \qquad . \qquad . \qquad . \qquad (3)$$

where P, L, and K are indices for output, manpower, and real capital respectively, α, β, and a are parameters, and $(1+\gamma)^n$ the 'trend factor'.[1] It is difficult to imagine that the 'trend factor' is of major importance in Africa or that it can be influenced appreciably by government expenditure, but it seems sensible to bear in mind the question of the quantity and quality of the labour force in considering the influence of fiscal policy on growth.

This slightly more sophisticated model still assumes that the incremental capital/output ratio, if not fixed, will not vary widely and will be positive. However, the little evidence we have suggests that the value of ratio may be subject to tremendous variations in the short run and that it may be impossible to discern any definite trend in its value. As 'conventional' development planning is divided up into five-year periods, this disturbing factor has an important bearing on fiscal policy. Table 4 illustrates this point :

TABLE 4

SHORT-RUN INCREMENTAL CAPITAL/OUTPUT RATIOS

	Nigeria	Ghana	Belgian Congo	Tangan-yika	Rhodesia and Nyasaland	Kenya	Uganda
1951	0·7	—	1·1	—	—	—	—
1952	0·9	—	16·4	—	—	—	—
1953	3·6	—	3·0	—	—	—	—
1954	1·1	—	49·0	—	—	—	—
1955	3·0	−3·3	3·6	36·6	14·8	2·7	2·6
1956	−5·6	1·5	9·8	10·9	1·9	7·0	1·9
1957	2·9	3·3	5·8	7·2	3·2	8·8	4·7
1958	—	−2·0	—	20·2	−16·2	57·0	−33·0
1959	—	—	—	3·2	—	—	18·0

These large variations can hardly be explained by statistical errors or by shifts in the composition of investment or in the size, structure, and quality of the labour force. It seems fairly safe to argue that they emphasize the importance of factors beyond the immediate control of these economies, notably, weather conditions and the international price level.

I have tried to bring together this argument in a simplified diagram. In Quadrant (I), we draw the investment function according

[1] For an interesting discussion of the use of such a model, with incidental reference to African conditions, see *The Economic World Balance*, by Thorkil Kristensen and others, chap. vii.

to the investment function embodied in Equation (1). Investment is a linear function of national income (although this is not a necessary assumption) and a rise in government investment increases the slope of the function. Quadrant (II) provides a device by which we can depict the increase in K produced by the increase in investment. In Quadrant (III), however, we draw a series of curves representing the relationship between K and D^R, on the assumption

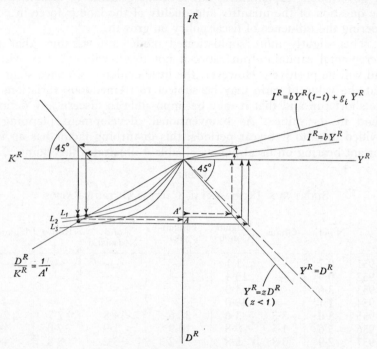

AA' = Terms of Trade "Correction"

of given amounts of labour such that $L_3 > L_2 > L_1$. In other words, for a given amount of capital, increasing the supply of labour increases D^R, but by a smaller percentage than the increase in labour. Alternatively, we can depict the relation between K^R and D^R on the assumption that the labour supply is fixed, such that the percentage increase in D^R gives us an approximation to Equation (3), except that we do not include the trend factor. It follows that D^R will only increase by the same percentage as K_d^R increases if $\alpha + \beta = 1$ and labour and capital increase by the same percentage.

If there were no further factors affecting real output, then the real increase in national product produced by the increase in investment would be derived via Quadrant (IV) by drawing a 45° line so that real domestic and real national product would be identical. However, real domestic product has first of all to be 'corrected' in order to allow for changes in the terms of trade which may exercise a major influence on the economy, and allowance must also be made for net incomes paid abroad, which are likely to be positive, so that real national product or income is less than real domestic product or income, as illustrated in Equation (2).

The firm lines depict the kind of situation assumed in the simple Domar case. The hatched line depicts an extreme case where the labour force does not grow at as fast a rate as capital, the terms of trade 'correction' is negative and the coefficient z in Equation (2) is less than unity. In other words, the nexus is severed between the acceleration in investment growth by fiscal means and the acceleration in income. Of course, these assumptions can be altered so that the rate of growth in income would be faster than the rate of growth in capital formation.

The important and rather disturbing conclusion of this analysis, if it is accepted as a fair indication of the kind of forces at work in African economies, is the fact that influential factors governing the pace of economic advance may be largely beyond the control of government policy as operated through the fiscal system.

Influencing the terms of trade depends upon international action of some kind and is beyond the scope of this study. Making the economy less dependent on weather conditions is certainly something which the public sector can concern itself with. The development of communications can bring about movements of goods and persons so that regional areas become less dependent on local production. Irrigation schemes can to some extent relieve periodic water shortages, and prevent flooding. Land conservation measures can prevent natural as well as man-made soil erosion. It is at least being realized that useful procedures can be developed for assessing the costs and benefits of such schemes using economic criteria, although there is bound to be a prodigious element of uncertainty embedded in such calculations.[1]

Even if it can be assumed that the 'exogenous' influences on the process of economic growth mentioned in the previous paragraph can be ignored, and discussion is confined to the influences on growth expressed in a Cobb-Douglas function of the kind described by Equation (3), then our analysis suggests that we should be somewhat sceptical of the notion that fiscal policy designed to accelerate growth

---

[1] For a good example of a calculation of this sort related to irrigation schemes see *The Economic Development of Tanganyika*, I.B.R.D., Mission, Johns Hopkins Press, Baltimore, 1961, Annex VII.

should concentrate solely on investment in fixed capital. In some of the territories considered, notably Nigeria and the Federation of the Rhodesias and Nyasaland, the growth in manpower will be very considerable over the next few years, and it seems sensible to consider how far fiscal measures might be used to encourage a more efficient use of this relatively abundant factor of production. Two common features of African fiscal policies are (i) encouragement of private investment through accelerated depreciation allowances and (ii) public investment in large-scale 'lumpy' projects such as the Kariba Dam scheme. So far as (i) is concerned, the alternatives forgone are possibly underrated, for example revenue which would finance further improvements in the quality of labour through education or tax relief for personal income receivers which might improve incentives. At least it is arguable that tax policy should not discriminate as between factor uses so that if enterprises are to be given some form of encouragement through fiscal measures, it should be through measures of the 'tax-holiday' kind rather than through discrimination in favour of capital-intensive production.[1]

It is realized that this argument must be qualified in order to take account of at least two complications. Imperfections in the labour market may mean that the relative abundance of labour is not reflected in low real wage rates in industry. It may also be the case that technical conditions may result in a low elasticity of substitution between capital and labour. However, some attention deserves to be paid to fiscal policies which place more emphasis on improving the quality and quantity of the one abundant factor available in African countries, policies which may be justified in any case on social and political grounds.

So far as (ii) is concerned, it is at least arguable that many forms of public expenditure for developmental purposes are not bound by technical conditions which demand capital-intensive production.[2] Construction work, notably the building of airfields and roads, produces an obvious example, and, as has been pointed out, these are major elements in government expenditure.

IV. FISCAL POLICY AND ECONOMIC STABILITY

So far it has been assumed that fiscal policy designed to influence the rate of growth is not adversely affected by changes in aggregate

[1] Given African conditions, I do not think I would go quite so far as Dr. Prest, who argues for subsidies to industry in order to increase labour-intensity. See his *Fiscal Survey of the British Caribbean*, 1957, Colonial Office Research Series, No. 27, p. 102.
[2] On this point, see the reference to conditions in the Central African Federation in *The Wealth of Three Nations*, Salisbury, 1960, prepared by the Phoenix Group.

demand. Aggregate expenditure, including expenditure by foreigners on exports, is not so low that resources are not fully utilized or so high that the expectation of continual price rises lowers the rate of saving and with it the 'desired' investment rate.

Fiscal policy designed to combine both stabilization and growth objectives is bound to be conditioned by two kinds of influence. The first is the relative priorities given to the objectives of policy and the second is the economic environment in which fiscal policy has to operate. In considering these two influences, it may be useful to contrast the position of African countries with that of developed countries.

The objective of stabilization must, of course, be matched with other objectives in developing as in developed countries which may place constraints on the type of tax and expenditure changes which are associated with control of prices and incomes. The first of these is the achievement of an 'equitable' distribution of the burdens and benefits of the government budget. The problem in this case is not only the obvious one of matching the desirable 'vertical' distribution of income with the requirements of an efficient stabilization policy, but also one of allowing for the 'equal treatment of equals' or the achievement of the desirable 'horizontal' equity. In developing countries in which a large part of income may be received in non-monetary form, the problem of horizontal equity is a very real one and it may be all too easy to 'pick on' those who can be easily 'got at' by the tax machine because of the difficulty of applying a general tax formula.[1]

The second of these objectives is concerned with political organization. There is a growing interest in federal government in Africa, but the price of federation may be limitations imposed on fiscal control at the centre.[2] The same problem is bound to arise in looser forms of economic union in which the political unit is still the individual territorial government.[3]

The first of these objectives has obvious implications not only for the distribution of the benefits of government expenditure but also for its level. The level of government expenditure will also be determined by the view taken of the government's responsibility for maintaining and possibly accelerating the rate of growth. Whether or not the government uses a fair proportion of national resources for these purposes, it is reasonable to suppose that its social and economic programmes will be based on the assumption that plans

[1] In time, a combination of popular government and a more educated electorate may make this kind of discriminatory action more difficult to execute.

[2] On this point, see particularly the *Report of the Advisory Committee on the Review of the Constitution of Rhodesia and Nyasaland*, Cmnd. 1148/1960, chapter 9, and the *Report of the Fiscal Commission of Nigeria*, Cmnd. 481/1958, para. 28.

[3] See *Report of the Economic and Fiscal Commission on East Africa*, Cmnd. 1279/61, paras. 200-2.

can be made for several years ahead. The important consequence for fiscal policy is that contra-cyclical variations in government expenditure may be difficult to operate if these expenditures are a large part of the total budget and if these plans are rigidly adhered to. In short, given these conditions, stabilization policy effected through the budget must be largely conducted through variations in tax yields which bring in their train budget surpluses or deficits. In the case of developed economies some element of flexibility exists in government expenditures which may make it possible to meet in part the demands of a contra-cyclical policy without requiring major modifications in long-term plans. Thus some transfer payments such as unemployment benefit and assistance payments will vary contra-cyclically without requiring changes in policy, and, with large investment already made in social overhead capital, the temporary postponement of a new capital project or of maintenance of existing projects in a boom may be put into operation without causing major damage to long-term plans. However, there are no automatic stabilizers of any consequence on the expenditure side of the budget of African economies comparable to those operating in developed economies, and the postponement or cutting back of projects as an anti-cyclical device may have major repercussions on development policy. As we shall see later, even if it were considered desirable in African economies to vary government expenditure in order to stabilize the economy in the short run, there are circumstances in which it would not be possible to do so because of the nature of the monetary system and also circumstances in which, even if it were possible, the policy would be largely ineffective.

While the pursuit of other objectives must modify the extent to which the budget can be used solely as an instrument of economic stabilization, it cannot be assumed, even if stabilization were the main objective, that there would not be major technical problems to be met. In considering the second set of influences on the operation of a compensatory fiscal policy, it is perhaps useful once again to compare and contrast developed and developing countries.

There is no need to underline the difficulties encountered in forecasting price and income movements in both developed and developing countries, especially in the case of countries relying heavily on foreign trade. Because of these difficulties, economists have often argued that the budget should be designed to act as an automatic compensator,[1] and that this form of compensation is best achieved by progressive taxes on incomes. Automatic compensators un-

---

[1] For a full account of the theory of 'built-in' budgetary flexibility, see R. A. Musgrave, *Theory of Public Finance*, chapter 21.

doubtedly exist in African countries and are likely to become more effective with the extension of the personal income tax combined with the introduction of speedier methods of collection through pay-as-you-go schemes. Moreover, measures designed to stabilize the incomes of primary producers and to tax incomes indirectly through export duties may have similar effects. However, in the short period at least, there will be obvious limits to the extension of tax measures designed to ensure automatic stabilization in economies in which a large proportion of the working population is engaged in subsistence agriculture, in petty trading, and in small-scale industry. Moreover, a crucial part is played in the system by companies. There are likely to be considerable delays in the settlement of tax liabilities of companies. The 'automatic' effect will work properly only if companies relate their current spending decisions to accruing tax liabilities and not to taxes actually being paid.

The main difference governing the operation of fiscal policy in developing as distinct from developed countries, lies in the monetary effects of budget surpluses or deficits. We can distinguish two kinds of monetary system in operation in African countries — the currency board system and the 'modified' system. In the first-named, which is usually in operation during the pre-independence period (an important exception being the Central African Federation), the currency has full sterling backing and it is not possible for the government to create money (at least to any appreciable extent); the banks are likely to be foreign-owned and their lending policies are designed to conform to the objective of making profits for the banking concern as a whole; the main savers are companies and government. In this situation the government is very much in the position of a local authority in the United Kingdom, except for the fact that it can impose taxes on goods crossing its borders and may exercise control over capital movements to countries outside the sterling area in collaboration with the British Treasury. Under the 'modified' system, the country, now independent, has its own Central Bank and, whether or not it is tied to any international currency or currency area, it is able to have a fiduciary issue. Generally speaking it would be reasonable to assume some control by the Central Bank over the commercial banking system either through the imposition of reserve requirements or the holding of a minimum of deposits with the Central Bank. A short-term bill market is likely to operate but is more doubtful if there will be much opportunity for conducting open-market operations to any extent.[1] With this very rough sketch

[1] For an up-to-date account of recent changes in African monetary systems, see *Economic Bulletin for Africa*, UN Economic Commission for Africa, Vol. 1, No. 1, chapter B/I.

of two different monetary systems in mind, the sequence of events which may confront an African country wishing to use the budget as a stabilizer will now be considered.

It seems sensible to associate the stabilization problem with changes in international economic conditions especially if the first monetary system is in operation. Given the level of households' income, it is fairly safe to argue that the variations possible in the marginal propensity to consume will be slight. The m.p.c. of households will probably be close to unity and the low standard of living must mean that the m.p.c. cannot move downwards to any marked extent. If the marginal propensity to invest by government or firms rises, then this must be associated with a rise in saving, unless the extra investment is financed by imported capital or from accumulated reserves. Thus if reserves are low and capital imports scarce, the initiating force in any change in incomes is likely to be a change in the economic fortunes of export industries.

The conflicts and difficulties in fiscal policy can now be illustrated by two examples. In both samples we assume for the sake of simplicity a fall in export prices. The difference between the examples lies in the assumptions about the type of monetary system.

Consider the case in which a currency board system obtains. Investment is being maintained at a constant rate as shown in our initial model, and then there is an unexpected fall in export prices. The incomes of exporters of primary products will fall, although the fall in national income may be cushioned by a more than proportionate fall in incomes in the form of profits paid abroad. Revenue from export duties or from other direct taxes on exporters falls off. In this kind of situation, if investment is to be maintained at the given constant rate, then companies and the government must be both, willing and able to draw on their currency reserves, or to draw on foreign borrowing. An alternative open to the government is to cut the rate of expenditure on current account, but this will simply reinforce the negative multiplier effects. It is clear that the fall in money incomes may be very difficult to offset in such a situation and that this fall may be a cumulative one if the government's reserves are slim. It is conceivable that a fall in money incomes might bring about a fall in prices, including wage rates, in which case the government might be able to maintain the same *real* rate of expenditure. This seems a doubtful argument. For one thing, government expenditure may have a large import content, and import prices will be completely beyond the control of the government. Further, it is doubtful if money wage rates paid by government would fall, except possibly in the case of the rates of pay for unskilled and casual labour. Administrators, technicians, and clerical staff are unlikely to be affected, at least in the short run.[1]

The sequence of events will be rather different in the second example with the introduction of the 'modified' monetary system. As before, a fall in export prices is assumed, and with it a fall in the incomes of primary producers and a fall in government revenue. However, it is now possible for the government to have a fiduciary issue so that it can adopt a policy of deficit spending. The rate of government spending can be maintained and a fall in the incomes of the private sector can be offset by tax reductions.

Two problems beset a government adopting this remedy. The first is that this policy may do little to restore the lost incomes of those most directly affected by the fall in export prices. Primary producers will only benefit appreciably from tax reliefs if they are able to substitute domestic sales of their produce for foreign sales or are able to grow other crops for the domestic market. Cocoa, coffee, cotton, and sisal are not likely to command domestic sales of anything like the magnitude necessary to offset the decline in export sales. Further, any shift to other lines of production will take a considerable time. It is beyond the scope of this contribution to consider in detail the problems of stabilizing the incomes of particular groups. However, this problem seems to reinforce the arguments for stabilization schemes related to producers' *incomes* and to cast doubt on the desirability of relying on export duties. A stabilization scheme based on incomes fits in with the general requirements of an automatic compensator. Moreover, it gets round the difficulties presented by the equity problem, because although producers have their incomes reduced at the margin in order to mitigate the domestic effects of a boom in export markets, they automatically become beneficiaries in a slump from their own previous efforts. If they are subjected to export duties, they may not only be discriminated against as taxpayers, but they will have no direct claim on the proceeds of the duties (or relief from these duties) in order to finance them through 'bad' times.[2]

The second problem is presented by the monetary effects of

---

[1] It is difficult to document this view, but in the case of Tanganyika, Mr. Dosser and I calculated that in 1954, the final demand for goods and services by government was divided percentagewise as follows : wages and salary payments 69 per cent ; domestic purchase of goods 1 per cent ; imports 30 per cent. See *The National Income of Tanganyika, 1952–54*, Colonial Research Studies, No. 26, Colonial Office, 1958, p. 46.

[2] For a fuller account of the relationship between stabilization schemes for primary and fiscal policy in general, see P. T. Bauer and F. W. Paish, 'The Reduction of Fluctuations in the Incomes of Primary Producers', *Economic Journal*, December 1952. But see also the subsequent discussion of this article in the same journal, September 1953 and December 1954.

deficit spending. The financing of deficits by the printing press in developed countries will usually mean that bank deposits increase and with it the possibility of a multiple expansion in credit. Whether or not economic conditions require this reinforcing effect to government deficit spending, the possibility exists in developed countries of refined methods of control through, for example, open-market operations. These methods are not possible in African countries, except to a very limited extent, because of the absence of a market in long-dated government bonds. However, it seems doubtful whether this problem is an important one at present. The argument presupposes a close link between changes in the supply of currency and bank deposits which may not be the case in countries where the use of the banking system by ordinary citizens, if increasing rapidly, is still limited. Further, it assumes that other methods of control over the supply of money do not operate. There is no need to do more than mention the possibilities of using variations in legal reserve requirements with or without compulsory investment by banks in government bills.[1] Finally, at the moment there seems to be a commendable desire by African governments to deny themselves the use of Central Bank credit as a means of finance, to the extent of defining the limits of such credit by statute. Whether they will show such restraint if development plans are jeopardized by lack of funds will depend upon the view taken not only of the internal effects of credit expansion but of the attitude to such methods adopted by foreign lenders.

V. SOME TENTATIVE CONCLUSIONS AND RECOMMENDATIONS

The analysis in III and IV has been designed to illustrate a way of thinking about the difficult problem of the place of fiscal policy in a development programme rather than to lay down any specific rules for action. The first conclusion is that, even if the assumptions of the analysis are not accepted or the empirical evidence on which it is based requires modification to meet particular circumstances, some kind of model-building, however crude, lies at the back of any development plan.

In the countries considered, the impact of economic thinking on development planning has been rather slight to say the least.

---

[1] For a full discussion of the use of variable reserve requirements, cf. Richard Goode and Richard S. Thorne, 'Variable Reserve Requirements Against Commercial Bank Deposits', International Monetary Fund, *Staff Papers*, April 1959.

Certainly, economic statistics have been improved out of all recognition over the last ten years and the professional examination of past economic trends, often pinned together with annual budget estimates or economic plans, is a welcome innovation. In the preparation of development plans, however, there is little evidence that developed economic techniques are used. Often a statement of a development plan consists of a statement of the cost of particular services arbitrarily classified as development expenditures by the government with an accompanying statement of the expected sources of finance.[1] No explicit attempt is made to explain the underlying assumptions of the plan such as, for example, the dependence of the finance of the plan on the rate of growth of national income and the weighing at the margin of the costs of particular forms of expenditure against the expected benefits.[2] This view of the application of economic analysis does not rely for its acceptance upon the adoption of any particular dogma about economic planning, including the view that the public sector should intervene as little as possible. Nor does it seek to minimize the difficulties involved in economic forecasting, especially under the conditions encountered in developing countries which demand the taking of a view about future international economic and political conditions. The advantage of the forecasting exercise based on economic reasoning is that it forces policy-makers to make clear the assumptions underlying future plans so that the consistency of the plans themselves can be tested.

Once granted the point that much more attention needs to be paid to the application of economic analysis to development planning, the next recommendation relates to the type of analysis to be employed. The analytical part of this contribution has stressed the view that a fiscal policy designed to accelerate economic growth by raising the rate of investment can only be effective in special circumstances which may not be typical of the kind of African countries considered. Much more attention needs to be paid to the other factors upon which economic growth depends. This is not to say that government investment in economic services is ineffective, but merely to stress that while these services may be a necessary condition for development, they are hardly a sufficient one. I have instanced a number of factors which can be brought within the scope of analysis provided by a more general type of aggregate production

---

[1] A typical example is the latest plan for Tanganyika, *Development Plan for Tanganyika 1961/62–1963/64*.

[2] For an interesting critical review of development plans in British Colonies as a whole, see Douglas G. M. Dosser, 'The Formulation of Development Plans in the British Colonies', *Economic Journal*, June 1959, pp. 255-66. Cf. also *Economic Bulletin for Africa*, Vol. 1, No. 1, chapter B/II.

function than the Domar type, but it may be that there are more fundamental influences on growth which need consideration and which are the concern of government action. It is unlikely that many of us would subscribe unconditionally to Adam Smith's dictum — 'little else is requisite to carry a state to the highest degree of opulence from the lowest barbarism, but peace, easy taxes, and a tolerable administration of justice'.[1] However, even in days when African countries demand a much faster rate of advance than Adam Smith had in mind, there is much to be said for emphasizing the importance of political stability and honest administration, not to speak of other non-fiscal aid to development such as land reform consistent with the creation of an efficient system of agriculture. In short, the place of fiscal policy as an aid to accelerated development must be seen as only one of a number of possible courses of action.

If these two recommendations have substance, then it is perhaps of some interest to consider their bearing on the question : what is the appropriate level and distribution of public expenditure in developing countries ? In a well-known article,[2] Professor Lewis and Miss Martin have advanced the proposition that developing countries have a useful frame of reference in a comparison of their distribution of public expenditure with the median expenditures in different functional groups for a selected number of countries. They are careful to stress that this comparison does not enable the planner to answer the question posed, but may stimulate him into inquiry into differences, and one is bound to agree with their view that personal assertion plays a major part in argument about 'appropriate' distribution of expenditure. However, it is doubtful if this kind of comparison has much more than academic value to policy-makers. The appropriate frame of reference of the policy-maker is the aims of policy, their order of priority, and the economic environment in which these aims are to be carried out. Granted differences in aim and differences in economic environment, it would be odd indeed if he did not expect very great differences in the pattern of expenditures. This suggests that if guidance is to be sought from experience of other countries, reference should be most appropriately made to those countries with roughly the same aims, the same ranking of aims in the scale of priorities, and with the same kinds of economic

[1] For the origin of this statement, see Edwin Cannan's Introduction to *The Wealth of Nations*, pp. xxxiv-xxxv.
[2] Alison Martin and W. Arthur Lewis, 'Patterns of Public Revenue and Expenditure', *Manchester School*, September 1956, pp. 203-44. See also comment on this article by E. A. G. Robinson, 'The Size of the Nation and the Cost of Administration', *The Economic Consequences of the Size of Nations* (edited for the International Economic Association by Austin Robinson), 1960.

constraints in operation, *e.g.* dependence on primary production, a population problem, and so on. Yet the sample of countries chosen by Miss Martin and Professor Lewis [1] contains countries at very different stages of development, with marked differences in policy aims and with striking differences in economic and political conditions.

The conclusions reached about the operation of a tolerably successful fiscal policy designed to mitigate fluctuations in incomes are probably unexceptional. The vital rôle of the balance of payments in the multiplier process in African countries immediately suggests that the prerequisite of such a policy is the existence of 'adequate' sterling or foreign exchange reserves built up during the boom periods for primary products and used to maintain the direct purchases of imports which, even in the long run, are likely to be essential for the investment programmes of both public and private enterprise, and which otherwise will be reduced during slumps, either because the government finds itself short of funds or because the primary and secondary falls in private incomes force a cut-back in import demand. If reserves are inadequate to deal with the problem, then government development plans have to be sufficiently flexible to allow for a cut in its import content *pari passu* with the decline in export earnings. These policies may place a considerable strain on the political system firstly because of the temptation to expand government programmes when revenues are buoyant, and secondly because the political prestige of Ministers is bound to be at stake when 'flexibility' requires a slowing-down of development plans which may affect some government departments more than others.

However, it is hardly fitting to lecture the governments of independent countries on the virtues of financial probity, when such virtues are not always conspicuous by their presence in developed countries and, in particular, when certain of the colonial territories, now independent, have suffered from depreciation of their reserves because of the requirement that investments should be held in the form of trustee securities.

While not much can be said by the economist about the problem of devising an efficient financial administration, perhaps something can be added by way of conclusion about the problem of preventing major upsets to development programmes because of international economic fluctuations. As we have seen, in the absence of a developed market for short- and long-term government borrowing at home, the countries considered have had to accumulate surpluses in advance

---

[1] Tanganyika, Uganda, India, Nigeria, Ceylon, Ghana, Jamaica, British Guiana, Colombia, Italy, Trinidad, France, United Kingdom, New Zealand, Sweden, and the U.S.A.

of a period of deficit spending. In periods of difficulty, it was always possible for a colonial territory to borrow from the Joint Colonial Fund or, as was nearly the case with Tanganyika in 1959, to become grant-aided by the British Treasury.

It might be argued that if Britain wishes to continue to take advantage of imports of capital from these countries (assuming they remain in the sterling area), then some kind of guarantee of short-term aid might have to be the corollary. Otherwise, it would be in the interests of these countries to support a scheme like the Triffin Plan which would enable them both to make interest-bearing deposits with the IMF guaranteed against devaluation and to obtain overdraft loans.

Chapter 25

MONETARY AND FISCAL POLICY IN RELATION TO AFRICAN DEVELOPMENT

BY

L. H. SAMUELS
University of the Witwatersrand,
Johannesburg

I. INTRODUCTORY

THE appropriate monetary and fiscal framework for highly organized economies has long been a topic of serious discussion among economists. The unsatisfactory state of the debate has been due to a serious difference of opinion regarding the rôle and working of monetary policy, the relative efficacy of credit and fiscal measures, as well as the objectives of policy. Fluctuations in economic thought are, of course, characteristic of every science, but the convolutions in emphasis during the past three decades in regard to the instruments and objectives of policy are not easy to parallel. The preoccupation of economists with cyclical fluctuations since the 'thirties has been superseded, to some extent by the contemporary interest in the growth of an economic system ; indeed, cyclical disturbances are now frequently treated as an outgrowth of a growing economy.

While the debate has proceeded, policy-makers in the less developed areas of the world have been faced with the practical problem of coping with fluctuations in economic activity and growing pressures for increasing output and standards of living of the local populations. Not unnaturally they have been forced to take action, often without a clear realization of the likely consequences of their policies. In the process, they have frequently appropriated ideas and instruments of policy devised for a different economic setting. Thus, in many African territories the potentialities of credit, budgetary, and other measures are frequently discussed in terms of categories of thought of the more 'capitalistic' countries of the West. There is no reason to believe that the expectations aroused by the transplantation of these ideas and weapons of control can be realized. On the contrary, they may simply deflect thought and energies from

677

dealing with the fundamental obstacles which impede the expansion of markets in areas in transition from still largely subsistence economies. The economic, financial, and physical environment of most of the African territories differs greatly from conditions prevailing in other continents or countries. For a large part of Africa the problem is less to regulate the column of activity, incomes, and employment than to enlarge existing growing points and create more productive work for the indigenous people. The majority of the African population is still engaged in traditional forms of activity with tenuous connections with the emerging money and market economies. The village and the countryside remain the core of African life and are likely to remain so for a considerable period of time.

There are great differences in the degree of sophistication in the economic and financial organization of even those territories, which are proceeding most rapidly to a more general use of money as a medium of exchange. At one end of the spectrum are the more advanced economies such as South Africa, which has enjoyed for a number of decades a well-developed commercial and central banking system, financial institutions specializing in different classes of debt, a fiscal system with considerable influence on the flow of aggregate incomes and spending, and, more recently, a rapidly evolving money market. In contrast are those territories which are still in the process of developing financial organizations with an increasing degree of control at the centre. In the Federation, Ghana, and Nigeria, the Currency Board system has in recent years been superseded by central banking institutions with wide powers of credit creation. The establishment of further central banks, which have become symbols of financial independence and maturity, can be increasingly expected as more and more African territories attain political independence.

Orthodox fiscal and central banking techniques devised for a fully monetized economy will be difficult to apply in conditions prevailing in most parts of the African continent. The bulk of the population is engaged in producing foodstuffs, mainly for its own needs, and make little use of monetary instruments. The small-scale nature of peasant farming and the absence of secure titles to land make the provision of rural credit difficult. The stock of money consists largely of currency ; the overdraft and cheque system are hardly known outside the main cities. The credit and capital resources available for the financing of domestic activities are limited by the poverty of most of the territories, while there is a dearth of suitable financial instruments for accumulation.

A proper appraisal of the potentialities of fiscal and credit policy in this environment would require a detailed study of the economic and financial conditions of the different regions and territories. This was out of the question. The present paper, therefore, confines itself to an analysis of certain fundamental problems arising from the still limited economic capacity of the indigenous peoples and their dependence on foreign trade and investment for improving their economic standards. The analysis is framed in general terms. This is, of course, a disadvantage because of the danger of over-simplification and facile generalization.

II. EXPORT INCOMES AND ECONOMIC DEVELOPMENT

The economic achievements of the African territories vary inversely with their success in establishing market economies and economic relations with the outside world. The areas most advanced economically are usually those with the highest volume of interregional and international trade per head of population. These are also the areas which have been most successful in attracting capital from abroad, or in providing, from their own resources, the funds required for building the network of roads, railways, and other forms of communication, the social overheads and all the productive devices necessary for increasing the income-creating capacity of the local populations. Indeed, the most characteristic feature of economic change in Africa is the scale on which customary ways of life are being disrupted as a result of the growth of commercialized and wage-earning activities.

The emergence of a wage-earning economy has proceeded furthest in South Africa. More than two-thirds of the African population is now engaged in modern economic production and the proportion is growing rapidly. The same tendencies are observable in Central, East, and West Africa. The growth of an urban, capitalistic, economic organization is producing serious problems of adjustment in the transition from a tribal to an industrial Western culture ; and the populations are being increasingly subjected to the political ambitions, intellectual influences, and economic incentives familiar in all urban civilizations. There is, in consequence, a growing impatience with present rates of growth and also a resentment against the increasing dependence of African economies on changes in the propensity to consume and invest of more advanced societies. In some of the African territories as much as 30 per cent, or more, of domestic incomes now depend on export production and associated activities. Strong pressures exist, therefore, to insulate the domestic economies against disturbances originating from abroad.

Fluctuations in foreign exchange receipts undoubtedly pose extremely serious political, social, and economic problems for the still largely 'under-developed' territories struggling to sustain the rising cultural and economic aspirations of growing numbers of their population. Whenever export earnings decline sharply, domestic money incomes fall and economic activity tends to slow down markedly. These tendencies are invariably accentuated because the higher export proceeds of a previous period usually give rise with a lag to increased demands for imports. As a result, the export economies are frequently caught in a scissors movement of rising demands for foreign exchange payments and falling export receipts. In the absence of adequate exchange reserves and/or a sufficient inflow of foreign funds, international reserves shrink rapidly and bank liquidity declines, leading to a destruction of bank deposits and a growing stringency in the credit and capital markets.

In periods of rising world demand, the 'terms of trade' of exporting territories shift rapidly in their favour because of relatively low short-run elasticities of supply. International reserves rise rapidly, replenishing the assets of the banks, and thereby increasing their willingness to expand credit. The higher export proceeds percolate throughout the economy through the mechanism of rising money incomes and prices. Domestic demands rise for locally produced products and especially for imports because of a high marginal propensity to import. This may be followed by a serious exchange problem, if large-scale importing happens to coincide with a decline in world demand for foodstuffs and industrial raw materials. This sequence of events has been typical of the post-war pattern in the developed and less developed territories on this continent. The subsequent phase of readjustment is all the more painful, if the inflationary effects of an export boom also stimulate a rising spiral of wages and prices.

III. FLUCTUATIONS IN EXPORT INCOMES : THE PROBLEM AND SOME SUGGESTED REMEDIES

Instability in foreign exchange receipts may be due to crop failures, financial extravagance at home, marketing and price policies which reduce the volume of exports, unfavourable shifts in the 'terms of trade', due to changes in relative demands or to changes in relative costs, adverse movements in capital account transactions, the creation of trade barriers, and so forth. All of these disturbing influences are of a highly complex character, each mutually reacting on one another and having their own 'causes' in an infinite regress. Since the war, the most usual cause of fluctuations has been the instability in export markets. To lend concreteness to the discussion I propose, therefore, to concentrate on this case.

Sharp movements in prices ruling on world markets would not be so serious if variations in crops, or in the output of mineral products, were inversely correlated with such price movements. Except for a few products, however, the terms of sale are beyond the control of the chief exporting countries, while the scope for domestic consumption of exportable goods is limited. A study sponsored by the United Nations [1] some years ago revealed that price and quantity changes have contributed about equally to variations in export earnings of the main commodities entering into international trade.

Improved farming techniques, the eradication of pests and diseases, and similar measures could conceivably eliminate some of the influences contributing to variations in output. But the prospects of mitigating the variety of adventitious factors, which plague the small peasant farmer or even the larger plantations, are not hopeful. On the other hand, a substantial contribution to greater stability in export earnings would be to reduce fluctuations in prices of export products. These price movements reflect, in the main, the variation in demand by the leading industrial countries as a result of sharp movements in fixed investment expenditures and/or fluctuations in stocks held for precautionary or speculative reasons. There is little evidence so far that the developed industrial countries have achieved any conspicuous success in stabilizing their aggregate level of monetary demand.

Proposals are therefore made from time to time for international commodity agreements which visualize the creation of buffer stocks of primary products. Despite the powerful arguments in favour of this idea, little progress has been made in promoting such arrangements. There are undoubtedly considerable financial, administrative and political difficulties in the way of implementing the principle, apart altogether from the difficulties in anticipating the future course of activity and prices. The main obstacle until now appears to have been the almost continuous expansion in demand for commodities, which has not been favourable for the accumulation of stocks on any

[1] See United Nations, *Instability in Exports of Underdeveloped Countries* (New York : United Nations, Department of Economic Affairs, 1952).

scale. If buffer stocks are to be accumulated, this ought to be done in periods of depressed trade and demands, not in times of boom.[1]

The failure to concert international measures for steadying movements in world commodity prices has led to a considerable volume of discussion on the national measures, which could be taken to reduce the effects of fluctuations in export earnings. There are, in principle, a number of devices for neutralizing the impact of variations in foreign exchange proceeds on domestic incomes and the level of employment. Some of these remedies, whatever their theoretical merits, either lack the requisite flexibility, such as changes in customs tariffs, or, like flexible exchange rates, are fraught with danger for a weak, dependent economy unable to maintain economic 'equilibrium'. Other possibilities, such as direct trade controls, are at best in the nature of pseudo-remedies. They cannot deal with the root causes of balance-of-payments difficulties, whether they are due to a fall in export proceeds, or to a level of internal expenditure which is too high in relation to a country's export earnings and the inflow of foreign funds. Indeed, they may perpetuate the very difficulties they seek to cure.

(a) *Import Restrictions*

Import controls, for example, tend to strengthen strong monopoly elements already existing in limited markets, aggravate inflationary tendencies, and reduce the competitive position of the export industries. They also distort existing patterns of spending and stimulate a propensity to import, whenever controls are lifted, in anticipation of a return to import restrcitions. In any case, severe import restrictions are bound to have a most dislocating effect on those African economies which depend heavily on imports for their development programmes and existing standards of consumption.

Except, therefore, as a crisis measure, there is little that can be said for such controls. It is sometimes argued that in the more economically advanced territories such restrictions on imports may stimulate the volume of domestic savings [2] or stimulate capital imports as a result of the fear of loss of markets by exporters. This is theoretically conceivable, but experience of such measures in South Africa is hardly encouraging. Such controls have stimulated not only the growth of foreign-controlled enterprises, but also a large range of local industries, which have increased and not reduced

---

[1] After a lapse of some years, further attempts are now being made to resuscitate the idea.

[2] Cf. *Report of Commission of Enquiry into Policy relating to the Protection of Industries*, U.G. No. 36/1958, p. 21.

the demand for imported raw materials, machinery, and other invest-ment goods. In consequence, South Africa has had to cope with a series of balance-of-payments crises during the post-war years whenever there has been an adverse shift in the 'terms of trade' or in capital account transactions.

(b) *Monetary and Fiscal Policy*

Equally limited are the possibilities of monetary and fiscal measures [1] when used to steady the flow of domestic money incomes, or the flow of external payments and receipts. One has merely to state the conditions for the successful functioning of these techniques of control to perceive their limitations. Ideally, fiscal policy could contribute to income stability by concentrating domestic investment expenditures and the raising or spending of external loans, where they largely finance them, in periods when export proceeds are declining. But the successful execution of such compensatory fiscal policy would require an exceptional degree of foresight in timing such expenditures, and good fortune in raising external loans in the least favourable periods.[2] It would be necessary to anticipate the future course of export prices, the marginal propensities to import, and the amounts likely to be raised from taxation and/or foreign issues. The expansion of bank credit should likewise be undertaken in a period of falling export incomes if the level of aggregate demand is to be sustained. But this is precisely a period when the banking system is least willing to deplete its liquidity further, and when an expansion in bank credit may do little in maintaining the level of economic activity.

The impotence of unwillingness to create credit is not, as is sometimes thought, due simply to the unorganized character of monetary institutions in many of the African territories, or because the largest of the banks are frequently under foreign control. The difficulties facing these economies are more deep-seated : they arise from a deficiency of foreign demand for the products of these territories and an excess demand for foreign currencies. Expansionist credit measures, introduced to offset the stringency in the credit and capital markets, only intensify demands for the scarce and dwindling

[1] Both kinds of policy may be needed and, indeed, are complementary. Except in conditions where the demand for credit is highly inelastic, with respect to move-ments in interest rates, fiscal policy cannot succeed unless it is supported by appropriate changes in credit policy.
[2] Historically, the most favourable opportunities for borrowing funds in the capital markets of the world have been in periods of low interest rates and favour-able changes in activity in the leading industrial countries. Cf. S. H. Frankel, *Capital Investment in Africa*, pp. 92 *et seq.*

supplies of foreign exchange reserves. They therefore accentuate the difficulties they are intended to cure. Domestic activity and incomes can only be maintained if the deficit in the current account of the balance-of-payments can be off-set by foreign borrowing, or if ample exchange reserves exist.

There is little in the experience of the more developed countries in Africa, or elsewhere, to encourage the belief that central banks or governments can be depended upon to pursue undeviatingly policies designed to eliminate cyclical disturbances. On the contrary, expansionist policies in times of an export boom, followed by exchange difficulties, when there is weakening or collapse in world demand, have been the usual pattern in all 'open' economies. Policies are not unalterable, but they are much influenced by the infectious optimism generated by an improving economic and financial climate, political pressure groups, and the absence of asceticism in the political rulers. There is, moreover, the difficulty that a small, dependent economy must necessarily adapt itself to the prevailing economic winds, and seize its opportunities for economic advancement whenever conditions are propitious. Unfortunately, when the boom has run the course there is a need for belated action frequently so drastic as to produce a recession.

(c) *The Stabilization of Producers' Prices*

The difficulties in the way of applying traditional fiscal and monetary techniques for moderating, or preventing, fluctuations in national money incomes, as a result of variations in exchange proceeds, have stimulated proposals for a variety of stabilization measures. Their common purpose is to break or weaken the link between fluctuations in external prices and export receipts and prices and incomes received by producers.[1] The criteria and objectives of such stabilization measures are not always precisely defined, or even clearly distinguished, for example, whether they should be used simply for stabilizing particular producers' prices or incomes, or some 'general level of prices' aggregate money incomes, output or employment; nor is there clarity in regard to the periods during which such stabilizing measures should operate. In suggesting the stabilization of one or more of these objectives, such as the stabilization of both real incomes and prices received by particular producers, there is frequently little recognition of the practical difficulties inherent in such proposals or their contradictory nature.[2]

[1] See Ragnar Nurkse, 'Fluctuations in Exports of Primary Products' in *Contribuições a Analise do Desenvolvimento Economico*, p. 257.

[2] There are also more sophisticated variants of these policies, such as the

Samuels — Monetary and Fiscal Policy in Development

In recent years there has been a revival of interest in the devices used in West Africa, South Africa, Uganda, and other African territories for stabilizing producers' prices. This is frequently achieved by the creation of state-regulated producer monopolies, which guarantee a price to domestic producers and arrange for the sale of products abroad at the prices prevailing in the export markets. Alternatively, the government can leave the marketing process in private hands and impose a system of variable export taxes, which rise sharply as export prices rise or pay subsidies when export prices slump. There are other possibilities of achieving the same end: for example, alteration in the rates at which exporters can sell their foreign exchange earnings to an authorized exchange dealer.

These price-stabilization measures, which have operated in Africa for cocoa, palm-oil, cotton, maize, wheat, and other agricultural products, amount to 'forced saving' in times of an export boom and a subsidy when world commodity prices fall. Implicit in these measures is the assumption that cultivators as a group are improvident or incapable of taking advantage of their prosperity to strengthen their resources, or their competitive ability, to meet an adverse turn in their economic circumstances. This is unlikely to be true of the well-organized farming units, or for that matter the large-scale producers of precious stones or base-metal products, who account for the bulk of the output in many African territories. Even if it is true that the smaller, peasant farmer is feckless and financially imprudent, it is still difficult to justify the imposition of a high rate of compulsory savings on people with limited resources. On the contrary, a higher standard of consumption is something to be encouraged if the indigenous people are to be induced to undertake change and participate in more specialized and diversified productive activities. An increase in consumption is, or ought to be, the object of growth and in a sense is the growth.

The case for a limited retention of export earnings for defined periods can be defended as a contribution to income stability. The repayment of such proceeds, when prices fall, serves to cushion the adverse effect on real incomes of an external deficit. But the case becomes extremely weak when discriminatory taxation of exporters' incomes becomes an accepted and permanent feature of the tax system in a period when prices tend to rise rather than fall. By paying

proposal for neutralizing the effect of changes in export and import prices upon domestic incomes and costs. One such proposal, favoured by Lord Keynes, was to devise an extra-budgetary system of taxes and bounties for exports and imports, worked in accordance with the principle of using increases in one set of prices to off-set increases in the other. The same result might be achieved by a system of multiple exchange rates. Cf. *Report of Committee on Finance and Industry*, Cmd. 3897, 1931, pp. 199-200.

producers much less than their products fetch on world markets, incentives to divert resources into the export industries are weakened. In this manner supplies are reduced when demand is most vigorous : *per contra* the payment of subsidies stimulates the volume of export production when export prices are low.

Naturally, much depends on producers' responses to price changes and their expectations regarding the future course of prices ruling on world markets. This is a complex matter ; it is affected by the interplay of the elasticities of the relevant supply and demand functions with respect to price and income changes. Thus, the elasticity of export supply depends on such factors as the gestation period of different crops, their variability due to climatic and other influences, producers' responses to price incentives, and the price elasticity of domestic demand for export goods. Again, much depends on the significance of domestic exports in relation to supplies coming on to world markets.[1]

It is difficult to believe that interference with the pricing functions of the marketing system will not lead to a less efficient allocation of resources, impair the competitive ability of the export industries, and produce a lower level of real incomes on the average during periods of rising and falling export prices. The losses in real incomes are likely to be great when the 'administered prices' lose touch with the underlying changes in the real conditions of supply and demand in world markets, and will fall with especial severity on the poorer territories. It is difficult not to agree with the judgment of the East African Royal Commission that the poverty of the African territories, which is due to their isolation from local and world markets, will increase as a result of attempts to cushion off producers from world markets.[2]

These considerations have prompted the suggestion that prices paid by marketing boards should be based on a moving-average formula to ensure that producer prices do not lose contact with world market trends.[3] This would undoubtedly be an improvement, though the effect on the volume of export production will depend on the weights assigned to prices in the different years comprised in the moving average. The greater the weight given to current prices in the formula, the greater will be the departure from a 'price

---

[1] Though the statistical evidence is by no means unambiguous, there are good reasons for thinking that, in both the developed and backward economies, producers of primary products respond positively to price movements. Cf. United Nations Study, *op. cit.*

[2] See *Report of East African Royal Commission, 1953–1955*, Cmd. 9475, p. 69. Cf. also P. T. Bauer, *West African Trade*, Cambridge University Press, 1954.

[3] P. T. Bauer and F. W. Paish, 'The Reduction of Fluctuations in the Income of Primary Producers', *Economic Journal*, December 1952.

stabilization' policy : the more important the influence of prices for past periods in the average, the more likely are real incomes to be smaller than the increase warranted by rising export prices.

Though easy to apply, the defects of variable export taxes are none the less great. Their discriminatory character would be lessened if they formed part of a broader mechanism of general taxation. The difficulties in using tax policies in the poorer territories to off-set temporary fluctuations in income are, of course, considerable. But it is not impossible to devise a tax system which will exact some contribution from small land and property owners or consumers of marketable products.[1] The introduction of a more widely based tax system is much easier in the more advanced territories which possess sufficient flexibility in their taxing arrangements to restrain to some extent fluctuations in money incomes.

Much depends on what is done with the tax proceeds, which are intended to reduce the impact on money incomes of price instability in the export markets. If they are used to repay foreign-held debt, or to strengthen the existing gold and foreign exchange reserves, they do indeed prevent an expansion of domestic money incomes. But if they are used to finance increased governmental expenditure, as so frequently happens, domestic money incomes will rise and the object of imposing increased taxation will be defeated. The buffer reserve of foreign exchange, which is theoretically being built up to enable a country to live beyond its foreign exchange earnings in depressed periods, will soon disappear. Subsidies to maintain producers' incomes in a time of falling commodity prices will then have to be financed by the sale of securities to the banking system or if possible to the public. The creation of credit in this manner can only accentuate the pressure on scarce exchange resources, and add to existing financial and economic difficulties.

IV. INFLATION AND INVESTMENT

Price stabilization schemes as a weapon of counter-cyclical policy and as an instrument of permanent financing, involve distinctly different objectives. In practice the line between the two has become extremely blurred : indeed, marketing control schemes and export levies are frequently defended because of their efficacy in providing capital resources for accelerating the rate of development. In these conditions export levies and other stabilizing devices tend to lose

[1] Such taxes have been the stock-in-trade of all countries which have depended on increased domestic savings for their development.

their essential purpose and become merged in general measures to extract from the indigenous peoples all the abstinence which governments in their wisdom think they should display.

The theory that a dependent economy can escape the backwash of unfavourable external changes through a policy of 'industrialization' has acquired a strong hold on policy-makers. It is certainly true that the more varied a country's resources, the less it is likely to be susceptible to every unfavourable turn in its economic fortunes. But it does not follow that it can escape its economic and financial difficulties by contracting out of the international economic order. Such a retreat to a policy of self-sufficiency would mean a reversal of the whole process, which has led to increased production, productivity, and incomes in the African territories. Had such a policy been consciously pursued the population of Africa would in all probability have been much less, and its well-being enormously less, than it is now.

The limited capacity of the African populations to save and invest is undoubtedly an important reason for their low productivity and the wasteful use of existing human and material resources.[1] It is tempting to conclude from this that, if savings could only be increased, additional demands could be created which would absorb, and employ more fully, the idle or under-employed resources. The case for artificially stimulating demands in these conditions through credit expansion or taxation has long been recognized.[2] In recent years the doctrine has been propounded in even more extreme forms [3] in which the expected increase in output will itself generate the saving required for the further expansion of economic activity. In such a context, the dog can grow, so to speak, by eating its own tail.

It is conceivable that this can happen in a period of depressed demands, when there are unemployed workers, large accumulations of stocks of goods, and a good deal of excess capacity. In such conditions expansionist credit and financial measures can be undertaken to revive demand without any serious inflationary dangers. Even though there is a time lag before the increased flow of goods comes on to the market, there is a sufficient hump of savings to support the demands of the newly employed workers. The real savings are available, all that is needed is an expansion in monetary demand to start the investment process.

---

[1] At any rate, as evaluated in terms of 'Western' values.

[2] R. A. Lehfeldt, *The National Resources of South Africa*, 1922, p. 4.

[3] Cf. W. A. Lewis, *Economic Development with Unlimited Supplies of Labour*, Manchester School, May 1954, pp. 139-91. See also the present writer's article, 'Some Aspects of Industrial Development in South Africa', *South African Journal of Economics*, September 1959, pp. 186-8.

The so-called 'disguised unemployment' in 'under-developed' territories cannot as a rule be so painlessly liquidated by an expansion in demand. The problem which exists is due less to a deficiency in demand as to the low productivity of *employed* labour. An expansion of effective demand by means of liberal credit policies is not only inadequate but may be harmful.[1] The phenomenon of 'under-employment' exists because of real causes, such as primitive methods of production in agriculture, unsatisfactory forms of land tenure, insufficient knowledge, capital, skill, and other complementary factors, institutional patterns of behaviour, which are resistant to economic change and impede the creation of new market opportunities and more efficient production, and so forth.

If these obstacles could be removed, and the conditions created for the more effective employment of the local population, substantial amounts of labour could doubtless be released, whether for investment, export, or other activities. But it is an illusion to suppose that such a reorganization of the economy can be brought about quickly or by techniques appropriate in more advanced societies. Substantial increases in the volume of saving, as well as in other co-operating factors, are necessary to facilitate the transition to a different economic structure, and this takes time. Without an expansion in the real volume of savings, credit and other inflationary techniques may accentuate the difficulties of these territories by weakening the competitive ability of their export industries which are the main engine of growth in most parts of Africa.

Nevertheless, it is tempting to believe that the barrier of time can be by-passed by compulsory saving. As a result, the 'forced saving' doctrine has attracted much support as the only feasible technique for reducing 'consumption' or, at any rate, preventing an increase in consumption by an inflationary rise in prices.[2] The objection that the resulting rise in prices is likely to increase the

[1] Cf. G. Haberler, 'Critical Observations on Some Current Notions in the Theory of Economic Development', in *L' industria riviata di economia politica*, Milano, 1957, p. 375.

[2] Models are frequently constructed which treat concepts such as 'consumption' and investment as if they are concrete quantities capable of manipulation at will for any length of time. These entities are in reality 'abstractions' which, when recorded by the national income statistician, simply reflect the outcome of complicated decisions to spend, save, or invest, as a result of a diversity of choices and circumstances in the past. There is no reason to expect that an alteration in 'consumption' will not simultaneously influence the whole economic process, including the scale and profitability of investment. Much of what is referred to as 'consumption' in advanced economies constitutes an important form of saving in the less-developed African territories : expenditures on durable consumption goods have, for example, been an important factor in raising standards of life in many parts of Africa and in releasing the inhabitants from much time-consuming labour.

inequality of income distribution, produce social unrest or intractable balance-of-payments problems, is recognized. But the need for higher investment is held to outweigh these evils. There are, indeed, supporters of this doctrine who welcome inflation on the ground that rising prices create a favourable climate for investment.

It is undoubtedly true that the prospect of profit and the large accumulations which are often possible for the propertied and entrepreneurial classes (and governments) in times of rising prices, are favourable for investment. But there are substantial reasons for doubting the historical interpretation that savings and investment have grown most rapidly in periods of inflation.[1] The nineteenth century was a notable period in the history of investment and in the material progress achieved in all the industrial countries, although the price level tended on the whole to decline after the Napoleonic War.[2]

It is an old story that in most situations an increase in total money expenditure, as a result of, say, deficit financing, will for a time produce an increase in investment and employment. But there is a further lesson to be drawn from the experience of these inflations, which ought not to be forgotten. They have not only shown that a sufficient increase of final demand can be achieved, but that in order to maintain the level of investment and activity, credit expansion has to go on at a certain progressive rate. This is shown particularly well by the great German inflation[3] during most of which the level of investment and employment was very high. But as soon and as often as the rate of inflation slowed down, unemployment reappeared, even though incomes and prices were still rising.

The investment projects undertaken in a period of rising prices and profits naturally tend to attract most attention, and they are frequently regarded as justifying a policy of inflationary finance. But these visible symbols of achievement throw little light on the economic costs involved in the inflationary process, or on the pro-

[1] See Earl J. Hamilton, 'American Treasure and the Rise of Modern Capitalism', *Economica*, November 1929, pp. 338-57 ; and J. M. Keynes, *Treatise on Money*, Macmillan, 1930, pp. 148 *et seq.* Compare the serious criticisms of these writings by J. U. Nef, 'Prices and Industrial Capitalism in France and England 1540–1640', *Economic History Review*, 1937, vii, pp. 155-85.

[2] Although prices fell and real wages rose during the years 1815–47, the rate of growth in industrial production during this period exceeded the rate of growth achieved during the whole era 1793–1914. See W. W. Rostow, *British Economy of the 19th Century*, Oxford, 1948, p. 8. Cf. also H. L. Beales 'The Great Depression in Industry and Trade', *Economic History Review*, October 1934, who stresses the impressive rate of economic growth in the period 1873–96, although prices and industrial profit margins were falling steadily.

[3] Cf. also G. Subercaseaux, *Le Papier-Monnaie*, Paris, 1920. It is also worth noting that countries such as Chile have remained poor in spite of a long history of inflation.

ductivity of the investment : the capital projects may have been undertaken less for their income-earning possibilities than as a hedge against further inflation. The history of investment is strewn with failures. Why should one assume that governments and local entrepreneurs possess the ability to invest 'forced saving' more wisely, or to avoid an expansion in productive facilities which may not be warranted by the consuming power of the population ?

The scope for extracting 'forced saving', through higher prices or taxation, from the poor communities in Africa is anyhow extremely limited. A large section of the population lives close to the margin of subsistence, and makes little use of money. The class most easily exploited, that is, those with relatively fixed money incomes, hardly exists. If wage earners and the small peasant cultivators find their real incomes considerably reduced by the rise in prices, there may be serious social unrest and the danger of political revolution. Productive efficiency will almost certainly decline seriously. Indeed, it is not even clear that the inflationary game yields worthwhile returns in the case of the small, exploitable groups in the population, such as the civil servants, petty traders, or the wealthier classes. Inflationary rises in prices distort the savings and investment process, lead to a wasteful use of resources in order to reap inflationary profits, encourage speculative hoarding, complicate the budgetary problem, weaken or destroy the domestic market for government bonds, and lead to recurrent balance-of-payments difficulties.

If economic growth was merely a matter of obtaining a sufficient volume of domestic saving and investment, improvements in the standard of living of the African peoples would necessarily be extremely slow. Even such modest progress could be threatened if the growth of population accelerated. Fortunately, there is no pre-ordained pace at which economic misery and poverty has to be endured or eradicated. Considerable additions to output are possible without much capital : simply by the more intelligent and intensive use of human labour.[1] Remarkable increases in labour productivity have been achieved in many African territories by the single device of consolidating farming lots, or by improved farming techniques such as crop rotation, contour cultivation, the more scientific selection of seeds, the use of suitable fertilisers, or improved farming implements.

Having said this it is as well to recognize the limits to these territories' capacity for self-improvement. African societies, with their still largely undifferentiated structures, lack the resources and

[1] See Sir Theodore Gregory, *India on the Eve of the Third Five-Year Plan*, the Associated Chambers of Commerce of India, Calcutta, 1961, p. 8.

the managerial and organizational skill to expand their limited markets and create new opportunities for specialized production. Whatever movement has taken place in this direction has been under the impact of Western influences : indeed, the economic achievements of the more advanced territories have been remarkable, considering their deficiency of savings and the prevalence of customary methods of production, and primitive techniques. It is possible that, with the passage of time, these territories will contribute increasingly to their own development. But for the forseeable future it is hard to believe that rapid progress can be achieved without passing the burden of development on to countries rich in capital skill and other resources.

There is, of course, nothing wrong with a policy of improving standards of living through the use of foreign capital or other forms of assistance. Foreign investment has long played a key rôle in the material progress of the more advanced territories in Africa. The benefits of such external financing have often been much greater than the net returns they have yielded, over and above repayments for interest or dividends because of their 'demonstration effect' : foreign-financed capital projects create and demonstrate valuable opportunities for profitable domestic investment, and introduce into a country the spirit, skill, and discipline necessary for successful business enterprise. Yet, it is sometimes thought that foreign investment is in some sense injurious to the borrowing country, because the debt has to be serviced, or profits and dividends have to be remitted to the foreign investor. Payments abroad can hardly be described as a 'burden' if they constitute a deduction from increased incomes flowing from the foreign investment. There may indeed be a 'transfer problem' if the foreign savings are not invested in ways which add directly to foreign exchange earnings or save foreign exchange through the replacement of imports. But this is merely to say that a country which is borrowing abroad to finance its development must maintain reserves which grow in keeping with the increased flow of domestic incomes.

The desirability of adequate reserves, even for developed countries, was first stressed a long time ago by Tooke : it was brushed aside then on the ground that reliance on the reserve might lead to a delayed response to adverse circumstances. The danger undoubtedly exists in the case of opportunistic and financially ambitious administrations who are unlikely to rank high a policy of reserve accumulation as compared with other forms of investment, or even consumption.[1] But this does not lessen the desirability of banking

[1] Cf. *Report of East African Commission*, pp. 68-9.

and fiscal measures to create such a form of investment. Adequate monetary reserves are necessary for economies exposed to adverse movements in world prices, and essential to attract the capital so necessary for the physical development of Africa.

V. THE CASE OF SOUTH AFRICA

There are clear limits to inflationary methods of financing even when economic and financial circumstances appear favourable for such an experiment. It is instructive, therefore, to compare the experience of South Africa, which is by far the most advanced part of Africa, accounting for possibly two-fifths or more of the domestic products of the territories south of the Sahara.

The rapid progress of the South African economy has been closely linked, over time, though not in any simple or direct manner, with the large-scale investment of foreign capital. The largest proportion of these foreign funds has been invested in the development of export production and activities connected with exports or the production of 'import substitutes'. According to the latest Census of South Africa's Foreign Liabilities and Assets, total foreign investments at the end of 1959 amounted to £1528 million, almost half this amount being due to the net capital inflow since the end of the war.

The substantial scale of foreign lending, especially in the earlier post-war years, was without question the primary catalytic agency in an investment boom, almost without parallel in South Africa's economic history. During the past fifteen years the ratio of her gross investment to the gross national product has averaged almost 24 per cent. Between 1946 and 1950 gross domestic savings financed about 55 per cent of gross domestic capital formation. Thereafter, domestic savings grew rapidly largely as a result of the expansion in output and an even more rapid growth in money incomes. During the years 1951–5 gross domestic savings rose to an annual average of about £350 million, more than twice the annual average figure for the previous five-year period, and financed about 82 per cent of domestic capital expenditures. Since 1956 gross domestic savings have increased even more remarkably, averaging more than £500 million a year, and were more than adequate to finance the whole of South Africa's capital outlay.

The conclusion sometimes drawn from these figures is that South Africa is now independent of foreign resources for her development. The growth in the recorded totals of 'savings' is undoubtedly impressive, but there are several weighty considerations for rejecting this view. Firstly, the savings as recorded by the national income statistician are an arithmetical result of the cessation of foreign lending after 1954/5 [1] and the continued high level of capital outlays. The mechanism by which savings *ex-post* have been brought into equality with requirements for further investment (and a reduction of international indebtedness in recent years) has been through higher taxation, compulsory loans, the intensification of import and exchange controls, and an increasing measure of profit inflation wherever the demand for savings increased. The growth in the so-called 'savings' is thus not wholly the result of decisions not to spend, but largely the consequence of involuntary abstention as a result of tax and inflationary policies. Secondly, these *ex-post* savings throw no light on the magnitude of the deficiency of savings, the margins of production which had to be contracted because of the scarcity of savings, or the productivity of investments financed by 'forced saving'. It is only possible to refer briefly to aspects of these intricate problems.

In spite of the high and increasing proportion of domestic incomes saved during the fifties, the rate of growth of the economy has shown a noticeable tendency to decline. These tendencies have become especially marked since the cessation of foreign lending. Since 1955 the real product per head of population has increased on the average by somewhat more than 1 per cent per annum, or approximately half the average annual rate of growth during the whole of the post-war period.

This slackening in the rate of economic expansion is surprising. It cannot be ascribed to a fall in exports or a decline in aggregate investment. On the contrary, the value of merchandise exports and gold production rose spectacularly during the fifties, while gross capital formation rose fairly steadily throughout this period. The answer must be sought, in part, in the use of domestic savings to reduce South Africa's foreign liabilities as a result of the outflow of capital, particularly since 1951, and, in part, in the large-scale diversion of savings to public investment. The 'public sector', which at present accounts for a little over one-fifth of the gross national product, now performs over two-fifths of the total gross investment. If we allow for 'capital consumption', net public capital investment as a proportion of the total net capital formation was as high as 49 per cent during the years 1956–9, as compared with about 34 per cent during the period 1948–51.

This loading of the capital investment programme in favour of the 'public sector' has evidently not added proportionately to the real

---

[1] There has in fact been a net capital outflow during the past five years.

income-creating capacity of the population. Could it be that such public outlays have been on projects which only promise a return in the distant future, or because they have led to a wasteful use of scarce capital resources ? What is certain is that many of the more grandiose and forward-looking projects would not have been undertaken if rates of interest had not been kept below their 'equilibrium' level by the substantial expansion of bank credit. Moreover, as a result of the diversion of resources for the expansion of public outlays, net private investment has contracted markedly in recent years and is now about one-half of the net investment undertaken during the years 1954/5. If we allow for the rise in prices of capital goods, the present scale of net investment in the private sector is below the level of private investment in the immediate post-war years.

There is a further reason for the slowing down in the economy's rate of growth, which is of some significance to countries with limited investible resources. Inflationary finance has not merely encouraged ambitious investment projects but has destroyed savings through the effect of rising prices on the funds accumulated to maintain the existing plant and other equipment required to sustain the present flow of goods. It is often forgotten that capital investment is a process requiring continuous human effort merely to maintain the corpus of existing real investment. During the past five years depreciation allowances have absorbed on the average about two-fifths of the recorded gross saving.

Had local prices risen less, or better still fallen, real investment would doubtless have been greater, and possibly too the rate of economic expansion. Instead, the net result of planning and controls, of priorities for the 'basic services', and of inflationary finance, has been that aggregate net investment in real terms is barely above the level attained during the immediate post-war years. To achieve even this result it has been necessary to impose 'forced levies' and other exactions on an unprecedented scale, reduce substantially private net investment, and run-down gold and foreign exchange assets to a dangerously low level, despite a threefold expansion in the value of export receipts.

VI. SOME CONCLUDING REFLECTIONS

The preceding discussion has indicated the limited possibilities of monetary and fiscal action in fostering economic development or in ironing out fluctuations in money incomes. This conclusion is not surprising in the present stage of economic development in Africa, and is not a consequence of the under-developed character of existing monetary or fiscal institutions. The absence of a well-developed financial system is rather a reflection of the poverty and economic backwardness of most of the African countries. As the productivity and income of these areas increase, more elaborate financial institutions will take root and facilitate the further expansion of the market economies and the growth in the volume of production. No ambitious scheme of financial reconstruction, with all the paraphernalia of central banks, money markets, and contra-cyclical fiscal policies can, however, alter the basic fact of poverty in the territories, or their dependence on external markets for the disposal of their surplus products, or for imports to sustain their development.[1]

The conclusion that little can be done through monetary or fiscal panaceas does not mean that fruitful possibilities of development do not exist in other directions. In the more backward territories the problem of low incomes and an inadequate margin for saving is frequently a consequence of institutional and social arrangements, which impede the mobility of resources and prevent the most productive use of land through out-moded legal systems relating to land tenure and property. Improvements in the administrative machinery and the removal of these social and legal obstacles, which inhibit opportunities for the productive use of saving, may actually yield higher returns than additional investments in specific industries. The chief cause of the alleged shortage of investible funds is frequently the failure to allow local populations an opportunity to exercise their initiative and participate fully in the process of mobilizing the real savings required for development.

Though average incomes may be low in Africa, some incomes are high and substantial accumulation of funds does not exist as a result of trading activities, the ownership of land, or other forms of investment. It is remarkable how rapidly savings multiply when there are a large number of small savers. The fact that owners of these savings prefer to invest them outside the territories, or hold them in forms which do not add significantly to the flow of output, is due, in the main, to the fear of inflation, or punitive taxation, or to a general sense of insecurity. The prime requisite for the productive investment of such savings is the strengthening of confidence in the policies of the executive and in the dependability of the administrative machine. Once these conditions have been established and there is some certainty that the monetary unit will retain its value (or, better still, increase its value) it is difficult not to believe that savings, small

[1] Cf. W. T. Newlyn and D. C. Rowan, *Money and Banking in British Colonial Africa*, Oxford, 1954.

though they may be in the beginning, will not accumulate at a rapid rate. Historically, all developed societies started with small savings which increased as new opportunities for profitable domestic investment were discovered.

The case is even clearer when applied to foreign investment. In a world of increasingly scarce capital resources the raising of fresh capital in the leading capital markets is becoming extremely difficult, even for borrowers with an unimpeachable financial record. Indeed, there is a disquietening tendency on the part of investors, with long-established ties with this continent, to withdraw their funds, or at any rate reduce their stake in Africa, because of fears, whether they are mistaken or not, regarding the safety of their investments. The recent experience of South Africa provides a grim warning of the speed with which long-established personal and financial ties can be severed.

In much modern economic writing thrift is relegated to a subsidiary and passive rôle. The centre-piece in the analysis is investment, which is thought to be strongly influenced by gently rising prices and the prospect of improving profits as a result of inflationary finance. But the fundamental lesson of history is that it is impossible to build up a viable, self-equilibriating society in conditions when the saver is plagued by fears regarding the stability and safety of his investments.[1] The preoccupation of the individual saver, in so far as he can save, becomes, then, the preservation of the immediate corpus of his investment rather than the long-term productivity of the economy. At any rate, for the poorer countries in Africa financial prudence and rectitude in the management of their economies are also likely to be the sure path to increasing accumulation and rising living standards.

DISCUSSION OF PAPERS BY PROFESSOR PEACOCK AND PROFESSOR SAMUELS

Mr. Beheiry, opening the discussion, in thanking Professor Peacock and Professor Samuels, commented that he had served for a good many years in the field of actual economic administration, where action could rarely be

---

[1] In earlier civilizations, the surplus, necessary in real terms for their development, was provided by the forcible application of human labour in the shape of slavery. The equivalent of classical slavery in the modern world is the involuntary enslavement of the saving classes by the process of inflation. But it may be added that these techniques of 'forced saving' are ceasing to be fruitful, at any rate so far as the working classes in the Western world are concerned, because of labour agreements by which wage scales are governed by changes in the cost of living.

guided by Western economic theory and where such theory rarely helped to explain practice. He proposed to try to indicate the main points put forward in the two papers and to give his own views where, he believed, they might be helpful.

The first question which the authors sought to answer was : Could fiscal and monetary techniques, as developed in the Western economies, be successfully applied in dealing with the problems of stability and economic growth in the African countries ? If not, could suitable fiscal and monetary techniques be devised under the existing fiscal and monetary structures of African countries, techniques capable of creating stability and promoting economic growth ?

The answer to the first question was more or less 'No', and we did not need to concern ourselves with it any longer for there could be little disagreement on that.

But it would be useful to recall the reasons given as they no doubt represent the basic problems of the African economies today. The reasons were : the largely subsistence nature of these economies ; the institutional inhibitions to development ; the dependence of these countries on the export earnings of their primary products, and their fluctuating nature ; the great propensity of these countries to import ; the limited credit and banking structure in these countries ; and finally, resulting from all these factors, their incapacity to provide from internal resources the capital and skill necessary for economic growth. Perhaps one should pause at this juncture and ask oneself the fundamental question : What, in the light of these practical limitations, should be the objects of fiscal and monetary policies in a given African country ?

The first objective must be to mobilize as much as possible of the internal resources for economic growth. In view of the limited dimensions of private savings, the state was perforce bound to make the maximum savings possible. The primary aim should therefore be to provide through the 'ordinary' annual budgets the maximum surpluses possible, to be in turn devoted to the financing of the capital or development projects decided upon.

Secondly, there was the problem of the fluctuations in the export earnings of the major products. This was a problem in which the external aspect was as important as the internal policies. In the absence of any international agreement capable at least of reducing such fluctuations (or in fact in the face of the difficulty, or perhaps the impossibility, of such an agreement) the policy should be to maximize the efficiencies of production by the search for new and better techniques to improve the competitiveness of such products, to diversify where possible, and to attempt where feasible to trade on really a global scale, especially in the markets of Eastern Europe, the Soviet Union, and China.

Thirdly, where reasonable economic prospects exist for the establishment of local industries essentially based on local products, the industrialization process should be started.

Fourthly, in the banking field the policy should be the establishment of specialized credit institutions, such as agricultural and industrial banks, which should at least be able to help in technical services and in the provision of capital where worthy private initiative exists.

The rôle of a central bank, where it is in operation, also needs discussion. Should it proceed along traditional lines known in most of the Western European countries, or should it embark upon commercial and other banking activities should that be necessary? From his own experience in a country where the cost of transferring money was prohibitively expensive, a network of branches in a great number of centres in the country coupled with flexible forms of credit should lead to the spreading of branches of commercial and other banks and in turn help in the opening up of new productive areas.

And finally, as to the institutional aspects of such as the different forms of land tenure, one could only say that their economic, social, and political importance was such that their change should not be entirely left to the process of time.

As a statement of objectives, what he had said might appear fine. But how would it produce the startling results which we are also so anxious to achieve? In view of the limitations of time, said *Mr. Beheiry*, he would attempt to give his own views without direct reference to the papers of Professors Samuels and Peacock.

First, he wished to dispute the inevitability of having to do everything at once, even though it cannot be physically done. The absorptive capacities of the countries concerned were limited and, within resources available, there should be wise allocation within a flexible framework of a plan capable of adjustments necessitated by the fortunes of each year.

Second, revenue-producing projects should always take precedence, not only to meet the rising bills of current expenditure but also to provide new money for new capital or development works. Transport to potential areas of production, research work, and education to meet the needs of the growing economy should occupy prominence in development plans.

Third, whenever private initiative could do the job, let it go ahead.

Fourth, the traditional tax structures were not as inflexible and unjust as they might sometimes appear. Import taxes and export duties could be manipulated to discourage imports or promote exports. The traditional taxes, such as tribute, poll-tax, house tax, were a form of income tax, however archaic, cheap, easy to run, and just. Fixed prices, unrelated to world prices, to producers need not penalize producers unless they are desired to do so. In countries where health, education, roads, and many other services were provided free, it was difficult to talk of injustice in the taxes levied. Even if an element of injustice was there, the sense of equity or duty must be tempered or subdued to expediency. This was not all to say that the introduction of income tax was not of high priority.

Fifth, a system of foreign exchange reserves budgeting could be evolved to help in the conscious utilization and conservation of such reserves.

Sixth, he believed that selective import control and liberal exchange control should be a feature of African economies for many years to come.

Seventh, it could not be over-emphasized what wise budget scrutiny and control of expenditure could lead to in terms of economies that could be used for development purposes.

He believed that these lines of action could produce good results, in spite of the fluctuating nature of export products, and with the help of foreign aid, when it could be found, the pace of progress could be greatly speeded up.

There were many other interesting and fundamental points raised by Professors Peacock and Samuels which should receive special consideration. Of particular importance were the rôle of deficit financing in African economic development, the problem of the holding of foreign reserves in the major currencies, the question of political instability, and the possible financial effects of some federal tendencies.

In conclusion, *Mr. Beheiry* said that in his view the process of economic development in Africa could not be helped by economic ideologies, whether pertaining to private enterprise or state ownership — what he felt that Africa most needed was self-help, flexibility in thought, and pragmatism in action, the various courses of which could only be settled in the light of conditions prevailing in the country concerned.

Professor Frankel emphasized the contrasts between theory and practice. The academic was not actually thinking of the problems of implementation. In order to implement policy it was necessary to create an elaborate chain of delegated authority ; this took time. The really fundamental point was that there was no simple substitute through monetary or fiscal policy for the investible surplus which had to be created for economic growth. The Union of South Africa had achieved high income levels through building up surpluses of exports to finance development, thanks to vigorous entrepreneurial action and vigorous government policies. They had adopted a fiscal policy which was simultaneously progressive and conservative. The earnings from exports had created the modern economy. Now the Union was trying to achieve, by means of credit, what it had formerly achieved through surpluses. The result was an exchange crisis. Fiscal and monetary policy could be an adjunct, but was no substitute for a surplus.

Mr. Vaizey drew attention to the ratios of government expenditure to national income, shown in Table 1 of Professor Peacock's paper, and the high figures by comparison with European standards that emerged. Was this because of very low values attached to the subsistence sector ? Had this been included in all cases ? Were there really differential prices operating in different sectors of the economy ? Did not these ratios suggest that the governments were paying prices without regard to the labour productivity of the services they were getting ? Were there possibilities for some African governments to push down prices in their own favour by stronger bargaining ?

Professor Robinson commented that government expenditure was composed largely of salaries of expatriates, and also of Africans commanding high salaries, because they possessed scarce professional qualifications. This meant that even a low real level of government expenditure represented a much higher proportion of national income in an African territory than it would do in a more advanced economy.

Mr. Onitiri asked how far a successful fiscal policy was possible under African conditions. He was afraid that the model that Professor Peacock had developed omitted certain important parameters that might be crucial to economic growth. If one tried to consider the ideal combination of types of investment in African countries, some were highly desirable but could not be dealt with in terms of product. Others were important in the long-run but short-term yields were low. They were dealing, in West Africa, with a situation in which the accumulated surpluses of the past were disappearing. It was imperative to ensure that such foreign investment as might come in would be used most effectively for long-term development. Thus it was necessary to give such investment a certain direction. Government fiscal policies had to provide incentives to use of the most abundant factors — that was to say, encourage labour intensive methods. How could they improve the relation between investment and output ? He thought that the same ideas regarding stabilization, as he had criticized in relation to Professor Bauer's paper, also affected Professor Samuels' paper. There was too much emphasis on equity. Progress, he thought, could not be achieved without inequities. He suggested that central banks in the advanced countries might take an overall view of the problems of stabilization and issue, when necessary, stabilization certificates — call them what one might — at high rates of interest. The cost to African countries of their own measures of stabilization had been very high. There had been a very heavy depreciation of the investments in their stabilization and reserve funds. Even now African central banks were reluctant to run down their reserves of foreign exchange. But need they be held in such vulnerable forms ? Could they not at least be invested in equities ? Was it necessary to sacrifice so much progress on the altar of stability ?

Professor Dupriez raised the question of the use of forced savings for development, making use of the inflationary process which could be so damaging to creditors. He thought it was important to realize the effects of forced saving on economic growth. Turning to fiscal policies, he commented that the classical system thought of import duties primarily from the point of view of the protection that they gave to industries. But in Africa import and export taxes were the main sources of revenue, and no African country could manage without them. The tax system operated by affecting the balance between domestic and international prices. But, while under-developed countries used both import and export duties, the developed countries confined themselves almost exclusively to import duties. In attempting to reduce export prices below world prices, the prices might be made too low and deprive countries of certain benefits. Was there not an economic and social danger in this?

Professor Walker said that one of the principal limitations on African development was the shortage of resources for government recurrent expenditures. Most African territories were already raising revenues which, having regard to average levels of real income, represented a substantial proportion of national income. The main problem was how their resources could most effectively be utilized. On the other hand, there was not, he thought, sufficient discussion of the problem of mobilizing small savings in Africa. More effective action was needed to channel into African uses even such savings as were already available. At the moment potential savings were going to waste. Government expenditure, he suggested, should be geared to create cash incomes which could in turn contribute through taxation to further development. He thought that a purely welfare approach to government expenditure was too negative. He believed that more consideration should be given to the scope, in African conditions, of credit creation and deficit finance. He felt that Professor Samuels' paper was perhaps a little too sound and orthodox. But it was all a question of orders of magnitude. Inflationary finance could certainly be carried to excess. But some measure of credit creation might be desirable.

He suggested that the rôle of deficit finance depended on three factors. Firstly, the magnitudes of the internal elasticities of supply, distinguishing between the agricultural and industrial sectors; during the period of restricted external supplies, agricultural output had increased remarkably; some African industries might also be working well below capacity. Secondly, the extent to which increased supplies might come from sources of which the incomes might be hoarded and escape the multiplier effect; it was impossible to know in advance, moreover, to what extent an increase of the prices of export products might stimulate exports, and thus exercise deflationary effects on the economy. Thirdly, the strength of the governmental machine and of the information at its disposal; improving statistical knowledge was making it easier to see how far incomes flowed back in the fiscal system.

He thought the order of magnitude of potential inflationary finance in a country like Uganda was around £5 m. a year — something like 1 per cent of national income and 5 per cent of government expenditure. It was large as compared with present expenditure on feeder roads, cattle dips, small dams, and could make a substantial contribution to economic development.

Dr. Singer argued that the change-over from the subsistence to the monetary economy opened up new opportunities for non-inflationary economic growth. As people came increasingly into the monetary economy they would want to hold assets in the form of money, and payment by means of the creation of additional money to that extent at least was non-inflationary. Studies that had been made of rates of growth and rates of inflation showed no strong correlation. The World Economic Survey had found that in the decade of the 1950s there had been no progress in the sense of increased government saving for the finance of economic development, and no increase in surpluses of government incomes in relation to national income. There had, however, been certain shifts in government expenditures in the direction of development — especially in respect of education. If he might comment on something said by Mr. Beheiry regarding the need for flexible planning, taking into account the fluctuations of foreign earnings, he himself thought there was no necessary inconsistency between fluctuations in commodity prices and development planning.

Professor Robinson was worried about the problem of controlling a variety of things with a limited set of macro-economic controls. These had to be used for three sometimes conflicting objectives : to control the rate of development of new activities ; to keep one's trade in step with other countries' trade ; to control inflation. The principal controls in most countries were the rate of interest and budgetary policy. Their use was mainly determined by the state of the gold or currency reserves and by one's fears of inflation. In an advanced country the objective of keeping one's foreign trade in balance was largely achieved by reducing the level of activity, and thus the level of imports. In an under-developed country one had to ask how the similar process operated. As he saw it, a primary producing country suffered an initial reduction of export earnings, which translated itself into reduced incomes and, through a multiplier effect, into a reduced national income, and ultimately into reduced imports. If, as was frequently the case, the fall of export earnings was heavy, the reduction of national income to recover a balance would equally be heavy. It seemed to him important, therefore, to ask whether, while adequate incentives to adjustment were required, something could be done to mitigate the extreme severity of the process. While he believed that buffer-stock and similar schemes had something valuable to contribute, he thought that it was even more important to improve methods of stabilizing the world economy itself. He thought that the advanced countries had a great responsibility to try to diminish the impacts of their mistakes and fluctuations on the less-advanced countries. In the nineteenth century, as it seemed to him, the process of keeping in step was relatively easier because there was, in effect, only one key-currency — sterling. The process was somewhat complicated when a second key-currency — the dollar — emerged. Now we had four or five key-currencies, with speculators hurrying their balances from one to another. He felt that this was making bold policies of stabilization increasingly difficult to operate. Indeed, he wondered whether there was an inherent conflict between the problems of keeping-in-step and those of achieving stabilization in a more far-reaching sense.

Professor Enke was sceptical of Professor Peacock's 'more sophisticated' model. He thought that the use that he had made of incremental capital/output ratios showed conclusively that this was a fruitless exercise. He agreed with Professor Peacock's conclusion (p. 673) as to the relative importance of fiscal policy. He thought it was of a fourth or fifth level of importance in most tropical African countries. He attached much more importance to a generous supply of agricultural economists and technicians. It was not a question of increasing credit in a country, but rather of who got the credit. What was wanted was a system that got the right amounts of credit to the right people, who could use it really effectively. Different people did not all use credit equally well.

Turning to the question of central banking in Africa, he argued that many of the conditions for its success were absent. African countries almost all lacked a money market and lacked the banking habit. He compared here the experience of Latin American countries. If credit creation was to become possible, the bank notes of individual commercial banks would need to be readily negotiable. Africa needed financial management as well as capital.

Professor Peacock intervened to draw attention to the cautions that he had given regarding the use of models (p. 660-6 of his paper). He had used the simple model only to draw attention to the dangers of assuming any simple relation between increments of capital and of output. He thought that in economics one could hardly escape using a model. Any statement of cause and effect involved a model.

Professor Leduc wondered whether it might not be useful to study the position of African countries south of the Sahara in respect of their monetary relations with outside countries. What was, in these days, the precise relationship of the Union of South Africa to the Sterling Area? Was there a special position? What were the connections between the Sterling and Franc Zones? Commenting on Professor Dupriez's remarks, he thought that fiscal measures must be regarded as essential instruments of economic policy. He believed that taxes on exports had resulted in a reduction of savings in international currencies. As he saw it, the efforts of governments to stimulate growth were closely associated with political issues. No development could be achieved without sacrifice and equally, he thought, without international assistance, which again was a political issue. In any agricultural country it was inevitably agriculture which had to bear the greatest burden. He thought there should be no timidity about using monetary policies as a factor in economic development.

Professor Houghton was convinced that in the long-term development of under-developed countries, the most important things were domestic capital formation and domestic savings as a means to it. Clearly, the volume of savings was affected by the distribution of incomes. Any more equal distribution of incomes would seem likely to increase consumption and diminish saving. In many parts of Africa, those Africans who received high incomes tended to spend them on conspicuous expenditure.

He thought that a high rate of progressive taxation might, with relatively small real sacrifice, drain some of this into productive expenditure. In fiscal policy emphasis should be placed on mobilizing resources for purposes of development. He thought it was almost equally true that some governments were guilty of conspicuous expenditure on over-lavish public buildings and the like. In the nineteenth century Great Britain had expanded, largely as a consequence of a spirit of frugality. Was it possible to create a similar spirit in Africa ?

Mr. Moran thought that before discussing tools one should discuss objectives. If one was to consider the problems of growth in the extraordinarily different countries of Africa, some framework to determine priorities had to be created.

Professor Williams suggested that it was valuable to study the experience of New Zealand. There had been a policy of insulation and exchange control, combined with attempts at industrialization. For the moment what had emerged was a position of great rigidity. There was heavy dependence on imported raw materials, with little value added. He thought that African countries might find themselves slipping into the same position. If imports were cut in New Zealand it meant unemployment. Consumer goods represented only 15 per cent of total imports and could not be wholly eliminated in a recession. Industrialization would not in itself make a country less dependent on foreign exchange requirements. There were limits to the central bank's control over trading banks in curbing inflationary policies. And even if, as in Australia, there were understandings about the remittance of profits, there were considerable potential liabilities in the form of remittances. He thought that what had been described as a sucking in of funds into London was not really a consequence of colonialism but of practical difficulties of expanding investment as fast as they would have liked. What was important was not the reserves of a central bank but the over-all assets of a government.

The discussion of Professor Samuels' and Professor Peacock's papers was continued in the afternoon session. In opening the resumed discussion, *Professor Walker* expressed scepticism of the possibility that income taxes could be made to play a central rôle in raising revenue in Africa. In advanced countries income taxes were unquestionably the most equitable means of raising revenue. But in African conditions there were two difficulties. First, they were expensive to collect ; in Africa there was a shortage of the skilled and responsible personnel that was required. Second, the problems of allowance raised by African family systems were very difficult to deal with. In Uganda, apart from the 10·6 per cent of revenue shown in Table 3 of Professor Peacock's paper as derived from income, there was about the same amount raised by poll-tax, levied by the local authorities. The large proportion of revenue — amounting to 34 per cent on average during the years 1949–59, and appreciably larger in individual years, was very burdensome and a powerful disincentive to the activities in which Uganda had a comparative advantage.

He thought that one must be very careful about pressing too hard the taxation of a country's leading sectors. Those who earned their income by trade paid, in contrast, very little in taxation, so that there was serious distortion. Import duties were, and would remain, a major source of revenue for all African territories. What were the maximum rates possible? He thought there was a tendency to underestimate the capacity of some imports for conspicuous expenditure to bear tax. Such taxation satisfied well the criterion of equity. He suggested that on certain imports tax rates in excess of 100 per cent were possible and with careful selection there were a number of imports which could bear as much as 75 per cent.

Mr. Dowuona said that it was suggested that African tax systems were out of date. But in Western countries the modern tax structure had been evolved only in recent years and after much experimentation. He thought that in Africa it would not have been possible to raise sufficient revenue without resource to the large import and export taxes that had been so severely criticized. But African countries were anxious to explore all avenues.

Professor Leduc argued that in Africa it was difficult to combine the imperative of economic development with present methods of raising taxes. In British territories there was a fiscal system based on direct taxation. In some British territories there was a para-fiscal system, raising development resources through commodity board buying and selling policies. In the French territories the main emphasis was on the taxation of imports. The impacts of these different systems on internal prices were different. In some parts of Africa it was difficult to choose between the two systems — a certain combination was necessary. As regards income taxes, some of the French territories had tried to introduce the system that operated in Metropolitan France. It was found that the cost of administration was very high, and it was feared that this policy could not be applied in many cases. The requirement of economic development was that there should be a tax system that was in keeping with practicalities — for example, taxes on equipment, trucks, and the like. Any export taxes should be levied only within limits that did not discourage producers. What was wanted was a carefully balanced equilibrium between different kinds of tax.

Dr. Singer had four points that he wished to make. First, he thought that in an under-developed country one should not be over-concerned with problems of equity in the raising of revenue. The problems of equity in government expenditure were, he thought, at least equally great and probably greater. In any case the two had to be considered together. Second, it was not only export taxes that discouraged exports. Brazil had no export taxes, but exports had been systematically discouraged by an over-valued currency; this had the same effect. African currencies, he thought, were under-valued. Official prices did not reflect local values. This meant that there was, in effect, a subsidy to exports. Third, he thought one should not be over-pessimistic about finding the resources required for development. There was a great untapped potential of private savings, given the right opportunities and incentives. Fourth, he thought that there were considerable opportunities to increase development expenditures by shifts within the total of existing government expenditures.

Mr. Ngcobo argued that poll-taxes were both regressive in character and inequitable in their effects. Since development expenditure had multiplier effects it was right to shift from hut and poll-taxes to a simple tax assessed on actual incomes. Poll-tax was only useful if it was supplemented by a number of other taxes which would redress its inequities. In Africa the practicable range of taxes was very limited. If one was driven to use import and export taxes one ought to be very careful to eliminate their regressive effects.

Professor Peacock suggested that it was very necessary to define what one meant by equity. One had to talk about equity as a whole, and not in every fragmentary part. On the tax side one should think both of vertical and of horizontal equity. There was no unanimity as to what was an equitable system. Thus equity was regarded as a political problem rather than a welfare problem. With economic development there might well be a desire to move away from the present system. He thought that the optimum level of revenue in relation to national income in many African territories had already been exceeded.

Dr. Wade could not help feeling that financial policies needed strengthening. Public expenditure in many of the French territories was very low as compared with gross national product. In West Africa they had to provide for elected legislatures, for increased government services, for diplomatic representation. All this was forcing government expenditure up. The coming of independence had considerably changed the scope of taxations. Non-exporting countries could only rely on some form of income tax or other. In Senegal they had a system of taxes, the revenue from which was related to specific expenditures. It was very difficult to find a single model that was appropriate to all the variety of conditions that existed in Africa.

Mr. Beheiry suggested that the apparent burden of taxation was least when there was identity of purpose between the people paying tax and the government collecting it. In that sense, independence and a democratic African government might reduce the apparent burden.

Mr. Bhouraskat (ECA) thought that too much was being made of the costs of collecting income tax. Countries like the United States and the United Kingdom had developed to the point where large volumes of tax could be collected cheaply. In Africa they had to make a start. For the time being it was better to think of the absolute cost of collecting tax rather than of its relation to national income.

Dr. Yudelman insisted that, if one of the basic needs of Africa was to develop the cash sector, it was most important that export taxes should not be so high as to drive people back into the subsistence sector. There was a need to examine fiscal policy in relation to the basic objectives of the economy.

Professor Enke thought that the extent of damage of conspicuous expenditure was being exaggerated. Was it really so bad ? Keeping up with the Joneses was as much a part of life in Africa as in any country. Nevertheless, he thought that there was still a possibility of reducing consumption by carefully selective import duties. At the time of its independence, the United States derived 99 per cent of its federal revenues from import duties. There were, however, difficulties in differentiating between different products for purposes of import duty. One had to remember the possibility of smuggling. In taxing exports, moreover, it was necessary to differentiate between minerals, which were usually produced by foreign enterprises, and agricultural products produced by domestic producers. Export taxes made an economy more vulnerable to external forces. A number of countries had used turn-over taxes, but these were rather difficult to administer. A poll-tax could only be considered as part of a general tax system. In under-developed countries part of the argument for a poll-tax was to provide an incentive to work. He wondered whether poll-tax could not be made more flexible. There was the possibility of allowing the poll-tax to be paid in kind or by labour, but this smacked of forced labour.

Professor Spengler wished to know whether expenditure taxes had been tried in Africa, or sumptuary taxes.

Professor Robinson wanted to return to a subject discussed earlier, the relatively low level of real services that could be financed in Africa by a relatively high level of revenue. This, as had been pointed out, was partly the consequence of the high levels of salaries paid to civil servants, both expatriates and Africans. Was there not a case for reconsidering the levels of civil service salaries in Africa to make them relate rather more nearly to average incomes in African territories ? In India after independence this had been done. Would it not be desirable to do the same in Africa ? During a transitional period any expatriates needed could continue to be paid the salaries to attract them. But was it necessary to pay African civil servants the salaries that would induce Europeans to take service in Africa ?

Mr. Bhouraskat (ECA) thought that average salaries in government employment should be related to *per capita* income for the territory concerned. As it was, the ratio of government expenditure to national income could be very misleading as an index of the services actually rendered. In Congo, for example, the ratio was considerably higher than in the Union of South Africa. The essential question was that of the standards of services provided.

Mr. Beheiry thought that government expenditures were high not because individual salaries were high but because the numbers employed were large. He thought that there was a great deal of scope for mechanization of accounting services ; saving should be made by reducing numbers and raising efficiency rather than by reducing individual salaries. It was most important to any African country that it should have a body of efficient and incorruptible civil servants. Good pay was a condition of that.

Dr. Okigbo was not sure that he agreed that large savings of staff were practicable. This was something that could only be discovered by experience. Public service with African governments was, moreover, a main and important source of employment.

Mr. Abbas (ECA) intervened to say that he thought that the levels of civil service salaries had to be studied country by country. This was a matter to which the ECA had given much thought. His own belief was that any economy should be secured by reduction in the numbers employed and increased efficiency, rather than by reduction of salaries.

Professor Peacock suggested that the market for some categories of administrative skills, such as Africa needed to buy, was international.

At the *Chairman's* suggestion, the last stages of the discussion were devoted to the monetary aspects of the problem. *Professor Dupriez* emphasized the important contribution of monetary policy to the stability of economic life, safeguarding the economy against disturbances. He thought one should pay more attention to this aspect than to regulating either incomes or expenditure. One should examine the functions of the banks in relation to the insulation of the country against fluctuations.

Mr. Onitiri argued that there were many advantages to be gained from breaking away from the Currency Board system. In Nigeria the Central Bank had inherited a great many rigidities from the former Currency Board. The extent to which a flexible monetary system could be operated depended on the power of the Central Bank to control all the reserves of the country. What ought to be done regarding the foreign exchange holdings, more particularly of expatriate banks? If a country could consolidate its entire foreign exchange holdings it would be possible to make economies in them. If monetary policy was to be successful, the Central Bank must also be in a position to exercise selective control over imports and the use of foreign currency. Since they were more concerned in the foreign trade, it was desirable to possess a more comprehensive control over expatriate banks than over indigenous banks.

Mr. Beheiry agreed that the currency board system was rather too rigid. In the Sudan they had found from experience, gained when they were no longer members of the Sterling Area, that the requirements of their country had outgrown the Currency Board system. From the objectives of administrative convenience and speed of action, they had reorganized their own system, pooling resources in a single agency. This had various advantages. It allowed a more systematic use of their reserves and a more remunerative investment of the reserves. Some regard to public confidence and public relations was necessary in determining investment policy. The nature of the reserve holdings was largely determined by the requirements of a particular country's foreign trade pattern.

The guiding policy regarding investments was determined by two factors : the need for liquidity and the need to get a return ; the latter was particularly important to the Sudan. From the point of view of safety, gold was obviously the best choice. Stocks and shares of different sorts introduced risks of varying degree, and the safety considerations might not be fulfilled. The real problem was to invest safely. Some form of assurance, such as might be achieved by an international scheme, was very desirable.

Turning to the problems of banking structure, *Mr. Beheiry* said that he thought that the creation of credit institutions was necessary as a preliminary to development. In setting up a central bank the fundamental question was whether one should follow traditional lines or try to adapt them to suit local requirements. He thought that this was a problem that needed a more thorough investigation. One very important question was what functions a central bank should perform : should it engage in ordinary commercial banking ? What collateral should it require ? All these were problems which needed very careful consideration.

Professor Bézy said that the systems of monetary areas had both advantages and disadvantages. In some under-developed countries he thought that such a system had been most valuable in promoting development. In other countries they seemed to have been an impediment. Within the French zone some prices were very far above world prices, and countries within the zone received a certain amount of protection.

Mr. Dowuona thought that it was much better that the developed countries should evolve trading and financial policies that would promote the economic development of the backward countries, rather than that they should give loans or aid. Within an under-developed country, the problem was how to get the most capital development. For this a careful conservation of foreign exchange was very important. He thought that there were considerable untapped resources of potential savings which could be evoked by suitable, if sometimes unorthodox, policies, such as compulsory premium bonds and other measures of that kind, some of which had been tried in Ghana.

Dr. Okigbo suggested that statistical returns relating to earnings from foreign trade were capable of a good deal of distortion and thought that policy prescriptions based upon their assumed accuracy might be ingenuous.

M. Rist commented on the very wide differences of tax systems and fiscal policies in different parts of the world. In regard to banks of issue, he thought that what was important was the policy they proposed to follow in future. Much might be learned from a study of South American financial history. The main objective should be to ensure that the major shocks caused by world events should be reduced in their effects on the country concerned by the appropriate use of the reserves. Continuity of growth was more important than maximum speed of growth at a particular moment. It was most important to use periods of good trade to strengthen reserves, and to husband them as carefully as possible.

Professor Peacock thought that the management of the reserves was the best test of the working of a monetary system. He suggested that most African countries needed much better monetary statistics than they yet possessed.

Chapter 26

THE CONTRIBUTION OF ECONOMIC
RESEARCH TO AFRICAN DEVELOPMENT

BY

W. F. STOLPER

Ministry of Economic Development, Lagos, Nigeria
and University of Michigan, Ann Arbor, Michigan

AFRICA is a big place, and economic research is a big subject. It is to be understood that I have limited first-hand experience of only a small part of Africa, and also that my research activities have dealt with only a few fields and that, in any case, I must be selective. The topic has a certain ambiguity. Presumably it should discuss the contributions that economics can make to economic development as against the contributions of other fields. It may be intended to discuss the contributions of economics as contrasted to political decisions. Or perhaps research may mean the discussion of as yet unresolved problems as compared to the application of more recent developments of economic theory.

Long ago Alfred Marshall defined theory as the machine for organizing facts. This definition, which has led in the past to a distinction between tool users and tool makers, has got somewhat into disrepute. Recent developments of theory, however, particularly the growth of empirical and quantitative economics, have blurred the distinction between tool users and tool makers and this has given new meaning to the Marshallian dictum.

Without overstressing the point, it is my feeling that the major obstacle to economic development from an economic standpoint is the lack of knowledge of facts, and it is therefore the main thesis of this paper that one of the major contributions to economic research consists in aiding the rational collection of data and the identification of our lacunae.

Economic development in Africa today is associated with economic planning, and it might be useful to use a planning framework to identify some of the contributions to be made by economic research as well as the relationships which economics has to other fields and policy decisions.

I. THE PLANNING FRAMEWORK

Planning in a non-centralized economy means, essentially, the giving of a central direction to development of an economy. The execution of the central direction may in fact be decentralized, and it may, to a large extent, be left to the play of market forces. In the African context, under-development means not only that the standard of living of the masses of the population has to be raised, but that obstacles have to be overcome which have impeded in the past the growth of the money economy, the increase in productivity, the increase in savings and investment ratios, the inter-communications amongst various sectors, etc. At the same time, all African economies suffer from a lack of skilled manpower which, in many cases, has probably been the real limit to possible investments. This is not to say that a shortage of investment funds has been unimportant. In all African economies, money has not penetrated the whole of the economy and it is almost a characteristic of under-developed economies that internal communications among various sectors are rudimentary and that they are primarily export oriented. These facts impose certain limitations on what can, or should, be done by economic planning.

Economic planning for economic development has essentially to go along three lines. First, there are capital budgets of ministries and public corporations which deal with such matters as road development, railroads, electricity, education. Secondly, provision has to be made for increasing recurrent budgets for economic development. For example, agricultural extension is essentially a question of providing manpower and recurrent expenditure. Thirdly, however, the very lack of skilled manpower and the very absence of a well-developed money economy make it essential that as many decisions as possible are decentralized, and that therefore as many decisions as possible are made in a semi-automatic manner. Whether or not this works depends in part on the responses of a population to economic incentives. I am told that in some parts of India or Pakistan it is extremely difficult to get increases in agricultural production by economic incentives. I know, on the other hand, that in the northern region of Nigeria it has in the past been sufficient to put in feeder roads and to distribute seeds in order to get substantial increases in agricultural production (though not necessarily agricultural productivity). Every plan must therefore include a section dealing with economic policies designed to establish markets, increase the scope of the money economy, and increase the area of decentralized decision making. I deliberately use this somewhat clumsy phrase because the problem to me seems essentially the same regardless of whether or not we deal with a socialist economy or a private economy. Certainly, there is some Russian or East German literature which stresses the need to make use of the economic incentive of the population and the need to use 'economic levers'.

All three parts of a plan raise the relation of economics to politics. It must be accepted without question that politics has primacy : in fact, the desire for economic development itself is primarily a political decision. I realize that many of the major capital-consuming expenditures of social overhead are not amenable to a strict economic calculus and are therefore particularly subject to the vagaries of political decisions. The only contributions an economist can make are twofold. First, he can point out to the politicians that resources are scarce and that they will be unable as a rule to satisfy all their 'legitimate' necessities. When the politician makes a choice, the economist can aid him in putting the available choices in straight opportunity cost terms : building a television station will cost so and so many schools, or so and so many tons of steel. Secondly, the economist has to point out that the sectors which do not have an economic payoff must be paid for from production originating in the directly productive sectors. Communist economists, as is well known, make this distinction between productive and non-productive sectors. There is evidence that communist writers have misunderstood Marx in identifying 'productive' with 'material', but we need not be concerned with the esoteric discussion on this point. The major point is that social overhead sectors must be financed from the payoffs of other sectors.

The major overall policy directive which can be given to the economist is the initial setting of a target for the rate of growth of total output. But this, of course, is not the only one. An economist will frequently be in a position to point out that the distribution of investment among sectors desired by politicians will not give the desired rate of growth, and he will frequently be in the disagreeable position where he has to point out that the savings ratio will have to be raised. The restricting of consumption is always more acceptable in abstraction than when a specific tax increase has to be voted.

While the discussion of capital and recurrent budgets brings up such questions as rate of growth of GNP, savings-investment ratios, or investment criteria, the discussion of economic policies is the place in which the other sister fields of economics come into their own. Under economic policies I would group two major topics. The first is the building of institutions, such as a central bank, money market, co-operative credit institutions, research institutes for agriculture

714

and industry, training institutes. The second is the development of policies to work through those institutions.

II. NATIONAL ACCOUNTING

Before a capital budget or any plan can be framed, it is useful to have an overall picture of the economy itself, recent developments, and its structure. The development of national accounting has been, perhaps, the most useful tool developed in recent years to give such an overall view. It becomes necessary to get some notion of what investment ratios have been and how they might develop in the future. It is of course agreed that the purpose of any planning exercise, and, indeed, of economic development, is to change the structure of the economy and to increase the rate of growth. It is therefore agreed that a simple extrapolation of the past into the future would only in rare cases be a meaningful procedure. It is, however, a useful starting-point : firstly, because it is essential to have some benchmark before the future can be sketched out ; secondly, because we are not starting our development from scratch but from an existing situation which has a considerable amount of inertia built into it — in fact, to a considerable extent, the future has already happened ; and thirdly, because the national accounting framework permits us to trace in a consistent manner the effects of certain supposed policy changes and, in particular, because it reminds us of the indirect repercussions on the rest of the economy which any governmental or private capital programme will have.

There are three topics in connection with national accounting which I wish to discuss somewhat more closely. One : the problem of the traditional sector. Two : the problem of the definition of investment. Three : the problem of the definition of the balance of payments. All three are as much statistical as theoretical problems.

(i) *The Traditional Sector*

In all African economies, a considerable amount of production, amounting to perhaps 30 or 40 per cent of the Gross Domestic Product, takes place in the so-called subsistence sector. The problems raised by measurement have been ably discussed by Phyllis Deane, Stewart and Prest, and, more recently, by Jackson and Okigbo, to mention just a few. I have nothing to add to the methodological problem of how to go about measuring the output by households of commodities for their own use. I am aware from reading the mentioned authors and others that all measurements of the traditional sector are extremely rough. The advice is sometimes found that, since the roughness of the estimates make the value of growth rates of GNP highly dubious (which is of course correct), it would be best to omit from all economic considerations a discussion of the subsistence sector. I cannot agree with this advice.

In the African context, the traditional sector is not only very big, but it is substantially intertwined with the money sector. The interrelation between the two sectors relates both to the products and to the people : the same person may be in and out of the money economy — which raises, among others, the problems of a stabilized labour force — and the same commodity may be inside and outside of the traditional sector. Moreover, it is not entirely correct to assume that the traditional sector is a sector outside the money economy. Thus, to use an example from my immediate knowledge, the eastern region and the western region of Nigeria export about the same amount of palm kernels, while the western region exports only a fraction of the amount of palm-oil exported from the eastern region. The difference must, presumably, be a greater consumption of palm-oil within the western region. But we do not know the nature of the consumption : to what extent it is traded on markets ; nor do we know exactly how much is actually so consumed ; nor do we know how much palm-oil is produced in the eastern region for domestic consumption. If, for example, it were desired to increase the ratio of exports to total production of palm-oil, we do not know how much of a price increase we would need, and, in fact, whether we would need a price increase at all. And we do not know whether increases in the exports of palm-oil in any particular year are due completely to greater production or whether they should be offset by decreases in palm-oil domestically consumed.

Similarly, we know, or at least so many surveys have told us, that when a man leaves his village to earn money, village production will be affected. We cannot assume in the African context that the marginal product of the labour in the country is zero. Therefore, we would make a mistake from a policy standpoint if we took any increase in the production of the money sector as the net increase in GDP without investigating whether or not there have been repercussions in the traditional sector.

An implication of this conclusion is that if we ever get to the stage where our data permits us a more sophisticated planning of an input-output type, it would be in the African context a mistake to put into the calculations the price of labour as zero, as Professor Tinbergen has suggested should be done in, say, India, and as, for example, Mr. Chakravarty does in his brilliant model of investment planning.

The discussion of the subsistence sector is also very closely linked with our very great ignorance of the nature of domestic trade. We know very little of how this trade is organized. We know very little of how efficient it is. We can gratefully accept Professor Bauer's analysis that the inefficiency of domestic trade is more apparent than real, and that its function is a continuous breaking of bulk, without accepting that this is a complete explanation. Similarly, we can gratefully accept the explanations of our sociologist and anthropologist colleagues that trading has a deep social function, without accepting that the petty trading system we meet in larger towns in, say, Nigeria, is necessarily the best system, and without having one's suspicions stilled that a more efficient organization of the system might set not insubstantial amounts of resources free for economic development.

(ii) *Investment*

In national accounting as developed by Western economists, investment is defined as the sum of expenditure on plant and equipment, land clearance and housing. These definitions are carried over to the national accounting as at present applied in such African countries which have any accounts at all. The factual questions which are raised even when this definition is accepted are again discussed by the authors I have mentioned, and others.

It should perhaps be remembered what the purpose of the definitions in a western context are. Investment, on the one hand, is supposed to provide for the enlargement of the productive capacity of an economy. Communist economists have distinguished between productive and unproductive accumulations which, in their context, may or may not make sense. I suggest that some of their distinction is meaningful in the African context. The reason why western economists include residential housing among investment expenses is, I believe, threefold. First, the expenditure can obviously produce a stream of services in the future, just as any investment produces a stream of payoffs. Second, given the social surroundings of a western economist, it would be considered impossible not to provide adequate housing for a work force in connection with new direct payoff investments. From that standpoint, the distinction between productive and non-productive accumulation to a western economist is simply another way of saying that real wages can be held down more easily in a socialist economy than in a capitalist economy by simply refusing the real income of adequate housing. Thirdly, however, most western economies have a Keynesian problem of inadequate demand on top of the ever-present classical problem of raising productivity. When there is a problem of inadequate demand, residential housing has an important stabilizing function and an important multiplier effect.

In the African context, the problem of inadequate demand does not seem to be of paramount importance. Most housing of the traditional type becomes durable only when tin roofs or other imported materials are used to protect the mud walls from the heavy rains. The modern type of housing, on the other hand, which is becoming an important incentive good, together with radios, bicycles, sewing-machines, and other imported durable goods, requires large amounts of imports. This means that it competes directly with development goods for scarce foreign exchange, and it means that it does not have the same stabilizing or multiplier effect, which it has in an advanced economy, because of the indirect effects which lead to further imports.

One implication of what I have said seems to be that, as long as a country does not have a building-materials industry, residential construction for policy purposes should be classified with consumption rather than investment. A second policy implication seems to be that the build-up of a building-materials industry should have high priority where possible, because this build-up makes it possible to convert residential housing from a leakage and a drain on scarce foreign resources into a motor for economic development. Once the building-material industries develop, construction can be used to absorb employment, to satisfy the needs for incentive goods, and to raise effective demand.

In a way, it is somewhat irrelevant whether residential construction is classified as consumption or investment as long as the statisticians give us sufficiently detailed figures. For international comparisons, however, it seems to me not as important that in all countries investment is defined to contain exactly the same categories but that it is defined to fulfil the same purpose : to raise productive capacity and to act as a motor for growth.

(iii) *Balance of Payments*

Many African economies are fortunate in having goods to export. The statistical information relating to export commodities and to imports is now most satisfactory in many of the African territories. (Actually, information on actual exports is satisfactory. Unfortunately, this is not the same as information on export commodities — see example of palm-oil ; groundnut is another example.) The difficulties arise along two lines. First, countries have become very conscious of the instability of raw material prices, and a great number of studies exist to prove the elasticity of demand for raw materials is low. In point of fact, less is known about elasticity of demand and terms of trade than seems to be the case. The recent drop in the price of cocoa, which has been associated with a very large increase in supply, has led to a much smaller reduction in export receipts for cocoa than was originally feared. In a period of less than a year the demand for cocoa has expanded beyond anticipation. This suggests that, in fact, elasticity is greater than expected. Secondly, many of the export products enter a highly competitive world market : hence the elasticity of demand for any particular commodity and for any particular supplier must be presumed to be larger than for the commodities as a whole. It follows from these two observations that commodity price stabilization and expansion of markets do not exhaust the possible reactions to raw material price fluctuations, and that a third must be to reduce the cost of production of these commodities to stay competitive. It is relevant that cost of production cannot, again, be defined in the same manner as it would be for a western economy. What really interests us are the out-of-pocket expenses of production for spreading fertilizer, new seedlings, etc., while the labour income should be considered as the payoff. Even substantial price falls can be easily absorbed if they are the result of relatively large increases in production, which are, in return, the result of relatively minor investment, as has been the case with cocoa and may easily be the case with the oil-palm products. Whether the foreign exchange earnings increase or decrease will depend, of course, on the elasticity which, for any particular country, cannot be assumed to be less than one. Moreover, even if it were true that the elasticity of demand for, say, cocoa is less than one, it still does not follow that an individual country should not expand its production since it would be even worse off by contracting it and thereby leaving the market to its competitors.

The terms of trade of a country will of course depend upon the structure of its imports and exports. For a long time to come African economies will be predominantly agricultural countries, unless they strike oil as has been the case in a few of them. It follows, therefore, that the countries might attempt to increase the number of agricultural products which they export. On the other hand, the movement of import prices will depend very much on the structure of imports which themselves depend on the level of consumption permitted and the structure of the investment programme envisaged. The fluctuations in the terms of trade of a country, such as Nigeria, seem to have had more to do with such events as the Korean War and the Suez crisis than with any supposed long-term trend of deteriorating terms of trade.

The major problems of the balance of payments deal, however, not with commodity trade but with capital movements. The knowledge of capital movements in large areas of Africa is extremely scant because of the colonial past of these territories, which has continued through association in monetary blocs and which is compounded by the fact that many of the major banking and trade institutions are expatriate.

In order not to be misunderstood, I wish to make it quite clear that I suspect that the former colonial territories probably benefit on balance from this fact of continued monetary association, and I would like to emphasize that I do not believe that exchange controls would solve any problems which cannot be solved better by other means. It is, however, a fact that a large number of transactions between an African country and its associated European country never go through the balance of payments, and that it is not always clear, for example, just how big sterling or franc reserves really are, or what its foreign assets are relative to its foreign liabilities. As long as there is no exchange control and as long as any legitimate foreign exchange needs of business, government, and private persons are met without any question, there is no real need to know the exact position. If, however, projections are to be made, or even if such policy questions are to be answered as to whether it is safe to expand domestic demand without running into a balance of payments crisis, more information on the nature of capital movement, the transfer of profits, the real influx of foreign capital, and the foreign asset position, becomes desirable. Yet even conceptually we are far from clear just what we want to know from large expatriate banks, say, or truly international corporations.

III. INTER-INDUSTRY FLOWS

In recent years there has been an expanding literature on investment criteria, and related to it has been a discussion of input-output models of inter-industry flows. This work, it must be stressed, has been of more direct relevance to the more sophisticated Asian economies. I believe, however, that the ideas, if not the techniques themselves, are immediately useful for the planning of economic development in African economies.

First, some sort of investment criteria must be developed for the allocation of funds amongst the competing governmental capital claims. For some of its sectors, direct cost/benefit calculations can be made ; for example, a broadcasting corporation will usually have some income available, or a road programme will lead to increased revenue from increased traffic. The issue whether or not all these programmes should actually be made to pay for themselves seems to me a different one from the issue whether they should be undertaken only if they can be made to pay. In other words, the allocation of resources and the distribution of the cost among various groups seem to me to involve two different decisions.[1] Such cost/benefit calculations have the added advantage of identifying possible sources of revenue, possible short-falls in financing, and the costs which are to be attached to non-economic factors. As we have learned from Professor Tinbergen, however, we have to look really beyond immediate cost/benefit calculations into the inter-relations in the economy. I have no hope of setting up an input-output table for, say, Nigeria which could be used for operational purposes (though it would give me great pleasure if I could produce even a crude one for academic purposes). But it is not beyond hope to try to identify for each particular programme what its material content is, whether the materials or labour have to be imported, what the major materials are which will be required, and when any payoffs may be expected to come in.

In this manner we cannot only approach an estimate of our foreign exchange needs and our manpower needs (information which may be expected to feed back into foreign exchange budgeting and into the educational programme), but we can identify those productions for which feasibility studies might profitably be undertaken.

Professor W. A. Lewis's study on the *Industrialization of the Gold Coast* is well known. In it he has used a combination of import statistics, location theory, and engineering studies, to identify possible industries for Ghana. Mr. Hirschman's proposition that imports are used to build up a market which, once it has reached a critical size, can then be pre-empted by domestic production, is along the same lines. The crude input-output statistics which can be collected for governmental programmes as well as the programmes of major public and private corporations can supplement the import

---

[1] As a sidelight, I have noticed that American economists when asked their income will give it before taxes, while German economists tend to state it after taxes !

information and make it dynamic, as it were, to identify which cells of the inter-industry table ought to be filled by domestic production.

This is obviously a far cry from the elegant system worked out by Mr. Chakravarty, or from the calculations of Mr. Chenery. Nevertheless, it is dubious whether we should have thought of collecting this kind of information in a systematic manner without the work they have done. We know, however, that in Russian planning, amazingly enough, the 'checkerboard' method of material balances has not apparently gone any further, although in that context one would have thought a fully fledged analysis would be essential.

In African economies, the number of firms employing five or more people and using relatively modern methods of production is limited. It should therefore be possible to carry through a census for such firms, with relatively limited staff and in limited time. In fact, I know of no such census which has been completed. Yet it would give us a great deal of important information which would be useful for development planning whether by government or the private sector. The information, for example, that a certain number of tons of cement would be needed for a certain number of years is equally useful to governments which wish to go into cement production themselves, or for a government which wishes to interest private investors into starting sufficient production.

Because we cannot get a complete picture of the economy, the inter-industry flow type of information must be integrated with the more aggregative national accounting in order to allow for indirect repercussions. In other words, I do not believe that we can build up at this stage a complete account of the need for, say, foreign exchange on the information available in inter-industry flows. We can, and must, use this information for the purpose of assessing investment criteria and therefore the allocation of funds, and for the purpose of identifying empty cells which should be filled by new production. I assume without going into it in this context that other conditions for production, such as availability of raw materials, are favourable. On the other hand, the fact that the requisite skilled labour must be available will feed back into the educational programme, may lead to the expenditure on foreign experts, and will have an important effect on the timing of investments.

IV. INSTITUTION BUILDING

I now turn to the building of institutions. It is natural for new countries to wish to have their own central bank or commercial banking system. However, to get more than an issuing of money, a money and capital market have to be developed. It is impossible to make monetary policy when no discountable paper exists, when there are no clearly understood signals in the economy, when commercial banks are run independent of the central bank, and when, in any case, there is relatively little business with commercial banks outside the foreign trade sector. The development of monetary policy requires that the banking system becomes more widespread. It requires that small and large savings are collected in the banks, that dealings in commercial paper, both private and governmental, develop. It is only a first step to set up central banking legislation and to define the relationship of commercial banks to the central bank. It then requires real imagination on the side of the monetary authorities to develop such papers which are acceptable to the business community outside of foreign trade.

The problem of developing the proper savings institutions probably requires the aid of sociologists and anthropologists. In any case, I do see the relationship of the other fields to economics, particularly in connection with the development of such institutions as co-operatives, agricultural credit organizations, public corporations, marketing boards. The problem there is not so much of the setting up of the legal framework as finding the methods of getting across to the public what the policy is intended to accomplish. If the policy deals with the problem of raising the savings ratio we have to know how to collect money from the small saver. This may require lotteries or a nationalized football pool ; it may require savings bonds with the lottery feature — which seem to me to make more sense in a country like Nigeria than in England where they are a success.

If the policy deals with expanding agricultural production, then we have already such institutions as agricultural extension services and, in many countries, marketing boards. But we still need agricultural co-operatives. And the agricultural extension service seems woefully understaffed and ineffective compared with what it is in the United States. The problem is frequently one of training supervisory staff, getting across that loans are for productive purposes rather than to help out the local bigshot, for inducing farmers to use methods which have been proven on large-scale experiments, and that in turn is a question of building up an agricultural extension staff and institution which can be kept reasonably free from political interference. There seems to be little use in saying that agricultural credit can be given only for productive purposes and not to personal and political friends when, in fact, the problem is how to train people to administer such a scheme and how to persuade people to accept such criteria as reasonable. The economist is trained primarily to set up the criteria, but not necessarily on how to get them across to a farmer or local politician.

The development of the private sector, as well as the efficient development of any public industrial sector if this should be desired, requires the training of managers and accountants. It also requires the training of skilled and supervisory manpower at the foreman level. Most countries seem to go in for education in general terms to build up a reservoir of manpower from which the skilled manpower will eventually be drawn. Technical education and business education is taking place either in special schools or in connection with the job.

It is no secret that in a country like Nigeria the educational programme has led to serious problems of the unemployability of school-leavers, and this is also true in other countries. In part, this problem has arisen because the expectations of the school-leavers are out of all proportion to their actual training. It is extremely difficult to get across in Africa that, in England or in the United States, say, it takes six to eight years of schooling before a man is allowed to be an unskilled worker, and even then he is not really expected to know anything directly useful to his job. We accept in the west the idea of general education in a liberal sense. In Africa, however, even the training of reading and writing seems to be considered professional education and the normal school-leaver expects the acquisition of such knowledge to free him from the drudgery of primitive farming and admit him automatically into the white-collar field. The fact is, however, that capital is simply not available to employ sufficient numbers of school-leavers outside of farming and, in any case, the idea originally was that he should be a more educated and hence more productive farmer.

The fact that the school-leaver problem has arisen, raises the question whether in fact curricula have been adapted imaginatively to local needs. Either the schools should be sold to the public as a means for liberal education and/or the means of making better citizens with no direct payoff, such as the right to expect a better job for the majority of school-leavers. Or else the school curriculum should be adapted so as to produce specifically the kind of people who will be needed. In which case, presumably, the amounts of money allocated to schooling would be drastically reduced. The school-leaver problem illustrates, in my opinion, the failure to integrate institutions properly into the developmental process.

On a different level, the problem of raw material price stabilization leads to the problem of institution building. The marketing boards in many African countries have in fact been used for taxation purposes rather than for price stabilization, even when there was no legal authority to do so. This is not said as a criticism. However, if in the future it should be decided that price stabilization cannot be achieved through marketing boards, it might become quite reasonable to abolish them and to transfer their marketing functions to a new agency, their taxation function directly to the ministries of finance, and their agricultural extension work — such as the distribution of seeds — directly to the departments of agriculture. I am not advocating the abolition of marketing boards, but merely use their case as another illustration for the need to build institutions which are adapted to the particular environment and which fulfil the purposes which they are intended to fulfil.

V. POLICIES

Many of the points which can be discussed in this section might also have been discussed in the preceding sections : such as, for example, the case for the stimulation of an industrial sector and manufacturing sector, including plantations and modern agriculture, through development corporations and/or development banks. One of the major policy problems is whether or not to have a large private sector. My personal answer would be that the development of a large private sector is essential, not for any particular ideological reason but, quite on the contrary, because the shortage of skilled manpower and of capital in African economies makes it imperative that no economic resource should be left unemployed for ideological reasons. One way of stimulating a private sector, which has a time-honoured history and which has recently been used effectively in the West German recovery, has been to pump public money into the private sector. This can be done in a number of ways. An indirect way is from tax concessions in which the public money is not collected in the first place. A second way is through a tariff policy which either gives special protection to particular industries deemed desirable, or which, preferably, protects certain types of industries. Since it is desirable to minimize personal administrative decisions and to have a maximum of certainty, it is probably preferable to have a graduated tariff starting with zero for raw materials and development goods and increasing for those kinds of industries dealing with certain kinds of manufactured consumer goods where domestic production might be feasible. A third method, which in some respects is more advisable since any industry which needs protection for any length of time is hardly a desirable industry for a poor country — it cannot be emphasized enough that making losses is no way of getting rich — is to establish government industries which, when successful, can be sold in part or in whole to the private sector. This has the advantage of starting initially a risky industry and then rolling over the capital possibly with a profit after the industry is established. An example would be the Nkalagu Cement factory in the eastern region of Nigeria. Some of their share capital is now held by the general public. An additional advantage of this particular method is to get the public used to the idea of buying shares, which is easier done for an established factory than for a new one, and which aids the collection of small savings.

The disadvantage is, of course, that in practice government is not well equipped to run a business enterprise and that bureaucrats, being human, would be loath to get rid of a profitable business because it looks good and an unprofitable business because it looks bad ! This should, however, not obscure the fact that in Japan or Germany this method has been successfully used and that it could be used also in Africa. Another function of development corporations would be, of course, to provide additional money where not sufficient private money comes in. A third one would be to make loans to private business rather than to provide equity capital. All of these methods have the political advantage that foreign funds can be channelled into the private sector through development corporations and/or banks, without the foreign interference feared by many of the newly independent countries.

I am, of course, aware that a development bank and a development corporation would have different policies and different investment criteria, but there is no point in going into this here.

A second set of policies refer to problems of taxation. The study of Lewis and Martin indicated that taxation in many under-developed countries is relatively low. Government consumption in Nigeria is well below 10 per cent of GDP. Now it would, of course, be absurd to claim that all that is needed is to raise the government sector to get increased development. Nevertheless, the justifiable development programmes do require both increased taxation and increased private savings. Many of the African countries must rely on indirect taxes for the bulk of their revenue, which means specifically export and import duties. I include marketing board profits among the export duties. At the same time, many of the African countries have become aware of equity considerations and like to raise additional taxes through direct income tax. The problems of administering a direct tax, other than a head tax, are, on the other hand, formidable, and the tax is likely to be more inequitable than the incidence of indirect taxation.

The tax problem raises also policy questions in respect to the development of the directly productive sector versus the social overhead, and toward the financing of the social overhead. It is, for example, by no means clear whether road systems must be subsidized. Fuel taxes and licence fees might just as well cover recurrent cost of a road system, including a reasonable interest charge and depreciation. It is by no means self-evident that elementary school systems must be 100 per cent supported by a central or provincial government, and in a poor country a good case can be made that local contributions should pay for a considerable share of the school system.

A fourth set of problems relates to the relative sizes of the social sector versus the directly productive sector. Mr. Hirschman has argued (on the basis of his Colombian experience) for letting the social sector lag and to let it emerge in response to the pressures generated by the development of the directly productive sector. My limited experience in Nigeria suggests that there is a good deal to be said for this view also in Africa. If the crude inter-industry approach to planning, which I have outlined, is used a certain amount of manpower planning can be built into the plan which itself gives one, but only one, criterion for the size and structure of the educational sector. The justly famous Ashby Report for Educational Development in Nigeria, and, in particular, Professor Harbison's contribution, specifically starts up from economic targets and attempts in a crude, but nevertheless the best possible manner to work out the manpower requirements. Similarly, although the transport system will always ultimately be determined politically, the politician nevertheless will be able to chose between roads which open up more of the hinterland, and those which just go nowhere ! Road priorities are already at present determined in many countries according to potential traffic which, in turn, is related to the hinterland and the expected agricultural production which is opened up by the roads. To the extent to which this is done the size of the social overhead itself is geared to the development of the directly productive sector. On the other hand, improving the health of the population will undoubtedly improve its productivity. Nevertheless, purely economic considerations are next to impossible to make for medical services, and are in any case repulsive to make.

On the other end of the spectrum is the theory, which seems to have been implicit in some development planning in the past, that the proper function of the government is to establish social overhead ; *i.e.* to establish physically the conditions for a market to exist and then hopefully wait for the private sector to develop the rest of the economy. The question in my mind is not whether the theory is correct — it is very likely correct. The question is that here as elsewhere in economics we do not as a rule deal with either-or propositions, but with more-or-less propositions. The social overhead had to be financed ; *i.e.* it must use real resources which must be taken away either from consumption or directly productive investments. Therefore, to the extent to which the financing of social overhead takes away from directly productive investment, it slows down the growth of the economy and future resources available for social overhead. Just as we can have, in the United States, a starving of the public sector to the benefit of the private sector, it seems to me that the danger in African economies is just the opposite : that too much will be drawn for roads, schools, and public buildings, and too little for the development of the directly productive sectors, particularly agriculture. This danger will be compounded by the fact that it is actually extremely difficult to spend large amounts successfully in the agricultural sector.

On the whole, I am inclined to agree with Mr. Hirschman's view, but unfortunately the problem is somewhat eased by the fact that a large part of the social sector actually is in the market nexus : electricity is actually sold ; bridges could be made toll bridges ; and a return from road users can be obtained from import duties and other taxation on vehicles and drivers. Hence the real problem relates only to those substantial sectors where such calculations cannot be made or where it would be repugnant to make them : primarily, health and education.

Another set of problems deals with the encouragement of foreign investment. This turns out to be a rather ticklish problem which is linked, on the one hand, with the question of private versus public ownership, and, on the other hand, with nationalistic sensibilities. The fact that a nation will have a large government sector in itself does not preclude the influx of foreign capital, as the case in India has shown. African nations have, however, still to live down their recent colonial past. On the one hand, it is quite clear that they will need large amounts of foreign capital and foreign know-how if they are to develop quickly ; on the other hand, there is an ever-present and quite understandable fear of 'colonialism' in a new guise. This is a phase through which many countries have gone. One way of dealing with this problem is to channel the foreign funds through a development corporation into the private indigenous sector, which can then be used to employ, where necessary, foreign experts and thus avoid being directly owned abroad. It is quite clear that a great deal of both research and education is needed to find a solution satisfactory at the same time to both the African statesman and the foreign investor.

DISCUSSION OF PROFESSOR STOLPER'S PAPER

Professor Robinson, opening the discussion, began by expressing his profound agreement with Professor Stolper's general approach. He thought that the most important thing was to know more of the facts — and especially the quantitative facts — about Africa. This was not that he believed in an anti-intellectual approach to African problems. The best theoretical work flowed from a thorough understanding of the facts. Alfred Marshall had compelled Pigou as a young man — a theorist if there ever was one — to begin by studying all the facts about wages. Starting from the facts he hoped that they would better understand some of the theoretical issues of African economies. He thought that much more knowledge was needed also of such subjects as motivations and incentives and their working in an African society — of what made an African economy 'tick'.

They needed more knowledge also to improve the powers of control over African economies. He had been asked a few years ago by the then Governor of Uganda to look at the East African organizations for statistical and economic research, because experience had shown that whenever a crisis hit East Africa not enough was known to deal with it effectively. Knowledge was power ; a clear factual analysis of a problem was more than half-way to its solution.

If they wanted facts about Africa, it was useful to think what were the instruments of knowledge. The richest were the population census, the census of production, crop yield estimates, mining returns, tax returns, government accounts, import and export data, employment data. Beyond these one had to depend largely on direct inquiries. Many of these were by-products of the administrative process. But they were there to be used more effectively.

In India, much use had been made of the population censuses. At each census some necessary piece of economic or social knowledge was made a matter of special inquiry, and questions were devised to throw light on it. *Professor Robinson* thought that African censuses could and should be similarly used. There were many things that were not known and which it was very important to know. Scarcity of qualified manpower was one of the problems of Africa. Yet virtually nothing was known in Central Africa about the numbers of people possessing certain qualifications, or as to the qualifications of immigrants. There were other instruments of knowledge which, in similar ways and at relatively small expense and trouble, could be made to add greatly to the available stock of knowledge.

He turned next to comparability. Some twenty-five years earlier he had worked with Lord Hailey on his great *African Survey*. Lord Hailey had added, to a chapter that Professor Robinson had drafted about trade returns, a phrase that he had never forgotten — 'it is enough to say that eccentricity, so interesting in social life, loses its charm when applied to the compilation of trade statistics'. It remained true that the trade returns of Africa retained many of their eccentricities regarding valuation, origin, and destination ; that every national income compiler had his own slightly varying definitions and methods of valuation — more particularly as regards subsistence income. Comparability was often more important than individual perfection. He hoped that the Economic Commission for Africa would exercise a beneficent stimulus to comparability.

But having said all this, *Professor Robinson* was convinced that there still remained in Africa wide scope for individual inquiry. It would be interesting to see studies of the transition from perfect self-subsistence to perfect market-economy in agriculture, which Dr. Yudelman had suggested. There was much room for more individual village studies which had formed the basis of so much of the economic knowledge of India in earlier years. He saw many opportunities for collaboration between economists and anthropologists in this field. There was room for much more quantitative study of the problems of location and of the relations between costs of manufacture, transport, and distributive handling. Some fascinating individual figures had been thrown out during the Conference by Professor Bézy and Professor Walker, but far too little quantitative information was available.

One could multiply examples of problems where quantitative research into facts and trends would be valuable. To take one example, better studies of the longer-term trends of individual primary product markets and of the rate of growth of substitutes would be of great value. Here he thought there was room for more collaboration between economists, scientists, and engineers. There had been some attempts at that in the United Kingdom.

Professor Robinson then turned to the problems of research into industrialization. He suggested that there was scope for very valuable research into the terms on which private enterprise could be attracted to Africa. This was partly a matter of financial terms. It was partly a matter of the terms of partnership with African governments. It would be valuable to know more as to whose function it had been to identify economically possible projects. Had this come from governments or from private enterprise? Who had made the feasibility studies? Not every private concern had the resources, or even the interest, to make feasibility

studies of the possibility of extending its activities into every country in
the world. It would be very interesting to see more case studies of how
all this had been successfully — or unsuccessfully — attempted. Was the
best division of labour the making of a 'grand jury' case for a development
by the African government, or by a United Nations agency, followed by a
firm's own private appraisal where prospects were good?

Here one came back to one's own private philosophy of African
development, and of the place of planning and government intervention
in it. He himself believed that, whether one liked it or not, most African
countries were going to have more planning and more government direction than one found in the United States, in the United Kingdom, or even
in the Union of South Africa. He himself believed that the important
thing was that government intervention should be helpful, working in the
same direction as the long-term economic forces, helping to remove bottlenecks by detecting them sufficiently in advance, helping the economy
along its own natural roads of progress, including, of course, roads, which
were in some measure politically determined. He believed that research
was valuable if it could help to show the longer-term trends, the reasonable expectations of growth in total and in various sectors, the bottlenecks
which might develop, the scarcities of particular inputs — particularly
foreign inputs — which might create obstacles. Such studies, he believed,
could speed up progress and increase the rate of growth, and he believed
that this was the biggest contribution that the economist could make to
African progress.

Professor Peacock asked whether facts or theories came first. Collection
of facts had to be within a frame of reference. This was not to suggest
that they should all become model-builders, but there was a need to have
models and to assign parameters. Much of the impetus to original
research in Africa had come from private sources. Professor Stolper had
seemed to concentrate on government investigations. Governments were
conservative about publishing data. Thus, there was need for a two-way
flow, and for government assistance in making information available for
research. He thought that there had not as yet been nearly enough
study of inter-industry flows. When he had been engaged on a national
income study in Tanganyika, they had tried to measure the input-output
relationships and made a modest attempt at constructing inter-industry
relationships. He thought that any thesis of balanced growth depended
on the identification of growing points. This might mean sustained aid
for a long time ahead.

Professor Leduc reminded the Conference that opportunities for the
systematic study of Africa had only existed for some ten or fifteen years
past. The anthropologists and sociologists had been first in the field.
The era of the economist was only just starting. But economists could
not conduct research without facts. Various agencies of the United
Nations and of the metropolitan countries were doing much to help
economists. It would be a good thing that economists should meet

regularly to review the progress of knowledge and to make scientific comparisons.

Dr. Yudelman thought that there should be more research at the field level. There was too little information at this level, and ignorance could lead to misallocation of resources. In Uganda, 10 per cent of the cotton crop had been left unpicked in some years — to a value of over £1 million. It was discovered that the picking season coincided with the planting of food crops. He pleaded for field studies, not only to find the facts, but also to establish the relations between different claims on resources.

Professor Enke argued the case for sample surveys in addition to the census. They could be used to fill in gaps in knowledge. He stressed the greater flexibility of private research, which did not have to conform to the rigid requirements of a government operation. Professor Robinson had mentioned data relating to location and transport costs ; there was a vast mass of data regarding this in the hands of businessmen. He thought one should ask how far economic theory could contribute to African progress. The developments of theory over the past fifty years had little applicability to African conditions. Simple linear programming might have more to offer. Africa was very heterogeneous. Regional studies were needed. He was sceptical of attempts to establish general propositions about Africa as a whole ; regional comparisons were likely to be more valuable.

Dr. Vopicka wished to say two things. First, he hoped that the socialist countries would be able to contribute increasingly to the study of the economic problems of Africa. In the Czechoslovak Socialist Republic, for example, they now had a special research centre for the economic and social problems of under-developed countries. Through this he hoped that they would be able both to increase their own knowledge of African problems and to give the most effective help to African countries.

Second, he thought that the experience of the socialist countries could be of great use to African countries, even though their social systems might be very different. He had in mind particularly the methodology of planning, the system of centralized financing, the foreign trade institutions, the methods of evaluating investments, the methods of education, and so on. They proposed to make their own experience more widely available by publishing books in English and French, with the needs of under-developed countries very much in mind. They also proposed to hold seminars for specialists from under-developed countries in Czechoslovakia, and already had plans for two on the financial systems of under-developed countries and on the planning of industrialization in their own backward areas. He thought such conferences as the present one helped to make it possible for them to contribute to thought about African development.

Dr. Okigbo said that those who were concerned with the day-to-day work of African Ministries found themselves so overwhelmed with work that economists from outside could make very important contributions to decisions that had far-reaching implications. He was anxious to support

Professor Peacock's argument that, however much one might decry theory, in the very choice of facts for collection there was need for a theoretical basis.

M. Wade believed that economic research had a twofold interest. It could improve economics. It could contribute to the welfare of a country. He questioned the value of much of the data that were already available. An economist could work only on accurate data. The work of the ECA, for example, could be useful only if the basic statistics were trustworthy. All African countries should take steps to improve their statistics.

Dr. Singer thought that one aspect had been neglected. Better information was wanted on the current economic situation in Africa. He agreed that better statistics were wanted as a means to better planning.

Professor Stolper summed up the discussion, saying that the main contribution of theory was the collection of facts in a systematic and not haphazard manner.

Mr. Abbas then gave the Conference a detailed description of the main lines of research that were currently being undertaken by the ECA. He emphasized the desire of the ECA to collaborate with economists from all parts of the world, and assured them of welcome and help from the ECA either in Addis Ababa itself or in the supply of necessary material that the ECA might possess.

Professor Robinson, in bringing the Conference to its conclusion, expressed the gratitude of the International Economic Association and of all participants to H.M. The Emperor and to the Government of Ethiopia and to the Economic Commission for Africa, for all that had been done by them to make the Conference enjoyable and stimulating. The Conference had particularly valued the opportunity to make use of the magnificent facilities provided, in Africa Hall by the Government of Ethiopia, for the use of the United Nations.

The Conference had been vigorous and hard-hitting. They had not always agreed. Indeed, an academic conference existed to bring to light differences of opinion rather than to gloss them over by meaningless phrases. At the end of their sessions they were thus probably more aware of differences of opinion than of agreements. In any case it was typical of economists to put one's views forcibly in public and to make one's concessions to other opinions only privately and later. It was difficult to say whether there had been a meeting of minds as distinct from a clash of minds. He was not sure that many would be going away wholly converted to other views. But they would all be going away more aware of other views and more aware of other conditions and problems than those with which they happened to be most familiar at home. There was much to be learned about Africa by the process of comparison and exchange of ideas. To that process he thought the Conference had greatly contributed.

INDEX

Entries in the Index in Black Type under the Names of Participants in the Conference indicate their Papers or Discussions of their Papers. Entries in Italics indicate Contributions by Participants to the Discussions

Abbai, B., and Ligthart, G. J., **3-47**

Abbas, M., *709, 733*

Abramovitz, M., 363 n.

Ady, P., and Courcier, M., 420, 655 n.

A.E.F. territories (former). *See* French Equatorial Africa

Africa, natural resources of, 49-52, 107-9, 188-9; special features of, 48-52

African development, aims and possibilities of, 3-47, 48-70; contribution of economic research to, 712-33

Agricultural development, 364-5, 554-587

Agriculture, African, 111-14; migration and, 293-300; non-African, 114-16, 134; problems of, 186-8; production systems in, 565-8; proportions engaged in, 9-11, 57-9, 74-7, 234-7, 250-65, 313, 556-9; self-subsistence, 189-92, 316-21, 336-7, 384-5, 398-406, 555-9; Swynnerton Plan, 104, 113, 114, 116, 117, 124, 463

Allais, Maurice, 159-60

Almond, G. A., and Coleman, J. S., 304 n.

Andic, S., 654 n.

Angola, exports of, 415, 489; external aid to development of, 446, 457; labour force in, 560; population and population density of, 50, 289, 292, 415, 562; problems of development of, 198-221

A.O.F. territories (former). *See* French West Africa

Asians, rôle of, in transfer of technical knowledge, 54-7, 65-70

Assistance, external, to development, 148-60, 444-73, 482-5

Aukrust, Odd, 340, 418

Badenhorst, L. T., 285 n., 286 n., 289 n., 290 n., 291 n. ; and Unterhalter, B., 286 n., 288 n., 289 n., 290 n.

Balandier, G., 297 n.

Baldwin, R. E., *528-9, 530-1, 582-3*

Bananas, terms of trade of, 516, 519. *See also* Agriculture

Banking and development, 262-3, 444-473, 722-3

Banton, M. P., 297 n., 299 n.

Barber, W. J., 243 n., 295 n.

Barbour, K. M., and Prothero, R. M., eds., 281 n., 282 n., 289 n., 294 n., 295 n., 296 n., 298 n., 300 n.

Bascom, William, 295 n.

Basutoland, exports of, 415; external aid to development of, 446; gross domestic product of, 415; population and population density of, 289, 292, 415

Bauer, P. T., 57, 388, 396 n., 404, 406, **532-53**, 686 n., 701, 717; and Paish, F. W., 544-5, 671 n., 686 n.

Beales, H. L., 690 n.

Bechuanaland, exports of, 415; external aid to development of, 446; gross domestic product of, 415; population and population density of, 289, 292, 415

Beheiry, M., *66, 70, 359, 401, 403, 441, 498, 586-7, 636, 652, 697-700, 707, 708-9, 709-10*

Belshaw, H., 631 n.

Benveniste, G., and Moran, W. E., 428 n., 431 n.

Berlin, Isaiah, 535

Bettelheim, C., 88 n.

Bézy, Fernand, *45, 68,* **71-88,** *308, 310, 336, 337, 338, 358, 377-8, 439-40, 530, 552, 634-5, 652-3, 710,* 730; and Lacroix, J. L., 86 n.

Bhouraskat, H., *707, 708*

Bilateral assistance, compared with multilateral, 448-67

Birth rates, 281-93, 305-11

Blacker, J. G. C., 286 n.

Blake, J., and Davis K., 286 n.

Blanc, R., and Théodore, G., 286 n., 288 n., 289 n., 291

735

Bohannan, P., 296 n.
Bournier, M., 140 n., 143
Boutillier, J. L., 289 n.
Branchu, M., 172
Brand, W., 631 n.
Brebent, V., 288 n., 289 n.
Bridger, D., *583-4*

Cairncross, A. K., 436, 543
Calloway, A., 191 n.
Cameroun (including former British and French Cameroons), agriculture in, 554-87 *pass.* ; capital formation in, 29, 170-2, external aid to, 446 ; education in, 27 ; energy consumption of, 21-2 ; gross domestic product of, 12 ; labour force in, 560-1 ; manufacturing in, 13-14, 16 ; population and population density of, 8, 50, 161, 289, 292, 414, 562 ; primary production sectors of, 10 ; rôle of government in development of, 33-8 ; trade of, 15-20, 146, 162-4, 414, 427 ; transport in, 23-4. *See also* French-language African countries
Cannan, Edwin, 417, 674 n.
Capet, Marcel, 387, 396, 397
Capital, imports of foreign, 261-2, 479-494, 692-3: *see also* Assistance, external ; the rôle of in African development, 61-4, 67-8, 407-43, 444-74, 625-7
Capital formation and development, 28-31, 61-70, 78-9, 140-3, 170-2, 225-33, 261-2, 271-2, 687-93, 717-18 ; incentives for, 371-4 ; institutions to promote in French Africa, 148-60, 444-74
Carbon, L. B. de, **138-83**
Central African Federation, agriculture in, 554-87 *pass.* ; capital formation in, 29-31, 225-33, external aid to, 446, 463 ; education in, 27, 236 ; energy consumption of, 21-2 ; gross domestic product of, 53, 226-7, 412-13, 414 ; industrial origin of gross domestic product in, 11-13, 57-8 ; Kariba Hydro-Electric Scheme, 231-2, 241-3, 463, 623, 666 ; labour force in, 420, 560-1 ; manufacturing in, 14, 237-42; population and population density of, 8, 50, 234-5, 288-92, 414, 562 ; primary production sectors of, 10 ; problems of development of, 222-45 ; rôle of government in development of, 33-8, 655-60 ; trade of, 15-20, 233-4,

238, 411, 414, 427, 489 ; transport in, 23-4
Central African Republic. *See* French-language African countries
Chad, exports of, 489 ; population and population density of,161,292. *See also* French-language African countries
Chakravarty, S., 717, 722
Chenery, H. B., 722
Chevalier, Louis, 289 n.
Church, R. J. H., 303 n.
Clark, Colin, 397 n., 409 n., 418-19, 437
Clark, Grover, 410 n.
Coale, A. J., 286 n., 289 n.
Cobb-Douglas type production function, 662-5
Cocoa, terms of trade of, 510-14, 519. *See also* Agriculture
Coffee, production of and trade in, 97-8, 99-100, 101-4, 132, 516, 518-20. *See also* Agriculture
Coleman, J. S., and Almond, G. A., 304 n.
Commodity policy, in Africa, 503-31
Commodity stabilization, issues of in Africa, 532-53, 679-86
Communications. *See* Transport
Congo (including former Belgian Congo and the Congo Republic), agriculture in, 554-87 *pass.*, capital formation in, 29-31, 78-82, external aid to, 446, 456-7, 463 ; consumption pattern of, 40 ; development planning in, 480-1, 495 ; education in, 27 ; energy consumption of, 21-2 ; gross domestic product of, 53, 412-13, 414, 420 ; industrial origin of gross domestic product in, 11-13, 57-8, 74-5 ; industry in, 14, 16, 74-5 ; labour force in, 76, 420, 560 ; population and population density of, 8, 50, 77, 161, 288-92, 308, 414, 562 ; primary production sectors of, 10 ; problems of development of, 71-87 ; rôle of government in development of, 33-8, 655 ; trade of, 15-20, 72-4, 411, 414, 427, 489, terms of, 480-1, 520-1, 523, 525-6 ; transport in, 22-5, 71. *See also* French-language African countries
Cookson, F., *311, 338, 403, 405, 499-500, 608-12, 653*
Copper, trade in, 238-9, 523, 525-6
Cotton, production of and trade in, 97, 99-100, 133, 520-3. *See also* Agriculture
Courcier, M., and Ady, P., 420, 655 n.

Dahomey, exports of, 145, 489 ; population and population density of, 161, 292. *See also* French-language African countries
Davidson, B. R., 115, 136
Davis, J. Merle, *ed.*, 222 n.
Davis, K., and Blake, J., 286 n.
Deane, Phyllis, 715
Death rates, 281-93, 305-11
De-colonialization, 66, 82-8
Demography. *See* Population
Development planning, impact of, 479-482
DeWitt, Nicholas, 343 n.
Dickman, A. B., and Palmer, G. F. D., 271 n.
Didier, Henri, 388 n.
Domar model, 661-2, 665, 674
Dorjahn, V. R., 287 n.
Dosser, D. G. M., 673 n. ; and Peacock, A. T., 671 n.
Dowuona, M., *359, 613-14, 706, 710*
Dual economy, 77-8
Dupriez, L. H., *44, 69, 308, 310, 358, 403, 406, 436, 498,* **503-31**, *586, 614, 637, 701-2, 709*

East Africa, problems of development of, 89-137
Economic research, contribution of to African development, 712-33
Education, for assimilation of modern techniques, 54-7, 192-6 ; content of, 343-6 ; rôle of in African development, 25-8, 54-7, 68-70, 340-60, 363-4, 727-9
Elkan, Walter, 295 n., 296 n., 297 n., 298 n., 299 n., 300 n., 322 n., 331-2, 576 n.
Ellis, H. S., and Wallich, H. C., *eds.*, 433 n., 434 n.
Employment, wage, 13-16, 57-9, 74-7, 234-7, 240-1, 252-3, 269-70, 420-422 ; of educated, 190-1, 724 ; in education, 346-54. *See also* Labour ; Wages
Energy in African countries, 21-2, 63, 241-2, 622-4
Enke, S., *66,* **361-81**, *381, 613, 634, 636-7, 704, 708, 732*
Entrepreneurs, rôle of in African development, 54-7, 196-7, 375-81, 630-1
Epstein, A. L., 299 n.
Ethiopia, capital formation in, 29, external aid to, 446 ; education in, 27 ; energy consumption of, 21 ; industrial

origin of gross domestic product in, 12 ; manufacturing in, 14 ; population and population density of, 8, 50, 292, 415 ; primary production sectors of, 10 ; rôle of government in development of, 32-3 ; trade of, 15-20, 415, 489 ; transport in, 23-4
Europeans, rôle of in transfer of technical knowledge, 54-7, 65-70
Exchange economy, the evolution of, 411-13
Export incomes, and development, 679-687, 698
Exports, composition of, 97-100, 109-111, 130-6, 143-6, 163-8, 233-4, 260, 272-4, 488-94, 494-502, 556-9 ; importance of mineral, 426-9 ; prices of, 392-4, 398-9 ; prospects for, 233-4. *See also* Trade

Fauvel, L., *497, 581, 653*
Fearn, Hugh, 416
Feldman, A. S., and Moore, W. F., 316, 320 n.
Fenn, D. H., *ed.*, 626 n.
Fernando Po Island, exports of, 415 ; population of, 289, 415
Fiscal policy, in relation to development, 31-8, 369-71, 389-91, 654-76, 677-92, 697-711, 726-7
Ford, C. S., 286 n.
Foreign aid. *See* Assistance
Fortes, Meyer, 296 n.
Frankel, S. H., *45, 46,* 61, *64-6, 67, 68, 70,* 140, *308, 311, 401-2, 405,* **407-43**, *437-8, 442-3,* 479, *651,* 683 n., *700*
Franzen, D. G., and Willers, J. J. D., 417-18, 422-3
French Equatorial Africa (former), agriculture in, 167 ; capital formation in, 170-2, external aid to, 446 ; gross domestic product of, 167, 414 ; labour force in, 560 ; population and population density of, 50, 161, 290-1, 562 ; trade of, 146-7, 162-4, 414, 427. *See also* French-language African countries
French franc area in Africa, bilateral assistance to, 448-54
French - language African countries, prices and price formation in, 382-406 ; problems of development of, 138-83
French West Africa (former), agriculture in, 167, 554-87 *pass.* ; capital

formation in, 170-2, external aid to
446 ; gross domestic product of, 53,
167, 414 ; labour force in, 560 ;
population and population density of,
50, 161, 562 ; trade of, 146-7, 162-4,
414, 427, terms of for staple products
of, 514-17, 519-20. *See also* French-
language African countries
Furtado, C., 433

Gabon, exports of, 489 ; population and
population density of, 161, 292. *See
also* French Equatorial Africa (former) ; French - language African
countries
Galbraith, J. K., 375
Gambia, exports of, 414, 489 ; external
aid to development of, 446 ; gross
domestic product of, 412-14 ; population of, 414
Gavrilov, N., *359, 380, 402, 442, 502,
584, 613, 653*
Gendarme, R., 142 n., 389 n.
Gezira Scheme, 60, 321, 574 n., 577,
586-7
Ghana, agriculture in, 186-8, 189-92,
554-87 *pass.* ; capital formation in,
29-31, external aid to, 446 ; education in, 27-8 ; energy consumption
of, 21 ; gross domestic product of,
53, 412-14, 420 ; industrial origin of
gross domestic product in, 12 ; labour
force in, 420, 560-1 ; manufacturing
in, 14, 16 ; population and population density of, 8, 50, 185-6, 288-92,
414, 420, 562 ; primary production
sectors of, 10 ; problems of development of, 184-97 ; rôle of government
in development of, 33-8, 655-60 ;
trade of, 15-20, 414, 427, 489, terms
of for staple products of, 510-14 ;
transport in, 22-4
Gold, importance of in South African
development, 247, 264-7
Goldsmith, R., and Saunders, C. T.,
eds., 417 n.
Goldthorpe, J. E., 288 n.
Goode, R., and Thorne, R. S., 672 n.
Government, impact of on development,
31-8, 116-19, 137, 654-711, 731 ;
rôle of in price determination, 389-92
Gregory, (Sir) Theodore, 691 n.
Gross domestic product, of African
countries, 52-4, 165-9, 226-7, 412-13 ;
industrial origin of gross domestic
product, 11-13, 57-9, 126-8

Groundnuts, terms of trade of, 511-12,
514, 516-17. *See also* Agriculture
Growth, basic barriers to, 433-5
Growth rates of African countries, 52-4,
156-7, 225-30, 418-21
Guinea (including Portuguese, Spanish
and the former French), education in,
27 ; energy consumption of, 21 ;
external aid to development of, 446 ;
gross domestic product of, 415 ; industrial origin of gross domestic product in, 12 ; manufacturing in, 14,
16 ; population and population density of, 8, 161, 288-92, 415 ; primary
production sectors of, 10 ; rôle of
government in development of, 33-8 ;
trade of, 15-20, 415 ; transport in,
23-4
Gulliver, P. H., 568 n.

Haberler, G., 689 n.
Hailey (Lord), 140-1, 282 n., 407, 730
Haines, C. G., *ed.*, 626 n., 627 n.
Hamilton, Earl J., 690 n.
Hammond, P. B., 320 n.
Hance, W. A., 622 n.
Harbison, F., 349, 727
Harris, M., 297 n., 298 n.
Healey, D. T., 148 n., 479
Heigham, J. B., 329
Herchenroder, M. V. M., 286 n.
Herskovits, M. J., 294 n.
Hirschman, A. O., 640, 721, 727, 728
Hogben, L., *ed.*, 283 n.
Holleaux, A., 150 n., 151 n.
Horst, Sheila v. d., 325 n.
Houghton, D. H., 55, *70*, 295 n., 298 n.,
300 n., **312-39**, *337, 338-9, 360, 378,
437, 581, 614, 634, 650, 704-5* ; as
ed., 326 n. ; and Walton, E. M.,
316 n., 318 n.
Hunter, Monica, 319 n.
Hutt, W. H., 547
Huybrechts, A., 508 n.

Import restrictions, 682-3
Imports, composition of, 15-20, 79,
130-6, 146-8, 163-8, 258-60 ; prices
of, 392-4. *See also* Trade
Incentives, in agriculture, 571-4, 584-5 ;
creation of for development, 361-81
Independence, effects of, ix-xvi, 429-33
Industry, innovation in, 364, 366-7 ;
inter-industry flows of, 720-2, 731 ;
large-scale in African development,
616-37 ; and migration, 293-300 ;

Index

output of, 254-7; small-scale in African development, 638-53
Industrialization, 11-16, 235-6; research into, 725-6, 730-1
Inflation and investment, 687-93
Infrastructures of African economies, 20-5, 31-5, 63-4
Innovation, acceleration of, 362-7
Institutions, creation of for development, 722-5
Institutions for development, in French Africa, 148-60, 444-74
Inter-industry flows, 720-2, 731
International Bank for Reconstruction and Development, contribution of to African development, 115, 117, 193, 232, 424-5, 440, 456, 462-4, 481, 606
International Development Association, contribution of to African development, 464-5
International Finance Corporation, contribution of to African development, 465-6
International Monetary Fund, contribution of to African development, 466
Investment. *See* Capital
Irvine, A. G., 425
Ivory Coast, education in, 27; energy consumption of, 21; population and population density of, 8, 161, 288-92 *pass.*; primary production sectors of, 10; rôle of government in development of, 32-8; trade of, 15-20, 145, 489; transport in, 22-4. *See also* French-language African countries

Jack, D. T., 412 n., 415 n.
Jackson, E. F., 715
Johnson, C. E., 571 n., 582
Johnson, H. G., 545 ; 50
Johnson, (Sir) Harry, 14
Johnston, B. F., 578 n.
Jones, W. O., 295 n., 303 n., 417 n.
Jones, W. R., 303 n.

Kamarck, A., 554 n.
Kariba Hydro-Electric Scheme, 231-2, 241-3, 463, 623, 666
Karp, Mark, 312 n., 322 n.; and Lorimer, F., 287 n.
Kenya, agriculture in, 35, 92, 101-4, 113-14, 115-16, 117, 124, 134, 136, 463, 554-87 *pass.*; capital formation in, 29-31, external aid to, 446, 455, 463; education in, 27; energy consumption of, 21-2; gross domestic

product of, 53, 412-13, 414, 420; industrial origin of gross domestic product in, 12-13, 57-8, 126; labour force in, 420, 560-1; manufacturing in, 14, 101-5, 121-2; population and population density of, 8, 50, 122-5, 288-92, 414, 562; primary production sectors of, 10; problems of development of, 89-137; rôle of government in development of, 33-8, 116-19, 137, 655-60; trade of, 15-20, 90-5, 101-5, 109-11, 119-21, 129-31, 134, 136, 414, 427, 489; transport in, 23-4, 101
Kerr, Clark, 316
Keynes, (Lord) J. M., 437, 443, 533-4, 690 n.
Keynesian concepts, 204, 718
Kiewiet, C. W. de, 320
Kimble, G. H. T., 293 n., 294 n., 300 n., 303 n., 422 n.
Kindleberger, C. P., 434, 531
Kirk-Greene, A. H. M., 297 n.
Korean War, effects of on African development, 527, 591
Krishna, K. G. V., *635*
Kristensen, T., 663 n.
Kuczynski, R. R., 282-3, 286 n.

Labour, incentives for, 367-71, 571-4; for large-scale industry, 624-5; problems of in African development, 312-339. *See also* Employment; Wages
Lacroix, J. L., and Bézy, F., 86 n.
Land. *See also* Agriculture
Land tenure, problems of, 122-5, 574-6
Land use, 568-70
Lardner, G., *67, 69*
Leclercq, H., 88 n.
Leduc, G., 153 n., 159 n., *307, 310, 337, 359, 376-7,* **382-406,** *406, 440-1, 497, 530, 552, 614, 651, 704, 706, 731-2*
Le Héragat, M., *393, 395*
Lehfeldt, R. A., 688 n.
Leibenstein, H., 305
Leurquin, P., 520 n.
Lewis, W. A., 4, 26 n., 27, 156, 201 n., 311, 356, 367, 617-18, 631 n., 688 n., 721; and Martin, Alison, 674-5, 726
Liberia, exports of, 415, 489; external aid to development of, 446; labour force in, 560; population and population density of, 292, 415, 562; problems of development of, 184-97

Ligthart, G. J., *45, 46-7* ; and Abbai, B., **3-47**
Little, K., 299 n.
Lockwood, W. W., 647 n.
Lorimer, Frank, 281 n. ; as *ed.*, 286 n., 287 n., 289 n. ; and Karp, M., 287 n.
Lugard, (Lord) F. D., 242
Lutolf, F., 554 n.

McKinney, Robert, *ed.*, 303 n.
Madagascar, gross domestic product of, 167, 414 ; population and population density of, 50, 161, 288, 292, 414, 562 ; trade of, 145-7, 162-4, 414, 427
Makings, S., and Yudelman, M., 571 n.
Malagasy Republic, external aid to development of, 446. *See also* French-language African countries
Maldant, M., 172
Mali, population and population density of, 161, 292. *See also* French-language African countries
Malthus, T. R., 281, 282, 305, 306
Malthusian concept, 504
Manley, Roy, 344 n.
Manpower, need to plan, 346-9 ; training of, 66, 329-30
Manufacturing, proportions engaged in, 13-16, 57-9, 74-7, 234-7, 250-65, 324-34
Markets, size of in Africa, 45, 627-30, 643-4. *See also* Trade
Marris, Peter, 299 n.
Marshall, Alfred, 340, 366 n., 712, 729
Martin, Alison, and Lewis, W. A., 674-5, 726
Martin, C. J., 282 n., 285 n., 289 n., 291
Marx, Karl, 68, 81, 313 n., 340, 714
Marzouk, G. A., 289 n.
Maud'huy, B. de, 138 n.
Mauretania, exports of, 489 ; population density of, 161, 292. *See also* French-language African countries
Mauritius, exports of, 414 ; fiscal structure of, 655-60 ; gross domestic product of, 412, 414 ; industrial origin of gross domestic product of, 57
Mayer, P., 315
Meade, J. E., 283 n.
Meek, C. K., 574 n.
Mel, Marinus van der, 444 n.
Menon, P. S., *308-9*
Mexico, as bench-mark of 'take-off' condition, 6, 11-31, 44-5
Migration, 293-300, 322-4

Minerals, rôle of in African development, 59-61, 188, 247, 426-9, 614-15
Mines, labour in, 321-4
Mining, for gold, 247, 264-7 ; problems of in Africa, 588-615
Mitchell, J. C., 290 n., 294 n., 295 n., 296 n., 298 n.
Monckton Commission, 225, 228, 232
Monetary policy, in relation to development, 654-76, 677-97, 697-711
Moore, W. F., and Feldman, A. S., 316, 320 n.
Moran, W. E., *45, 67, 69-70, 309, 311, 357, 378, 402,* **475-502***, 502, 551, 582, 612, 648-50, 653, 705*; and Benveniste, G., 428 n., 431 n.
Morgan, W. B., 296 n.
Mortality, 281-93, 305-11
Moussa, P., 157, 159 n.
Mozambique, exports of, 415 ; external aid to development of, 446, 457 ; labour force in, 560 ; population and population density of, 50, 289, 292, 415, 562
Multilateral assistance, compared with bilateral, 448-67
Murdock, G. P., 294 n.
Musgrave, R. A., 668 n.
Myburgh, C. A. L., 289 n., 291 ; and Shaul, J. R. H., 289 n.
Myint, H., 567

Nadel, S. F., 290 n.
Nadler, L. F., 290 n.
Natality, 281-93, 305-11
National incomes of African countries, 51, 84, 126-8, 165-9, 237-8, 250-2, 412-15, 556-9, 715-17
Natural resources, 49-52, 107-9, 188-9
Nef, J. U., 690 n.
Newlyn, W. T., and Rowan, D. C., 696 n.
Ngcobo, S. B., *45, 336-7, 338, 400, 585, 707*
Niger, exports of, 489 ; population and population density of, 161, 292. *See also* French-language African countries
Nigeria, agriculture in, 186-8, 189-92, 554-87 *pass.* ; capital formation in, 29-31 ; education in, 27 ; energy consumption of, 21 ; external aid to development of, 446, 455, 456, 464 ; gross domestic product of, 53, 412-13, 414 ; industrial origin of gross domestic product of, 12, 57-8 ; labour

force in, 420, 560 ; population and population density of, 8, 50, 185-6, 288-92, 414, 562 ; primary production sectors of, 10 ; problems of development of, 184-97 ; rôle of government in development of, 32-8, 655-60 ; trade of, 15-20, 414, 427, 489, terms of for staple products of, 510-12, 514 ; transport in, 22-5

Niven, C. R., 294 n.

Northcott, C. H., 324

Nurkse, R., 391 n., 684 n.

Nyasaland, problems of development of, 222-45. *See also* Central African Federation

Nye, P. H., 569 n.

Okigbo, P. N. C., *359, 377, 402, 403-4, 440, 500, 552, 583, 636, 650, 651-2, 709, 710,* 715, *732-3*

Onitiri, H. M. A., *46, 310, 311, 339, 403, 497-8, 527-8, 551, 635, 701, 709*

Oppenheimer, H. F., 274 n.

Owen Falls Hydro-Electric Scheme, 63, 98, 623

Paish, F. W., and Bauer, P. T., 544-5, 671 n., 686 n.

Palm oil and palm nuts, terms of trade of, 515, 516, 517

Palmer, G. F. D., and Dickman, A. B., 271 n.

Peacock, A. T., *67, 304-7, 310,* 347-8, 356, *404-5, 438-9, 552, 651,* **654-76, 697-711,** *704, 707, 709, 711, 731* ; and Dosser, D. G. M., 671 n.

Perroux, François, 391

Phillips, John, 570 n.

Piercy, Mary, 246 n., 270 n. ; and Richards, C. S., 252 n.

Pigou, A. C., 366 n., 534, 729

Pinto, L. M. Teixeira, and Santos, R. Martins dos, **198-221**

Poleman, T. T., 299 n.

Poles, of development, 205-21

Population, densities of, 161, 185-6, 292, 562 ; movements and problems of in Africa, 122-5, 281-311

Population growth, economic implications of, 301-11

Populations of African countries, 7-8, 49-50, 76-7, 161, 249-50, 268-9, 413

Postel-Vinay, A., 152 n., 154 n.

Pré, Roland, *69, 310, 335-6, 380, 441, 499, 551-2, 584,* **588-615,** *612-13, 614, 615, 635, 650*

Prebisch, R., 504

Prest, A. R., 666 n., 715

Price formation, in African economies, 382-406

Price indexes, 261

Prices. *See also* Commodity policy ; Commodity stabilization

Private investment, foreign, 225-32, 271-2, 485-7, 422-6, 467-9

Prothero, R. M., 296 n., 300 n. ; and Barbour, K. M., *eds.,* 281 n., 282 n., 289 n., 294 n., 295 n., 296 n., 298 n., 300 n.

Quevrin, E., 504 n.

Raeburn, J. R., 573 n.

Railways. *See* Transport

Raisman Commission, 120, 122

Rao, Badri, 444 n.

Rao, K. N., 647 n., 648 n.

Raw materials, for industry, 619-21

Reader, D. H., 329 n., 330 n.

Reddaway, W. B., and Smith, A. D., 436

Reproduction rates, 281-93, 305-11

Rey, L., 154, 155, 157 n.

Rhodesias, problems of development of, 222-45. *See also* Central African Federation

Richards, A. I., *ed.,* 297 n., 300 n., 314 n.

Richards, C. S., **246-78** ; and Piercy, Mary, 252 n.

Rist, Leonard B., *359-60,* **444-74,** 581 n., *615, 710-11*

Rivlin, Alice, 344 n.

Roads. *See* Transport

Roberts, D. F., and Tanner, R. E. S., 290 n.

Robertson, H. M., 319 n.

Robinson, E. A. G. R., ix-xvi, *43-4, 45, 46,* **48-70,** *67-8, 69, 70,* 222 n., 243 n., *307, 309, 357-8, 359, 379, 380, 405, 436-7, 438, 442, 498-9, 531, 550-1, 586, 612, 613, 614, 635-6, 650-1, 701, 703, 708, 729-31, 733* ; as *ed.,* 302 n., 674 n.

Rostow, W. W., 3-5, 20, 30, 43-4, 638, 690 n.

Rouch, Jean, 300 n.

Rowan, D. C., and Newlyn, W. T., 696 n.

Royer, Jean, 491

Ruanda-Urundi, external aid to development of, 446, 456-7 ; gross domestic product of, 414 ; labour force in, 560; population and population density of,

50, 288, 292, 414, 562 ; trade of, 411, 414, 427, 489, terms of for staple products of, 516, 518

Sadie, J. L., 289 n., 290-1, 299 n.
Samuels, L. H., *45, 68-9, 337*, 418, *494-7*, **677-711**
Santos, R. Martins dos, and Pinto, L. M. Teixeira, **198-221**
Saunders, C. T., and Goldsmith, R., *eds.*, 417 n.
Sauvy, A., 303 n.
Saving. *See* Capital formation
Schapera, I., 296 n., 297 n., 300 n., 314 n., 568 n.
Schlote, W., 509
Schumpeter, J., 436, 509
Scitovsky, T., 366 n.
Scott, Peter, 300 n.
Scott, R., and Thomas, H. B., 131
Seklani, M., 288 n.
Self-subsistence agriculture, 189-92, 316-21, 336-7, 384-5, 398-406, 555-9
Senegal, exports of, 145, 489 ; population and population density of, 161, 288-92 *pass. See also* French-language African countries
Shaul, J. R. H., 289 n., 290 n. ; and Myburgh, C. A. L., 289 n.
Shaw, William, 319 n.
Shoup, C. S., 303 n.
Sierra Leone, agriculture in, 186-8, 189-192 ; exports of, 414, 489 ; external aid to development of, 446 ; gross domestic product of, 412-13, 414 ; labour force in, 560 ; population and population density of, 50, 185-6, 292, 414, 562 ; problems of development of, 184-97
Simoons, F. J., 289 n.
Singer, H. W., *44, 45-6, 66-7, 69, 70, 309, 310, 339, 356, 358, 378, 401, 437, 442, 500, 529-30, 531, 551, 582, 613, 632-3,* **638-53**, *653, 702-3, 706-7, 733*
Skinner teaching machines, 345
Skorov, G., *439, 501*
Smith, A. D., and Reddaway, W. B., 436
Smith, Adam, 66, 506, 674
Smith, R. H., 325 n.
Smith, T. E., 286 n.
Social obstacles to growth, 41-3, 68-70
Somali Republic (including French Somaliland, former British and Italian Somaliland), capital formation in, 170, external aid to, 446 ; exports of,

414, 415 ; population of, 161, 414, 415
Sorel, Marcel, 290 n.
Soudan. *See* Mali
South Africa, Republic of, capital formation in, 261-2, 271-2, 422-4 ; gold mining in, 247, 264-7 ; gross domestic product of, 53, 412-13, 415, 420 ; industrial origin of gross domestic product in, 57-8 ; industry in, 254-7, 267-72 ; labour force in, 252-3, 420, 560-1 ; monetary and fiscal policy of, 693-5 ; population and population density of, 50, 249-50, 268-9, 288-92 *pass.*, 415, 562 ; problems of development of, 246-78 ; trade of, 258-60, 272-4, 411, 415 ; transport in, 263
South West Africa, exports of, 415 ; gross domestic product of, 415 ; population of, 289-92 *pass.*, 415
Spanish territories, problems of development of, 184-97
Spengler, J. J., **281-311**, *309, 311, 338, 355-7, 380-1, 437, 551, 612, 614-15, 636, 708*
Stability, fiscal policy and, 666-72, 698
Stabilization, commodity, in Africa, 532-53, 679-86
Staley, Eugene, 653
Stamp, L. D., 296 n., 303 n.
Stanley, S., *379-80, 440, 584, 636, 652*
Staple products, terms of trade for various, 510-26
Stenning, D. J., 290 n.
Stephens, R. W., 569 n.
Stewart, I. G., 654 n., 715
Stigler, G., 349
Stolper, W. F., **712-33**, *733*
Structural imbalance, 39-41
Structures of African economies, 6-20, 57-9
Subercaseaux, G., 690 n.
Sudan, agriculture in, 401, 554, 559 ; exports of, 415, 489 ; external aid to development of, 446, 465 ; population and population density of, 50, 288-92 *pass.*, 415
Sutter, Jean, and Tabah, Léon, 303 n.
Swaziland, exports of, 415 ; external aid to development of, 446 ; gross domestic product of, 415 ; population and population density of, 289, 415
Swynnerton Plan, 104, 113, 114, 116, 117, 124, 463

Index

Tabah, Léon, and Sutter, Jean, 303 n.

'Take-off', applicability of concept of to African economies, 3-6, 11, 43-7

Tanganyika, agriculture in, 105-7, 111-112, 114-15, 554-87 pass. ; external aid to development of, 446, 464 ; government finance and fiscal structure of, 135, 655-60 ; gross domestic product of, 53, 412-13, 414, 420 ; industrial origin of gross domestic product in, 57-8, 127 ; labour force in, 420, 560-1 ; population and population density of, 50, 122-5, 288, 292, 414, 562 ; problems of development of, 89-137 ; rôle of government in development of, 116-19, 137 ; trade of, 90-5, 105-7, 109-11, 119-21, 129-31, 135-6, 414, 427, 489 ; transport in, 105

Tanner, R. E. S., and Roberts, D. F., 290 n.

Taussig, F. W., 498

Taxation. See Fiscal policy

Taylor, W. L., 222-45

Techniques, choice of in mining, 601-4, 608-12 ; modern, problems of transfer, 54-7, 192-6

Terms of trade, in Africa, 146, 162, 164, 503-31 ; effects of on development, 480-1, 494-502; for specific products, 510-26. See also Trade

Théodore, G., and Blanc, R., 286 n., 288 n., 289 n., 291

Thomas, H. B., and Scott, R., 131

Thorne, R. S., and Goode, R., 672 n.

Tietze, C., 287 n.

Tinbergen, J., 716, 721

Togoland, Republic of, agriculture in, 557 ; capital formation in, 170 ; exports of, 414 ; population and population density of, 161, 288-92 pass., 414, 562. See also French-language African countries

Trade, foreign, of African countries, 93-4, 102-3, 129-32, 135-6, 143-8, 161-4, 258-60, 272-4, 488-92, 496-7, 499-500, 501-2, 603-4, 718-20 ; and price formation, 384-8, 398-9 ; structure of, 6-20. See also Exports; Imports ; Markets ; Terms of Trade

Trade policy, in Africa, 503-31

Transport, and development, 22-5, 32-4, 96-7, 242-3, 263, 602, 621-2 ; effects of cost of, on prices and trade, 388-9, 399, 506-8

Trewatha, G. T., and Zelinsky, W., 293 n.

Uganda, agriculture in, 92, 97-9, 111-12, 114-15, 554-87 pass. ; external aid to development of, 446, 464 ; gross domestic product of, 53, 128, 412, 414, 420 ; labour force in, 420, 560 ; Owen Falls Hydro-Electric Scheme, 63, 98, 623 ; population and population density of, 50, 122-5, 288-92 pass., 414, 562 ; problems of development of, 89-137 ; rôle of government in development of, 99-100, 116-19, 137, 655-60 ; trade of, 90-5, 97-8, 109-11, 119-21, 129-33, 414, 427, 489, terms of, for staple products of, 522-3 ; transport in, 96-7

United Nations, contribution of, to African development, 461-2

Unspecified factor, in economic growth, 418-21, 435-43

Unterhalter, B., and Badenhorst, L. T. 286 n., 288 n., 289 n., 290 n.

Urbanization, migration and, 293-300 ; problems of, 77

Vaizey, John, 340-60, 360, 378, 380, 700-1

Van Velsen, J., 299 n.

Viljoen, D. J., 616-37

Viljoen, S. P., 299 n.

Vincent, P., 287 n.

Viner, J., 504

Volta, population and population density of, 161. See also French-language African countries

Vopicka, E., 310-11, 379, 652, 732

Waasdijk, T. van, 273 n.

Wade, A., 68, 308, 310, 311, 337, 377, 402, 551, 583, 613, 651, 707, 733

Wages, in African countries, 81, 90, 256, 258, 270, 332-4, 400. See also Employment

Walker, David, 45, 89-137, 307-8, 337-338, 339, 398-400, 441, 500-1, 530, 553, 583, 702, 705-6, 730

Wallich, H. C., and Ellis, H. S., eds., 433 n., 434 n.

Walton, Edith M., and Houghton, D. H., 316 n., 318 n.

Watson, W., 296 n., 297 n.

Wertheim, W. F., 288 n.

West Africa, problems of development of, 184-97

Economic Development for Africa South of the Sahara

White, C. M. N., 290 n.

Willers, J. J. D., and Franzen, D. G., 417-18, 422-3

Williams, J. W., *44-5*, **184-97**, *309, 375-6, 378-9, 400, 402, 404, 405-6, 585-6, 636, 652, 705*

Wilson, Godfrey and Monica, 313 n.

Winklé, F. F., 273 n.

World economy, Africa and the, 475-502

World wars, effects of two, on Africa, 102, 105, 139, 140, 514, 629

Wrigley, C. C., 565 n.

Yamey, B. S., 532 n., 542 n.

Yudelman, M., *45, 69, 311, 379, 401, 405, 435-6, 440, 442, 501-2, 530, 551,* **554-87**, 564 n., *584-5, 613, 614, 634, 653, 707-8, 730, 732* ; and Makings, S., 571 n.

Zanzibar and Pemba, external aid to development of, 446 ; exports of, 414 ; population of, 289-92 *pass.*, 414

Zelinsky, W., and Trewatha, G. T., 293 n.

THE END

PRINTED BY R. & R. CLARK, LTD., EDINBURGH